THE YALE EDITION

OF

HORACE WALPOLE'S

CORRESPONDENCE

EDITED BY W. S. LEWIS

VOLUME FORTY-TWO

HORACE WALPOLE'S MISCELLANEOUS CORRESPONDENCE

III

EDITED BY W. S. LEWIS

AND

JOHN RIELY

WITH THE ASSISTANCE OF

EDWINE M. MARTZ

AND

RUTH K. McCLURE

NEW HAVEN

YALE UNIVERSITY PRESS

OXFORD · OXFORD UNIVERSITY PRESS

1980

TABLE OF CONTENTS

VOLUME III

LIST OF ILLUSTRATIONS

VOLUME III

HORACE WALPOLE'S CORRESPONDENCE

From EDMOND MALONE, Monday 4 February 1782

Printed from the MS in the Yale University Library. First printed, Toynbee *Supp.* ii. 163. Reprinted in J. M. Osborn, 'Horace Walpole and Edmond Malone,' in *Horace Walpole: Writer, Politician, and Connoisseur*, ed. W. H. Smith, New Haven, 1967, p. 307. Damer-Waller; the MS was sold Sotheby's 5 Dec. 1921 (first Waller Sale), lot 157, to Dobell; acquired in 1935 by Russell G. Pruden, of New Haven, who bequeathed it to the Yale Library in 1949.

Feb. 4.

MR Malone presents his compliments to Mr Walpole, and takes the liberty of sending him a very hasty essay[1] on the Chatterton business, which for obvious reasons he does not publicly avow.[2]

To EDMOND MALONE, Monday 4 February 1782

Printed from the MS now WSL. First printed, Cunningham ix. 492–4. Reprinted, Toynbee xii. 152–4; J. M. Osborn, 'Horace Walpole and Edmond Malone,' in *Horace Walpole: Writer, Politician, and Connoisseur*, ed. W. H. Smith, New Haven, 1967, pp. 307–9. The MS is untraced until sold Sotheby's 3 Aug. 1858 (S. W. Singer Sale), lot 103, to Peter Cunningham; resold Sotheby's 17 March 1876 (W. Ashley Sale), lot 446 (with another letter), to Waller; offered by Waller, Cat. No. 120 (1878), lot 289; sold Sotheby's 28 May 1946 (Lord Cunliffe Sale), lot 888, to Maggs for WSL.

Berkeley Square, Feb. 4, 1782.

YOU have made me a very valuable present,[1] Sir, for which I was earnestly wishing, as your criticisms are far too good to be committed only to the few hours of life of a newspaper. You have produced many new and very forcible arguments against the champions of Rowley, and pointed their own artillery against them victoriously. Indeed I wonder so acute a writer as Mr Bryant[2] could relax into

1. *Cursory Observations on the Poems Attributed to Thomas Rowley, a Priest of the Fifteenth Century: with Some Remarks on the Commentaries on those Poems, by the Rev. Dr Jeremiah Milles, Dean of Exeter, and Jacob Bryant, Esq.; and a Salutary Proposal Addressed to the Friends of those Gentlemen*, 1782. Malone sent HW a copy of the second edition, 'revised and augmented' (now WSL; Hazen, *Cat. of HW's Lib.*, No. 3690:16). The pamphlet is an enlarged version of the article signed 'Misopiclerus' that appeared in GM 1781, li. 555–9, 609–15. See *ante* ca Dec. 1781 and CHATTERTON 363.

2. The pamphlet was published anonymously. For HW's opinion of it see following letter.

1. See previous letter, n. 1.

2. Jacob Bryant (1715–1804), fellow of King's College, Cambridge; classical schol-

so many assumptions—but when he set out with begging the question that Rowley wrote in all sorts of provincial dialects (which a monk confined to his convent was of all men the least likely to be conversant in) I do not believe he expected that you would discover that Rowley not only employed every *patois,* but the language of two entire centuries. This is foiling him at his own weapons. So you have in the specimens you have produced of commencements of such a series of old poems[3] both prior and subsequent to the supposed era,[4] and which no more resemble the modulation of the imaginary Rowley, than the first leathern waggons that were called coaches, are like to a modern varnished chariot. In fact, if there is any such discriminating faculty in us by which we distinguish between the hobble of a rhymer of the 15th century, and a poet of the 18th, we cannot be in doubt a moment.

Mr Bryant and Dr Milles[5] have in vain resorted to the fastnesses of uncouth old story, as the Welsh did into the precipices of Wales, and thought nobody would follow them but such persevering climbers into the clouds as themselves—yet, Sir, you have baffled them there too; and I own I am flattered, that the same argument struck me in a letter I wrote to Mr Cole[6] of Milton, on the first publication of Mr Bryant's book, namely, that the MS the most likely to have been found in one of Canning's[7] six chests, was a diary[8]—nay, I find since that, that there was such a diary by Turgot.[9]

ar; author of *Observations upon the Poems of Thomas Rowley: in which the Authenticity of those Poems Is Ascertained* (in two parts), 1781. HW's copy, now WSL, is Hazen, *Cat. of HW's Lib.* No. 3690:5,6. HW's annotations in this copy are printed in CHATTERTON 351–7.

3. Malone quotes the opening lines of fifteen medieval and early Renaissance poems, beginning with *Piers Plowman* and ending with verses by Skelton.

4. The fifteenth century, when the fictitious priest Thomas Rowley was alleged to have written the poems composed by Chatterton.

5. See *ante* 20 Oct. 1767, n. 1. Milles was the editor of *Poems, Supposed to Have Been Written . . . by Thomas Rowley . . . with a Commentary in which the Antiquity of them is Considered, and Defended,* 1782. HW's copy, now in the BM, is Hazen, op. cit., No. 3690:1. HW's notes in this copy are printed in CHATTERTON 331–43.

6. HW to William Cole 30 Dec. 1781 (COLE ii. 286–9).

7. William Canynges (ca 1399–1474), merchant and sometime mayor of Bristol. He rebuilt the church of St Mary Redcliff at Bristol; in Chatterton's fiction he was a friend and patron of Thomas Rowley.

8. 'It appears by the evidence that Canninge left six chests of MSS, and that Chatterton got possession of some or several. Now what was therein *so probably* as a diary drawn up by Canninge himself or some churchwarden, or wardens, or by a monk or monks? . . . Hypothesis for hypothesis, I am sure this is as rational an one, as the supposition that six chests were filled with poems never else heard of' (HW to Cole 30 Dec. 1781, COLE ii. 289).

9. (d. 1115), Bp of St Andrews, 1109. Chatterton alleged that *A Discorse on Brystowe* was Rowley's translation of Turgot's 'Saxonnes Latyn' history of Bristol,

Of all the forgeries, the most preposterous to be sure is that of Canning's *cabinet* of curiosities;[10] the poor lad,[11] before he came to London, might be ignorant enough to write it—but ignorance is not a term coarse enough for any one past fifteen who can swallow so gross and clumsy an imposture. A picture by Vandyck in that collection, as you say, Sir, could not augment the absurdity, it is already so complete—nor is any man who credits it, fit to be reasoned with. It would be flattering him with seeming to take him for a rational being.

I observed the other day in the first volume of the *Biographia Dramatica* that Mr Thomas Broughton,[12] who wrote in the *Biogr[aphia] Britann[ica]*[13] was possessed of the cure of St Mary Ratcliffe in 1744, and was buried in that church in 1774.[14] Is it credible that so literary a man should have never heard of the famous MSS? He wrote a play[15] too, and consequently was something [of] a poet—and yet did he never take the least notice of such treasures! Is it possible that he never should have heard of them, though they passed into so many hands? Mr Broughton lived between the period when Vertue copied the painter's bill,[16] and that in which Chatterton first saw this mine of poetry.

I beg your pardon, Sir, for troubling you with so long a letter. I intended only to thank you—but the pleasure your book gave me[17]—in which I fear your kindness to me had a little share too—

containing Rowley's 'emendals' (emendations). The *Discorse* was entirely Chatterton's invention, there being no such 'diary' account by Turgot (E. H. W. Meyerstein, *A Life of Thomas Chatterton*, 1930, pp. 109, 547).

10. Described in the *Yellow Roll* (dated '1451'), a parchment fabricated by Chatterton. Malone, in his *Cursory Observations on the Poems Attributed to Thomas Rowley*, 1782, p. 25, had written: 'Cannynge too must be furnished with a cabinet of coins and other rarities; and there being a private printing press at Strawberry Hill (the only one perhaps in England), the Bristol mayor must likewise have one.'

11. Chatterton.

12. (1704–74), vicar of Bedminster and of St Mary Redcliff 1744–72; prebendary of Salisbury 1744–74; miscellaneous writer and divine.

13. Broughton contributed the articles signed 'T' in the first edition of the *Biographia Britannica*, 7 vols, 1747–66.

14. See D. E. Baker, *Biographia Dramatica*, rev. and enl. Isaac Reed, 1782, i. 47.

15. His musical drama *Hercules*, 1745, was the libretto for Handel's oratorio (P. H. Lang, *George Frideric Handel*, New York, 1966, pp. 421–2).

16. HW mistakenly believed that a passage transcribed by George Vertue 'from a book belonging to the church of St Mary Ratcliffe at Bristol' was an early painter's bill, and he printed the passage in *Anecdotes of Painting* (*Works* iii. 46). Chatterton forged an imitation of the passage; both were later printed together in Chatterton's *Works*, 1803, iii. 303–6. But there is no evidence that Vertue ever visited Bristol. See CHATTERTON 133 and nn. 107, 109.

17. George Steevens, the Shakespeare scholar, wrote Malone 18 Jan. 1782 that his *Cursory Observations* ridiculing Bryant and Milles 'afforded me a hearty laugh. I had the honour of a conversation this

drew me into a conversation beyond what was fair. I have the honour
to be with great gratitude and respect Sir

Your most obedient humble servant

Hor. Walpole

To John Henderson, Monday 4 March 1782

Printed from a copy of the MS in the possession of Mr Martin Heath, Ashton
House, Worton, Devizes, Wilts, kindly supplied by the late Roland Heath. First
printed, Cunningham viii. 172. Reprinted, Toynbee xii. 186–7. For the history
of the MS see *ante* 16 April 1781.
Address: To Mr Henderson in Buckingham Street.

Berkeley Square, March 4, 1782.

I AM afraid, dear Sir, that I am not robust enough to bustle through
the great crowd that, I hope, you will have at your benefit;[1] but
as I am not deaf as well as lame, it is very hard that I am not to
hear you repeat your *own* verses,[2] which I had rather hear than those
of others, though you do more justice to the latter, for your modesty
was so great that if your own had not been excellent, I should not
have discovered their merit by your repetition of them. I will certainly search for the book[3] you want, if I have it, the first moment
I can go to Strawberry Hill, which I doubt will not be for a week
or ten days.[4] I shall be extremely glad to contribute a mite to a poem
I like so much; and when we are better acquainted, as I hope we

morning with Mr Walpole, whose sentiments perfectly coincide with yours' (MS
in the Osborn Collection, Yale University
Library).

1. 'For the benefit of Mr Henderson.
At the Theatre Royal in Covent Garden,
Tuesday March 19 will be revived *The
Double Dealer*. Written by Congreve; and
now carefully revised and corrected, by
expunging the exceptionable passages.
. . . Tickets to be had of Mr Henderson,
at his house in Buckingham Street, York
Buildings' (*Public Adv.* 2 March). See
London Stage Pt V, i. 505.
2. Presumably verses that Henderson

had composed to be spoken at his benefit
performance on 19 March. He was the
author of various occasional poems, some
of which were published, with biographical anecdotes by John Ireland, in *Letters
and Poems by the late Mr John Henderson*, 1786.
3. *Palladis Tamia; Wit's Treasury Being the Second Part of Wits Common-
wealth*, by Francis Meres, 1598. HW's copy
(untraced) is Hazen, *Cat. of HW's Lib.*,
No. 1755. See following letter and n. 2.
4. He was at SH on 11 March (Mann
ix. 253), returning to Berkeley Square by
the 14th.

shall be, you will know that I am no flatterer; nor would I do so base an act as to commend verses highly that I thought indifferent. It would be flattery, if never having seen you on the stage but twice,[5] I should tell you that you excel Mr Garrick. It is very sincere, when I protest that I admired your verses extremely, and that I thought him a very indifferent poet, or rather no poet at all—I shall be very impatient to be confirmed in this preference: in the meantime give me leave to thank you for *The School for Scandal*,[6] for your ticket,[7] and for the real obligation I have to you for saving my scenes from the *Biographia Dramatica*[8]—but pray do not imagine that I think I have paid all my debts by the enclosed little note.[9] I am Sir

Your grateful humble servant

Hor. Walpole

To John Henderson, Thursday 14 March 1782

Printed from a copy of the MS in the possession of Mr Martin Heath, Ashton House, Worton, Devizes, Wilts, kindly supplied by the late Roland Heath. First printed, Cunningham viii. 177. Reprinted, Toynbee xii. 193–4. For the history of the MS see *ante* 16 April 1781.

Address: Mr Henderson in Buckingham Street, Strand.

Berkeley Square, March 14, 1782.

Dear Sir,

I WAS at Strawberry Hill yesterday and hunted all over my library for *Palladis Tamia*, the book you wanted,[1] but could not find it.

5. In Dec. 1777, when Henderson appeared as Brutus in William Shirley's *The Roman Sacrifice*, and on 17 Nov. 1781, when he played Austin in *The Count of Narbonne*. HW wrote Lady Ossory 23 Dec. 1777: 'I have been at another new play, *The Roman Sacrifice*. . . . I went to see it, as I had never seen Henderson, and thought I could judge him better in a new part—but either the part was so bad, or he wants to copy, that I should not have found out that he was at all superior to all the other actors' (Ossory i. 409–10).

6. A political satire dealing with the American war, written in imitation of Sheridan's play but not intended for the stage; published in London in 1779. HW's copy (probably the copy presented to him by Henderson, although it lacks an inscription) is now wsl; Hazen, op. cit., No. 1810:29:5.

7. A ticket to Henderson's benefit.

8. See *ante* 16 April 1781 and n. 9.

9. Missing.

1. See previous letter.

I did not remember having it, nor is it in the catalogue of my books,[2] though that is no certain rule, as I have bought a great many since the catalogue was made, and have neglected to enter them.[3] However, I do believe that Mr Malone is mistaken in thinking I bought a book, of which I have not the least idea, though I do not pretend that my memory is as good as it was. I hope this non-possession will not make me forfeit a sight of your poem, by the specimens of which you did not seem to want assistance from an old author. Will you ask Mr Malone what the size is of *Palladis Tamia,* and whether in verse or prose? I hope I never looked into it, or that it is very bad, since I recollect nothing about it—and if it is not good, you will have no loss. Still if you can describe it to me, I will search again.

Yours most sincerely

Hor. Walpole

To Robert Henry,[1] Saturday 16 March 1782

Printed from a photostat of the MS among the Moncreiff of Tulliebole papers deposited in the Scottish Record Office. First printed in R. S. Woof, 'Some Horace Walpole Letters,' N & Q 1965, ccx. 24–5 (misdated 'March 15, 1782'). The MS presumably came into the possession of Sir Henry Moncreiff Wellwood (1750–1827), 8th Bt, one of Robert Henry's executors, at the time he was writing his short 'Life of Robert Henry' for the sixth volume of Henry's *History of Great Britain,* published posthumously in 1793; it remained among the Moncreiff family papers, now the property of the 5th Baron Moncreiff of Tulliebole.

Address: To the Reverend Dr Henry at Edinburgh. *Postmark:* 16 ⟨MR⟩.

Berkeley Square, March 16, 1782.

I SHOULD receive with great pleasure, Sir, the honour you do me, if I had any title to it, or were I not conscious that I have very slender pretensions to it on the foundation on which you are

2. The Manuscript Catalogue of the Main Library at SH, compiled early in 1763 by an unidentified clerk. *Palladis Tamia* was entered in the catalogue as 'Mere's Wit's Treasury,' which probably explains why HW was unable to locate it (Hazen, *Cat. of HW's Lib.* i. xxii; ii. 83, 251). See *ante* 9 Nov. 1776, headnote.
3. HW himself entered books in the Manuscript Catalogue from 1763 to 1766;

later additions were made by his printer and secretary, Thomas Kirgate (ibid. i. xxi).

———

1. (1718–90), D.D., 1771; historian and divine (Dalrymple 168 n. 1). This is the earliest known letter in HW's correspondence with Henry; the MS came to light after the rest was printed in Dalrymple.

so obliging as to say[2] you send me your *History*;[3] but I am too well acquainted with that, and with my own superficial writings, to suppose that such straws could have contributed to so deep-laid and solid a structure. I have only flitted over parts of our story here and there, and, I doubt, on those least material. It would not sound mere grateful flattery, if I were to expatiate on the various new lights in which you have placed our annals, and in which I may say you have expounded them by searching to the source, and looking for the origin of actions in the manners and usages of the several ages, less than in imaginary politics, at which we rather guess, than of which any evidences are preserved. I do not mean that princes in all ages have not their politics; but when we judge of them by our own, we may follow very erroneous guides, for undoubtedly even the modes of thinking are influenced in part by the complexion and habits of the times: nor would the ablest monarch or minister accomplish his views, if he was totally unacquainted with the cast of thought in those he is to govern or put in action. You have helped us, Sir, to read every period of our story with a map of the understandings of each age in our hands; and the plan of your work[4] is so new and so just, that whencesoever you took materials, the design, arrangement and utility can be claimed by no man; and though I should be proud to have furnished a hint, it would be strange vanity in me to claim any relation to your work, though you should be candid enough to pay a passenger who had removed a pebble out of your way, and that only for his own amusement. Thus, Sir, while I must deny your having any debt to me, the larger is mine to you; and it is with great gratitude I own that I am

     Sir

Your most obliged and obedient humble servant

HOR. WALPOLE

PS. I wrote this six days ago, Sir, on receiving the honour of yours, but kept it back till I should receive your volumes. However I have

2. Henry's letter to HW is missing.

3. *The History of Great Britain, from the First Invasion of It by the Romans under Julius Caesar, Written on a New Plan*, 6 vols, 1771–93. The first four volumes were published 1771–81. HW's copy (untraced) is Hazen, *Cat. of HW's Lib.*, No. 543.

4. Henry's *History* is divided into periods, beginning with Roman invasions and ending with the death of Henry VIII. Each period is treated in seven different areas: civil and military affairs, religion, government and law, education, the arts, commerce, and manners.

determined now to send it away, lest you should think me remiss, or indifferent to the valuable present you make me.

I hope it will not look like vanity if I suppose that my doubts on the story of Richard III[5] may have struck you[6]—yet instead of suffering myself to be flattered by that imagination, I very sincerely beg you, Sir, to examine the question impartially, and be assured that I wish to have everybody decide by his own judgment, to which an historian is especially obliged. I did call my work nothing but *Doubts*. They are still so on some points, though I have found very corroborating circumstances since on the side to which I incline.[7] I will own fairly, that, at first, opposition and the petulance of controversy carried me, prejudiced me farther than was fitting, and I did make replies to my antagonists[8] with less tenderness than I ought, both from finding their answers[9] very weak, and from *knowing* that the motives of some of them were personal to *me* not to the question. However, I did not publish my replies,[10] though I am sure that the matter, if not the manner, would strengthen the side to which I incline. I have no doubt of Richard being a bad man, but as there is not the smallest reason for thinking him a fool, I cannot believe the silly stories that are told of him, and the still sillier steps which Henry VII took to prove them true,[11] for though he was not a fool neither, power, which knows itself too strong to be contradicted, is apt to make use of looser logic, than men dare have recourse to, who dispute on equal terms—but I fear I am rather trying to draw you to my opinion, than doing what I really desire, persuade you to remember your own dignity, and speak impartially.

5. In *Historic Doubts on the Life and Reign of King Richard the Third*, 1768.

6. Henry wrote HW 3 March 1783: 'Your *Doubts* put me upon my guard, and if there is anything commendable in my short sketch, it is really owing to them' (Dalrymple 169).

7. In the Preface to *Historic Doubts* HW writes: 'Many of the crimes imputed to Richard seemed improbable; and, what was stronger, contrary to his interest. . . . as it was easy to perceive, under all the glare of encomiums which historians have heaped on the wisdom of Henry the Seventh, that he was a mean and unfeeling tyrant, I suspected that they had blackened his rival, till Henry, by the contrast, should appear in a kind of amiable light' (*Works* ii. 109).

8. See *ante* 29 March 1772, n. 2.

9. For their titles and dates see Hazen, *Bibl. of HW* 72–3.

10. They were published posthumously in HW's *Works*, 1798.

11. HW wrote Henry 15 March 1783: 'There can be no doubt of Henry VII having done his utmost to suppress all truth of the preceding period, and to blacken the lawful line [of royal succession], that of York. One is warranted then to receive with caution the partial evidence he gave or tolerated, and to suspect that he who fabricated false, stifled or corrupted genuine evidence' (Dalrymple 174).

To John Nichols, April 1782

Printed from the MS now wsl. First printed, Nichols, *Lit. Anec.* iii. 301. Reprinted, Toynbee xii. 219. The MS is untraced until sold by Walter T. Spencer to wsl, Sept. 1932.

Dated approximately by the endorsement.

Endorsed by Nichols: (This from Mr Walpole) April 1782.

As it is said to be so much desired, the author consents to let the whole of the letter on Chatterton be printed in the *Gentleman's Magazine*,[1] but not in a separate pamphlet.

To Charles Rogers, Thursday 18 April 1782

Printed for the first time from the MS now wsl. The MS is untraced until sold Parke-Bernet 1 Nov. 1950 (Oliver Barrett Sale), lot 1118, to Brick Row for wsl.

Address: To Charles Rogers Esq. in Lawrence Poutney Lane. *Postmark:* SHAW.

Berkeley Square, April 18, 1782.

MR H. Walpole has been out of town[1] or should have thanked Mr Rogers sooner for his obliging present of his *Dante.*[2]

---

1. The complete text of HW's *Letter to the Editor of the Miscellanies of Thomas Chatterton*, SH, 1779, was reprinted serially in GM 1782, lii. 189–95, 247–50, 300, 347–8. 'We are happy,' Nichols wrote (p. 189), 'in obliging our numerous readers by presenting it to them entire, with the full permission of the author.'

1. He was at SH 14–16 April (Mason ii. 233, 236).

2. *The Inferno of Dante Translated,* 1782. Rogers's English translation into blank verse was dedicated to Sir Edward Walpole. HW's copy is Hazen, *Cat. of HW's Lib.,* No. 3222:18:3.

To John Baynes,[1] Friday 24 May 1782

Printed from the MS now WSL. First printed, Toynbee xii. 255. The MS is untraced until sold Sotheby's 19 June 1899 (William Wright Sale), lot 1439; *penes* Maggs Bros., 1904; later acquired by Charles Sessler, Philadelphia, and sold by Sessler to WSL, Aug. 1957.

Endorsed by Baynes on the address leaf: Mr Hor. Walpole. May 25th 1782.

Address: To John Baines Esq. in Coney Court No. 11, Gray's Inn. *Postmark:* PENNY POST PAID.

Berkeley Square, May 24, 1782.

I AM ashamed to trouble you with a letter to no purpose, Sir, but Mr Mason having desired me to resolve a question in which you want information,[2] I thought it would look like neglect, if I was silent upon it. It seems you wish to know where is to be found a ballad by the Duke of Wharton,[3] of which I have quoted two lines in the *Royal and Noble Authors.*[4] I am ashamed to say, Sir, that I cannot tell you, nor can recollect at this late period whether I transcribed them from any book, or retained them by memory. The latter is most probable, for though I was but an infant when the Duke left England,[5] his exploits were so recent, and I heard so much about him in my childhood and youth, that when I wrote his article,[6] his story was perfectly fresh in my memory. The case is very different now, and I cannot at all recollect whether I ever saw the ballad either in print or manuscript.[7] It is possible that Mr Nichols[8] the

1. (1758–87), fellow of Trinity College, Cambridge, 1778–87; lawyer and miscellaneous writer (GM 1787, lvii pt ii. 742–3; Nichols, *Lit. Anec.* viii. 113–15).

2. Mason wrote HW 18 May 1782: 'The *one* Baines whom you mentioned in your last but one is an ingenious young Yorkshire man, a student in Gray's Inn, who . . . wants much to know whether that ballad of the Duke of Wharton's which you have quoted in your *Noble Authors* . . . be in print or in MS, if in print where he can find it. I should be much obliged to you, if you will give him a single line of intelligence on this matter. . . . I know not why he wants it, but I wish to oblige him as he has been very useful to me, and may be more so' (MASON ii. 247).

3. Philip Wharton (1698–1731), 2d M. of Wharton, 1715; cr. (1718) D. of Wharton; rake and Jacobite.

4. The duke he drew out half his sword.
——the guard drew out the rest.

HW says that the lines were 'in a song he [Wharton] made on being seized by the guard in Saint James's Park, for singing the Jacobite air, *The king shall have his own again*' (*A Catalogue of the Royal and Noble Authors of England, Works* i. 443).

5. Wharton left England to attend the court of the exiled Pretender at Vienna in June 1725, when HW was seven years old.

6. In 1757 ('Short Notes,' GRAY i. 29).

7. HW wrote Mason 25 May 1782: 'I did write a few lines last night to Mr Baines

printer can tell you where it is to be found, if in print.⁹ I wish I could give you any more sure direction, and am Sir

Your most obedient humble servant

Hor. Walpole

To the Earl of Buchan,¹ Sunday 2 June 1782

Printed for the first time from a photostat of an 'Extract of a letter from the Honourable Horace Walpole to the Earl of Buchan' in Buchan's hand in the University of Glasgow Library (MS Murray 502/69). The MS is untraced until it was acquired by the Glasgow lawyer and book collector David Murray, who presented his library of printed books and MSS to the University of Glasgow in 1927. The 'Extract' was kindly brought to our attention in 1959 by Mr James G. Lamb. The punctuation has been modernized. The original letter is missing.

Berkeley Square, June 2d 1782.

A PROPOS the Lady Margaret Douglas,² mother of the Lord Darnley,³ I did mean to ask your Lordship a question. I have somewhere read, I do not recollect where,⁴ that she [was] married to

that *you* might lose no merit with him, but I could give him no satisfaction. I have utterly forgot every circumstance relative to that ballad. Probably as I lived in that century, I retained the lines by memory, but whether I did or not I cannot tell now' (Mason ii. 249–50).

8. John Nichols, printer and bookseller; HW's occasional correspondent.

9. The *Gentleman's Magazine* 1791, lxi pt i. 536, printed a letter of inquiry signed 'G. G.' addressed to the editor: 'Did any of your correspondents ever meet with this ballad [by Wharton]? Mr Walpole, who has been applied to, can recollect nothing more of it.' The source of the ballad has not been found.

1. David Steuart Erskine (1742–1829), styled Lord Cardross 1747–67; 11th E. of Buchan, 1767; antiquary; founder of the Society of the Antiquaries of Scotland. Another letter to Buchan is printed *post* 2 Oct. 1783; the rest of HW's correspon-

dence with him is included in Dalrymple.

2. (1515–78), dau. of Margaret Queen of Scots by her second husband, Archibald Douglas, 6th E. of Angus, m. (1544) Matthew Stuart, 4th E. of Lennox; niece of Henry VIII.

3. Henry Stuart (1545–67), eldest surviving son of the 4th E. of Lennox; styled Lord Darnley; second husband of Mary Queen of Scots.

4. Possibly in Holinshed's *Chronicles,* where it is related that on 'The eight[h] of June [1536] began the Parliament, during which the Lord Thomas Howard, without the King's assent, affi[anc]ed the Lady Margaret Douglas, daughter to the Queen of Scots, and niece to the King, for which act he was attainted of treason, . . . and so he died in the Tower, and she remained long there as prisoner' (*The Chronicles of England, Scotland, and Ireland,* 1587, iii. 940). HW's copy of this edition is Hazen, *Cat. of HW's Lib.,* No. 597.

her second husband Lord Thomas Howard[5] and by him was mother of the remarkable Lady Douglas Sheffield,[6] wife of the famous Leicester.[7]—Pray, my Lord, was this so?—I have lately purchased out of Scotland a most precious historic jewel,[8] a golden heart enamel, with [a] variety of emblematic devices and Scottish mottoes, made by order of Lady Margaret on the murder of her husband, the Regent Lenox, and worn (probably) about her neck by a chain of gold or pearls. Your Lordship, it is likely, has seen this curiosity, which came this winter to England on sale.[9]

The portrait of Dr Arbuthnot[10] belongs to the Earl of Bristol[11] and I shall inform myself about it as early as I can find an opportunity. Whence Larrey[12] took his portrait of James IV of the Scots[13] I cannot tell; he has not specified any of his authorities.[14] Your Gambarini[15] picture of the Countess of Desmond[16] I very much suspect; all the pictures said to be hers are of Rembrandt's mother. Mr Pennant[17] gave a print of one of them (because he had it engraved[18])

5. (d. 1536), second son of Thomas Howard, 2d D. of Norfolk, by his second marriage to Agnes, dau. of Hugh Tilney (Collins, *Peerage*, 1812, i. 81; GEC).

6. See *ante* 29 Jan. 1777, n. 1. She was daughter of William Howard (ca 1510–73), cr. (1554) Bn Howard of Effingham, and the niece of the Lord Thomas Howard referred to by HW.

7. Robert Dudley (1532 *or* 1533–88), cr. (1564) E. of Leicester.

8. 'A golden heart set with jewels, and ornamented with emblematic figures enamelled, and Scottish mottos; made by order of the Lady Margaret Douglas, mother of Henry Lord Darnley, in memory of her husband Matthew Stuart, Earl of Lenox and Regent of Scotland, murdered by the papists' ('Des. of SH,' *Works* ii. 477). The jewel was bought for Queen Victoria at the SH Sale (xv. 60) and is now in the Royal Collection. A print entitled 'The Lennox Jewel in the Tribune, Strawberry Hill' appears in Thomas Mackinlay's extra-illustrated copy of the SH Sale Catalogue, ii. 154 (now WSL). The jewel is described in Joan Evans, *A History of Jewellery 1100–1870*, 1953, and illustrated facing pp. 102, 126. See HW to Buchan 29 Nov. 1792 (DALRYMPLE 233–4).

9. We do not know from whom HW purchased the jewel.

10. John Arbuthnot (1667–1735), phy-

sician and author; friend of Pope and Swift. The portrait, by an unidentified artist, is still at Ickworth, Suffolk; see ibid. 164 n. 3.

11. Frederick Augustus Hervey (1730–1803), Bp of Derry, 1768; 4th E. of Bristol, 1779.

12. Isaac de Larrey (ca 1638–1719), sieur de Granchamp et de Courménil; French historian.

13. (1473–1513), K. of Scotland 1488–1513.

14. 'From the exact resemblance of Larrey's portrait of this king to Lord Buchan's picture of him, it seems to have been taken from an original bust or figure in stone' (note in Buchan's hand in the 'Extract'). Larrey's *Histoire d'Angleterre, d'Ecosse, et d'Irlande*, Rotterdam, 1697–1713, i. 21, contains an engraving by Gerard Valck after Adriaen van der Werff's portrait of James IV. HW did not own a copy of Larrey's work.

15. Giuseppe Gambarini (1680–1725), Italian painter.

16. See *ante* 17 Sept. 1757, n. 3.

17. Thomas Pennant, HW's correspondent.

18. The engraving, after the picture at Dupplin Castle, seat of the Earl of Kinnoull, appears in Pennant's *A Tour in Scotland; MDCCLXIX*, 3d edn, Warrington, 1774, plate VI, facing p. 74.

after I had convinced him it was spurious. They all are copied from the one at Windsor, on the back of which I found, *Rembrandt's mother given to the King by Sir Robert Kerr*.[19] In King Charles's *Catalogue*[20] it is called so too and said to be *given by the Earl of Ancram,* which was afterwards Sir Robert Kerr's title.[21]

I much applaud your Lordship's intention of securing your collection by a perpetual trust, which we could not easily do in England.[22] Collections seldom sell for what they cost an[d] when once sold and dispersed, most of the articles perish or are sold for next to nothing. The chief utility of collections consists in their being kept together where they may be consulted. When they are scattered they become no better than the scattered leaves of a book. This is particularly the case with respect to libraries and collections in natural history: nay, of portraits too, more liable to be undervalued and the names to be forgotten or misapplied.

With regard to the controversy on Rowley, it is one of those problems, my Lord, that I believe will never be cleared, so as to unite mankind in one opinion. Though I have been forced to declare myself on one side,[23] yet as Chatterton destroyed the proofs of the authenticity of the poems, if such he ever had:[24] and as, if an impostor, he was a greater wonder himself, it is not to be supposed but belief will fluctuate, and prejudice adhere to the party it has espoused, since the first cannot receive proofs, and the other certainly will not be convinced by circumstantial evidence alone. However, the ingenuity of Mr Bryant[25] will always give weight to the

19. (1578–1654), cr. (1633) E. of Ancram.

20. *A Catalogue and Description of King Charles the First's Capital Collection of Pictures . . . and other Curiosities,* compiled by Abraham Van Der Doort, 1757, p. 150, No. 101. HW's copy (now wsl) of the *Catalogue,* which was prepared for publication by George Vertue and seen through the press by HW, is Hazen, op. cit., No. 2478.

21. HW printed this information as a 'Note' on an unpaged leaf that he had inserted in the remaining copies of his *Fugitive Pieces,* 1758; see *Works* i. 217. HW's presentation copy to Pennant, dated 'April 14th 1774' (now wsl), lacks the leaf (Hazen, *SH Bibl.* 41). For Pennant's rejection of HW's theory see COLE i. 329, 332, 339.

22. Since Lord Buchan's letter to HW

is missing, the details of his plan for creating a perpetual trust of his collection are not known. Possibly it formed part of his scheme for creating a 'Temple of Caledonian Fame' to be administered by the Society of the Antiquaries of Scotland, which he had founded in 1780 (DALRYMPLE 138 n. 2). Unlike English law, with its rules against perpetuities, Scots law took a benevolent attitude towards them; see T. B. Smith, *The United Kingdom: The Development of its Laws and Constitutions,* 1955, ii. 899–900.

23. See *ante* 11 Jan. 1779 and nn. 1, 2.

24. HW never saw any of Chatterton's forgeries, many of which are now in the British Museum.

25. See HW to Edmond Malone *ante* 4 Feb. 1782, n. 2.

Rowleyans, though the wit of the *Archæologic Epistle*[26] will have still greater weight with most men, and not suffer the Rowleians to be popular. The controversy about Ossian[27] will not be more easily or sooner decided; nor does it much signify whether either is. The world is fortunate, when agitated only by the bloodless, though abusive squabbles of literary men. Their best termination is ridicule, a more lasting umpire than a conqueror or an inquisitor. I have the honour of being with great respect, my Lord,

Your Lordship's most obedient humble servant

Hor. Walpole

To Benjamin Ibbot, Sunday 2 June 1782

Printed for the first time from a photostat of the MS among the Fletcher of Saltoun papers deposited in the National Library of Scotland, kindly furnished by Mr Alan S. Bell. The MS is untraced until sold Sotheby's 25 April 1843 (Jeremiah Milles Sale), lot 186, to Bagiter; probably resold Sotheby's 13 Dec. 1854 ('Another Property'), lot 419, to Waller; later added to a collection of autographs that is now part of the Fletcher of Saltoun papers.

Address: To Benjamin Ibbott Esq. in Dartmouth Street, Westminster.

Berkeley Square, June 2d 1782.

IT is so long, Sir, since I had the pleasure of hearing of you,[1] that I concluded you was retired into the country and never came to London. I am sorry to hear that you are much more disagreeably confined. I cannot say that I am totally a prisoner, though now and frequently laid up with the gout. You are in the right, Sir; we must submit, and in old age cannot expect to be free from all disorders.

I will certainly show your letter[2] and your son's[3] to General Con-

26. *An Archæological Epistle to the Reverend . . . Jeremiah Milles,* a verse satire published anonymously by William Mason in March 1782, lampooning Milles's defense of Chatterton's Rowley poems. For HW's good opinion of it see Mason ii. 199–200.

27. That is, the Ossianic epic *Fingal,* written by James Macpherson and published in 1761. HW believed that 'the success of Ossian's poems had suggested the idea [of the Rowley poems]' (HW to William Bewley 23 May 1778, Chatterton 124).

———

1. The most recent letter in their surviving correspondence is printed *ante* 18 Nov. 1773.

2. Missing.

3. Doubtless Henry Ibbot, commissioned as a second lieutenant in the Royal Artillery 20 Jan. 1780, at this time stationed at Gibraltar (*Army Lists,* 1782, p. 282). His letter is also missing.

way[4] the first moment I see him, which probably will be in a day or two.[5] I shall recommend your suit[6] warmly, though, if he can grant, I am sure very little solicitation will be necessary. I say *if,* because I am quite ignorant whether it is a common or extraordinary case. In the former, General Conway is so humane, that he will want no incitement—if improper for him to grant, I could not be so unjust to him as to press it. I might have stayed till I had spoken to him, but I would not seem a moment to neglect answering a letter from so old an acquaintance.

I am Sir

Your obedient humble servant

Hor. Walpole

To Benjamin Ibbot, Sunday 9 June 1782

Printed from a photostat of the MS in the Pierpont Morgan Library. First printed, Toynbee *Supp.* i. 285–6. For the history of the MS see *ante* 24 Sept. 1773.

Toynbee dated the letter 'June 30, 1782.' However, HW's letter to Ibbot *ante* 2 June 1782 states that he expected to see Conway 'probably . . . in a day or two,' and his letter of 10 June to Sir Horace Mann indicates that a meeting had recently taken place (Mann ix. 286). 'Sunday evening' in the present letter must therefore be 9 June, and the meeting 'five days ago' must have occurred on 4 June, as HW had predicted.

Address: To Benjamin Ibbott Esq. in Dartmouth Street, Westminster. *Postmark:* PENNY POST PAID. 3 O'CLOCK.

Sunday evening.

GENERAL Conway has been so very busy, Sir, that though I gave him your letter and your son's[1] five days ago, I could not see him again till today, when he told me how glad he should have been to have obliged you, and how concerned he is that he cannot, but that it is impossible for him to give leave for a person to leave Gibraltar just now on account of illness, as the Governor of Gibraltar[2] can only be the proper judge whether it is fit, and not the Com-

---

4. Conway, HW's first cousin and intimate friend, had been appointed commander-in-chief when the new administration was formed in March of this year.

5. HW probably saw Conway on Tuesday, 4 June; see following letter.

6. A request 'to leave Gibraltar . . . on account of illness' (ibid.).

———

1. See previous letter.

2. George Augustus Eliott (1717–90), K.B., 1783; cr. (1787) Bn Heathfield; Gen., 1778; Gov. of Gibraltar 1776–87.

mander-in-Chief at this distance. I am truly sorry, Sir, that my application has been so fruitless, as I should have been very happy to have obliged you,[3] had it been in the power of

Sir

Your obedient humble servant

Hor. Walpole

To Thomas Pennant, Thursday 13 June 1782

Printed for the first time from the MS now wsl. For the history of the MS see *ante* 25 May 1773.
Address: To Thomas Pennant Esq. at Downing, Flintshire. *Postmark:* 13 IV. GC.

Berkeley Square, June 13, 1782.

I HAD read your new *Journey*,[1] dear Sir, with great pleasure and entertainment, before I received the favour of your letter,[2] in which you was so good as to send me the order for the six portraits,[3] for which I return you a thousand thanks. I hope I have not taken too great a liberty in begging Mr White[4] to add the bust of Lady Digby[5]—but as I would not be too impertinent, I would not tell him

3. See *post* 3 July 1782.

———

1. *The Journey from Chester to London*, 1782. See *ante* 25 May 1773, n. 2. HW wrote Cole 1 June 1782: 'I have just finished Mr Pennant's new volume, parts of which amused me though I knew every syllable that was worth knowing before, for there is not a word of novelty' (Cole ii. 323). HW's copy (untraced), part of a nine-volume collection of Pennant's works, is Hazen, *Cat. of HW's Lib.*, No. 547.

2. Missing.

3. These six engraved 'heads' were among the twenty-two plates executed by various engravers for Pennant's *Journey*. The subjects are Catherine, Countess of Suffolk, second wife of Thomas Howard, cr. (1603) E. of Suffolk (pl. XI, after the picture at Gorhambury); George Calvert, cr. (1625) Bn Baltimore (pl. XII, after the picture at Gorhambury); Margaret, Count-

ess of Cumberland, wife of the 3d E. of Cumberland (pl. XIII, after the picture at Gorhambury); John Talbot, cr. (1442) E. of Shrewsbury, and his wife Margaret, Countess of Shrewsbury (pls XVIII and XIX, after the portraits at Castle Ashby); and Lady Digby (n. 5 below).

4. Benjamin White (1725–94), bookseller in Fleet Street; publisher of Pennant's *Journey*. He was a younger brother of Gilbert White, the naturalist, who was a close friend of Pennant.

5. Venetia Anastasia Stanley (1600–33), m. (1625) Sir Kenelm Digby. The bust of Lady Digby, which was at Gothurst in Buckinghamshire, is described by William Cole in a letter to HW ca 25 Sept. 1762 (Cole i 27–8; see also ibid. i. 9, ii. 43). HW and Cole saw it at Gothurst in July 1763 (*Country Seats* 52). The engraving of the bust is pl. XXI in Pennant's *Journey*.

that I should be happy to have too the prints of Gorhambury,[6] Gothurst,[7] Castle Ashby[8] and Houghton:[9] but I shall be still more obliged, if you will give me leave to ask them.

I am ashamed to be more importunate and to give you more trouble, but I think you flattered me with hopes that Dr Nash[10] would give me the portraits in his *Worcestershire*.[11] I will not ask you to remind him; but if you think I might take that freedom, I would write to him myself to beg them and those in his new volume.[12] All I will trouble you for, is his direction.[13] I hope you have not concluded your own tours, ⟨and⟩ that you will not suffer much by the influenza. I had it badly and then the gout,[14] but am much better, and always

Your most obliged humble servant

HOR. WALPOLE

PS. I find Lady Digby was one of the six portraits.

6. The seat of Lord Grimston, near St Albans, Herts. The sixteenth-century house built by Sir Nicholas Bacon is described by HW in *Country Seats* 21–2; see *ante* 8 May 1761, n. 2. The 3d Viscount Grimston pulled down the house and replaced it with a Palladian mansion built 1777–84 (OSSORY ii. 571 n. 16). The engraving of the old house is pl. X in Pennant's *Journey*.

7. Gothurst or Gayhurst House, near Newport Pagnell, Bucks, was the seat of George Wright (or Wrighte), M.P., when HW visited it in 1763 (n. 5 above); formerly the seat of Sir Kenelm Digby. The engraving is pl. XX in Pennant's *Journey*.

8. In Northants, the seat of the Earl of Northampton; visited by HW in July 1763 (*Country Seats* 53–4). The engraving is pl. XVII in Pennant's *Journey*.

9. Houghton Park Hall, Bedfordshire, one of the seats of the Duke of Bedford; visited by HW in June 1771 (*Country Seats* 69). The engraving is pl. XXII in Pennant's *Journey*.

10. Treadway Russell Nash (1725–1811), D.D.; historian.

11. *Collections for the History of Worcestershire*, 2 vols, folio, 1781–2, edited by Richard Gough and printed by John Nichols. Benjamin White was one of the booksellers authorized to sell the book. HW wrote Cole 29 March 1781: 'Dr Nash has just published the first volume of his *Worcestershire*. It is a folio of prodigious corpulence, and yet dry enough—but then it is finely dressed, and has many heads and views' (COLE ii. 266). HW's copy (untraced) is Hazen, op. cit., No. 6. HW noted in his copy (now WSL) of the *Supplement*, 1774, to Granger's *Biographical History of England* that 'Several [portraits never before engraved are] in Nash's *History of Worcestershire*, and others in Mr Pennant's *Journeys* over England, Wales and Scotland.'

12. That is, the second volume of Nash's *Worcestershire*.

13. Nash lived at Bevere, Claines, Worcs.

14. These illnesses are mentioned in HW's letter to Mann 21 July 1782 (MANN ix. 297).

To John Nichols, Wednesday 19 June 1782

Printed from the MS now WSL. First printed, Nichols, *Lit. Anec.* iii. 301–2 (closing omitted). Reprinted, Wright vi. 174; Cunningham viii. 233 (closing and signature omitted in Wright and Cunningham); Toynbee xii. 267–8 (closing omitted). The MS was formerly in the collection of William Upcott (1779–1845); later in the collection of William K. Bixby; sold Anderson Galleries 1 March 1917 (Bixby Sale), lot 1078, to Walter R. Benjamin; resold American Art Association 8 Nov. 1934 (Roderick Terry Sale, Part II), lot 340, to Brick Row for WSL.

Address (in Thomas Kirgate's hand): To Mr Nichols, Red Lyon Passage.

Berkeley Square, June 19, 1782.

Sir,

JUST this moment on opening your fifth volume of miscellaneous poems,[1] I find the translation of Cato's speech[2] into Latin, attributed (by common fame) to Bishop Atterbury.[3] I can most positively assure you that that translation was the work of Dr Henry Bland,[4] afterwards headmaster of Eton School, provost of the College there and Dean of Durham. I have more than once heard my father Sir Robert Walpole say, that it was he himself who gave that translation to Mr Addison, who was extremely surprised at the fidelity and beauty of it. It may be worthwhile, Sir, on some future occasion to mention this fact in some one of your valuable and curious publications.[5] I am Sir with great regard

Your very humble servant

HOR. WALPOLE

To Mr Nichols.

1. *A Select Collection of Poems, with Notes, Biographical and Historical,* 8 vols, 1780–2. Nichols was the editor of this miscellany. HW's set (in the Dyce collection, Victoria and Albert Museum) is Hazen, *Cat. of HW's Lib.,* No. 348.

2. The soliloquy which opens the last act of Addison's *Cato* (V. i. 1–40).

3. Francis Atterbury (1662–1732), Bp of Rochester 1713–23. See *A Select Collection of Poems* v. 6–8, where Nichols appends a note from the *Biographia Britannica,* 2d edn, 1778–93, i. 50: 'Fame has attrib-

uted this [translation] to the late Bishop Atterbury; and as it was superlatively fine, the world thought fame in the right, and so it proved.'

4. See *ante* 2 Nov. 1737 OS, n. 3.

5. The 'Additional Remarks and Corrections' in *A Select Collection of Poems* viii. 302 states: 'The [Latin] version of the famous soliloquy in *Cato* is ascribed to Bishop Atterbury on the authority of the *Biographia,* and of oral tradition in the University of Oxford (as a correspondent informs me). It should have been

To Thomas Pennant, Sunday 23 June 1782

Printed for the first time from the MS now WSL. For the history of the MS see *ante* 25 May 1773.
Address: To Thomas Pennant Esq. at Downing, Flintshire. *Postmark:* 24 IV.

Strawberry Hill, June 23, 1782.

I GIVE you many thanks, dear Sir, for the new order for the prints,[1] which I have received from Mr White, and for your kind intentions about Dr Nash, who I do not doubt forgot what he was [so] good as to intend for me, and which I shall at any time receive with gratitude.

I wish I could tell you any anecdotes of Queen Catherine[2] and Owen Tudor. On the contrary I must expect some from you. Their story is certainly very obscure. I think I have read in some authors that *he* was beheaded during the Wars of the Roses;[3] and in another, at least, though I forget where, that it was his son of both his names.[4] Such a son, I suppose, was by a former or later wife,[5] for Owen's sons by the Queen, if I recollect rightly, were Edmund of Hadham[6] and Jasper Duke of Bedford.[7] I should think there must be some traces of that descent in the Herald's office; your countrymen, and I may call them mine by the Philipps's,[8] were not wont to be careless of their genealogies. It is a point worth scrutinizing.

mentioned that it is also supposed to have been the production of Dr Bland, Dean of Durham.' Nichols goes on to say that Johnson, in his *Life of Addison*, refers to a Latin version by Bland. The fact that Nichols's edition of *The Epistolary Correspondence . . . and Miscellanies of the Right Reverend Francis Atterbury, D.D.*, 1783–9, does not contain the Latin translation may indicate that he came to accept the attribution to Bland. See *post* 30 June 1782.

1. In his letter to Pennant *ante* 13 June 1782, HW had requested separate 'prints of Gorhambury, Gothurst, Castle Ashby and Houghton' from Pennant's *The Journey from Chester to London*, 1782.
2. Catherine of Valois (1401–37), dau. of Charles VI of France, m. 1 (1420) Henry V of England; m. 2 (ca 1429) Owen

Tudor (d. 1461), grandfather of Henry VII.
3. A faithful Lancastrian, he was taken prisoner at the Battle of Mortimer's Cross 4 Feb. 1461 and, by order of Edward of York (later Edward IV), was beheaded at Hereford.
4. Owen Tudor (d. 1501), monk at Westminster (Isenburg, *Stammtafeln*, II, taf. 63).
5. He was a son by Queen Catherine (see below).
6. Edmund Tudor (ca 1430–56), styled Edmund of Hadham; cr. (1452) E. of Richmond; Henry VII's father.
7. Jasper Tudor (ca 1431–95), cr. (1453) E. of Pembroke and (1485) D. of Bedford.
8. HW's maternal grandmother, Elizabeth Philipps (d. 1728), was the daughter of Sir Erasmus Philipps, 3d Bt, of Picton Castle, Pembrokeshire.

The new edition of the *Anecdotes of Painting*[9] were published by my direction, though not printed at Strawberry Hill. It is a smaller edition in octavo, and without prints, to make it a cheap purchase especially to artists. In short, Sir, I am so ashamed of the ridiculous prices to which the Strawberry editions have risen, merely on account of their being scarce, that I determined people should have the *Anecdotes* (the most useful) at an easy price, if they choose it— Collectors, I know, prefer dear rarities. There are a few new articles, not many, nor any novelty that is curious, but about three pages of supplement to the first volume,[10] with an account of a very considerable architect,[11] till now quite unknown, but a volume of whose drawings[12] are in Lord Warwick's[13] possession.

Since I wrote the above, I have turned to Sandford[14] and Milles.[15] They both give Catherine of Valois a third son called Owen, and both make him a monk at Westminster and nothing more.[16] I much doubt that, for as Henry VI created his other maternal brothers,[17] Edmund and Jasper, earls, he would scarce have suffered the third to be a simple monk, but would have made him a bishop or abbot at least. Sandford says[18] that Edmund was transferred to St David's and had an inscription on his tomb there;[19] does it remain? Methinks his son Henry VII might have bestowed more than a stone on his father. I shall hope to learn a good deal about the Tudors at least from your

9. See *ante* 23 Nov. 1781, n. 10.

10. See *Anecdotes of Painting, Works* iii. 144–5.

11. John Thorpe (ca 1565–1655), surveyor and architect (Ossory ii. 248 n. 18).

12. See *ante* 10 Aug. 1773, n. 21.

13. George Greville (1746–1816), 2d E. Brooke of Warwick Castle and E. of Warwick, 1773.

14. Francis Sandford, *A Genealogical History of the Kings of England*, 1677. HW's copy (now wsl) is Hazen, *Cat. of HW's Lib.*, No. 581.

15. Thomas Milles, *The Catalogue of Honor or Treasury of True Nobility, Peculiar and Proper to the Isle of Great Britaine*, 1610. HW's copy (untraced) is ibid. No. 605.

16. Sandford, p. 285; Milles, p. 193.

17. That is, half-brothers, Henry VI being Queen Catherine's only son by her first marriage to Henry V.

18. Sandford, op. cit. 283–4.

19. He died 3 Nov. 1456 at Carmarthen and was buried there in the Greyfriars church. At the dissolution of the monasteries in 1536, the altar-tomb containing his remains was transferred to St David's Cathedral. Both the inscription and the effigy were apparently removed before HW's time; the tomb has since been restored, and the present inscription is said to follow the original one, which Sandford gives as follows: 'Under this marble stone here inclosed, resteth the bones of that most noble lord Edmond Earl of Richmond, father and brother to kings. The which departed out of this world in the year of Our Lord God 1456, the first [*sic*] of the month of November, on whose soul Almighty Jeshu have mercy. Amen.' See Royal Commission on Ancient and Historical Monuments, *An Inventory of the Ancient Monuments in Wales and Monmouthshire*, 1911–25, vii. 350–1 and fig. 295.

researches, dear Sir, in their own province in which you are so deeply versed. I am with great regard, dear Sir,

Your much obliged and obedient humble servant

HOR. WALPOLE

To JOHN NICHOLS, Sunday 30 June 1782

Printed from a copy by the late Sir Shane Leslie, Bt, in 1941, from the MS then in the possession of the Hon. Mrs Clive Pearson, Parham Park, Pulborough, Sussex. First printed, Nichols, *Lit. Anec.* iii. 302 (text incomplete; see n. 5 below). Reprinted, Toynbee xii. 275. The MS was sold Sotheby's 9 July 1878 (George Manners Sale), lot 312, to Naylor; resold Sotheby's 13 March 1903 (Autograph Letters and Historical Documents Sale), lot 785, to W. V. Daniell; acquired by Sir Herbert H. Raphael, Bt, who inserted it in an extra-illustrated copy of Cunningham's edition of HW's *Letters*, 18 vols, folio; this copy was sold Sotheby's 4 Feb. 1919 (Raphael Sale), lot 311, to Bumpus for Lord Cowdray, the father of the Hon. Clive Pearson; bequeathed by his widow, the Hon. Mrs Pearson, to her daughter, Mrs P. A. Tritton, of Parham Park, in 1974.

June 30, 1782.

MR Walpole is much obliged to Mr Nichols for the prints,[1] and will beg another of Mr Bowyer[2] for his collection of heads as he shall put the one he has received [in]to Mr Bowyer's life.[3]

Mr W. has no objection to being named for the anecdote of Dr Bland's translation,[4] as it is right to authenticate it[5]—but the other corrections[6] are too trifling to require authority.

In p. 190 of the royal *Wills*[7] are two errors.[8] Richard de Coningsburgh[9] was only Earl of Cambridge and never Duke of York: but he

1. Not identified except for the print of William Bowyer (see below).

2. William Bowyer, the younger (1699–1777), printer.

3. *Biographical and Literary Anecdotes of William Bowyer*, 1782. HW's copy (now WSL) is Hazen, *Cat. of HW's Lib.*, No. 3349. A print of Bowyer engraved by James Basire is bound in this copy, but whether by HW or a later owner of the book is unclear.

4. See *ante* 19 June 1782.

5. The rest of the letter was omitted by Nichols.

6. Not identified.

7. *A Collection of All the Wills, Now Known to Be Extant, of the Kings and Queens of England*, 1780. Nichols was the editor of this work. HW's copy (untraced) is Hazen, op. cit., No. 3350.

8. Nichols had written: 'Richard de Coningsburgh Duke of York, father of Edward, slain at the Battle of Wakefield, 1460' (*A Collection of All the Wills*, p. 190).

9. Richard (ca 1375–1415) of Coningsburgh, also styled Richard of York; cr. (1414) E. of Cambridge.

was father of *Richard* Duke of York[10] slain at Wakefield, whose son *Edward* was Edward IV.[11]

To Benjamin Ibbot, Wednesday 3 July 1782

Printed from a photostat of the MS in the Pierpont Morgan Library. First printed, Toynbee *Supp.* i. 286. For the history of the MS see *ante* 24 Sept. 1773.
Address: To Benjamin Ibbott Esq. Dartmouth Street, Westminster. *Postmark:* PENNY POST PAID.

Berkeley Square, July 3d 1782.

YOU are much too generous, Sir, in paying me so liberally for being an unsuccessful solicitor;[1] and I should blush to receive your presents,[2] if I had not satisfaction in them as marks of your good heart. I am therefore obliged to you for them, and for the notes[3] that accompany them. I could only wish that your own portrait[4] had more resemblance, and that you could give me a better account of yourself. If your health mends, I should be happy to see you at Strawberry Hill, and am, Sir,

Your much obliged humble servant

Hor. Walpole

---

10. Richard (Plantagenet) (1411–60), only son of Richard of Coningsburgh by his first marriage to Anne de Mortimer; 3d D. of York, 1415; killed at the Battle of Wakefield 30 Dec. 1460.
11. Edward IV (1442–83), eldest surviving son of Richard, Duke of York; K. of England 1461–83.

———

1. See *ante* 9 June 1782.
2. The engraved portrait of Ibbot (n. 4 below) and, presumably, the item of pottery described in 'Des. of SH,' *Works* ii. 406, as 'An earthenware dish, with the heads of Charles II and Queen Catherine in blue and white; a present from Mr Ibbot.'
3. Missing.
4. A stipple engraving by D. P. Pariset, after the drawing (now in the BM) by the same artist, described as 'bust, right profile, in circular frame, with tablet below; 1776' (*BM Cat. of Engraved British Portraits* ii. 600).

From EDMUND BURKE, Sunday 7 July 1782

Printed from the MS now WSL. First printed, Cunningham ix. 523 (as 'Richard Burke to the Hon. Horace Walpole'). Reprinted in Dixon Wecter, 'Horace Walpole and Edmund Burke,' *Modern Language Notes*, 1939, liv. 126 n. 4; *The Correspondence of Edmund Burke*, ed. T. W. Copeland, Chicago, 1958–78, v. 10. This letter and the following one from Richard Burke, along with HW's 'Copy of Mr Burke's proposal' and his own notes, were preserved in a wrapper that HW docketed 'Papers relating to Mr Burke's application for Clerk of the Pells.' These MSS were probably among those sold by the Waldegrave family to Richard Bentley, the publisher, ca 1843, and descended to his grandson, Richard Bentley the younger. The letter from Richard Burke, the 'Copy of Mr Burke's proposal,' and HW's notes were acquired from the Bentley estate by WSL in 1937; the letter from Edmund Burke was sold Hodgson's 28 April 1939, lot 556; to Colbeck Radford and Co., who sold it to WSL in May 1939.

For the dating of the letter see n. 1 below.

Sunday morning.[1]

MR Burke presents his compliments to Mr Walpole and will have the honour of waiting on Mr Walpole for the purpose of a few minutes conversation with him at any hour he will please to appoint this forenoon.[2]

1. HW has written 'July 7th 1782' below 'Sunday morning' in the MS.

2. HW wrote in *Last Journals* ii. 453–6: 'I received a letter from him [Burke] to desire an interview with me. . . . Burke's business with me was to desire me to propose to my brother Sir Edward Walpole, Clerk of the Pells (an employment for life, which during the [American] war had been stated by the Commissioners of Accounts to produce to him 7000*l.* a year), to resign that office, in consideration of receiving the full yearly value of it during Sir Edward's life (and I think there was an additional offer to Sir Edward of the disposal of the junior Burke's place). The resignation was to be made that very day, that Lord [John] Cavendish might bestow it on Edmund Burke the father, before his Lordship resigned his office. Full security, Burke assured me, should be given to Sir Edward that he should be no loser, unless the office should be reduced by Parliament, as it probably would be, and then Sir Edward should receive the full of the reduced value.

'So frantic a proposal I suppose was never made. . . . However, astonished as I was at the absurdity of the request, I commanded myself enough to make the following temperate answer—that I would acquaint my brother with Mr Burke's request, though I would not bind myself to advise it; . . . he must do on it as he should please: he was not in town, but at Isleworth, whither I must go to him. . . . And I added, that I must be so frank as to tell Mr Burke that Sir Edward was a most warm anti-American, and did not speak with much patience on those who disapproved the American war.

'Mr Burke was much disheartened at so unexpected a state of the case, and chose to say no more himself on the subject, but he made his son write to me that night and come to me the next morning to persuade me of the goodness of the security.' See following letter.

From RICHARD BURKE,[1] Sunday 7 July 1782

Printed from the MS now WSL. First printed, Cunningham ix. 523–4. Re-printed in *The Correspondence of Edmund Burke,* ed. T. W. Copeland, Chicago, 1958–78, v. 11–14; extract quoted in Dixon Wecter, 'Horace Walpole and Edmund Burke,' *Modern Language Notes,* 1939, liv, 126 n. 4. For the history of the MS see the headnote to the previous letter.

Address: To the Honourable Horatio Walpole, Berkely Square.

Whitehall, July 7, 1782.

Dear Sir,

I TOOK the liberty of calling on you this evening[2] by my father's desire, he being confined at home by business, to trouble you with a second part of his conversation with you this morning. I do not know what excuse he made for trespassing so much on your friendship.[3] I know there is none sufficient for my presumption and can only beg of you to extend to me your indulgence to my father. You have, enclosed, the proposal in writing, somewhat altered from what you heard it in the morning, but, as I think it is, and intended it to be, more favourable to the present possessor.[4] If, however, a gross sum should be preferred to a rateable share, as stated in the second condition, it will be easy to alter it back again. I will with your per-mission, since you have suffered me to proceed so far, call on you in the morning, that I may explain anything that is defective in what I now trouble you with, as well as in the written proposal. My idea is that this proposal should be laid before your brother. My father has informed [me] of your very great kindness in offering to undertake that office. If the advantage strikes his mind, or that of those whom he consults about the business, immediately and as clearly as it does me, I shall then be happy to proceed upon it. I will then take the liberty of informing you of a method by which the business may be concluded with the greatest facility and the *most perfect security* to

1. (1758–94), only surviving son of Ed-mund Burke; lawyer; M.P., but died be-fore taking his seat.

2. HW was apparently not at home when he called, so that the meeting did not take place.

3. 'I had at no time lived in friendship with Mr Burke, and latterly we had had no intercourse, though always on civil

terms when we met by accident' (*Last Journals* ii. 454).

4. Sir Edward Walpole had held the office of Clerk of the Pells since 1739. According to the editors of the Burke *Correspondence,* the post was worth about £3000 a year (*The Correspondence of Ed-mund Burke,* Chicago, 1958–78, v. 12 n. 1).

Sir Edward Walpole. If, on the contrary, it does not strike him, I should wish to drop the matter entirely. I need not inform you that the peculiarity of the present conjuncture,[5] which is indeed my apology to you, if I can have any, does not permit a long intercourse upon the subject. Therefore, if it does not pretty soon meet your brother's concurrence, I wish the proposal to be withdrawn. Till it does, I must request of you to conceal the name.[6] I must conclude this letter by throwing myself entirely upon your good and kind feelings for my apology in this letter and the whole proceeding.

I have the honour to be, with great respect,

Your most obedient humble servant,

RICHD. BURKE

[Enclosure][7]

July 7, 1782.

If it suits Sir E. W. the following proposal is submitted to him relative to his office of Clerk of the Pells.

But first let it be understood that if Sir E. has made any arrangement by which the succession to the office may be continued to his family, the proposer requests Sir E. to consider this proposal as not made. If no such arrangement has taken place, he is to determine whether it will be for his advantage to accept this proposal.

It is proposed to Sir E. W. to resign his place of etc. on two conditions:

First, that the person in whose favour he shall resign, shall pay to Sir E. W. during the term of his life the whole and entire profits of the office. Securing to Sir E. the entire profits of the office during his life, another person having the nominal possession, appears at first

---

5. The change in government caused by the sudden death of Lord Rockingham on 1 July gave Lord John Cavendish, the chancellor of the Exchequer, the power to bestow whatever places became vacant before the new administration took office.

6. HW recorded in *Last Journals* ii. 455–6 that Richard Burke came 'to me the next morning to persuade me of the goodness of the security; but I so amply exposed to him the improbability of a man's resigning 7000*l*. a year for no rea-

son, and merely on a *promise* of indemnification, that the son saw the folly of the proposal and gave it up.'

7. The MS is in HW's hand and is endorsed by him 'Copy of Mr Burke's proposal.' The original MS is missing; possibly it was given by HW to Sir Edward Walpole (although there is no evidence that he communicated the Burkes' proposal to Sir Edward) or was returned to Richard Burke. Words abbreviated by HW in the 'Copy' have been expanded.

sight to be no disadvantage at all to Sir E. W. But the fact is otherwise. A reduction of the Exchequer places is now in agitation.[8] It is
very probable, but not quite certain, that no reduction will take
place while the present possessors hold those offices. If another has
the nominal possession, it is very probable, but not quite certain,
that there will be a reduction. Therefore if Sir Edward was now to
resign in favour of another person, though he, Sir Edward, were to
receive the whole profits of the place, he might still be a considerable
loser. To counterbalance that disadvantage it is proposed in the second place,

That after the demise of Sir E. one third of the profits accruing
from the place (whether reduced or not reduced[9]) should be paid to
any person named by Sir E. W. during the life of the person, who on
his resignation would now succeed him, a person under twenty-five
years old.[10] Upon this proposal the question will be simply this,

Whether it is more advantageous for Sir E. W. to have his place
on its present establishment during his life only, or to take the
chance of the reduction of the profits of the office (whatever that may
be) in order to secure one-third part of that office for any of his
family during the life of a person under twenty-five.

If this proposal should meet with Sir Edward's approbation, the
most indisputable security will be given for the performance of the
conditions.

It will be found upon a calculation that the reduction of the office
must be great indeed not to leave Sir Edward a considerable advantage (as the proposer imagines) by this scheme.

A proper method will be taken to ascertain the profits both now

8. In connection with the Bill for Eco-
nomical Reform, which Edmund Burke
had introduced in 1780 and 1781, the
House of Commons in committee on
18 June considered resolutions concerning certain places in the Exchequer and
other government offices. The committee
adopted resolutions stating that 'the income and emoluments arising from the
several offices of . . . Clerk of the Pells
. . . and usher of the Exchequer have
. . . become unreasonable and excessive,
and that the same require some regulation in future' (see Cobbett, *Parl. Hist.*
xxiii. 120). The Commissioners for Examining the Public Accounts later concluded
that the Clerk of the Pells, among other
offices in the Exchequer, received fees
and emoluments that were excessive. By
the Act of 23 Geo. III, c. 82, these payments were to cease on the death of the
present Clerk of the Pells (Sir Edward
Walpole), and thereafter the Clerk of the
Pells was to receive a flat sum of £3000
a year (*Statutes at Large,* ed. Owen Ruffhead, 1763–1800, xiv. 401–2).

9. The MS reads 'deduced.'

10. Richard Burke was then twenty-
four. Since Sir Edward Walpole (b. 1706)
was over seventy-five, a sinecure for life
was likely to be worth far more if held
by Burke.

and hereafter in order that, if this scheme should take place, there may be no doubt that the sum accounted for is equal to the sum received.

[HW's notes on the Burkes' proposal][11]

I said I would not promise.

Sir Edward must appoint to all the places

If transferred, more likely to be a reduction*[11a]

No arrangement certainly intended.

Great delicacy in my proposing on account of Sir Edward['s] age.

Is it credit[able] to Mr B. to propose? It must be known.

(to be concluded afterwards *on articles*)

My father always intended to get this for me—therefore the Clerk of Pells omitted.[12]

You won't mention this—I hope Sir I have shown you that I have been persuading you not to let it be mentioned.

Would any man alive do a deed that would shake the best security possible of his property, in order to have a third part of that property at his disposal after his death?

Would he do a deed that not only would shake that security, but provoke danger to it?

And as that provocation may occasion a great diminution, nay a loss of the whole, and as he would be entitled only to a third of it when so reduced,[13] and to nothing if the whole were taken away,

11. These notes are HW's record of his conversations with Edmund and Richard Burke concerning their proposal.

11a. The asterisk is HW's.

12. HW has written on another portion of the wrapper: 'Young Burke told me his father had always intended to get him Clerk of Pells—therefore it was omitted in new bill.' He elaborated on this point in *Last Journals* ii. 456: 'One passage the son [Richard] dropped that was very memorable. He said his father had always intended to get the office of Clerk of the Pells. This struck me, and explained what I had never comprehended, which was why in Mr Burke's reforming bill that office had not been mentioned among the great sinecures that were to be annihilated on the deaths of

the present incumbents. Can one but smile at a reformer of abuses reserving the second greatest abuse for himself?' The Burke editors point out, however, that HW 'may have misunderstood what Richard said, and he certainly oversimplified the principles on which Edmund was acting. Edmund had not pledged himself to destroy all sinecures, some of which he insisted were useful as the reward of merit. . . . He was particularly ready to defend sinecures held for life, since these enabled their holders to become politically independent of the Crown' (*Correspondence* v. 14 n. 1).

13. At this point in the MS 'would it be advantageous to him to risk the whole for the third of nothing?' is crossed out.

would it be advantageous to risk the whole[14] in order to have the disposal after his death of the third of nothing?

From RICHARD GOUGH[1] and JOHN NICHOLS, Tuesday 9 July 1782

Printed for the first time from a photostat of the MS draft in Richard Gough's hand in the Pierpont Morgan Library. This MS and that of HW's reply *post* 10 July 1782 were presumably in the collection of John Nichols until the Nichols sale at Sotheby's 16–19 April 1828; not further traced until acquired by Morgan. The original letter is missing.

July 9, [17]82.

MR Gough and Mr Nichols present their respectful compliments to Mr Walpole, and propose themselves the pleasure of waiting on him at Strawberry Hill on any Saturday morning in this month[2] which may be most convenient to him.

To RICHARD GOUGH and JOHN NICHOLS, Wednesday 10 July 1782

Printed for the first time from a photostat of the MS in the Pierpont Morgan Library. For the history of the MS see *ante* 9 July 1782.
Dated by the endorsement.
Endorsed by Nichols: (Received July 10, 1782) J.N. [written over 'Received *July 10* at night.']
Endorsed in pencil in a later hand on the mount: From John Nichols' coll. 1832.

MR Walpole shall be very glad of the favour of seeing Mr Gough and Mr Nichols at Strawberry Hill on Saturday July 20th but

---

14. 'for the third of nothing?' is crossed out in the MS.

1. (1735–1809), antiquary.

2. Gough first wrote 'next Saturday morning or the Saturday following,' then crossed out all but 'Saturday morning' and inserted words to complete the sentence as printed here.

hopes they will be so good as to dine with him that day,[1] that they may not hurry themselves, but have time to see whatever they please.[2]

From GEORGE ROSE,[1] Saturday 10 August 1782

First printed, *Works* ii. 387. The history of the MS and its present whereabouts are not known. The text is included in the following letter to Charles Bedford.

To CHARLES BEDFORD, Monday 12 August 1782

Printed from Cunningham viii. 263–4, where the letter was first printed. Reprinted, Toynbee xii. 308–9. The history of the MS and its present whereabouts are not known.

Strawberry Hill, Aug. 12, 1782.

Dear Sir,

I YESTERDAY received from Mr Rose the following order:

Treasury Chambers, 10th Aug., 1782.

Sir,

I am commanded by the Lords Commissioners of His Majesty's Treasury to desire you will forthwith cause to be made out and transmitted to me for their Lordships' information,

An account of the ordinary allowance of stationery delivered into this office in the year 1780; together with the prices of each article, and the amount of the whole.[1]

---

1. HW wrote Cole 23 July 1782: 'Mr Gough and Mr Nichols dined with me on Saturday last [20 July]. I lent the former three and twenty drawings of monuments out of Mr Lethuillier's books, for his large work, which will be a magnificent one' (COLE ii. 331). Gough was at work compiling his *Sepulchral Monuments in Great Britain*, 2 vols, 1786–96.
2. William Cole wrote Gough 25 July: 'I find you and Mr Nichols dined at Strawberry Hill on Saturday; and I make no doubt of your entertainment; as I was

well pleased to hear Mr Walpole communicated to you so many of Mr Lethieullier's drawings. He seems much pleased with your plan' (Nichols, *Lit. Anec.* i. 696).

---

1. (1744–1818), secretary to the Treasury 1782–3; M.P.

---

1. As usher of the Exchequer, HW supplied the Exchequer and the Treasury with various articles of stationery. See *ante* 9 June 1777.

An account of the extraordinary allowance of stationery, and all other necessaries whatsoever, delivered to the Lords, Secretary, Clerks, or any other person in this office, within the same time; together with the prices of each article, and the amount of the whole.

I am Sir,
Your most humble servant,[2]

GEORGE ROSE

I beg, dear Sir, that you will immediately make out the accounts required with the most rigid exactness and truth. I have, you know, nothing to disguise or palliate, and I wish you to be over-minute rather than omit anything. The whole world is welcome to know everything relating to my office. I have never, in above forty years that I have enjoyed the office, made or sought to make the smallest advantage of it beyond my just and legal dues. I have never solicited any favour in it, and, as you know, constantly ordered your father[3] and you to take care that the office was served in the best manner, and that the goods I supplied should be purchased of the most substantial tradesmen, and for which I constantly paid the best prices.[4] In short, I have always acted in my office in a manner so much to my credit, that I should be glad to have my conduct scrutinized in the most rigid way; but of that say nothing—I desire no parade or ostentation.

When you have drawn up the accounts as faithfully as you can possibly, pray bring them hither to me before you deliver them. In the meantime I would have you call immediately on Mr Rose, and tell him, with my compliments, that the orders shall be obeyed as fast as you can, and *that I have directed you to be as minute, exact, and particular as possible*. Say those very words.

Yours most sincerely,

HOR. WALPOLE

2. The complete closing is printed here from *Works* ii. 387.

3. Grosvenor Bedford, HW's deputy usher of the Exchequer 1755–71, was succeeded by Joseph Tullie 1771–4, and then by Charles Bedford 1774–97 (see *ante* 27 Feb. 1771, n. 1).

4. In his 'Account of My Conduct Relative to the Places I Hold under Government, and towards Ministers' (dated 30 March 1782), HW wrote: 'I believe no man will accuse me of having ever paid court or even attendance on a first lord of the Treasury. . . . All the goods I

From GEORGE ROSE, Friday 16 August 1782

Printed from *Works* ii. 387, where the letter was first printed. Reprinted, Cunningham viii. 264 n. 2; Toynbee *Supp.* iii. 38 n. 2. The history of the MS and its present whereabouts are not known.

Duke Street, Westminster, August 16, 1782.

Sir,

I WAS very much concerned to understand yesterday, from Mr Bedford, that you had considered my letter to him[1] as leading towards an inquiry into the conduct of your office; it was merely to know what the consumption of stationery at the Treasury has been, which I could not learn with correctness there. This I begged Mr Bedford would assure you of in the strongest terms, to prevent a possibility of your continuing under a mistake with respect to my intention in writing to him;[2] and when I mentioned the misapprehension to Lord Shelburne,[3] he expressed the utmost anxiety to have it set right, and desired I would write to you myself for that purpose, with assurances that it would give him very great pain to have occasioned the smallest uneasiness to you, which I hope you will admit as an apology for my having given you this trouble. I have the honour to be,

Sir,

Your most obedient and very humble servant,

GEORGE ROSE

furnish have always been purchased by me at the highest prices. . . . my steadfast purpose [has been] not to interfere with the public examination of places, nor take the smallest step to mitigate my own fate, which I submit implicitly to the discretion of the legislature' (*Works* ii. 369–70).

1. Doubtless the letter *ante* 10 Aug. 1782 addressed to HW, not to Bedford.

2. HW had grounds for suspicion in view of the recent agitation in Parliament concerning economic reforms. See *post* 19 June 1783 and 16 June 1791.

3. First lord of the Treasury July 1782 – April 1783.

To George Rose, Sunday 18 August 1782

Printed from *Works* ii. 388–9, where the letter was first printed. Reprinted, Toynbee xii. 314–15. The history of the MS and its present whereabouts are not known. HW's MS draft of the letter (endorsed by him 'not sent') is in the Pierpont Morgan Library; the text is printed in *Extracts from the Journals and Correspondence of Miss Berry*, ed. Lady Theresa Lewis, 2d edn, 1866, ii. 42–3; Toynbee *Supp.* iii. 38–40. Extracts from the draft are quoted in the notes below.

Strawberry Hill, August 18, 1782.

THOUGH I am very sorry, Sir, that you have had so much trouble on my account, I cannot entirely lament it, both as it has procured me a most obliging letter from you, and as it gives me an opportunity of explaining my expressions by Mr Bedford, which, if I had had the pleasure of being better known to you, would not have surprised you.

As a very subordinate officer of the Exchequer, I have always known it was my duty to receive the commands of my superiors, the Lords of the Treasury, with respect and obedience, and to give them any information that they please to demand of me. I owe everything I have to the Crown and the public, and certainly by no merit of my own;[1] the servants of the Crown and the public are entitled to any lights that can fall to my province to furnish; and so far from having any secrets in my office, I would not keep it an hour, by any mystery, subterfuge, or disguise. I once received an inquiry from Mr Robinson[2] something parallel, Sir, to yours, and, as Mr Bedford can tell you, immediately complied with his request.[3]

When the Commissioners of Accounts sent for Mr Bedford, I gave him the most positive orders to lay before them the most minute details of my office, and answer their every question circumstantially.

Forgive my troubling you, Sir, with these particulars about myself: they are only meant to show you that so far from entertaining any jealousy about my office, I think myself accountable for every part of it, and should blush if I were not ready and willing to give it:

1. 'I should deserve to lose all, were I capable of any deceit' (HW's draft).

2. See HW to John Robinson *ante* 9 June 1777.

3. 'It is very true, Sir, that at first I did imagine that there might be a farther view in your inquiry; but I was not less ready to obey it' (HW's draft).

perhaps that delicacy made me express myself a little more eagerly than the case deserved.[4]

With regard to Lord Shelburne's or your own desire of information, I beg both will command me or Mr Bedford on any occasion without ceremony.[5] I feel extremely obliged to you, Sir, for your readiness in explaining your orders; and I must entreat you to present my most respectful thanks to Lord Shelburne for his Lordship's condescension and attention, to which my insignificance had no pretensions, but which must increase my gratitude. I would take the liberty of thanking his Lordship myself, but he cannot have time to read complimentary letters. I fear, Sir, I have taken up but too much of yours, for which I beg your pardon, and have the honour to be with great regard, Sir,

Your most obedient and most obliged humble servant,

Horace Walpole

To John Nichols, Sunday 18 August 1782

Printed from Nichols, *Lit. Anec.* iii. 302. Reprinted, Toynbee xii. 315. The history of the MS and its present whereabouts are not known.

Strawberry Hill, Aug. 18, 1782.

MR Walpole is extremely obliged to Mr Nichols for the books and prints;[1] and begs, when he sees Mr Gough, to thank him for his obliging present of Mr Brown's tract.[2]

4. 'When there has been any question on patent places, I have thought it most respectful to await the determination of the legislature in silence; and therefore resolved neither to make interest to save myself from what should be thought necessary for the public; nor, as I have great contempt for ostentation, not to affect to be willing to give up my right, as I do not believe that any man really desires to have his fortune lessened; though I flatter myself that nobody is less disposed to prefer his private interest to that of the public' (HW's draft).

5. See *post* 23 Aug. 1782.

1. Not identified.

2. *Adenochoiradelogia; or an Anatomick-Chirurgical Treatise of Glandules and Strumaes, or Kings-Evil-Swellings. Together with the Royal Gift of Healing,* 1684, by John Brown, surgeon-in-ordinary to Charles II. HW's copy (untraced) is Hazen, *Cat. of HW's Lib.,* No. 2655.

To CHARLES BEDFORD, Friday 23 August 1782

Printed from Cunningham viii. 271, where the letter was first printed. Reprinted, Toynbee xii. 319–20. The history of the MS and its present whereabouts are not known.

Strawberry Hill, Aug. 23, 1782.

Dear Sir,

I HAVE received so very civil and obliging a letter from Mr Rose,[1] that I will not give you the trouble of bringing the account[2] down hither, but will desire you to deliver it to him on Monday morning,[3] and tell him that I have ordered you to give him at any time any information that he wishes to have, as far as you have it, or can be informed yourself.

I believe I shall not be able to be in town before the end of next week,[4] but you shall know on what day as soon as I can fix it.

I am, dear Sir, yours most sincerely,

HOR. WALPOLE

1. Either Rose's letter *ante* 16 Aug. 1782 or possibly a more recent (missing) letter.
2. Rose's letter to HW *ante* 10 Aug. 1782 ordered HW to furnish an account of the allowance, prices, and total amount of stationery supplied by the usher of the Exchequer to the Treasury during the year 1780.

3. 26 August.
4. HW wrote Lady Ossory 31 Aug. 1782: 'I did mean to go to town today on purpose, but I have had the gout . . . I propose in two or three days to make my appearance' (OSSORY ii. 352).

TO EDWARD KING,[1] Tuesday 27 August 1782

Printed from Toynbee *Supp.* iii. 40–1, where the letter was first printed. The MS is untraced until sold Sotheby's 12 April 1921 (Miscellaneous Sale), lot 411, to Dobell; offered by Maggs, Cat. Nos 417 (Christmas 1921), lot 3258, and 457 (Christmas 1924), lot 3063; resold American Art Association-Anderson Galleries 25 Nov. 1936 (property of Mrs Milton E. Getz), lot 1593 (with another letter), to Brick Row for WSL. The MS was inadvertently destroyed on arrival at Farmington. The letter is misdated 1784 in Maggs' catalogues and 1762 in the American Art Association-Anderson Galleries catalogue.

Strawberry Hill, Aug. 27, 1782.

IT is very true, Sir, that I was extremely pleased with your account of ancient castles,[2] and thought it the most sensible and satisfactory of all the papers published by the Antiquarian Society; but though I dare to say that better judges are of the same opinion, my sanction, I fear, can add no weight to it. My knowledge is very superficial, and little deserved the attention of a gentleman of your accurate observation. But though I had little claim to such a compliment, Sir, I am not the less grateful for it, and beg leave to return you my most sincere thanks.

In cutting the leaves of your book,[3] Sir, for I have but this moment received it, I observed a description of Haddon House.[4] Many years ago I was much struck with that very ancient seat, and had a drawing made of the angle of, I think, the first court, the irregular patch-

1. (ca 1735–1807), F.R.S., 1767; F.S.A., 1770; P.S.A., 1784; miscellaneous writer and antiquary.

2. 'Observations on Ancient Castles . . . Read at the Society of Antiquaries, March 21, 28, and April 18, 1776,' in *Archæologia,* 1777, iv. 364–413; 'Sequel to the Observations on Ancient Castles . . . Read January 17, 1782,' in *Archæologia,* 1782, vi. 231–375. HW wrote Mason 6 July 1777: 'I must tell you that at the end of the new *Archæologia* there is a very good essay on ancient castles, with very curious matter, by a Mr King. I don't know who he is' (MASON i. 320).

3. *Observations on Ancient Castles. Sequel to the Observations on Ancient Castles,* 1782. 'Reprinted with the original Plates from Vols 4 and 6 of the "Archæ-

ologia."' HW's copy (untraced) is Hazen, *Cat. of HW's Lib.,* No. 544. HW wrote Lady Ossory 31 Aug. 1782: 'I have just been reading a most entertaining book, which I will recommend to you . . . the author sent it to me. Part was published some time ago in the *Archæologia,* and is almost the only paper in that mass of rubbish that has a grain of common sense. It is Mr E. King on ancient castles' (OSSORY ii. 353).

4. Haddon Hall, near Bakewell, Derbyshire, a seat of the Duke of Rutland. King described it as 'castellated and embattled, in all the apparent forms of regular defense; but yet really without the least means of resistance, even in its original construction' (*Observations on Ancient Castles,* pp. 170–1).

work of which is remarkable.⁵ If it should at any time lie in your road, I should be glad of the honour of seeing you here⁶ and showing you that drawing, or any other pieces of antiquity in my possession that may be worthy of your notice. It will give me an agreeable opportunity of assuring you in person with how much respect and gratitude I am, Sir,

Your most obedient and most obliged humble servant,

Hor. Walpole

From Giuseppe Cardini,¹ Friday 30 August 1782

Printed for the first time from the MS now wsl. The MS is untraced until acquired by wsl from an unrecorded source ca 1924.

Address: To the Honourable Horace Walpole.

Eccellenza,

SONO giunto in questa mattina a ore una alla casa di Milord Grantham,² da Firenze con dei dispacci consegniatimi per il medesimo da Sir Horace Mann a Firenze, e avendomi egli reccomandata questa lettera³ per v[ostra] e[ccellenza]. La consegno in sua casa in Berkeley Square per mandargliela subito in campagna,⁴ ho consegniato subito i miei dispacci a Milord Grantham e devo tornare al suo uffizio in Cleveland Row⁵ questa mattina per ricevere ordini che

5. See *ante* 2 September 1760 and n. 10. HW visited Haddon in August 1760 (*Country Seats* 29).

6. There is no record of a visit by King to SH.

———

1. Diplomatic courier. In his letter to HW 10 Jan. 1767, Sir Horace Mann mentions Cardini as being a servant to 'Mr Worsely' (?Thomas Worsley, of Pidford, Isle of Wight) and describes him as 'a very diligent man' (Mann vi. 476–7). Cardini served as messenger between Britain and the garrison at Minorca in 1781–2. Mann occasionally employed him to carry letters to HW.

2. Thomas Robinson (1738–86), 2d Bn Grantham, 1770; diplomatist. He had become secretary of state for foreign affairs in July (ibid. ix. 296 n. 1).

3. Mann to HW 19 Aug. 1782 (ibid. ix. 305–6). HW replied on 'Friday evening,' 30 Aug.: 'I have this moment received from London your letter which Cardini brought, and shall send one of my servants to town tomorrow morning with this answer, and conclude he will not be set out on his return' (ibid. ix. 309).

4. That is, SH.

5. The passage in front of St James's Palace in which Grantham had his office as secretary of state.

non so quali saranno. Ho lasciato Sir Horace Mann a Firenze lunedì del dì 19 del corrente a ore 4 dopo pranzo in perfetta salute.[6]

Se devo servirla io saro reperibile 'at Mr Badiote,[7] No. 3, Haymarket' e con tutto l'ossequio sono di v[ostra] e[ccellenza], Londra venerdì mattina a ore 8, 30 agosto, devotissimo e obbedientissimo servo,

GIUSEPPE CARDINI

To THOMAS PENNANT, Tuesday 15 October 1782

Printed for the first time from the MS now WSL. For the history of the MS see *ante* 25 May 1773.

Strawberry Hill, Oct. 15, 1782.

I DOUBT, dear Sir, whether you have not a higher opinion of my sagacity as an antiquary, and a lower of your own, than either of us deserve[s]. I could not have made more happy conjectures on the persons in the Froissart[1] than you have done; and I am sure I cannot discover the rest with equal felicity. Indeed how is it possible to guess at personages with no insignia and with no attendant circumstances, especially of that age, of which scarce any portraits are preserved but of kings and queens and a few higher clergymen? I know there are some in a few MSS, but then are they not described, or specified, in the chapters to which they relate? It is still more impracticable for me to guess at portraits without seeing them. Your note[2] only specifies four men, of which one has a red cap—and three men. Among the attendants on two or three princes how can I guess who

6. 'Cardini assured me by a line that he left you [well], which he knew would be the most welcome news he could give me' (HW to Mann 30 Aug. 1782, ibid. ix. 312).

7. Not identified.

---

1. An illuminated manuscript of Froissart's *Chronicles*, presumed to have been executed ca 1460–70 by an unknown artist for Philippe de Comines, the historian (H. N. Humphreys, *Illuminated Illustrations of Froissart*, 1845, 'Advertisement'; J. M. B. Kervyn de Lettenhove, ed.,

Œuvres de Froissart, Brussels, 1867–77, i pt iii. 323–5). This is Harleian MS 4380, now in the British Museum. HW refers to an illuminated miniature at f. 141, depicting the challenge between the Duke of Hereford (later Henry IV) and the Duke of Norfolk before Richard II in 1398. This miniature was engraved for Pennant's *The Journey from Chester to London*, 1782, pl. IX, facing p. 167, and is reproduced in G. G. Coulton, *The Chronicler of European Chivalry*, 1930, p. 94.

2. On the miniature in the Froissart manuscript. Pennant's note is missing.

the individuals meant are? I may guess at hazard—but it is ten to one but I am wrong. I may turn to history and choose at will the great officers of the time; and after all, the seven attendants may only mean courtiers or guards. One ought to know in what precise year the MS was written and where presented, and still one could only conjecture. Nay, those little faces in illuminated MSS are so small and indistinct, that they give little notion of the features and less of the characters: nor when one does know whom they represent, has one any precise idea of the countenances. Turn over Strut's *Regal and Ecclesiastic Antiquities*,[3] and tell me whether almost every one of the personages might not serve for any of the rest. Those illuminators drew, in their manner, men and women, palaces, churches, castles, battles; but with so little exactitude or discrimination, that one knows no more than one knew without them, that there were men, women and buildings in those times.

With regard, Sir, to your guess at Joan Princess of Wales,[4] though it is a very probable one, I doubt whether your reason for concluding so is a just one, her being in *black*. I am not at all clear that *black* in that age was used for mourning: I rather think *white* was; but I do not assert it.

I am very glad to hear that the remainder of your Welsh *Tour*[5] is in the press, and thank you much for the offer of the prints.[6] I should be ungrateful indeed, Sir, if I had been making presents of my *Description* of this place,[7] and had neglected to beg your acceptance of

3. Joseph Strutt, *The Regal and Ecclesiastical Antiquities of England*, 1773. HW's copy (untraced) is Hazen, *Cat. of HW's Lib.*, No. 3847. The original drawings for Strutt's work (formerly in the collection of HW's correspondent Richard Bull) are now WSL.

4. Joan (ca 1328–85), Cts of Kent, m. 1 (ca 1339) Sir Thomas Holand; m. 2 (before 1343) William de Montagu, 2d E. of Salisbury, 1344; m. 3 (1361) Edward, P. of Wales.

5. *A Tour in Wales*, vol. II, 1783. The first volume of Pennant's Welsh *Tour* was published in 1778. *The Journey to Snowdon* appeared in 1781; in his 'Advertisement' to this work, dated 1 March 1781, Pennant says that 'This *Journey* is the continuation of my *Tour in Wales*. Another part will appear with all conve-

nient speed . . . which will complete the second volume.' The other part was that published in 1783. The second volume thus consists of two parts, and the complete *Tour in Wales* is variously listed as two or three volumes; some copies of the second volume have a title-page dated 1783. HW's copy, part of a nine-volume collection of Pennant's works, is Hazen, op. cit., No. 547.

6. The plates to be included in the final part of the Welsh *Tour*. The first volume contains 26 plates, the *Journey to Snowdon* 11 plates, plus 10 'supplemental plates.' The second part of the *Journey* contains 15 plates, making a total of 36 plates in vol. II of *A Tour in Wales*.

7. *A Description of the Villa of Horace Walpole*, SH, 1774. 100 copies were printed (Hazen, *SH Bibl.* 107–10).

one. The case is exactly this. I have long had such a design in hand, but it is not finished, nor are half the prints executed, nor even begun. I did print a few copies of part,[7a] some years ago, for the use of the housekeeper[8] and those who come to see the house. Of those very imperfect catalogues Mr Cole and Dr Lort each begged one,[9] without a single print. No others have gone out of my hands, nor are those, imperfect as they are, any longer of the least value, as the disposition of many of the pictures has been since changed, and two or three rooms were not then built.[10] I certainly did not think of offering you such a fragment. I hope in about a year, if I live, to beg your acceptance of a complete one with the prints;[11] for I assure you, Sir, I shall always be happy of returning your great civilities, though inadequately, for I am, Sir,

Your much obliged and obedient humble servant,

H. WALPOLE

PS. I do not quite understand, Sir, your question about Gibson[12] and his wife, as I do not recollect the circumstances of the picture, which I think I once saw, but several years ago.

7a. Only two copies have been located, the Storer copy at Eton and the one that Mrs Damer gave Lord Harcourt in 1801. This second copy passed to Lord Waldegrave and is now WSL (ibid. 105).

8. Margaret Young (fl. 1760–85).

9. Cole's copy, presented to him 29 Oct. 1774 on his visit to SH, is now WSL; Lort's copy is missing.

10. HW wrote Cole 19 Dec. 1780 that 'many articles have been added to my collection since the *Description* was made . . . and . . . the positions of many of the pictures have been changed' (COLE ii. 254). The Beauclerk Tower, completed in 1776, was the only main addition to the house between 1774 and 1782 (W. S. Lewis, 'The Genesis of Strawberry Hill,' *Metropolitan Museum Studies*, 1934, v pt i. 82).

11. In 1784 HW printed at SH 200 copies of *A Description of the Villa of Mr Horace Walpole*. This edition, without the later appendix and additions, contained 25 plates (Hazen, *SH Bibl.* 123).

12. Perhaps Richard Gibson (ca 1615–90), painter. An account of him and his wife, Anne Shepherd, together with engraved portraits of both, is given in *Anecdotes of Painting, Works* iii. 327–8.

TO MRS GARRICK,[1] November 1782

Printed for the first time from a photostat of the MS in the possession of Mr George Milne, New York City. The MS is untraced until sold Sotheby's 23 July 1962 (property of Lt-Col. R. Solly), lot 293, to Quaritch; acquired jointly from Quaritch by Mr Milne and the late E. L. McAdam, Jr, in Nov. 1962.

Dated approximately by the publication of Stratford's *Fontenoy* (see n. 2 below).

MR WALPOLE has the pleasure of sending Mrs Garrick Mr Stratford's *Poem*,[2] for which she was so good as to subscribe; and he is ashamed to trouble her with two others, for Mrs Bouverie[3] and Miss More,[4] Mr Walpole not knowing how to convey them to those ladies.

TO BENJAMIN IBBOT, Tuesday 19 November 1782

Printed from a photostat of the MS in the Pierpont Morgan Library. First printed, Toynbee *Supp.* i. 287. For the history of the MS see *ante* 24 Sept. 1773.

Address: To Benjamin Ibbot Esq. in Dartmouth Street, Westminster. *Postmark:* PENNY POST PAID.

Berkeley Square, Nov. 19th 1782.

YOU will give me leave, Sir, to hope that you have now received by the fleet good news[1] of your son,[2] which I shall have great pleasure to hear. I was so hurt at not being able to obtain the leave

1. Eva Maria Veigel (1724–1822), called 'Violette,' m. (1749) David Garrick; dancer.

2. *The First Book of Fontenoy, a Poem in Nine Books*, 1782, by the Rev. Thomas Stratford (1735–86). Although this work was not officially published until 25 Dec. 1782 (*Public Adv.* 25 Dec.), subscription copies were evidently available a month earlier. HW subscribed to ten copies in order to help the author, 'a poor worthy Irish clergyman' (MASON ii. 233). The title-page of HW's copy bound in his 'Poems of Geo. 3' at Harvard is dated by him 'November' (Hazen, *Cat. of HW's Lib.*, No. 3222:18:14).

3. Elizabeth Bouverie (ca 1726–98), of Teston, Kent; friend of Mrs Garrick and Hannah More (MORE 294 n. 3).

4. Hannah More, HW's correspondent.

1. 'Yesterday some letters were received from Plymouth, with advice of Lord Howe, with the major part of his fleet, being safe arrived at Plymouth from Gibraltar, and his Lordship was last night expected in town' (*Daily Adv.* 16 Nov.). Howe had relieved and victualled the British garrison at Gibraltar, which had been under siege by the combined French and Spanish fleet; his 'sedate triumph' is heralded in HW's letter to Mann 10 Nov. 1782 (MANN ix. 337–8).

2. See HW to Ibbot *ante* 2 June 1782, n. 3.

that you desired for him, that it prevented my answering the favour of your last³ and the obliging offer of a visit to Strawberry Hill, which however I should have asked,⁴ if I had not gone thither very late, and been much out of order⁵ since. I shall be very glad of the favour of your dining there next summer and am, Sir, with great regard

Your most obedient humble servant

Hor. Walpole

To Benjamin Ibbot, Friday 22 November 1782

Printed from a photostat of the MS in the Pierpont Morgan Library. First printed, Toynbee *Supp.* i. 287–8. For the history of the MS see *ante* 24 Sept. 1773.
Address: To Benjamin Ibbott Esq. in Dartmouth Street, Westminster. *Postmark:* PENNY POST PAID.

Berkeley Square, Nov. 22d 1782.

Dear Sir,

I SPOKE to General Conway last night, who will ask Captain Vallaton,¹ when he sees him, about your son; but in the meantime I flatter myself that I can make you easy, as General Conway's aide-de-camp² told me your son must be living,³ or there would be application to fill up the vacancy. I am very glad to give you this satisfaction, and am Sir,

Your obliged humble servant

Hor. Walpole

3. Missing.
4. In his letter to Ibbot *ante* 3 July 1782, HW wrote that 'I should be happy to see you at Strawberry Hill,' but he named no day.
5. Presumably with gout, although HW does not mention it in his letters of this time.

1. Charles Vallotton (d. 1793), Capt. 56th Foot, stationed at Gibraltar (GM 1793, lxiii pt ii. 674; *Army Lists*, 1782, p. 127). 'The officer who arrived on Thursday [14 Nov.]

at Mr Secretary Townshend's office from Gibraltar is Capt. Valatton, of the 56th Regiment, Gen. Elliott's first aide-de-camp. He took his passage in the *Buffalo*, lately arrived at Penzance, but, it is said, brings no dispatches' (*Daily Adv.* 16 Nov.).
2. Not identified.
3. The *Daily Adv.* 18 Nov. printed 'Extracts of the Returns of the Killed and Wounded in the several Corps at Gibraltar, from the 9th of August to the 17th of October, 1782, inclusive.' Henry Ibbot's name does not appear in the list.

From JOHN BOWLE, Saturday 28 December 1782

Printed for the first time from a photostat of Bowle's MS draft, bound in his 'Green Book' (letter copybook) in the Bowle-Evans Collection, University of Cape Town Library. For the history of this collection see *ante* 6 Feb. 1764. The original letter is missing.

Endorsed by Bowle: Wrote Dec. 12, 13, 1782. Honourable Horace Walpole.

London, Dec. 28, 1782.

Sir,

AS no man sets a higher value on your learned labours than myself, and the last volume of the *Anecdotes of Painting*,[1] and several other detached pieces of yours now lie by me in order for binding, from the common wish of collectors to complete their pursuits, and from your former civilities, I am induced to beg, what by other methods I cannot obtain, a copy of your observations on Chatterton.[2] As in the new edition of the painters[3] you have added some supplementary matter, it may not yet be amiss to mention an artist who merited the notice and elogium of that honest and sensible monk *Matthew Paris*.[4] This was *Walter de Colchester*,[5] Sacrist of St Albans, whom he speaks of as *pictor & sculptor incomparabilis*. As it is much more satisfactory to make use of our own eyes than to trust to another's transcript, it seems more eligible barely to refer you to Dr Watt's[6] edition of the *Vitæ 23 Abbatum S. Albani*, p. 108, 21, 2, 4, Lond. 1640:[7] more especially as the name is not to be found in the in-

1. Printed at SH in 1771 but not published until 1780; see *ante* 4 Oct. 1780, n. 2.

2. *A Letter to the Editor of the Miscellanies of Thomas Chatterton*, SH, 1779. Bowle could not obtain a copy from a bookseller because the work was printed for private distribution only (*ante* 11 Jan. 1779, n. 4).

3. 'The third edition, with additions' (vol. iv, 'Second edition') was published in 5 vols, 8vo, in May 1782 (*ante* 31 Oct. 1781 and nn. 16, 20).

4. (ca 1200–59), monk of St Albans Abbey; historian.

5. Walter (ca 1180–1248) of Colchester; monk of St Albans Abbey; painter and

carver in wood and stone (Thieme and Becker xxxv. 120).

6. William Watts (ca 1590–1649), D.D., 1639; chaplain to Prince Rupert of the Palatinate; scholar and divine.

7. Watts's edition of Matthew Paris's *Vitæ . . . viginti trium abbatum Sancti Albani* is in the second part (title-page dated 1639) of his edition of Paris's *Historia major*, London, 1640, folio. Walter of Colchester is referred to as 'pictor & sculptor incomparabilis' on p. 122 of the *Vitæ*; other references to him occur on pp. 108, 121, and 124, as Bowle indicates. HW owned a copy of Watts's edition of the *Historia major* published in London in 1686 (Hazen, *Cat. of HW's Lib.*, No. 607).

dex. Permit me to say a word or two of the print of Lord Herbert of Chirbury,[8] which I mentioned when you favoured me with a sight of your invaluable collection of curiosities.[9] We have in it the truest picture of chivalry, *la cavalleria andantesca,*[10] anywhere to be met with. The several particulars are selected with much judgment. The scene a forest, the lake and bank at a distance, the esquire, and armour merit notice. But the principal figure is the knight, who is partly armed—his sword by his side, his shield on his arm. The flame of fire and the sparks on the same may be considered as the *empresa.*[11] He is habited in his hose and doublet, and his recumbent posture is that of the Cavallero de los Espejos[12] in *Don Quixote,* P[art] 2, C[hapter] 12, whose first act when he is discovered is 'él tenderse en el suelo, y arrojarse.'[13] The customary arms of knights mentioned in the 52d chapter,[14] the lance, shield, and coat-armour, hanging as a trophy, the lance resting against a tree,[15] a circumstance mentioned four times by Cervantes, the helmet with plumes, and the caparisoned horses fastened by the reins to the tree, were probably suggested to the painter by Lord Herbert himself. The death of Oliver [16] in 1617 will furnish some hints for guessing at the time of the picture. What the relation was betwixt him and *Isaac Olivier,*[17] whose name is so

8. The engraving by Anthony Walker, after the painting of Lord Herbert by Isaac Oliver (still at Powis Castle in Wales), is the frontispiece to *The Life of Edward Lord Herbert of Cherbury, Written by Himself,* SH, 1764.

9. The date of Bowle's visit to SH is not known, but it was probably not long after HW began to correspond with him in 1764. In his letter to HW *ante* 16 Feb. 1764, Bowle wrote that 'some time this spring . . . I may visit London'; in his reply *ante* 25 Feb. 1764, HW urged Bowle to 'let me have the satisfaction of being acquainted with you when you come to London.'

10. 'Knight-errantry.'

11. Heraldic device.

12. Knight of the Mirrors.

13. 'He stretched himself out on the ground, and flung himself down.' This is an abridged quotation from Part II, chapter xii, of *Don Quixote (Historia del famoso cavallero, Don Quixote de la Mancha,* ed. John Bowle, London and Salisbury, 1781, iii. 85).

14. *Las armas las acostumbradas de los Cavalleros, lanza, y escudo, y arnés tranzado, con todas las demás piezas:* 'the customary arms of knights, lance and shield and coat of mail, with all the other accoutrements' (ibid. iv. 406).

15. These arms and accoutrements of the knight are so depicted on the engraved title-pages of Bowle's edition of *Don Quixote.*

16. Isaac Oliver (ca 1565–1617), miniature painter. He was the son of Pierre Ollivier, a Huguenot who lived at Rouen (Edwina Brett, *A Kind of Gentle Painting,* Edinburgh, 1975; Daphne Foskett, *A Dictionary of British Miniature Painters,* 1972, i. 427–9).

17. Isaac Oliver (or Olivier, or Ollivier) (d. 1687), probably a son of Isaac Oliver, the painter; educ. Eton ca 1626–30 and King's College, Cambridge; fellow of King's 1633–86; lived for many years at Isleworth, Middlesex; became insane (Sir Wasey Sterry, *The Eton College Register 1441–1698,* Eton, 1943, pp. 250–1).

spelt and subscribed to a copy of thirty-two English verses in the *Obsequies to the Memorie of Mr Edward King*, Cambridge, 1638, 4to,[18] is not clear. Among the Latin poems on the birth of the fifth child of Charles,[19] of the same place, I find a copy signed *Is. Olivier, Coll. Regal.*[20] In the *Rex Redux*, Cant[abrigiæ], 1633, *Isaac Ollivier, Coll. Regal.*[21] In the list of the Eton alumni, A.D. 1630, Isaac Oliver appears, with a note: MSS. *Olivier.*[22] From whence we may infer that he was fellow of King's.[23] Among the *Elegies on the Death of the last Lord Stafford* in 1640, 4to, is one signed *B. Ollivier.*[24] The connection betwixt these, if any, must be obscure. Sir John Harington,[25] a lover and judge of painting and engraving, in the notes to the 33d book of his *Orlando*,[26] makes very honourable mention of *Hilliard.*[27] 'For takyng the true lynes of the face,' he says, 'I think our countryman Mr *Hilliard* is inferior to none that lives at this day: (1591)[28] as among other things of his doing, myselfe have seen him, in white and blacke in foure lynes only set downe the feature of the Queenes Majesties countenaunce; that it was even thereby to be knowne; and he is so perfect therein (as I have heard others tell) that he can set it down by the Idea he hath, without any paterne.'[29] Your having once hinted, that any information on the subject of painting, which,

18. Oliver's elegy of thirty-two lines is the eighth poem (pp. 15–16) in *Obsequies to the Memorie of Mr Edward King*, Cambridge, 1638, which forms the second part of *Justa Edovardo King naufrago, ab amicis mœrentibus, amoris & μνείας χάριν*, Cambridge, 1638.

19. Anne (1637–40), fifth child and third dau. of Charles I and Queen Henrietta Maria; died of consumption, aged three (M.A.E. Green, *Lives of the Princesses of England*, 1849–55, vi. 393–5).

20. Συνῳδία, *sive musarum Cantabrigiensium concentus et congratulatio, ad serenissimum Britanniarum regem Carolum, de quinta sua sobole, clarissima principe, sibi nuper felicissime nata*, Cambridge, 1637, sig. I2.

21. *Rex redux, sive musa Cantabrigiensis voti damnas de incolumitate & felici reditu regis Caroli post receptam coronam, comitiaq; peracta in Scotia*, Cambridge, 1633, pp. 35–6 (a Latin poem by Oliver).

22. *Catalogus alumnorum, e collegio regali Beatæ Mariæ de Etona in collegium regale Beatæ Mariæ & Sancti Nicolai apud Cantabrigienses cooptatorum, ab anno Domini 1444 . . . usque ad annum 1730*, compiled by Joseph Pote, Eton, 1730, p. 20. HW's copy (untraced) is Hazen, op. cit., No. 3175:2.

23. See n. 17 above.

24. B. Ollivier's 'On the Memory of the late Lord Stafford' appears on sig. T2 of *Elegies upon the Death of the last Lord Stafford*, in Anthony Stafford's *Honour and Vertue, Triumphing over the Grave*, 1640. The poems eulogize Henry Stafford (1621–37), 5th Bn Stafford, 1625. 'B. Ollivier' has not been identified.

25. (1561–1612), Kt, 1599; author and translator of Ariosto.

26. *Orlando Furioso in English Heroical Verse*, 1591, folio.

27. Nicholas Hilliard (ca 1547–1619), miniature painter.

28. Harington's translation was published in 1591; the parenthesis is Bowle's.

29. See *Ludovico Ariosto's Orlando Furioso Translated into English Heroical Verse by Sir John Harington (1591)*, ed. Robert McNulty, Oxford, 1972, p. 385 (Book XXXIII, 'Historie').

from the general opinion of mankind, you have so properly illustrated, would not be unacceptable,[30] must be the excuse for my present intrusion. I am, Sir,

Your most obedient, and most humble servant,

John Bowle

PS. John Rose,[31] Gent., chief gardener (so styled in his epitaph, *New View of London*, 1708, 350[32]), who died September 1677, was the founder of a charity school for a certain number of children to be taught to read and write at Ambrosebury,[33] the place of his nativity.

Honourable Mr Horace Walpole, Berkley Square.

If you will permit your servant to leave a copy for me with Mr Dodsley,[34] or, if more convenient, with Mr Blake[35] at Twickenham, I shall ever retain a grateful sense of the favour.[36]

30. In his letter to Bowle *ante* 11 Feb. 1764, HW wrote: 'If these volumes [*Anecdotes of Painting*], Sir, should ever fall in your way, you would add to the obligation you have already conferred on me, by either pointing out any errors, or contributing to the collection.'

31. (1619–77), gardener to the Duchess of Somerset, afterwards to the Duchess of Cleveland and Charles II (Mason ii. 45 n. 21).

32. The inscription on his monument in St Martin-in-the-Fields church, London, reads in part: 'In memory of John Rose, Gent. late chief gardener to King Charles II. Born at Ambrosbury, in the county of Wilts, October 1619. Deceased in this parish, September 1677 . . .' ([Edward Hatton], *A New View of London*, 1708, i. 350).

33. That is, Amesbury, Wilts, 7½ miles N of Salisbury. A charity school at Amesbury is not recorded in *An Account of Charity Schools lately Erected in Great Britain and Ireland*, 9th edn, 1710, but 'A subscription towards a school' to be set up there is mentioned (p. 14).

34. James Dodsley, the London bookseller.

35. Doubtless John Blake, an attorney who lived at Cross Deep Lodge, Twickenham (R. S. Cobbett, *Memorials of Twickenham*, 1872, p. 262; Berry ii. 237, 240; Chute 358 n. 14).

36. 'In consequence of the above Mr Walpole sent me the book accompanied with a polite letter' (Bowle's note in his MS draft). HW's letter is missing.

To William Suckling,[1] Friday 31 January 1783

Printed from *Works* ii. 389, where the letter was first printed. Reprinted, Toynbee xii. 397. The history of the MS and its present whereabouts are not known.

Berkeley Square, January 31, 1783.

Dear Sir,

THE more I reflect on what you said to me yesterday, the stronger is my opinion that the most faithful and exact account should be given of all the fees and profits belonging to the office.[2] There can be no right to anything that it is necessary to conceal from those who have authority to ask an account[3]: and as this is my opinion, I must beg you will observe it as far as I have any title to interfere, and to keep it as a record of my sentiments, if they do not prevail in other offices.[4] I do not pretend to judge for others, but I am very solicitous to preserve my own conduct uniform with what it has always been. I have no notion of holding a public office and not being ready to give an account of it at a minute's warning. I am, dear Sir,

Yours most sincerely,

Hor. Walpole

1. (1730–98), deputy collector of customs 1772–98; HW's first cousin once removed (Mann viii. 178 n. 7).

2. The office of collector of customs London port inwards. The office was nominally held by Sir Horace Mann, but HW and Sir Edward Walpole received large shares of the profits. See HW to Edward Louisa Mann *ante* 28 July 1771, n. 6.

3. The Act of 20 Geo. III (1780), c. 54, and subsequent amendments, 'appointing and enabling commissioners to examine, take, and state the public accounts of the kingdom; and to report what balances are in the hands of accountants, which may be applied to the public service,' made all offices in the Customs subject to inquiry (*Statutes at Large,* ed. Owen Ruffhead, 1763–1800, xiii. 590–2). The results of the investigation were published in *The Thirteenth Report of the Commissioners Appointed to Examine . . . the Public Accounts,* 1785, and the *Fourteenth Report,* 1786.

4. See following letter.

From William Suckling, Saturday 1 February 1783

Printed from *Works* ii. 389–90, where the letter was first printed. The history of the MS and its present whereabouts are not known.

February 1, 1783.

Dear Sir,

BE pleased to accept my most humble thanks for your speedy compliance with my request in applying to the Commander-in-Chief[1] for purchasing a commission; the young man I wish to introduce into the service is my son,[2] aged twenty, about five feet, ten inches high.

Since I had the honour of waiting upon you, [I] have received a letter from Mr Adair's[3] office of a cornetcy to be sold in Lord Southampton's[4] regiment of dragoons,[5] which I am in treaty for. If any difficulty should arise in the business, your very kind offer of speaking again to the Commander-in-Chief shall be embraced by me.

It gives me the fullest satisfaction to find you more and more strengthened in your opinion as to the propriety of rendering the accounts called for.[6] Sir Edward[7] entirely agreed therein, as he also did in the new arrangement of the warehouse officers.[8] I have the honour to inform you that the Duke of Manchester[9] sees the necessity of a compliance, and has ordered his deputies[10] to make suitable returns to the accounts called for. I am with great respect, dear Sir,

Your most obliged and humble servant,

WILLIAM SUCKLING

1. General Conway.

2. William Suckling, Jr (1762–1833), appointed Cornet, 3d Dragoon Guards, 5 March 1783 (*Army Lists*, 1784, p. 36). He attained the rank of Lt-Col. in his regiment and was made a barrack-master of Great Britain 5 Sept. 1801 (J. J. Muskett, *Suffolk Manorial Families*, Exeter, 1900–10, ii. 205; GM 1801, lxxi pt ii. 954).

3. 'Mr Adair, Chidley Court, Pall Mall,' was the army agent for the 3d Dragoon Guards, in which the younger William Suckling obtained his commission (*Army Lists*, 1784, p. 36).

4. Charles Fitzroy (1737–97), cr. (1780) Bn Southampton.

5. The 3d (King's Own) Dragoons.

Southampton had been Col. of the regiment since 1772. Since the cornetcy that Suckling purchased for his son was in the 3d (Prince of Wales's) Dragoon Guards, he may have been confusing the two regiments.

6. See previous letter.

7. Sir Edward Walpole.

8. For the 'Arrangement of the Officers . . . in the King's Warehouses' see *The Fourteenth Report of the Commissioners Appointed to Examine . . . the Public Accounts*, 1786, pp. 6, 54-5; Appendix VI, p. 71.

9. George Montagu (1737–88), 4th D. of Manchester, 1762; collector of customs London port outwards 1762–88.

To Benjamin Ibbot, Wednesday 19 March 1783

Printed from a photostat of the MS in the Pierpont Morgan Library. First printed, Toynbee *Supp.* ii. 1–2. For the history of the MS see *ante* 24 Sept. 1773.

Address: To Benjamin Ibbott Esq. in Dartmouth Street, Westminster. *Postmark:* ⟨P⟩ENNY ⟨POST PAID⟩.

Memorandum (in ink, in an unidentified hand, on the address leaf): Edmonds.

Berkeley Square, March 19, 1783.

I FEAR, dear Sir, you have thought my silence very blameable or negligent—yet I assure you I have not been in fault: I have neither forgotten nor neglected what you desired.[1] Yet after all I can give you little satisfaction. General Conway at the very first gave your letter[2] to the Duke of Richmond,[3] who said he thought your son would come home, unless removed to some other garrison. I then twice pressed the Duke himself to give me a letter to General Elliot for leave: the Duke said, he believed it would not be minded, and seemed unwilling to give it—yet I flattered myself he would—however as I find no hopes of obtaining it,[4] I could not refrain any longer from acquainting you with what I knew before, that I have little interest, and can only be your useless, though

Sincere humble servant

Hor. Walpole

10. James Meller, deputy collector; William Bates, deputy for foreign business (*Court and City Register*, 1783, p. 116).

1. Since the previous June, Ibbot had been trying to obtain a medical leave of absence for his son, an officer in the Royal Artillery stationed at Gibraltar. He had asked HW to intercede with General Conway, the commander-in-chief, but Conway insisted that the Governor of Gibraltar, General Eliott, was the only proper judge of whether leave should be granted (*ante* 2 and 9 June 1782).

2. A letter (missing) requesting leave for Ibbot's son.

3. Richmond was master general of the Ordnance from March 1782 to April 1783 (Mann ix. 262, 392).

4. Leave was subsequently granted, however, and Ibbot's son returned to England. In March 1784 HW was 'instrumental' in obtaining an extended leave of three months (*post* 12 March 1784).

To RICHARD BULL, Wednesday 26 March 1783

Printed for the first time from the MS pasted in Bull's extra-illustrated copy of Hentzner's *A Journey into England*, SH, 1757, now WSL. This copy (Hazen, *SH Bibl.* 33, copy 4) remained in Bull's library at North Court, Shorwell, Isle of Wight, eventually passing by family descent into the possession of the 5th Lord Burgh (1866–1926); sold Sotheby's 29 June 1926 (Burgh Sale), lot 159, to Quaritch; offered by Quaritch, Cat. No. 405 (Jan. 1927), lot 3061; sold by them to Frank B. Bemis, of Boston, Feb. 1927; acquired from Bemis's estate (through Goodspeed) by WSL, Dec. 1937.

Address: To R. Bull Esq.

March 26th 1783.[1]

Dear Sir,

I COULD not go to Strawberry Hill till Saturday last, when I looked for a Hentzner,[2] which I thought I had, and did find, and send you; but I am sorry it is bound, which perhaps you would wish it were not;[3] yet I have no other,[4] and must therefore beg you to accept this.

Your much obliged

H. WALPOLE

1. '1783' is in Bull's hand.
2. *A Journey into England. By Paul Hentzner, in the Year MDXCVIII*, SH, 1757. 220 copies were printed (Hazen, *SH Bibl.* 31).
3. Bull had the copy rebound in blue morocco in two volumes, which are interleaved and extra-illustrated.
4. That is, to give away. HW's library contained two copies, one of them now WSL and the other in the Dyce Collection, Victoria and Albert Museum (Hazen, *Cat. of HW's Lib.*, Nos 2395 and 2513).

To George Colman, Saturday 10 May 1783

Printed from a photostat of the MS inserted in vol. I of HW's 'Poems of Geo. 3' in the Harvard College Library. First printed in George Colman, the younger, *Posthumous Letters . . . Addressed to Francis Colman, and George Colman, the Elder*, 1820, pp. 123–5. Reprinted in R. B. Peake, *Memoirs of the Colman Family*, 1841, ii. 151–2; Wright vi. 185–6 (closing misquoted and signature omitted); Cunningham viii. 364–5; Toynbee xii. 444–5 (closing and signature omitted in Cunningham and Toynbee); extract printed in E. R. Page, *George Colman the Elder*, New York, 1935, p. 277. The MS apparently passed to George Colman, the younger, after his father's death; sold Wheatley 10 July 1833 (Miscellaneous Autographs Sale), lot 65 (with other letters to Colman); offered by Thomas Thorpe, Cat. of Autographs of Illustrious Personages, 1833, lot 1585; not further traced until sold Sotheby's 26 July 1921 (various properties), lot 490, to Maggs; offered by Maggs, Cat. No. 417 (Christmas 1921), lot 3257; acquired by Augustin Hamilton Parker and given by him (with 'Poems of Geo 3') to Harvard, 1924.

Strawberry Hill, May 10, 1783.

Dear Sir,

FOR *so* you must allow me to call you, after your being so kind as to send me so valuable and agreeable a present as your translation of Horace,[1] I wish compliment had left any terms uninvaded, of which sincerity could make use without suspicion. Those would be precisely what I would employ in commending your poem; and if they proved too simple to content my gratitude, I would be satisfied with an offering to truth, and wait for a nobler opportunity of sacrificing to the warmer virtue.

If I have not lost my memory, your translation is the best I have ever seen of that difficult epistle. Your expression is easy and natural, and when requisite, poetic. In short, it has a prime merit, it has the air of an original.

Your hypothesis in your commentary[2] is very ingenious. I do not know whether it is true, which *now* cannot be known; but if the

1. *The Art of Poetry: An Epistle to the Pisos*, translated, with notes, by George Colman, the elder, 1783. HW's annotated copy, bound in his 'Poems of Geo. 3' at Harvard, is Hazen, *Cat. of HW's Lib.*, No. 3222:19:7.

2. In his introductory dedication to Joseph and Thomas Warton, Colman opposed the view of Richard Hurd, Bishop of Worcester, who had stated that 'the proper and sole purpose of the author

was . . . simply to criticize the Roman drama' (*Ars Poetica. Epistola ad Pisones, with an English Commentary and Notes* [by Hurd], 1749, pp. iv–v). Colman maintained that 'one of the sons of Piso, undoubtedly the elder, had either written, or meditated, a poetical work, most probably a tragedy; and . . . he had, with the knowledge of the family, communicated his piece, or intention, to Horace: but Horace, either disapproving of the work,

scope of the epistle was, as you suppose, to hint in a delicate and friendly manner to the elder of Piso's sons, that he had written a bad tragedy, Horace had certainly executed his plan with great address; and, I think, nobody will be able to show that anything in the poem clashes with your idea. Nay, if he went farther, and meant to disguise his object, by giving his epistle the air of general rules on poetry and tragedy,[3] he achieved both purposes, and while the youth his friend was at once corrected and put to no shame, all other readers were kept in the dark, except you, and diverted to different scents.

Excuse my commenting your comment, but I had no other way of proving that I really approve both your version and criticism than by stating the grounds of my applause. If you have wrested the sense of the original to favour your own hypothesis, I have not been able to discover your art, for I do not perceive where it has been employed.[4] If you have given Horace more meaning than he was entitled to, you have conferred a favour on him, for you have made his whole epistle consistent, a beauty all the spectacles of all his commentators could not find out—but indeed *they* proceed on the profound laws of criticism, *you* by the laws of common sense,[5] which marching on a plain natural path is very apt to arrive sooner at the goal, than they who travel on the Appian Way, which was a very costly and durable work, but is very uneasy, and at present does not lead to a quarter of the places to which it was originally directed. I am Sir, with great regard

Your much obliged (and not for the first time)[6]
and most obed[ient] humble servant

Hor. Walpole

or doubting of the poetical faculties of the elder Piso, or both, wished to dissuade him from all thoughts of publication. With this view he formed the design of writing this *Epistle,* addressing it . . . indifferently to the whole family, the father and his two sons' (Colman, op. cit. vi).

3. Colman argued, contrary to Bishop Hurd, that the opening section of the *Epistle* 'certainly contains general rules and reflections on poetry, but surely with no particular reference to the drama' (ibid. v).

4. 'Of the following version I shall only say, that I have not, knowingly, adopted a single expression, tending to warp the judgment of the learned or unlearned reader, in favour of my own hypothesis' (ibid. ix).

5. 'I do not wish to dazzle with the lustre of a new hypothesis, which requires, I think, neither the strong optics, nor powerful glasses, of a critical Herschel, to ascertain the truth of it; but is a system, that lies level to common apprehension, and a luminary, discoverable by the naked eye' (ibid. vi).

6. In 1778 Colman had produced HW's one-act 'moral entertainment' *Nature Will Prevail* at the Little Theatre in the Haymarket; see *ante* 2 March 1778.

To the Hon. Thomas Fitzwilliam,[1]
Friday 16 May 1783

Printed from a photostat of the MS in the University of Reading Library, kindly furnished by the Archivist, Mr J. A. Edwards. First printed, Cunningham viii. 369. Reprinted, Toynbee xii. 449–50. The MS, along with that of HW to Fitzwilliam *post* 28 May 1787, was apparently 'found among the papers of the late Viscount Fitzwilliam'; owned by Henry Castleman, of Beech House, near Ringwood, Hants, in 1857; not further traced until presented by Mr S. Smith, of Stoneham School, Cockney Hill, Reading, to the University of Reading Library in 1965.

Endorsed in an unidentified hand: The original of the letter printed in p. 369.[2]

Berkeley Square, May 16, 1783.

I FEAR, Sir, that I must have appeared very ungrateful and negligent for not thanking you the instant I had the honour of receiving your letter;[3] but the truth is, that lest I should give you the double trouble of two letters from me, I waited till your present[4] arrived, which the carrier brought to me but half an hour ago.

The beauty and curiosity of the basin, great as they are, scarce could add to my confusion. It was considerable enough before! How could I suppose myself entitled to such a favour? such an honour? I must ever be partial to my house and inconsiderable collection, since they were curious enough to amuse you, Sir, and to make you recollect their still more inconsiderable possessor. Since you have been so favourable to all three, I must flatter myself that whenever you are at Richmond,[5] you will condescend to visit once more a house to which you have added so rare an ornament, and a person who will be very impatient to thank you in person.

The basin which is perfect, is I believe, Turkish. I have a small plate, but very inferior in beauty and preservation, which was given to me for Turkish;[6] and the characters on the outside of your basin, Sir, seem to me Eastern—but I question very much whether the

1. (1755–1833), 9th Vct Fitzwilliam, 1830.
2. That is, Cunningham viii. 369.
3. Missing.
4. 'A basin of Turkish earthenware, gilt within; a present from Mr Fitzwilliam,' kept in the China Room at SH ('Des. of SH,' *Works* ii. 416).
5. Fitzwilliam's mother, the Dowager Viscountess Fitzwilliam, lived at Richmond in Surrey (see n. 8 below).
6. In the China Room, 'a Turkish earthenware plate, brown and gold, a present from Mrs Griffith the authoress' ('Des. of SH,' *Works* ii. 416).

art of gilding the composition is not only, extremely ancient, but an art lost. It resembles those Moorish mosaics which are said to adorn the Alhambra in Spain.[7]

You have added to this great favour, Sir, by giving me a pretense for asking the honour of a visit from Lady Fitzwilliam;[8] and if you and Mrs Fitzwilliam[9] are ever so good as to meet her at Strawberry Hill,[10] you will make completely happy one who has the honour to be with the highest respect and gratitude,

Sir,

Your most obliged and most obedient humble servant

HORACE WALPOLE

From RICHARD BULL, Friday 30 May 1783

Printed for the first time from the MS now WSL, pasted in the second volume of HW's *Collection of Prints, Engraved by Various Persons of Quality*. For the history of this volume see Hazen, *Cat. of HW's Lib.*, No. 3588.

Address: Hon. Mr Walpole, Berkeley Square.

May 30, 1783.

MR Bull sends the enclosed[1] for Mr Walpole to put into his book[2] or into his fire, as he pleases. They are engraved by

7. HW also had in his collection at SH 'three pieces of Moorish mosaic; on one a shield, with the name or title of a Moorish king; bought at the auction of Mr Carter, who published an account of Spain' (ibid. ii. 417).

8. Catherine Decker (d. 1786), m. (1744) Richard Fitzwilliam (1711–76), 6th Vct Fitzwilliam, 1743.

9. Agnes Macclesfield (d. 1817), m. (1780) the Hon. Thomas Fitzwilliam.

10. HW's 'Book of Visitors,' begun in 1784, records visits to SH by Thomas Fitzwilliam on 5 Aug. 1794 and 4 May 1796 (BERRY ii. 246, 250).

———

1. Nine etchings, some signed 'E H' or 'H' and dated between 1761 and 1765.

Among them are views of the church of St Victor and Peter Abelard's Paraclete (dated 'Parisiis Jun. 13, 1763'), 'Vieux Calais,' 'W. End of the Church of Dunmore Priory, Essex, E H fec. Dec. 31, 1765'; also a bust-length portrait with HW's MS note 'Sir Thos. Bodley, from his portrait' and three prints of heads and figures, two of them dated 'Feb. 11, 1761.'

2. *A Collection of Prints, Engraved by Various Persons of Quality* (see headnote).

3. Edward Haistwell (or Hastewell) (ca 1736–83), son of Edward Haistwell, of the Middle Temple, barrister at law; F.S.A.; friend of Richard Gough (GM 1783, liii pt i. 181; 1800, lxx pt i. 87; Nichols, *Lit. Anec.* vi. 268, 615–16).

Mr Haistwell,[3] formerly a fellow commoner of C.C.C. College,[4] Cambridge.[5]

Mr Bull will be in town again soon.

To the REV. CHRISTOPHER ALDERSON,[1]
Sunday 1 June 1783

Printed for the first time from the MS now WSL. The MS passed by family descent into the possession of Mrs Helen G. Mott, who sold it (through the good offices of her brother, Mr G. F. J. Cumberlege) to WSL in Jan. 1960.

Address: To the Reverend Mr Alderson at the Countess of Holderness's[2] in Hertford Street, London. *Postmark:* 2 IV. ISLEWORTH.

Strawberry Hill, June 1st 1783.

I WAS vexed on Friday, Sir, to hear you had called at my house without letting me know you was there. I was just coming hither, but should certainly have been glad to see you. I did write immediately to Gen. Conway,[3] though I did not know your friend's[4] name which Mr Mason does not mention,[5] to inquire if there was any probability of his being served soon.[6] Mr C. replies[7] that he finds on his list a Mr Anderton[8] recommended by Lady Holderness, and

4. Corpus Christi College. Haistwell was admitted as a pensioner in 1753, as a fellow commoner in 1758 (Venn, *Alumni Cantab.* Pt II, iii. 284).

5. 'He married Miss Brickenden of New-bury and died in his 47th year at the Hotwells, Bristol, 1783' (MS note in an unidentified hand on Bull's letter). Richard Gough's 'Epithalamium, On the Marriage of Edward Haistwell, Esq. F.S.A.' is printed in Nichols, *Lit. Anec.* vi. 338.

1. (ca 1737–1814), William Mason's curate at Aston, Yorks; rector of Aston 1797–1814 in succession to Mason (MASON i. 43 n. 10).

2. Lady Holdernesse's late husband, the 4th Earl (1718–78), was Mason's patron; he had given Mason the living of Aston in 1754.

3. As commander-in-chief.

4. Not identified, but apparently a relative also named Alderson.

5. Mason wrote HW 19 May 1783: 'I should be greatly obliged to you if you would permit [Alderson] to give you a memorandum relating to an application which Lady Holdernesse made to General Conway some time ago for a young relation of his about an ensigncy. I know he put him on his list' (MASON ii. 303).

6. HW's letter of 30 May to Conway is missing. He informed Mason 31 May: 'I wrote a line immediately to General Conway, desiring he would look over his memoranda for a recommendation of Lady Holderness (for you did not even tell me the young gentleman's name) and send me word whether anything was likely to be done for him soon' (ibid. ii. 304).

7. Conway's reply of 31 May is missing; HW received it 1 June (ibid. ii. 307).

8. The name was spelled 'Alderton' on Conway's list, as HW states correctly in his letter to Mason 31 May (ibid. ii. 307, *sub* 'Sunday, June 1').

asks if it is the person I mean. I shall tell him, if you do not contradict me, that it is within a letter.[9] He says indeed, that when Lady H.
applied it was before the close of the war,[10] when he thought it
would rain ensigncies; and that he is now left with above an hundred engagements, the difficulty of performing which is increased by
the plan adopted of seconding two companies with their officers on
all the corps.[11]

I shall be in town on Thursday, Sir, and if you will be so good as
to call on me on Friday, I shall have seen Gen. Conway, and will let
you know if there are any better hopes of serving your friend soon.[12]
I am Sir

Your most obed[ient] servant

HOR. WALPOLE

9. That is, within one letter of the correct spelling, Alderson.

10. With America.

11. 'Seconding' is a military term for
the temporary removal of an officer from
his regiment or corps (OED *sub* 'second'
v. 2). The plan for reducing the size of
the Army was outlined by the secretary-
at-war, the Hon. Richard Fitzpatrick, in
a speech 13 June 1783 in the House of
Commons. He announced that 'it had
been determined to reduce the companies
from ten to eight, except in the guards
and household troops,' and it was proposed 'that the captains of the two reduced companies should remain on full
pay, so that in each regiment there would
be eight companies, and ten captains . . .
the two captains *en second* were to succeed to such companies as should become
vacant; and . . . no others were to be appointed captains in their stead' (Debrett's
Parliamentary Register, 1781–96, x. 165–6).

12. HW reported to Mason on Monday,
9 June: 'I have seen Mr Alderson and
told him what General Conway says, to
whom I have spoken again, and who will
serve his friend when he can, though it
will not be soon from the circumstances I
mentioned, and of which Mr Alderson
allows the force' (MASON ii. 308). The
Army Lists for the next ten years include neither an Alderson nor an
Alderton.

To ? Thomas Cadell, Wednesday 11 June 1783

Printed for the first time from the MS in Thomas Kirgate's hand, now wsl. The MS is untraced until acquired by Lewis Buddy, III; sold by his family (in a collection of Walpoliana) to wsl, Feb. 1946.

The addressee is conjecturally identified as Thomas Cadell, one of the two publishers of Hugh Blair's *Lectures on Rhetoric and Belles Lettres*, 1783, which contained the engraved portrait of Blair. HW, who was acquainted with Cadell, probably saw the advertisement for the *Lectures* in the *London Chronicle sub* 7 June, liii. 542, and had Kirgate write to Cadell to request a separate impression of the engraving (see n. 2 below).

Strawberry Hill, June 11, 1783.

Sir,

MR Horace Walpole will be much obliged to you if you will let him have one of Dr Hugh Blair's[1] head,[2] and will send it to his house in Berkeley Square tomorrow or Friday when he will be in town.

To George Colman, ? Wednesday 11 June ?1783

Printed from an extract quoted in Thomas Thorpe's Catalogue of Autographs of Illustrious Personages, 1833, lot 1584. The MS, described as a note dated 'Strawberry Hill, June 11' thanking Colman for the present of a book, has not been further traced. The book is conjecturally identified as George Lillo's *Fatal Curiosity*, altered by Colman and published in 1783 (Hazen, *Cat. of HW's Lib.*, No. 1810:36:1).

Strawberry Hill, June 11.

[Mr Walpole] is concerned that though they are such near neighbours,[1] they meet so seldom.

1. (1718–1800), D.D., Scottish literary critic and divine.

2. An engraving by James Caldwall, after the painting by David Martin, executed for the frontispiece to Blair's *Lectures on Rhetoric and Belles Lettres*, 2 vols, published ca 7 June 1783 by Cadell and by William Strahan (*BM Cat. of Engraved British Portraits* i. 197; Ossory ii. 416 n. 13). The book does not appear in the SH records, but HW doubtless wanted a separate impression of the print for his collection of 'heads.' He apparently received it, for an engraved portrait of Blair was sold London 626 (with other prints) to Evans for 13s.

1. Colman lived across the Thames in Richmond, where he had built a villa in 1766 (Ossory i. 31 n. 18).

To Lord Shelburne,[1] Thursday 19 June 1783

Printed from *Works* ii. 390–1, where the letter was first printed. Reprinted, Toynbee xiii. 9–11. The history of the MS and its present whereabouts are not known.

June 19, 1783.

My Lord,

NOTHING but the dread of ostentation would have prevented me long ago from taking the step I am now going to take, and which obliges me to give your Lordship this trouble, which I flatter myself you will excuse in pity to the feelings of a man who has long suffered in silence under the painful sensation of being reckoned in any manner a burthen to the public.

From the moment that the necessities of this country made reformation of expense called for,[2] I not only approved of such a design, but was most ready to be an object of it. So far from any wish of being exempted, I did everything that became me as a benefited servant of the public to lay open my situation to those delegated to inquire into the state of offices. I ordered my deputy [3] to give the most minute account of my advantages, and to offer to the Commissioners every light that it was possible for me to give about my own office.[4] I can boldly say, that every Board of Treasury that has been employed since reformation was started, must bear me witness that publicly or privately they never heard my name to any application for favour or mitigation of my lot. I could go farther, if the repugnance I have to saying anything of myself did not enjoin me silence, as it has during a long period of very irksome reflections on my standing in the light of one chargeable to the public, without any merit on my part.

But, my Lord, when I read in the papers on coming to town today that my office of usher of the Exchequer has not only been alleged in the House of Commons as an expensive one, but as a bar to the

1. William Petty (1737–1805), styled Vct Fitzmaurice; 2d E. of Shelburne, n.c., 1761; cr. (1784) M. of Lansdowne; first lord of the Treasury July 1782–April 1783.
2. See Richard Burke to HW *ante* 7 July 1782, n. 8.

3. Charles Bedford, deputy usher of the Exchequer.
4. HW's letter to Bedford, instructing him to furnish the accounts of his office requested by the Treasury commissioners, is *ante* 12 Aug. 1782.

correction of great waste,⁵ I can no longer be silent. I must sacrifice my aversion for parade to my duty; and must beg leave to say to your Lordship, that I entreat that my patent may be no obstacle to any necessary reformation. I am ready to consent to anything that Parliament shall think it proper to do. The legislature without my consent may do what it pleases, but it will have my perfect and cheerful acquiescence in whatever it shall please to ordain about me and my office. I am ready to surrender my patent, and shall be content with whatever shall be thought enough for me by a new regulation. I wish my age of sixty-six and my infirmities did not reduce this tender to a very immeritorious one, for to give up what I have very little time to enjoy is no very heroic effort.

But though I am little solicitous about myself, I do feel for my deputy and clerk,⁶ who have long faithfully executed all the trouble of my office, and have wives and families unprovided for, but during my life. I should hope to have them considered; and though I have no merit to plead myself, I flatter myself that this testimonial to their integrity will have a little weight.

The great confidence I have in your Lordship's goodness and honour makes me take the liberty of addressing this letter to you, for two reasons; one to authorize your Lordship to take what step you please with regard to my office,⁷ and the other, that you would

5. The *London Chronicle* 17–19 June, liii. 579–80, reported the debate in the House of Commons 17 June on the bill for reform of abuses in public offices. William Pitt 'said he would state a few facts . . . which would convince them . . . that abuses did exist in several public offices'; he asserted that 'many [abuses] existed in the very Treasury itself. . . . The House would, probably, be surprised to hear, how much [Lord North] had cost the public the last year he presided at that Board, for stationery ware.' Lord North replied that 'as to . . . stationery for his use, £40 per cent. must be taken off, as the due of the usher of the Exchequer . . . the 40 per cent. perquisites to another officer [HW], would bring the consumption to about £600 a year; and on this he must say, that as the Treasury was served by patent, it was not served as well, or as cheaply, as it might otherwise be.'

6. William Harris (*ante* 27 Feb. 1771, n. 2).

7. 'Lord John Cavendish [the chancellor of the Exchequer] called on me on [June] 22d; said, if I resigned, my place must go to [Samuel] Martin. He said he should, when he had time, bring in a bill for taking away Exchequer places, but should give possessors the same salaries as stated by the Commissioners of Accounts. I said I could not take mine at that rate; they had stated mine at 4100 *l.* a year; which I thought hard: they had taken a very high year when I had received more than a yearly payment (indeed three quarters); that I had not complained, because I would not seem to lower my place; yet, as I had thought myself ill-treated by its being overcharged, I could not in conscience not tell him the truth; and that so far from desiring 4000 *l.* a year, I should be content with half: that I had much rather have a provision made for my deputy and clerk for their lives' (HW's note at the conclusion of 'Letters

not produce this letter unless necessary to my vindication. I had still rather bear the vexation of what has been said on my place in public, than seem to affect any vainglorious self-denial. It shall suffice me to have deposited my justification in so honourable a bosom as your Lordship's, unless I should be called on to clear myself more publicly.

I have the honour to be with the greatest respect, my Lord,

Your Lordship's most obedient humble servant,

HOR. WALPOLE

From RICHARD GOUGH, Wednesday 25 June 1783

Printed from Nichols, *Lit. Anec.* vi. 286, where the letter was first printed. The history of the MS and its present whereabouts are not known.

June 25, 1783.

MR Gough presents his respectful compliments to Mr Walpole, with many thanks for the use of the monumental drawings[1] now returned, hopes the execution of the plates[2] will be an apology

to and from Ministers,' *Works* ii. 392). The Commissioners for Examining the Public Accounts subsequently concluded that the usher of the Exchequer received fees and emoluments that were excessive. By the Act of 23 Geo. III, c. 82, the office was to be abolished upon the death of the present holder and the holder of the reversion (*Statutes at Large*, ed. Owen Ruffhead, 1763–1800, xiv. 401–2). Since Samuel Martin, who had the reversion of the office, predeceased HW, the ushership was not abolished until HW's death in 1797. See J. E. D. Binney, *British Public Finance and Administration 1774–92*, Oxford, 1958, p. 232.

1. Twenty-three drawings of monuments from the three-volume collection of Smart Lethieullier that HW had purchased in 1761. HW had lent the drawings to Gough in July 1782 for use in preparing his *Sepulchral Monuments in Great Britain*, 2 vols. 1786–96 (*ante* 10 July 1782,

n. 1). The collection is now BM Add. MSS 27,348–50; see Hazen, *Cat. of HW's Lib.*, No. 3503.

2. Part I of *Sepulchral Monuments*, published in 1786, contains numerous plates plus engravings in text, as detailed in the List of Plates, pp. 11–12. The drawings from the Lethieullier collection that interested Gough were chiefly those of the tombs of the Earls of Oxford in Earls Colne Priory, Essex. These drawings, which were made by Daniel King in 1653 and formerly belonged to Lord Fairfax, were engraved for *Sepulchral Monuments* i. 32, 36 (pl. IX, two subjects), 68 (pl. XXIV), and 130 (pl. LII); others are mentioned, though not engraved, ibid. ii. 50. King's drawings are reproduced in F. H. Fairweather, 'Colne Priory, Essex, and the Burials of the Earls of Oxford,' *Archæologia*, 1938, lxxxvii. 292–3, pls LXXXVI–LXXXIX. In addition to those by King, other drawings lent by HW from the collection were engraved for *Sepulchral Mon-*

for so long detaining the draughts and designs. Mr Walpole is requested to accept of the proofs.[3]

From Mrs John Duncombe,[1] Wednesday 25 June 1783

Printed for the first time from the MS pasted in a bound volume of drawings, notes by HW, and other Walpole oddments, now WSL. These materials, along with eighty-five drawings by Michael Burghers, were originally in an album composed by Sir Jonathan Wathen Waller, Bt, from the papers bequeathed to him by Mrs Damer in 1828; the album was sold Sotheby's 5 Dec. 1921 (first Waller Sale), lot 244, to John Johnson of the Oxford University Press; Johnson kept the Burghers drawings and sold the Walpole oddments in Aug. 1931 to WSL, who had the oddments bound in the present volume.

Herne, near Canterbury,[2] June 25, 1783.

AS a small acknowledgment of the pleasure she has received from *The Castle of Otranto*,[3] Mrs Duncombe desires Mr Walpole's acceptance of the enclosed sketch of a principal scene.[4]

uments i. 16 (pl. II*), *36 (pl. XII), 122 (pl. XLVI), and 133 (pl. LIII, two subjects); ibid. ii. 93 (pl. XXX) and 223 (pl. LXXXVII); and in the Introduction (published 1799) to vol. II, p. cccxxx (pl. XL). Gough acknowledges HW's help in the Preface, p. 10, and on p. *36 of Part I.

3. That is, proof impressions of the plates. On 7 Feb. 1782 William Cole had sent HW a specimen (proof sheets) of Gough's work (COLE ii. 294). See *post* 5 July 1783.

1. Susanna Highmore (ca 1730–1812), only dau. of Joseph Highmore, the painter; m. (1761) the Rev. John Duncombe (1729–86), rector of St Andrew and St Mary Bredman, Canterbury, 1757–86 and vicar of Herne, Kent, 1773–86; poet and artist. She was eulogized by her husband as Eugenia in *The Feminiad*, 1754, where she is described in a note (p. 28) as a lady who 'has successfully applied herself to the two sister arts of drawing and poetry.' See GM 1761, xxxi. 188; 1786, lvi pt i. 85, 187–9.

2. In 1773 John Duncombe obtained from Archbishop Cornwallis the living of Herne, about six miles from Canterbury, 'which afforded him a pleasant recess in the summer months' (GM 1786, lvi pt i. 189).

3. The fourth edition was published in 1782, but we have no record that HW presented a copy of this or of an earlier edition to Mrs Duncombe.

4. See illustration. The drawing was made by Mrs Duncombe's brother, Anthony Highmore; see following letter. A very similar drawing, inscribed 'S. Duncombe invt' and bound in a copy (now WSL) of the first edition of *The Castle of Otranto* containing the signature of John Willyams (1707–79), may be Mrs Duncombe's original sketch.

SCENE FROM 'THE CASTLE OF OTRANTO,'
BY ANTHONY HIGHMORE

To Anthony Highmore,[1] Saturday 28 June 1783

Printed from GM 1816, lxxxvi pt i. 578, where the letter was first printed. Reprinted, Cunningham viii. 384; Toynbee xiii. 17. The history of the MS and its present whereabouts are not known.

Strawberry Hill, June 28, 1783.

I AM much obliged to you, Sir, for the favour of your drawing;[2] an honour I could not expect from a gentleman with whom I have not the pleasure of being acquainted; which last circumstance, I hope, will be my excuse if I do not direct this letter properly.

You have expressed well, Sir, what I meant, except one particular, in which, perhaps, I have not delivered myself clearly.[3] I intended to describe the figure as detaching itself not only from the frame, but from the ground; for, as I have said, the figure retired into the chamber at the end of the gallery: it would be more awkward to suppose the whole picture walking, and not the mere figure itself. You will, I flatter myself, Sir, forgive this observation, and be assured that I am with great respect, etc.

Horace Walpole

1. (1719–99), only son of Joseph Highmore, the painter; draughtsman (DNB *sub* Joseph Highmore).

2. See previous letter.

3. The episode occurs in chapter I of *The Castle of Otranto:* 'At that instant the portrait of his [Manfred's] grandfather, which hung over the bench where they [Manfred and Isabella] had been sitting, uttered a deep sigh and heaved its breast. . . . the picture . . . began to move . . . he saw it quit its panel, and descend on the floor with a grave and melancholy air. . . . the vision sighed again, and made a sign to Manfred to follow him. . . . The spectre marched sedately, but dejected, to the end of the gallery, and turned into a chamber on the right hand' (*Works* ii. 20–1).

To Richard Gough, Saturday 5 July 1783

Printed from the MS now wsl. First printed, Nichols, *Lit. Anec.* vi. 286. Reprinted, Toynbee xiii. 17–18. The MS was apparently part of a three-volume collection of autograph letters formed by Miss Anne Nichols that became the property of William Upcott (1779–1845); not further traced until the third volume of letters was sold Sotheby's 18 Nov. 1929 (John Gough Nichols Sale), lot 197, to Rosenbach, whose successor in business, John Fleming, sold the letter (removed from the volume) to wsl in Jan. 1956.

Strawberry Hill, July 5th 1783.

MR Walpole is extremely obliged to Mr Gough for his magnificent present,[1] and very glad to have had any opportunity of contributing to so beautiful and valuable a work. Mr Walpole should have thanked Mr Gough sooner, but did not know how to direct, till he had sent to Mr Nichols.[2]

To Unknown, Wednesday 16 July 1783

Printed for the first time from the MS in Thomas Kirgate's hand, now wsl. The MS is untraced until acquired by Lewis Buddy, III; sold by his family (in a collection of Walpoliana) to wsl, Feb. 1946. The dateline is on a separate slip of paper pasted in the upper right corner of the MS.

Strawberry Hill, July 16, 1783.

Sir,

MR Horace Walpole will be obliged to you if you will inform him where Mrs Macauley Graham[1] lives.[2]

I am, Sir,
Your humble servant,

T. Kirgate

---

1. A set of proof impressions of plates for Part I of Gough's *Sepulchral Monuments*. See *ante* 25 June 1783.
2. John Nichols, HW's occasional correspondent and Gough's intimate friend. After Gough's death, Nichols wrote of him: 'The loss of Mr Gough was the loss

of more than a brother—it was losing a part of [my]self' (*Lit. Anec.* vi. 315).

———

1. Catharine Sawbridge (1731–91), m. 1 (1760) George Macaulay, M.D.; m. 2 (1778) William Graham; historian. The eighth and final volume of her *History*

From JEAN-BAPTISTE-LOUIS-GEORGES SEROUX D'AGINCOURT,[1] Sunday 20 July 1783

Printed from the MS now WSL. First printed, Toynbee *Supp.* iii. 284–8. Damer-Waller; the MS was sold Sotheby's 5 Dec. 1921 (first Waller Sale), lot 88, bought in; resold Christie's 15 Dec. 1947 (second Waller Sale), lot 55, to Maggs for WSL.

Except for the closing and signature, the MS is in the hand of a secretary or amanuensis.

Rome 20 juillet 1783.

Monsieur,

J'ESPÈRE que M. Byres,[2] arrivé à bon port en Angleterre, vous aura remis le paquet dont il s'était chargé,[3] et je vous adresse celui-ci,[4] comme j'ai eu l'honneur de vous en prévenir, chez M. Woolett,[5] graveur.

of England from the Accession of James I to that of the Brunswick Line, 1763–83, was published before 11 July 1783 (MASON ii. 102 n. 15). HW's set (untraced) is Hazen, *Cat. of HW's Lib.*, No. 3197. The date of this letter suggests that Mrs Graham had sent HW her last volume.

2. After her second marriage to William Graham, younger brother of the Scottish quack James Graham, 'she retired to a cottage in Leicestershire.' At the time of her death she was living at Binfield, Berks (GM 1791, lxi pt i. 589).

1. (1730–1814), French archæologist and numismatist; author of *Histoire de l'art par les monuments*, 6 vols, 1823 (A.-J. Dumesnil, *Histoire des plus célèbres amateurs français*, 1857–8, iii. 1–58; *Enciclopedia italiana*, Rome, 1929–39, xxxi. 445; NBG). HW referred to him as 'M. le Chevalier d'Azincourt, a French antiquary, long settled in Italy.' D'Agincourt visited HW at SH in July 1777 (CONWAY iii. 291 and n. 3).

2. James Byres (1734–1817), Scottish architect, antiquary, and art dealer, who sold to Sir William Hamilton the celebrated Barberini vase, later acquired by the Duchess of Portland. He lived in Rome during his active career, retiring in 1790 to his family estate of Tonley in

Aberdeenshire (GM 1817, lxxxvii pt ii. 378; Brinsley Ford, 'James Byres, Principal Antiquarian for the English Visitors to Rome,' *Apollo*, 1974, xcix. 446–61).

3. HW may never have received this parcel, which apparently contained a MS copy of d'Agincourt's 'Recherches sur l'ancien style de l'architecture en Angleterre.' Fearing that the parcel had gone astray, d'Agincourt had another copy made and sent it to HW with his letter *post* 29 June 1784; that copy is presumably the one endorsed by Byres 'Envoyé le 4 juin 1783 à Mr Walpole par M. Byres' and bound, along with the letter and a MS copy of d'Agincourt's 'Recherches relatives à l'origine de l'ogive ou *arco acuto, the pointed arch*,' in a volume (labelled on the spine 'Architecture') now in Sir John Soane's Museum, London. The volume was possibly given away by HW between 1784 and 1797; it is Hazen, *Cat. of HW's Lib.*, No. 3994.

4. That this second parcel arrived safely is apparent by the letter's descending to Mrs Damer (see headnote), but the engravings were not kept with the letter.

5. William Woollett (1735–85), engraver; appointed engraver in ordinary to George III in 1775. He lived in Upper Brook Street, Rathbone Place (GM 1785, lv pt i. 406).

Il contient les différentes gravures que je vous ai annoncées.[6]

Vous verrez pour celles que je destine à l'histoire de l'art[7] que je me borne à donner le trait et les contours, parce que ne pouvant mettre sous les yeux le coloris que la gravure ne rend pas, j'ai cru que pour faire connaître le style de ces temps sur la composition et les formes du dessein, il suffisait de montrer le simple trait des figures. Vous observerez que pour ne donner que des exemples authentiques, je n'ai choisi que des peintures qui portent le nom du peintre ou le millésime de la peinture et de celles dont l'époque est assurée d'une manière historique ou incontestable. Vous voudrez bien m'en dire votre sentiment.

Je vous envoie le dessein d'un médaillon d'Aristote que j'ai trouvé ici dans un collège anglais,[8] que peut-être d'après ce que dit la notice au-bas, vous croirez fondu pour H[enri] VIII par Holbeins[9] et qui entrerait dans la collection singulière que vous avez, de tous les genres de travaux de cet artiste, et dans la liste de ses talents divers que vous donnez, p. 92.[10]

J'y joins trois pièces que je me suis amusé dernièrement à graver: l'une est le portrait du Duc de Chartres,[11] voyageant en Italie sous le nom du Comte de Joinville[12] et qui depuis a passé en Angleterre. L'autre est celui de mon vieux valet de place,[13] le doyen des ciceroni

6. D'Agincourt presumably mentioned them, 4 June, in entrusting to Byres the previous parcel.

7. Published posthumously in 1823 as *Histoire de l'art par les monuments, depuis sa décadence au quatrième siècle jusqu'à son renouvellement au seizième. Ouvrage enrichi de 325 planches*, 6 vols, folio.

8. Roger Baynes (1546–1623), secretary to Cardinal Allen, bequeathed to the English College in Rome a bronze portrait plaque of Aristotle that had once belonged to Henry VIII. This plaque was a replica of the original relief portrait (not a genuine likeness of the philosopher) probably executed by an Italian artist during the second half of the fifteenth century. The replica remained in the library of the English College until the time of the French Revolution; in 1920 the plaque was in the possession of Mr Maurice Rosenheim. A sketch of the plaque made by d'Agincourt, with a note in his hand concerning its history, is in

Vatican Library MS 9846, f. 98 (Cardinal Gasquet, *A History of the Venerable English College, Rome*, 1920, pp. 91–2, 267–71; illustration facing p. 92).

9. Hans Holbein, the younger.

10. 'Holbein's talents were not confined to his pictures; he was an architect, he modelled, carved, was excellent in designing ornaments, and gave draughts of prints for several books, some of which it is supposed he cut himself. . . . He invented patterns for goldsmith's work, for enamellers and chasers of plate, arts much countenanced by Henry VIII' (*Anecdotes of Painting*, SH, 1762–71, i. 92).

11. Louis-Philippe-Joseph de Bourbon (1747–93), Duc de Chartres, 1752; Duc d'Orléans, 1785; 'Philippe Égalité.'

12. He often used the name of the Comte de Joinville when travelling in order to avoid the ceremonies, civic welcomes, and other formalities accorded to a prince of the blood (E. S. Scudder, *Prince of the Blood*, 1937, p. 60).

13. Not idéntified.

ou nomenclatori des Romains. La troisième offre des ornements. Permettez-moi d'ajouter ici quelques observations.

Sur l'histoire[13a] de la peinture et de la sculpture d'après le premier volume de vos *Anecdotes of Painting in England*,[14] qui vous montreront l'attention et le plaisir avec lesquels je les ai lues, et que je regarde la manière dont vous avez traité cette partie, comme propre à servir de modèle.

Les recherches que j'ai faites dans les différentes villes de l'Italie[15] et les monuments des temps reculés que j'y ai fait dessiner, m'ont prouvé que rien de plus vrai, et plus sagement pensé, que ce que vous avez observé au commencement du premier chapitre sur l'inutilité des prétentions à la priorité du renouvellement de l'art, objet perpétuel de contestation dans toutes les villes et les diverses écoles de ce pays.[16]

Le style des commencements pour la composition et pour le choix des sujets est à peu près le même que celui indiqué aux p[ages] 3, 4, 5, et 6.[17]

L'époque de l'invention de la peinture à l'huile éprouve en Italie les mêmes difficultés et par les mêmes raisons que celles discutées aux p[ages] 8, 24, 25, 26, et 27.

Les tableaux qu'on dit peints à l'huile antérieurement à Jean d'Eyck[18] le sont avec un vernis gras couché sur une peinture en détrempe qui au premier aspect les fait croire à l'huile.

13a. The MS reads 'l'historique.'

14. D'Agincourt's *Histoire de l'art* contains numerous references to the *Anecdotes*. Speaking of the fine arts in England, he observes that 'cette nation est soigneuse de conserver les monuments des arts qui peuvent en montrer l'état successif et en illustrer les maîtres. Ceux qui voudront recueillir des matériaux de ce genre, en auront beaucoup de moyens. L'ordre en est parfaitement indiqué dans l'ouvrage de M. Horace Walpole . . . qui mérite d'être honorablement distingué, à cause de l'exactitude du goût et de la critique éclairée avec lesquels il est exécuté' ('Peinture,' *Histoire de l'art* ii. 137).

15. In 1781 d'Agincourt visited Naples, Pæstum, Herculaneum, Pompeii, Mount Vesuvius, and Monte Cassino before returning to Rome to begin work on the *Histoire de l'art* (NBG).

16. 'Mr Vertue had taken great pains to prove that painting existed in England before the restoration of it in Italy by Cimabue. If what we possessed of it in those ignorant times could be called painting, I suppose Italy and every nation in Europe retained enough of the deformity of the art to contest with us in point of antiquity' (*Anecdotes of Painting* i. 1).

17. HW quotes entries from early manuscript records consulted by Vertue.

18. Jan Van Eyck (ca 1390–1441), Flemish painter. He is traditionally credited with the discovery of the technique of modern oil painting, although recent scholarship has tended to define the 'discovery' as his perfecting of the technique. HW doubted the tradition and suggested that oil colours had been in use long before Van Eyck's time (ibid. i. 24–7). He refers to Van Eyck as 'the supposed inventor of painting in oil, which he was said to discover in a search for varnish' (ibid. i. 6n).

On savait dans les derniers temps si bien employer la détrempe perfectionée qu'on lui donnait un moelleux qui la fait prendre pour une peinture à l'huile; d'une autre côté, le défaut de pratique dans les premiers temps où l'on employa l'huile, laisse à ces tableaux une sécheresse qui les fait croire en détrempe, de sorte que je finirais par dire que si Jean d'Eyck n'est pas l'inventeur de la peinture à l'huile, il l'est au moins de l'emploi le plus heureux de l'huile dans la peinture. En effet ce tableau célèbre qu'il envoya au Roi Alphonse[19] et que vous citez, Monsieur, page 27,[20] est encore aujourd'hui du coloris le plus frais, le plus moelleux et le plus harmonieux que l'usage de l'huile ait jamais procuré à la peinture; il est au Château Neuf à Naples; il représente l'adoration des Mages.[21] Je l'ai fait graver; j'en joins ici une épreuve. J'en ai fait graver un autre qui se trouve dans la même ville et sur lequel l'école de Naples réclame la priorité de l'invention à l'huile; il est daté de 1371, porte le nom du peintre, représente St Antoine Abbé,[22] et véritablement paraît peint à l'huile, mais évaporée et séchée de manière à faire croire plutôt, qu'il est en détrempe sous un vernis qui fut gras. La gravure en est ci-jointe. Vous aurez vu sans doute *A Critical Essay on Oil Painting by R. E. Raspe, London, Cadell, in-quarto*,[23] et je vous serai obligé de me dire ce que vous en pensez.

Les difficultés et les erreurs que présente l'article Cavallini,[24] p[ages] 17, 18, et 19, se rencontrent à chaque pas à l'égard des anciens artistes. J'ai sous les yeux les éditions de Vasari[25] dont l'une fait mourir Cavallini à 75 ans et l'autre à 85. L'une dit qu'il fleurissait en 1344, et l'autre en 1364. Elles disent toutes deux qu'il fit le portrait d'Urbain V,[26] mais suivant la p[age] 17 *at that time*[27] . . .

19. Alfonso V (1394–1458), K. of Aragon 1416–58, of Naples 1442–58.

20. 'Some of John ab Eyck's pictures were carried to Alphonso King of Naples' (ibid. i. 27).

21. This 'Adoration of the Magi,' sometimes attributed to Van Eyck, was formerly in the church of Santa Barbara in the Castel Nuovo; it was transferred before 1893 to the Palazzo Reale. The picture has been assigned by Bernard Berenson to Francesco Napoletano, ca 1520 (Felice de Filippis, *La Reggia di Napoli*, Naples, 1942, pp. 63–4; illustrated pl. LXV).

22. 'St Anthony Abbot accompanied by angels and cherubims,' by Colantonio del Fiore, in the church of San Antonio del Borgo, Naples. D'Agincourt's engraving

of it is in *Histoire de l'art* iii. pl. CXXX.

23. For HW's rôle in the printing of this work see *ante* 13 Aug. 1781, n. 3.

24. Pietro Cavallini (fl. 1270–1330), Italian painter and sculptor.

25. Giorgio Vasari (1511–74), author of *Le Vite de' più eccellenti architetti, pittori, e scultori italiani*, Florence, 1550. Later editions of his work were published at Florence (1568), Bologna (1647), Rome (1759–60), and Livorno (1767–72).

26. Guillaume de Grimoard (1310–70), pope 1362–70 as Urban V.

27. 'At that time [1260], says Vasari, flourished there [Rome] Peter Cavalini, a painter and the inventor of mosaic, who had performed several costly works in that city' (*Anecdotes of Painting* i. 17).

il paraît que la vôtre parle d'Urbain IV,[28] qui regnait un siècle avant.

J'ai trouvé encore quelques-unes des histoires de l'ancien testament que Vasari dit que Cavallini peignit dans la nef du milieu de l'église de St Paul;[29] je vous en envoie une copie afin qu'en la comparant à celles de la Chapelle de St Édouard[30] que Virtue, comme vous le dites, p[age] 18,[31] lui attribue, vous puissiez juger.

En parlant des tableaux peints sur bois, permettez-moi de vous demander si pour réunir les différentes pièces qui forment celui dont vous avez cru devoir faire une description particulîère, p[age] 31,[32] il s'y trouve une toile collée, ce que j'ai remarqué à plusieurs de cette espèce longtemps avant que l'usage de peintre sur le toile fut pratiqué, on mettait encore sur cette toile plusieurs couches de plâtre fin, ensuite une couche d'or épaisse, sur laquelle enfin on posait la couleur; cette diversité de matière et d'usage me donne quelque peine pour entendre le catalogue de la page 58.[33]

La compagnie des peintres dont la notice se trouve dans une chartre d'Édouard IV forme une anecdote intéressante,[34] parce que je ne sais s'il en est d'antérieure à cette époque en Italie. M. Strutt dans ses *Antiquités*[35] cite des MSS saxons avec miniature du dixième et du douzième siècle.[36]

28. Jacques Pantaléon (d. 1264), pope 1261–4 as Urban IV. It is unlikely that Cavallini painted a portrait of either Urban IV or Urban V.

29. The early Christian basilica of San Paolo fuori le Mura, almost entirely destroyed by fire in 1823 but subsequently restored. Probably ca 1277–90, Cavallini decorated the walls of the main nave of the basilica with scenes from the Old Testament and from the life of St Paul. These mosaics were severely damaged when an attempt was made to transfer them to the interior of the church after the fire (John White, 'Cavallini and the Lost Frescoes in S. Paolo,' *Journal of the Warburg and Courtauld Institutes*, 1956, xix. 84–95; E. Lavagnino, 'Pietro Cavallini,' *Encyclopedia of World Art*, New York, 1959–68, iii. 171). Several of the scenes were engraved for d'Agincourt's *Histoire de l'art* iii. pl. CXXV.

30. The shrine of Edward the Confessor in Westminster Abbey, erected by Henry III in 1269.

31. 'The old paintings round the chapel of St Edward, and those, in a very beau-

tiful and superior style, though much decayed, over the ragged regiment, Vertue ascribes to the same Cavalini' (*Anecdotes of Painting* i. 18).

32. HW describes an altarpiece, then in the collection of James West, depicting Henry V and his family, 'painted on several boards joined' (ibid. i. 31).

33. 'In the inventory in the augmentation office . . . containing an account of goods, pictures and furniture in the palace of Westminster . . . it appears that they called a picture, *a table with a picture;* prints, *cloths stained with a picture;* and models and bas reliefs, they termed *pictures of earth*' (ibid. i. 58). HW quotes eleven entries from the inventory as examples.

34. 'Their first charter in which they are styled Peyntours, was granted in the 6th of Edward IV but they had existed as a fraternity long before' (ibid. i. 59).

35. Joseph Strutt, *The Regal and Ecclesiastical Antiquities of England*, 1773. HW's copy (untraced) is Hazen, *Cat. of HW's Lib.*, No. 3847.

36. Strutt cites a 'curious and ancient

Sans trouver que vous ayez donné des dates positives à la sculpture, il me semble qu'elle est ancienne en Angleterre et qu'on la travaillait en bois, puisqu'à la p[age] 10, Henri III ordonne de délivrer trois chênes pour faire des images.[37] Je ne sais si en lisant page 6, *columnis marmoreis bene et decenter incisis,*[38] cela veut dire que les colonnes étaient sculptées ou canallées.

Le No. VIII de la collection publiée par cahiers par M. Thomas Hearne[39] parle d'une statue d'albâtre de Jean, Duc de Suffolk, et de sa femme Élisabeth,[40] sœur d'Édouard IV, et le No. VII cite une statue du Roi David I[41] et du Prince Henri[42] dans l'église de Melrose, bâtie peu après 1322.[43]

illumination . . . taken from a book of grants, given by King Edgar himself to Winchester Cathedral (dated *anno* 966). It is written entirely . . . in the old Saxon character.' He also mentions an illumination depicting the murder of Thomas à Becket: 'The original is a frontispiece to the life of that prelate. The book is very old, and was most probably written soon after his death' (*The Regal and Ecclesiastical Antiquities of England*, pp. 5, 9). Both items are in the Cottonian Library in the British Museum.

37. 'The next [record transcribed by Vertue], dated in the same year [34 Henry III, m. 7], exhibits a donation of three oaks for making images' (*Anecdotes of Painting* i. 10). HW quotes the entry in Latin.

38. 'Marble columns well and handsomely cut.'

39. (1744–1817), topographical draftsman and watercolourist. In 1777 Hearne began a collaboration with the engraver William Byrne (1743–1805) on a series of topographical views (mostly of Gothic buildings) in England and Scotland. The views were engraved by Byrne and others, after Hearne's drawings, and were published serially, four plates to a number, each with a letterpress description in English and French, beginning in 1778. In 1786 the numbers were collected and published in a volume of 52 plates entitled *Antiquities of Great-Britain, Illustrated in Views of Monasteries, Castles, and Churches, now Existing.* HW was a subscriber to this work and may have owned more than one copy; see Hazen, *Cat. of*

HW's Lib., Nos 3429 and 3645. A second volume containing 32 plates was published in 1807.

40. Elizabeth (Plantagenet) (1444–ca 1503), sister of Edward IV and Richard III, m. (before Oct. 1460) John de la Pole (1442–ca 1491), 2d D. of Suffolk, 1450. 'There are but few monuments remaining in the Church [of Wingfield in Suffolk] . . . the monument of John, Duke of Suffolk, and Elizabeth his duchess (sister to King Edward IV), whose figures cut in alabaster, are placed upon the tomb at full length, with their coronets and robes of state' (*Antiquities of Great-Britain*, 1786, pl. XXX, Wingfield Castle).

41. (1084–1153), K. of Scotland 1124–53.

42. Henry (ca 1114–52) of Scotland, only son of David I. 'Over the east window [of Melrose Abbey] is the statue of an old man, having a globe in his left hand, and a young man standing by him on his right, with a crown over their heads: these are supposed to be King David, founder of this monastery, and his son, Prince Henry' (ibid. pl. XXVII, Melrose Abbey).

43. Melrose Abbey in Roxburghshire was founded by David I in 1136. One of its side chapels contains a carved head of David I, and there are also two figures (above the arch of the great east window) said to represent the King and his Queen, Matilda. The statue of Prince Henry has not been verified. In 1322 Edward II's army, retreating from Scotland, sacked the Abbey (J. Wass, *Melrose Abbey, with Notes Descriptive and Historical*, 14th edn, Edinburgh, 1890, pp. 10, 23, 26–7).

J'ai entendu parler d'un *Abecedario pittorico*[44] en anglais; je vous prierais de me dire ce que c'est:[45] on y aura sans doute fait entrer les noms des peintres et autres artistes que vous avez découverts et dont vous donnez une liste et des notices intéressantes. Le No. VII des cahiers par M. Th[omas] Hearne fait mention de Jean Murdo[46] dont le nom se trouve dans une inscription de l'église de Melrose, et qui avait été chargé de la maçonnerie des diverses cathédrales.[47]

Je vous assure, Monsieur, de tout mon respect

D'Agincourt

44. Pellegrino Antonio Orlandi, *Abcedario pittorico*, Bologna, 1704. HW's copy (untraced) of the edition published at Bologna in 1719 is Hazen, *Cat. of HW's Lib.*, No. 2082.

45. A small portion of Orlandi's work had been translated into English as *Repertorium sculptile-typicum: or A Complete Collection and Explanation of the Several Marks and Cyphers by which the Prints of the Best Engravers are Distinguished*, 1730.

46. John Morvo (or Morrow), a mason who worked on the south transept of Melrose Abbey. 'The remains of two interesting inscriptions in Gothic lettering are to be seen on the west wall; both have reference to a master mason named John Morvo (Moreau), who was born in Paris and who was probably responsible for detailing the features of the south

gable' (J. S. Richardson and Marguerite Wood, *Melrose Abbey, Roxburghshire*, Edinburgh, 1932, pp. 12–13; inscriptions quoted p. 13).

47. 'To the right of the south window in the print is a door, leading to a curious winding turnpike staircase, over which is a compass with an inscription alluding to the form of the staircase, with the name of John Murdo annexed to it: and nearly adjoining, on a stone fixed into the wall, are some uncouth lines, which import that this John Murdo had the care and direction of all the mason's work in the cathedral churches of St Andrew's, and Glasgow, the abbey churches of Melrose, and of Paisley, as likewise, in those of Niddisdale and Galloway' (*Antiquities of Great-Britain*, 1786, pl. XXVII, Melrose Abbey).

From Charles James Fox, ?August 1783

Printed from an extract quoted in Maggs Bros. Catalogue 405 (summer 1921), lot 870. The MS is described as an autograph letter signed by Fox, one page, quarto, written from Grafton Street, London; its present whereabouts is not known.

Maggs conjecturally dated the letter 'April 1782' (when Fox was for the first time secretary of state for foreign affairs), but it was more likely written between April 1783 (when he regained the office in the new coalition government) and 10 Sept. 1783, the date of his letter to HW concerning an employment for Thomas Walpole the younger. In his letter to the Hon. Thomas Walpole 23 July 1783, HW says he will seize any chance 'to be useful to my cousin Thomas . . . but I am so useless and of so little consequence to ministers, that it is not very likely; nor are there many from whom I would ask a favour' (FAMILY 211).

I . . . can only say that I shall be very happy upon all occasions to obey your commands. In this instance the regard I have for Mr Thos. Walpole[1] would certainly be a strong additional motive. . . . whenever a proper occasion presents itself I shall be very glad to employ young Mr Walpole[2] in the way that you seem to wish for him.[3]

---

1. See *ante* 30 April 1772, n. 2.
2. Thomas Walpole (1755–1840), eldest son of HW's first cousin the Hon. Thomas Walpole; minister plenipotentiary 1784–8 and envoy extraordinary and plenipotentiary 1788–96 to the Court of the Elector Palatine at Munich, and envoy extraordinary and minister plenipotentiary to Bavaria 1784–96; minister to the Imperial Diet at Ratisbon 1784, 1795–6 (D. B. Horn, *British Diplomatic Representatives 1689–1789*, 1932, Camden Society, 3d ser., xlvi. 43, 62–3; S. T. Bindoff, E. F. Malcolm Smith, and C. K. Webster, *British Diplomatic Representatives 1789–1852*, 1934, Camden Society, 3d ser., l. 21, 106).
3. See *post* 10 Sept. 1783.

To Edward Edwards,[1] Wednesday 13 August 1783

Printed for the first time from a photostat of the MS in Thomas Kirgate's hand in the British Museum (Stowe MS 755, f. 81). On the same sheet, below the note, are two pencil sketches by HW of the east front of SH before and after he altered it.[2] The sketches are numbered by Edwards, with his memoranda in pencil underneath: '1. The house when first taken by Mr Walpole. 2. After the alterations.' A pencil note in a different hand reads: 'Sketch by H. Walpole.' In the lower left corner there is a pencil sketch of a shield and two ornamental borders. The MS was given by Edwards to George Baker (1747–1811) in 1797 (see n. 2 below); sold Sotheby's 18 June 1825 (Baker Sale), lot 314 (with other SH items), to Colnaghi; later acquired by the 2d Duke of Buckingham and Chandos, who sold the Stowe MSS to the 4th Earl of Ashburnham in 1849; sold by the 5th Lord Ashburnham to the British Museum in 1883.

Address: Mr E. Edwards, Windmill Street near Rathbone Place, London.
Postmark: 14 AV.

Strawberry Hill, Aug. 13, 1783.

MR Walpole will be glad to see Mr Edwards and Mr Humphrie[3] on Friday.[4]

1. (1738–1806), A.R.A., 1773; painter and engraver. He was frequently employed at SH in 1781–3 to make drawings (now WSL) that were engraved for the *Description of SH*, 1784. He wrote a continuation of HW's *Anecdotes of Painting* that was published in 1808.

2. Edwards wrote to the collector George Baker 26 Sept. 1797: 'E[dwards] also sends the note containing the sketch of the east front of the house as it was when Mr Walpole first took it. As E. saw him make the sketch in his presence and for him, he thinks it a curiosity' (BM Stowe MS 755, f. 88).

3. Probably Ozias Humphry (1743–1810), R.A., 1791; portrait painter and miniaturist. In his bedchamber at SH, HW had a portrait by Humphry of Prince William and Princess Sophia, children of the Duchess of Gloucester, 'done when infants at Rome, in chalks' (HW's MS note in his copy, now WSL, of the *Description of SH*, 1784, p. 41). HW gave Humphry a copy of the third edition of *Anecdotes of Painting*, 1782.

4. We have found no record of this meeting.

To Lord Dacre, Sunday 31 August 1783

Printed from a copy kindly supplied by the late Sir Shane Leslie, Bt, in 1941 from the MS then in the possession of the Hon. Mrs Clive Pearson, Parham Park, Pulborough, Sussex. First printed, Toynbee xiii. 50. The MS is untraced until sold Sotheby's 13 March 1903 (Autograph Letters and Historical Documents Sale), lot 597, to W. V. Daniell; acquired by Sir Herbert H. Raphael, Bt, who inserted it in an extra-illustrated copy of Cunningham's edition of HW's *Letters*, 18 vols, folio; this copy was sold Sotheby's 4 Feb. 1919 (Raphael Sale), lot 311, to Bumpus for Lord Cowdray, the father of the Hon. Clive Pearson; bequeathed by his widow, the Hon. Mrs Pearson, to her daughter, Mrs P. A. Tritton, of Parham Park.

Strawberry Hill, Aug. 31, 1783.

My best Lord,

HOW very kind you always are to me! I have now to thank your Lordship for the print of Copthall,[1] as well as for the list of Scotch painters,[2] which I return with gratitude. I shall add them to my own Catalogue,[3] but I shall certainly not think of another edition;[4] there have surely been enough printed. I do lament that your Lordship had so much trouble in getting the paper[5]—but there is no end of my obligations. Your Lordship's and Lady Dacre's goodness to me at Belhouse[6] I can never forget, nor cease to be her Ladyship's and your Lordship's

Most devoted humble servant

Hor. Walpole

1. Copt, or Copped, Hall, 2 miles SW of Epping, Essex, the seat of John Conyers (d. 1818) (GM 1818, lxxxviii pt i. 476; [Elizabeth Ogborne], *The History of Essex*, 1814, pp. 209–12). His father, John Conyers (1717–75), M.P., pulled down the old Elizabethan mansion and built a smaller house there 1753–7 (Montagu i. 92 n. 16).

2. HW pasted in vol. iv of his extra-illustrated copy (now wsl) of *Anecdotes of Painting* an eight-page transcript in Thomas Kirgate's hand entitled 'Anec-

dotes of Painting in Scotland. From the *Weekly Magazine, or Edinburgh Amusement*. Thursday, Jan. 16, 1772.' This was probably the 'list of Scotch painters' mentioned in the letter.

3. That is, *Anecdotes of Painting*.

4. HW called the third edition, 1782, 'my *last*' (*post* 14 July 1784), but a fourth edition was published in 1786.

5. Not identified.

6. Belhus, Lord Dacre's seat near Aveley, Essex.

From CHARLES JAMES FOX,
Wednesday 10 September 1783

Printed from the MS now wsl. First printed, Toynbee *Supp.* iii. 288–9. Damer-Waller; the MS was sold Sotheby's 5 Dec. 1921 (first Waller Sale), lot 126, bought in; resold Christie's 15 Dec. 1947 (second Waller Sale), lot 14, to Maggs for wsl.

St James's, 10 September 1783.

My dear Sir,

I DO assure you that I had not forgot your application in favour of your cousin,[1] and that in consequence of it I told the Duke of Portland[2] that the thing I should *like* best to do upon Maddison's[3] death[4] would be to appoint Mr Walpole[5] to it; but I need not tell you how much what one likes is out of the question when a place[6] is so much and so earnestly solicited as this is. However, it is not yet impossible, though I confess I think it unlikely, that I may be able to follow my own inclination in this instance, in which case you may be assured your cousin will be appointed.[7] I do assure you that

---

1. Hon. Thomas Walpole. See *ante* ? Aug. 1783.

2. William Henry Cavendish Bentinck (1738–1809), styled M. of Titchfield 1738–62; 3d D. of Portland, 1762; first lord of the Treasury April – Dec. 1783 in the coalition ministry of Fox and Lord North.

3. George Maddison (d. 1783). After serving for a time with the Post Office, he became Sir Joseph Yorke's private secretary when Yorke was ambassador at The Hague. He was under-secretary to Lord Grantham while the latter was secretary of state in 1782–3. He was appointed secretary of embassy at Paris 23 April 1783 and died there four months later (D. B. Horn, *The British Diplomatic Service 1689–1789*, Oxford, 1961, p. 140; idem, *British Diplomatic Representatives 1689–1789*, 1932, Camden Society, 3d ser., xlvi. 26, 166).

4. On 27 Aug. 1783, 'at Paris, after a few days illness . . . supposed to have been accidentally poisoned' (GM 1783, liii pt ii. 805).

5. Thomas Walpole, the younger.

6. The secretaryship of embassy at Paris.

7. The Duke of Portland wrote to the Duke of Manchester, the British ambassador at Paris, 4 Sept. 1783: 'Gibbon, Dudley Long, Tom Walpole's son, Mr William Ponsonby, Mr Charles O'Hara, and [William Augustus] Fawkener . . . were all objects of our discussion. . . . With respect to Walpole, Fox is somewhat embarrassed by a sort of promise he made to Lord Camden when they were in administration together, to find out some foreign employment for this young man, but his opinion preponderates greatly in favour of O'Hara. . . .' Fox himself wrote Manchester 17 Sept.: 'The Duke of Portland has, I know, mentioned several persons to you to succeed Maddison; there is another, Mr [Anthony Morris] Storer, who is very strongly recommended, and the disposition of whose place here would be very remarkably convenient.' Fox wrote to him again on the 21st: 'After considering all the circumstances of the case, it was impossible for [me] to avoid naming Mr Storer to succeed Mr Maddison, and you will accordingly hear of his appointment in my next letter. . . . The only thing that concerns me in this business is that I am not able to oblige Lord Camden,

I shall always feel how infinitely I am obliged to you for the conversation we had in Berkeley Square[8] and I am very happy to say that I already find less cause of complaint than I did. General Conway has behaved in the kindest manner in Major Stanhope's[9] business,[10] and I should be very sorry he should not know how sensible I am of this obligation.

I am with great regard, my dear Sir,

Yours ever,

C. J. Fox

To LORD BUCHAN, Thursday 2 October 1783

Printed for the first time from the MS laid in a scrapbook collection of SH Press proofs, now WSL. The collection was acquired by Lowe Bros. (Birmingham) Ltd. with the library of the late Mrs Astley and her late son, Colonel Astley, of Brinsop Court, Herefordshire; offered by them, Cat. No. 1201, lot 762; sold by them to WSL, March 1961.

Endorsed in an unidentified hand: Hor. Walpole. Spurious portrait of David Rizzio.

Address: To the Earl of Buchan at Edinburgh.

Strawberry Hill, Oct. 2d 1783.

I AM very sorry to hear, my Lord, that your Lordship has been out of order.[1] The season indeed has been uncommonly unhealthy, and produced several sorts of epidemic disorders. I have been scared

and Mr Thomas Walpole, to both of whom I feel myself very much engaged; but they may depend upon it that it shall not be long before I find some opportunity' (Hist. MSS Comm., 8th Report, App. ii [*Manchester MSS*], 1881, pp. 131–3). The younger Thomas Walpole was appointed to diplomatic posts in Germany a few months later; see *ante* ? Aug. 1783, n. 2, and FAMILY 214, 219.

8. We have no record of this conversation, but it almost certainly concerned the 'Expostulation of Charles Fox with General Conway on not obliging him with promotions in the army, nor acquainting him and the Ministers with his measures' (*Last Journals* ii. 531, *sub* Aug. 1783). Conway was at this time the commander-in-chief. HW wrote him 15 Aug. 1783: 'I have a high opinion of Mr F[ox] and

believe that by frankness you may become real friends . . . F[ox] is the minister with whom I most wish you united' (CONWAY iii. 406).

9. Hon. Henry Fitzroy Stanhope (1754–1828), younger son of the 2d E. of Harrington; Major 86th Foot, 1779 (Collins, *Peerage*, 1812, iv. 289; GM 1828, xcviii pt ii. 283; *Army Lists*, 1783, p. 163).

10. Stanhope was transferred 12 Sept. 1783 from the 86th Foot to the 1st Foot Guards and promoted to Captain-Lieutenant in the regiment, Lieutenant-Colonel in the army (*Army Lists*, 1784, p. 56). The colonel of the 1st Foot Guards was the Duke of Gloucester, whose wife was HW's niece and Conway's cousin.

———

1. Buchan's letter to HW is missing.

these two months by the rheumatism;[2] but though it was, I believe, produced by the season, my age makes me little expect to get rid of it; though as it adds to my lameness from the gout, I am more earnest than perhaps is reasonable to find a remedy for it. Both together they make me very unfit for anything but quiet.

I know nothing of the picture of David Rizzio,[3] nor indeed of the reputed possessor—nor in truth do I give much credit to the account. I believe it may be above twenty years ago that there was on sale[4] in London a half length picture said to be of Rizzio. I went to see it, but neither could discover any circumstance that appropriated it to him, nor could the proprietor give any reason why he called it so. It was long exposed to sale, yet I do not remember to hear that it was purchased. It is very common in this country for housekeepers, and even for their masters, to baptize pictures without authority.

I sent your Lordship's enclosed letter[5] as you ordered; and shall be very happy to pay my respects to your Lordship this winter in London. I have the honour to be

My Lord
Your Lordship's most obed[ient] humble servant

Hor. Walpole

2. HW mentions his 'poor rheumatic shoulder' in his letter to Lady Ossory 4 Aug. 1783 (OSSORY ii. 412). He wrote Mann 10 Sept. 1783: 'I have the rheumatism in my right arm' (MANN ix. 432).

3. (or Riccio) (ca 1533–66), secretary and alleged lover of Mary, Queen of Scots; he was murdered by her husband and others. The only reference we have found to a portrait of Rizzio is in Some Particulars of the Life of David Riccio, 1815 (included in vol. i of Miscellanea Antiqua Anglicana, 1816), where the frontispiece engraved by C. Wilkin is identified as 'David Rizio. From an original picture painted in 1564, in the possession of H. C. Jennings Esqr.'

4. Not identified.

5. Presumably to a correspondent in London.

From THOMAS POWNALL,[1] ca Saturday 25 October 1783

Printed for the first time from a photostat of the MS in the British Museum (Add. MS 35,335, f. 65). This letter, a copy in Thomas Kirgate's hand of HW's reply *post* 27 Oct. 1783, and the revised draft of Pownall's character sketch of Sir Robert Walpole were endorsed by HW (f. 66): 'Governor Pownall's letters, and my answer, etc. to be preserved. H. W.' They are included in a volume of letters, political verses, and miscellaneous papers, chiefly relating to Sir Robert Walpole, that was in HW's possession; at some time after his death, the volume was acquired by the antiquary John Caley (ca 1763–1834); sold Evans 31 July 1834 (Caley Sale), lot 2245; acquired by Sir Thomas Phillipps (1792–1872), 1st Bt (Phillipps MS 6798); resold Sotheby's 5–10 June 1899 (Phillipps Sale), lot 1175, to the British Museum.

Dated approximately by HW's reply *post* 27 Oct. 1783. The MS bears the date 'Oct. 30, 83' in an unidentified hand, but this is clearly an error.

Richmond, Surrey.

Sir, ——

I VENTURE to submit to your perusal a sketch of the character of your father as a great minister.[2] I mentioned it to you as Lady Mary[3] saw me drawing it and I thought she might possibly mention it. I venture to submit to your eye, as I have the pride to feel that I never do flatter any man, and never did mean anything in any one line I ever wrote but direct truth. My view in this draught in particular was to meet misrepresentation with truth opposed to it, and to bring forward some knowledge of that character (which wants only to be understood) in contrast to the total ignorance under which hitherto it hath been received by the generality of those who presume to be judges.

If there appears to you anything in this sketch, either trifling below the scale of the character, anything that is a misprising of it, any error in fact—the only favour I beg is that you will throw it into the fire.[4] I retain no copy of it and there let it end—this is not a copy of my countenance. I really mean what I say.

1. (1722–1805), lt-governor of New Jersey May 1755; governor of Massachusetts Bay 1757–9, of South Carolina 1760 (did not assume the post); M.P.

2. This character sketch was subsequently revised at HW's request (see *post* 27 Oct. and 7 Nov. 1783) and published as 'On the Conduct and Principles of Sir Robert Walpole, by Governor Pownall' in William Coxe's *Memoirs of the Life and Administration of Sir Robert Walpole, Earl of Orford*, 1798, iii. 615–20.

3. Lady Mary Churchill. See *ante* 25 Aug. 1744 OS, n. 9.

4. HW returned the draught to Pownall with his comments; see following letter.

Whatever there be in it—I may err or fall short in the execution of my hand, but I can never deviate from the reverence I bear to the character of Lord Orford—nor from respect and esteem with which I have the honour to be,

Sir,
Your most obedient and most humble servant,

T. POWNALL

The Honourable Mr Walpole.

PS. I wish you would read Hume's character[5] before you read the enclosed.

To THOMAS POWNALL, Monday 27 October 1783

Printed from the MS now WSL. First printed, GM 1798, lxviii pt ii. 1018–19. Reprinted, Nichols, *Lit. Anec.* iv. 709–11; Wright vi. 204–8; Cunningham viii. 420–4; Toynbee xiii. 73–7 (closing and postscript omitted by Wright and Cunningham, postscript omitted by Toynbee); extract printed in *Letters of Eminent Persons Addressed to David Hume*, ed. J. H. Burton, Edinburgh and London, 1849, p. 1, n. 1. The MS apparently passed from Pownall to John Nichols (see *Lit. Anec.* iv. 709n); sold Sotheby's 18 Nov. 1929 (John Gough Nichols Sale), lot 240, to Maggs; offered by Maggs, Cat. No. 568 (Dec. 1931), lot 1451; sold by them to WSL, June 1932. A copy of the letter in Thomas Kirgate's hand, signed and endorsed by HW 'To Governor T. Pownall, on sending me a sketch of a character of my father, Sir Robert Walpole,' is in the British Museum (Add. MS 35,335, ff. 67–8); for its history see *ante* ca 25 Oct. 1783.

Strawberry Hill, Oct. 27th 1783.

I AM extremely obliged to you, Sir, for the valuable communication you have made to me.[1] It is extremely so to me, as it does justice to a memory that I revere to the highest degree; and I flatter

5. 'A Character of Sir Robert Walpole' in vol. ii of Hume's *Essays, Moral and Political*, Edinburgh, 1741–2. HW did not own a copy of this edition, but he had Hume's *Essays and Treatises on Several Subjects*, 1753–6, which reprinted the 4th edition, 1753, in vol. i (Hazen, *Cat. of HW's Lib.*, No. 1523). In subsequent editions of the *Essays, Moral and Political*, up to and including the edition of 1768, the 'Character' was relegated to a footnote in the essay 'That Politics may be reduced to a Science'; thereafter Hume omitted it entirely (T. E. Jessop, *A Bibliography of David Hume and of Scottish Philosophy*, 1938, pp. 16–17).

1. Pownall had sent HW a draught of his character sketch of Sir Robert Walpole; see previous letter.

myself that it would be acceptable to that part of the world that loves truth—and that part will be the majority, as fast as *they* pass away, who have an interest in preferring falsehood. Happily truth is longer-lived than the passions of individuals; and when mankind are not misled, they can distinguish white from black.

I myself do not pretend to be unprejudiced; I must be so to the best of fathers; I should be ashamed to be quite impartial. No wonder then, Sir, if I am greatly pleased with so able a justification. Yet I am not so blinded but that I can discern solid reasons for admiring your defence. You have placed that defence on sound and *new* grounds; and though very briefly, have very learnedly stated and distinguished the landmarks of our constitution, and the encroachments made on it, by justly referring the principles of liberty to the Saxon system, and imputing the corruptions of it to the Norman.[2] This was a great deal too deep for that superficial mountebank Hume to go[3]— for a mountebank he was. He mounted a *tréteau* in the garb of a philosophic empiric, but dispensed no drugs but what he was authorized to vend by a royal patent, and which were full of Turkish opium. He had studied nothing relative to the English constitution before Queen Elizabeth, and had selected her most arbitrary acts to countenance those of the Stuarts; and even hers he misrepresented, for her worst deeds were levelled against the nobility; those of the Stuarts against the people: Hers consequently were rather an obligation to the people, for the most heinous part of common despotism is, that it produces a thousand despots instead of one. Muley Moloch[4] cannot lop off many heads with his own hand—at least, he takes those in his way, those of his courtiers—but his bashaws and viceroys spread destruction everywhere.

The flimsy, ignorant, blundering manner in which Hume executed the reigns preceding Henry VII[5] is a proof of how little he had examined the history of our constitution.

2. Pownall argued that English kings and 'abettors of regal power' had always favoured the Norman system of government, while the 'genuine English' always resisted it and preferred the Saxon system. The former he associated with present-day Tories, the latter with Whigs (BM Add. MS 35,335, ff. 69–71; see n. 6 below).

3. In his *History of England*, 6 vols, 1754–62. But after the first two volumes

had appeared, HW flatteringly told Hume that his was 'the best history of England' (*ante* 15 July 1758).

4. See Cole i. 289 n. 3.

5. Hume's completed *History of England, from the Invasion of Julius Cæsar to the Revolution in 1688*, 'A New Edition Corrected,' 6 vols, 1762, covered the period from the Roman invasions to the accession of Henry VII in the first two volumes.

I could say much, much more, Sir, in commendation of your work, were I not apprehensive of being biased by the subject. Still that it would not be from flattery, I will prove, by taking the liberty of making two objections, and they are only to the last page but one[6]— perhaps you will think that my first objection does show that I *am* too much biased.

I own I am sorry to see my father compared to Sylla,[7] the latter was a sanguinary usurper, a monster—the former, the mildest, most forgiving, best natured of men, and a *legal* minister. Nor, I fear, will the only light in which you compare them, stand the test. Sylla resigned his power, voluntarily, insolently—perhaps timidly, as he might think he had a better chance of dying in his bed, if retreated, than by continuing to rule by force.[8] My father did not retire by his own option. He had lost the majority of the House of Commons. Sylla, you say, Sir, retired unimpeached—it is true, but covered with blood. My father was not *impeached*, in our strict sense of the word, but, to my great joy, he was in effect. A secret committee, a worse in-quisition than a jury, was named—not to try him—but to sift his life for crimes—and out of such a jury, chosen in the dark, and not one of whom he might challenge, he had some determined enemies, many opponents, and but two he could suppose his friends—and what was the consequence—a man charged with every state crime almost, for twenty years, was proved to have done—what? Paid some writers much more than they deserved for having defended him against ten thousand and ten thousand libels (some of which had been written by his inquisitors) all which libels were confessed to have been lies by his inquisitors themselves—for they could not produce a shadow of one of the crimes, with which they had charged him![9]—I must

6. The revised draught of Pownall's character sketch of Sir Robert Walpole is in the British Museum (Add. MS 35,335, ff. 69–81).

7. Lucius Cornelius Sulla (138–78 B.C.), ruthless dictator of Rome 82–79 B.C.

8. In 79 B.C., at the height of his power, Sulla abdicated his dictatorship for no known reason and retired to Puteoli, where he died the following year.

9. 'Thus Sir Robert Walpole lost the majority of the House of Commons and was driven from his post . . . . They ap-pointed a committee of inquisition to search for proof of crimes which for twenty years they had imputed to him without proof. Proofs light as air would have served to conviction but even these could not be found, and the imputed crimes themselves were so unsubstantial that they vanished upon the touch. His enemies to their eternal infamy and dis-honour could establish no one fact but the one which came now glaring forward in the face of mankind, their falsehood, on which they had been writing, speaking, and acting for twenty years' (Pownall's revised draught, f. 79).

own, Sir, I think that Sylla and my father ought to be set in opposition rather than paralleled.

My other objection is still more serious; and if I am so happy as to convince you, I shall hope that you will alter the paragraph, as it seems to impute something to Sir Robert, of which he was not only most innocent, but of which if he had been guilty, I should think him extremely so, for he would have been very ungrateful.

You say 'he had not the comfort to see that he had established his own family by anything which he received from the gratitude of that Hanover-family, or from the gratitude of that country which he had saved and served.'[10]—Good Sir, what does this sentence seem to imply, but that, either Sir Robert himself, or his family, thought or think, that the Kings George I and II, or England, were ungrateful in not rewarding his services!—Defend him and us from such a charge! He nor we ever had such a thought. Was it not rewarding him to make him prime minister, and maintain and support him against all his enemies for twenty years together! Did not George I make his eldest son[11] a peer, and give to the father and son a valuable patent place in the Custom House for three lives![12] did not George II give my elder brother the Auditor's place,[13] and to my other brother and me other rich places for our lives[14]—for though in the gift of the first Lord of the Treasury, do we not owe them to the King who made him so? did not the late King make my father an earl, and dismiss him with a pension of £4000 a year for his life? Could he or we not think these ample rewards? What rapacious sordid wretches must he and we have been and be, could we entertain such an idea? As far have we all been from thinking him neglected by his country.

10. Pownall's revised draught reads (f. 80): 'He retired with a fortune not greater than his fame . . . . His fame expanded and became more and more illustrious in the eyes of men, while they could not but make the comparison, that the minister, if he had been the man he was represented to be by his opponents, might have amassed millions, left the fortunes of his family unequal to the support of the honours with which he had graced and adorned it.'

11. Robert Walpole (1701–51), cr. (1723) Bn Walpole; 2d E. of Orford, 1745.

12. 'King George the First had graciously bestowed on my father the patent place of Collector of the Customs for his own life, and for the lives of his two elder sons Robert and Edward' (HW's 'Account of my Conduct relative to the Places I hold under Government, and towards Ministers,' *Works* ii. 364).

13. Robert Walpole held 'the great place of Auditor of the Exchequer' (ibid.).

14. Sir Edward Walpole was made Clerk of the Pells and Master of Pleas and Escheats, in addition to his place in the Customs. HW shared the income from the Customs place (1739–84) and was also made usher of the Exchequer, comptroller of the Pipe, and clerk of the Estreats.

Did not his country see and know those rewards? and could it think those rewards inadequate! Besides, Sir, great as I hold my father's services, they were solid and silent, not ostensible. They were of a kind to which I hold your justification a more suitable reward than pecuniary recompenses. To have fixed the House of Hanover on the throne, to have maintained this country in peace and affluence for twenty years, with the other services you record, Sir, were actions the *éclat* of which must be illustrated by time and reflection, and whose splendour has been brought forwarder, than I wish it had, by comparison with a period very dissimilar!

If Sir Robert had not the comfort of leaving his family in affluence, it was not imputable to his king or his country. Perhaps I am proud that he did not. He died forty thousand pounds in debt—That was the wealth of a man that had been taxed as the plunderer of his country! yet with all my adoration of my father, I am just enough to own that it was his own fault if he died so poor. He had made Houghton much too magnificent for the moderate estate which he left to support it; and as he never, I repeat it with truth, *never* got any money but in the South Sea and while he was Paymaster,[15] his fondness for his paternal seat, and his boundless generosity were too expensive for his fortune. I will mention one instance, which will show how little he was disposed to turn the favour of the Crown to his own profit. He laid out fourteen thousand pounds of his own money on Richmond New Park.[16]

I could produce other reasons too why Sir Robert's family were not in so comfortable a situation, as the world, deluded by misrepresentation, might expect to see them at his death. My eldest brother had been a very bad economist during his father's life, and died himself fifty thousand pounds in debt, or more; so that to this day neither Sir Edward nor I have received the five thousand pounds apiece which Sir Robert left us as our fortunes.[17] I do not love to charge the dead,

15. He was paymaster of the Forces 1714–15 and 1720–1. For details of his profits from stockholding in the South Sea Company see J. H. Plumb, *Sir Robert Walpole: The Making of a Statesman*, Boston, 1956, pp. 306–9.

16. 'As soon as he obtained the Rangership of Richmond Park for his eldest son, in 1726, he became his deputy and set about the Old Lodge. An army of carpenters, plasterers, furnishers made short work of £14,000 and Walpole had another comfortable, extravagant house where he could indulge his friends with good food, good wine and excellent hunting at the weekend' (idem, *Sir Robert Walpole: The King's Minister*, 1960, p. 90). See MANN i. 164 n. 1.

17. 'He gave to my brother Edward and me only 5,000 *l.* apiece, of which I have

therefore will only say that Lady Orford,[18] reckoned a vast fortune, which till she died she never proved, wasted vast sums; nor did my brother or father *ever* receive but the twenty thousand pounds which she brought at first, and which were spent on the wedding and christening, I mean including her jewels.[19]

I beg your pardon, Sir, for this tedious detail, which is minutely, perhaps too minutely true—but when I took the liberty of contesting any part of a work which I admire so much, I owed it to you and to myself to assign my reasons. I trust they will satisfy you; and if they do, I am sure you will alter a paragraph, against which it is the duty of the family to exclaim.[20] Dear as my father's memory is to my soul, I can never subscribe to the position that he was unrewarded by the House of Hanover. I have the honour to be, Sir, with great respect and gratitude

Your most obliged and obedient humble servant

Hor. Walpole

PS. I did not take the liberty of retaining your essay, Sir, but should be very happy to have a copy of it at your leisure.

never received but 1,000 *l.* and none of the interest' ('Account of my Conduct,' *Works* ii. 365). See n. 19 below.

18. See *ante* mid-October 1773, n. 3.

19. HW complained to Mann 8 Sept. 1782 that 'To this moment [Lady Orford's son, the 3d Earl] has not paid my brother or me a shilling of our fortunes, though bound by bond to pay us on his mother's death [in 1781]' (Mann ix. 315–16). In 1786 Lord Orford paid HW the remaining £4,000, but without all of the interest due from the date of the bond (ibid. ix. 637).

20. Pownall altered the paragraph to HW's satisfaction; see *post* 7 Nov. 1783.

To Elizabeth Montagu,[1] Thursday ?30 October 1783

Printed for the first time from the MS now wsl, removed from a copy of *Odes by Mr Gray*, SH, 1757, bound by Rivière. This copy is untraced until sold Parke-Bernet 5 April 1949 (property of Mrs Meredith Hare), lot 411, to Brick Row for wsl.

Dated conjecturally by the reference to Mrs Montagu's visiting Mrs Garrick at Hampton. Such a visit occurred in late October 1783; see *Mrs Montagu, 'Queen of the Blues,'* ed. Reginald Blunt, 1923, ii. 138. Mrs Montagu wrote Elizabeth Carter on Friday, 24 Oct. 1783: 'I propose to take a trip to Hampton the first fine morn next week, and shall then perhaps have the pleasure of finding Miss [Hannah] More with Mrs Garrick' (Henry E. Huntington Library MS MO 3559).

Endorsed in an unidentified hand: Lord Orford.

Thursday.

BY the stupidity of a new servant[2] Mr Walpole did not know that Mrs Montagu had done him the honour of calling on him the other day with Mrs Garrick, nor that she was in the neighbourhood till last night, Mr Walpole not having looked at the card that was left, nor perceived the writing with a pencil. If Mrs Montagu should remain at Hampton[3] tomorrow, Mr W. would be very happy if she and Mrs Garrick would do him the honour of breakfasting at Strawberry Hill.[4]

1. Elizabeth Robinson (1720–1800), m. (1742) Edward Montagu; author of *An Essay on the Writings and Genius of Shakespear*, 1769; bluestocking.

2. Not identified.
3. See *ante* 3 Aug. 1757, n. 2.
4. It is not known whether they came.

To Thomas Pownall, Friday 7 November 1783

Printed from a photostat of the MS in the possession of Mr Robert H. Taylor, Princeton, New Jersey. First printed, GM 1798, lxviii pt ii. 1020. Reprinted, Nichols, *Lit. Anec.* iv. 712; Wright vi. 208; Cunningham viii. 424 (closing and signature omitted in Wright and Cunningham); Toynbee xiii. 78. The MS was apparently owned by John Nichols in 1812 and was later bound in a volume of autographs in the collection of the Rev. John Wild, of Whitehill, Newton Abbot; by 1935 it was in the possession of Wild's great-grandson, R. N. Carew Hunt, 14 Vincent Square Mansions, London, who sold it to the Seven Gables Bookshop for Mr Taylor in 1953.

Endorsed by Pownall: Mr H. Walpole. Letter to me upon my writing a character of his father Sir R. Walpole.

Address: To Governor Pownall at Richmond, Surry. *Postmark:* 7 NO.

Berkeley Square, Nov. 7th 1783.

YOU must allow me, Sir, to repeat my thanks for the second copy of your tract on my father, and for your great condescension in altering the two passages to which I presumed to object, and which are now not only more consonant to exactness, but I hope no disparagement to the piece.[1] To me they are quite satisfactory; and it is a comfort to me too, that what I begged to have changed, was not any reflection prejudicial to his memory, but in the first point, a parallel not entirely similar in circumstances; and in the other, a sort of censure on others to which I could not subscribe. With all my veneration for my father's memory, I should not remonstrate against just censure on him. Happily, to do justice to him, most iniquitous calumnies ought to be removed—and then there would remain virtues and merits enough, far to outweigh human errors, from which the best men, like him, cannot be exempt. Let his enemies, aye, and his *friends,* be compared with him—and then justice would be done!

Your essay, Sir, will, I hope, some time or other clear the way to his vindication.[2] It points out the true way of examining his character; and is itself, as far as it goes, unanswerable. As such, what an obligation must it be to

Sir

Your most grateful and obedient humble servant

HOR. WALPOLE

1. See *ante* 27 Oct. 1783 and n. 6. Pownall's letter enclosing the revised draught of his 'tract' is missing.   2. See *ante* ca 25 Oct. 1783, n. 2.

To Henry Sampson Woodfall,
Saturday 8 November 1783

Printed from the MS now wsl. First printed in *The General Biographical Dictionary*, ed. Alexander Chalmers, new edn, 1812–17, xxxi. 61–2. Reprinted, Toynbee *Supp.* iii. 447–8. The MS is untraced until it was offered by Maggs, Cat. No. 258 (1910), lot 701; owned by the Rosenbach Company in 1926; acquired in 1928 from George Barr McCutcheon by James F. Drake, Inc., New York; offered by Drake, Cat. No. 234 (1933), lot 297, and sold by them to wsl, Feb. 1933.

Address: To Mr H. S. Woodfall at the corner of Ivy Lane, Paternoster Row.

Berkeley Square, Nov. 8, 1783.

MR H. Walpole sends his compliments to Mr Woodfall, and does entreat him to print no more of the *Mysterious Mother,* which it is a little hard on the author to see retailed without his consent.[1] Mr Walpole is willing to make Mr Woodfall amends for any imaginary benefit he might receive from the impression, though as copies of the play have been spread,[2] there can be little novelty in it; and at this time the public must be curious to see more interesting articles than scenes of an old tragedy on a disgusting subject, which the author thinks so little worthy of being published, that after the first small impression, he has endeavoured to suppress it as much as lies in his power;[3] and which he assures Mr Woodfall he would not suffer to be represented on the stage, if any manager was injudicious enough to think of it.[4] Mr Walpole is very sorry Mr Wood-

1. Extracts from HW's play appeared in the *Public Advertiser,* of which Woodfall was the printer. HW wrote Lady Ossory 8 Nov.: 'this morning at breakfast I was saluted with the first scene of my old tragedy, all sugared over with comfits like a Twelfth-cake. I have been writing to Mr Woodfall, to beg to buy myself out of his claws, and to lecture him for his gross compliments. I have ever laughed when I have seen little men called *great,* and I will not bear to be made ridiculous in the same way' (Ossory ii. 429).

2. HW printed only fifty copies at the SH Press in 1768. He gave away very few of them, but seven contemporary MS copies have been found, and there were doubtless others. In 1781 HW arranged to have the play reprinted by Dodsley in

order to forestall an unauthorized edition. The plan succeeded, and although the reprint was never distributed by Dodsley, HW presented a few copies of this edition to his friends (Hazen, *SH Bibl.* 79–83).

3. For another instance of HW's efforts to suppress the play see *ante* 16 April 1781.

4. Writing to Robert Jephson *ante* 24 Feb. 1775, HW said he had 'written a tragedy that can never appear on any stage.' He wrote Mason 22 May 1781: 'As to *The Mysterious Mother* being acted I am perfectly secure, at least while Lord Hertford is Lord Chamberlain, nay, whoever should succeed him I think would not license it without my consent' (Mason ii. 144).

fall dropped such a hint, as well as the extravagant preference given to him over other gentlemen of great merit, which preference Mr Walpole utterly disclaims, as well as the other high-flown compliments which he is not so ridiculous as to like.

Mr Walpole trusts that Mr Woodfall will not communicate this letter to anybody, and will be much obliged to him if he will let him know what satisfaction Mr Woodfall will expect for suppressing all farther mention of him and his play.[5]

To EDWARD JERNINGHAM, before 1784

Printed from a photostat of the MS in the Henry E. Huntington Library. First printed in Lewis Bettany, *Edward Jerningham and his Friends*, 1919, p. 45. Reprinted, Toynbee *Supp.* iii. 41. For the history of the MS see *ante* 13 Feb. 1778.

Dated approximately by the reference to HW's 'private party . . . for the Veseys.' Agmondesham Vesey died ca 3 June 1785 (MORE 230 and n. 1) and he was ill during the previous year, having had a series of apoplectic seizures (*Mrs Montagu, 'Queen of the Blues,'* ed. Reginald Blunt, 1923, ii. 183, 190). The party probably took place during the early 1780s, when HW was frequently in company with Mrs Vesey, and Mr Vesey was still in good health.

Address: To Edw. Jerningham Esq.

Monday.

I KNOW how awkward it is to *prier* a man of the world on an opera night; however as you cannot be so much awkwarder as to go thither before it is over, I must tell you that I shall have a private party tomorrow night for the Veseys,[1] which will begin at the beginning, and you may go to the Haymarket[2] afterwards and complain that you have been forced to go to a place, where everybody was come before it was time for them to go away;[3] but indeed it was at

5. No reply from Woodfall has been found; he apparently heeded HW's admonition and nothing more came of the incident.

---

1. See headnote and *post* 18 June 1784, n. 1.

2. The King's Opera House, Haymarket. Operas were performed there regularly throughout the season, which lasted from November to late June or early July.

3. HW commented on the fashion of going late to public amusements in his letter to Mason 19 Feb. 1781: 'They who are called *the people of fashion* or *the ton* have contributed nothing of their own but *being too late;* nay, actually do go to most public diversions after they are over' (MASON ii. 109). 'To be crowded to death in a waiting room at the end of an entertainment is the whole joy,' he wrote to Mary and Agnes Berry 23 June 1789, 'for who goes to any diversion till the last minute of it?' (BERRY i. 15).

an old gentleman's of the last century, who had lived long before the world had found out that there is no real diversion upon earth but in being too late for everyone.

To John Nichols, ?1784

Printed for the first time from a photostat of the MS fragment in the Bodleian Library. The MS is untraced until sold in a collection of Nichols family papers at Sotheby's 29 Oct. 1975 ('Other Properties'), lot 147, to the Bodleian.

Dated conjecturally by the reference to Nichols's *Bibliotheca Topographica Britannica*, No. 20 (see n. 4 below). HW, who owned a set of the *Bibliotheca*, probably queried Nichols soon after the publication of this number.

. . . to ask Mr Nichols who Earl of P——[1] and what his poem on Mr[2] Howard,[3] in p. 32. of No. XX. of *Biblioth. Topograph.*[4]

Mr Walpole will be much obliged to Mr Nichols for two or three impressions of the seal of W. Fitz Otho in p. 63. of that number.[5] In Mr Walpole's *Anecd. of Painting* chap. 1. Mr Nichols ⟨will⟩ find accounts of Edw. Fitz Otho.[6]

---

1. 'Peterborough' added parenthetically by Nichols in the MS. Charles Mordaunt (ca 1658–1735), cr. (1689) E. of Monmouth; 3d E. of Peterborough, 1697.

2. 'Mrs' added parenthetically by Nichols in the MS.

3. Henrietta Hobart (ca 1688–1767), m. 1 (1706) Charles Howard, 9th E. of Suffolk, 1731; m. 2 (1735) Hon. George Berkeley; mistress of George II; HW's correspondent.

4. 'A Greek translation in Anacreontics of the Earl of P——'s poem upon Mr Howard, by the treasurer, was communicated' ⟨*An Account of the Gentlemen's Society at Spalding*, 1784, p. 32 [*Bibliotheca Topographica Britannica*, No. 20, included in vol. iii of the collected *Bibliotheca*, 1790]). The poem, attributed to Lord Peterborough, begins, 'I said to my heart, between sleeping and waking,' and ends, 'Who'd have thought Mrs Howard ne'er dreamt it was she!' HW, who mentions the poem in the article on

Peterborough in his *Catalogue of the Royal and Noble Authors* (*Works* i. 439), probably wanted to know if this was the same poem referred to in the *Bibliotheca*. HW's set of the *Bibliotheca* is Hazen, *Cat. of HW's Lib.*, No. 3348. See Gray ii. 243 and n. 8.

5. 'On Otho's son's seal to an instrument in King's College, 30 E[dward] I 1302, are his insignia as *monetarius* or master of the mint, the coining hammer in his right, and sword as on St Martin's money in his left. He is seated on a throne or large circular seat of judicature, as *Cuneator*' (Maurice Johnson, 'A Dissertation on the Mint at Lincoln,' in *An Account of the Gentlemen's Society at Spalding*, p. 63). 'William Fitz Othes was a goldsmith and *Cuneator*, was lord of Mendlesham in Suffolk, and is represented in the above plate, copied from an engraving by Mr Vertue' (ibid. 63n).

6. See *Anecdotes of Painting, Works* iii. 17–18, and *ante* ca March 1762, n. 6.

From the HON. CHARLES HAMILTON,[1]
Saturday 31 January 1784

Printed from the MS now WSL. First printed, Toynbee *Supp*. iii. 289–92. For the history of the MS see *ante* 14 Feb. 1759.

Lansdown Road, Bath, Jan. 31, 1784.

Sir,

I AM sadly afraid you will think me very impertinent for giving you this trouble, but when I consider your great desire that everything which comes from you should be perfectly accurate, I flatter myself you will pardon my setting you right in one particular, which it was extremely difficult for you to know, and almost impossible for me not to know: I mean my own family.

In your *Memoires de Grammont*, pages 75[2] and 273,[3] you seem at a loss to account for the two Hamiltons: Anthony,[4] the author, was certainly not one of them;[5] all that is said of him is that he received his materials from the Comte de Grammont; the eldest of the Hamiltons was my grandfather, his name James,[6] who never came to the earldom of Abercorn, which was possessed by an elder branch

1. (1704–86), 9th son of James, 6th E. of Abercorn; M.P. He lived formerly at Pains-hill, near Cobham, Surrey, 'where he has really made a fine place out of a most cursed hill' (HW to Montagu 11 Aug. 1748, MONTAGU i. 71). On his death, HW referred to him as 'one of my patriarchs of modern gardening' (OSSORY ii. 527).

2. Hamilton refers to Dodsley's 1783 reprint of Anthony Hamilton's *Mémoires du Comte de Grammont*, which HW had printed at the SH Press in 1772: 'George et Antoine Hamilton étaient les fils cadets du Chevalier George Hamilton, quatrième fils du Comte d'Abercorn, et de Marie, troisième fille de Thomas Vicomte de Thurles, fils aîné de Gaultier Butler Comte d'Ormond, et sœur de Jacques, premier Duc d'Ormand' (p. 75n).

3. 'Tout ce qui regarde Georges Hamilton . . . doit, à ce que je crois, se rapporter à son frère Antoine: car il est évident, que ce qui regarde Mad. de Chesterfield appartient à Georges, qui était l'aîné des frères; et qui, comme l'auteur qui était le cadet dit p. 75 fût tué, comme Milord Falmouth. De reste, il n'est pas vraisemblable, que l'auteur se fut tant loué lui-même dans cette page là. Selon le texte, voilà deux frères, et cependant toutes les aventures sont mises sur le compte du seul Georges. Il est clair aussi que l'auteur peint un nouveau caractère, quand il parle de Hamilton qui était l'amant de Mad. Wetenhall, et dont il dit modestement, "c'est celui qu'on a vu servir en France avec distinction." Or Georges n'avait point servi en France' (ibid. 273n).

4. See *ante* late Dec. 1781, n. 4.

5. That is, one of the two eldest sons of Sir George Hamilton (ca 1607–79). Anthony was the third son; his elder brothers were James (n. 6 below) and George (n. 14 below).

6. James Hamilton (d. 1673), Col. of a regiment of foot; groom of the Bedchamber to Charles II; M.P. (Ireland) (*Scots Peerage* i. 56–7).

during his life,[7] and did not descend to my father[8] till 1701; he married Lord Colpeper's daughter[9] the year of the Restoration, and was King Charles' great favourite (as described) who gave him a patent of peerage (which I have in my possession) which was to have been perfected at his return from that fatal expedition with the Duke of York,[10] where a cannonball took off one of his legs, and soon after his life;[11] the King out of regard to him sent for my father and made him a Groom of his Bedchamber though but 17 years old, just come from West[minster] School.

I had a beautiful miniature portrait of him finely done by Cooper,[12] which I gave to the present Lord Abercorn,[13] and have now a small one in oil, done I should think from Cooper's; if it would give you any satisfaction to see it, as it is small I could very easily send it in a little box, for you to look at.

George[14] who was the second son (as you rightly observe, page 75) followed King James to France at the Revolution, where he was made lieutenant general and a count;[15] he had three daughters by Mlle Jennings,[16] sister to the Duchess of Marlbro', who after his death married the Duke of Tyrconnell.

The three daughters were married to Lord Dillon,[17] Lord Kingsland[18] and Lord Ross;[19] Lord Beaulieu[20] is grandson to Lady Ross,

7. His contemporary, George Hamilton (ca 1636 – before 1683), 3d E. of Abercorn, died unmarried at Padua. The title descended to Claud Hamilton (d. 1690), Lord Strabane, who was a first cousin once removed of Col. James Hamilton (GEC i. 4–5).

8. James Hamilton (1656–1734), 6th E. of Abercorn, 1701.

9. Elizabeth Colepeper (ca 1637–1709), eldest dau. of John Colepeper (ca 1600–60), cr. (1644) Bn Colepeper; m. (1661) Col. James Hamilton (Scots Peerage i. 57).

10. Afterwards K. of England 1685–8 as James II.

11. 'His regiment being embarked on board the navy, in one of the expeditions of the Duke of York against the Dutch, Colonel Hamilton had one of his legs taken off by a cannonball, of which wound he died 6 June 1673, and was buried 7 June in Westminster Abbey' (ibid.).

12. Samuel Cooper (1609–72), miniature painter.

13. James Hamilton (1712–89), 8th E. of Abercorn, 1744. He was the Hon. Charles Hamilton's nephew.

14. George Hamilton (d. 1676), styled 'Sir George' and, in France, 'Comte' Hamilton.

15. Not so. He was an officer in the Horse Guards until 1667, afterwards entering the French army. Several years later he raised the so-called Régiment d'Hamilton of Irish soldiers in the service of Louis XIV. He earned military distinction for himself and was made maréchal de camp, or major-general, on 25 Feb. 1676; he had the rank of count. He was killed at the Battle of Saverne (ibid. i. 53–4).

16. See ante ?March 1773 bis, nn. 5, 6.

17. Frances Hamilton (d. 1751), 2d dau. of Sir George Hamilton, m. 1 (1687) Henry Dillon (d. 1714), 8th Vct Dillon, 1691; m. 2 Patrick Bellew (d. 1720).

18. Mary Hamilton (d. 1736), 3d and youngest dau. of Sir George Hamilton,

and has, I believe, portraits of several of the *dramatis personæ* of the *Memoirs*.[21]

I was acquainted with Count Grammont's two daughters; Lady Stafford[22] lived several years in England; and when I was at the Academy in Lorraine, Prince Craon[23] carried me to visit the Abbess of Poussay,[24] where his daughter Princess Shimay,[25] younger sister of the Duchess of Mirepoix,[26] was then a chanoinesse. I passed a week there most agreeably, and she showed me the portraits of all my great uncles and aunts, and amongst them her father and mother, the Count and Countess of Grammont, if I remember right at this great distance of time (1725). What became of those portraits at her death I am not certain, but believe she left them to a daughter[27] of her uncle Richard Hamilton[28] who had been a chanoinesse of Poussay, but was then married to the Comte de Marmière in Champagne, and was upon a visit at Poussay all the time I was there.

Now, Sir, if I could, I would make you a proper apology for troubling you with this dry genealogical epistle; my real motives were,

m. (1688) Nicholas Barnewall (1668–1725), 3d Vct Barnewall of Kingsland, 1688.

19. Elizabeth Hamilton (d. 1724), eldest dau. of Sir George Hamilton, m. (1685) Richard Parsons (d. 1703), cr. (1681) Vct Rosse.

20. Edward Hussey (after 1749, Hussey Montagu) (1721–1802), cr. (1762) Bn Beaulieu and (1784) E. of Beaulieu. His mother was Catherine Parsons, dau. of Richard, 1st Vct Rosse, by Elizabeth, Lady Rosse.

21. There were portraits of Anthony Hamilton and his brother, Sir George Hamilton, at Ditton Park, Lord Beaulieu's house in Buckinghamshire; other versions of these portraits were probably at one time in the possession of Mary, Lady Kingsland (n. 18 above) and are now in the National Portrait Gallery (David Piper, *Catalogue of Seventeenth-Century Portraits in the National Portrait Gallery 1625–1714*, Cambridge, 1963, pp. 153–5).

22. Claude-Charlotte de Gramont (ca 1659–1739), elder dau. of Philibert (1621–1707), Comte de Gramont, by Elizabeth (1641–1708), eldest dau. of Sir George Hamilton (ca 1607–79); m. (1694) Henry Stafford Howard, cr. (1688) E. of Stafford.

23. See *ante* 9 July 1742 NS, n. 1.

24. Marie-Élisabeth de Gramont (1667–1735), younger dau. of Philibert, Comte de Gramont; Abbesse de Poussai, 1695 (MONTAGU i. 119 n. 10).

25. Gabrielle-Françoise de Beauvau (1708–58), m. (1725) Alexandre-Gabriel-Joseph d'Alsace-Hénin-Liétard, Prince de Chimay; Chanoinesse de Poussai (La Chenaye-Desbois and Badier, *Dictionnaire de la noblesse*, 3d edn, 1863–76, ii. 741).

26. See *ante* 19 Oct. 1765, n. 26.

27. Margaret Emily Hamilton, m. (1718) François-Philippe de Marmier (1681–1736), Comte de Marmier (La Chenaye-Desbois and Badier, op. cit. xiii. 274). She was the daughter of John Hamilton (d. 1691), 6th and youngest son of Sir George Hamilton (ca 1607–79). Before marrying the Comte de Marmier, she lived for a time with her cousin, the Abbess of Poussai (Ruth Clark, *Anthony Hamilton*, 1921, pp. 107 n. 5, 168).

28. Richard Hamilton (d. 1717), 5th son of Sir George Hamilton (ca 1607–79). He served bravely in James II's army during the war in Ireland, afterwards retiring to France with the exiled king and becoming a lieutenant-general in the French service. He died in poverty at Poussai, where he had gone to live with his niece, the Abbess (ibid. 161–2; *Scots Peerage* i. 55).

the knowing your love of accuracy, and as everything that comes from you, will undoubtedly go through many, many editions, possibly you might like that in future ones,[29] the notes relative to this subject might be set right: at all events you may be assured I do it with the best intentions, and that I am always with the sincerest regard,

Sir,

Your most obedient humble servant,

CHA. HAMILTON

PS. The above particulars are very truly and clearly stated in Douglass's[30] *Peerage of Scotland.*[31]

To BENJAMIN IBBOT, Monday 8 March 1784

Printed from a photostat of the MS in the Pierpont Morgan Library. First printed, Toynbee *Supp.* i. 288 (misdated 'March 8, 1783'). For the history of the MS see *ante* 24 Sept. 1773.

Address: To Benjamin Ibbott Esq., Dartmouth Street, Westminster.

Berkeley Square, March 8, 1784.

Sir,

I SENT your application and the certificate[1] to the Duke of Richmond,[2] who thinks them very reasonable, and will speak to the commanding officer[3] for farther leave. As the time presses, I will put him in mind again today[4]—but I was very glad to give you this notice.

Your obedient servant

HOR. WALPOLE

29. Dodsley's 1783 edition was the only one that is specifically a reprint of the SH edition, although the *Mémoires* have been frequently reprinted by later editors.

30. Sir Robert Douglas (1694–1770), 6th Bt, 1764.

31. *The Peerage of Scotland, Containing an Historical and Genealogical Account of the Nobility of that Kingdom, from their Origin to the Present Generation,* Edinburgh, 1764, folio. HW did not own a copy of this work. Douglas correctly states (p. 4) that Sir George Hamilton (d. 1676) 'was a count and major-general in France, and was killed at the battle of Saverne.' See n. 15 above.

1. Doubtless an application requesting an extended medical leave of absence from the army for his son, along with a physician's certificate attesting to his son's ill health. See *ante* 19 March 1783.

2. Richmond was master general of the Ordnance.

3. Not identified.

4. See following letter.

To Benjamin Ibbot, Monday 8 March 1784 *bis*

Printed from a photostat of the MS in the Pierpont Morgan Library. First printed, Toynbee *Supp.* i. 288 (misdated by Dr Toynbee 'March 10, 1783' on the assumption that the previous letter was written in 1783). For the history of the MS see *ante* 24 Sept. 1773.

Address: To Benjamin Ibbott Esq. in Dartmouth Street, Westminster.

Monday past one.

I HAVE just had a message[1] from the Duke of Richmond, Sir, to tell me that he has no doubt of obtaining farther leave of absence for your son,[2] and that in the meantime you may stop his coming to town.

Yours etc.

H. Walpole

1. Missing.

2. See *post* 12 March 1784.

From JOSEPH WHITE,[1] Thursday 11 March 1784

Printed from the MS pasted in HW's 'Book of Materials,' 1771, p. 97, now WSL. First printed, Toynbee *Supp.* ii. 165–6. Reprinted, Toynbee *Supp.* iii. 292. Damer-Waller; the 'Book of Materials' was sold Sotheby's 5 Dec. 1921 (first Waller Sale), lot 54, to Maggs for Henry C. Folger; acquired by WSL in exchange with the Folger Shakespeare Library, July 1950.

Paris, 11 mars 1784.

JOSEPH White presents his duty to Mr H. Walpole[2] and begs leave to inform him that the Bedford missal,[3] King René prayer book[4] and the greatest part of the manuscripts were bought by his *Most Christian Majesty*[5] for the use of his public Library[6] at Paris. N.B. The *Guirlande of Julia*,[7] No. 3247, sold for 14,510 livres.[8]

1. (d. 1791), bookseller in 43 Holborn; formerly in Serle Street, Lincoln's Inn Fields (GM 1791, lxi pt ii. 1161; Ian Maxted, *The London Book Trades 1775–1800*, 1977, p. 245). He was among the recipients of a copy of the Duc de Nivernais's French translation of HW's *Essay on Modern Gardening* in 1785 (BERRY ii. 259).

2. HW wrote the Hon. Thomas Walpole 3 Jan. 1784: 'Mr White . . . goes [to Paris] to purchase books at the Duc de la Valière's sale. I have given him some commissions at a very high rate, and yet do not expect, indeed almost hope not, to obtain the articles, especially as I have never seen them and may be much disappointed when I do' (FAMILY 216). The sale of the Duc de la Valière's collection of books and MSS took place 12 Jan.– 5 May 1784. HW had a copy of the *Catalogue des livres de la bibliothèque de feu M. le duc de la Valière*, compiled by Guillaume de Bure, 3 vols, 1783 (Hazen, *Cat. of HW's Lib.*, No. 3335), and he presumably entrusted White with bids for the items mentioned in this letter. But feeling the need to be 'more economic now than formerly,' he changed his mind and cancelled the commissions (HW to Thomas Walpole 6 Jan., 1 Feb. 1784, FAMILY 217, 223).

3. The 'Sarum' or 'Bedford' Breviary, a fifteenth-century illuminated MS including scenes from early English church history, executed for John, Duke of Bedford (1389–1435). It was sold as lot 273 (*Catalogue* i. 85–90) to Louis XVI for 5,000 livres and is now MS Latin 17294 in the Bibliothèque Nationale (David Diringer, *The Illuminated Book*, 1958, pp. 405–6; Victor Leroquais, *Les Bréviaires manuscrits des bibliothèques publiques de France*, 1934, iii. 271–348).

4. The 'Anjou Hours,' a fifteenth-century illuminated book of hours executed for René d'Anjou (1409–80), titular King of Sicily 1435–80. It was sold as lot 285 (*Catalogue* i. 98–103) to Louis XVI for 1200 livres and is now MS Latin 1156A in the Bibliothèque Nationale (Diringer, op. cit. 403; Victor Leroquais, *Les Livres d'heures manuscrits de la Bibliothèque Nationale*, 1927, i. 64–7).

5. Louis XVI.

6. The Bibliothèque Royale, now the Bibliothèque Nationale.

7. 'La Guirlande de Julie,' the celebrated seventeenth-century illuminated MS with calligraphy by Nicolas Jarry and miniatures by Nicolas Robert, executed for the Duc de Montausier (1610–90) and given by him in 1641 to Julie-Lucine d'Angennes, Mlle de Rambouillet. It was sold as lot 3247 (*Catalogue* ii. 382–4) to the London bookseller Thomas Payne for 14,510 livres; in 1925 it was in the possession of the Duchesse d'Uzès (J. W. Bradley, *A Dictionary of Miniaturists, Illuminators, Calligraphers, and Copyists*, 1887–9, ii. 144, iii. 160–1; Toynbee *Supp.* iii. 292 n. 3).

8. These books were sold at the Duc de la Valière's sale. The *Guirlande de Julie*

TO BENJAMIN IBBOT, Friday 12 March 1784

Printed from a photostat of the MS in the Pierpont Morgan Library. First printed, Toynbee *Supp.* ii. 1 (misdated 'March 12, 1783'). For the history of the MS see *ante* 24 Sept. 1773.

Address: To Benjamin Ibbott Esq. in Dartmouth Street, Westminster. *Postmark:* 5 O'CLOCK.

Berkeley Square, March 12, 1784.

Sir,

I HAVE this minute received a favour of your letter[1] just as I was going to write another to tell you that your son's leave of absence for *three* months longer is granted.[2] I am very happy to have been instrumental to it, and hope that Bath will quite set him up.

I am Sir
Your obedient humble servant

HOR. WALPOLE

was, I suppose, the dearest book ever sold (HW).

1. Missing.
2. See *ante* 8 March 1784 *bis.*

To John Fenn,[1] Friday 7 May 1784

Printed from a photostat of the MS in the Norwich Central Library, Norfolk. First printed in R. W. Ketton-Cremer, 'Some New Letters of Horace Walpole,' *Times Literary Supplement,* 15 March 1957, lvi. 164; extracts printed in *Paston Letters,* ed. Norman Davis, Oxford, 1958, p. xxv; *Paston Letters and Papers of the Fifteenth Century,* ed. Davis, Oxford, 1971, p. xxiv. This MS and those of six other letters between HW and John Fenn and Mrs Fenn, bound by Fenn in two quarto volumes of correspondence concerning the publication of the Paston letters in 1787, came to light too late to be included in CHATTERTON. The volumes presumably passed to Fenn's brother-in-law, John Frere (1740–1807), in the bequest of his library, and descended to John Tudor Frere (1843–1918); sold Sotheby's 14–18 Feb. 1896 (J. T. Frere Sale), lots 988–9, to Levine; later in the library formed by J. J. Colman and his son, Russell J. Colman (1861–1946), at Crown Point, Norwich; given by their family representatives to the City of Norwich in 1955.

Berkeley Square, May 7th 1784.

Dear Sir,

I HAVE brought you back your MSS[2] myself, for I was afraid of keeping them they are so valuable, especially the Paston letters, which are the most curious papers of the sort I ever saw, and the oldest original letters I believe extant in this country.[3] The historic picture they give of the reign of Hen[ry] VI[4] makes them invaluable, and more satisfactory than any cold narrative. It were a thousand pities they should not be published, which I should be glad I could persuade you to do. I flatter myself with the pleasure of seeing you again before you leave town, and am with the greatest regard, Sir,

Your much obliged humble servant

HOR. WALPOLE

1. Sir John Fenn (1739–94), of East Dereham, Norfolk; F.S.A., 1771; Kt, 1787; sheriff of Norfolk, 1791; antiquary (CHATTERTON 231 n. 1).

2. Letters and other documents of antiquarian interest, including those first published by Fenn in *Original Letters, Written during the Reigns of Henry VI, Edward IV, and Richard III, by Various Persons of Rank or Consequence,* 2 vols, 1787. Fenn's edition of the Paston letters was dedicated to George III; the MSS were presented by Fenn to the King in 1787, and most of them were later acquired by the British Museum.

3. HW wrote Fenn 15 May 1782: 'I did not know that there was so much as a *private* letter extant of that very turbulent period. This gives me, Sir, a high idea of your treasure. . . . you would much oblige literary virtuosos, especially were you to print the letters themselves, or the interesting extracts' (CHATTERTON 243).

4. King of England 1422–61, 1470–1.

To Edmond Malone, Thursday 13 May 1784

Printed from Toynbee *Supp.* ii. 3, where the MS was first printed. Reprinted in J. M. Osborn, 'Horace Walpole and Edmond Malone,' in *Horace Walpole: Writer, Politician, and Connoisseur,* ed. W. H. Smith, New Haven, 1967, pp. 311–12. The MS was owned by Dodd and Livingston, New York, in 1918; its earlier and later history is not known.

Berkeley Square, May 13th 1784.

MR Walpole is always very ready and happy to obey Mr Malone's commands, and will do it in the present instance as far as it is in his power, though he cannot exactly in the manner desired.[1] Mr Walpole having been obliged from many disagreeable adventures to restrain the number to *four* on the same day,[2] and being desired to admit a larger company of H.R.H. Princess Amelie's[3] family, did presume to represent his situation, and her Royal Highness was so good as to say he was in the right, and sent only four of her servants[4] at a time.[5] Since that time Mr Walpole has been obliged to be very strict, but he will willingly send Mr Malone three tickets for four each for any days that he will please to name after next Monday, if Mr Malone will be so good as to let him know those days before next Sunday morning.[6]

1. Malone's letter, asking HW's permission to bring a large group of people to visit SH, is missing.
2. See *ante* 7 Sept. 1781 and n. 1.
3. Amelia Sophia Eleanora (1711–86), Princess, second dau. of George II.
4. That is, members of her royal household or establishment.

5. We have found no record of this visit.
6. 16 May. HW's 'Book of Visitors' records the visit of 'Mr Malone' on 20 May, but makes no mention of others accompanying him (Berry ii. 221).

From JOHN FENN, Monday 14 June 1784

Printed from a photostat of Fenn's MS draft in the Norwich Central Library, Norfolk. First printed in R. W. Ketton-Cremer, 'Some New Letters of Horace Walpole,' *Times Literary Supplement*, 15 March 1957, lvi. 164. For the history of the MS draft see *ante* 7 May 1784. The original letter is missing.

Bedford Row,[1] 14 June 1784.

Dear Sir,

I HAVE called two or three times in Berkeley Square, hoping to have found you in town, that I might have presented Mr and Mrs Frere's[2] compliments and thanks for your polite attention to them and for the great pleasure they received at Strawberry Hill.[3]

Mrs Fenn[4] likewise joins with me in respectful acknowledgments on the same occasion.

We *reviewed* your Cabinet[5] etc. on our way to town, with infinite satisfaction, and the various curiosities we saw afforded us agreeable conversation for many days.

Since I was with you, I have been informed that you had drawn up and printed a descriptive catalogue of your pictures and curiosities,[6] and as I hope a petition for a copy will not be impertinent, I own the possessing one would be a great satisfaction both to Mrs Fenn and myself.[7]

I have enclosed a slight engraving of a well known antiquary,[8] taken from a sketch made by me in 1770. The countenance and profile are like him—that is the only merit it can boast; but being a private plate of my own, I hope the impression will find a place in your collection of portraits.[9]

1. Fenn was staying with his brother-in-law, John Frere, at No. 26 Bedford Row (CHATTERTON 246 and n. 1).

2. John Frere (1740–1807), of Roydon Hall, Norfolk; high sheriff of Suffolk, 1766; F.R.S., 1771; M.P. He married in 1768 Jane Hookham (ca 1746–1813), only dau. of John Hookham of London (GM 1813, lxxxiii pt i. 388).

3. We have found no record of their visit.

4. Eleanor Frere (1744–1813), dau. of Sheppard Frere of Roydon Hall, Norfolk, m. (1766) John Fenn; author of books for children.

5. The Chapel, which was later called the Cabinet and still later the Tribune.

The objects in it are listed in 'Des. of SH,' *Works* ii. 470–93.

6. See *ante* 15 Oct. 1782 and n. 7.

7. See John Fenn to HW *post* 3 July 1784 and n. 2.

8. Sir William Hamilton, HW's correspondent.

9. Fenn's etching, inscribed 'J. F. Sc[ulpsit] 1776,' was pasted by HW in his *Collection of Prints, Engraved by Various Persons of Quality*, now WSL; it is reproduced in CHUTE 403. Fenn's sketch, if taken from life, could not have been made before August 1771, when Hamilton returned to England from Naples (*London Chronicle* 8–10 Aug. 1771, xxx. 138).

I told you of (and would have shown you if I had lately happened of⁹ᵃ you at home) the original drawing of Henry VI which I have in my possession. This, since I came to town, I have had engraven and intend it for a frontispiece to my original letters, should I ever publish them¹⁰—Do you think it will answer that purpose?—I intend to amuse myself this summer in transcribing such of those letters as are not already done, rendering them into more modern English and adding historical notes where necessary—And should I meet with any difficulties in my progress, a permission to apply to your learned and ingenious pen would be an honour I should most highly esteem.

I cannot help thinking but that I can discover a likeness between the portrait of this prince in your picture of his marriage¹¹ and this drawing of him—it struck me in comparing it with your plate in the *Anecdotes of Painting*¹²—Can you discover the same or is it only a fancy of my own?¹³

Of this plate I shall at present give away only two or three impressions, as I intend it for use, but I could not have such a thing in my possession, without requesting your acceptance of one, as a small token of acknowledgment for the many civilities conferred by you upon

Your obedient respectful humble servant,

JNO. FENN

PS. I shall leave town on Friday and I expect to be at Dereham in about ten days.

Honourable Horace Walpole.

9a. So in MS; a slip for 'on.'

10. The drawing was engraved by Thomas Cook (ca 1744–1818) for the frontispiece to the first volume of Fenn's *Original Letters*, 1787 (*ante* 7 May 1784, n. 2).

11. HW had purchased ca 1754 an anonymous fifteenth-century painting on wood, supposedly representing the marriage of Henry VI to Margaret of Anjou. The picture hung over the chimney in the Library at SH, and was sold SH xx.

25 to the Duke of Sutherland; it is now in the Toledo Museum of Art. HW's identification of the subject has been disputed. See GRAY ii. 68 n. 12 and illustration.

12. 'The Marriage of Henry VI' was engraved by Charles Grignion for *Anecdotes of Painting*, where it is discussed by HW (*Anecdotes*, 1762–71, i. 33–5; *Works* iii. 37–9).

13. See HW to Fenn *post* 29 June 1784.

To Elizabeth Vesey,[1] Friday 18 June 1784

Printed from the MS now WSL. First printed, Toynbee xiii. 159. The MS descended from Mary (Hamilton) Dickenson to her great-granddaughter, Elizabeth Georgiana Anson; sold Sotheby's 31 May 1927 (property of Miss Elizabeth G. Anson), lot 506, to W. T. Spencer, from whom WSL acquired it in Sept. 1932.

The letter was sent by Mrs Vesey to Mary Hamilton, as is indicated by the second address 'To Miss Hamilton' in Mrs Vesey's hand on the verso.

Address: To Mrs Vesey in Clarges Street, Piccadilly, London. *Postmark:* 19 IV. ISLEWORTH.

Strawberry Hill, June 18th 1784.

My dear Madam,

AS I delight in showing attention to you and Miss Hamilton,[2] it is come into my head that very likely the two Misses Clarkes[3] who live with Miss Hamilton, would not be sorry to see my baby-house[4] in such agreeable company. If you both think so, and that it would not be impertinent in me to invite them on so little acquaintance and such short notice, will you take upon you to invite them?[5]

Your devoted and ever obliged

Hor. Walpole

1. Elizabeth Vesey (ca 1715–91), m. 1 William Handcock; m. 2 (before 1746) Agmondesham Vesey (d. 1785); bluestocking.

2. Mary Hamilton (1756–1816), only child of Charles Hamilton (1721–71), of Northampton; m. (1785) John Dickenson (More 205 n. 1).

3. Isabella and Anna Maria Clarke (living 1806). They lived with Mary Hamilton in Clarges Street, in a house opposite the Veseys, from Feb. 1783 until Miss Hamilton's marriage in 1785 (ibid. 214 n. 1).

4. Strawberry Hill.

5. Mary Hamilton wrote in her journal: 'In a very polite note Mr Walpole had written to say: if it would give me pleasure, and the Miss Clarkes, he should be happy to see them with me on Monday [21 June]. . . . I wrote by this post to A[nna] Maria but I told her I feared she would not get the intelligence time enough to go to Strawberry Hill' (*Mary Hamilton, afterwards Mrs John Dickenson, at Court and at Home,* ed. Elizabeth and Florence Anson, 1925, p. 209). The invitation presumably did not reach the Clarke sisters in time, as the visitors at SH on the 21st were only Mr and Mrs Vesey, Miss Hamilton, and Mrs Garrick (ibid. 209–10).

To John Fenn, Tuesday 29 June 1784

Printed from a photostat of the MS in the Norwich Central Library, Norfolk. First printed in R. W. Ketton-Cremer, 'Some New Letters of Horace Walpole,' *Times Literary Supplement*, 15 March 1957, lvi. 164; extract printed in *Paston Letters*, ed. Norman Davis, Oxford, 1958, p. xxv. For the history of the MS see *ante* 7 May 1784.

Address: To John Fenn Esq. at East Dereham, Norfolk. *Postmark:* 29 IV.

Strawberry Hill, June 29, 1784.

I AM much mortified, Sir, that by my absence from London I have missed the opportunity of thanking you personally for all your favours and late presents. The portraits I have already pasted into my *Collection*,[1] and I agree with you in finding great resemblance between your Henry VI and mine, and shall have the more confidence in mine as representing that prince. I did not flatter you, Sir, I do assure you, in my declarations of the value I set on your Paston letters. I know nothing of that dark period[2] so curious; nay, I shall think the public a little obliged to me if I can persuade you to print them. If this age, which affects so much to deal in historic anecdotes, is not struck with your present, its pretensions must be very false, and its taste very undiscerning. Barrows, and cromlechs, and fragments of Roman camps, give us no ideas which we had not perfectly before—but familiar letters written by eyewitnesses, and that, without design, disclose circumstances that let us more intimately into important events, are genuine history; and as far as they go, more satisfactory than formal premeditated narratives. My poor assistance, Sir, to the elucidation *you* cannot want. My knowledge is very superficial: yours, accurate and well-digested. Not that I would waive any pains that you should think I could contribute. I am too zealous for the publication to decline any office in my power towards its appearance.

It is a great satisfaction to me, Sir, that Mrs Fenn and you and Mr and Mrs Frere were amused at Strawberry Hill; but I shall never forgive myself for having been so engrossed by showing it, that it put it quite out of my head to thank Mrs Fenn for her very useful, lively and engaging present[3] on education. I am too seriously ashamed of

1. See *ante* 14 June 1784 and n. 9.
2. The fifteenth century.
3. A copy of her *Cobwebs to Catch Flies: or, Dialogues in Short Sentences,* *Adapted to Children,* 2 vols, 1784. HW's copy is untraced; see Hazen, *Cat. of HW's Lib.,* No. 2414, and CHATTERTON 244 n. 1.

myself not to confess the truth and my own selfish ill breeding, for which I have no excuse—and yet I assure you, Sir, the merit of her work was by no means lost on me—though it is plain that I am too old to be taught—I hope she will meet with more deserving scholars, whose virtues will be the better for hers. She too will learn not to throw pearls before the superannuated who have lost their eyes or memories, or both, as was the case of her and

Your most obedient and obliged humble servant

HOR. WALPOLE

From JEAN-BAPTISTE-LOUIS-GEORGES SEROUX D'AGINCOURT
Tuesday 29 June 1784

Printed for the first time from a photostat of the MS bound in a volume (labelled 'Architecture' on the spine) in Sir John Soane's Museum, London, kindly furnished by Sir John Summerson. For the full contents of this volume and its history see Hazen, *Cat. of HW's Lib.*, No. 3994.

Roma, 29 juin 1784.

Monsieur,

IL Signor Bonomi,[1] architecte romain établi en Angleterre depuis longtemps et où il a épousé une parente de la célèbre Angelica,[2] s'est chargé de vous remettre ce paquet autant pour avoir une occasion de connaître quelqu'un aussi capable que vous d'apprécier ses talents, que pour m'obliger. J'espère que le sort en sera plus heureux que celui de deux autres que j'ai eu l'honneur de vous adresser l'année dernière. L'un le 4 juin par M. Byres, gentilhomme écossais qui depuis plusieurs années s'occupe d'antiquités à Rome et des mains de qui il a été retiré en entrant en France, et l'autre dans une

1. Giuseppe Bonomi (1739–1808), A.R.A., 1789; Italian architect. He came to England in 1767 at the invitation of Robert and James Adam, with whom he remained for several years, and became well known as a master of perspective and as a fashionable designer of country houses. He visited Italy in 1783–4 (Howard Colvin, *A Biographical Dictionary of British Architects 1600–1840*, 1978, pp. 123–5).

2. Maria Anna Angelica Caterina Kauffmann (1741–1807), m. (1781) Antonio Zucchi; painter. Her cousin, Rosa Florini, married Giuseppe Bonomi in 1775 (Adeline Hartcup, *Angelica: The Portrait of an Eighteenth-Century Artist*, 1954, pp. 124–5).

caisse contenant plusieurs estampes que j'avais adressée chez M. Wool-ett,[3] graveur à Londres et qui était chargée sur le navire dont trois grecs se sont emparé après avoir égorgé presque tout l'équipage.

On m'a bien dit que le premier paquet avait été mis à la porte de Nice pour l'Angleterre et que le second se retrouvera puisque le navire avait été repris et les brigands punis, mais dans la crainte que rien ne vous soit encore parvenu, pardonnez-moi de vous répéter une partie de ce que je vous disais.

Je vous rappelais, Monsieur, la bonté avec laquelle vous voulûtes bien au printemps de 1777, à la recommandation de Milady Hamil-ton,[4] qu'à présent, nous regrettons tous deux, me recevoir à Straw-berry Hill.[5] Je vous y fis part du projet que j'avais de rassembler pendant le voyage que j'allais faire en Italie, les monuments ⟨de⟩ l'architecture, de la peinture et de la sculpture, dep⟨uis⟩ la décadence au 4e siècle jusqu'au renouvellemen⟨t⟩ au 16e pour les faire graver. Afin qu'en les joignan⟨t⟩ aux monuments qui le sont sur la première époque, c'est à dire, depuis l'invention de l'art jusqu'à la décadence, et à ceux qui le sont aussi pour la troisiè⟨me⟩ époque, c'est à dire, depuis le renouvellement jusqu'à nos jours, on puisse avoir *par les monuments* une histoire complète de l'art.[6] Vous me parûtes ap-prouver cette idée et depuis plus de quatre ans que je parcours l'Italie, je l'ai exécuté en partie.

Quoique ce soit de l'état des arts, en Italie, comme dans leur vérita⟨ble⟩ patrie, où il semble plus juste de prendre les exemples, cepend⟨ant⟩ je ne me refuserais pas à montrer ce qu'ils ont été dans les autres pays au moins en général, sauf à laisser à chaque nati⟨on⟩ le soin d'en faire l'histoire en détail; c'est surtout pour l'architec-tu⟨re⟩ comme celui des trois arts le plus généralement et le plus anciennem⟨ent⟩ pratiqué que j'aurais désiré de donner quelques monuments pour chaque pays, mais quand je m'en suis occupé pour l'Angleterre, par exemple, j'ai éprouvé ce que vous en dites, Mon-

3. See *ante* 20 July 1783 and nn. 2–5.

4. Catherine Barlow (d. 1782), dau. of Hugh Barlow, of Lawrenny Hall, Pem-broke; m. (1758), as his first wife, Sir Wil-liam Hamilton, K.B., 1772.

5. HW wrote Conway 10 July 1777: 'Pray tell her [Lady Hamlton] I have seen *Monsieur la Bataille d'Agincourt*. He brought me her letter yesterday: and I kept him to sup, *sleep* in the modern

phrase, and breakfast here this morning; and flatter myself he was, and she will be, content with the regard I paid to her letter' (CONWAY iii. 291).

6. Hence the title of d'Agincourt's great work: *Histoire de l'art par les monu-ments, depuis sa décadence au quatrième siècle jusqu'à son renouvellement au seizième*, 6 vols, folio, 1823.

sieur, pages 106 et 112 du premier volume des *Anecdotes*.[7] Dans cet
embarras j'ai fait *deux notices*[8] que je vous adressais et dont je
prends la liberté de vous envoyer *ci-joint des copies* en vous priant
de me dire ce que vous en pensez et s'il vous serait possible de m'indiquer avec votre justesse et votre précision ordinaire, les monuments que je pourrais choisir et où je les pourrais trouver gravés,
pour donner les exemples du style de l'architecture en Angleterre,
aux trois époques que j'indique. Je crois que vous les avez parfaitement bien disposées et fait distinguer dans la boiserie des différents
appartements de votre maison à Strawberry Hill. Si vous en aviez
des desseins[9] et que cela vous convint, je pourrais les faire graver, en
y joignant les observations que vous auriez la complaisance de
m'envoyer relativement à chaque genre d'architecture et à son âge.
Dans la crainte de ne pas trouver ce que je vous demande et pour
aller en avant, j'ai fait graver quatre planches dont je vous envoie des
épreuves dans mon premier paquet et dont je joins ici d'autres exem-
plaires, dans la crainte que les premiers ne soient perdus. Je les ai
choisis dans les cahiers donnés par Hearne et Byrne depuis 1778.[10]
Je m'appuie pour leurs dates sur les notices qu'ils y ont jointes et
quoiqu'elles ne soient peut-être pas d'une authenticité telle que je le
désire, faute de mieux, elles indiqueront au moins quelque chose.
Vous m'obligerez beaucoup de me dire jusqu'à quel degré vous croyez
qu'on peut y prendre confiance, surtout s'il ne vous était pas possible

7. In *Anecdotes of Painting*, 1762–71,
i. 106, HW gives his reasons 'for not
going very far back into the history of
our architecture. Vertue and several other
curious persons have taken great pains to
enlighten the obscure ages of that science;
they find no names of architects, nay
little more, than what they might have
known without inquiring; that our ancestors had buildings.' 'I have myself turned
over most of our histories of churches,
and can find nothing like the names of
artists. With respect to the builders of
Gothic, it is a real loss: there is beauty,
genius and invention enough in their
works to make one wish to know the authors' (ibid. i. 112–13).

8. 'Recherches relatives à l'origine de
l'ogive ou *arco acuto*, the *pointed arch*'
(4 pp.) and 'Recherches sur l'ancien style
de l'architecture en Angleterre' (8 pp.).

MS copies of these two essays are bound
with this letter in the 'Architecture' volume mentioned in the headnote. At the
end of the first essay are the following
notes in HW's hand (probably for his
[missing] reply to d'Agincourt):
    Byers
    Grose's Views
    Mr King on Castles
    Archæologia
    Mr Warton not the sufferer, but phy-
        sician
    Warton's poetry
    Carter
    have Saxon [sketch of overlapping
        arches]
9. Most of the original designs for the
interiors at SH, executed by John Chute
and Richard Bentley, are now WSL (Hazen,
Cat. of HW's Lib., Nos 3490, 3585).

10. See *ante* 20 July 1783, n. 39.

de m'indiquer aucun monument plus décidé pour le style et qui soit plus incontestable pour la date.

Quant à la peinture et à la sculpture: j'ai de même fait une collection de tout ce qu'elles ont produit depuis le 4ᵉ jusqu'au 16ᵉ siècle par ordre chronologique. J'ai puisé dans les Catacombes de Rome, dans les mosaïques des églises, dans les manuscrits, et depuis Cimabue jusqu'à Raffael dans les églises et dans les cabinets. Je vous en ai rendu un compte plus détaillé et vous ai envoyé quelques épreuves des peintures et des sculptures de ces temps reculés, que j'ai commencé à faire graver, dans le paquet adressé chez Woolett que vous pourrez faire retirer de chez ce graveur. Si avec les autres effets repris, ainsi que le vaisseau qui les portait, sur les pirates qui s'en étaient empar⟨és⟩ il y est enfin arrivé, sinon je pourrai vous en faire repasser d'autres. Je vous prie de m'adresser votre réponse[11] à Rome chez M. le Cardinal de Bernis,[12] ambassadeur de France, et s'il s'agissait de paquets plus considérables qu'une lettre, de les remettre à M. Bonomi, qui vous donnera son adresse.

Je vous renouvelle, Monsieur, toutes mes excuses pour tant d'importunités et les assurances de mon respect.

D'Agincourt

Je n'ai point nouvelles du Chev. Hamilton[13] depuis qu'il est repassé en Angleterre[14] où il s'était chargé de me rappeler à votre souvenir. M. de Cholmondelly[15] et le jeune M. Conway[16] m'ont dit qu'ils auraient la même bonté.

---

11. Missing.

12. François-Joachim de Pierre (1715–94), Cardinal de Bernis, 1758; French ambassador to the Holy See, 1769; statesman and author.

13. Sir William Hamilton, HW's correspondent.

14. Hamilton left Naples 24 May 1783 on a leave of absence, arriving in England in early August; he remained there until Sept. 1784 (Brian Fothergill, *Sir William Hamilton, Envoy Extraordinary,* New York, 1969, pp. 186, 191; Mann ix. 427).

15. George James Cholmondeley (1752–

1830), HW's grandnephew (Berry i. 83 n. 41). During the autumn of 1783 he was travelling on the Continent and visited Sir Horace Mann at Florence in October (Mann ix. 435–6).

16. Hon. (after 1793, Lord) Hugh Seymour-Conway (after 1794, Seymour) (1759–1801), Capt. R.N., 1779; Vice-Adm., 1799; M.P.; HW's first cousin once removed. He went to France with the Duke of Richmond in July 1783, returning to England from the Continent in Dec. 1784 (Coke, 'MS Journals' 12 July 1783, 20 Dec. 1784).

From JOHN FENN and MRS FENN, Saturday 3 July 1784

Printed from a photostat of the MS draft in the Norwich Central Library, Norfolk. First printed in R. W. Ketton-Cremer, 'Some New Letters of Horace Walpole,' *Times Literary Supplement*, 15 March 1957, lvi. 164. For the history of the MS draft see *ante* 7 May 1784. The original letter is missing.

East Dereham, 3 July 1784.

Dear Sir,

I AM exceedingly obliged to you for your letter[1] which I received yesterday and I shall employ myself this summer in copying, translating (if I may so call it) ⟨and⟩ adding notes where necessary to my Paston letters—Your good opinion ⟨of⟩ them will spur me on to make them as deserving of the public eye as I can, and your permission to consult you on any emergency as to any historical fact or person mentioned will ever be esteemed a particular favour.

I am glad that the resemblance between your picture of Henry VI and my original drawing of that prince struck you.

Since we were favoured with a sight of Strawberry Hill, I have heard that some time ago there was a descriptive catalogue of the various pictures, curiosities etc. printed. I made several inquiries when in town after it, but could not gain any satisfactory account. I fear therefore that my information was not authentic—I was the more earnest in my inquiries, as I should have esteemed such a publication as a treasure.[2]

Mrs Fenn thinks herself highly honoured by your approbation of her 'School Dialogues'[3] and has taken the liberty of acknowledging her obligation on the next page.

She joins in respectful compliment[s] to you with your obliged, obedient humble servant,

JNO. FENN

1. *Ante* 29 June 1784.
2. HW wrote in his reply to Mrs Fenn 7 July 1784: 'Not to trouble Mr Fenn again unnecessarily, may I beg you, Madam, to tell him, that I have long begun a description of my collection, and a very imperfect list was printed several years ago, but was suppressed. I have not yet completed it, but whenever it shall be ready and appear, a copy shall certainly be at Mr Fenn's command' (CHATTERTON 245). Fenn's name appears in Charles Bedford's list of persons to whom HW bequeathed copies of the 1784 *Description of SH*, but because Fenn predeceased HW, a copy may have been sent to Mrs (after 1787, Lady) Fenn; it has not been traced.
3. See *ante* 29 June 1784, n. 3.

Honourable Horace Walpole
Strawberry Hill
Twickenham
Surry

[Mrs Fenn's letter][4]

I do indeed, Sir, think myself highly honoured by your approbation of my little vols. Your silence on the subject I imputed to that politeness which shone so conspicuously in your whole behaviour and spared those blushes which must have arisen had you recalled to my mind the liberty I had taken in offering to your acceptance such trifles. My attention was too much engrossed by the beautiful objects around me to allow my thoughts to wander even for a moment, so that I never recollected the confusion which I escaped except when Mr Fenn pointed out to me that picture of Lord Falkland[5] in the gallery which you mention as having given rise to an incident in *The Castle of Otranto*[6]—now as I have selected from that delightful work a few passages to insert in a little volume[7] which is now in the press, an obvious train of ideas brought my 'School Dialogues' for an instant to my mind—but they were soon banished by the agreeable scene and I forgot the presumption[8] of which I had been guilty in striving to procure for my books the honour to be presented by Mr Walpole to the use of some friend of his.

I am gratified with the hope that my works may have afforded a few hours' innocent amusement in the Royal Nursery, as I ventured to send them to Lady C. Finch[9] and was honoured with a polite letter in return—but your smile is still more flattering 'for sure your smiles are fame.'[10]

---

4. The MS draft is in Mrs Fenn's hand.

5. Henry Carey (ca 1575–1633), cr. (1620) Vct of Falkland; Lord Deputy of Ireland 1622–9; M.P.

6. The portrait of Lord Falkland, dressed in white, by Van Somer hung on the window side of the Gallery at SH. 'The idea of the picture walking out of its frame in *The Castle of Otranto*, was suggested by this portrait' ('Des of SH,' *Works* ii. 466n). See COLE i. 88 and n. 3; *ante* 28 June 1783, n. 3.

7. *The Female Guardian*, 1784, containing brief extracts from *The Castle of Otranto*, with Mrs Fenn's edifying com-

mentary. See CHATTERTON 245 n. 2 and Hazen, *Cat. of HW's Lib.*, No. 2414.

8. At this point in the MS draft 'Lady C. Finch' is written in large letters (see following note).

9. Lady Charlotte Fermor (1725–1813), m. (1746) Hon. William Finch; governess of the royal nursery 1762–93 (OSSORY ii. 232 n. 1).

10. 'For sure thy smiles are fame' is the concluding line of HW's sonnet to Lady Mary Coke, which he wrote as a dedication to the second edition of *The Castle of Otranto*, 1765 (Appendix 6, MORE 429).

To Richard Bull, Wednesday 14 July 1784

Printed for the first time from the MS pasted in the front of Bull's album of 'Drawings,' now WSL (see n. 2 below). This volume passed by family descent into the collections of Lady Jane Ashburnham and Miss Julia Swinburne, and was later owned by Sir Francis Colchester-Wemyss; sold Sotheby's 20 July 1954 (property of a Gentleman), lot 426, to Maggs for WSL.

July 14, 1784.

I RETURN the books,[1] dear Sir, with many thanks. The drawings are very curious and admirable, and though Mary Merian's[2] are very fine, Mrs Luther's[3] are worthy of a place near them; though I am not such a flatterer, as to say they are equal.

I am sorry I did not know of Gunter[4] before my last edition;[5] but as it is my *last,* I cannot profit by the communication.

The Lucan[6] does but add to my shame, as a new proof of the expense I have so often (though unwittingly) put you to. What joy

1. An album labelled 'Drawings,' an album of designs for jewelry by Marcus Gunter, and Bull's copy of the SH Lucan bound by Edwards of Halifax (see nn. 2, 4, and 6 below).

2. Maria Sibylla Merian (1647–1717), m. (1665) Johann Andreas Graff; German watercolourist and engraver. Her exquisitely detailed drawings of insects, fish, and reptiles are contained in a quarto album bound in red morocco, labelled 'Drawings' on the spine; the album also includes numerous portrait drawings (many of them copies) by other hands.

3. Levina Bennet (living 1819), m. (1762) John Luther (?1739–86), M.P.; Richard Bull's step-daughter (Conway ii. 348 n. 27; N & Q 1913, 11th ser., vii. 170).

4. Marcus Gunter, a painter 'descended from a good family in Leicestershire' who passed most of his life on the Continent, where he 'gained some knowledge of enamelling for goldsmiths' while undertaking alchemical experiments. In his old age he returned to England and 'attempted to restore the taste for painting on glass; but being totally unknown and unprotected, he died in great poverty' (HW's 'Book of Materials,' 1771, p. 96, now WSL). 'Mr Bull has . . . several drawings by Gunter, designs for goldsmiths

and for enamelling ornaments, for jewels, as earrings, handles of swords, buckles, badges of knighthood etc. They are exceedingly neat, in the manner of Gribelin, but in better taste. Some are dated 1702, 1703, 1729, 1734, 1689, and some are dated at Amsterdam, La Haye' (ibid.). There were 111 drawings in this collection, most of them signed and dated between 1684 and 1753, mounted in a small folio album given to Bull by the antiquary Francis Grose; the album was sold Sotheby's 20 July 1954 (property of a Gentleman), lot 241, to Eisemann; not further traced. In his copy of the *Description of SH,* 1774, 'More additions,' HW listed a portrait of 'Marc Gunter, a painter, in a fine enamelled case; a present from Rd. Bull Esq.' It was sold SH xiv. 101 to Baldock for £3.3.0

5. Of *Anecdotes of Painting.* The third edition, 5 vols, octavo, without plates, was published in 1782. A fourth edition appeared in 1786, but makes no mention of Gunter.

6. A copy of Lucan's *Pharsalia,* SH, 1760, handsomely bound in vellum for Bull by Edwards of Halifax, with a foreedge painting of SH and another view of it on the spine; it is now WSL (Hazen, *SH Bibl.,* 1973 edn, pp. xv, 50, copy 6).

would Cicero, who said to his friend, *Orna me*,[7] have felt, if *his* friend had been as partial and as magnificent as Mr Bull! As I have no more of Cicero's vanity than of his abilities, I beseech you to have done adorning me.

It was a disappointment to me on opening the parcel, not to find a copy of a little MS[8] you showed me at Strawberry Hill, and promised me. It is not fair to have given me so many valuable presents, and to have broken your word on the only one I had the confidence to ask. Even modesty is not excuse for breach of promise—and yet I must still be

Your ever much obliged humble servant

Hor. Walpole

To Benjamin Ibbot, Wednesday 4 August 1784

Printed from a photostat of the MS in the Pierpont Morgan Library. First printed, Toynbee *Supp.* ii. 4. For the history of the MS see *ante* 24 Sept. 1773.

Address: To Benjamin Ibbott Esq. in Dartmouth Street, Westminster. *Postmark:* 5 AV. ISLEWORTH.

Strawberry Hill, Aug. 4, 1784.

IT is very uneasy to me, Sir, to decline complying with your request; but indeed I have no title to ask of the Duke of Richmond the favour you desire.[1] I have no doubt but it is a reasonable one, and being so, and what you say very few would desire, I can only advise that your son should present a memorial to his Grace setting forth the grounds of his suit, and that his sufferings have been caused or increased by his strict performance of his severe duty. The Duke is so just and compassionate, that I flatter myself he will do what is right, and rather from the reason of the solicitation, than from

7. *Neque tamen ignoro, quam impudenter faciam, qui primum tibi tantum oneris imponam . . . deinde etiam, ut ornes mea, postulem:* 'And yet I am quite sensible of my presumption, first, in laying such a burden upon you . . . and then in demanding actually that you should eulogize [adorn] my achievements' (*Epistulæ ad familiares* V. xii. 2, Cicero to Lucius Lucceius).

8. Not identified.

1. HW had previously interceded with Richmond to obtain an extended medical leave of absence from the army for Ibbot's son (*ante* 8 March *bis*, 12 March 1784). He had doubtless been asked by Ibbot to do so once again.

partiality to any other person—and if he does not think it right, I confess I should not care to ask it, even if I expected that he would mind my interposition—but indeed I have no claim to take any such liberty, and must beg to be excused. Lord Edgcumbe[2] perhaps might have more weight.[3]

I am Sir
Your obedient humble servant

HOR. WALPOLE

To EDWARD JERNINGHAM, Friday 6 August 1784

Printed from a photostat of the MS in the Henry E. Huntington Library. First printed in Lewis Bettany, *Edward Jerningham and his Friends*, 1919, pp. 47–8. Reprinted, Toynbee *Supp.* iii. 42. For the history of the MS see *ante* 13 Feb. 1778.

Dated by the postmark and by the reference to an air balloon, which places the letter in the mid-1780s. Between 1779 and 1790, 6 August fell on a Friday only in 1784.

Address: To Edward Jerningham Esq. in Grosvenor Square, London. *Postmark:* 7 AV.

Strawberry Hill, Friday 6th.

I TAKE your intention of coming hither on Sunday so kindly, dear Sir, that I write to accept it, on purpose that you may not think yourself at liberty to change your mind—you must not venture to return at night, for there is a body of 200 footpads between this place and Isleworth, three regiments of housebreakers at Brentford, between three and four thousand highwaymen encamped at Turnham-Green,[1] and a whole army of nabobs at Knightsbridge who plunder and murder without any treachery.[2] I can send you safely back the next day to Lady Jerningham:[3] an air-balloon sets out every morning

2. See *ante* 23 May 1767, n. 2.
3. Possibly because of his long experience and position (Admiral of the White, 1782) in the navy.

1. Between Brentford and Hammersmith, the scene of frequent highway robberies. HW wrote Conway 14 Aug. 1784 that he had heard of 'nothing but robberies and house-breaking. . . . I do not believe there have been above threescore highway robberies within this week,

fifty-seven houses that have been broken open, and two hundred and thirty that are to be stripped on the first opportunity' (CONWAY iii. 420). 'The forests that overspread the heath of Turnham are infested by banditti' (HW to Mrs Dickenson 31 July 1785, MORE 234–5).
2. Like Turnham Green, Knightsbridge was notorious as a lurkingplace for footpads and highwaymen.
3. Jerningham's mother (*ante* late Dec. 1781, n. 6).

from the Mun Gulph's head,[4] and puts up at the Moon in Moor-fields.

Your affectionate cousin

H. Fitzosbert[5]

To James Dodsley,[1] Sunday 8 August 1784

Printed from a photostat of the MS in the Harvard College Library. First printed in *The Literary Correspondence of John Pinkerton, Esq.*, ed. Dawson Turner, 1830, i. 46 (closing, signature, and postscript omitted). Reprinted, Wright vi. 223–4; Cunningham viii. 491; Toynbee xiii. 173 (signature and postscript omitted in all three editions). The MS was among Pinkerton's papers acquired after his death in 1826 by Dawson Turner; probably sold Puttick and Simpson 10 June 1859 (Dawson Turner Sale), lot 679 (in a 52-volume collection of autographs); not further traced until given to Harvard by 'a lady' in Feb. 1960.

Endorsed by Pinkerton: Mr Walpole 8 Aug. 1784.

Address: To Mr Dodsley in Pall Mall, London. *Postmark:* 9 AV. ISLE-WORTH.

Strawberry Hill, Aug. 8, 1784.

I MUST beg, Sir, that you will tell Mr Pinkerton[2] that I am much obliged to him for the honour he is willing to do me, though I must desire his leave to decline it. His book[3] deserves an eminent patron: I am too inconsiderable to give any relief to it; and even in its own line am very unworthy to be distinguished. One of my first pursuits was a collection of medals, but I early gave it over, as I could not afford many branches of virtù; and have since changed or

4. An allusion to the Montgolfier brothers, who invented the first hot-air balloon (*montgolfière*) and launched it at Annonay, France, on 5 June 1783 (Mann ix. 450 n. 8; Conway iii. 425 n. 11). The 'Mun Gulph's head' is an imaginary dockyard for balloons.

5. HW claimed to have discovered an ancient kinship between the Walpole and the Jerningham (Jernegan) families, by virtue of Isabel Fitz-Osbert's having been married first to Sir Henry de Walpole and later to Sir Walter Jernegan. See Cole i. 375 n. 8, ii. 3.

1. (1724–97), younger brother of Robert Dodsley; bookseller in Pall Mall.

2. John Pinkerton (1758–1826), antiquary and historian; HW's correspondent.

3. *An Essay on Medals*, 1784, published anonymously by Dodsley. Pinkerton had asked permission to dedicate the book to HW even though they had never met. In his copy HW identified the author and noted the publication date as 14 July (Hazen, *Cat. of HW's Lib.*, No. 278). The second edition, 2 vols, 1789, was dedicated to HW.

given away several of my best Greek and Roman medals.⁴ What remain I shall be glad to show Mr Pinkerton; and if it would not be
inconvenient to him to come hither any morning by eleven o'clock
after next Thursday that he will appoint,⁵ he shall not only see my
medals, but any other baubles here that can amuse him.

I am Sir
Your humble servant

HOR. WALPOLE

PS. Pray send me a *Grammont*⁶ bound by the coach.

To JOHN PINKERTON,¹ Sunday 5 September 1784

Printed for the first time from a copy of the MS in the Lloyd W. Smith
Collection, Morristown National Historical Park, Morristown, New Jersey,
kindly supplied by Mr Francis S. Ronalds. The MS is untraced until sold
Sotheby's 16 July 1891 (Phillipps Sale), lot 513, to Barker; resold Sotheby's
20 Dec. 1905 (Barker Sale), lot 834, to Benjamin; later in the possession of
Lloyd W. Smith, whose collection of manuscripts was acquired by Morristown
National Historical Park in 1955. This is the first of four letters to Pinkerton
that came to light too late to be included in CHATTERTON.

Address: To John Pinkerton, Esq. at Knightsbridge.

Strawberry Hill, Sept. 5, 1784.

Sir,

I CANNOT fix a precise day for the pleasure of seeing you, as I
am expecting General Conway and Lady Aylesbury and their
family, who have been prevented by Lady William Campbell's² ex-

---

4. HW collected coins and medals while
on the Grand Tour in Italy in 1739–41.
In 1772 he gave Lord Rockingham several medals in exchange for the Cellini
bell (MANN vii. 383), but kept some thousands that were sold on the ninth and
tenth days of the SH sale in 1842. The
most valuable of those he kept are listed
in the 'Catalogue of the 25 most precious
coins and medals in the rosewood case,'
'Des. of SH,' *Works* ii. 449–51.
5. The date of Pinkerton's first visit to
SH has not been found, but it is clear

from HW's letter to him 24 Aug. 1784
that the visit had taken place before that
date (CHATTERTON 251–2).
6. Dodsley was the publisher of the 1783
reprint of *Mémoires du Comte de Grammont*, SH, 1772.

———

1. (1758–1826), antiquary and historian;
HW's correspondent.
2. Sarah Izard (d. 1784), m. (1763) Lord
William Campbell, the younger brother
of the 5th Duke of Argyll and Lady Ailesbury (OSSORY ii. 50 n. 9).

treme danger.³ As soon as I am certain about them,⁴ I will let you know and am

Your obedient humble servant

HOR. WALPOLE

From WILLIAM FERMOR,¹ Wednesday 8 September 1784

Printed from Toynbee *Supp.* ii. 5 n. 1, where the letter was first printed. Damer-Waller; the MS was sold Sotheby's 5 Dec. 1921 (first Waller Sale), lot 123 (with Fermor to HW 26 Sept. 1784), to Brocklehurst; not further traced. Mr A. E. Salmon has kindly informed us that the two letters from Fermor to HW are apparently no longer in the Brocklehurst family collection at Sudeley Castle.

This letter was probably enclosed in a letter (missing) from Fermor's mother, Lady Browne, to HW (MORE 217).

T[u]smore, Sept. the 8th 1784.

Sir,

I FLATTER myself that the following curious anecdotes will help to make my apology for troubling you with a detail of them. I have had great satisfaction in collecting the particulars, which will be sensibly increased should they prove of the least entertainment to yourself.

In 1782 Mr Lucas,² a gentleman of fortune and veracity, in company with several others, now residing at Sudeley Castle³ in Gloucestershire, opened the grave where Catherine Parr⁴ was buried.⁵ She

3. She died the previous day, 4 Sept. (GM 1784, liv pt ii. 717).

4. No record of their visit has been found, but HW may have been referring to it when he wrote William Fermor *post* 16 Sept. 1784 that 'I have a set of company with me for two or three days.' Pinkerton was at SH 19–20 Sept. (CHATTERTON 252).

1. (1737–1806), of Tusmore and Somerton, Oxon.; son of HW's Twickenham neighbour and correspondent Lady Browne by her first marriage to Henry Fermor (ca 1715–47); D.C.L. (Oxon.), 1792 (Foster, *Alumni Oxon.* ii. 457; MORE 192 n. 1; GM 1827, xcvii pt i. 114, 580).

2. John Lucas; see DNB *sub* Catherine Parr.

3. About seven miles NE of Cheltenham. It was then in ruins, but was restored in the nineteenth century (BERRY ii. 165 n. 16).

4. (1512–48), m. 1 (ca 1529) Sir Edward Burgh (d. ca 1533); m. 2 (1533) John Nevill, 3d Bn Latimer, 1530; m. 3 (1543) Henry VIII of England; m. 4 (1547) Thomas Seymour, cr. (1547) Bn Seymour of Sudeley.

5. According to Treadway Russell Nash's 'Observation on the Time of the Death and Place of Burial of Queen Katharine Parr,' *Archæologia*, 1789, ix. 1–9, the grave was opened by 'some ladies, who happened to be at the castle in May 1782.'

lay about two feet from the surface of the ground, as it now is, a pavement having been removed some years ago for the purpose of repairs. The following was the appearance of the body—it was of a light brown colour, the flesh soft and moist, and the weight of the hand and arm as those of a living body of the same size. The appearance of the features was rather pleasing than otherwise, Mr Lucas remarking that he had seen many bodies recently dead wearing a much more unpleasing aspect. The teeth were perfect and of the best sort, and the nails in great preservation. She was rather of a low stature. The body was perfectly sweet and showed no marks of decay. She was clad, one may say, in a leaden doublet, which was made to fit exactly her body, arms, and legs, and entirely covered her face. Between this lead and the body was a thickness of linen cloths, twelve or fourteen double, which appeared to have been dipped in some composition, in order to preserve them, which had answered the end so completely, that it was with difficulty they could be separated with a large knife. There were neither earrings in the ears, nor any ring upon the fingers of the hand they examined; the other hand they did not remove from its leaden case. She had the following inscription in very ill-formed letters on the upper part of the lead over her breast:

'K. P. 6th and last wife to Henry the 8th and after that married to Ld. Thos. Seymer,[6] Baron of Sudeley, and High Admirall of Englond.'

On the body being again opened about twelve months after, it appeared to be in a putrid state, and highly offensive.[7] This I apprehend to have arisen from the free admission of air, it having been previously, one may say, in a vacuum, in consequence of the linen wrappers and the close coat of lead. It was laid in a very handsome Gothic chapel,[8] now fallen to decay, and is the property of Lord Rivers.[9] There appears to have been a white marble monument over

6. Thomas Seymour (ca 1508–49), younger brother of Edward, Duke of Somerset, and of Jane, third wife of Henry VIII; cr. (1547) Bn Seymour of Sudeley; Lord High Admiral, 1547; K.G., 1547.

7. 'In May 1784 some persons having curiosity again to open the grave, found that the air, rain, and dirt, having come to the face, it was entirely destroyed, and nothing left but the bones' (Nash, op. cit.

3). In 1786 Nash himself, with two others, examined the grave and 'found the face totally decayed. . . . The body, I believe, is perfect, as it has never been opened' (ibid.). When the coffin was opened in 1817, nothing remained but the skeleton (Toynbee *Supp*. ii. 5 n. 1).

8. The chapel is illustrated (plate I) in Nash's account.

9. George Pitt (1721–1803), cr. (1776) Bn Rivers; M.P.

her, from some fragments still remaining in the wall, part of which marble I now have in my possession. She died in childbed at this castle in 1548, at the age of 48,[10] having had four husbands. The particulars of her death, and funeral in the chapel of this castle, are to be seen in the *History of Gloucestershire*,[11] which I examined at Sudeley Castle the 6th of September, and at the same time had the above recited account from Mr Lucas himself.

I have the honour to be, Sir,

Your much obliged and very obedient humble servant,

WM. FERMOR

To WILLIAM FERMOR, Thursday 16 September 1784

Printed from Toynbee *Supp.* ii. 5–7, where the letter was first printed. The MS is untraced until sold Sotheby's 1 March 1851 (Interesting Autograph Letters Sale), lot 90 (with two other letters), to C. Jones; resold Sotheby's 31 May 1912 (Autograph Letters and Historical Documents Sale), lot 77 (with other Walpolian items), to Maggs; offered by Maggs, Cat. Nos 295 (1912), lot 3681; 317 (1913), lot 3697; 337 (Whitsuntide 1915), lot 1018; 360 (autumn 1917), lot 2343; 381 (autumn 1919), lot 2220; 417 (Christmas 1921), lot 3254; 457 (Christmas 1924), lot 3062; not further traced.

This letter was enclosed in a covering letter addressed to Fermor's mother, Lady Browne (see n. 1 below).

Strawberry Hill, Sept. 16, 1784.

I AM extremely obliged to you, Sir, for the trouble you have been so kind as to take in giving me such very curious information.[1] I had never heard of that discovery of Queen Catherine Parr's corpse, and am ignorant of its having ever been published. If it was not, it was depriving the public of a very singular event: and it is much pity that no drawing was made of her Majesty's face; nor any precautions taken to preserve the body in the state it was found.

---

10. She died at the age of thirty-six, having been born in 1512.

11. Samuel Rudder, *A New History of Gloucestershire*, Cirencester, 1779, pp. 719–20. HW's copy (untraced) is Hazen, *Cat. of HW's Lib.*, No. 530.

1. See previous letter. HW wrote Lady Browne the same day, 16 Sept.: 'I am vastly obliged to Mr Fermor, Madam, for the curious account he has been so good as to send me: and I have written this letter to thank him the first moment I had time' (MORE 217).

I would by no means neglect an early opportunity of returning you my thanks, Sir, for so obliging a favour; but as I have a set of company[2] with me for two or three days, I have not the time to say more at present, though perfectly sensible of your goodness.

I have the honour of being with great respect, Sir,

Your most obliged and most obedient humble servant,

HOR. WALPOLE

From WILLIAM FERMOR, Sunday 26 September 1784

Printed from Toynbee *Supp.* ii. 7 n. 2, where the letter was first printed. Damer-Waller; the MS was sold Sotheby's 5 Dec. 1921 (first Waller Sale), lot 123 (with Fermor to HW 8 Sept. 1784), to Brocklehurst; not further traced.

T[u]smore, Sep[t]. 26th 1784.

Sir,

I AM honoured with your letter of the 16th inst[ant], for which I beg leave to return you many thanks. No account has ever been published, I believe, of the discovery of Catherine Parr's corpse, as the particulars of so singular an event have been known to few. A circumstance so striking in the history of preservation excited my curiosity when in Gloucestershire, and induced me to go to the spot to inquire into the truth of what I had heard asserted by some friends living in that neighbourhood; the result of my inquiries and the testimonials of creditable living witnesses, I had the honour of transmitting to you, and I am happy to find, Sir, they afforded you the least entertainment.

The particulars of Queen Catherine's funeral may be seen in Rodder's *History of Gloucestershire*,[1] which is a continuation of Atkins's.[2]

As a further confirmation of the truth of Queen Catherine's death in childbed, I beg leave to transcribe a curious letter written to her by Queen Elizabeth[3] on the last day of July 1548: which serves as a

2. Perhaps Henry Conway and Lady Ailesbury; see *ante* 5 Sept. 1784 and MORE 217 n. 3.

1. See *ante* 8 Sept. 1784, n. 11.

2. Sir Robert Atkyns, *The Ancient and Present State of Glocestershire*, 1712. HW's copy (untraced) of the 2d edn, 1768, is Hazen, *Cat. of HW's Lib.*, No. 423.

3. At that time Princess Elizabeth.

testimonial of the great regard the Queen had for her, and of her then pregnant state, to which the Queen unequivocally alludes.

The Lady Elizabeth's letter to the Queen Dowager Parr, then married to the Lord Admiral Seymour. Cotton Lib[rary] Otho C. x, fol. 462, A.D. 1548.[4]

'Although your Higness letters be most joyful to me in absence,[5] yet considering what pain it is to you to write, your Grace being so great with child, and so sickly, your commendation were enough in my *Lords*[6] letter. I much rejoice at your health, with the well liking of the country, with my humble thanks that your Grace wished me as with you, till I were weary of that country. Your Higness were like to be combered, if I should not depart till I were weary being with you. Altho' it were in the worst soil in the world, your presence wou'd make it pleasant. I can not reprove my Lord for not doing your commendations in his letter, for he did it; and altho' he had not, yet I will not complain on him for that he shall be diligent to give me knowledge from time to time, how *his* busie child doth; and if I were at his birth no doubt I would see him beaten, for the trouble he has put you to. Mr Denny[7] and my Lady[8] with humble thanks, prayeth most entirely for your Grace, praying the Almighty God to send you a lucky delivrance. And my mistress[9] wisheth no less, giving your Highness most humble thanks for her commendations. Written with very little leisure, this last day of July.

Your humble daughter[10]

ELIZABETH'

I beg leave to remark here, that we probably owe the high preservation of the body amongst other circumstances to that state she was

4. *The Letters of Queen Elizabeth,* ed. G. B. Harrison, 1935, pp. 8–9, follows the text printed in Agnes Strickland's *Lives of the Queens of England,* 1842–8, v. 116–17, which was taken from Hearne's *Sylloge* rather than from the MS in the Cottonian Library; there are a few minor differences.

5. After Queen Catherine's marriage to Thomas Seymour, Elizabeth went to live in their household. But scandalous rumours of her familiarities with the Lord Admiral caused Elizabeth to leave her stepmother shortly after Whitsun 1548 and establish her own household at Cheshunt (Harrison, op. cit. 3, 7).

6. Thomas, Lord Seymour.

7. Sir Anthony Denny (1501–49), of Cheshunt, Herts; Kt, ca 1545; King's Remembrancer; Groom of the Stole; M.P. (GRAY ii. 148 n. 7).

8. Lady Denny.

9. Mistress Kate Ashley, Elizabeth's governess.

10. That is, stepdaughter.

taken off in, as we may reasonably suppose she was in perfect health; before disorder had destroyed or impaired materially any part of the structure which very probably was committed to the earth, as indeed most of the bodies of Henry VIII's wives were, with little or no blood remaining.

I have the honour to be with great respect,

Sir,

Your much obliged and obedient humble servant,

WM. FERMOR

To LADY LYTTELTON,[1] Saturday 27 November 1784

Printed from a photostat of the MS in the Robert C. Waterston Collection, Massachusetts Historical Society. First printed, Toynbee xvi. xi-xii (misdated 'Nov. 25, 1784'). Reprinted, Toynbee *Supp.* ii. 8–9; *Horace Walpole's Fugitive Verses*, ed. W. S. Lewis, 1931, pp. 178–9. The MS is in the autograph collection of Robert C. Waterston, acquired with his library by the Massachusetts Historical Society in 1899; its earlier history is not known.

HW apparently composed these verses on 27 Nov. but misdated them 'Nov. 28, 1784.' His transcript of the verses in his 'Miscellany' is headed: 'A card sent from Strawberry Hill to Eliz. Rich, Baroness Dowager Lyttelton, to inquire when she will be in town, Nov. 27, 1784' (*Horace Walpole's Miscellany 1786–1795*, ed. L. E. Troide, New Haven, 1978, pp. 24–5). This transcript includes 'Lady Lyttelton's answer the next day,' dated 'Ripley Cottage, Nov. 28th.' A copy (in Lady Lyttelton's hand) of her answer is written below HW's verses in the MS (see following letter). HW quoted the verses in his letter to Conway 28 Nov., explaining that 'It came into my head yesterday to send a card to Lady Lyttelton, to ask when she would be in town—here it is in an heroic epistle' (CONWAY iii. 430).

Address: To the Right Honourable the Lady Dowager Lyttelton at the Cottage at Ripley. *Postmark:* ISLEWORTH.

Strawberry Hill, Nov. 28, 1784.

From a castle[2] as vast—as the castles on signs,
From a hill that an African—molehill[3] outshines,

---

1. Elizabeth Rich (ca 1716–95), m. (1749), as his second wife, George Lyttelton (1709–73), 5th Bt, 1751, cr. (1756) Bn Lyttelton.
2. Strawberry Hill.

3. 'all Africa's—ant-hills' in the transcript in HW's 'Miscellany'; 'all Africa's—mole-hills' in the letter to Conway (see headnote).

This epistle is sent to a cottage so small,
That the door cannot ope, should you stand in the hall,
To a lady, who would be fifteen, if her knight
And old swain were as young—as Methusalem quite,[4]
It comes to inquire, not whether her eyes
Are as radiant as ever, but how many sighs
He must vent to the rocks and the echoes around
(Though no echo nor rock in the parish is found)
Before she obdurate his passion will meet—
His passion to see her in Portugal Street.[5]

From Lady Lyttelton, Sunday 28 November 1784

Printed from a photostat of a copy in Lady Lyttelton's hand, written on the MS of HW's verses addressed to her (see previous letter). First printed, *Works* v. 236 n. 1. Reprinted, Toynbee xiii. 222 n. 4; *Horace Walpole's Fugitive Verses*, ed. W. S. Lewis, 1931, p. 179. Lady Lyttelton's copy is headed 'Answer' (that is, her answer to HW's verses). The original MS of her reply to HW is missing.

Ripley Cottage, Nov. 28th.[1]

Remember'd (tho' old) by a wit, and a beau!
I shall fancy, e'er long, I'm a Ninon L'Enclos![2]
I *must* feel impatient such kindness to meet,
And shall hasten my flight into Portugal Street.

4. HW was then sixty-seven years old. 'As the sixth line goes rather too near the core, do not give a copy of it: however, I should be sorry if it displeased; though I do not believe it will, but be taken with good humour as it was meant' (HW to Conway 28 Nov. 1784, Conway iii. 430). According to Mary Berry, 'It was taken in perfect good humour; and she returned the following answer, which Mr Walpole owned was better than his address' (*Works* v. 236 n. 1). See following letter.

5. Where Lady Lyttelton lived in London.

1. The dateline is supplied from the transcript in HW's 'Miscellany' (see headnote to the previous letter).

2. See *ante* 22 July 1757, n. 5.

To Lady Lyttelton, Thursday 2 December 1784

Printed from a photostat of the MS in the Robert C. Waterston Collection, Massachusetts Historical Society. First printed, Toynbee xvi. xii. Reprinted, Toynbee *Supp.* ii. 9. For the history of the MS see *ante* 27 Nov. 1784.

Address: To the Right Honourable Lady Lyttelton at the Cottage at Ripley. *Postmark:* 2 DE.

Berkeley Square, Dec. 2d 1784.

I CANNOT be ashamed of being an old simpleton, since I have given occasion to your Ladyship to show so much cleverness and good humour; I am the more pleased as they imply your being in health and spirits. I knew you had a thousand talents, but did not suspect your being so ready at capping verses, and congratulate myself on making the discovery. I thought my *beaux jours*[1] had long been over, but I will rhyme to anything that can show how much I am dear Lady Lyttelton's

Most faithful humble servant

Hor. Walpole

PS. I believe I made my own lines still more foolish by writing *nor* how many sighs, for *but* how many sighs[2]—no matter, since they drew so good an answer.

1. Cf. the first line of Lady Lyttelton's verses: 'Remember'd (tho' old) by a wit and a beau!'

2. Not so: line 8 of his verses to Lady Lyttelton reads 'but how many sighs' (*ante* 27 Nov. 1784).

To SAMUEL IRELAND,[1] Thursday 2 December 1784

Printed from a photostat of the MS in the Harvard College Library. First printed Toynbee xiii. 227. The MS is untraced until sold Puttick and Simpson 6 June 1867 (Collection of Unusually Interesting . . . Autograph Letters Sale), lot 1037, to Locker (i.e. Frederick Locker-Lampson; listed in *The Rowfant Library, A Catalogue of the Printed Books, Manuscripts, Autograph Letters, Drawings and Pictures Collected by Frederick Locker-Lampson*, 1886, p. 219); owned by Godfrey Locker-Lampson, Rowfant, Crawley, Sussex, in 1905; not further traced until acquired by Harvard in 1953. There is a facsimile of the MS in the Melbourne Public Library.

Address: To —— Ireland Esq. at No. 3 in Arundel Street in the Strand.

Berkeley Square, Dec. 2, 1784.

Sir,

I CAME to town but yesterday evening and found the favour of your letter[2] and the two beautiful prints,[3] for which I give you many thanks. I am very grateful too for the honour you offer me of an inscription,[4] which you will forgive me for declining. They deserve far more illustrious names, than that of an obsolete old man, who lives quite out of the world, and has had no connection with an university for half a century.[5] The offer and this request granted will be a double obligation, Sir, to

Your most obedient and most grateful humble servant

HOR. WALPOLE

1. (d. 1800), author, engraver, and collector; father of William Henry Ireland, the forger of Shakespeare manuscripts.
2. Missing.
3. Not identified, but doubtless engraved by Ireland himself.
4. Ireland had apparently proposed an inscription dedicating the prints to HW.
5. HW was an undergraduate at King's College, Cambridge, 1735–8 ('Short Notes,' GRAY i. 5, 8).

To the Rev. Joseph Warton,
Thursday 9 December 1784

Printed from a photostat of the MS in the possession of Mr Robert H. Taylor, Princeton, New Jersey, kindly furnished by its former owner, the late Sir John Murray. First printed, Cunningham viii. 532–4. Reprinted, Toynbee xiii. 230–2; extract printed in M. B. Finch and E. A. Peers, 'Walpole's Relations with Voltaire,' *Modern Philology*, 1920–1, xviii. 200. The MS was acquired by Sir John Murray, 50 Albemarle Street, London, before 1936; sold Sotheby's 11 May 1970 (property of Sir John Murray), lot 232, to Hofmann and Freeman, from whom Mr Taylor acquired it in Sept. 1970.

Berkeley Square, Dec. 9th 1784.

I AM very much obliged to you, Sir, for your repeated kindness and communications:[1] and was much pleased at the sight of both the letters of Voltaire[2] and Mr Windham,[3] which I return with thanks and gratitude. Both are curious in different ways. Voltaire's English would be good English for any other foreigner—but a man who gave himself the air of criticizing our—and I will say, the world's, greatest author,[4] ought to have been a better master of our language, though both this letter and his commentary prove that he could neither write it nor read it accurately and intelligently.

That little triumph however I shall decline; I mean, I will make no use of his letter. It would be a still poorer scrap than it is, if curtailed, and I would by no means be accessory to printing the first part, in which I am happy to find you agree with me. Indeed it would be publishing scandal, and to the vexation of an innocent gentleman.[5] I condemn exceedingly all publication of private letters, in which living persons are named. I thought it scandalous to print Lord Chesterfield's and President Montesquieu's letters.[6] It is cruel

1. Missing.
2. Apparently a letter by Voltaire in Warton's possession, but not addressed to him. The late Theodore Besterman informed us that 'there is no trace of Warton anywhere in Voltaire' and that 'there was nothing by Warton in Voltaire's library.'
3. Doubtless either Thomas Wyndham (1696–1777), M.P., George Bubb Dodington's first cousin and residuary heir, or

Wyndham's nephew, Henry Penruddocke Wyndham (1736–1819), M.P., the topographer and editor of Bubb Dodington's *Diary* (MANN ix. 503 n. 9). See n. 13 below.
4. Shakespeare. See *ante* 5 Feb. 1765, n. 13.
5. Not identified.
6. Many of the political figures mentioned in Chesterfield's *Letters . . . to His Son*, 2 vols, 1774, were still living when Mrs Stanhope (n. 8 below) pub-

to the writers, cruel to the persons named, and it is a practice that
would destroy private intercourse in a great measure. What father
could venture to warn his son against the company of such or such a
person, if it were likely that a Curl[7] or a Mrs Stanhope[8] would print
his letter with the names at length? I detained my own fourth volume of painters for nine years, though there is certainly no abuse in
it, lest it should not satisfy the children of some of those artists.[9]

Still I am far, Sir, from carrying this delicacy so far as some expect.
I would respect the characters of the living, and the feelings of
their children. I should not have so much management for their
grandchildren, who may have a full portion of pride about their
ancestry, but certainly have very rarely a grain of affectionate tenderness for them. I did give much offence to some persons who
yearned with those genealogic duties, by my *Catalogue of Royal and
Noble Authors*[10]—but I did not care a straw. Indeed if every bad
man who has had the honour of being great-grandfather to someone
or other, was to be spared for fear of shocking his noble descendants,
history would be as fulsome as dedications were some years ago.
Philip the Second[11] was ancestor to half the monarchs of Europe.
May not he be branded as a monster without offence to their majesties?

The anecdote on Pollio[12] in the other letter did not at all surprise

lished the letters. *Lettres familières du
Président de Montesquieu Baron de la
Brède à divers amis d'Italie* was published at Florence in 1767 by the Abbé
Guasco. HW wrote Mann 30 May 1767
concerning the *Lettres familières:* 'I am a
little scandalized at the notes, which
though very true, are too bitter, considering the persons are alive. . . . I
think it cruel to publish private letters,
while the persons concerned in them are
living. Nobody has a right to publish
what the author certainly did not mean
such persons should ever see. It is making
him inflict a wound against his intention,
and such publications must frighten people from writing their private sentiments
of others to their most intimate friends'
(MANN vi. 523–4).

7. Edmund Curll (1675–1747), bookseller and editor; antagonist of Alexander
Pope. His unauthorized edition of *Mr*

Pope's Literary Correspondence, 5 vols,
was published in 1735–7.

8. Eugenia Peters (d. 1783), m. (before
1757) Philip Stanhope, Lord Chesterfield's
illegitimate son. See n. 6 above.

9. The final volume of *Anecdotes of
Painting,* though printed by 1771, was
not published until 1780. See *ante* 21 Jan.
1773 and n. 4.

10. *A Catalogue of the Royal and Noble
Authors of England,* SH, 1758. Lady Cardigan (later Duchess of Montagu) was
offended by HW's remarks on the avarice
of her grandfather, the Duke of Marlborough; see MONTAGU ii. 89 n. 14.

11. (1527–98), K. of Spain 1556–98.

12. Gaius Asinius Pollio (76 B.C.–A.D.
5), protector and patron of Virgil. In *A
Poetical Epistle from the late Lord Melcombe to the Earl of Bute: with Corrections, by the Author of the Night
Thoughts,* 1776, Bute is addressed as
Pollio. See MASON i. 242 and n. 7.

me. Indeed, does not the late *Diary*[13] teem with instances of similar growth? Nor is it any longer strange that Lord Melcombe should leave such a proof of his own—I know not what to call it! Has not he seemed proud of recording his own variations and contradictions and flattery?

I will say no more on that subject, Sir, but turn to another in which *you* are more interested. In the *Gentleman's Magazine* for last month, there is a pretended discovery of the name of the unfortunate lady to whose memory Mr Pope wrote his beautiful elegy[14]—the writer of that communication corroborates too the circumstance of the sword—but I believe he is quite mistaken in both[15]—at least my Lady Hervey, who was well acquainted with Pope, and who lived at the time, gave me a very different name, and told me the exit was made in a less dignified manner, by the rope.[16] I have never spread this, from the reasons I have given you in the former part of the letter: I do not know but some of the family may be living—nor is one bound to tell the world all one knows. I shall not have the same reserve to you, Sir, when I have the pleasure of seeing you, which I am glad to hear will be soon.[17] I am, Sir,

Your grateful and most obedient servant

Hor. Walpole

13. *The Diary of the late George Bubb Dodington, Baron of Melcombe Regis: from March 8, 1748–9, to February 6, 1761,* ed. Henry Penruddocke Wyndham, Salisbury, 1784. HW's two copies are Hazen, *Cat. of HW's Lib.,* Nos 429 and 2837.

14. 'Elegy to the Memory of an Unfortunate Lady,' first published in Pope's *Works,* 1717.

15. The writer of the letter, dated 16 Nov. 1784 and signed 'Parvus,' says that he received his information 'long ago, from a very worthy, but obscure, country parson.' He identifies the lady's name as 'Scudamore' and relates that 'she somehow or other procured a sword, and put an end to her life' (GM 1784, liv pt ii. 807).

16. HW noted in his copy (now WSL) of Pope's *Works,* 1741–3: 'The name of this lady was *Withinbury*, pronounced *Winbury*: the seat of her family was Chiras Court, vulgarly Cheyney's Court, situated under Frome Hill and forming nearly a triangle with Home Lacey and Hampton Lacey. It is said that she did not stab, but hang herself' (Hazen, op. cit., No. 2453). William Mason transcribed HW's note in his copy of Warburton's edition of Pope, 1751 (also now WSL), and added: 'This anecdote I copied from Mr H. Walpole who had it from Lady Hervey.' Warton wrote that 'If this Elegy be so excellent, it may be ascribed to this cause; that the occasion of it was real' (*An Essay on the Writings and Genius of Pope,* 1756, p. 253). The consensus among recent editors is that Pope's 'unfortunate lady' was probably a fiction.

17. We have found no record of this meeting.

TO EDMOND MALONE, Sunday 26 December 1784

Printed from a photostat of the MS in Thomas Kirgate's hand in the Hornby Library, Liverpool City Libraries. First printed in J. M. Osborn, 'Horace Walpole and Edmond Malone,' in *Horace Walpole: Writer, Politician, and Connoisseur,* ed. W. H. Smith, New Haven, 1967, p. 312. The MS is untraced until sold Sotheby's 22 March 1890 (Hayward Sale), lot 377, to Barker; acquired by the Liverpool City Libraries in 1899.

Berkeley Square, December 26, 1784.

MR Walpole is much mortified that he could not have the pleasure of seeing Mr Malone when so good as to call on him, Mr Walpole being confined to his bed by a severe fit of the gout.[1] He is almost as sorry to receive Mr Jephson's play,[2] when incapable of tasting the beauties of it; being only able to give it a slight reading at snatches in a most uneasy posture; and yet he thought some of the incidents very striking, though no play ever had so little justice done to it in the perusal. Mr Walpole begs Mr Malone will be so good as to represent his suffering state to Mr Jephson.

TO SIR WILLIAM MUSGRAVE, 1785

Printed for the first time from a photostat of the MS fragment in Sir William Musgrave's collection of autographs in the British Museum (Add. MS 5726A, f. 175).
Dated by the endorsement.
Endorsed by Musgrave: 1785.

MR Walpole begs Sir William Musgrave to let him know what Sir William desired . . .

1. This attack, followed by several relapses, lasted until March 1785. HW wrote Mann 5 March 1785 that it had confined him 'above three entire months, the longest fit I ever had, but one' (MANN ix. 561).
2. Presumably Jephson's farce *The Hotel; or, The Servant with Two Masters,* first produced at the Smock Alley Theatre in Dublin on 8 May 1783; published in Dublin in 1784 (*London Stage* Pt V, ii. 1322; BM Cat.). There was no copy of the play in HW's 'Theatre of Geo. 3.'

To Edmond Malone, ?early 1785

Printed from a photostat of the MS copy by John Singleton Copley in the Chamberlain Collection, Boston Public Library. First printed in J. M. Osborn, 'Horace Walpole and Edmond Malone,' in *Horace Walpole: Writer, Politician, and Connoisseur*, ed. W. H. Smith, New Haven, 1967, p. 313 (last paragraph omitted); extract printed in *More Books: The Bulletin of the Boston Public Library*, 1930, v. 201.

The copy is part of a fourteen-page MS entirely in Copley's hand, containing transcripts of letters and Copley's own notes on pictorial sources for his historical painting 'Charles I Demanding in the House of Commons the Five Impeached Members.' Copley apparently drew up the MS in anticipation of the trip he made during the summer of 1785 to investigate these sources in various English collections. The MS includes a transcript of Malone's long letter to Copley 4 Jan. 1782, supplying detailed information about the subject of the painting and the persons to be represented in it. Malone later consulted HW on Copley's behalf and allowed Copley to make a copy of HW's reply to him (the original letter is missing). Since HW's letter to Malone refers to an event that took place in April 1784 (see n. 7 below), it must have been written after that time but before Copley began preparations for his trip the following year.

MR Walpole sends Mr Malone a few short notes of what little information he can give him about the portraits he wants.[1]

Mr W. has a drawing in Indian ink of Speaker Lenthall[2] which he believes was done by Captain Brown.[3]

Mr W. has an enamel by Boit[4] of Oliver Cromwell, from the fine miniature by Cooper[5] that was Sir Thomas Frankland's, and since, his widow's,[6] but since her death Mr W. does not know what is become of it, it was not in Lady Frankland's sale.[7] Mr W. once heard that she had sold it to the Duchess of Kingston.

Sir Robert Walpole gave the original picture by Lely of Sir Henry

---

1. In his letter to Copley 4 Jan. 1782, Malone appended a list of persons to be represented in 'Charles I Demanding in the House of Commons the Five Impeached Members,' with notes on existing portraits of these persons. Lacking information about several portraits, Malone later called upon HW's extensive knowledge of English iconography and received this reply. Copley's painting is now in the Boston Public Library. See J. D. Prown, *John Singleton Copley*, Cambridge, Mass., 1966, ii. 343–50; illustrated fig. 599.

2. William Lenthall (1591–1662), Speaker of the House of Commons 1640–53.

3. Not identified.

4. Charles Boit (1662–1727), painter of portraits in enamel.

5. 'Oliver Cromwell; by Boit, after Cooper; given to Mr Walpole by his brother Lord Orford' ('Des. of SH,' *Works* ii. 476).

6. See *ante* 24 Sept. 1773, n. 9. She died 14 Oct. 1783 (GM 1783, liii pt ii. 895).

7. At Christie's 19–20 April 1784 (Frits Lugt, *Répertoire des catalogues de ventes publiques, 1600–1825*, The Hague, 1938, No. 3712). For the later provenance of

Vane, junior,[8] which had been in the Wharton Collection[9] to the late Earl of Darlington,[10] and most probably the present Earl[11] has it.[12]

The present Lord Bolinbroke[13] had a portrait of Oliver St John,[14] but Mr Walpole does not know what is become of it, but will inquire.

The print of Endymion Porter[15] by Faithorne[16] is the second Earl of Essex,[17] with only the inscription changed.[18] The King has certainly that which was at Carlton House,[19] but Mr W. is not sure that it is the portrait of E. Porter.[20]

the miniature by Cooper see *ante* 24 Sept. 1773, n. 6.

8. (1613–62), eldest son of Sir Henry Vane, the elder; Kt, 1640; M.P.; statesman and author.

9. In his will HW records that Sir Robert 'bought the fine collection of Vandycks and Lelys' from Philip, Duke of Wharton, whose father, Thomas Wharton (1648–1715), cr. (1706) E. and (1715) M. of Wharton, had formed the collection at Winchendon House (SELWYN 371).

10. Henry Vane (ca 1705–58), 3d Bn Barnard, 1753; cr. (1754) E. of Darlington; M.P.

11. Henry Vane (1726–92), 2d E. of Darlington, 1758.

12. Copley acknowledged his source to be the 'interesting portrait by Lely, in the possession of the Countess Dowager of Darlington' (Prown, op. cit. ii. 433, *sub* Sir Henry Vane, Jr). Lely's original portrait is probaby one of the three or four versions now in the Vane family collection at Raby Castle, Durham (David Piper, *Catalogue of the Seventeenth-Century Portraits in the National Portrait Gallery*, Cambridge, 1963, p. 360; R. B. Beckett, *Lely*, 1951, No. 543).

13. Frederick St John (1734–87), 2d Vct Bolingbroke, 1751. He lived at Lydiard Tregoze, near Swindon, Wilts.

14. (ca 1598–1673), lord chief justice of the Common Pleas; politician.

15. (1587–1649), poet and courtier.

16. William Faithorne (1616–91), engraver.

17. HW doubtless has in mind not the 2d E. of Essex, but rather his son Robert Devereux (1591–1646), 3d E. of Essex, 1604.

18. The first state of Faithorne's engraving (after the painting by William Dobson) is inscribed: 'The true and lively Pourtraicture of Endimmyon Porter of his Ma[jes]ties Bedchamber Esquire.' In the second state, the moustache is larger and the inscription reads: 'The true and lively Pourtraicture of Robert Earle of Essex his Excellence Generall of the Army etc.' (Louis Fagan, *A Descriptive Catalogue of the Engraved Works of William Faithorne*, 1888, pp. 54–5).

19. Formerly the official residence of the Dowager Princess of Wales, mother of George III, until her death in 1772; in 1783 it became the residence of the Prince of Wales, later George IV.

20. Dobson's portrait is now in the Tate Gallery (Piper, op. cit. 281; Martin Davies, *The British School* [National Gallery catalogue], 1946, pp. 49–50; illustrated in Gervas Huxley, *Endymion Porter: The Life of a Courtier 1587–1649*, 1959, facing p. 284).

To Lord Sandwich, Saturday 1 January 1785

Printed from a photostat of the MS copy by Mark Noble in the Bodleian Library (MS Eng. misc. d. 150, f. 3). First printed, Toynbee *Supp*. iii. 329–31. The MS copy was formerly in the possession of Noble's great-grandson, the Rev. R. H. Cresswell, and was acquired with Noble's correspondence by the Bodleian in 1927; the original letter is missing.

Endorsed by Noble: A copy of a letter from the Hon. Horace Walpole which Lord Sandwich did Mr Noble the honour to send; but with a desire to have it returned.

N.B. The letter was not written by Mr Walpole but it was signed by him.

Berkeley Square, Jan. 1st 1785.

My Lord,

I AM so incapable of writing with my own hand, or indeed of even dictating[1] much, having been laid up above this fortnight with a sharp fit of the gout,[2] that I will not only decline all thanks for the honour of your Lordship's letter,[3] but without further preface, say what I can at present on the subject of it. I have turned to the volume of my *Anecdotes,* where Cromwell's funeral is mentioned;[4] and though my memory is not so good as it was, especially on matters of which I had long ago discharged it, the passage convinces me, as I thought before I looked at it, that I took my information from Vertue's MSS and not from my own knowledge. I quote him there as saying he had seen an office-book,[5] whence he probably took the particulars.[6] I have not the smallest recollection myself of having ever seen any other account of Oliver's funeral. If any print of it exists Mr Rich[ard] Bull is more likely to know of it than anybody: but he is in the Isle of Wight,[7] and not likely to be in London this winter. It

1. To his secretary, Thomas Kirgate.
2. See *ante* 26 Dec. 1784, n. 1.
3. Missing.
4. *Anecdotes of Painting,* SH, 1762–71, ii. 158.
5. 'There is an entry in an office-book of a payment to him [Francis Carter] of 63*l.* 13*s.* 4*d.*' (ibid.).
6. HW took his information from George Vertue's MS notebooks, which he had purchased from Vertue's widow in 1758 (*ante* 29 Aug. 1758, n. 5). The list of officers who walked at Cromwell's funeral was copied by Vertue from a MS in the

collection of James West (Vertue Note Books, *Walpole Society* 1935–6, xxiv. 68). For the 'office-book' entry, Vertue had consulted 'A Declaration of his Majesty's Revenue' in *Truth Brought to Light: or, The History of the First 14 Years of King James I,* 1692 (ibid. 1929–30, xviii. 57–8).
7. In 1783 Bull began visiting the Isle of Wight and staying at North Court, a Jacobean manor house in the parish of Shorwell; he bought the house in 1795 (J. M. Pinkerton, 'Richard Bull of Ongar, Essex,' *Book Collector,* 1978, xxvii. 43–5).

is possible that there may be one in the library of the Antiquarian Society, but they were too foolish even for me, or I not foolish enough even for them, and so I have long had no more connection with them.[8]

My Lord, I did this summer read Mr Noble's[9] book[10] with much satisfaction, and as I frequently do by books that interest me, I scribbled many notes on the margins, and remarked some omissions. My copy is at Strawberry Hill, but if I am able to go thither before your Lordship comes to town I will bring it back with me, and if I find anything worth notice, I will communicate it to your Lordship when I have the honour of seeing you.[11] Forgive me for concluding abruptly, for I have not breath to say more; and am, with great respect and gratitude

Your Lordship's most obedient humble servant

HOR. WALPOLE

To the DUC DE NIVERNAIS, Thursday 6 January 1785

Printed from a photostat of the MS draft in Thomas Kirgate's hand in the Junius S. Morgan Collection, Princeton University Library. First printed, Toynbee xiii. 236–40. This MS and that of HW to Nivernais 1 Feb. 1785 are inserted in Kirgate's copy of Nivernais' French translation of the *Essay on Modern Gardening*, SH, 1785; for the history of this copy see Hazen, *SH Bibl.* 132, copy 7. The letter sent to Nivernais is missing.

Berkeley Square, Jan. 6, 1785.

Monsieur le Duc,

THOUGH painful illness[1] has been all my real crime, still I almost feel the unhappiness of the guilty on not having yet at-

---

8. HW was elected a fellow of the Society of Antiquaries on 19 April 1753, but resigned his membership in July 1772 because other members of the Society wrote attacks on his *Historic Doubts of . . . Richard the Third* ('Short Notes,' GRAY i. 28, 47).

9. Rev. Mark Noble (1754–1827), antiquary and divine; HW's correspondent (*post* 11 Jan. 1785, n. 1).

10. *Memoirs of the Protectorate-House*

of *Cromwell*, 2 vols, Birmingham, 1784. HW's copy, containing numerous notes, corrections, and markings by him (now WSL), is Hazen, *Cat. of HW's Lib.*, No. 2913. Sandwich became Noble's patron as a result of the book (see *post* 2 April 1785, n. 2).

11. The meeting did not take place until 31 Jan. (*post* ca 26 Jan. 1785, n. 2).

---

1. See *ante* 26 Dec. 1784, n. 1.

tempted to express my thanks for the honour you have done me[2]—
but surely you cannot have thought me intentionally culpable. If ill-
breeding or indolence neglect their duty on receiving obligations,
yet vanity is never ungrateful; it finds its own interest gratified in
proclaiming the favours it receives. You have done more for me than
I could achieve for myself; you have made me speak the universal
language[3]—would not a Carthaginian author have been proud to
have had his work familiarized at Rome by the pen of Scipio?[4]

As you have proved, M. le Duc, how perfectly you understand
English, it would be very ungrateful in me to mangle your language
in return; and though my own will not furnish me with terms adequate to my sensations, I will not weaken them by turning them
into French; you alone can improve what you translate.

My surprise, my satisfaction, at finding my own composition make
so agreeable an appearance, are not to be described. I *was* surprised,
though acquainted with the talents of the Duc de Nivernois:[5] but
though I knew how eloquently he could express his own thoughts,
could I imagine that he could transmute mine into gold too?—
Oh! but I found as I proceeded, that he could effect much more;
he could make Milton, our great Milton, write as correct and
beautiful French verse as Boileau himself—If I was ashamed that the
successor of La Fontaine should have thrown away some valuable
moments on translating me, how much more did I regret that those
moments had not been employed on larger versions of the beautiful
parts of *Paradise Lost!*[6] Yes, M. le Duc—Milton himself, when you
meet in Elysium, will reproach you with not having made all Europe
acquainted with his sublime poetry—and if he is just, he will confess that you could have accomplished what he failed in, you could
have *Regained Paradise* to all who do not understand English.

These reflections have sometimes augmented, sometimes soothed

---

2. Nivernais had sent HW his French
translation of HW's *Essay on Modern
Gardening;* his letter to HW is missing.
3. That is, the French language.
4. Publius Cornelius Scipio Africanus
(237–183 B.C.).
5. During his visit to Paris in 1765–6,
HW had heard Nivernais read some of
his fables (*ante* 11 May 1766, n. 10). HW
wrote Mason 15 May 1773 that Nivernais
had 'written an hundred or two of fables,
and read some of them to the Academy,

but told me it was thought wrong for a
nobleman in France to publish. . . . The
fables are good, as far as anything can
be so, that gives one no pleasure' (MASON
i. 84).
6. In the *Essay on Modern Gardening*
HW quoted passages from Milton's description of the Garden of Eden (*Paradise
Lost* iv. 134–42, 223–30, 237–47); Nivernais
rendered Milton's lines in French couplets
(*Essay*, SH, 1785, pp. 30–4).

my sufferings for three weeks. The very night on which Mrs Buller[7] delivered your invaluable present to me, I was forced to leave her abruptly from increase of pain, having been seized by the gout three days before: and though self-love and impatience could not prevent my reading the whole the next morning, my hands have been ever since so swelled and incapable of writing, and my head so little in a state of application for more than a few minutes at a time, that after begging Mrs Buller to represent my misfortune, I preferred waiting till I could dictate a few lines for myself.

You are so modest, M. le Duc, as to ask my pardon—What is it possible I should resent, but your conferring an obligation, which I can never return? A jeweller can give lustre to rude stones by cutting them into brilliants; but brilliants can receive no farther splendour, and can owe nothing to any new setting.

With equal condescension, M. le Duc, you give me leave to make corrections in your version of my essay. As a proof of my obedience, I will point out the single passage in your translation, in which, on the strictest comparison, I can discover that you have not completely rendered my meaning. It is in p. 26, in these words, 'heureusement Kent[8] et quelques autres n'ont pas été tout à fait si timides, et nous pourrons à présent monter et descendre par des rampes en plein air.' Instead of the last phrase, I meant to say, 'sans quoi nous aurions encore aujourd'hui à monter et à descendre par des rampes en plein air.' You will correct my French, if I have made myself understood.[9]

There is one other little alteration in the disposition of my words, which, though no error, makes me give an opinion which I did not mean. I have said that *Fountains and cypresses peculiarly become buildings;* the translation says, *les fontaines entourées de cypres*[10]— but though each separately are graceful ornaments to architecture, I should not recommend the latter to surround the former.

These slight changes are all that the partial eye of self-love could wish made in so beautiful a translation—but that eye, to be strictly just, ought to point out several passages which have been improved

<hr/>

7. Mary Coxe (ca 1744–1812), second dau. and coheir of John Hippisley Coxe of Ston Easton, Somerset, m. (1770) James Buller (1740–72) of Downes, Devonshire (BERRY i. 122 n. 2). She was a veteran traveller abroad and had presumably just returned from France with the MS (now missing) of Nivernais' translation.

8. William Kent (1684–1748).

9. Nivernais closely followed HW's suggestion; the printed translation reads: 'sans quoi nous aurions peut-être encore à monter et à descendre par des rampes en plein air' (*Essay*, p. 46).

10. Nivernais did not alter the phrase (ibid. 72).

and embellished by the translator, but it would be writing a commentary, not a letter, were I to specify all the particulars.

There are a few trifling errors in the notes, that in conformity to your commands, M. le Duc, I will remark.

In p. 8, it should be said that Theobalds[11] belonged to James the First, not James II.[12]

P. 9, Warwick Castle is situated *au bout de la ville* de Warwick.[13]

P. 14, Au lieu de, *Quand mon père s'est marié,* lisez, *Quand mon frère.*[14]

P. 27, *Sir Harry Beaumont,* nom supposé que prit M. Spence[15] dans plusieurs de ses ouvrages.[16]

P. 31, Le jardin de mon père fut planté par M. Eyre[17] il y a plus de *soixante* ans.[18]

P. 47. Monsieur *Whateley*[19] was the author of the *Observations on Gardening.*[20]

P. 49, Petworth[21] is in *Sussex,* not *Surrey.*[22]

P. 54, Lord *Nuneham* is now Lord *Harcourt.*[23] Park Place[24] is near *Henley,* not Chatham.[25]

These, M. le Duc, are all the changes I can discover as necessary: unless, perhaps, a note were added towards the conclusion, to explain

11. The house near Cheshunt, Herts, built by William Cecil, Lord Burleigh, during Queen Elizabeth's reign; it became the property of James I, who made it his hunting-seat and died there. In the eighteenth century it was sold to George William Prescott, 1st Bt, who pulled down the old palace and replaced it with a large modern house (William Angus, *The Seats of the Nobility and Gentry in Great Britain and Wales,* Islington, 1787, text facing pl. XXXI).
12. The corrected note reads 'Jacques I' (*Essay,* p. 14n).
13. Nivernais' note reads: 'Warwick castle est situé dans la province et près de la ville de Warwick' (ibid. 16n).
14. The correction was made (ibid. 26).
15. Rev. Joseph Spence, HW's occasional correspondent.
16. Nivernais' note reads: 'Joseph Spence était un sçavant, homme d'esprit et de goût. . . . Henry Beaumont est un nom supposé' (ibid. 48n).
17. According to HW, one of the earliest examples of the ha-ha boundary

was in the garden at Houghton in Norfolk, 'laid out by Mr Eyre an imitator of [Charles] Bridgman' (ibid. 53, 55).
18. Nivernais ignored the correction; his note reads 'à peu près cinquante ans' (ibid. 54n).
19. Thomas Whately (ca 1728–72), M.P.; author of *Observations on Modern Gardening,* 1770. HW's copy is Hazen, *Cat. of HW's Lib.,* No. 2307:1.
20. Nivernais' note identifying 'L'ingénieux auteur des Observations sur l'art des Jardins modernes' reads: 'Mr Whately mort il y a environ douze ans' (*Essay,* p. 82n).
21. The ancient seat of the Percy family, at this time owned by the 3d Earl of Egremont.
22. The correction was made (ibid. 84n).
23. George Simon Harcourt (1736–1809), styled Vct Nuneham 1749–77; 2d E. Harcourt, 1777; HW's correspondent.
24. The seat of HW's first cousin Henry Conway.
25. Both corrections were made (ibid. 92n).

that the essay is but part of a larger work on painting, or else the recapitulation seems to have nothing to do with the history of gardening.[26]

I wish the Duc de Nivernois would baptize the new style by a simple term. I confess I could never please myself with one. I have suggested one for a designer of modern gardens, and which has been approved, and will suit as well in French and English. To distinguish him from the *gardener,* I would call him *gardenist,* in French *jardiniste.*[27]

I fear I have said too much, though I can never satisfy myself or think I have sufficiently expressed my gratitude for the honour I have received—yet how unreasonable is vanity when once the bridle is thrown on its neck! Can it resist so natural an impulse as that of wishing that this charming translation was published?[28]—But no! it would be presumption to hope it when the author of so many exquisite fables still withholds them from the press![29] True genius, like virtue and charity, is content with the consciousness of its own merits—in virtue it is allowable—but ought not charity to contribute to the felicity of others?

Forgive this tedious discourse, M. le Duc, and impute some of its faults to my present weakness, and to a mind uneasy till it had expressed a little of its gratitude and admiration, and who knew not whether it should ever have an opportunity of even returning its thanks. I have the honour to be with the highest respect, M. le Duc,

Your most obliged and most devoted humble servant

[Hor. Walpole]

26. No such note was added.
27. Nivernais used the word 'artistes' (ibid. 68).

28. See *post* 1 Feb. 1785.
29. See *ante* 11 May 1766, n. 10.

To the Rev. Mark Noble,[1] Tuesday 11 January 1785

Printed from a photostat of the MS in Thomas Kirgate's hand in the Bodleian Library (MS Eng. misc. d.150, f.25). First printed, Toynbee *Supp*. iii. 331–2. For the history of the MS see *ante* 1 Jan. 1785.

Berkeley Square, Jan. 11, 1785.

Sir,

I DOUBT you have entertained much too favourable an idea of the assistance I can give you towards a new edition of your *Cromwell*.[2] I did make some remarks on the first edition; but it was without any view or intention of making any use of my notes; and as they were occasioned by a very cursory reading, I little remember what they were; I am sure, not many and perhaps of no value, and as probably, some anecdotes that you may since have gathered yourself. Such as they are, you shall see them, and will be at full liberty to reject them, if very trifling and insignificant.

I am not so indifferent about the excessive compliments you pay me:[3] I am in no light entitled to them. Both my reading and writings have been of a very idle desultory kind. They have told the world nothing but what it might have collected without my information; and as I am well aware of what class of authors I belong to, I must very seriously protest against the rank to which you would raise me. It would injure you to have it supposed your opinion, and would make me ridiculous if I should be believed capable of thinking it due to me.

I must as earnestly beg that you would not mention my desire of assisting you. I am far from thinking I shall contribute anything of consequence to your work; and I should blush to be thanked for having contributed a peg or two to a large edifice. I am old, and have a very precarious state of health, and desire to pass my little remainder in tranquillity and forgotten; and though very ready to

1. (1754–1827), vicar of Badesley Clinton and Packwood, Warwickshire, 1781; rector of Barming, Kent, 1786–1827; F.S.A., 1781; author of biographical and antiquarian works. His *Memoirs of the Protectorate-House of Cromwell*, Birmingham, 1784, gained him the patronage of Lord Sandwich and Lord Leicester (later 2d Marquess Townshend).

2. See *ante* 1 Jan. 1785, n. 10. Having gained the patronage of Lord Sandwich, Noble sought HW's acquaintance. Sandwich had written Noble 3 Jan. 1785 that 'the approbation and assistance of so eminent a character in the literary world as Mr Walpole, cannot but be extremely flattering and advantageous to you' (Bodleian MS Eng. misc. d.150, f. 4).

3. Noble's letter to HW is missing.

contribute to the encouragement of rising authors of parts, as far as my small power would go, I had rather be numbered with my co-temporaries who have had their little day of attention, than be held out as still an object worthy of notice. I shall be obliged to you, therefore, if you will accept my literary mite, without thinking yourself called on for any return—and be assured that this is no affected modesty, but the sincere request of, Sir,

Your obedient humble servant

HOR. WALPOLE[4]

To LORD SANDWICH, ca Wednesday 26 January 1785

Printed from a photostat of the MS in Thomas Kirgate's hand in the Bodleian Library (MS Eng. misc. d.150, f.45). First printed, Toynbee *Supp.* iii. 333. For the history of the MS see *ante* 1 Jan. 1785.

The date of the letter is approximate and was assigned by Mark Noble, to whom Sandwich had sent the letter. Other mentions of a 'relapse' of gout in letters to Mann 2 Feb. and to Lady Ossory 5 Feb. support Noble's dating (MANN ix. 555; OSSORY ii. 459).

MR Walpole is exceedingly sorry he cannot receive the honour of Lord Sandwich's visit, having had a very severe relapse, attended by so great a weakness on his breast, that Sir John Eliot[1] has forbidden his seeing anybody for a few days. Mr Walpole will desire the honour of Lord Sandwich's company as soon as he is able to speak without giving his Lordship trouble.[2]

4. The signature is in HW's hand.

1. Sir John Elliott (1736–86), Kt, 1776; cr. (1778) Bt; M.D. (St Andrews), 1759; physician to the Prince of Wales. His attendance on HW during this illness is described in HW's letter to Lady Ossory 5 Feb. (OSSORY ii. 459–60).
2. Sandwich wrote Mark Noble 31 Jan. 1785: 'I have this morning had a long interview with Mr Walpole, he is every-thing you could wish with regard to your business, but an absolute cripple with the gout, and confined to his chair' (Bodleian MS Eng. misc. d.150, f. 50). Sandwich also visited HW in Berkeley Square on 6 Feb., 19 Feb., and 9 March; the information he received for Noble's second edition of his work on Cromwell was promptly communicated to Noble (Bodleian MS Eng. misc. d.150, ff. 91, 99, 152, 215, 228). See *post* 2 April 1785.

To the Duc de Nivernais, Tuesday 1 February 1785

Printed from a photostat of the MS copy in Thomas Kirgate's hand in the Junius S. Morgan Collection, Princeton University Library. First printed, Toynbee xiii. 242–4. For the history of the MS see *ante* 6 Jan. 1785. The letter sent to Nivernais is missing.

London, Berkeley Square, Feb. 1st 1785.

HAVING had a dangerous relapse, it was impossible for me, M. le Duc, to express my thanks, as soon as I wished, for the great pleasure I felt at the gracious consent[1] you have condescended to give to my press being honoured by printing your translation.[2] I had, I confess, formed that ambitious wish—but my vanity was not bold enough to let it pass my lips. I was conscious that I was already but too nobly distinguished by having the Duc de Nivernois for my translator, and the author's pride was humbly content to flatter itself that some time or other the beautiful merit of the version would dispel all impediments and break out and shine in public.

Intoxicated as I am with this new condescension, believe me, M. le Duc, self-love is not the sole ingredient of my satisfaction. You intimate some intention of bestowing more of your happy talent in translation on an English author, infinitely more worthy of employing your pen; and more congenial, as he was a capital poet. When the specimens you have given from Milton shall appear in the *Essay on Gardening*, France will demand more from your hand,[3] and I shall be pardoned for having misemployed your moments, since I have been the occasion of your country's hearing that you owe it the brightest use of all your powers—and your country never did, nor ever will ask services from you in vain.

It would be superfluous to say with how much joy I embrace the offer of printing the translation at Strawberry Hill—though aware of all the difficulties that will attend the execution in the manner I would wish. My printer[4] is totally ignorant of the French language, which must make him proceed very slowly.[5] I not only ought but will revise and correct every page myself, which, besides my printing-

1. Nivernais' letter to HW is missing.
2. See *ante* 6 Jan. 1785.
3. Nivernais discusses his translation of the whole of *Paradise Lost* in his letter to HW *post* 29 Feb. 1792.

4. Thomas Kirgate (1734–1810).
5. HW employed an assistant to Kirgate, Edward Yardley, for printing the translation (*Journal of the Printing-Office*, pp. 20, 68).

house being in the country, will prevent my beginning the impression till I am settled at Strawberry Hill, whither I go in June.[6]

The interval, however, allows me to ask a great favour, in order that I may produce an edition as little unworthy of the work as shall be in my power. The copy I had the honour of receiving is written in such very small characters, that my printer, unaccustomed to French manuscript, would make endless mistakes and confusion. Might I take the liberty of begging that the Duc de Nivernois would order one of his secretaries to send me another copy transcribed in a very large and distinct hand of both the text and notes, with stops and accents exactly as he would please to have the whole printed?[7] I could not even trust my own diligence and attention without this assistance.

Perhaps I am going to use greater and too great freedom: Mrs Buller[8] communicated to me a correction of four of the lines translated from Milton.[9] I do not at all pretend to judge which are the better, as French poetry—but an English ear cannot help being prejudiced in favour of the first translation. *Canal,* I am aware, has not the same precise signification in French as in English. In the former, I know, it implies no more than a current—with us it is confined to signify *a straight pond,* which is one of the ingredients of ancient gardens which the modern taste most condemns; and when followed by the words *qui sans se détourner,* seems more strongly to convey the idea of a lineal canal. This, I confess, is a mere English objection; yet, I own too, that *un fleuve profond* sounds to me more nobly poetic than *un large canal. Clôture du jardin* is also to my imagination more bold and Miltonic than *se perd sous un mont*[10]—but this criticism I offer with timidity and humility; and submit with proper deference to the better judgment of a true French poet and critic.

6. Printing began at SH on 5 July 1785; the work was finished the last week in August (ibid. 20).

7. Nivernais sent HW a beautifully executed copy in April (*post* 30 April 1785).

8. Who had delivered the original MS to HW in Dec. 1784.

9. *Paradise Lost* iv. 223–7:

Southward through Eden went a river large,
Nor changed his course, but through the shaggy hill
Passed underneath ingulphed, for God had thrown

That mountain as his garden mould, high raised
Upon the rapid current . . . .

10. The printed translation reads:

L'Eden est traversé par un fleuve profond,
Qui suit un même cours et se perd sous un mont,
Clôture du jardin que l'artisan du monde
Posa comme un rempart sur le courant de l'onde
(*Essay on Modern Gardening,* SH, 1785, p. 30).

I have the honour to be, with the utmost respect and gratitude, the Duc de Nivernois's

Most obliged and most devoted humble servant

Hor. Walpole

To Edmond Malone, Friday 11 February 1785

Printed from a photostat of the MS in Thomas Kirgate's hand in the Hyde Collection, Somerville, New Jersey. First printed, Toynbee xiii. 249. Reprinted in *The R. B. Adam Library Relating to Dr Samuel Johnson and his Era*, 1929–30, iii. 252; J. M. Osborn, 'Horace Walpole and Edmond Malone,' in *Horace Walpole: Writer, Politician, and Connoisseur*, ed. W. H. Smith, New Haven, 1967, pp. 313–14; extract quoted in Sir James Prior, *Life of Edmond Malone*, 1860, p. 120; *Notes by Horace Walpole on Several Characters of Shakespeare*, ed. W. S. Lewis, Farmington, Connecticut, privately printed, 1940, p. [v]. The MS is untraced until sold Puttick and Simpson 14 Feb. 1873 (Interesting Collection of Autograph Letters Sale), lot 214, to E. Knight; resold Sotheby's 17 June 1875 (Euing Sale), lot 251 (with another HW letter), to Harvey; acquired before 1905 by R. B. Adam; sold with the Adam collection to Donald F. Hyde, 1948.

Endorsed by Malone: Mr Walpole.

Address: To Edmund Malone, Esquire.

Berkeley Square, Feb. 11, 1785.

MR Walpole is very sorry he cannot answer the favour of Mr Malone's obliging letter[1] with his own hand, having had two relapses of the gout, and being still much out of order.

Mr Walpole knows he has notes on several of the characters of Shakespeare, but they are at Strawberry Hill,[2] and till he can go thither they cannot be got at, but as soon as he is recovered enough to go there, he will certainly look them out, and will send them to Mr Malone, and hopes they will not be too late for his edition.[3]

1. Missing.

2. HW had written various notes on Shakespeare in his two 'Books of Materials' begun in 1759 and 1771; they have been published in *Notes by Horace Walpole on Several Characters of Shakespeare*, ed. W. S. Lewis. But HW's letter to Malone *post* 30 March 1785 makes it clear that the notes he had in mind were those 'made to Rowe's edition' of Shakespeare's *Works*, 6 vols, 1709.

3. *The Plays and Poems of William Shakespeare*, ed. Edmond Malone, 10 vols, 1790. HW's copy (now wsl) is Hazen, *Cat. of HW's Lib.*, No. 1360. He disparaged Malone's edition in his letter to Mary Berry 14 June 1791 (Berry i. 291).

To Edmond Malone, Wednesday 30 March 1785

Printed from a photostat of the MS in the Osborn Collection, Yale University Library, kindly furnished by the late James M. Osborn. First printed in J. M. Osborn, 'Horace Walpole and Edmond Malone,' in *Horace Walpole: Writer, Politician, and Connoisseur,* ed. W. H. Smith, New Haven, 1967, pp. 314–15. The MS was among the correspondence and literary papers of Malone given to James Boswell, the younger, by Malone's sisters after his death in 1812; sold Sotheby's 24 May 1825 (James Boswell, Jr, Sale), lot 3177, to Thorpe; not further traced until resold Sotheby's 10 Nov. 1964 (property of M. V. Whitmore), lot 443, to Dobell for Mr Osborn.

Address: To Edmond Malone Esq., Queen Anne Street East.

Berkeley Square, March 30, 1785.

MR Walpole having been confined the whole winter by the gout, was not able till a few days ago to go to Strawberry Hill and examine his Shakespeare for the notes which Mr Malone desired. They are merely on the historic personages in two or three of the plays, and being made to Rowe's edition,[1] he finds that a few errors he had remarked there, have been since corrected in later editions.[2] One only remains unamended; in the Dramatis Personas of *Hen[ry] V* Edward Duke of York[3] is called uncle to the King, but was only his cousin.

In *Richard II the Duke of York* was Edmund[4] son of Edward III.

—*Aumerle,* was Edward,[5] eldest son of the preceding, whom he succeeded in the title, and was killed at Agencourt.

Salisbury was John Montacute Earl of,[6]

Northumberland, Henry Percy Earl of,[7]

1. *The Works of Mr William Shakespeare,* ed. Nicholas Rowe, 6 vols, 1709. This work does not appear in the SH records, but it seems certain from the present letter that HW owned a copy and annotated it.

2. Of Shakespeare, not of Rowe.

3. Edward (Plantagenet) (1373–1415), eldest son of Edmund of Langley, 1st D. of York; cr. (1397) D. of Aumale; 2d D. of York, 1402; killed at the Battle of Agincourt, 1415.

4. Edmund (Plantagenet) (1341–1402) of Langley, fifth son of Edward III; cr. (1385) D. of York.

5. See n. 3 above.

6. John de Montagu (ca 1350–1400), 3d E. of Salisbury, 1397. HW published an account of him in the *Postscript to the Royal and Noble Authors,* SH, 1786.

7. Henry de Percy (1341–1408), cr. (1377) E. of Northumberland.

—*Willoughby* was William Lord Willoughby of Eresby,[8] who afterwards married Joan[9] widow of Edmund Duke of York.

—*Duchess of Gloucester* was Eleanor Bohun[10] widow of Duke Thomas, son of Edward III.

the Bishop of Carlisle was Merks.[11]

Lord Fitzwalter's Christ[ian] name was Walter.[12]

—*Ross*, was William Lord *Roos* (and so should be printed) of Hamlake,[13] afterwards Lord Treasurer to Henry IV.

It should be observed that Anne Queen of Richard II was dead, before the play commences, and Isabella, his second wife, was a child at the time of his death.[14]

In *Hen[ry] V*

the Earl of Cambridge, was Richard de Coninsburg, younger son of Edmund of Langley Duke of York, and was father of Richard Duke of York, father of Edward IV.[15]

Henry Lord Scrope[16] was a third husband of Joan Duchess of York (she had four) mother-in-law[17] of Richard Earl of Cambridge.

Mr Walpole is aware that these notes are very trifling, but he chose to send them, not to neglect any commands of Mr Malone,[18] and would have waited on him with them, but has a little return of the gout by the cold on Sunday.

---

8. William de Willoughby (ca 1370–1409), 5th Bn Willoughby, 1396.

9. Joan de Holand (ca 1380–1434), m. 1 Edmund, 1st D. of York; m. 2 (between 1402 and 1404) William de Willoughby, 5th Bn Willoughby; m. 3 (1410) Henry le Scrope (ca 1373–1415), 3d Bn Scrope of Masham, 1406; m. 4 (1415 or 1416) Henry Bromflete, Bn Vessy (GEC *sub* William de Willoughby).

10. Eleanor de Bohun (d. 1399), m. (ca 1376) Thomas (1355–97) of Woodstock, seventh and youngest son of Edward III, cr. (1385) D. of Gloucester.

11. Thomas Merke (d. 1409), Bp of Carlisle 1397–1409.

12. Walter Fitzwalter (1368–1406), 5th Bn Fitzwalter, 1386.

13. William de Ros (d. 1414), 6th Bn Ros, 1394; lord treasurer 1403–4. The ancient Barony of Ros or Roos held the

estate of Helmsley, otherwise called Hamlake (GEC).

14. Anne died in 1394; Isabella was ten years old in 1399, the year Richard resigned the crown.

15. See *ante* 30 June 1782, nn. 9–11.

16. See n. 9 above.

17. That is, stepmother.

18. 'Malone incorporated much of this genealogical information into his notes to *Richard II* in the 1790 edition, with proper acknowledgments to Walpole. . . . Malone also utilized Walpole's identification of Richard, Earl of Cambridge and Henry, Lord Scrope, in *Henry V* act ii. The other history plays show no new notes quoting Walpole, indicating that Malone applied to him for information only for *Richard II*' (J. M. Osborn, 'Horace Walpole and Edmond Malone,' p. 315).

Mr Walpole has Marshall's[19] print of Shakespeare with the laurel,[20] but it is pasted into a volume of prints[21] too large to be brought to town.

To Lord Sandwich, Saturday 2 April 1785

Printed from a photostat of the MS in the Bodleian Library (MS Eng. misc. d.150, f.255b). First printed, Toynbee *Supp.* iii. 333. The letter was enclosed in Sandwich's letter to the Rev. Mark Noble 2 April 1785, which reads in part: 'Mr Walpole called here this morning when I was from home, and left the enclosed card with your two volumes marked by him in the margin, which I will send to you as soon as you inform me by what conveyance you would wish me to forward them' (Bodleian MS Eng. misc. d.150, f. 255a). For the history of the MS see *ante* 1 Jan. 1785.

M R Walpole has brought to town his volumes of Cromwells,[1] and has the honour of waiting on Lord Sandwich with them; but he finds his own notes so few and trifling, that he should certainly not have troubled his Lordship with them, but to mark attention to his commands.[2]

19. William Marshall (fl. 1630–50), engraver.

20. HW noted in his *Catalogue of Engravers* that 'Marshal had the felicity too of engraving Shakespeare for an edition of his poems in duodecimo, 1640, representing him with a square stiff band and a laurel in his hand' (*Works* iv. 33). This is *BM Cat. of Engraved British Portraits* iv. 62, No. 16. The portrait was adapted from the famous engraving by Martin Droeshout in the First Folio, but HW believed that 'Marshal's print is genuine' and 'probably drawn from the life' (MS note in his copy, now WSL, of James Granger's *A Biographical History of England*, 1769, i. 185).

21. Doubtless one of HW's nineteen folio volumes of engraved English portraits (Hazen, *Cat. of HW's Lib.*, No. 3636).

1. See *ante* 1 Jan. 1785, n. 10.

2. Sandwich wrote Noble 11 April, 'the books with Mr Walpole's corrections will come to you' and cautioned that an anecdote related by HW in one of his marginal notes should not be published in the second edition of Noble's work (Bodleian MS Eng. misc. d.151, f. 4). Sandwich visited HW at SH on 20 June 1785 and 'brought Mr Noble with him, the author of the history of the Cromwells. . . . Lord Sandwich has taken the patronage of Mr Noble, as Hinchinbrook was the residence of Oliver, and the second edition will be much more accurate and curious than the first' (HW to Lady Ossory 20 June 1785, Ossory ii. 468). See *post* ca 8 March 1787.

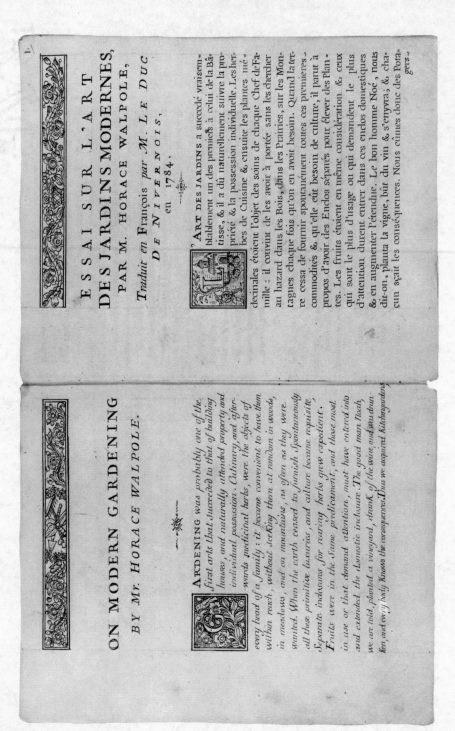

ON MODERN GARDENING

BY Mr. HORACE WALPOLE.

GARDENING was probably one of the first arts that succeeded to that of building houses and naturally attended property and individual possession. Culinary, and afterwards medicinal herbs, were the objects of every head of a family: it became convenient to have them within reach, without seeking them at random in woods, in meadows, and on mountains, as often as they were wanted. When the earth ceased to furnish spontaneously all these primitive luxuries, and culture became requisite, separate inclosures for rearing herbs grew expedient. Fruits were in the same predicament, and those most in use or that demand attention, must have entered into and extended the domestic inclosure. The good man Noah, we are told, planted a vineyard, drank of the wine, and was drunken; and every body knows the consequences. Thus we acquired kitchen-gardens

ESSAI SUR L'ART DES JARDINS MODERNES,

PAR M. HORACE WALPOLE,

Traduit en François par M. LE DUC DE NIVERNOIS, en 1784.

L'ART DES JARDINS a succédé vraisemblablement un des premiers à celui de la Bâtisse, & il a dû naturellement suivre la propriété & la possession individuelle. Les herbes de Cuisine & ensuite les plantes médecinales étoient l'objet des soins de chaque Chef de Famille : il convint de les avoir à portée sans les chercher au hazard dans les Bois, dans les Prairies, sur les Montagnes chaque fois qu'on en avoit besoin. Quand la terre cessa de fournir spontanément toutes ces premières commodités & qu'elle eût besoin de culture, il parut à propos d'avoir des Enclos séparés pour élever des Plantes. Les fruits étoient en même considération & ceux qui sont le plus d'usage ou qui demandent le plus d'attention durent entrer dans ces enclos domestiques & en augmenter l'étendue. Le bon homme Noé, nous dit-on, planta la vigne, bût du vin & s'enyvra; & chacun sçait les conséquences. Nous eûmes donc des Potagers.

WALPOLE'S ESSAY 'ON MODERN GARDENING,' TRANSLATED BY THE DUC DE NIVERNAIS

From the DUC DE NIVERNAIS, Saturday 30 April 1785

Printed from the MS now WSL. First printed, Toynbee *Supp.* ii. 170. Damer-Waller; the MS was sold Sotheby's 5 Dec. 1921 (first Waller Sale), lot 165 (with three other letters from Nivernais to HW), to Wells; offered by Quaritch, Cat. No. 415 with Nivernais to HW 29 Feb. 1792 (April 1928), lot 987, in a collection of Walpoliana, inserted in William Parsons's presentation copy of the *Essay on Modern Gardening*, SH, 1785; sold by Quaritch in Aug. 1936 to WSL, who has since removed the two letters from the volume. The MS (excepting the signature) is in the hand of a secretary.

À Paris, le 30 avril 1785.

M. le Comte de Sarsfield[1] qui va à Londres veut bien se charger de porter à Monsieur Horace Walpole la nouvelle copie que j'ai fait faire du charmant morceau *On Modern Gardening*.[2] La copie est faite avec soin et j'espère que Monsieur Horace Walpole en sera content; mais il lui faudra bien plus d'indulgence pour être satisfait de la traduction. J'ai profité, Monsieur, de toutes les observations dont vous avez bien voulu me faire part,[3] et je trouve la copie encore si loin de l'original que ce qu'il y aurait de mieux à en faire serait, ce me semble, de la jeter au feu. Monsieur Horace Walpole en sera bien le maître; c'est son bien, et c'est assez pour moi d'avoir tenté d'approcher d'un pareil modèle autant que ma mediocrité a pu me le permettre. Il me suffit de vous avoir donné par là, Monsieur, une preuve du prix que je sais mettre à vos ouvrages.

Je n'en mets pas moins aux bontés dont vous avez bien voulu m'honorer jusqu'à présent; je vous en demande avec instance la continuation, et je vous supplie de croire que j'en suis digne par l'inviolable attachement et la consideration distinguée avec lesquels j'ai l'honneur d'être plus parfaitement que personne, Monsieur, votre très humble et très obéissant serviteur,

LE DUC DE NIVERNOIS

M. Horace Walpole.

1. Probably Guy-Claude (1718–89), Comte de Sarsfield.

2. This elegant example of the calligrapher's art is now WSL (Hazen, *Cat. of HW's Lib.*, No. 2617). A label on the cover reads: 'Pour remettre à Monsieur Horace Walpole.' HW wrote on the inside cover: 'This beautiful manuscript was written at Paris in 1785 by order of the Duc de Nivernois, Mr Walpole having

desired to have a very accurate and legible copy of the Duke's translation, that the printer at Strawberry Hill, who was not accustomed to print French, nor indeed understood it, might make no mistakes. From this MS the edition was printed.' See illustration.

3. Nivernais did not adopt all of the corrections suggested by HW in his letters *ante* 6 Jan. and 1 Feb. 1785.

To John Fenn, Monday 2 May 1785

Enclosure only; printed from a photostat of the MS in the Norwich Central Library, Norfolk. First printed in R. W. Ketton-Cremer, 'Some New Letters of Horace Walpole,' *Times Literary Supplement*, 15 March 1957, lvi. 164. For the history of the MS see *ante* 7 May 1784. This 'certificate' was presumably enclosed by HW in a letter of the same date (missing) to Fenn.

[Enclosure]

I HAVE no doubt of the originals of these letters[1] being most genuine; and I think them not only very valuable for their antiquity, but full of curious matter both historic, and as illustrating ancient manners and usages; and the more precious, as the period at which they were written, has, from the turbulence and distractions of the times, furnished fewer materials than almost any portion of our story. Private familiar letters too of so dark an age are very uncommon curiosities. The method employed by the possessor and editor in arranging and illustrating the materials seems most judicious; and the labour he has bestowed on transcribing the letters, and on imitating the autographs and even the paper marks etc. on ascertaining the dates, are additional obligations to the public.

Horace Walpole   May 2d 1785.[2]

1. The Paston letters; see *ante* 7 May 1784, n. 2.
2. Two similar documents signed by Sir John Cullum and Edward King, testifying to the authenticity of the Paston letters, are preserved with this one in the volumes of Fenn's correspondence. Fenn had presumably intended to print these 'certificates' in the preface to his edition of the Paston letters, but he did not do so and merely thanked the three men for their help and encouragement. See *post* 1 Feb. 1787.

To Edmond Malone, early July 1785

Printed from a photostat of the MS in the possession (1940) of Mrs Augustus Loring, Boston, Massachusetts. First printed in J. M. Osborn, 'Horace Walpole and Edmond Malone,' in *Horace Walpole: Writer, Politician, and Connoisseur*, ed. W. H. Smith, New Haven, 1967, p. 315. HW's note is written on the blank leaf of a copy of HW's rules for admission to SH (Hazen, *SH Bibl.* 228); underneath the note is pasted a small slip of paper (probably cut from a book that HW had at Eton) signed 'Hor. Walpole 1731.' The history of the MS is not known.

Dated approximately by Malone's visit to SH on 7 July 1785 (see n. 1 below).

MR Walpole will not refuse Mr Malone's company,[1] but as he has been forced to print these rules,[2] he fears he shall disoblige others, and therefore must beg it may not be mentioned.[3]

To Edmond Malone, Sunday 10 July 1785

Printed from a photostat of the MS in the Pierpont Morgan Library, removed from an extra-illustrated copy of *Letters of James Boswell, Addressed to the Rev. W. J. Temple*, 1857. First printed in Sir James Prior, *Life of Edmond Malone*, 1860, p. 121. Reprinted, Toynbee xiii. 293–4; J. M. Osborn, 'Horace Walpole and Edmond Malone,' in *Horace Walpole: Writer, Politician, and Connoisseur*, ed. W. H. Smith, New Haven, 1967, p. 317 (closing and signature omitted in all previous printings). The history of the MS is not known.

Strawberry Hill, July 10, 1785.

I AM much obliged to you, Sir, for the favour of your letter,[1] to which I was extremely sorry to have given any occasion, and of which I beg you will give me leave to send you this account.

I live here in so numerous and gossiping a neighbourhood, that

1. HW's 'Book of Visitors' shows that 'Mr Malone and 3' were admitted at SH on 7 July 1785 (BERRY ii. 223). The visit is recorded in Boswell's Journal for 7 July: 'Another rural party; Courtney [John Courtenay] and the ladies in coach, Malone and I in chaise. Went and saw Strawberry Hill, Hampton Court, dined in Bushy Park in the air, saw Pope's Grotto' (*Private Papers of James Boswell from Malahide Castle*, ed. Geoffrey Scott and F. A. Pottle, Mt Vernon, New York, privately printed, 1928–34, xvi. 106). The 'ladies' were presumably Malone's two sisters, Catherine and Henrietta, and his sister-in-law, Lady Sunderlin. From the following letter it appears that only four members of the party of six saw the house.

2. See headnote.
3. See following letter.
———
1. Missing.

I am not only tormented daily by applications for tickets, but several persons have quarrelled with me for not complying with all their demands. Nay, I have received letters reproaching me with indulging some of my particular friends with a greater latitude than four, for they are so idle as to watch and count the number of carriages at my gate. The very day you was here last,[2] Sir, a gentleman and his wife,[3] who came from a neighbour's, were in the house, and I knew would report that I had admitted six,[4] if the carriages[5] were seen—and yet out of regard to you, Sir, I could not think of disappointing your friends. You was extremely good to favour me,[6] and I hope by this relation will see how much I am distressed, though very desirous of obliging. As numbers come to see my house, whose names I do not even know, I must limit the number—and I offend, if I break my rule; therefore last year I printed those rules,[7] and now should give still greater offence, if I did not adhere to them, while the only advantage that accrues to myself, is, that my evenings are free, and that I keep the month of October for myself.

I beg your pardon, Sir, for troubling you with this detail, but it was due to your politeness, and will I hope convince you that I am Sir

> Your much obliged and obedient humble servant
>
> Hor. Walpole

---

2. 7 July. See previous letter, n. 1.
3. Not identified.
4. That is, all six members of Malone's party.
5. A coach and a chaise.

6. Malone and his friends had apparently abided by HW's rule of admitting no more than four persons on the same day.
7. See *ante* 7 Sept. 1781, n. 1.

To Thomas Astle, Tuesday 19 July 1785

Printed from Toynbee xiii. 295, where the letter was first printed. The MS is untraced until sold Sotheby's 5 July 1900 (Autograph Letters and Historical Documents Sale), lot 323, to Edgar; resold Sotheby's 13 Dec. 1902 (Autograph Letters and Historical Documents Sale), lot 806, to Bowler; resold Puttick and Simpson 16 April 1903, lot 206, to unknown; resold Sotheby's 20 Nov. 1903 (Autograph Letters and Historical Documents Sale), lot 465, to Johnston; later acquired by Frederick Barker, of London; resold Sotheby's 20 Dec. 1905 (Barker Sale), lot 836, to B. F. Stevens; resold American Art Association 4 March 1925 (William F. Gable Sale, Part VII), lot 1044, to unknown; resold American Art Association-Anderson Galleries 30 Oct. 1929 (Geddes Sale), lot 218, to E. J. Heise; not further traced.

Strawberry Hill, July 19, 1785.

Sir,

AS your great knowledge makes you an oracle, you must excuse your being consulted, and will forgive me, I hope, for troubling you. An acquaintance[1] of mine has a lawsuit for an estate *in Staffordshire*, under a grant of Humphrey Earl of Buckingham[2] to Ralph Macclesfield[3] in tail *of the manor of Meir or Mere* in Staffordshire dated 21st of Henry VI.[4] This manor of Meir is claimed by a grant of Henry VIII in his 26th year[5] to Rowland Lee,[6] Bishop of Litchfield, and it says the *Priory of St Thomas near Stafford* was endowed with it.[7] What is wished to be known is, by whom and at what time that priory was so endowed?[8]

---

1. Hon. Thomas Fitzwilliam (1755–1833), 9th Vct Fitzwilliam, 1830; HW's occasional correspondent.

2. Humphrey Stafford (1402–60), 2d E. of Buckingham, ?1438; cr. (1444) D. of Buckingham.

3. Not identified. In 1780 Thomas Fitzwilliam had married Agnes Macclesfield (d. 1817); she was doubtless a descendant of Ralph Macclesfield. The outcome of the lawsuit was 'entirely successful' for Fitzwilliam; see *post* 5 Aug. 1785.

4. 1442/3. No record of this grant has been found. However, on 10 Oct. 1474 (14 Edward IV) the Crown granted the manor of Mere (now Meir), near Newport, Staffs, to Humphrey Stafford of Grafton and his heirs (*Calendar of the Patent Rolls . . . 1467–1477*, 1900, pp. 470–1). This Humphrey Stafford was doubtless related to

the Duke of Buckingham of the same name. See n. 7 below.

5. 1534/5.

6. Rowland Lee (or Legh) (d. 1543), Bp of Coventry and Lichfield 1534–43; lord president of the Council in the Marches of Wales, 1534.

7. The Augustinian priory of St Thomas the Martyr, near Stafford, had among its temporal estates in the sixteenth century the manor of Maer, near Newcastle-under-Lyme. On 13 Oct. 1539 Bishop Lee, the priory's patron, obtained a grant of the priory and all its landed possessions and churches from the Crown, to which they had been previously surrendered. On Lee's death in 1543, the property passed to his nephews (*Vict. Co. Hist. Staffs* iii. 265–6; DNB *sub* Rowland Lee). In the early nineteenth century the manor was

If you, Sir, can be so good as to give any information on this head, you will do great service to the gentleman in possession, and will much oblige

Your most obedient humble servant,

HOR. WALPOLE

TO MRS ANDERSON,[1] August 1785

Printed for the first time from the MS pasted in Mrs Anderson's presentation copy of HW's *Essay on Modern Gardening*, SH, 1785, now WSL. This copy came into the possession of the 4th Earl of Orford, n.c. (1813–94), and descended to his granddaughter, Mrs Scott Murray (later Mrs Colin Davy), of Heckfield Place, Basingstoke, Hants; sold Christie's 17 Dec. 1957 (Mrs Colin Davy Sale), lot 73, to Maggs for WSL (Hazen, *SH Bibl.*, 1973 edn, p. xxviii, copy 14).

Dated approximately by the endorsement.

Endorsed by Mrs Anderson: August 1785. Strawberry Hill.

Mon enfant,

I SEND you not only the *Royal and Noble Authors*[2] which you wanted, but another noble author of whom you may not have heard, the Duc de Nivernois. There are but few printed,[3] but you are a favourite of the printer.

H. W.

purchased by Josiah Wedgwood, son of the famous potter (William Pitt, *A Topographical History of Staffordshire*, 1817, p. 332).

8. At the *quo warranto* inquiry of 1293 the prior, Nicholas of Aspley, claimed the right of free warren in Maer as well as in various other properties (*Vict. Co. Hist. Staffs* iii. 263). The priory probably acquired the manor of Maer (as opposed to Mere) in the later thirteenth century. HW confuses the manor of Mere with the manor of Maer in this letter.

----

1. Caroline Georgina Johnston (ca 1764–1823), only surviving dau. of Gen. James and Lady Cecilia Johnston, m. (1780), after eloping with him, Francis Evelyn

Anderson (1752–1821), M.P. For a full note on her see BERRY i. 23 n. 38.

2. *A Catalogue of the Royal and Noble Authors of England*, 2 vols, SH, 1758; 2d edn, 2 vols, 1759. Mrs Anderson's copy has not been located.

3. 400 copies of Nivernais' French translation of HW's *Essay on Modern Gardening* were printed at SH in July and August 1785; 200 copies were sent to Paris for Nivernais' use (Hazen, *SH Bibl.* 129). Mrs Anderson's name appears in HW's list of persons to whom he presented copies of the book (BERRY ii. 259). Her copy is inscribed on the verso of the title-page: 'C. G. Anderson. Given me by the Author 1785' (see headnote).

To Edward Jerningham, Wednesday 3 August 1785

Printed from a photostat of the MS in the Henry E. Huntington Library. First printed in Lewis Bettany, *Edward Jerningham and his Friends*, 1919, p. 46. Reprinted, Toynbee *Supp.* iii. 43. For the history of the MS see *ante* 13 Feb. 1778.

Address: To Edward Jerningham Esq. in Grosvenor Square, London. *Postmark:* 4 AU. ISLEWORTH.

Strawberry Hill, Aug. 3d 1785.

I AM rejoiced, dear Sir, to hear that Lady Jerningham[1] is revived, and that her amendment will procure me the pleasure of your company to Park Place, where I am sure you will be most welcome, as you will be here on Friday morning[2] to

Your obedient servant

H. WALPOLE

To Thomas Astle, Friday 5 August 1785

Printed from the MS now WSL. First printed, Toynbee xiii. 303. The MS is untraced until sold Sotheby's 8 Feb. 1901 (Autograph Letters and Historical Documents Sale), lot 219, to Gardyner; resold Sotheby's 20 Dec. 1905 (Frederick Barker Sale), lot 835, to B. F. Stevens; owned in 1934 by Daniel Berkeley Updike of the Merrymount Press, who later gave it to the Providence Public Library; presented by the Library, through the kindness of the Librarian, Mr Stuart C. Sherman, and the Trustees, to WSL, April 1968.

Endorsed by Astle: August 5th 1785. The Honourable Mr Walpole. [On the recto:] *310.*

Address: To Thomas Astle Esq. at Battersea Rise. *Postmark:* 6 AU. 2 ⟨O'C⟩LOCK. ISLEWORTH.

Strawberry Hill, Aug. 5th 1785.

I DEFERRED my thanks, Sir, for the very ready and obliging manner with which you was so good as to comply with my late request,[1] till I could tell you the event of Mr Fitzwilliam's cause,

1. Jerningham's mother (*ante* late Dec. 1781, n. 6). She died in Grosvenor Square 23 Sept. 1785 (GM 1785, lv pt ii. 751).

2. HW and Jerningham left for Park Place, the seat of HW's cousin Henry Conway, on Friday, 5 Aug.; HW was back at SH by the 10th (OSSORY ii. 484).

1. See *ante* 19 July 1785.

which has been entirely successful, and to which I believe your very clear information contributed.[2] If you was pass[ing] this way any time this season after the beginning of next week, I shall be very happy to have the pleasure of thanking you in person, as I have the honour to be with great regard, Sir,

Your much obliged and obedient humble servant

Hor. Walpole

To Edward Jerningham, late August 1785

Printed from a photostat of the MS in the Henry E. Huntington Library. First printed in Lewis Bettany, *Edward Jerningham and his Friends*, 1919, p. 47. Reprinted, Toynbee *Supp.* iii. 43–4. For the history of the MS see *ante* 13 Feb. 1778.

Dated approximately by the reference to Cardinal de Rohan's arrest for forgery, which took place on 15 Aug. 1785. HW's letters to Mann 26 Aug. and to Lady Ossory 29 Aug. also mention the arrest (Mann ix. 603–4; Ossory ii. 494–5); the present letter was doubtless written about this time.

Address: To Edward Jerningham Esq., Grosvenor Square.

THANK you, dear Sir, for your curious news.[1] I am rather sorry for it, as I suppose it will please the Emperor[2] to hear that a cardinal[3] is sent to prison for forgery[4]—and his Imperial Rapacity[5] is such a tyrant, that he will commit new injustice on pretence of punishing your Church.[6] I was not acquainted with the Cardinal de Rohan—pray was he not a cousin of that capital swindler the Prince

2. Mrs Toynbee printed 'Mr Fitzwilliam's cause' and 'I believe your very clear information contributed' in italics; we have not done so because we believe that the underscoring in the MS was done by the person who numbered the letter '*310*' (see headnote).

1. Jerningham's letter is missing.
2. Joseph II (1741–90), Holy Roman Emperor 1765–90.
3. Louis-René-Édouard (1734–1803), Cardinal-Prince de Rohan-Guéménée.
4. He was arrested 15 Aug. 1785 and imprisoned in the Bastille for allegedly forging a letter from Marie Antoinette to

obtain a diamond necklace; he was later acquitted as being the victim rather than the perpetrator of the fraud (Mann ix. 603 nn. 3–6; Ossory ii. 495 n. 23).
5. HW also refers to the Emperor in this way in his letter to Lady Ossory 10 Aug. 1785 (ibid. ii. 486).
6. Jerningham was a Roman Catholic. In 1781–2 Joseph II had issued various orders designed to reduce Rome's influence in ecclesiastical matters; among his reforms was the suppression of numerous religious houses in his territories (Mason ii. 181 n. 40; Mann ix. 236 n. 7; Ossory ii. 487 n. 13).

de Guéméné?⁷ The manners of nations seem to cross over and figure in. In France two Rohans and a cardinal punished for petty larceny! In England—oh, I will not incur the penalty of Scandalum Magnatum—but at least the greatest rogues are not sent to Newgate.⁸

To Dr Charles Burney,¹ Tuesday 6 September 1785

Printed from a copy of the MS kindly furnished by its owner, Mr John R. G. Comyn, The Cross House, Vowchurch, Turnastone, Herefordshire. First printed in *Diary and Letters of Madame d'Arblay*, ed. Austin Dobson, 1904–5, ii. 483. Reprinted, Toynbee xiii. 317. The MS descended in the Burney family to Mr Comyn, a direct descendant of Dr Burney (see Joyce Hemlow, *A Catalogue of the Burney Family Correspondence 1749–1878*, New York and Montreal, 1971, p. xvi).

Address: To Dr Burney in St Martin's Street, Leicester Square, London.

Strawberry Hill, Sept. 6, 1785.

MR Walpole is very happy that Dr Burney can oblige him with his company on Thursday evening, but shall certainly not let him sleep anywhere else, nor consent to his going away the next day, if he can possibly keep him.²

If it is not too much to ask, Mr Walpole would be exceedingly flattered, if Dr Burney would bring Miss Burney³ with him. Her

7. Henri-Louis-Marie de Rohan (1745–1808), styled Prince de Guéménée (MANN ix. 513 n. 13). He was Cardinal de Rohan's nephew. In 1782 he went bankrupt, 'breaking for 28 millions of *livres*' (HW to Lady Ossory 5 Nov. 1782, OSSORY ii. 366).

8. 'He [Cardinal de Rohan] might not have been sent to Newgate here for using the Queen's name to get diamonds' (HW to Lady Ossory 29 Aug. 1785, ibid. ii. 495).

1. (1726–1814), Mus.D. (Oxon.), 1769; F.R.S.; historian of music.

2. HW wrote Lady Ossory 17 Sept. 1785: 'Dr Burney and his daughter Evelina Cecilia have passed a day and half with me. He is lively and agreeable; she, half and half sense and modesty, which possess her so entirely, that not a cranny is left for affectation or pretensions'

(OSSORY ii. 498). Fanny Burney's account in her *Memoirs of Dr Burney*, 1832, iii. 64–70, calls this 'a visit of some days' in 1786. See following note.

3. Frances Burney (1752–1840), m. (1793) Alexandre d'Arblay; novelist and diarist. HW's 'Book of Visitors' shows that Miss Burney had visited SH on 4 Sept. 1784 and that HW showed her the house himself (BERRY ii. 222). She wrote Hester Maria Thrale 10 Oct. 1785: 'I have been spending some time with my Father at Mr Walpole's at Strawberry Hill, and much to my satisfaction. I don't know if you ever saw his extraordinary collection of *out of the way* things? The house and every thing in it is curious, interesting, or historical: and he is himself all three into the bargain' (*The Queeney Letters*, ed. the Marquis of Lansdowne, 1934, p. 114).

maid[4] shall be lodged too or Mr W's housekeeper[5] shall attend her: and if Dr Burney and Cecilia[6] will grant him this favour, he shall think it as great an one as if Dorset's self had blessed his roof.[7]

To George Colman, Monday 19 September 1785

Printed from a photostat of the MS in the National Library of Scotland. First printed in George Colman, the younger, *Posthumous Letters . . . Addressed to Francis Colman, and George Colman, the Elder*, 1820, pp. 135–6. Reprinted in R. B. Peake, *Memoirs of the Colman Family*, 1841, ii. 197–8; Wright vi. 256 (closing and signature omitted); Cunningham ix. 16; Toynbee xiii. 325–6. The MS was acquired by the National Library of Scotland before 1936; its earlier history is not known.

Strawberry Hill, Sept. 19, 1785.

Sir,

I BEG your acceptance of a little work[1] just printed here; and I offer it as a token of my gratitude, not as pretending to pay you for your last present[2]—a translation, however excellent, from a very inferior Horace would be a most inadequate return: but there is so much merit in the enclosed version, the language is so pure, and the imitations of our poets so extraordinary, so much more faithful and harmonious than I thought the French tongue could achieve,[3] that I flatter myself you will excuse my troubling you with an old performance of my own,[4] when newly dressed by a master hand. As

4. Professor Joyce Hemlow informs us that to her knowledge Fanny Burney had no maid prior to her years at Court.

5. Margaret Young (fl. 1760–85).

6. *Cecilia; or, Memoirs of an Heiress* (5 vols, 1782) is the title of Miss Burney's second novel. HW's copy is Hazen, *Cat. of HW's Lib.*, No. 2812.

7. An allusion to Matthew Prior's 'An Extempore Invitation to the Earl of Oxford, Lord High Treasurer,' 1712, ll. 11–14:

Among the guests, which e'er my house
Receiv'd, it never can produce
Of honour a more glorious proof—
Tho' Dorset us'd to bless the roof.

Charles Sackville (1638–1706), 6th E. of Dorset, 1677, was Prior's friend and patron.

1. The French translation by the Duc de Nivernais of HW's *Essay on Modern Gardening*, SH, 1785. 'Mr Colman' is the twelfth name on HW's list of persons to whom he presented copies of the book (Berry ii. 259); his copy has not been traced.

2. Colman's translation of Horace's *Ars poetica*. See *ante* 10 May 1783 and n. 1.

3. 'The versions of Milton and Pope are wonderfully exact and poetic and elegant, and the fidelity of the whole translation, extraordinary' (HW to Lady Ossory 17 Sept. 1785, Ossory ii. 496).

4. The *Essay*, dated 'August 2, 1770,' first appeared in the fourth volume of *Anecdotes of Painting* (printed 1771; published 1780).

too there are not a great many copies printed, and those only for presents,[5] I have particular pleasure in making you one of the earliest compliments and am Sir

Your most obliged and obedient humble servant

Horace Walpole

To George Colman Esq.

A MS fragment in HW's hand, consisting only of the dateline of a letter ('Strawberry Hill, Oct. 14th 1785') and, on the verso, part of one sentence ('There have undoubtedly bee⟨n⟩ . . . have given annuities for life'), is now WSL. No letter by HW of this date has been found, and HW's correspondent has not been identified.

To Sir John Elliott,[1] Thursday 27 October 1785

Printed from the MS pasted in vol. II of Sir John Elliott's copy of *Curiosités historiques*, Amsterdam, 1759, now WSL (see n. 2 below). First printed, Toynbee xiii. 338. This copy of *Curiosités historiques* is part of a two-volume set owned by Lord Mowbray and Stourton in 1905; acquired by WSL from Winifred A. Myers Ltd in Aug. 1966.

Strawberry Hill, Oct. 27, 1785.

Dear Sir,

I RETURN your books[2] with a thousand thanks. They not only contain curious pieces, but are exactly to my taste: I can read almost any book, if it has but a comfortable quantity of proper names in it. I do not insist upon their great actions or profound wisdoms;

---

5. See HW to Mrs Anderson *ante* Aug. 1785, n. 3.

———

1. (1736–86), Kt, 1776; cr. (1778) Bt; M.D. (St Andrews), 1759; physician to the Prince of Wales. He attended HW during his severe attack of gout earlier in 1785 (*ante* ca 26 Jan. 1785 and n. 1).

2. A set of *Curiosités historiques, ou recueil de pièces utiles à l'histoire de France, et qui n'ont jamais paru*, 2 vols, Amsterdam, 1759. HW owned a copy of the first volume only (Hazen, *Cat. of HW's Lib.*, No. 3006).

I had rather see them in their *robes de chambre,* when neither they nor I are upon our good behaviours.

The second volume has a merit for which I have often declared I would read any book in the world through—that is, if it pays me with one superlative passage. Pray turn to page 74, in the account of the death of Louis treize,[3] when he receives the *saint viatique* with *grosses larmes et des élévations d'esprit qui faisaient connaître évidemment un commerce d'amour entre leurs Majestés divines et humaines.*[4] Don't you think that this true French *valet de chambre* would have been shocked if he could have supposed that God would not receive his Majesty at the top of the stairs and give him a *fauteuil à bras?*[5]

If you have any more such *patients,* I beg you will lend them to me. I had rather see them, and should learn more of human nature than if I knew all the policy exerted at the Treaty of Westphalia.[6]

Yours sincerely

H. WALPOLE

From LORD CHARLEMONT, mid-November 1785

Printed from a photostat of Charlemont's MS draft in the Royal Irish Academy, Dublin. First printed in Hist. MSS Comm., 13th Report, App. viii (*Charlemont MSS*), 1894, ii. 385–6 (salutation, closing and signature omitted). For the history of the MS draft see *ante* 20 Oct. 1770. The original letter is missing.

Dated approximately by HW's reply *post* 23 Nov. 1785.

My dear Sir,

AS I have the best reason to be confident that to put it in your power to oblige is at all times to give you pleasure, my letters are usually the vehicles of request. In the present instance, however, as indeed in all others, I must beg that I may be positively refused if a compliance with my desire should be in any degree disagreeable

3. (1601–43), K. of France 1610–43.
4. 'grosses larmes qui lui tombaient des yeux, avec des élévations d'esprit continuelles, qui faisaient . . .' ('Mémoire fidèle des choses qui se sont passées à la mort de Louis XIII . . . fait par Dubois, l'un des valets de chambre de sa Majesté, le 14 mai 1643,' in *Curiosités historiques* ii. 74).

5. HW makes a similar comment on this passage in his letter to Lady Ossory the same day (OSSORY ii. 503).
6. The treaties that established the Peace of Westphalia in 1648, ending the Thirty Years' War, were preceded by years of complicated negotiations.

or inconvenient. Mr Livesay,[1] a painter of whom possibly you may have heard, has been employed by me to perfect my collection of the works of *your* Hogarth—I call him yours because you have established his fame by that account of him,[2] in which you have secured credit with posterity for his excellencies by candidly acknowledging his imperfections. Two or three of his prints are not to be met with, and Livesay will desire leave in my name to make sketches from the originals, which are in your possession.[3] This request would seem sufficient for one letter, and yet I cannot rest here. My audacity must add a still more important one. The maxim is as true as it is trite that bounty usually creates importunity, one reason of which I take to be that we are the more apt to ask when we hope to have our desires gratified. You have, as I am informed, printed a new edition of the *Mysterious Mother* with notes.[4] Your kind bounty gave me the power, and therein lies the whole of my pretension. I say no more, for in truth I am ashamed of having said so much. Though a beggar, I am not an impudent one. If however most sensibly to feel the merit of that work, and to entertain the most entire esteem, and grateful affection for its author, can any way excuse the presumption of my more than insinuated request, no man, I am bold to say, has a better apology than,

My dear Sir,
Your ever faithful, most obliged
and most obedient humble servant,
CHARLEM[ONT]

1. Richard Livesay (d. ?1823), portrait and landscape painter. In the early 1780s, when Charlemont began to form a comprehensive collection of Hogarth's works, Livesay lodged with Mrs Hogarth in Leicester Fields; he was employed there as a copyist of Hogarth's prints and drawings, executing a series of facsimiles to be sold by Mrs Hogarth (Thieme and Becker xxiii. 294; DNB).

2. In the fourth volume of *Anecdotes of Painting*, published in 1780 (*Works* iii. 453–73).

3. Richard Livesay wrote Charlemont 25 Oct. 1785: 'I must now inform your Lordship [of] the progress I have made in the little commissions of prints I undertook for you.

'Of the Hogarths I have nearly got all that it is ever likely I shall get. Of those not to be obtained there are a few that I think so valuable in a collection that I am persuaded you will not think too much of having sketches from and which if agreeable I believe I can get permission to do from Lord Exeter's and Mr Walpole's collections.'

'The prints I here refer to are, *The Discovery, A Just View of the British Stage*, Frontispiece to Dr Sharp's pamphlet, *A Masquerade*, two prints for [*Paradise Lost* by] Milton, and *Hell Gate*. . . . With sketches from these and the prints I have got I don't think there will remain anything unpossessed in the collection that need be regretted' (MS in the Royal Irish Academy, Dublin).

4. See *ante* 8 Nov. 1783, n. 2.

To Lord Charlemont, Wednesday 23 November 1785

Printed from a photostat of the MS in the Royal Irish Academy, Dublin. First printed in Hist. MSS Comm., 13th Report, App. viii (*Charlemont MSS*), 1894, ii. 29–30. Reprinted, Toynbee xiii. 346–8 (closing and signature omitted in both printings); extract printed in Francis Hardy, *Memoirs of the Political and Private Life of James Caulfield, Earl of Charlemont*, 2d edn, 1812, ii. 72–3; Wright vi. 263–4; Cunningham ix. 30–1. For the history of the MS see *ante* 20 Oct. 1770.

Strawberry Hill, Nov. 23d 1785.

NOTHING, my Lord, could honour me more than your Lord-ship's commands, nor make me happier than obeying them. Mr Livesay shall be welcome to make the transcripts you desire, with only a single reservation, which I am sure your Lordship will allow me to make, when I tell you the cause of my making it, and add, that I believe my reserve will not deprive your Lordship of a copy, as I have heard that another proof has been found. In a word, my Lord, I have an emblematic print[1] by Hogarth, of which no other was known. I have twice positively refused to let mine be copied[2]— not from the narrow selfishness of a collector who envies others a similar possession; but I had a very particular reason for my refusal, which I would tell your Lordship if I had the honour of seeing you. As it is, I should now give great offence if I granted what I absolutely denied before—and I am persuaded Lord Charlemont does not wish me to make personal enemies. I heard last winter that Mr Gulston,[3] I think it was, had discovered another proof. His collection is going to be sold, and I am told will employ forty days.[4] If he had such a print, it will most probably be copied, unless sold at an extravagant price,[5] which I am sorry to say I have partly been the cause of his worst works bearing.

1. Probably the 'emblematic print representing Agriculture and Arts. Seems to be a ticket for some society' listed in HW's 'Catalogue of Mr Hogarth's Prints,' *Anecdotes of Painting, Works* iii. 463. This is possibly the print known as *Harrison's Tobacco Paper,* now considered to be a questionable attribution to Hogarth (Ronald Paulson, *Hogarth's Graphic Works,* rev. edn, New Haven, 1970, i. 301 [No. 279], 319).

2. The occasions of these refusals are not known.

3. See *ante* 30 Jan. 1772, n. 13.

4. Gulston's vast collection of prints was sold by Greenwood 16 Jan. – 15 March 1786, shortly before his death on 14 July (Frits Lugt, *Répertoire des catalogues de ventes publiques,* The Hague, 1938, No. 3975).

5. Livesay wrote Charlemont 10 March 1786: 'There is now just concluded a very

The new edition of the tragedy,[6] for which your Lordship is pleased to express a wish, shall be at your command as soon as I go to London, as I have not a copy here—but this edition has not the merit of the first impression, I mean, of being printed here, and of being a rarity.[7] I was forced to make Dodsley print in haste a sufficient number for sale, to prevent a spurious edition that was advertised. My advertisement fortunately did stop the other impression, as I had hoped—and having done so, I never published my own. Notes I believe there are none, but the references to two or three passages alluded to, and which were also in the first edition; but in the second I omitted the Postscript, which contained a kind of apology for the offensiveness of the subject; and I thought it more decent and respectful to the public, to plead guilty, than to attempt to defend what I knew was so faulty. If your Lordship will be so good as to let me know how I may convey the play, I will take the liberty of adding another piece,[8] which though in some measure mine too, will carry with it a full compensation; though I doubt that compensation will be a proof of my own vanity.

As your Lordship has given me this opportunity, I cannot resist saying what I was exceedingly tempted to mention two or three years ago, but had not the confidence. In short, my Lord, when the Order of St Patrick was instituted,[9] I had a mind to hint to your Lordship that it was exactly the moment for seizing an occasion that has been irretrievably lost to this country. When I was at Paris, I found in the convent of Les Grands Augustins three vast chambers filled with the portraits (and their names and titles beneath) of all the Knights of the Saint-Esprit from the foundation of the Order.[10] Every new

capital sale of prints, the property of a Mr Gulstone. . . . Among them is a collection of Hogarths, all of which bring very great prices, and the scarce ones go at astonishing rates' (MS in the Royal Irish Academy, Dublin). Livesay managed to purchase several rare Hogarth prints for Charlemont at the sale. It further appears from Livesay's letter that he planned to make the copies of prints desired by Charlemont from impressions in Lord Exter's collection rather than HW's.

6. *The Mysterious Mother.*

7. Only 50 copies of the SH edition were printed in 1768 (Hazen, *SH Bibl.* 79).

8. The French translation by the Duc de Nivernais of HW's *Essay on Modern Gardening*, SH, 1785. Charlemont's name appears in HW's list of persons to whom he gave the translation (BERRY ii. 260), but his copy has not been traced. See *post* 9 Dec. 1785.

9. The first knights companions of the Order of St Patrick, founded by George III, were installed in St Patrick's Cathedral 17 March 1783 (*Daily Adv.* 21 March 1783; MANN ix. 365 and n. 24). Charlemont was one of the original fifteen knights; see GEC i. 227–8.

10. On 28 Nov. 1765 HW visited the convent, then situated in the Quai des

knight, with few exceptions, gives his own portrait, on his creation. Of the Order of St Patrick I think but one founder[11] is dead yet, and his picture perhaps may be retrieved. I will not make any apology to so good a patriot as your Lordship for proposing a plan that tends to the honour of his country, which I will presume to call mine too, as it is both by union and by my affection for it. I should wish the name of the painter inscribed too, which would incite emulation in your artists—but it is unnecessary to dilate on the subject to your Lordship, who as a patron of the arts as well as a patriot, will improve on my imperfect thoughts, and if you approve of them, can give them stability. I have the honour to be with the greatest respect

> My Lord
>> Your Lordship's most obedient humble servant
>>> HOR. WALPOLE

From LORD CHARLEMONT, early December 1785

Printed from an extract quoted in Francis Hardy, *Memoirs of the Political and Private Life of James Caulfield, Earl of Charlemont*, 2d edn, 1812, ii. 74. The text is there described as 'part of a short note or letter to Mr Walpole.' The original letter is missing.

Dated approximately by the previous letter and by HW's reply *post* 9 Dec. 1785.

. . . I should be glad to know whether the Knights of the St-Esprit are drawn in their robes of ceremony? The reason of my question is, that, if such dress were not necessary, as I doubt it is, a series of fashion, as well as of portraits, might be transmitted to posterity. . . .

Grands-Augustins, and viewed two large chambers containing portraits of the knights of the Ordre du St-Esprit; he was especially delighted to find a portrait of Philibert, Comte de Gramont ('Paris Journals,' DU DEFFAND v. 276; MORE 77–8).

11. Henry Loftus (1709–83), cr. (1771) E. of Ely. He was nominated 5 Feb. 1783 as one of the original fifteen Knights of St Patrick, but was neither invested nor installed, being out of the Kingdom at the time of the first installation and dying soon afterwards (GEC).

To Lord Charlemont, Friday 9 December 1785

Printed from a photostat of the MS in Thomas Kirgate's hand in the Royal Irish Academy, Dublin. First printed in Francis Hardy, *Memoirs of the Political and Private Life of James Caulfield, Earl of Charlemont,* 2d edn, 1812, ii. 74–5 (two sentences omitted). Reprinted in Hist. MSS Comm., 13th Report, App. viii (*Charlemont MSS*), 1894, ii. 30; Toynbee xiii. 350 (last sentence omitted in both printings). For the history of the MS see *ante* 20 Oct. 1770.

Berkeley Square, December the 9th.

MR Walpole has received the honour of Lord Charlemont's letter,[1] but is quite incapable of answering it, being laid up by a severe attack of the gout in his whole right arm and hand.[2] He sends the enclosed two books,[3] of which he begs his Lordship's acceptance, to Mr Malone,[4] with whom he has the pleasure of being acquainted.

The portraits of the Knights of the St-Esprit at Paris, are only heads on panel, which touch one another. The head of the Comte de Grammont, of which Mr Walpole has a copy,[5] is in armour. Perhaps the Grand Masters might be whole or half lengths, in the dress of the order to show the habit. Other knights in their own robes of peers, or in the dress of the times: but it ought to be an inviolable rule that no fantastic dresses should be allowed in a national and historic monument. If the whole present number would consent to sit at once, it might be worth the while of a good painter to go from London to paint them.[6]

Mr Walpole is not able to say more at present.

1. See previous letter.
2. HW wrote Mann 8 Jan. 1786: 'I am getting free from my parenthesis of gout, which . . . has confined me above six weeks, and for a few days was very near being quite serious. It began by my middle finger of this hand, with which I am now writing, discharging a volley of chalk, which brought on gout and an inflammation, and both together swelled my arm almost to my shoulder. In short, I was forced to have a surgeon—but last week my finger was delivered of a chalk-stone as big as a large pea—and now I trust the wound will soon heal; and in every other respect I am quite well' (MANN ix. 617–18).

3. *The Mysterious Mother,* 1781 edn, and the *Essay on Modern Gardening,* SH, 1785 (*ante* 23 Nov. 1785).
4. Malone informed Charlemont 17 Dec. 1785: 'Mr Walpole two days ago sent me a small parcel for you, which Mr Rigge takes the charge of' (MS in the Royal Irish Academy, Dublin).
5. See MORE 78 n. 14.
6. Charlemont seems to have shared HW's enthusiasm for instituting such a series of portraits, but nothing apparently came of the idea (Francis Hardy, *Memoirs of the Political and Private Life of James Caulfield, Earl of Charlemont,* 2d edn, 1812, ii. 73–4).

From JAMES RAFTOR,[1] ? early 1786

Printed from the catalogue issued by William Strong of Bristol, 1843, lot 3410, where the letter was first printed. Lot 3410 is described as 'A white and gold snuff box, enamelled: it originally belonged to the celebrated Colley Cibber, and was presented to Mr Walpole by Mr Rafter, with letter enclosed, £4.4.'

For the dating of the letter, see n. 4 below.

Address: To the Honourable H. Walpole, Esq.

Sir,

I TAKE the liberty to send you old Mr Cibber's[2] snuff box, which he used in his fop characters;[3] it is as old as the last century, and therefore I think ought to have a place in your museum,[4] as a sort of rarity; I hope you will honour it with your acceptance, and forgive the liberty I have taken. I am, with the greatest regard, etc., etc.,

J. RAFTER

1. (d. 1790), actor; Kitty Clive's brother or half-brother, with whom she lived at Little Strawberry Hill (*ante* 19 Aug. 1777, n. 4).

2. Colley Cibber (1671–1757), actor and dramatist.

3. Among Cibber's most famous fop rôles were Sir Novelty Fashion in his own *Love's Last Shift*, Lord Foppington in Vanbrugh's sequel *The Relapse,* and Sir Fopling Flutter in Etherege's *The Man of Mode*.

4. The snuff box was probably kept in the glass closet in the Great North Bedchamber, but it is not listed in the 1784 *Description of SH.* However, the *Description* does mention (in the final version printed in *Works* ii. 404) a bust of Cibber, given by Cibber to Mrs Clive and presented by her brother, James Raftor, to HW after her death on 6 Dec. 1785. It seems likely that the snuff box was also in Mrs Clive's possession and was given to HW by Raftor soon after her death. It was sold SH xv. 111 to Strong of Bristol for £2.12.6. See headnote.

To Edmond Malone, January 1786

Printed from a photostat of the MS in the British Museum (Add. MS 54,226, f. 211). First printed in Sir James Prior, *Life of Edmond Malone*, 1860, pp. 126–7. Reprinted, Toynbee xiii. 356. The letter is untraced until sold Puttick and Simpson 7 Aug. 1872 (A Few Autograph Letters Sale), lot 57 (with other letters), to Bussiere; resold Sotheby's 20 Dec. 1877 (Collection of Autograph Letters Sale), lot 145, to Waller; later acquired by the National Portrait Gallery and presented by the Trustees of the Gallery, in a collection of autograph letters and documents, to the British Museum in Dec. 1967.

According to Prior, op. cit. 126, this letter is one of 'Two or three notes from Walpole [that] occur early in this year [1786].'

Address: To Edmund Malone Esq. in Queen Anne Street East. *Postmark:* PENNY POST PAID.

MR WALPOLE sends his compliments to Mr Malone and assures him he has looked for the source whence he mentioned a picture of Lord Roscommon[1] by Carlo Maratti,[2] but cannot find it. He concludes that it was from some note of Vertue, but at the distance of so many years cannot be sure; and as all Vertue's memorandums were indigested, and written down successively, as he made them, in forty volumes[3] and often on loose scraps of paper, it is next to impossible to find the particular note; nor, were it found, does it probably contain more than Mr W. has copied into the *Anecdotes*.[4]

---

1. Wentworth Dillon (ca 1637–85), 4th E. of Roscommon, 1649; poet.

2. (1625–1713), painter. The following extract is taken from 'Maloniana': 'I this day (July 24, 1789) perused Wentworth Lord Roscommon's will at Doctors' Commons. He having been once the owner of my estate in Westmeath, in Ireland, I feel an interest about him, and should be glad to meet with his picture by Carlo Maratti which is somewhere extant' (Sir James Prior, *Life of Edmond Malone*, 1860, p. 404).

3. See *ante* 10 May 1766 and n. 2.

4. 'Several English sat to that master [Carlo Maratti] at Rome, particularly the Earls of Sunderland, Exeter, and Roscommon, Sir Thomas Isham, Mr Charles Fox, and Mr Edward Herbert of Packington, a great virtuoso' (*Anecdotes of Painting*, SH, 1762–71, ii. 51n). HW's source for this note was an entry in Vertue's notebooks, where it is recorded that 'afterwards he [Maratti] did several Nobles particularly of England who came to Rome, amongst others . . . My Lord Roscommon standing holding in his hand a General's Staff . . . freely disposed in a picturesque manner à l'antique' (Vertue Note Books, *Walpole Society* 1937–8, xxvi. 64). Vertue had taken the information from Ottavio Lioni's *Ritratti di alcuni celebri pittori del secolo XVII. . . . Si è aggiunta la vita di Carlo Maratti, scritta da Gio[vanni] Pietro Bellori . . .* , Rome, 1731.

To Princess Amelia,[1] Sunday 2 April 1786

Printed from a photostat of the MS in the Royal Archives, Windsor Castle (RA 53082). First printed, Toynbee *Supp.* ii. 12 (part of one sentence omitted). The letter was enclosed by Princess Amelia in her letter to the Prince of Wales 2 April 1786, also preserved in the Royal Archives (see n. 6 below). A copy of the letter in HW's hand, headed 'Paper delivered to Princess Amalie April 2d ⟨by H.W.⟩' and followed by a note quoted in n. 6, is now wsl; this MS was offered by Thomas Thorpe, Catalogue of Autographs, 1843, lot 3932; not further traced until sold Sotheby's 27 Nov. 1891 (Several Important . . . Autograph Collections Sale), lot 337, to Depray; later inserted in an extra-illustrated eighteen-volume set of Peter Cunningham's edition of HW's *Letters* that belonged to Frederick S. Peck ('Wm. P. Sheffield' on the title-page of Vol. I); this set was sold Parke-Bernet 22 March 1961 (Charles H. Morse Sale), lot 445, to Seven Gables for wsl.

April 2d 1786.

LEST I should not find words, Madam, ready to express sufficiently my deep sense of your Royal Highness's goodness in graciously offering me the distinguished honour of dining with the Prince of Wales[2] at your Royal Highness's,[3] I presume, Madam, to present in writing my most humble thanks for so signal a mark of favour.

It is with deep concern, Madam, that I feel myself so circumstanced, as to be forced to beg leave to decline that honour. Your Royal Highness once asked me if I had been at his Royal Highness's levee? I replied, that as I was unfortunately precluded from paying my duty to his Majesty,[4] I thought it did not become me to present myself before the Prince; and your Royal Highness was pleased to say that I acted properly.

Having therefore never had the honour of kissing his Royal Highness's hand,[5] and not being in a situation of paying my duty to him,

1. Amelia Sophia Eleanora (1711–86), dau. of George II.
2. George (1762–1830), P. of Wales; K. of England 1820–30 as George IV; Ps Amelia's great-nephew.
3. Her town house was in Cavendish Square at the corner of Harley Street (Ossory ii. 535 n. 20).
4. Because of the secret marriage in 1766 of HW's niece, the Dowager Countess Waldegrave, to the Duke of Gloucester, the King refused to receive at Court the Duchess of Gloucester or those who visited

her (Family 73, 74 n. 2; *Last Journals* i. 150, 175–6). When the marriage was made public in 1772, HW sent word through Lord Hertford 'that, concluding the new Duchess's family could not be very welcome at St James's, I should not presume to present myself there without leave.' After hearing the King's response, HW 'went no more to St James's' (ibid. i. 136–7).
5. HW had apparently declined Princess Amelia's invitation to dine with the Prince of Wales 28 July 1783 for the same reason (Ossory ii. 416 and n. 8).

it appears to me that the greatest mark of respect that I can show to his Royal Highness, is to make a sacrifice of an honour so extremely flattering to me, rather than be wanting in any expression of reverence to his Majesty and to the Prince: and as your Royal Highness knows how proud I am of your Royal Highness's constant graciousness towards me, you must be sure, Madam, that I should not waive receiving so precious a mark of your favour, if I did not think that a scrupulous respect to your royal family was the properest way of expressing my gratitude to your Royal Highness.[6]

From Mrs Buller,[1] Thursday 6 April 1786

Printed for the first time from the MS now wsl. The MS was offered by Thomas Thorpe, Catalogue of Autographs, 1843, lot 516; 1844, lot 232; not further traced until acquired by Maggs in a 'very miscellaneous private collection' and sold to wsl, Nov. 1963.

Dated by the following letter.

Address: The Honourable Mr Walpole, Berkeley Square.

Duchess St, Thursday.

MRS BULLER has the honour to present her respects to Mr Walpole and to convey to him a sort of request from a crowned head,[2] of which Mr Walpole will take what notice he pleases. The

6. Princess Amelia wrote the Prince of Wales 2 April 1786, enclosing HW's letter: 'As you choose to dine with me a Tuesday, and that I have nothing but Methusalems like myself at my table of that day, for commerce, and cribbage, I send you Mr Walpole's answer in writing to my invitation, but as you have been so polite as to make some of your gentlemen kiss my hand before you, may I desire to do the same by you, in Mr Walpole's having the honour of being presented by me, to you, next Tuesday [4 April] at four o'clock' (MS RA 53081 in the Royal Archives, Windsor Castle). HW noted at the end of his copy of his letter to the Princess: 'On the Princess sending the Prince this letter, he wrote to her in return, that he thought himself particularly fortunate in having this opportunity of being introduced especially by her to Mr W. whose

distinguished abilities and universal good qualities have long gained him not only the admiration but the esteem of the whole world. The Princess sent his letter to Mr W. who transcribed these words and returned it' (MS now wsl). After being presented, HW dined with the Prince at Lord Hertford's on 13 May, at the Prince's (Carlton House) on 28 May, and again at Princess Amelia's at Gunnersbury on 16 June (Conway iii. 438 n. 4; Lady Mary Coke, 'MS Journals' 28 May 1786; More 298–9; Ossory ii. 517).

1. Mary Coxe (ca 1744–1812), second dau. and coheir of John Hippisley Coxe of Ston Easton, Somerset, m. (1770) James Buller (1740–72) of Downes, Devonshire (Berry i. 122 n. 2).

2. Stanislas II (1732–98), K. of Poland 1764–95.

Count Potocki[3] dined yesterday with Mrs Buller and showed her a letter from the King of Poland, in which are these words—Si vous voyez M. Horace Walpole, vous lui direz que je lis actuellement avec un grand plaisir, le quatrième tome de ses *Anecdotes* sur la peinture,[4] mais que je ne sais où trouver les trois premiers;—vous seriez charmant de me les apporter de sa part.[5]

M. Potocki waited on Mr Walpole last night[6]—He is just arrived from Paris,[7] and his abode here will be only for a few days.

Mrs Buller begs leave to add for herself, that she is infinitely grateful to Mr Walpole for his polite condescension to her on many occasions; and in this case she takes no farther interest than merely as relating a circumstance, of which Mr Walpole would be otherwise uninformed.

To Stanislas II,[1] Friday 7 April 1786

Printed from a photostat of HW's MS draft inserted in John Morris's extra-illustrated copy of *The Works of Thomas Gray*, ed. T. J. Mathias, 1814 (Vol. I, Pt ii. 535–6), now in the Eton College Library. First printed, Toynbee *Supp.* iii. 44–5. The MS draft was offered by Thomas Thorpe, Cat. of Autograph Letters, 1843, lot 3930; not further traced until acquired by John Morris for the extra-illustrated *Works of Gray*. The original letter is missing.

Endorsed by HW: To the King of Poland.

London, April 7th 1786.

Sire,

IMPLICIT submission[2] to your Majesty's commands[3] must stand me in lieu of the modesty and repugnance which I must feel before I can presume to lay at your feet anything so unworthy of your

3. Probably Comte Ignacy Potocki (1750–1809), grand marshal of Lithuania, son-in-law of the Princess Lubomirska, who was Stanislas II's cousin and who visited HW at SH in 1787 (Family 281 n. 6).

4. The fourth volume of *Anecdotes of Painting* was printed at SH in 1771 but not published until 1780.

5. See following letter.

6. Doubtless in Berkeley Square, but HW may have been at SH.

7. He was possibly one of the 'two foreign noblemen, who have come upon their travels to make the tour of England, [and]

were at Court and presented to their Majesties by the French ambassador' on 30 March (*Morning Herald* 31 March 1786). No specific notice of Count Potocki's arrival in England has been found.

————

1. Stanislas II (Stanislas Augustus Poniatowski) (1732–98), K. of Poland 1764–95. HW had met him during his visit to England in 1754 (n. 12 below; Chute 82).

2. 'obedience' crossed out in the MS draft.

3. See previous letter.

royal notice as my trifling writings. But your Majesty will forgive me, I flatter myself, for saying that the sacrifice[4] I make of my confusion to obedience will cost me dear, for how, Sire, can I ever recover any humility after receiving so distinguished an honour, as that of your Majesty not only condescending[5] to read, but commanding me to send you any work of mine? Titus[6] was so excellent a prince that he regretted the loss of a day which had not been well employed.[7] Your Majesty, who has not yet been so criminal, will (besides the charge of intoxicating with vanity me, who never offended you[8]) be[9] guilty of throwing away at least the value of two days, if you peruse the volumes[10] which I dare not but[11] consign to Count Potocki,[12] and for which the only atonement I can make is by begging your Majesty's gracious acceptance of a translation made from a small part of those volumes by M. le Duc de Nivernois,[13] who by his beautiful language and poetry has stamped a merit on those pages which[14] it was not in my power to infuse into the original.

I will not, Sire, steal more of those precious moments which your Majesty consecrates to all the[15] virtues of beneficence, nor attempt to paint[16] the sentiments with which I am penetrated. The goodness of your own heart, Sire, will tell you that gratitude is the most natural

4. 'that' and 'which' crossed out in the MS draft.

5. HW first wrote 'as that your Majesty should condescend.'

6. Titus (Titus Flavius Vespasianus) (A.D. 39–81), Emperor of Rome 79–81.

7. HW has somewhat confused the anecdote recorded in Suetonius's Lives of the Cæsars, Book VIII ('Divus Titus'), where Titus, remembering at dinner that he had made no gift to anyone that day, remarked, 'Amici, diem perdidi.'

8. HW first wrote 'intoxicating me, who never offended you, with vanity.'

9. 'will' crossed out in the MS draft.

10. The four quarto volumes of Anecdotes of Painting and the Catalogue of Engravers, SH, 1762–71. See HW to Thomas Walpole the younger 8 April 1786 (FAMILY 238).

11. HW first wrote 'transmit to your hands,' then 'deliver to Count Potocki,' and finally substituted 'consign' for 'deliver.'

12. HW's copy of his letter in French to Comte Potocki 7 April 1786 was of-

fered by Thomas Thorpe, Catalogue of Autograph Letters, 1843, lot 3931; not further traced. He wrote Thomas Walpole the younger 26 June 1792: 'Count Potocki brought me a message from the present King of Poland, with whom I had been acquainted when he was in England, desiring my Anecdotes of Painting—It distressed me, as they were out of print—and I had only my own set. In short, I was reduced to buy a second hand set (yet in good condition) and though the original set sold for less than thirty shillings, I was forced to pay thirteen guineas, from their scarcity. In return, I received a letter of thanks in his Majesty's own hand' (FAMILY 281). See following letter.

13. Nivernais' French translation of HW's Essay on Modern Gardening was published at SH in 1785; see ante 6 Jan. 1785.

14. 'I could have' crossed out in the MS draft.

15. 'virtues beneficent' crossed out in the MS draft.

16. 'express' crossed out in the MS draft.

and best counterpart to exalted obligations; nor is it necessary to be your subject to feel the strongest warmth of attachment to, and the most respectful affection for your royal person: your Majesty's great qualities extend your empire over the dominions of other princes; the only amiable kind of usurpation; and the less claim I, an inconsiderable stranger, can possibly have to your gracious patronage, the more I am bound to be with every sentiment of humble reverence

Sire
Your Majesty's most highly honoured
and most respectfully devoted servant

HOR. WALPOLE

From STANISLAS II, Wednesday 7 June 1786

Printed for the first time from a photostat of the MS in the possession (1960) of Mr Boleslaw Mastai, New York City. A photographic facsimile of the MS was published in Aleksander Janta, 'Listy i portrety Stanisława Augusta w zbiorach amerykańskich,' *Wiadomości* (London), 10–17 April 1960, p. 1. The MS was probably sold SH vi. 112 (with another letter of Stanislas II and one of Peter the Great) to J. Young; not further traced until acquired by Mr Mastai before 1940.

Warsaw, the 7 June 1786.

I HAVE received, but since few days, with the greatest pleasure, your letter of the 7 April[1] together with the anecdotes of painting and engraving, and an essay on the art of gardening, for the author of which I felt long ago a sympathy, formed by the analogy of our tastes. You will be glad, I think, to be informed that your lessons do thrive in this country: and as it is but a few years since we do here creep out of the servitude of symmetry,[2] we have not yet had time to come to the opposite excess, against which you endeavour to guard your country.

Please to God, you may, Sir, still for many years, embellish and instruct it by your taste and writings.

These are the wishes of

Your much affectionate

STANISLAUS AUGUSTUS KING

1. See previous letter.
2. An allusion to the 'symmetrical and unnatural gardens' that preceded the 'modern' landscape garden in England; see HW's *Essay on Modern Gardening*, *Works* ii. esp. 524–7.

From ROBERT FULLARTON UDNY,[1]
Saturday 10 June 1786

Printed for the first time from a photostat of the MS in the John Carter Brown Library, Providence, Rhode Island. The letter was almost certainly kept by HW with the psalter illuminated by Giulio Clovio; for its presumed later history see n. 3 below.

Berners Street,[2] 10 June 1786.

MR UDNY presents his compliments to Mr Walpole and congratulates him on the purchase he has made of the Duchess of Portland's missal,[3] which he has the pleasure to assure him is not only the best preserved but he thinks the most beautiful of six he has seen.[4] Mr Udny would be happy to show Mr Walpole some acquisition of capital pictures he has lately met which he knows would give Mr Walpole pleasure.

1. (1722–1802), West India merchant of London and later (1792) of Udny Castle, Aberdeenshire; F.R.S., 1785; HW's neighbour at Teddington (BERRY i. 89 n. 37; *The Genealogist*, 1878, ii. 89–90). Udny was well known for his collection of paintings, chiefly Italian.

2. No. 23 Berners Street (*The Universal British Directory of Trade, Commerce, and Manufacture*, 1791, p. 319).

3. 'The book of Pslams, with 21 inimitable illuminations by Don Julio Clovio, scholar of Julio Romano. If anything can excel the figures, it is the execution of the borders, which are of the purest antique taste, and unrivalled for the lustre and harmony of the colours, as well as for the preservation, which is allowed to be more perfect than any of the few works of this extraordinary master. It was painted, as is said on one of the illuminations, Principi Andegavensi, 1537; was afterwards in the Arundelian collection; on the dispersion of which it was purchased by the Earl of Oxford in 1720, who bequeathed it to his daughter the Duchess of Portland, at whose sale Mr Walpole bought it in 1786' ('Des. of SH,' *Works* ii. 505). The psalter was lot 2952 in the Duchess of Portland's sale 24 April–8 June 1786, purchased by HW for £169.1.0; bought in at the SH sale xv. 90 by the Earl Waldegrave for £441; acquired by Mrs John Carter Brown after 1874 and now in the John Carter Brown Library, Providence, Rhode Island.

4. HW wrote Conway 18 June 1786: 'Do you know that I have bought . . . the Julio Clovio! Mr Udny assures me he has seen six of the hand, and not one of them so fine or so well preserved' (CONWAY iii. 442). HW also quoted Udny's opinion in a MS note in his copy of the Portland sale catalogue, now WSL; see OSSORY ii. 518 n. 11.

To Princess Amelia, Friday 16 June 1786

Printed from a photostat of the MS in the possession of Mr Robert H. Taylor, Princeton, New Jersey. The MS is probably HW's copy of the verses he sent to Princess Amelia. HW quoted the verses in his letters to Conway 18 June (Conway iii. 441–2) and to Lady Ossory 5 July (Ossory ii. 517); the verses are reprinted in *Horace Walpole's Fugitive Verses*, ed. W. S. Lewis, 1931, p. 181. The MS was formerly in the Penzance Library; later acquired by Paul C. Richards, Brookline, Mass., who sold it to Hofmann and Freeman, May 1970; sold by them to Mr Taylor, Sept. 1970.

To her Royal Highness the Princess Amelia commanding me
to write something in praise of Gunnersbury[1] June 16, 1786[2]

1.

In deathless odes for ever green
Augustus' laurels blow;
Nor e'er was grateful duty seen
In warmer strains to flow.

2.

Oh! Why is Flaccus[3] not alive
Your fav'rite scene to sing?
To Gunnersbury's charms could give
His lyre immortal spring.

3.

As warm as his my zeal for you,
Great Princess, could I show it:
But though you have a Horace too,
Ah! Madam, he's no poet.

1. Princess Amelia's summer residence at Ealing, Middlesex.

2. HW wrote Conway 18 June 1786: 'I was sent for again to dine at Gunnersbury on Friday [16 June]. . . . The Princess, Lady Barrymore, and the rest of us, played three pools at commerce till ten. I am afraid I was tired and gaped. While we were at the dairy, the Princess insisted on my making some verses on Gunnersbury. I pleaded being superannuated. She would not excuse me. I promised she should have an ode on her next birthday; which diverted the Prince [of Wales]—but all would not do—so, as I came home, I made the following stanzas, and sent them to her breakfast next morning. . . . If they are but poor verses, consider I am sixty-nine, was half asleep, and made them almost extempore—and by command! However, they succeeded, and I received this gracious answer' (Conway iii. 441–2). See following letter.

3. Horace (Quintus Horatius Flaccus).

From Princess Amelia, Saturday 17 June 1786

Printed from a photostat of the MS in the Princeton University Library. First printed in A. M. Broadley, *Chats on Autographs*, New York, [1910], p. 134. HW quoted the letter in his letters to Conway 18 June (Conway iii. 442) and to Lady Ossory 5 July (Ossory ii. 517–18). Reprinted in *Horace Walpole's Fugitive Verses*, ed. W. S. Lewis, New York, 1931, p. 181. The MS was sold SH vi. 114 (with two other letters) to Sholto V. Hare; not further traced until acquired before 1910 by A. M. Broadley, who inserted it in an extra-illustrated copy of John Doran's *A Lady of the Last Century (Mrs Elizabeth Montagu)*, 1873 (Vol. IX, facing p. 279); resold Scott and O'Shaughnessy 20 Feb. 1917 (Miscellaneous Collection Sale), lot 115; acquired by Dickson Q. Brown and given by him to the Princeton University Library in 1924. The letter has since been removed from the extra-illustrated volume.

Endorsed by HW: From her R. H. Princess Amelia June 17, 1786.
Address: To Mr Walpole.

17 of June.

I WISH I had a name that could answer your pretty verses.[1] Your yawning yesterday[2] opened your vein for pleasing me, and I return you my thanks, my good Mr Walpole, and remain sincerely your friend,

Amelia

1. In his verses addressed to Princess Amelia, HW played on the name Horace.
2. See previous letter, n. 2. 'The moment the Princess came hither [SH] t'other morning and spied the shield with Medusa's head on the staircase, she said "Oh! now I see where you learnt to yawn"' (HW to Lady Ossory 5 July 1786 Ossory ii. 518).

To Richard Gough, Wednesday 21 June 1786

Printed from the MS now wsl. First printed, Nichols, *Lit. Anec.* vi. 289–90. Reprinted, Wright vi. 269–70; Cunningham ix. 56–7 (closing, signature, and postscript omitted in both editions); Toynbee xiii. 388–90; extract printed in *Minor Lives,* ed. E. L. Hart, Cambridge, Mass., 1971, p. 89. The MS presumably came into the possession of John Nichols about the time of the publication of *Literary Anecdotes,* vol. vi (1812), and descended in the Nichols family; sold Sotheby's 18 Nov. 1929 (John Gough Nichols Sale), lot 233, to Francis Edwards, from whom wsl acquired it in Sept. 1932.

Endorsed by John Bowyer Nichols: To Richard Gough Esq. (Printed in *Literary Anecdotes.*)

Berkeley Square, June 21st 1786.

ON COMING to town yesterday upon business, I found, Sir, your very magnificent and most valuable present,[1] for which I beg you will accept my most grateful thanks. I am impatient to return to Twickenham to read it tranquilly. As yet I have only had time to turn the prints over and to read the preface; but I see already that it is both a noble and laborious work, and will do great honour both to you and to your country. Yet one apprehension it has given me—I fear not living to see the second part![2] yet I shall presume to keep it unbound, not only till it is perfectly dry and secure; but as I mean the binding should be as fine as it deserves, I should be afraid of not having both volumes exactly alike.[3]

Your partiality, I doubt, Sir, has induced you to insert a paper not so worthy of the public regard, as the rest of your splendid performance. My letter to Mr Cole,[4] which I am sure I had utterly forgot-

1. A copy of Gough's *Sepulchral Monuments in Great Britain Applied to Illustrate the History of Families, Manners, Habits, and Arts, at the Different Periods from the Norman Conquest to the Seventeenth Century,* Part I, 1786. HW had lent many drawings for Gough to use in this work; see *ante* 25 June 1783.

2. Part II was published in 1796; see *post* 5 Dec. 1796.

3. HW's set of *Sepulchral Monuments,* Parts I and II, was still uncut and in boards when it was sold in 1842; it is Hazen, *Cat. of HW's Lib.,* No. 3644.

4. In his Preface, pp. 2–3, Gough included a long passage ('With regard to a history of Gothic architecture . . . an idea worth pursuing') from HW's letter to William Cole 11 Aug. 1769 (Cole i. 190–2), introducing it as follows: 'Mr Walpole cannot be displeased at the circulation of his own most laudable intention, as I find it in a letter addressed by him to the late Mr Cole of Milton, in 1769.' The passage, which is somewhat inaccurately transcribed, was doubtless given to Gough by Cole (their correspondence is printed in Nichols, *Lit. Anec.* i. 673–97).

ten to have ever written, was a hasty indigested sketch, like the rest of my scribblings, and never calculated to lead such well-meditated and accurate works as yours. Having lived familiarly with Mr Cole from our boyhood, I used to write to him carelessly on the occasions that occurred, and as it was always on subjects of no importance, I never thought of enjoining secrecy. I could not foresee that such idle communications would find a place in a great and national work, or I should have been more attentive to what I said. Your taste, Sir, I fear, has for once been misled, and I shall be sorry for having innocently blemished a single page.

Since your partiality (for such it certainly was) has gone so far, I flatter myself you will have retained enough to accept—not a retribution—but a trifling mark of my regard, in the little volume[5] that accompanies this, in which you will find that another too favourable reader has bestowed on me more distinction than I could procure for myself, by turning my slight *Essay on Gardening* into the pure French of the last age; and, which is wonderful, has not debased Milton by French poetry[6]—on the contrary, I think, Milton has given a dignity to French poetry—nay and harmony, both which I thought that language almost incapable of receiving. As I would wish to give all the value I can to my offering, I will mention that I have printed but 400 copies, half of which went to France—and as this is an age in which mere rarities are preferred to commoner things of intrinsic worth,[7] as I have found by the ridiculous prices given for some of my insignificant publications merely because they are scarce,[8] I hope under the title of a kind of curiosity, my thin piece will be admitted into your library.

If you would indulge me so far, Sir, as to tell me when I might hope to see the second part, I would calculate how many more fits of the gout I may weather, and would be still more strict in my regimen. I hope at least that you will not wait for the engravers,[9] but will accomplish the text for the sake of the world (in this I speak disinterestedly). Though you are much younger than I am,[10] I would

5. The French translation by the Duc de Nivernais of HW's *Essay on Modern Gardening*, SH, 1785.

6. See *ante* 6 Jan. 1785 and n. 6.

7. The MS reads 'work.'

8. In April 1786 HW had been forced to pay thirteen guineas for a secondhand copy of *Anecdotes of Painting* to give to the King of Poland; see *ante* 7 April 1786, n. 12.

9. Gough employed several engravers, but the majority of the plates in both parts of *Sepulchral Monuments* were the work of James Basire (1730–1802).

10. Gough was eighteen years younger than HW, who was then sixty-eight.

have your part of the work secure: engravers may always proceed or be found—Another *author* cannot.

I have the honour to be with great gratitude, Sir,

Your much obliged and obedient humble servant

Hor. Walpole

PS. I add a little piece[11] which is also rare here; Sir Hor. Mann sent me four,[12] and I beg your acceptance of one.

To Dr Charles Burney, Thursday 6 July 1786

Printed from a copy of the MS kindly furnished by its owner, Mr John R. G. Comyn, The Cross House, Vowchurch, Turnastone, Herefordshire. First printed in *Diary and Letters of Madame d'Arblay*, ed. Austin Dobson, 1904–5, ii. 487–8. Reprinted, Toynbee xiii. 397–8. For the history of the MS see *ante* 6 Sept. 1785. *Address:* To Dr Burney in St Martin's Street, Leicester Fields, London.

Strawberry Hill, July 6th 1786.

YOU cannot imagine, dear Sir, how I rejoice for her sake and yours on the preferment of Miss Burney;[1] which indeed is a very generous proceeding on my side, as I fear she will now not stoop

from the stately brow
Of Windsor's heights to the expanse below,[2]

and condescend to visit *the veteran of Strawberry Hill*, though he were as *well preserved* as the newspapers flatter him he is.[3]

11. *Elogio del Capitano Giacomo Cook* or *Elogy of Captain James Cook*, Florence, 1785, by Michelangiolo Gianetti, with an English translation by Robert Merry, dedicated to Sir Horace Mann. HW's copy is Hazen, op. cit., No. 4006.

12. HW thanked Mann for the copies in his letter of 28 March 1786 (Mann ix. 635–6 and n. 3).

1. In June Fanny Burney had accepted appointment as Second Keeper of the Robes to Queen Charlotte. She began her service at Court on 17 July 1786 (Joyce Hemlow, *The History of Fanny Burney*, Oxford, 1958, pp. 195–9).

2. Thomas Gray, *Ode on a Distant Prospect of Eton College*, ll. 5–7:
And ye, that from the stately brow
Of Windsor's heights th'expanse below
Of grove, of lawn, of mead survey.

3. The *Morning Herald* 30 June 1786 printed the following paragraph: 'The illustrious monarch of Prussia, the venerable chief of the Court of King's Bench, and Mr Macklin, the comedian, have been often mentioned as instances in whom the mental faculties, as well as the corporeal powers, were unimpaired by age. Should we not add to these, the veteran of Strawberry Hill, and Colonel Lascelles, the latter of whom, particularly, still enjoys society with all the vivacity of youth.'

I certainly will not detract from your daughter's merit, nor from the judgment and goodness of the Queen; yet I do suspect that Mrs Delany[4] has a little contributed to the success by her recommendation.[5] My good friend in truth is but a baby of a courtier,[6] or she would not introduce a young favourite to supplant herself—but she will grow wiser in time; and as Miss Burney has a vast way to go before she learns to have a bad heart, I trust she will not undermine Mrs Delany, but be content with succeeding her,[7] and with living as long and as honourably. This is still more generous than my former generosity, since I cannot possibly live to be witness to the whole career of her triumphs, as I am to her brilliant dawn.

As you, dear Sir, may still find a day of leisure, I hope you will bestow it on

Yours most sincerely

H. Walpole

From Dr Charles Burney, Thursday 20 July 1786

Printed for the first time from Burney's MS draft, now WSL. The MS draft was presumably in Fanny Burney d'Arblay's possession at the time of her death in 1840; not further traced until acquired by WSL from the dealer G. F. Sims in May 1955. The letter sent to HW is missing.

Endorsed by Burney: Copy of letter to the Honourable Hor. Walpole 1786.

Endorsed by Fanny Burney d'Arblay: To Horace Walpole afterwards Lord Orford. / On Dr B's 2d daughter being called to the household establishment of Queen Charlotte.

St Martin's Street, July 20th 1786.

FEW consequences of the honour so graciously conferred on my daughter by her Majesty have afforded either of us more

4. See *ante* after 7 April 1774, n. 1.

5. Though Mrs Delany had been instrumental in laying the ground for Fanny Burney's 'preferment,' she wrote Frances Hamilton 3 July 1786 that Fanny had 'in the course of *this last year* [1785] . . . been so good as to pass a few weeks with me at Windsor, which gave the Queen an opportunity of seeing and speaking to her,' and that Fanny was 'chosen by the Queen without any particular recommendation from anybody' (*The Autobiography*

and Correspondence of Mary Granville, Mrs Delany, ed. Lady Llanover, 1861–2, vi. 366). See following letter.

6. In Sept. 1785, at the age of eighty-five, Mrs Delany went to live at Windsor in a house that the King and Queen had provided for her, with an annuity of £300 (ibid. vi. 280, 286–8; Hemlow, op. cit. 195).

7. Mrs Delany died in London in 1788; Fanny Burney remained at Court until 1791.

pleasure than the letter[1] it has produced from Strawberry Hill, and for which my best acknowledgments would have been much sooner offered, had I not waited till she was actually *inducted* to her new *living* at Windsor. This ceremony being happily over last Monday,[2] my doubts and indeed almost total incredulity which a long series of disappointments had generated are put to flight, and I now begin to think the transaction *real*, and no part of 'the baseless fabric of a vision.'[3]

The good and unsuspecting Mrs Delany is indeed still more a *baby of a courtier*[4] than you can imagine: for without the least apprehension that her Majesty's new attendant should ever arrive at *diabolism*, she obstinately goes on in treating her with such kindness and parental affection[5] as if she thought it impossible she should ever avail herself of the frequent opportunities which her situation will afford her, of rendering evil for good.

To be sure, my ingenious daughter has hitherto unaccountably kept me and her most intimate acquaintance ignorant of her ingratitude and other wicked practices; and all I have to wish, is, that she may continue to throw such an artful veil over them, as shall not only deceive her friends, but the most subtle and penetrating courtier of them all. At present indeed she seems so much pleased and flattered by the congratulations of her friends, that one would almost swear she was in earnest. And though the benign Mrs Delany, with all her zeal and kindness, never presumed to recommend her as a fit person to supply the place of Mademoiselle Hagerdorn,[6] or any other place whatever, yet her deceitful friend puts on all the semblance of gratitude, reverence, and affection for Mrs D. which could be due to the most munificent patroness upon earth.

If it be true, as some sour satirists pretend, that all mankind are

1. *Ante* 6 July 1786.
2. 17 July. The events of the day are fully described by Fanny Burney in a journal letter addressed to her sister Susanna Phillips (*Diary and Letters of Madame d'Arblay*, ed. Austin Dobson, 1904–5, ii. 378–87).
3. 'And, like the baseless fabric of this vision' (*The Tempest* IV. i. 151).
4. HW used this phrase in his letter of 6 July.
5. Fanny Burney relates that when she first arrived at Windsor, Mrs Delany

showed a 'chastened satisfaction . . . she rejoiced in the prospect before me; she was happy we should now be so much united, but she felt for my deprivations, she saw the hard conflict within me, and the tenderest pity checked her delight' (*Diary and Letters* ii. 379).
6. Mrs Hagerdorn (fl. 1761–86). She came to England from Germany with the Queen in 1761; in 1786 she resigned her post as Second Keeper of the Queen's Robes and returned to Germany.

equally wicked at heart, and that the difference is only in being good or bad *actors*, Mrs Siddons,[7] *I will be bold to say*, is a *baby of an actress* to my daughter. I believe, dear Sir, that we had better not probe these matters too deeply, but still suppose it just possible for people to have those imposing and *amiable weaknesses*, vulgarly called gratitude, sensibility, goodness of heart, affection, benevolence etc. At least I must beg of you to push these romantic ideas so far, as to imagine that I greatly deceive myself, if I am not with the utmost respect and regard, dear Sir,

Your most obliged and most devoted servant,

CHAS. BURNEY

Though my filial companion has now taken the *veil*, and is *devoted* elsewhere, I shall hope, during the course of the summer, to do myself the honour of waiting upon you at Strawberry Hill.[8]

To JOSHUA SHARPE,[1] Monday 21 August 1786

Printed for the first time from a photostat of the MS among the Seymour of Ragley papers in the Warwickshire County Record Office, Priory Park, Cape Road, Warwick, by kind permission of the Marquess of Hertford, through the good offices of Mr Randolph Trumbach. The MS doubtless passed from Sharpe to Lord Hugh Seymour (n. 2 below), whose grandson, Francis Hugh George Seymour, became the 5th Marquess of Hertford in 1870; the Seymour of Ragley papers were deposited on loan in the Warwickshire County Record Office by the 7th Marquess of Hertford in 1936-8.

Berkeley Square, Aug. 21st 1786.

Sir,

AS I was to come to town last night, I deferred returning you the proposed settlement on my niece,[2] till I could send it by my own servant.

---

7. Sarah Kemble (1755-1831), m. (1773) William Siddons; actress.

8. We have found no record of a meeting between HW and Burney during the summer of 1786.

---

1. (d. 1788), lawyer of Lincoln's Inn; attorney and legal adviser to the Countess of Orford (MANN iv. 547 n. 5). He was at this time employed by Lord Hertford to draw up the marriage settlement between the Hon. Hugh Seymour-Conway and Lady Anna Horatia Waldegrave (see following note).

2. Lady Anna Horatia Waldegrave (1762-1801), HW's great-niece, m. (3 April 1786) the Hon. (after 1793, Lord) Hugh Seymour-Conway (after 1794, Seymour)

You know full well, Sir, that I am no lawyer, and therefore can only conclude that the draught is very proper, as it seems agreeable to what was agreed on.[3] I am also persuaded that Lord Hertford and Captain Conway mean everything that is right and kind by Lady Horatia; and as I flatter myself that she will always continue to deserve her husband's affection and esteem, I have so full reliance on Mr Hugh Conway's honour, that I am persuaded he will leave her in as good a situation as he can, if she should have the misfortune to lose him.[4] I am, Sir,

Your most obedient humble servant

Hor. Walpole

(1759–1801), 5th son of Lord Hertford, Capt. R.N., 1779; Vice-Adm., 1799; M.P. 'Heads of a proposed Marriage Settlement,' a four-page document drawn up by Sharpe, is among the Seymour of Ragley papers in the Warwickshire County Record Office. One of the memoranda on the document reads: '14 Aug. [1786]. 3 copies as altered [made], to send to Mr [Hugh Seymour] Conway, Lord Hertford and Mr Hor. Walpole.' Although the basic terms of the settlement were agreed upon by treaty before the marriage, the legal document was not executed until afterwards. The two families were related, Lady Horatia being Hugh Seymour-Conway's second cousin once removed. HW was presumably asked to approve the proposed settlement because Lady Horatia's father (the 2d Earl Waldegrave) and grandfather (Sir Edward Walpole) were both dead by this time. The actual marriage settlement, written on ten parchment sheets, is also among the Seymour of Ragley papers.

3. In the 'Heads of a proposed Marriage Settlement' it is stated that 'the fortune of the said Lady Anne Horatia Waldegrave consisted of the sum of £14000 reduced 3 p[er] cent annuities then standing in her name and also of the sum of £200 by the year of long annuities then also standing in her name and that she was also entitled to one undivided 3d part or share of certain messuages, lands and tenements in the counties of Cambridge and Huntingdon as tenant in common thereof with her two sisters.' It is also stated that 'the said Earl of Hertford had proposed to give unto his said son Hugh Seymour Conway the sum of £6000 for his portion' and that 'on the treaty for the said marriage it was proposed and agreed that the sum of £12000 reduced bank annuities and part of the said £14000 reduced annuities and the said £200 long annuities should be transferred into the names of trustees to pay interest, dividends and annual produce thereof to the said Hugh Seymour Conway during his life and after his decease as a provision for the said Lady Anne Horatia Conway in case she should survive the said Hugh Seymour Conway, and the issue of the marriage and other trusts in [the] manner after mentioned.'

4. She died 12 July 1801, two months before his death 11 Sept. 1801 (Violet Biddulph, *The Three Ladies Waldegrave*, 1938, pp. 244–5).

To Samuel Ireland, Sunday 27 August 1786

Printed for the first time from the MS now WSL. The MS is untraced until sold Sotheby's 17 Dec. 1973 ('Other Properties'), lot 272, to John Wilson; offered by Wilson, Cat. No. 11 (Jan. 1974), lot 121, and sold by him to Kenneth W. Rendell, Inc.; offered by Rendell, Cat. No. 95 (1974), lot 159, and sold by them to WSL, May 1974. The separate address leaf, which bears Ireland's endorsement, was inserted in William Upcott's extra-illustrated copy of Boswell's *Life of Johnson*, ed. J. W. Croker, 1831; this copy was sold Sotheby's 25 March 1974 (property of a Gentleman), lot 176, to Owen for Mrs Donald F. Hyde, who removed the leaf and gave it to WSL, Dec. 1974.

Endorsed by Ireland: Mr Walpole Aug. 27, [17]86.

Address: To Mr Ireland in Arundel Street in the Strand, London. *Postmark:* ISLEWORTH.

M R WALPOLE was in Berkshire[1] when Mr Ireland's card[2] came, and returned too late to send a ticket for the day he desired, but Mr Ireland may have one for Friday next,[3] if he will let Mr Walpole know by Tuesday's post; or for Sunday next: Saturday is engaged. Mr Walpole desires an answer,[4] as he cannot keep two days unengaged.

1. HW visited Conway and Lady Ailesbury at Park Place 'for a few days' in late August (OSSORY ii. 524) and returned to SH by 27 August, when he received Prince Oginski (BERRY ii. 226; CHUTE 386).

2. Missing; apparently requesting a ticket to visit SH.

3. 1 Sept.   HW recorded in his 'Book of Visitors' for this date: 'Mr Ireland and 3—he brought 7, but only 4 admitted'

(BERRY ii. 226). In his diary *sub* 4 April 1797, Joseph Farington described a visit (possibly the same visit) by Ireland to SH: 'Mr Aytoun once went to Strawberry Hill with P. Sandby and Ireland. Mr Walpole was very obliging to them—and permitted Ireland and Sandby to trace rare prints of Hogarth, while he showed the house to Aytoun' (DALRYMPLE 338).

4. Missing.

To Lady Craven, Monday 27 November 1786

Printed from *Works* v. 662–4, where the letter was first printed. Reprinted, Wright vi. 274–6; Cunningham ix. 75–6; Toynbee xiii. 418–20; *The Beautiful Lady Craven*, ed. A. M. Broadley and Lewis Melville, 1914, i. xlvi–xlviii (closing and signature omitted in Wright, Cunningham, and Broadley and Melville). The history of the MS and its present whereabouts are not known.

Berkeley Square, November 27, 1786.

TO MY extreme surprise, Madam, when I knew not in what quarter of the known or unknown world you was resident or existent, my maid[1] in Berkeley Square sent me to Strawberry Hill a note[2] from your Ladyship, offering to call on me for a moment—for a whirlwind, I suppose, was waiting at your door to carry you to Japan; and, as balloons have not yet settled any post offices in the air, you could not, at least did not, give me any direction where to address you—though you did kindly reproach me with my silence. I must enter into a little justification before I proceed. I heard from you from Venice,[3] then from Poland,[4] and then, having whisked through Tartary, from Petersburgh[5]—but still with no directions. I said to myself, 'I will write to Grand Cairo, which, probably, will be her next stage.' Nor was I totally in the wrong—for there came a letter from Constantinople,[6] with a design mentioned of going to the Greek islands,[7] and orders to write to you at Vienna,[8] but with no banker or other address specified.

1. Possibly Mary, HW's maid when he lived in Arlington Street, who probably moved with him to Berkeley Square (OS-SORY i. 84, 330).

2. Missing. Lady Craven sailed from Holland for England 1 Oct. 1786; she visited her mother, Lady Nugent, in London (whence she presumably wrote to HW) and her brother George (n. 15 below) in Sussex; she was on the Continent again, in Paris, by 26 Nov. (*The Beautiful Lady Craven*, ed. A. M. Broadley and Lewis Melville, 1914, i. xliv–xlv).

3. This letter, probably written in Nov. 1785, is mentioned in HW's letter to Mann 16 March 1786 (MANN ix. 632 and n. 23). All of Lady Craven's letters mentioned in this paragraph are missing. Her itinerary can be traced from her letters to the Margrave of Brandenburg-Ansbach, printed in her *Journey through the Crimea to Constantinople*, 1789.

4. She was in Warsaw in Jan. 1786 (MANN ix. 632 n. 26).

5. She arrived at St Petersburg 29 Jan. 1786 OS; from there she went to Moscow (ibid. ix. 632 n. 22; Broadley and Melville, op. cit. i. xxxviii).

6. Where she arrived 20 April 1786 (ibid. i. xxxix; MANN ix. 9). HW apparently wrote, but did not send, a reply to this letter; an extract from it appears in his 'Miscellany,' 1786–95. See Appendix 5.

7. She visited Athens and Smyrna, then travelled by boat to Varna and by land to Vienna (MANN ix. 654–5 and n. 13; Broadley and Melville, op. cit. i. xl–xlii; *Memoirs of the Margravine of Anspach. Written by Herself*, 1826, i. 172).

The real Castle of Otranto as existing on the eastern coast of Italy taken from the spot. 1785.

REVELEY'S DRAWING OF THE CASTLE OF OTRANTO
AS IT EXISTED IN 1785

For a great while I had even stronger reasons than these for silence. For several months I was disabled by the gout⁹ from holding a pen; and you must know, Madam, that one can't write when one cannot write. Then, how write to *la Fiancée du Roi de Garbe?*¹⁰ You had been in the tent of the Cham of Tartary,¹¹ and in the harem of the Captain Pacha,¹² and, during your navigation of the Ægean, were possibly fallen into the terrible power of a corsair. How could I suppose that so many despotic infidels would part with your charms? I never expected you again on Christian ground. I did not doubt your having a talisman to make people in love with you; but anti-talismans are quite a new specific.

Well, while I was in this quandary, I received a delightful drawing of the Castle of Otranto¹³—but still provokingly without any address. However, my gratitude for so very agreeable and obliging a present could not rest till I found you out. I wrote to the Duchess of Richmond,¹⁴ to beg she would ask your brother Captain Berkeley¹⁵ for a

8. Which she visited in Sept. (MANN ix. 655 n. 14). In a letter to Dr Budd 1 Feb. 1786 from St Petersburg, she asked that letters at the end of the summer be directed to her in care of Sir Robert Murray Keith at Vienna (Broadley and Melville, op. cit. i. xxxv–xxxvi).

9. See *ante* 9 Dec. 1785, n. 2.

10. The text in *Works* reads '*Financée.*' La Fontaine's 'Fiancée du Roi de Garbe' is a *nouvelle* in verse about a heroine who has amatory experiences on her way to marry the Roi de Garbe. HW also makes this allusion in his letter to Mann 22 June 1786 (MANN ix. 655).

11. Probably mentioned in her missing letter from Constantinople.

12. Hassan Bey, 'the Captain Pacha, or high admiral' at Constantinople (*Memoirs of the Margravine of Anspach* i. 167–8).

13. A watercolour drawing executed in March 1785 by Willey Reveley (1760–99). 'Here [at Constantinople] I met with Sir Richard Worsley, who had a person [Reveley] with him to take views. He showed me a coloured drawing of the Castle of Otranto, which he proposed as a present to Horace Walpole. I then asked him, whether he were an acquaintance of his. Upon his replying in the negative, I did not hesitate to ask him for it, that I might, as a friend of Mr Walpole's, have the pleasure of giving it to him' (*Memoirs of the Margravine of Anspach* i. 170–1). The drawing was sold SH xvi. 117 (with another drawing) to Forster for £1.13.0 and is now bound in HW's copy of *The Castle of Otranto*, 2d edn, 1765, in the British Museum (Hazen, *Cat. of HW's Lib.*, No. 2486). The drawing is inscribed by HW: 'The real Castle of Otranto as existing on the eastern coast of Naples, taken from the spot 1785.' See illustration. Reveley's drawing was engraved by Barlow for the frontispiece to the sixth edition of *The Castle of Otranto*, Parma, 1791, printed by Bodoni for James Edwards of London. See also OSSORY iii. 36 n. 15 and CHUTE 435–6. Watercolour copies of Reveley's view were inserted by Richard Bull in his copies of *The Castle of Otranto* and the *Description of SH*, 1784, both now WSL (Hazen, *Bibl. of HW* 61).

14. Lady Mary Bruce (1740–96), m. (1757) Charles Lennox, 3d D. of Richmond, 1750. HW's letter to her is missing.

15. Hon. George Cranfield Berkeley (1753–1818), Capt. R.N., 1780; Admiral, 1810; K.B., 1813; M.P. He was a cousin of the Duke of Richmond and in 1784 had married the Duke's niece, Emily Charlotte Lennox.

direction to you;[16] and he has this very day been so good as to send me one,[17] and I do not lose a moment in making use of it.

I give your Ladyship a million of thanks for the drawing, which was really a very valuable gift to me. I did not even know that there was a Castle of Otranto. When the story was finished, I looked into the map of the kingdom of Naples for a well-sounding name, and that of Otranto was very sonorous. Nay, but the drawing is so satisfactory, that there are two small windows, one over another, and looking into the country, that suit exactly to the small chambers from one of which Matilda heard the young peasant singing beneath her.[18] Judge how welcome this must be to the author; and thence judge, Madam, how much you must have obliged him!

When you take another flight towards the bounds of the western ocean, remember to leave a direction. One cannot always shoot flying. Lord Chesterfield directed a letter to the late Lord Pembroke,[19] who was always swimming, 'To the Earl of Pembroke in the Thames, over against Whitehall.'[20] That was sure of finding him within a certain number of fathom; but your Ladyship's longitude varies so rapidly, that one must be a good bowler indeed, to take one's ground so judiciously that by casting wide of the mark one may come in near to the jack.[21]

I have the honour to be, with gratitude and respect,
Your Ladyship's most obliged humble servant,

HOR. WALPOLE

16. 'Chez le Chevalier Lambert, Banquier, à Paris,' according to Lady Craven's letter to Sir Robert Murray Keith 26 Nov. 1786 (Broadley and Melville, op. cit. i. xlvi).

17. Berkeley's letter to HW is missing.

18. *The Castle of Otranto, Works* ii. 33-4.

19. Henry Herbert (ca 1689–1750), 9th E. of Pembroke, 1733.

20. See MORE 402 and n. 3.

21. 'In the game of *Bowls,* a smaller bowl placed as a mark for the players to aim at' (OED *sub* 'jack,' sb. 18).

To Mrs Delany, Tuesday 28 November 1786

Printed from the MS inserted in vol. I of Mrs Delany's presentation copy of *Anecdotes of Painting*, 2d edn, SH, 1765–71, now WSL. First printed in *The Autobiography and Correspondence of Mary Granville, Mrs Delany*, ed. Lady Llanover, 1861–2, vi. 416. Reprinted, Toynbee xiii. 420–1. The presentation copy of the *Anecdotes* (inscribed 'M. Delany/ given me by the author') descended in the Granville family and was sold Sotheby's 19 July 1955 (Bevil Granville Sale), lot 475, to Maggs for WSL.

Berkeley Square, Nov. 28, 1786.

M R WALPOLE having been called upon for a new edition of the *Anecdotes of Painting*,[1] could not in a history of English arts resist the agreeable occasion of doing justice to one who has founded a new branch. He hopes therefore that Mrs Delany will forgive the liberty he has taken of recording her name in vol. 2, p. 242;[2] and that she will please to consider how cruel it would have been for him to be denied the satisfaction of mentioning her, only because he has the honour and happiness of her acquaintance.

1. 'The fourth edition, with additions' was published by James Dodsley and advertised in the *London Chronicle* 4–7 Nov. 1786, lx. 445, *sub* 6 Nov.: 'This day was published, in five volumes . . . a new edition, corrected, of *Anecdotes of Painting in England*. By Mr Horace Walpole. Printed for J. Dodsley . . . and sold by all other booksellers.' HW sent Mrs Delany a set; see *post* 30 Nov. 1786.

2. HW appended the following footnote to a passage mentioning the self-portrait of Jean Petitot that was purchased by the Duchess of Portland from one of Petitot's descendants living in Dublin: 'This portrait the Duchess [of Portland] at her death, in 1785, bequeathed to her friend, the widow of Doctor Delany and correspondent of Swift; a lady of excellent sense and taste, a paintress in oil, and who, at the age of 75, invented the art of paper-mosaic, with which material coloured, she, in eight years, executed within twenty of a thousand various flowers and flowering shrubs, with a precision and truth unparalleled.' For an account of her paper mosaics of flowers see *The Autobiography and Correspondence of Mary Granville, Mrs Delany*, ed. Lady Llanover, 1861–2, vi. 94–8. Many of her flower mosaics are in the British Museum.

To Lord Duncannon,[1] Wednesday 29 November 1786

Printed from the MS now WSL. First printed, Toynbee *Supp.* iii. 46–7. The MS apparently descended in the Ponsonby family and was sold Sotheby's 15 Dec. 1920 (property of Claude A. C. Ponsonby), lot 591, to Francis Edwards; resold Sotheby's 4 April 1955 (property of Major H. T. H. Foley, of Stoke Edith, Herefordshire), lot 226 (with other Walpolian items), to Maggs for WSL.

Endorsed in an unidentified hand: Hor. Walpole.

Address: To the Right Honourable the Lord Viscount Duncannon in Cavendish Square, London. *Postmark:* 30 NO. ISLEWORTH. FREE.

Strawberry Hill, Nov. 29th 1786.

My Lord,

I AM going to ask a favour of your Lordship, which I must preface by begging you to refuse without the least difficulty or ceremony, if you have the smallest objection to granting it.

Over the chimney in her library Princess Amelie[2] had a portrait of her grandmother,[3] the wife of King George the First, of whom there is certainly no other picture in England. I should be very glad to have a drawing made of it before it goes abroad, as I conclude it is left to the Landgrave[4] or one of his brothers.[5] If I might have leave, I would send a painter to make a drawing,[6] as I have a passion

1. Frederick Ponsonby (1758–1844), styled Vct Duncannon 1758–93; 3d E. of Bessborough, 1793; M.P.

2. Who had died 31 Oct. 1786. Lord Duncannon's father, the Earl of Bessborough, was one of Princess Amelia's executors, but as he was not well, Lord Duncannon acted for him (see Ossory ii. 535).

3. Sophia Dorothea (1666–1726) of Celle (Zell), m. (1682) George of Hanover (afterwards George I of England), from whom she was later divorced. HW described the portrait of her in his 'Book of Materials,' 1759, p. 146 (now WSL): 'Princess Emily has a portrait of her grandmother, wife of King George I. It is a round face with very dark hair. A blue velvet mantle edged with ermine lies on her knee, and she rests her left arm on a red cushion with a gold tassel. The portrait is sitting, not whole length.' See *Reminiscences Written by Mr Horace Walpole in 1788*, ed. Paget Toynbee, Oxford, 1924, pp. 22–4.

4. Georg Wilhelm (1743–1821), son of George II's daughter, Princess Mary, by Frederick II, Landgrave of Hesse-Cassel; Landgrave of Hesse-Cassel as Wilhelm IX, 1785; Elector of Hesse as Wilhelm I, 1803. He was Princess Amelia's nephew.

5. Charles (1744–1836), Prince of Hesse-Cassel, regent of Schleswig-Holstein; and Frederick (1747–1837), Prince of Hesse-Cassel. They were Princess Amelia's residuary legatees (Ossory ii. 534 and n. 14).

6. HW received permission, as is evident from the MS note he made concerning the drawing in one of his copies of the *Description of SH*, 1774, p. 158 (now WSL): 'Sophia Dorothea, wife of K. George I, copied in watercolours by Hardinge [Silvester Harding (1745–1809)] in 1786 from the original which belonged to King George II and which was bequeathed by his daughter Princess Amelie to her nephew the Landgrave of Hesse' (Hazen, *SH Bibl.* 109, copy 1). The drawing hung in the Red Bedchamber at SH ('Des. of SH,' *Works* ii. 438); it was sold SH xxii. 62 to Town and Emanuel for £1.0.0.

for English historic portraits; but I can easily waive that wish, if it would put your Lordship to any inconvenience in indulging me. I have the honour to be with great respect, my Lord,

Your Lordship's most obedient humble servant

Hor. Walpole

From Mrs Delany, Thursday 30 November 1786

Printed from *The Autobiography and Correspondence of Mary Granville, Mrs Delany*, ed. Lady Llanover, 1861–2, vi. 416–17, where the letter was first printed. The MS was presumably in the possession of Lady Llanover, a descendant of Mrs Delany's only sister, Ann Granville (later Mrs John Dewes), in 1861; not further traced.

Windsor,[1] November 30th 1786.

MRS DELANY presents her compliments to Mr Walpole, and her acknowledgments for the very kind and acceptable present he has made her (which she received last night) of his new edition of his *Anecdotes on Painting*[2]—nor is she insensible of the honour done her in mentioning her name in so ingenious and valuable a work with so much delicacy as to reconcile her to a publication that would have been rather painful from any other hand.

To Lady Craven, Tuesday 2 January 1787

Printed from *Works* v. 664–5, where the letter was first printed. Reprinted, Wright vi. 277–9; Cunningham ix. 86–8; Toynbee xiii. 435–7; *The Beautiful Lady Craven*, ed. A. M. Broadley and Lewis Melville, 1914, i. li–liii (closing and signature omitted in Wright, Cunningham, and Broadley and Melville). The history of the MS and its present whereabouts are not known.

Berkeley Square, January 2, 1787.

YOUR Ladyship tells me that you have kept a journal of your travels—you know not when your friends at Paris[1] will give you

---

1. See *ante* 6 July 1786, n. 6.
2. See *ante* 28 Nov. 1786. Mrs Delany's set of the fourth edition is untraced. Her presentation copy of the second is now WSL.

1. Where Lady Craven was then staying, *en route* to Ansbach. Her letter of 25 Dec. 1786 to the Marquess of Carmar-

time to put it *au net*—that is, I conclude and hope, prepare it for the press.[2] I do not wonder that those friends, whether talismanic or others, are so assiduous, if you indulge them; but unless they are of the former description, they are unpardonable, if they know what they interrupt—and deserve much more that you should wish they had fallen into a ditch, than the poor gentlemen who sigh more to see you in sheets of Holland[3] than of paper. To me the mischief is enormous. How proud I should be to register a noble authoress of my own country, who has travelled over more regions and farther than any female in print! Your Ladyship has visited those islands and shores,[4] whence formerly issued those travelling sages and legislators who sought and imported wisdom, laws and religion into Greece; and though we are so perfect as to want none of those commodities, the fame of those philosophers is certainly diminished when a fair lady has gone as far in quest of knowledge. You have gone in an age when travels are brought to a juster standard, by narrations being limited to truth.

Formerly the performers of the longest voyages destroyed half the merit of their expeditions, by relating not what they had, but had *not* seen; a sort of communication that they might have imparted without stirring a foot from home. Such exaggerations drew discredit on travels, till people would not believe that there existed in other countries anything very different from what they saw in their own: and because no Patagonians, or gentry seven or eight feet high, were really discovered,[5] they would not believe that there were Laplanders

then was written from the Hôtel de l'Empereur (*The Beautiful Lady Craven*, ed. A. M. Broadley and Lewis Melville, 1914, i. l).

2. Her 'journal,' in the form of letters addressed to the Margrave of Brandenburg-Ansbach, was published 7 Feb. 1789 as *A Journey through the Crimea to Constantinople* (Ossory iii. 35 n. 5). HW wrote Lady Ossory 6 Feb. 1789: 'Lady Craven's Travels I received from Robson two hours ago. Dodsley brought the MS to me before I came to town [in Oct. 1788]; but I positively refused to open it, though he told me my name was mentioned in it several times—but I was conscious how grievous it would be to her family and poor daughters, and therefore persisted in

having nothing to do with it. . . . I fear she may come to wish, or should, that *she* had not been born with a propensity to writing' (ibid. iii. 36–7).

3. 'A linen fabric, originally called, from the province of Holland in the Netherlands, Holland cloth' (OED *sub* 'Holland' 2).

4. See *ante* 27 Nov. 1786 and n. 7.

5. In 1766 HW had written and published *An Account of the Giants lately Discovered; In a Letter to a Friend in the Country*, a satire on the extravagant newspaper accounts of the Patagonians, as reported by the Hon. John Byron, captain of the *Dolphin* (Hazen, *Bibl. of HW* 67–9; Cole i. 126 n. 4).

or pigmies of three and four. Incredulity went so far, that at last it was doubted whether China as much as existed; and our country-man Sir John Mandeville[6] got an ill name, because, though he gave an account of it, he had not brought back its right name—at least, if I do not mistake, this was the case[7]—But it is long since I read anything about the matter; and I am willing to begin my travels again under your Ladyship's auspices. I am sorry to hear, Madam, that by your account Lady Mary Wortley[8] was not so accurate and faithful as modern travellers.[9] The invaluable art of inoculation, which she brought from Constantinople,[10] so dear to all admirers of beauty, and to which we owe perhaps the preservation of yours, stamps her an universal benefactress; and as you rival her in poetic talents, I had rather you would employ them to celebrate her for her nostrum, than detect her for romancing. However, genuine accounts of the interior of seraglios would be precious; and I was in hopes would become the greater rarities, as I flattered myself that your friends the Empress of Russia[11] and the Emperor[12] were determined

6. The fourteenth-century author of *The Voyages and Travels of Sir John Mandeville, Knight,* a famous collection of travel narratives of the Near and Far East and elsewhere, purporting to describe Mandeville's own adventures but actually based on accounts written by other (genuine) travellers. There were many early editions in English of Mandeville's *Travels;* HW's copy of an edition described in the SH sale catalogue as 'Sir John Mandeville's Travels, in black letter, very rare,' is Hazen, *Cat. of HW's Lib.,* No. 2412.

7. For a variety of reasons the authenticity of Mandeville's *Travels* was gradually discredited; by the beginning of the seventeenth century his name had become a byword for the lying traveller (J. W. Bennett, *The Rediscovery of Sir John Mandeville,* New York, 1954, p. 251).

8. Lady Mary Pierrepont (1689–1762), m. (1712) Edward Wortley Montagu.

9. Her so-called Embassy Letters, published posthumously as *Letters of the Right Honourable Lady M—y W——y M——e,* 3 vols, 1763, describe her experiences during her husband's diplomatic mission to Turkey in 1716–18. HW wrote to Mann 10 May 1763: 'These letters, though pretty well guarded, have certain marks of originality—not bating freedoms,

both of opinion, and with regard to truth, for which you know she had little partiality' (MANN vi. 141). Her biographer, Robert Halsband, comments: 'Although their form is partially fiction, the Embassy Letters tell the substance of her life abroad' (*The Life of Lady Mary Wortley Montagu,* Oxford, 1956, p. 59).

10. At Adrianople Lady Mary observed the practice of smallpox inoculation, and she had her son inoculated at Constantinople in March 1718; her daughter was inoculated in England three years later. She defended inoculation in 'A Plain Account of the Inoculating of the Small Pox by a Turkey Merchant,' published in *The Flying-Post: or, Post-Master* 11–13 Sept. 1722. This activity popularized smallpox inoculation and gained her credit for having brought it into England, although accounts of the practice had been published there several years earlier (ibid. 71–2, 80–1, 104–5, 109–12, 121, 255).

11. Catherine the Great, Empress of Russia 1762–96. Lady Craven was received by the Empress at the Hermitage in St Petersburg on 29 January 1786 OS (*Memoirs of the Margravine of Anspach. Written by Herself,* 1826, i. 148–50, 157–8; Broadley and Melville, op. cit. i. xxxvii).

12. Joseph II, Holy Roman Emperor

to level Ottoman tyranny. His Imperial Majesty, who has demolished the prison bars of so many nunneries,[13] would perform a still more Christian act in setting free so many useless sultanas; and her Czarish Majesty, I trust, would be as great a benefactress to our sex, by abolishing the barbarous practice that reduces us to be of none.[14] Your Ladyship's indefatigable peregrinations should have such great objects in view, when you have the ear of sovereigns.

Peter the Hermit[15] conjured up the first crusadoes against the infidels by running about from monarch to monarch. Lady Craven should be as zealous and as renowned; and every fair Circassian would acknowledge that one English lady had repaid their country for the secret which another had given to Europe from their practice.

> I have the honour to be, Madam,
> Your Ladyship's most obedient humble servant,
>
> Hor. Walpole

To Richard Bull, Wednesday 10 January 1787

Printed for the first time from the MS pasted in Bull's presentation copy of the *Postscript to the Royal and Noble Authors*, SH, 1786, now wsl. This copy (Hazen, *SH Bibl.* 137, copy 2) remained in Bull's library at North Court, Shorwell, Isle of Wight, eventually passing by family descent into the possession of the 5th Lord Burgh (1866–1926); sold Sotheby's 29 June 1926 (Burgh Sale), lot 165, to Maggs for wsl.
Endorsed by Bull: Mr Bull.

Berkeley Square, Jan. 10, 1787.

I HAD a person[1] with me on business, dear Sir, and could not answer your kind note[2] by your servant. I am much obliged to you for the game, and very sorry you are not quite well—when you

1765–90. He gave a private audience to Lady Craven at Vienna in Sept. 1786 and showed her further attentions (Lady Craven's *Memoirs* i. 130–3; *ante* 27 Nov. 1786, n. 8).

13. See *ante* late Aug. 1785, n. 6. HW wrote Mann 17 Jan. 1782: 'We hear with some surprise of the Emperor's very rapid suffocation of nunneries' (Mann ix. 236).

14. Eunuchs were employed as harem attendants.

15. (Peter of Amiens) (ca 1050–1115), an enthusiastic and very successful preacher of the First Crusade; he led one of its bands.

1. Not identified.
2. Missing.

are I hope to see you. I enclose a little piece[3] of which I beg your acceptance, and must desire too that you will not speak of it, not only that I do not mean it for the public, but I have printed only forty copies which I destine for presents, and have allotted them all,[4] and therefore wish not to be asked for what I shall not have to give. Your extreme and unmerited partiality entitle you to everything that you can think worth possessing of mine or from my press.[5]

Yours most faithfully

Hor. Walpole

To Richard Bull, ?late January 1787

Printed for the first time from a photostat of the MS inserted in Bull's presentation copy of HW's *A Letter to the Editor of the Miscellanies of Thomas Chatterton*, SH, 1779, now in the McGill University Library. This copy (Hazen, *SH Bibl.* 119, copy 6) was sold Sotheby's 1 May 1880 (Bull Sale), lot 732, to Harvey; resold Sotheby's 12 July 1910 (G. F. Smith Sale), lot 119, to Dobell; later acquired by Mr F. Cleveland Morgan, of Montreal, who presented it to McGill University ca 1954.

Dated conjecturally by the previous letter, in which Bull is said to be 'not quite well' and HW tells him he is entitled to 'everything that you can think worth possessing of mine or from my press.'

MR WALPOLE is very sorry that Mr Bull is still indisposed. Mr W. thought Mr Bull had one of the *Letters to Chatterton*,[1] or should certainly have begged his acceptance of one, as he now does.

---

3. A copy of the *Postscript to the Royal and Noble Authors*, SH, 1786 (see headnote).

4. HW wrote Lady Ossory 9 Jan. 1787: 'I have printed but forty copies, and merely for presents . . . and as I have appropriated all the rest, I shall not have another copy but my own left' (OSSORY ii. 552).

5. Bull was the chief contemporary collector of Walpoliana. Many of his handsomely bound and extra-illustrated copies of SH Press books are now WSL; a list of them is given in J. M. Pinkerton, 'Richard Bull of Ongar, Essex,' *Book Collector*, 1978, xxvii. 56–9. See following letter.

---

1. *A Letter to the Editor of the Miscellanies of Thomas Chatterton*, SH, 1779 (see headnote).

To Anna Maria Clarke,[1] Saturday 27 January 1787

Printed from the MS now WSL. First printed, Toynbee *Supp.* iii. 345–6. Reprinted in *Mary Hamilton, afterwards Mrs John Dickenson, at Court and at Home. From Letters and Diaries 1756 to 1816,* ed. Elizabeth and Florence Anson, 1925, p. 285. The MS apparently passed from Miss Clarke to Mary (Hamilton) Dickenson, and descended to Mrs Dickenson's great-granddaughter, Elizabeth Georgiana Anson; probably sold Sotheby's 31 May 1927 (property of Miss Elizabeth G. Anson), lot 514 (with seven other HW letters), to W. T. Spencer, from whom WSL acquired it in Sept. 1932.

Dated by the endorsements.

Endorsed, probably by Anna Maria Clarke: January 27, 1787.

Endorsed in a different hand: January 27th 1787. Honourable Horace Walpole.

Address: To Miss Anne Clarke, Piccadilly.

MR WALPOLE is extremely sensible of Miss A. Clarke's kindness in giving him the pleasure of knowing Mrs Dickenson[2] is so safe and well;[3] and he rejoices in it on Miss Clarke's own account too, and sincerely wishes her joy.

Mr Walpole begs Miss Clarke to congratulate Mr and Mrs Dickenson from him: he takes a sincere part in their happiness, though he loses so much satisfaction by it: and cannot envy what is so justly deserved.

---

1. (living 1806). She and her sister, Isabella, were friends of Mary Hamilton, and the three lived together in a house in Clarges Street from Feb. 1783 until Miss Hamilton's marriage to John Dickenson in June 1785 (MORE 214 n. 1).

2. See *ante* 18 June 1784, n. 2.

3. She had given birth the day before to a daughter (her only child), Louisa Frances Mary Dickenson (1787–1837), who married in 1815 Gen. Sir William Anson, K.C.B., cr. (1831) Bt (*Mary Hamilton, afterwards Mrs John Dickenson, at Court and at Home. From Letters and Diaries 1756 to 1816,* ed. Elizabeth and Florence Anson, 1925, p. 284; Burke, *Peerage and Baronetage,* 1928, p. 118).

To Richard Cosway,[1] Tuesday 30 January 1787

Printed from the MS now wsl. First printed, Toynbee *Supp*. iii. 47–8. The MS is untraced until offered by Maggs, Cat. Nos 396 (autumn 1920), lot 2669; 439 (summer 1923), lot 1167; acquired from B. Garnett by wsl, Sept. 1932.
Address: To Mr Cosway, Pall Mall.

Jan. 30th 1787.

YOU have too good an opinion, dear Sir, of my antiquarian knowledge; I cannot expound the letters of the ring[2]—but I can send you to the fount of explication, Mr Astle[3]—nay, I dare to say that half of the initiated of *the Society*[4] can decipher the letters, though they may not be able to read anything else.

The engraving of the stone is certainly not antiquarian, but antique, and contains one of those chimeras formed of heads of Minerva and Socrates. Our ancestors frequently adopted Grecian or Roman intaglios for seals. I think I have seen somewhere that an archbishop[5] made use of one of those triple chimeras, where there was a Mercury too, for an emblem of the Trinity.

I return the ring, but have retained the impression, which I will show to the first wizard I meet.

Yours etc.

H. Walpole

1. (1742–1821), miniature-painter. He and his wife Maria, who was also a painter, visited SH on 17 Aug. 1787 and were shown the house by HW himself (Berry ii. 228). HW commissioned portraits of Mrs Damer and Elizabeth Farren, the actress, from him in 1789 (Ossory iii. 84 n. 31).
2. An intaglio seal ring engraved with the heads of Minerva and Socrates, as described below, but not further identified.
3. Thomas Astle (1735–1803), the antiquary; HW's correspondent (*ante* 3 Aug. 1767, n. 1).
4. The Society of Antiquaries. In 1772 HW had resigned his membership in the Society because other members wrote attacks on his *Historic Doubts of . . . Richard the Third* ('Short Notes,' Gray i. 47).
5. Not identified.

To John Fenn, Thursday 1 February 1787

Printed from a photostat of the MS in the Norwich Central Library, Norfolk. First printed in R. W. Ketton-Cremer, 'Some New Letters of Horace Walpole,' *Times Literary Supplement*, 15 March 1957, lvi. 164. For the history of the MS see *ante* 7 May 1784.
Dated by the endorsement.
Endorsed by Fenn: February 1, 1787.

MR WALPOLE came to thank Mr Fenn for his most valuable present,[1] and to inquire after the health of Mrs Fenn.[2]

From George, Prince of Wales,[1] Wednesday 21 February 1787

Printed for the first time from the MS now WSL. The MS was sold SH vi. 114 (with letters of Princess Amelia and the Duke of Buckingham) to Sholto V. Hare; not further traced until sold Sotheby's 11 May 1970 ('Other Properties'), lot 156, to Seven Gables for WSL.

Carlton House,[2] February 21st 1787.

My dear Mr Walpole,

YOUR friend Lord Hertford[3] and his family dine at my house tomorrow. May I hope that you will make one of us.[4]

Ever most sincerely
Yours

George P.

1. A copy of Fenn's edition of the Paston letters, entitled *Original Letters, Written during the Reigns of Henry VI, Edward IV, and Richard III, by Various Persons of Rank or Consequence,* 2 vols, published 3 Feb. 1787 (*Morning Chronicle* 3 Feb.). HW's copy, which included the two additional volumes published by Fenn in 1789, is Hazen, *Cat. of HW's Lib.,* No. 3251. In the Preface, pp. xxxii–xxxiii, Fenn acknowledged 'the assistance, which he has received from the Honourable Horace Walpole, the Reverend Sir John Cullum, Bart. and Edward King, Esq. men who are so well known in the world of literature, that their names (whenever they are permitted to be used) will stamp a value upon any work, which they may honour with their approbation.' HW

wrote Lady Ossory 1 Feb. 1787: 'The *Letters of Henry VI's Reign,* etc., are come out, and *to me* make all other letters not worth reading. I have gone through above one volume, and cannot bear to be writing, when I am so eager to be reading' (Ossory ii. 558–9). See *ante* 2 May 1785.
2. See *ante* 14 June 1784, n. 4.

1. George (1762–1830), P. of Wales; King of England 1820–30 as George IV.
2. The official residence of George, Prince of Wales, since 1783. In Sept. 1785 HW visited Carlton House to see the new alterations by Henry Holland (Ossory ii. 498–500).
3. Who was also HW's first cousin.
4. 'Yesterday [22 Feb.] a grand dinner was given by the Prince of Wales at Carl-

To the Rev. Mark Noble, ?Thursday 8 March 1787

Printed from a photostat of the MS in the Bodleian Library (MS Eng. misc. d.153, f. 38a). First printed, Toynbee *Supp.* iii. 334. For the history of the MS see *ante* 1 Jan. 1785.

The date of the letter is approximate and was assigned by Noble.

M R WALPOLE is extremely obliged to Mr Noble for his kind present,[1] and will be very glad of the favour of seeing him in Berkeley Square any morning at eleven o'clock.

To the Rev. Mark Noble, March 1787

Printed from a photostat of the MS in the Bodleian Library (MS Eng. misc. d.153, f. 39b), First printed, Toynbee *Supp.* iii. 334. For the history of the MS see *ante* 1 Jan. 1785.

The approximate date of the letter is that assigned to it by Noble.

M R WALPOLE returns Mr Noble the volume[1] with many thanks for the entertainment; and should not have kept it so long, but the faintness of the ink prevented his being able to read it by candlelight. He shall be glad to see the second volume.[2]

ton House to several of the nobility' (*Daily Adv.* 23 Feb.). We do not know whether HW accepted the Prince's invitation.

1. Dr Toynbee suggested that this was a copy of Noble's *Memoirs of the Proctectoral-House of Cromwell,* 2d edn, 2 vols, published at Birmingham in this year, but HW was a subscriber to it. Noble's present may have been his *Two Dis-*

sertations upon the Mint and Coins of the Episcopal-Palatines of Durham, Birmingham, 1780 (Hazen, *Cat. of HW's Lib.,* No. 243).

1. Probably the first volume in MS of Noble's *Memoirs of the Illustrious House of Medici,* published in 1797.
2. See following letter.

To the Rev. Mark Noble, Thursday 22 March 1787

Printed from a photostat of the MS in the Bodleian Library (MS Eng. misc. d.153, f. 46). First printed, Toynbee *Supp.* iii. 334–5. For the history of the MS see *ante* 1 Jan. 1785.

March 22d 1787.

Sir,

YOUR volumes,[1] which I return, are very entertaining, and as the history of the Medici is little known in this country, I dare to say, would please much.[2] Indeed I wonder how without knowledge of Italian, you could collect[3] so much information about them. Still it is pity you cannot examine the new authentic history[4] published by order of the present Great Duke.[5]

You are not quite accurate in a few facts, and the style sometimes wants correction, and the whole will want some notes. The third Great Duke[6] should be called only Francis or Francesco, not Francesco *Maria*, for though he might be so christened, he never was called so; and the last Great Duke[7] should always be called John Gastone, or Giovanne Gastone, not simply Giovanne.

I beg you will be so kind to omit *the celebrated* to my name, and if you think the fact[8] worth mentioning, be so good as to put an as-

1. Presumably the remaining volumes in MS of Noble's *Memoirs of the Illustrious House of Medici, from Giovanni, the Founder of their Greatness, who Died in the Year 1428, to the Death of Giovanni-Gaston, the last Grand Duke of Tuscany, in 1737*, published in 1797. From the previous letter to Noble *ante* March 1787, it seems likely that HW had already read the first volume in MS of the *Memoirs*.

2. HW had once thought of writing a history of the Medici himself, but was dissuaded by Sir Horace Mann (Mann v. 278, 291; Dalrymple 53 and n. 6).

3. The MS reads 'collection.'

4. *Istoria del Granducato di Toscana sotto il governo della Casa Medici*, 5 vols, Florence, 1781, by Iacopo Riguccio Galluzzi (1739–1801), historian and politician. HW's two copies are Hazen, *Cat. of HW's Lib.*, Nos 32 and 3097.

5. Leopold II (1747–92), Grand Duke of

Tuscany 1765–90; Holy Roman Emperor 1790–2.

6. Francesco I (Francesco Maria) (1541–87) de' Medici, Grand Duke of Tuscany 1574–87. He was the son of Cosimo I, whom he succeeded as the second Grand Duke.

7. Giovanni Gastone (1671–1737) de' Medici, Grand Duke of Tuscany 1723–37. He was the last Grand Duke of the Medici family.

8. HW had an audience with the Dowager Electress Palatine, Anna Maria Luisa (1667–1743) de' Medici, in Florence in Dec. 1739, while he was on the Grand Tour. She was the last of the Medici family, being the daughter of Cosimo III, Grand Duke of Tuscany 1670–1723, and the sister of Giovanni Gastone (n. 7 above); she married in 1691 Johann Wilhelm (1658–1716), Elector Palatine, and returned to live in Florence after his death.

terisk, and in a note to say, v. Gray's letters,[9] which will exculpate me from being thought to have supposed my audience of any importance. I am Sir with great regard

Your obedient humble servant

H. Walpole

To John Fenn, Saturday 31 March 1787

Printed from a photostat of the MS in the Norwich Central Library, Norfolk. First printed in R. W. Ketton-Cremer, 'Some New Letters of Horace Walpole,' *Times Literary Supplement*, 15 March 1957, lvi. 164. For the history of the MS see *ante* 7 May 1784.

Address: To John Fenn Esq. at East Dereham, Norfolk. *Postmark:* 31 M⟨R⟩.

Berkeley Square, March 31st 1787.

I HAVE been confined so long, dear Sir, by a great cold and cough, that till today I could not go to Carter's[1] and see your pictures[2] as you desired. They are certainly in a woeful condition, but I think

---

9. Thomas Gray wrote to his mother from Florence 19 Dec. 1739 NS: 'Mr Walpole is just come from being presented to the Electress Palatine Dowager; she is a sister of the late Great Duke's; a stately old lady, that never goes out but to church, and then she has guards, and eight horses to her coach. She received him with much ceremony, standing under a huge black canopy, and, after a few minutes talking, she assured him of her good will, and dismissed him: She never sees anybody but thus in form; and so she passes her life, poor woman!' (*Correspondence of Thomas Gray*, ed. Paget Toynbee and Leonard Whibley, Oxford, 1935, i. 136). This letter was first printed in *The Poems of Mr Gray. To which Are Prefixed Memoirs of his Life and Writings by W. Mason, M.A.*, York, 1775, pp. 72–4. Noble mentioned HW's audience in his account of Giovanni Gastone: 'She [Anna Maria Luisa] was extremely fond of pomp, and very stately. When . . . she alone remained of all her family, she resided in the Palace Pitti. . . . She never went out

for some years before her death, except to church, or sometimes to see Florence in the evening; at these times she was drawn by eight horses, and attended by a guard. The present Earl of Orford informed the author, that he once had the honour to pay his respects to her. She received him under a large black canopy, she stood indeed, but after a few minutes talking, she assured him of her good wishes, and then dismissed him; nor did she see anyone but in this ridiculous way' (*Memoirs of the Illustrious House of Medici*, pp. 449–50). Noble did not add a note referring to Gray's letter.

---

1. Probably John Carter (1748–1817), draftsman and architect, who was employed by HW to make drawings of SH (Chatterton 192 n. 2). He lived at No. 3 Wood Street 1784–86, No. 2 College Street, Westminster 1787–88, and No. 2 Hamilton Place, Hyde Park 1789–94 (Algernon Graves, *The Royal Academy of Arts*, 1905–6, ii. 4).

2. Not identified.

never could have been good in colouring, no more than they are in drawing. They no doubt contain some popish legend or legends, but probably no true history.

But though I cannot explain your pictures, I have accidentally met with a curious passage that throws great light on one of the most remarkable letters in your late valuable publication;[3] I mean on the circumstance of the Earl of Warwick[4] borrowing 10 pounds of Sir John Paston.[5]

In the new edition of ancient French *mémoires* which they are republishing at Paris,[6] I found in the *Mémoires* of Olivier de la Marche[7] (Vol. IX, p. 125) who writes the history of Philip Duke of Burgundy[8] and of his son Charles the Bold,[9] an account of the Duke of Clarence[10] and the Earl of Warwick, coming to Louis XI,[11] when they were driven out of England,[12] and of the latter he gives this very memorable account;

'Cestuy Comte de Warwich fut homme sage, & subtil en ses affaires, & entretint la cité de Londres & le royaume d'Angleterre par trois voyes. La première, par caperonnées & par humilité feinte au peuple de Londres, dont il étoit moult aimé. Secondement, il estoit maître des cinq ports d'Angleterre, où il souffroit grand dommage faire; & jamais de son tems on ne fit droit en Angleterre à aucun étranger de perte qu'il luy fut faicte, parquoy il estoit aimé par les pillars d'Angleterre, qu'il vouloit bien entretenir. Et tiercement il entretint la ville de Londres par tousjours y debvoir trois ou quatre cens mille escus à diverses gens, & à diverses parties, & ceux à qui il devoit desiroyent sa vie & sa prosperité, afin d'être une fois payez de leur deu.'[13]

3. Fenn's edition of the Paston letters (*ante* 1 Feb. 1787, n. 1).

4. Sir Richard Nevill (1428–71), 16th E. of Warwick, 1449; called the 'king-maker.'

5. (1442–79), Kt, 1463; courtier and letter-writer. The letter in which Warwick asked to borrow ten or twenty pounds, to make up a sum to complete the purchase of an estate, is actually addressed to Sir Thomas Tuddenham (*Original Letters, Written during the Reigns of Henry VI, Edward IV, and Richard III, by Various Persons of Rank or Consequence*, 1787, i. 84–7).

6. *Collection universelle des mémoires particuliers relatifs à l'histoire de France*, ed. J.-A. Roucher, A.-C. Bellier-Duchesnay, and Antoine Perrin, London and Paris, 1785–1807. HW eventually owned 67 volumes in the series, 1785–91 (Hazen, *Cat. of HW's Lib.*, No. 3084); see MORE 245.

7. (ca 1426–1502), French chronicler and man of letters. La Marche's *Mémoires* are printed in vols VIII and IX of the *Collection universelle*.

8. Philippe III (1396–1467), D. of Burgundy, 1419.

9. Charles (1433–77) the Bold, D. of Burgundy, 1467.

10. George (Plantagenet) (1449–78), cr. (1461) D. of Clarence and (1472) E. of Warwick and Salisbury; elder brother of Richard III.

11. (1423–83), K. of France 1461–83.

12. By Edward IV in April 1470, after being proclaimed traitors on 31 March.

13. HW's quotation from the *Collection universelle* ix. 125 is accurate except for

If this notice, Sir, should come to you in time, perhaps you would not be sorry to insert it as a note to the letter in question.[14] At least I flatter myself that the information will be satisfactory to yourself, as elucidating the character of so remarkable a man, whom it shows to have been as shrewd a politician as he was a great soldier.

I beg my respects to Mrs Fenn, and am with great regard, Sir,

Your obedient humble servant

Hor. Walpole

To Sir Joseph Banks,[1] Saturday 31 March 1787

Printed from a photostat of a MS copy in the General Library of the British Museum (Natural History), South Kensington (Banksian Correspondence, vol. V, f. 147). This MS copy was made by one of the daughters of Dawson Turner (1775–1858), the botanist and antiquary, or by one of his clerks. Turner was at one time the owner of the original MS, which was probably sold Puttick and Simpson 10 June 1859 (Dawson Turner Sale), lot 680 (in a 54-volume collection of autographs); resold Puttick and Simpson 28 June 1893 (Brabourne Sale), lot 984; not further traced.

Berkeley Square, March 31st 1787.

I RETURN you the book,[2] with many thanks. It is a most curious one; and as I readily lent my Ceres[3] to be drawn for it,[4] I confess I should have been much pleased if it had been thought fit to give me one.

a few minor differences in spelling and punctuation; accent marks have been normalized here.

14. Fenn did not add such a note to the letter in the second edition of the Paston letters, published later in 1787.

———

1. (1744–1820), cr. (1781) Bt; K.B., 1795; F.R.S., 1766; P.R.S., 1778–1820; traveller and naturalist.

2. *An Account of the Remains of the Worship of Priapus, lately Existing at Isernia, in the Kingdom of Naples . . . to which Is Added, A Discourse on the Worship of Priapus, and its Connection with the Mystic Theology of the Ancients*, 1786, by Richard Payne Knight (1750–1824), M.P., numismatist and antiquary. The publication of this work was sponsored by

the Society of Dilettanti. Banks, as Secretary of the Society, was given custody of all copies of the book and could distribute them only by an order made at a regular meeting of the Society (Lionel Cust and Sidney Colvin, *History of the Society of Dilettanti*, 1898, pp. 122–3; F. J. Messmann, *Richard Payne Knight: the Twilight of Virtuosity*, The Hague, 1974, pp. 42–4).

3. Described in Knight's *Priapus* as follows (p. 124): 'In an ancient bronze at Strawberry Hill this goddess [Ceres] is represented sitting, with a cup in one hand, and various sorts of fruits in the other; and the bull, the emblem of the power of the Creator, in her lap.' It was displayed in one of the windows of the Gallery at

I should still be very glad at least, if I could obtain one or two impressions of my Ceres; as I gather as many prints as I can of the pictures and curiosities in my collection. I have not the pleasure of knowing Mr Knights;[5] but I think he would not refuse me such a trifling request;[6] and you are always so good to me, that if it would not be disagreeable to you to mention it, I should be still more

Your much obliged and most obedient humble servant

HOR. WALPOLE

To Sir Joseph Banks, Thursday 3 May 1787

Printed for the first time from a photostat of the MS in Thomas Kirgate's hand in the Pierpont Morgan Library. The history of the MS is not known.

Berkeley Square, May 3d 1787.

Sir,

I HAVE been laid up for these three weeks by a sharp fit of the gout, and am still confined to my couch in so uneasy a posture that I cannot write with my own hand;[1] you will therefore excuse my returning you, in this manner, my most sincere thanks for your very obliging compliance with my request;[2] and I must entreat you, Sir, as I am incapable of writing myself, to allow me to beg you to present my most respectful thanks and gratitude to Mr Knight, and to the gentlemen of the Society of Dilettanti, for the honour of their very valuable present:[3] I would wait on Mr Knight myself, if I were able.

SH ('Des. of SH,' *Works* ii. 467) and was sold SH xxiii. 109 to Cope for £73.10.0.

4. The drawing was made at SH ca July 1785 by D'Hancarville, the French antiquary; it was engraved for Knight's *Priapus*, plate VIII, fig. 1, following p. 195. See OSSORY ii. 479 and n. 15.

5. *Sic* in the MS copy. HW wrote Mason 22 March 1796: 'He [Knight] is a great favourite of a very near relation of mine and intimate friend [probably Mrs Damer] . . . through whom I have received several civilities from the person himself' (MASON ii. 339). In the same letter HW refers to Knight as 'a trumpery prosaic po-

etaster,' 'this pretended and ill-warranted dictator to all taste,' 'this knight of the brazen milk-pot' (ibid. ii. 338–40).

6. See following letter.

———

1. The letter was dictated to HW's secretary, Thomas Kirgate.

2. See previous letter. Since HW does not mention receiving separate impressions of the engraving of his bronze Ceres, it seems probable that none was sent to him.

3. HW's copy of Knight's *Account of the Remains of the Worship of Priapus* was presented to him by a vote of the

I should be very happy, Sir, to have the honour of seeing you, when you pass this way, as I am impatient to repeat to you, how very sincerely I am

Sir,

        Your most obliged and most obedient humble servant

Horace Walpole

To the Hon. Thomas Fitzwilliam,
Monday 28 May 1787

Printed for the first time from a photostat of the MS in the University of Reading Library, kindly furnished by the Archivist, Mr J. A. Edwards. For the history of the MS see *ante* 16 May 1783.

Endorsed in an unidentified hand: Original letter of Horace Walpole, found among the papers of the late Viscount Fitzwilliam.

Berkeley Square, May 28, 1787.

MR WALPOLE is this moment come to town and finds the honour of Mr Fitzwilliam's letter,[1] but is extremely sorry he cannot obey his commands. There is a company to go to his house tomorrow;[2] and Mr Walpole having been forced by several disagreeable accidents to adhere to the enclosed printed rules,[3] it is not in his power to dispense with them without disobliging many persons, to whom he has sent them, and consequently he cannot admit more than four persons in one day.

If Wednesday will suit Mr Fitzwilliam's friends, Mr Walpole encloses a ticket for that purpose, which he must beg to have returned,

Society of Dilettanti 'as an acknowledgment of the useful assistance received from him by the author in the prosecution of this work' (inscription on the verso of the title-page by Banks, Secretary of the Society, dated 1 April 1787). The copy is now wsL (Hazen, *Cat. of HW's Lib.*, No. 2404). HW noted on the fly-leaf: 'Few copies of this book were printed, and only for the members of the Society of Dilettanti, and for presents. This copy was sent to me for having permitted Mr Knight the author to make a drawing of my bronze of Ceres, which is engraved in Table VIII. H.W.'

---

1. Missing; it was a request that friends of Fitzwilliam be allowed to visit SH on Tuesday, 29 May.

2. HW's 'Book of Visitors' shows that 'Mr Demainbray and 3' were admitted at SH on 29 May 1787 (Berry ii. 227).

3. See *ante* 7 Sept. 1781, n. 1. The copy of HW's rules for admission to SH is preserved with the letter.

if it will not:[4] or he can send one for Friday, but Thursday is also engaged.[5]

Mr Walpole is much mortified that he cannot oblige Mr Fitzwilliam more completely, as he should be happy to do.

To the Hon. Mrs Boyle Walsingham,[1]
Thursday 26 July 1787

Printed from a photostat of the MS in the possession (1963) of Col. W. H. S. Byng, Kenton Cottage, Furzebrook, Wareham, Dorset. First printed, Toynbee xiv. 9. The MS passed by family descent to Mrs Walsingham's great-granddaughter, the Hon. Mrs J. R. Swinton, who bequeathed it in a collection of letters to her goddaughter, the Hon. Mrs Schomberg Byng, the mother of Col. Byng.

Strawberry Hill, July 26, 1787.

MR WALPOLE was much mortified on his return from London[2] at finding the great and flattering entertainment Mrs Walsingham had been so good as to offer him[3]—charmed he is sure he should have been, for does not he know Miss Boyle's[4] genius?[5] He would have attempted to forestall the lark and the carpenter yesterday morning, but most unfortunately the Princess Lubomirski[6] had

4. Wednesday, 30 May, presumably did not suit Fitzwilliam's friends, for the 'Book of Visitors' records that '4 persons from Mr Thomas Fitzwilliam' were at SH on the 28th, the same day that this letter was written (ibid.).

5. 'Mrs Davison and 3 from Mr Carr' were admitted on Thursday, 31 May (ibid.).

1. Charlotte Hanbury Williams (1738–90), second dau. of HW's correspondent Sir Charles Hanbury Williams, m. (1759) Hon. Robert Boyle (later Boyle Walsingham) (1736–80), 5th son of the 1st E. of Shannon, naval officer and M.P.

2. HW wrote Conway 20 July 1787 that 'on Monday [23 July] I must go to town on business of my own' (Conway iii. 453).

3. The 'entertainment' was apparently to have been a puppet show devised by

Mrs Boyle Walsingham's daughter (see following note).

4. Charlotte Boyle (1769–1831), m. (1791) Lord Henry Fitzgerald (1761–1829), 4th son of the 1st D. of Leinster; Bns Ros or Roos, s.j., 1806.

5. HW wrote Lord Strafford 28 July 1787: 'Mrs Walsingham is making her house at Ditton (now baptized Boyle Farm) very orthodox. Her daughter Miss Boyle, who has real genius, has carved three tablets in marble with boys designed by herself. Those sculptures are for a chimney-piece; and she is painting panels in grotesque for the library, with pilasters of glass in black and gold' (Chute 390). See also More 251 and nn. 3, 4.

6. Isabella (Elizabeth) Helene Anne Czartoriska (1736–1816), m. 1 (1753) Stanislas (1722–83), Prince Lubomirski; m. 2 (1786) Michael, Count Oginski (Ossory ii. 565 n. 27).

engaged to breakfast with him, and instead of seeing a sight, he was forced to show one: and Mrs Walsingham may think what she will, but if she and Miss Boyle make Boyle Farm⁷ as delightful as they are capable of doing, they will live to repent it. The wise men will come from the East, and all the foolish men and women in Europe, to visit it, and Miss Boyle will have made a *puppet-show*, that for once she did not intend. It cannot be wonderful that I complain of such visitation, when it has cost me so dear today! but I trust that Mrs Walsingham's own impatience to see her chimney-piece⁸ again and again, will soon aid Mr Walpole's, and make him amends for yesterday's vexation.

To John Pinkerton, Monday 30 July 1787

Printed from an extract quoted in *A Catalogue of Holograph and Autograph Letters . . . and Important Unpublished Correspondence*, n. d. (probably mid-nineteenth century), p. 120, issued by John Waller, Bookseller, 58 Fleet Street, London. The MS is described as an autograph letter signed by HW, one page, quarto; it has not been further traced.

[Strawberry Hill, July 30, 1787.]

I ENCLOSED the order¹ you desired, and you will be so good as to inform the gentleman that no more than four can be admitted.² If you will come and dine, and take a bed here, on Sunday,³ I shall be very glad of your company; bring me a sufficient account of Lord Elibank's⁴ publications, as now my printer⁵ waits for them.⁶

7. Mrs Boyle Walsingham's house at Thames Ditton, Surrey, which she had purchased from Lord Hertford apparently in 1783 (CONWAY iii. 416 n. 4).

8. See n. 5 above.

1. A ticket of admission to SH, in the form of a written order addressed to HW's housekeeper.

2. HW's 'Book of Visitors' records that 'Mr R. Ingram and 3 from Mr Pinkerton' were admitted at SH on 8 Aug. 1787 (BERRY ii. 228). The same Mr Ingram visited SH again on 25 July 1792 (ibid. ii. 241).

3. 5 August. See n. 6 below.

4. 'D'Elibank's' in Waller's *Catalogue* (see headnote), doubtless a misreading of 'Ld Elibank's.' Patrick Murray (1703–78),

5th Bn Elibank, 1736; lawyer, soldier, and patron of literature.

5. Thomas Kirgate.

6. On 6 July 1787 HW 'resumed printing my works in quarto, with additions to *Royal and Noble Authors*' (*Journal of the Printing-Office* 20). A week earlier, on 29 June, HW had written to Pinkerton, asking him to send 'a list of the writings of Lord Elibank' that Pinkerton had promised to furnish (CHATTERTON 292). We do not know whether Pinkerton went to SH on Sunday, 5 August, but he wrote Lord Buchan 20 Sept. 1787 that he was at SH 'about a month ago' (ibid. 293 n. 12). HW made no use of any information from Pinkerton in his account of Lord Elibank (*Works* i. 542).

To Charles Bedford, Thursday 9 August 1787

Printed from the MS now wsl. First printed, Toynbee *Supp.* ii. 19–20. The MS was in the possession of Dodd and Livingston, New York City, in 1918; sold American Art Association—Anderson Galleries 14 Jan. 1937 (Various Properties), lot 548, to Brick Row for wsl; its earlier history is not known.

Address: To Charles Bedford Esq. at the Exchequer, Westminster. *Postmark:* AU 9 87.

Strawberry Hill, Aug. 9, 1787.

Dear Sir,

IT IS very true that I did say to Mr Harris,[1] that you might bring me the money[2] hither, but I do think it is better you should not, as I do not love to keep a sum here, and I do not know when I can be in town. As I know that you do not love to keep it, I will beg you to pay it to Mr Croft[3] the banker in Pall Mall, and let him give you a receipt in my name; and be so good as to send me word what the sum is. I hope you are quite well, as I am, and

Yours most sincerely

H. Walpole

To Thomas Pennant, Wednesday 10 October 1787

Printed for the first time from the MS now wsl. For the history of the MS see *ante* 25 May 1773.

Strawberry Hill, Oct. 10, 1787.

Dear Sir,

I RETURN your paper of queries[1] with such answers as I am capable of giving to them. If they are not quite as satisfactory as I

1. William Harris, HW's clerk in the Exchequer (*ante* 27 Feb. 1771, n. 2).
2. Presumably a regular payment due to HW as usher of the Exchequer.
3. Richard Croft (d. 1793), banker in Pall Mall, with whom HW and Sir Horace Mann had various dealings (Mann vi. 278 n. 1).

1. Missing.

should wish, they may at least assist you in leading to more authentic information.[2]

I do not know the age of Sir Henry Lee[3] nor year of his death; but I am very glad you mean, Sir, to give a print of him.[4] If I were not so old myself, I should more lament your talking of your concluding labours—yet I have such kind wishes for posterity, that at least I am glad you design them a legacy.[5]

I have the honour to be with great regard, Sir,

Your most obedient humble servant

Hor. Walpole

To Lady Lyttelton, Sunday 28 October 1787

Printed from a photostat of the MS in the Harvard College Library. First printed, Cunningham ix. 116–17. Reprinted, Toynbee xiv. 29–31. The MS is untraced until acquired by Ellis Gray Loring, of Boston, Massachusetts, before 1877; later in the autograph collection of James Freeman Clarke, which was deposited in the Harvard College Library in Feb. 1946 and given in Dec. 1956.

The MS is damaged by two large holes that have made a number of lacunæ in the text; conjectural readings are supplied within angle brackets.

Address: To the Right Honourable the Lady Dowager Lyttelton at the Cottage, Ripley. *Postmark:* OC 29 ⟨87⟩. ISLEWORTH.

Strawberry Hill, Oct. 28, 1787.

IT IS very kind in you, my dear Madam, even to reproach me with my silence.[6] Alas! I have no excuse to plead but one that I cannot help; I am grown so old, and insipid to myself, that I never think of troubling anybody with my nullity. I know and do nothing that is

2. Pennant was at work on his *Of London*, published in 1790, with *Additions and Corrections* the following year. HW, who for many years had been collecting materials for a similar work on the streets of London (never written), answered other queries from Pennant and sent him various items of information for his book. See *post* 30 April 1788, 30 March 1789, 10 April 1789; Berry i. 93–4.

3. (1530–1610), Kt, 1553; K.G., 1597; master of the Ordnance; president of the Society of Knights Tilters.

4. An engraved portrait of Lee by James Basire, after a drawing by Moses Griffith, is the frontispiece to Pennant's *Of Lon-*

don, 1790. Griffith's drawing was made from the 'original in possession of the late Mrs Sydney Lee, of Chester' (ibid. 97). Pennant states that Lee 'died aged 80, in the year 1611, and was interred in the once elegant little church of Quarendon, near Aylesbury' (ibid.).

5. Pennant wrote in the Advertisement to *Of London,* p. v: 'I feel within myself a certain monitor that warns me to hang up my pen in time, before its powers are weakened, and rendered visibly impaired. . . . My literary bequests to future times, and more serious concerns, must occupy the remnant of my days. This closes my public labours.'

worth repeating, and therefore scarce ever write a letter. I heard with pleasure from Lady Cecilia[1] that you are well and very much employed, which is a proof of health; and as you have been thinning your forest, I expect to see you return to town[2] with a pair of ⟨cheeks as⟩ hale as a woodman's: and shall have great pleasure ⟨in listening⟩ to the babel of compliments that will be made to you on y⟨our goo⟩d looks by the representatives of all the princes in Europe at Mrs Cosway's[3] Diet.[4] That, I doubt, will not be so soon as I wish; indeed I am ignorant whether the signora[5] is returned from Paris— but I shall know at the end of the week, when I shall remove to Lond⟨on to gr⟩eet the Court of Gloucester in London the beginning ⟨of the mont⟩h.[6] Besides, the smoke of the capital is more congenial to my ⟨   7th⟩an the damp winter,[8] and the late deluges alarm my gout.

I know, my good Lady, you never read a newspaper till it is old-enough to be incorporated into the history of England,[9] and therefore probably do not know that we have been going to war (no matter to you with whom) and that we are to have peace,[10] of which I wish you joy, as *that* does concern you, for we could not quarrel with any part of Europe, without your losing some *diplomatique,* and they are all in succession your friends, as they are Sir Clement

1. Lady Cecilia Johnston (HW to Lady Henrietta Cecilia West *ante* before 4 May 1762, n. 1).
2. Lady Lyttelton had a house in Portugal Street.
3. Maria Louisa Catherine Cecilia Hadfield (1759–1838), m. (1781) Richard Cosway; miniature-painter.
4. Mrs Cosway was well known for her elaborate concerts and entertainments, which HW occasionally attended. At this time she lived with her husband at Schomberg House, Pall Mall (BERRY i. 285 n. 14).
5. Mrs Cosway was born and brought up in Italy.
6. The Duke and Duchess of Gloucester landed at Dover 10 Nov. and arrived at Gloucester House 11 Nov. after an absence from England of five and a half years (OSSORY ii. 581 n. 2). HW wrote Lady Ossory 3 Dec. 1787: 'The return of the Duke and Duchess of Gloucester engaged me but the first two or three days' (ibid. ii. 581–2).
7. An earlier owner of the MS has writ-
ten 'eyes' in the blank space, but this reading seems doubtful. HW to Mann 3 April 1777 (MANN viii. 289), says that damp 'affects my nerves,' and drives him to town.
8. 'I came to town the middle of last week to quit the damps that made me much out of order, but the smoke of London soon recovered me' (HW to Lady Ossory 12 Dec. 1786, OSSORY ii. 543–4).
9. HW told Conway 22 May 1779: 'If you hear of us no oftener than we of you, you will be as much behindhand in news as my Lady Lyttelton' (CONWAY iii. 320).
10. The Stadtholder (the Prince of Orange) was engaged in a struggle with the Patriot party. The British government offered financial and military assistance to the King of Prussia in his efforts to support the Stadtholder. The intervention of Prussian troops in Holland helped the Prince to regain control, and on 27 Oct. declarations were signed discontinuing 'all warlike preparations.' See ibid. iii. 450 n. 13, 455 n. 12, 457 n. 4, 459 n. 5.

Cotterel's[11]—I am not sure that he is the present introductor, or his grandson;[12] but like your Ladyship I am more familiar with the images of the last reign than of the present, and we understand one another best by the old vocabulary.

You see, I hope, my dear Madam, by these old jokes that[13] I am rejoiced to hear from you,[14] and answer in my ancient style. I care little for new friends and new acquaintance; they t⟨ake no r⟩oot in my veteran heart; but I am constant to those tha⟨t are register⟩ed in my first almanacs. Mr Conway is gone to Jersey,[15] but I t⟨rust the paci⟩fication will bring him back incontinently, and that he will see ⟨no fir⟩e but those he kindles in his own lime-kilns.[16] The Churchills[17] are in town tending Mrs Walpole[18] and expecting another grandbabe.[19] This is all I know of the current century, and I fear it proves how little I had to say; though, silent or tattling, I am always equally

Your Ladyship's sincere old friend and servant

Hor. Walpole

---

11. Sir Clement Cottrell Dormer (1686–1758), Kt, 1710; Master of the Ceremonies. The office of Master of the Ceremonies was hereditary in Sir Clement's family from 1640 (More 10 n. 6).

12. Sir Clement Cottrell Dormer (d. 1808), Kt, 1779; Master of the Ceremonies, 1779.

13. The MS reads 'than.'

14. Lady Lyttelton's letter to HW is missing.

15. Henry Conway had been governor of Jersey since 1772 (Conway iii. 164 n. 1). HW wrote to him 11 Nov. 1787: 'I find you knew nothing of the pacification when you wrote. When I saw your letter [missing], I hoped it would tell me you was coming back, as your island is as safe as if it was situated in the Pacific Ocean. . . . Well, I enjoy both your safety and your great success, which is enhanced by its being owing to your character and abilities' (Conway iii. 459).

16. Conway had a distillery on the grounds of his estate, Park Place, and carried on experiments with coke-ovens. In 1782 he obtained a patent for a 'Kiln and oven for burning lime, also for distilling and brewing purposes' (ibid. iii. 392 n. 6, 551–2).

17. See ante 25 Oct. 1744 OS, n. 9.

18. Sophia Churchill (d. 1797), younger dau. of Charles and Lady Mary Churchill, m. (1781) Hon. Horatio Walpole (1752–1822), 2d E. of Orford, n.c., 1809.

19. A fourth son, John (1787–1859), was born to the Walpoles on 17 Nov. He was later a lt-colonel in the army and chargé d'affaires in Chile (Burke, Peerage and Baronetage, 1928, p. 1786).

To Dr Charles Burney,
Wednesday 19 December 1787

Printed from the MS now wsl. First printed, Toynbee *Supp.* ii. 20–1. The MS passed by family descent to Dr Burney's great-great-grandson, Charles Burney (1840–1912), whose widow owned it in 1918; not further traced until acquired by wsl from Peter Murray Hill (Rare Books) Ltd, Jan. 1954.

Berkeley Square, Dec. 19, 1787.

Dear Sir,

I HAVE been very unlucky twice when you have been so good as to call on me, particularly today, for as I came home, I saw across the square a chariot stop at my door, and go away because I was not here. When I learnt who it was, I sent after, but could not overtake you. I very seldom do go out before dinner, and as I find, besides being unpleasant, that it brings me bad luck, I will leave off such a foolish custom, and trust to my Penates for rewarding my piety by bringing you again soon. However, not to draw my household gods into a scrape, I will let them into a secret; I am to keep my Christmas with my rural Lares, and shall certainly not be in town after Sunday for a few days;[1] therefore should you have any inspiration to visit me in the beginning of next week, be sure it is at the instigation of the Wicked One, and I advise you to drive him away like Saul's evil spirit;[2] *you* well know how.[3]

Yours most sincerely

Hor. Walpole

1. HW was still in town on Saturday, 22 Dec., when he wrote to Mrs Dickenson (More 256); he had returned to Berkeley Square from SH by the 28th (see following letter).

2. I Samuel 16. 23: 'And it came to pass, when the evil spirit from God was upon Saul, that David took an harp, and played with his hand: so Saul was refreshed, and was well, and the evil spirit departed from him.'

3. Dr Burney was an accomplished musician.

To the Hon. Mrs Boyle Walsingham,
Friday 28 December 1787

Printed for the first time from a photostat of the MS in the possession of the Hon. John William Boyle, Craigantaggart, Dunkeld, Perthshire. The MS passed by family descent to Mrs Boyle Walsingham's great-great-granddaughter, Lady Evelyn Boyle (d. 1965, unmarried), who left it to her nephew, the present owner.

Berkeley Square, Dec. 28, 1787.

THE SNOW delayed the post so late yesterday,[1] dear Madam, that I was at dinner and could not answer your letter before today.

I should be extremely ashamed to have you think of taking the trouble to carry the Cowley[2] yourself to Strawberry Hill. I am persuaded it would go very safely by itself in your chaise, if only laid flat at the bottom, with nobody in the chaise. When there, will you please to order it to be delivered to my housekeeper,[3] and set in the Blue Room,[4] but not put into the frame till I come there myself.

I long, Madam, to see your copy, and as much to see your library,[5] though I have seen so many of your works, and so many proofs of your and Miss Boyle's taste,[6] and such samples of the library, that my impatience is moderated by my faith, and both are chained by the bad weather, and by a less changeable tyrant, the gout, with which I have had various skirmishes, in some of which I have been made prisoner, though I soon made my escape each time.[7] I came to town with an inflammation in my eye from the same enemy. It is but just gone, after falling on my lip and cheek, and giving me what sounds ridiculous for me, a *swelled face*. I remember that a thousand years

1. The *Daily Adv.* 26 Dec. reported: 'Not above half the mails arrived yesterday at the General Post Office, being kept out by the great fall of snow. . . . A person who came from Highgate yesterday morning on foot says, that in several places he was up to the middle in snow, and that further up the country it is in many places near two yards deep.'

2. A portrait of Abraham Cowley (1618–67), the poet, by Sir Peter Lely. HW acquired it at the sale of Edward Lovibond in 1776; it hung in the Breakfast Room at SH (OSSORY i. 294 n. 11). HW had lent the portrait to Mrs Boyle Walsingham to copy.

3. Ann Bransom.

4. HW doubtless means the Breakfast Room, which was 'furnished with blue paper, and blue and white linen,' rather than the Blue Bedchamber ('Des. of SH,' *Works* ii. 421).

5. At Boyle Farm, Thames Ditton, Surrey. See n. 14 below.

6. See *ante* 26 July 1787 and n. 5.

7. 'I have had no formal gout, but several skirmishes with it that have confined me for two or three days at a time' (HW to Lady Ossory 16 Dec. 1787, OSSORY ii. 586).

ago when I was at Reggio I caught a distemper of the country,[8] which dilated my whole head to a monstrous size. It came on rapidly and retired so precipitately, that when the Italian physician,[9] who had only seen me in bed with such chuffy cheeks, found me sitting in my chair in open day with my pale meager face, he thought a trick was playing on him, and would not believe I had been his real patient.

As my constitution has not at present the same bladder-like activity, I dare not gratify my curiosity, great as it is, yet. Nay, Madam, I conclude you will be in town, before I shall venture into the country. However the late sultry weather may have persuaded you that July was come six months before its time, the deuce is in it if from Sunday night[10] you have not been fetched back to the almanac's true reckoning.

For Miss Boyle's despair of copying the family of Digby,[11] I don't value it of a rush. Don't tell me, Madam; Miss Boyle can do what she pleases; nay, she can do what *you* please. If you bid her paint your whole house, make all the furniture, carve all the chimney-pieces, cast waxen babies, build a theatre for *fantoccini*,[12] write a pantomime, and dance the figures, copy all the Duke of Marlborough's gems[13] in a breath—why, she does all and more.[14] Well, if I cannot

---

8. In May 1741, while travelling in Italy on the Grand Tour, HW 'fell ill at Reggio of a kind of quinsy, and was given over for fifteen hours, escaping with great difficulty' ('Short Notes,' GRAY i. 10 and n. 62).

9. Antonio Cocchi (1695–1758), Florentine physician (ibid. i. 231 n. 9).

10. 23 Dec.

11. HW owned sixteen miniatures of the Digby family, purchased in two lots from descendants of the family in 1771 and 1775 (*ante* 25 May 1773, nn. 22, 23). The miniature that Miss Boyle copied was probably the family group of Sir Kenelm Digby, his wife, and two sons, by Peter Oliver, after Van Dyck ('Des. of SH,' *Works* ii. 426); her copy is preserved along with the MS of the letter (see headnote).

12. Puppets.

13. The celebrated collection of gems formed by George Spencer (1739–1817), 3d (4th) Duke of Marlborough, 1758. Most of the gems came from the Arundelian collection of cameos and intaglios, presented by Lady Elizabeth Germain to the Duke's brother, Lord Charles Spencer, who gave them (as intended) to the Duke. The Duke purchased for £5000 Lord Bessborough's collection of gems and, in 1761, most of those in the collection of Conte Antonio Maria Zanetti of Venice (HW's 'Book of Materials,' 1759, p. 178 *bis*, now WSL; MANN v. 561). The Duke's collection is described in *Gemmarum antiquarum delectus; ex præstantioribus desumptus, quæ in Dactyliothecis Ducis Marlburiensis conservantur*, privately printed, 2 vols, folio, 1781–90. HW's copy of this work, now WSL, is Hazen, *Cat of HW's Lib.*, No. 3625; it contains an extended note by HW in Kirgate's hand concerning the history of the collection.

14. Hannah More wrote to one of her sisters in Dec. 1787: 'I never was so astonished as to see this large and very elegant house already completely furnished; all the beautiful purple and gold pilasters of the magnificent library, the chimney pieces, sculpture as well as painting, both

DR ANTONIO COCCHI, AFTER JOSEPH WILTON

almost believe, your house was built in such a twinkling, that you sometimes made her scramble up a ladder with a hod of mortar on her shoulder. Positively I shall think it is your fault by setting her on some such day-labour, that she has not yet finished her copy of the Digbys in perfection.

Miss Anti-Lactilla[15] is mighty cunning, after a parenthesis of three months of silence,[16] to promise me a letter soon—but she will be caught, for I am to dine with her at Mrs Montagu's on Tuesday next,[17] and then I will snap her nose off, unless perhaps when I come so near her face, I may soften my movement, and make a less violent attack.

Your Christmas I don't doubt, Madam, has been very agreeable with Mrs Garrick and Miss Moore[18] (for *you* are in charity with the latter) but I cannot find in my heart to wish you so happy a New Year, since, as I have just told you, I am to profit by your loss. Bating the first day, you have my best wishes for the rest of the whole twelvemonth, and I have the honour to be with great regard

> Dear Madam,
> Your most obedient humble servant
>
> HOR. WALPOLE

designed and executed by Miss Boyle. The doors are adorned with rich paintings, copied from the Vatican; the panels, pictures emblematical of the arts and sciences, from the Herculaneum, all done by that young lady in the short space of a year!' (William Roberts, *Memoirs of the Life and Correspondence of Mrs Hannah More*, 1834, ii. 94).

15. Hannah More. During the summer of 1786 a quarrel had arisen between her and Ann Yearsley, the poetical milkwoman of Bristol, whose *Poems on Several Occasions*, 1785, had been sponsored by Miss More and Mrs Montagu; HW referred to Mrs Yearsley as 'Lactilla' in letters to Miss More (MORE 218 n. 1, 244 and n. 3, 253–4 and n. 12).

16. Hannah More's most recent letter to HW was written in early October (ibid. 251).

17. This 'very select little party in Portman Square' on New Year's Day is described in a letter from Hannah More to one of her sisters 11 Jan. 1788, quoted ibid. 258. See also *Mrs Montagu, 'Queen of the Blues,'* ed. Reginald Blunt, 1923, ii. 218.

18. Hannah More was by this time in the habit of spending the winter with Mrs Garrick at Hampton (MORE 348 and n. 3). HW wrote Miss More 14 Oct 1787: 'I hope it will not be long before you remove [from Cowslip Green] to Hampton' (ibid. 256).

To Edward Gibbon, ?early 1788

Printed for the first time from a photostat of the MS in the British Museum (Add. MS 34,886, f. 55). For the history of the MS see *ante* ca 12 Feb. 1776.

The letter was written between 9 Jan. 1781, when Gibbon's friend J. B. Holroyd was created Lord Sheffield, and 5 Dec. 1791, the day that HW succeeded his nephew as 4th Earl of Orford. The only two periods within these dates when Gibbon and the Duchess of Gloucester were in England at the same time were from 1781 to the summer of 1782 (when the Duke and Duchess embarked on a Continental journey that lasted five and a half years), and from 10 Nov. 1787 (the date of their return) to July 1788 (when Gibbon went back to Lausanne). The handwriting of the MS is clearly of the later period.

I WAS extremely sorry, dear Sir, that I could not receive the honour of your visit yesterday, as the Duchess of Gloucester was come to speak to me on a little business.[1]

I am as sorry that I cannot satisfy you or Lord Sheffield[2] about the portrait,[3] whose face I do not know. Nor am I much wiser about the painter—most of the information I gave of our artists[4] was transcribed from Vertue's notes,[5] and few of them deserved to have their manner studied or remembered. The face, and especially, the right hand, in the picture you have sent me, are very well painted, and by what I can recollect of a few of his works, I should think the painter was Sir John Medina.[6] I have a portrait of Lord Rochester[7] in the same kind of dress, *mi-partie*, Roman and Common Pleas, but mine is by Greenhill[8] and not near so well coloured. I am ashamed whenever I am consulted, for I ought to understand better than I do the trifling branches about which I have employed myself.

Yours most obediently

Hor. Walpole

1. Not explained.
2. John Baker Holroyd (1735–1821), cr. (1781, 1783, and 1802) Bn Sheffield and (1816) E. of Sheffield; M.P.; Gibbon's intimate friend and literary executor.
3. Not identified.
4. In *Anecdotes of Painting in England*.
5. See *ante* 29 Aug. 1758, n. 5.
6. Sir John Baptist Medina (ca 1660–1710), Kt, 1707; portrait painter. HW included an article on him in *Anecdotes of Painting, Works* iii. 375–6. For a recent account see John Fleming, 'Sir John Medina and his "Postures",' *Connoisseur*, 1961, cxlviii. 22–5.

7. John Wilmot (1647–80), 2d E. of Rochester, 1658; poet. HW's portrait of 'Wilmot, Earl of Rochester' was at his house in Berkeley Square and is included in the 'List of Pictures in London to be sent to Houghton' appended to HW's will (Selwyn 370). HW may have been mistaken about the subject of the portrait; no portrait of Rochester is mentioned in later accounts of the pictures at Houghton.
8. John Greenhill (1649–76), painter.

To ?Bishop Percy, Wednesday 2 January 1788

Printed for the first time from a photostat of the MS in the Henry E. Huntington Library. The MS is untraced until acquired by Maggs in a collection from a member of the Hastings family; sold by Maggs with the Hastings Collection to Huntington in 1927.

The addressee, either a nobleman or a bishop, is tentatively identified as Thomas Percy, who became Bishop of Dromore in 1782. Percy's interest in historical and antiquarian subjects, along with his eagerness to communicate scholarly curiosities, makes him the most likely candidate among HW's acquaintance at this date.

Berkeley Square, Jan. 2d 1788.

My Lord,

I was gone out to have the honour of waiting on your Lordship, when you was so good as to send me the papal bull,[1] which I return with many thanks.

It is very curious and remarkable, since it not only records the title by victory, but the King had got crowded into it every other kind of claim, however contradictory; for *right, conquest,* and *election*[2] are rather repugnant than confirmative—but impudent power does not give itself the trouble of reasoning consequentially; and the Holy Father himself[3] was no better a logician; for after granting the bull to confirm the marriage between Henry and Elizabeth *for the conservation of universal peace and eschewing of slanders*[4] by the union of the two houses, he opens a door to the

1. The papal bull issued by Innocent VIII, confirming the marriage of Henry VII and Elizabeth of York in 1486. The original bull, dated 27 March 1486, is in the Public Record Office; the text is printed in Thomas Rymer's *Fœdera, conventiones, literæ, et cujuscunque generis acta publica,* 1703–35, xii. 297–9. HW, who did not own a set of the *Fœdera,* was apparently sent a copy of Henry VII's proclamation in English summarizing the papal bull. The proclamation was printed on a single folio sheet by W. de Machlinia in London sometime after 13 June 1486; the text is given in *Tudor Royal Proclamations,* ed. P. L. Hughes and J. F. Larkin, New Haven, 1964–9, i. 6–7.

2. 'And in likewise His Holiness confirmeth, establisheth, and approveth the right and title to the crown of E[ngland] of the said our sovereign lord Henry VII . . . as well by reason of his nighest and undoubted title of succession as by the right of his most noble [victory], and by election of the lords spiritual and temporal and other nobles of his realm, and by the [ordi]nance and authority of parliament made by the three estates of this land' (ibid. i. 6).

3. Innocent VIII (Giovanni Battista Cibò) (1432–92), pope 1484–92.

4. The exact words of the proclamation are: 'for conservation of the universal peace and eschewing of slanders' (ibid. i. 6).

renewal of the quarrel by settling the crown, in case the Queen should die without issue, on the children of Henry by any other wife,[5] though the Queen left sisters,[6] who would have an equal right to the crown that she had had[7]—but both Henry VII and his son[8] took a surer way of preventing competitors, by beheading all the princes and princesses of the House of York that they could get into their power.[9] *Being nighest to the crown,*[10] which Henry, though falsely, pretended was his own title, he held, in the case of others, a reason for cutting off their heads.

I should beg your Lordship's pardon for troubling you with these observations, if I did not think it more respectful to show your Lordship how attentively I have examined the curiosity with which you have been pleased to favour,

My Lord
Your Lordship's most respectful obedient
and obliged humble servant

Horace Walpole

5. 'Furthermore he approveth, confirmeth, and declareth that if it please God that the said Eli[zabeth], which God forbid, should decease without issue between our sovereign lord and her of their bodies bor[n and had], then such issue as between him and her whom after that God shall join him to shall be had and born [shall be] heritors to the same crown and realm of England' (ibid. i. 7).

6. Elizabeth's surviving sisters at her death in 1503 were Cecily (or Cecilia) (1469–1507), m. 1 (1487) John Welles, Lord Welles, 1485, cr. (1486) Vct Welles; m. 2 (ca 1503) Thomas Kyme; Anne (1475–?1511), m. (1495) Lord Thomas Howard; Katherine (1479–1527), m. (?1495) William Courtenay, cr. (1511) E. of Devon; and Bridget (1480–before 1513) (M. A. E. Green, *Lives of the Princesses of England*, 1850–55, iii. 395–437, iv. 1–48; GEC).

7. Since, as sisters, they were all daughters of Edward IV.

8. Henry VIII.

9. Edward, Earl of Warwick (*ante* 29 Dec. 1767, nn. 15, 17), eldest son of George, Duke of Clarence, and nephew of Edward IV and Richard III, was imprisoned in the Tower by Henry VII in 1485 and finally executed in 1499. In the same year

Henry did away with Perkin Warbeck (ibid. n. 23), pretender to the throne, whom some people (including HW) believed to be the true Duke of York, younger son of Edward IV. Edmund de la Pole (ca 1471–1513), Earl of Suffolk, who, after Warwick, was the lineal heir to the pretensions of the House of York, was imprisoned in the Tower by Henry VII in 1506 and executed by Henry VIII in 1513. Edward IV's grandson Henry Courtenay (ca 1498–1539), Marquess of Exeter, whose father had been imprisoned 1503–9 by Henry VII, was executed for high treason by Henry VIII in 1539, along with Henry Pole (ca 1492–1539), Lord Montagu, the grandson and eldest representative of George, Duke of Clarence. Montagu's mother, Margaret (1473–1541), Countess of Salisbury, daughter of George, Duke of Clarence, was beheaded in 1541 (Montagu i. 98 n. 25). Henry VIII also executed in 1521 Edward Stafford (1478–1521), 3d Duke of Buckingham, who, as a descendant of Edward III, was a potential rival for the throne. See S. B. Chrimes, *Lancastrians, Yorkists, and Henry VII*, 2d edn, 1966, pp. 158–63.

10. See n. 2 above.

To the REV. JOSEPH WARTON, Friday 18 January 1788

Printed for the first time from the MS now WSL. The MS was formerly owned by John Mitford (1781–1859), the editor of Gray's *Works;* sold Sotheby's 9 July 1860 (Mitford Sale), lot 5 (with HW to Warton 19 July 1789, in a large collection of letters), to Boone; later in the possession of Sir Thomas Phillipps (Phillipps MS 1778); acquired from the Phillipps collection by William H. Robinson Ltd, who sold it to James M. Osborn in 1955; given by Osborn to WSL, May 1955.
Endorsed by Warton: Mr Walpole's note—

Berkeley Square, Jan. 18, 1788.

MR WALPOLE waited on Dr Warton yesterday; and now begs him to thank the gentleman[1] who has been so obliging as to send him the essay on mezzotinto,[2] which however Mr Walpole has possessed for some time,[3] and did read with much pleasure and satisfaction, as a very sensible, modest, and candid tract—perhaps too candid, as it mentions the writer of this with more indulgence than he deserves,[4] his *Anecdotes* being frequently erroneous, and compiled[5] with too little attention and care.

As the gentleman proposes a new edition,[6] Mr Walpole will be very glad to see him, or to assist him with any little information in his power.

1. Rev. James Chelsum (1738–1801), D.D., 1773; rector of Droxford, Hants, vicar of Lathbury, Bucks, and rector of Badger, Salop; author of works attacking Gibbon's *Decline and Fall of the Roman Empire* (Foster, *Alumni Oxon.;* DNB).
2. *A History of the Art of Engraving in Mezzotinto,* Winchester, 1786, published anonymously by Chelsum.
3. HW's copy (untraced) is Hazen, *Cat. of HW's Lib.,* No. 288:5.
4. Chelsum wrote in his *History* (p. 2) that 'much may be found respecting this

art [of engraving in mezzotinto] both in Mr Walpole's elegant *Catalogue of English Engravers* compiled from the papers of Vertue, and in the well-known *Biographical History of England* by Mr Granger.' On p. 6, n. 6, he refers to HW as 'this distinguished author.' There are numerous references throughout the book to HW's *Anecdotes of Painting in England,* including the *Catalogue of Engravers.*
5. The MS reads 'complied.'
6. This was apparently never published.

TO EDWARD KING, Saturday 26 January 1788

Printed for the first time from a photostat of the MS in the Fitzwilliam Museum, Cambridge. The MS is untraced until acquired by the Fitzwilliam Museum as part of the Ashcombe Collection (I. 77), presented by the 2d Baron Ashcombe in Aug. 1917.

Berkeley Square, Jan. 26, 1788.

MR WALPOLE begs leave to thank Mr King for the honour he has done him by his valuable present,[1] which Mr Walpole is sure he shall read with great pleasure and instruction.

Mr Walpole was extremely sorry he was just going to Gloucester House[2] by appointment,[3] when Mr King did him the honour of calling last.

TO EDMOND MALONE, Sunday 3 February 1788

Printed from the MS now WSL, removed from an extra-illustrated copy of HW's *Reminiscences* that belonged to Malone. First printed in J. M. Osborn, 'Horace Walpole and Edmond Malone,' in *Horace Walpole: Writer, Politician, and Connoisseur,* ed. W. H. Smith, New Haven, 1967, p. 318. The copy of *Reminiscences* was sold by W. Heffer and Sons, Ltd, to WSL in Aug. 1950; its earlier history is not known.
Dated by the endorsement.
Endorsed by Malone: (Feb. 3, 1788.)
Address: To Edmond Malone Esq.

MR WALPOLE begs Mr Malone a thousand pardons, but will own fairly that he had forgotten Mr Malone's commands,[1] but hopes it will be imputed to the badness of his memory at seventy.

1. A copy of King's *Morsels of Criticism, Tending to Illustrate Some Few Passages in the Holy Scriptures upon Philosophical Principles and an Enlarged View of Things*, 1788; it is Hazen, *Cat. of HW's Lib.*, No. 3241. See MORE 281 and n. 14.
2. The Duke of Gloucester's house in London.
3. Doubtless to see his niece, the Duchess of Gloucester.

1. Malone wished to borrow (for use in his edition of Shakespeare) the original mortgage deed, signed by Shakespeare and dated 11 March 1613, relating to the purchase of a gate-house in Blackfriars, London. The deed had been discovered in 1768 by Albany Wallis, David Garrick's friend and lawyer, among the title deeds of the Rev. Utrick Fetherstonhaugh, of Oxted, Surrey; Fetherstonhaugh presented

Mr Walpole will endeavour to make amends for his fault without delay.[2]

To Edmond Malone, Thursday 7 February 1788

Printed from a photostat of the MS in the British Museum (Add. MS 33,964, f. 16). First printed in J. M. Osborn, 'Horace Walpole and Edmond Malone,' in *Horace Walpole: Writer, Politician, and Connoisseur,* ed. W. H. Smith, New Haven, 1967, p. 319, n. 36. The MS is untraced until acquired by the British Museum in a collection of letters of sovereigns, noblemen, and others in 1891 (bequest of Andrew George Kurtz, of Liverpool).

Although HW dated the letter 'Feb. 7th 1789,' it clearly belongs with his letter of 3 Feb. 1788 to Malone.

Berkeley Square, Feb. 7th 178[8].[1]

Sir,

MRS GARRICK is at Hampton,[2] but I have written to her,[3] and[4] she has been so obliging as to promise[5] to bring the deed to town in [a] few days and to lend it to me for you; but she was afraid of sending it by the coach. You shall have it as soon as I receive it.[6]

I am Sir
Your most obedient humble servant

Hor. Walpole

the deed to Garrick in April of that year. See S. Schoenbaum, *William Shakespeare: A Documentary Life,* New York, 1975, pp. 224–5, No. 183; *The Letters of David Garrick,* ed. D. M. Little and G. M. Kahrl, Cambridge, Mass., 1963, ii. 604. See *post* 7 Feb. 1788.

2. The next day, 4 Feb. 1788, HW wrote to Hannah More: 'Mr Malone, who is *about* Shakespeare, desired me, before you came to town, to ask Mrs Garrick to lend him for a few days the deed in her possession to which Shakespeare's name is subcribed, wishing, I suppose, to have a *facsimile* engraved from it. . . . Mr Malone . . . is such a man of honour, and so true a devotee, that Mrs Garrick may

safely trust the deed with him' (More 259–60). See following letter.

———

1. See headnote.
2. See *ante* 3 Aug. 1757, n. 2.
3. HW actually wrote to Hannah More, who was spending the winter at Hampton with Mrs Garrick. See previous letter, n. 2.
4. 'but' crossed out in the MS.
5. No letter from Mrs Garrick to HW around this time has been found.
6. Shakespeare's mortgage deed, along with an explanatory letter from Albany Wallis to David Garrick 18 April 1768, was delivered to Malone on 13 Feb. See More 259–60 nn. 4, 5, where Malone's use of the deed in his edition of Shakespeare is discussed.

To Sir Joseph Banks, Saturday 9 February 1788

Printed from a photostat of the MS inserted in an extra-illustrated copy of James T. Fields, *Yesterdays with Authors*, Boston, 1887, now in the Massachusetts Historical Society. First printed, Toynbee *Supp.* iii. 337. The MS was formerly owned by Dawson Turner (1775–1858), the botanist and antiquary, and was probably sold Puttick and Simpson 10 June 1859 (Dawson Turner Sale), lot 680 (in a 54-volume collection of autographs); later acquired by Curtis Guild, Jr (1827–1911), who extra-illustrated the copy of *Yesterdays with Authors;* acquired with Guild's library by the Massachusetts Historical Society in Dec. 1949. A MS copy of the letter, made by one of Dawson Turner's daughters or by one of his clerks, is in the General Library of the British Museum (Natural History), South Kensington (Banksian Correspondence, vol. VI, f. 10).

Berkeley Square, Feb. 9, 1788.

I HAVE no right, dear Sir, to ask a favour of you—but I could not refuse to lend my name, of however little weight, to a recommendation, when it was solicited by a most ingenious and worthy man. Mr Pinkerton[1] is very ambitious to succeed the gentleman,[2] who, he hears, is likely to attain Mr Planta's[3] place at the Museum, if the latter quits it;[4] and Mr Pinkerton imagines that my asking your interest,[5] if not engaged,[6] might be serviceable to him. If his own merit were not a much better plea, I am sure I should not think my canvassing for him would be worth a straw; and without his merit, I should not wish it were, as the post ought to be properly

1. John Pinkerton, HW's friend and correspondent.
2. Probably the Rev. Richard Southgate (1729–95), collector and numismatist; assistant keeper of the MSS and medals at the British Museum 1784–95 (CHATTERTON 325 n. 2). Southgate assisted Pinkerton in preparing the second edition (1789) of his *Essay on Medals.*
3. Joseph Planta (1744–1827), assistant keeper of the printed books at the British Museum 1773–6; under librarian and keeper of the MSS and medals 1776–99; principal librarian 1799–1827 (ibid. 295 n. 4).
4. Planta had sought the permission of the principal trustees of the British Museum to go abroad, but was refused. He did not resign his post, as Pinkerton believed he might. See n. 6 below.

5. As president of the Royal Society, Banks was a trustee *ex-officio* of the British Museum (*Royal Kalendar*, 1788, p. 213).
6. HW wrote Pinkerton 11 Feb. 1788: 'I wrote a letter to Sir Joseph Banks soliciting his interest for you, should there be a vacancy at the Museum. He answered . . . that he is positively engaged to Mr Torkelyn [Grimur Jonsson Thorkelin (1752–1829), antiquary and editor], should Mr Planta resign; but that the Chancellor having refused to sign the permission for the latter, who will not go abroad without that indulgence, no vacancy is likely to happen from that event. Sir Joseph has since called on me to make excuses for not complying with my request' (CHATTERTON 294–5). Banks's reply to HW's letter is missing.

filled.[7] I look upon myself therefore as only the mouth of his modesty; ⟨and⟩ if I want the latter myself, I hope my zeal for merit will excuse ⟨m⟩y impertinence in taking the liberty. I have the honour to be ⟨wi⟩th great respect, Sir,

Your most obedient humble servant

Hor. Walpole

To Unknown, Saturday 15 March 1788

Printed for the first time from the MS now wsl. The MS is untraced until sold Hodgson's 20 Oct. 1938 (property of the late Thomas A. Gilbert), lot 527, to Maggs for wsl.
Endorsed in pencil in a later hand: Mrs Gilbert.

March 15, 1788.

I RETURN you the plays, Madam, with thanks: I saw this French *Hamlet*[1] when it was first acted at Paris some years ago;[2] and though the author talks of its success, I am much mistaken if it was acted above twice,[3] nor could Mlle Dumesnil[4] and Molé[5] save it. The author says he does not understand English;[6] he is still farther from having conceived Shakespeare! How happy for us that Shakespeare was as ignorant of the ridiculous etiquettes of the French

7. When Southgate (n. 2 above) died in 1795, Pinkerton again asked HW to recommend him for the vacant position at the British Museum; see ibid. 325–6.

1. An adaptation of Shakespeare's tragedy by Jean-François Ducis (1733–1817), based on the French translation by Pierre-Antoine de la Place.
2. Ducis's *Hamlet* was first acted by the Comédie-Française in Paris on 30 Sept. 1769. HW attended the opening performance with Mme du Deffand and other friends ('Paris Journals,' du Deffand v. 332). See Chute 121.
3. There were nine performances at the Comédie-Française in 1769 and three performances in 1770. At all of these performances the rôle of Hamlet was played by Molé and the rôle of Gertrude by Mlle

du Mesnil. Ducis's *Hamlet* was considered to be a great success; it had 208 performances in France between 1769 and 1851 (Sylvie Chevalley, 'Ducis, Shakespeare et les Comédiens français, I,' *Revue d'histoire du théâtre,* 1964, No. 4, 327–50).
4. Marie-Françoise Marchand (1713–1803), called Mlle du Mesnil; actress.
5. François-René Molé (1734–1802), actor.
6. In the 'Avertissement' to *Hamlet, tragédie, imitée de l'anglais,* 1770, Ducis writes: 'Je n'entends point l'anglais et j'ai osé faire paraître *Hamlet* sur la scène française. Tout le monde connaît le mérite du *Théâtre anglois* de M. de la Place. C'est d'après cet ouvrage précieux à la littérature que j'ai entrepris de rendre une des plus singulières tragédies de S[h]akespeare.'

stage! What marvellous beauties should we have lost, if he had learnt to ride in a Parisian *manège!*

I like the *École des pères*[7] pretty well—I wish it was natural and probable! The *Amis à l'épreuve*[8] is very feeble.

Your most obedient servant

HOR. WALPOLE

To THOMAS PENNANT, Sunday 20 April 1788

Printed from the MS now WSL. First printed, Toynbee *Supp.* iii. 50–2. The MS is untraced until offered by Maggs, Cat. Nos 333 (spring 1915), lot 435; 360 (autumn 1917), lot 2344; 386 (Christmas 1919), lot 3162; 425 (summer 1922), lot 1841; 497 (Christmas 1927), lot 2612; 560 (summer 1931), lot 726; sold by them to Miss Abby L. Tallmadge, of Evanston, Illinois; given by her in Nov. 1950 to R. W. Chapman, who gave it to WSL, 21 Nov. 1950.

Address: To Thomas Pennant Esq. at Downing, Flintshire. *Postmark:* AP 21 88.

Strawberry Hill, April 20, 1788.

I HAVE received, dear Sir, the favour of your letter,[1] and the agreeable present of your tract on the Patagonians,[2] which is very curious and informing, and for which I return you many thanks.

I am much obliged to you too, Sir, for your kind inquiries after my health; it is tolerably returned, though I had a very severe attack of the gout this winter.[3]

I do not remember what my last letter was,[4] but am very sorry if it gave you any cause to think that I am not grateful for all your favours. My age and decays might be in fault, not my intention. Of them and of my perishing memory I am very sensible; and they have brought on, not only idolence, but a fear of trusting to my

---

7. A comedy in five acts in verse by Pierre-Alexandre Pieyre (1752–1830), first acted at the Théâtre Français 1 June 1787 (*Journal de Paris*, 1787, pt i. 669).

8. A comedy in one act in verse, also by Pieyre, first acted at the Théâtre Français 19 July 1787 (ibid., 1787, pt ii. 887).

1. Missing.

2. *Of the Patagonians. Formed from the Relation of Father Falkener, a Jesuit who*

Had Resided among them Thirty Eight Years, Darlington, 1788. Forty copies only were printed for Pennant by George Allan at his private press at Blackwell Grange, near Darlington, Durham. HW's copy (untraced) is Hazen, *Cat. of HW's Lib.,* No. 2443. See *ante* 2 Jan. 1787, n. 5.

3. See *ante* 28 Dec. 1787.

4. It was presumably his letter *ante* 10 Oct. 1787.

recollection. I have very little knowledge but of trifles; and not refreshing that idle store, I cannot depend on myself, and therefore am cautious lest I mislead others. The lameness of my fingers contributes to the shortness of my letters and has made me reduce my correspondence to little or none.[5] If therefore I was too brief in my last, you will have the goodness, dear Sir, to excuse a very old man, who is not only past 70, but has been afflicted with fits of the gout for a third of that time, and who is consequently very unfit to make a pleasant correspondent. I am conscious of my defects, but ingratitude is not of the number, and I am very sincerely

Dear Sir
    Your most obliged and most obedient humble servant

HOR. WALPOLE

PS. I do not know whether Col. Mydelton[6] told you, Sir, what a valuable present he has been so kind as to send me of the picture of Prince Arthur and Q[ueen] Katherine.[7] I not only ought not to be silent on it, but must add that his desiring a portrait of my father[8] in return, and the letter[9] I have since had the pleasure of receiving from him, are favours still more grateful to me than the picture, curious as it is; for my father's memory is much dearer to me than the greatest rarity.

5. HW certainly wrote fewer letters now than in the past, but he continued to correspond fairly regularly with Lady Ossory and with newer friends such as Hannah More.
6. Richard Myddelton (1726–95), of Chirk Castle, Denbighshire; M.P. He was for some time Colonel of the Denbighshire militia (*Chirk Castle Accounts A.D. 1666–1753*, ed. W. M. Myddelton, Manchester, 1931, p. 467, n. 2578).
7. Catherine (1485–1536) of Aragon, m. 1

(1501) Arthur (1486–1502), P. of Wales; m. 2 (1509) Henry VIII of England. The picture of 'Prince Arthur and Catharine of Arragon, on board, in the original frame; a present from Colonel Myddelton of Denbighshire, in which county it had remained from the death of the Prince at Ludlow,' was hung in the Yellow Bedchamber, or Beauty Room, at SH ('Des. of SH,' *Works* ii. 420).
8. Sir Robert Walpole.
9. Missing.

To Thomas Pennant, Wednesday 30 April 1788

Printed for the first time from the MS now wsl. For the history of the MS see *ante* 25 May 1773.
Address: To Thomas Pennant Esq. at Downing, Flintshire. *Postmark:* AP 30 88.

Berkeley Square, April 30, 1789[8].

NICHOLS the printer has just published two enormous quartos, and meditates a third, on the progresses of Queen Elizabeth.[1] Few of the pieces are quite new, and scarce any of the prints[2]—but all together they form (and they should only be together) no history of her reign, but a vast mass both of her pomp and economy. They prove too that she was as fond of flattery as Louis Quatorze; and if his flatterers had more taste, hers were more excusable, as Venus, Ceres, Bacchus, Mars, Diana etc. were newer to the age than they were a century later.

My reason, dear Sir, for giving you this notice, is, that having turned the volumes over (for I did not attempt to read the Latin verses of Cambridge and Oxford,[3] nor Churchyard's English[4]) I found in the second volume a list of the London-houses of the nobility in Elizabeth's time, from a MS by Norden in the British Museum,[5] which will be of use to you[6]—as other passages up and

1. *The Progresses, and Public Processions, of Queen Elizabeth,* 2 vols, 1788, by John Nichols, HW's occasional correspondent. HW's copy (untraced) is Hazen, *Cat. of HW's Lib.,* No. 3353. At the end of the Preface (i. xxxii) Nichols solicited other 'particulars' concerning Elizabeth's progresses, noting that 'at a proper period they shall certainly be published in a future volume.' A third volume appeared in 1805.

2. The two volumes contain forty-five plates, including the frontispiece to vol. I and several engravings in the text.

3. In the first volume Nichols reprinted various poems in Latin celebrating Queen Elizabeth's visits to Cambridge in August 1564 and to Oxford in August–Sept. 1566; the second volume contains verses on her visit to Oxford in Sept. 1592.

4. In the second volume Nichols included three pieces by Thomas Churchyard (?1520–1604): *A Discourse of the Queenes Majesties Entertainment in Suffolk and Norffolk* (1578), *A Rebuke to Rebellion* (1588), and *A Pleasant Conceite Penned in Verse . . . Presented, on New-Yeeres-Day last, to the Queenes Majestie, at Hampton Court* (1593).

5. 'The Houses of Noblemen betwene Charinge-Crosse and Temple-Barr briefly recompted' is part of 'Norden's Description of Queen Elizabeth's Palaces. (From A MS in the British Museum.)' The MS is presumably Harleian MS 570, which is the original MS of *Speculum Britanniæ. The First Parte. An Historicall, and Chorographicall Discription of Middlesex,* 1593, by John Norden (1548–1625), topographer.

6. Pennant was gathering materials for his *Of London,* published in 1790. See *ante* 10 Oct. 1787, n. 2.

down those volumes will also be. I cannot easily direct you to the page, for never was book so absurdly paged—each year recommencing the paging—but when you see the book, you must look for page 42, after the accounts of the Queen's sickness and death.[7] I hope this zeal will atone for my brevity of which you complained,[8] and show how much I interest myself in your works, and that I am, dear Sir

Your obedient servant

HORACE WALPOLE

To Richard Gough, Thursday 8 May 1788

Printed from the MS now WSL. First printed, Nichols, *Lit. Anec.* vi. 291 (enclosure omitted). Reprinted, Toynbee xiv. 46 (enclosure omitted). The MS presumably came into the possession of John Nichols about the time of the publication of *Literary Anecdotes,* vol. vi (1812), and descended in the Nichols family; sold Sotheby's 18 Nov. 1929 (John Gough Nichols Sale), lot 234, to Maggs; later acquired by Walter T. Spencer, who sold it to WSL, Sept. 1932.

Endorsed by John Bowyer Nichols: To Richard Gough Esq. (Printed in 'Literary Anecdotes.')

Address: To Richard Gough Esq. at Enfield.

Berkeley Square, May 8th 1788.

SINCE your draftsman[1] was with me, Sir, I can give you a little better answer to your queries, than I could then extempore, especially as I had then a person[2] with me on business. I have since been at Strawberry Hill and thought I recollected a rude sketch of the head of Charles VI[3] in Vertue's MSS.[4] I was so lucky as to find it, and enclose a still ruder sketch (for I never could draw well, and my

---

7. 'The Houses of Noblemen . . .' appears on pp. 42–3 of the section beginning with 'The Queen's last Sickness and Death, 1602' in the second volume of Nichols's *Progresses.*

8. See previous letter.

———

1. Probably Jacob Schnebbelie (1760–92), who made many drawings for Part II

of Gough's *Sepulchral Monuments in Great Britain,* published in 1796.

2. Not identified.

3. (1368–1422), K. of France 1380–1422.

4. See *ante* 29 Aug. 1758, n. 5. Vertue's sketch of Charles VI is reproduced in Vertue Note Books, *Walpole Society* 1931–2, xx. 46.

lame fingers are yet more incapable now). The attire of the head is precisely the same with that of our fourth Henry.[5] Vertue's account I have transcribed too.[6]

I was very sure I had seen somewhere an account of Joan of Navarre[7] being suspected by Henry V. I looked into Stowe,[8] Hollingshed[9] and Hall,[10] but they mention no such thing.[11] Nor can I recollect where I found it—but Rapin does touch on it briefly in the place I have set down.[12] Still I am positive I have seen rather a fuller account of it, though I cannot recall where.

I hope, Sir, you received the letter[13] in which I told you of my imperfect negotiation with Lord Monson[14] about the pictures at Brox-

5. The head-dress is very similar to that in Vertue's engraving of Henry IV 'taken from a picture at Hampton Court, Herefordshire' (Paul de Rapin-Thoyras, *The History of England*, trans. Nicholas Tindal, 3d edn, 1743-7, i. facing 484). HW mentions this portrait of Henry IV in *Anecdotes of Painting*, calling it 'an undoubted original' (*Works* iii. 31). According to Gough, 'Mr Walpole has a copy of this portrait, which is very rude indeed' (*Sepulchral Monuments* ii. 71), but no copy is mentioned in HW's *Description of SH*.

6. This is no longer preserved with the letter. For Vertue's brief comments on the resemblance noted by HW, see *Walpole Society* 1931-2, xx. 46.

7. Joan (ca 1370-1437) of Navarre, m. 1 (1386) John V of Brittany; m. 2 (1403) Henry IV of England.

8. There is an account of the supposed conspiracy in *The Annales, or Generall Chronicle of England, begun first by maister John Stow, and after him continued and augmented . . . unto the ende of this present yeere 1614 by Edmond Howes, gentleman*, 1615, p. 358: 'This yeere [1419] Queene Joane mother to the Duke of Brytaine, and the King's stepmother being defamed of some wicked practise, by witchcraft, or sorcery, that she had devised the King's death, by the counsell of John Randolph Doctor of Divinitie, of the order of the Fryars minors, . . . her confessor, forfeited all her lands and goods by Parliament, and having all her servants

put from her, was committed to the custodie of J. Pellam, and by him sent to the Castle of Leeds in Kent.' HW's copy of Stow's *Annales* (now WSL) is Hazen, *Cat. of HW's Lib.*, No. 610.

9. Holinshed's *The Chronicles of England, Scotland, and Ireland*, [1587], iii. 568, gives this account: 'In this sixt yeare [of Henry V's reign] . . . Queene Jone late wife of King Henrie the Fourth, and mother in law to this King, was arested by the Duke of Bedford the King's lieutenant in his absence, and by him committed to safe keeping in the Castell of Leeds in Kent, there to abide the King's pleasure. About the same time, one Frier Randoll . . . confessor to the same Queene, was taken in the Isle of Gernesey. . . . It was reported that he had conspired with the Queene by sorcerie and necromancie to destroie the King.' HW's copy of the 1587 edition is Hazen, op. cit., No. 597.

10. *The Union of the Two Noble and Illustre Famelies of Lancastre and Yorke*, 1548, by Edward Hall (d. 1547). A continuation of Hall's chronicle, up to the end of Henry VIII's reign, was published by Richard Grafton in 1550. Neither work appears in the SH records.

11. Gough does not mention the conspiracy in his account of Joan in *Sepulchral Monuments* ii. 31, 34.

12. See the enclosure printed below.

13. Missing.

14. John Monson (1753-1806), 3d Bn Monson, 1774.

bourne,[15] which I sent the day before your draftsman was with me, and directed to you, as you ordered, at Enfield.[16]

I am Sir
Your most obedient humble servant

HOR. WALPOLE

[Enclosure]
Promptuarium Iconum, 4° Latin, publ[ishe]d at Lyons, 1553,[17] by Gulielm. Rouillius,[18] with some additions in Italian, 1577.[19]
p. 187. Carolus 6, Rex Franciae.[20]
V[ide] Vertue's MSS, fol. 1, p. 51 verso.[21]

Rapin in the reign of Henry V under the year 1417, mentions Joan of Navarre (whom he calls Blanche) being accused of conspiring against Henry.[22]

15. That is, Broxbournbury, Monson's seat at Broxbourne, Herts, which he sold in 1789 to Jacob Bosanquet (J. E. Cussans, *History of Hertfordshire*, 1870–81, ii ['Hundred of Hertford'], 175). The 'old portraits' at Broxbournbury were removed to Monson's house in Albemarle Street, London, where Gough was later given permission to inspect them; see HW to Gough *post* 17 May 1790.
16. Gough's residence in Middlesex, north of London.
17. *Prima pars Promptuarii iconum insigniorum a seculo hominum . . . Promptuarii iconum pars secunda . . .* , Lyons, 1553.
18. Guillaume Rouillé (or de Roville) (1518–89), French printer (Bibl. Nat. Cat.; NBG).
19. Rouillé published at Lyons in 1577 a *Secunda editione, nella quale sono agionti i personaggi insigni dopoi la*

prima (BM Cat.); also, in the same year, a second edition in French (Bibl. Nat. Cat.). Besides the Latin edition, there were French and Italian editions published by Rouillé in 1553. HW owned a copy of the first edition in French, 1553; it is Hazen, op. cit., No. 490.
20. Gough, presumably following HW's note, included the reference in *Sepulchral Monuments* ii. 71, but mistakenly connected it with Henry V instead of Henry IV.
21. The meaning of '1' is not clear, since the reference is not in the earliest of Vertue's folio notebooks. Vertue lettered this notebook 'A.g.' (now BM Add. MS 23,070). See *Walpole Society* 1929–30, xviii. xix.
22. 'On trouve dans quelques histoires, que dans cette même année [1417] la Reine Blanche de Navarre, veuve de Henri IV et belle-mère du Roi regnant, fut accusée d'avoir, avec son confesseur, conspiré

To Thomas Barret,[1] Thursday 5 June 1788

Printed from *Works* v. 668–9, where the letter was first printed. Reprinted, Wright vi. 289–91; Cunningham ix. 126–7 (closing and signature omitted in Wright and Cunningham); Toynbee xiv. 47–8; extract quoted in Antony Dale, *James Wyatt*, Oxford, 1956, p. 138. The history of the MS and its present whereabouts are not known.

Berkeley Square, June 5, 1788.

I WISH I could charge myself with any merit, which I always wish to have, towards you, dear Sir, in letting Mr Matthew[2] see Strawberry;[3] but in truth he has so much merit and modesty and taste himself, that I gave him the ticket with pleasure—which it seldom happens to me to do; for most of those who go thither, go because it is the fashion, and because *a party* is a prevailing custom too; and my tranquillity is disturbed, because nobody likes to stay at home. If Mr Matthew was really entertained, I am glad—but Mr Wyatt[4] has made him too correct a Goth not to have seen all the imperfections and bad execution of my attempts; for neither Mr Bentley[5] nor my workmen had *studied* the science, and I was always too desultory and impatient to consider that I should please myself more by allowing time, than by hurrying my plans into execution before they were ripe. My house therefore is but a sketch by beginners; yours[6] is fin-

contre le Roi. Quelques-uns ont ajouté, qu'elle fut condamnée à dix ans de prison, et que son confesseur fut tué par un chapelain de la Tour, avec lequel il avait pris querelle sur ce sujet. C'est tout ce qu'on peut dire sur cette accusation, dont les historiens ne parlent que fort confusément' (Paul de Rapin-Thoyras, *Histoire d'Angleterre*, 2d edn, The Hague, 1727, iii. 470). HW's copy of the first edition, 1724–7, is Hazen, op. cit., No. 1144. The English translation by Tindal (n. 5 above) refers to the Queen as 'Joanna of Navarre' (i. 520).

1. (?1743–1803), of Lee Priory, near Canterbury, Kent; M.P.
2. James Wyatt's building foreman; not further identified.
3. HW's 'Book of Visitors' records that 'Mr Matthew, Mr Wyat's foreman and one'

were at SH on 25 May 1788 (Berry ii. 229).
4. James Wyatt, the architect, whom HW commissioned to build the Offices at SH in 1790. HW greatly admired Wyatt's work even before he began designing in the Gothic style; see *ante* 26 July 1772.
5. Richard Bentley, HW's correspondent.
6. Lee Priory, about four miles from Canterbury. HW's example probably inspired Barret to Gothicize his house; the remodelling began under Wyatt's direction about 1782 and was completed by 1790. HW called Lee Priory 'a child of Strawberry prettier than the parent,' 'the quintessence of Gothic taste, exquisitely executed' (Berry ii. 111; More 342). For an illustrated account see Hugh Honour, 'A House of the Gothic Revival,' *Country Life*, 1952, cxi. 1665–6.

ished by a great master—and if Mr Matthew liked mine, it was *en virtuose*, who loves the dawnings of an art, or the glimmerings of its restoration.

I finished Mr Gibbon[7] a full fortnight ago, and was extremely pleased. It is a most wonderful mass of information, not only on history, but almost on all the ingredients of history, as war, government, commerce, coin, and what not. If it has a fault, it is in embracing too much, and consequently in not detailing enough, and in striding backwards and forwards from one set of princes to another, and from one subject to another; so that, without much historic knowledge, and without much memory, and much method in one's memory, it is almost impossible not to be sometimes bewildered: nay, his own impatience to tell what he knows, makes the author, though commonly so explicit, not perfectly clear in his expressions. The last chapter of the fourth volume, I own, made me recoil, and I could scarcely push through it. So far from being Catholic or heretic, I wished Mr Gibbon had never heard of Monophysites, Nestorians,[8] or any such fools!—But the sixth volume made ample amends; Mahomet and the popes were gentlemen and good company.[9]—I abominate fractions of theology and reformation.

Mr Sheridan,[10] I hear, did not quite satisfy the passionate expectation that had been raised[11]—But it was impossible he could, when people had worked themselves up into an enthusiasm of offering

7. The concluding volumes (IV–VI) of Edward Gibbon's *History of the Decline and Fall of the Roman Empire* were published 8 May 1788 (J. E. Norton, *A Bibliography of the Works of Edward Gibbon*, Oxford, 1940, p. 61).

8. Gibbon's account of the Monophysites (a faction later revived as the Jacobites) and the Nestorians is in chapter xlvii, pp. 593–605, of vol. IV of the *Decline and Fall*.

9. The sixth volume covers the period from 1095 (the First Crusade) to the end of the fifteenth century. HW wrote Lady Ossory 10 Feb. 1789: 'I am a little surprised, I confess, at your Ladyship's finding it laborious to finish Mr Gibbon, especially the last volume, which I own too, delighted me the most—perhaps because I was best acquainted with the subjects of it. In the other volumes I was a little confounded by his leaping backwards and forwards, and I could not recollect all

those *fainéant* emperors of Constantinople. . . . How he could traverse such acres of ill-written histories, even to collect such a great work, astonishes me' (OSSORY iii. 39–40).

10. Richard Brinsley Sheridan.

11. Of his speech in .Westminster Hall, upon bringing forward one of the charges against Mr Hastings (HW). On 3 June Sheridan, one of the managers in the trial of Warren Hastings, began his speech on the charge of Hastings's cruelty to the Begums of the province of Benares; the speech was continued on 6 and 10 June, and concluded on 13 June. Seats in Westminster Hall sold for as high as £50 (MORE 265 n. 7; CHUTE 391 n. 7). HW wrote Lord Strafford 17 June 1788: 'General Conway, Mrs Damer, and everybody else are drowned by Mr Sheridan, whose renown has engrossed all fame's tongues and trumpets' (ibid. 391).

fifty—aye, *fifty* guineas for a ticket to hear him. Well! we are sunk and deplorable in many points—yet not absolutely gone, when history and eloquence throw out such shoots! I thought I had outlived my country; I am glad not to leave it desperate! Adieu, dear Sir!

Yours most sincerely,

Hor. Walpole

To the Hon. Mrs Boyle Walsingham,
Tuesday 10 June 1788

Printed for the first time from a photostat of the MS among the De Ros family papers in the Public Record Office of Northern Ireland, Belfast, by kind permission of the late Baroness De Ros through the good offices of Mr G. Heatly and Mr Anthony Malcomson. The MS passed by family descent to Mrs Boyle Walsingham's great-great-great-granddaughter, Una Mary, *suo jure* Baroness De Ros (1879–1956), who deposited the De Ros family papers in the Public Record Office of Northern Ireland in 1952; the papers are now the property of her eldest granddaughter, the present Baroness De Ros.

Endorsed, probably by Mrs Boyle Walsingham: Mr Walpole—

Address: To the Honourable Mrs Walsingham at Boyle Farm, Thames Ditton.

Postmark: JU 10 88.

Berkeley Square, June 10, 1788.

MR WALPOLE will have the honour of waiting on Mrs Walsingham on Friday;[1] but as he should be vexed to see Cowley[2] for the first time by twilight, he hopes she will excuse his coming a little before the time appointed; and as she needs not do the honours to him before the curtain draws up, he will on the contrary help to light the lamps, squeeze lemons, or take a pot with Phillis at the alehouse, till he is wanted for a cotillon.

1. 13 June, the date of Mrs Boyle Walsingham's ball at Boyle Farm, Thames Ditton. HW wrote Lord Strafford 17 June 1788: 'Last Friday [I] came hither to look for a minute at a ball at Mrs Walsingham's at Ditton; which would have been very pretty, for she had stuck coloured lamps in the hair of all her trees and bushes, if the east wind had not danced a reel all the time by the side of the river' (Chute 391). Mrs Boscawen gives a brief account in a letter to Fanny Sayer: 'Mrs Walsingham's ball was charming, abounding with dancing men and with great ladies, as the Duchess of Buccleuch and her daughter, Lady Weymouth and hers, Lady Mornington and hers, Lady Clarendon and hers; though the prince got away from her the Marlboro's, Manchesters, Ladies Salisbury and Sefton, and I suppose many others' (Cecil Aspinall-Oglander, *Admiral's Widow: Being the Life and Letters of the Hon. Mrs Edward Boscawen from 1761 to 1785*, 1943, pp. 131–2).

2. A portrait of the poet Abraham Cowley, copied from Lely's original in HW's collection at SH. See *ante* 28 Dec. 1787 and n. 2.

To Thomas Astle, Tuesday 29 July 1788

Printed from the MS now WSL. First printed in N & Q 1869, 4th ser., iii. 216. Reprinted, Toynbee xiv. 64. The MS passed to Astle's descendant, Robert Hills, of Colne Park, Essex, who owned it in 1869; later acquired by Louis I. Haber, of New York City; sold Anderson Auction Co. 10 Dec. 1909 (Haber Sale, Part III), lot 371; *penes* F. T. Sabin, London, in 1918; purchased from Gabriel Wells by WSL July 1932.

Endorsed by Astle: July 29th 1788 Mr Walpole. [in another hand on the recto:] No. 132.

Address: To Thomas Astle Esq. at Battersea Rise near Clapham. *Postmark:* JY 30 88. 2 O'CLOCK.

Strawberry Hill, July 29, 1788.

A THOUSAND thanks to you, dear Sir, for *King Alfred's Will*,[1] and for the most superb of all royal locks[2]—nay, and for the most secure one, for I am sure it could not be picked but by a pick-axe. There is mechanism enough about it to lift the drawbridge of a citadel, and one grieves that such complicated ingenuity should have been employed for so simple an operation as unlocking a door. By the beauty of the Gothic border, and by the rose and crown I imagine it to have been manufactured in the reign of Henry VII; and by the prodigious weight of metal and involved machinery, I should think his Majesty had set half a dozen of the strongest Cyclopses of his Board of Works, to fashion this lock for the door of his exchequer and hoard at Shene.[3]

I have company[4] with me, and expect another party when they are gone, or I would wait on you with my thanks in person, as I will as soon as I am at liberty, being with great gratitude and regard

Dear Sir
Your much obliged and obedient humble servant

HOR. WALPOLE

1. *The Will of King Alfred*, Oxford, 1788. Astle was editor of this work; the English and Latin translations of the Anglo-Saxon text (from a register of Newminster Abbey, Winchester, then deposited in Astle's manuscript library) were supplied by the Rev. Owen Manning. The book does not appear in the SH records.
2. 'A curious royal lock, made as early as in the reign of Henry VII, from one of the palaces; a present from Thomas Astle, Esq.' ('Des. of SH,' *Works* ii. 442). The lock was kept in the Armoury at SH; it was sold SH xix. 91 to Webb of Old Bond Street for £2.12.6.
3. Shene (or Sheen), the old royal palace at Richmond.
4. Not identified.

From WELBORE ELLIS,[1] Saturday ?23 August 1788

Printed for the first time from the MS now WSL. For a history of the MS see *ante* 15 March 1763.

Dated conjecturally by the entry in HW's 'Book of Visitors' *sub* 28 Aug. 1788 (see n. 4 below).

Address: To the Honourable Mr Walpole.

Memoranda:[2]

Unfeeling
Insincere
Cunning
Trifling [all crossed out]
not pious [crossed out] Pr[ince]
not avaricious
not generous
children only when young nor Q[ueen] [crossed out]
no love of glory
no taste
not firm but persevering [crossed out]
pride not virtue [crossed out]
temperance [crossed out]

He was not avaricious, yet had not a speck of generosity; and if he ever made a present, of which I never heard but one instance, it never amounted to the value of ten guineas, for though he had ⟨not⟩ love for money, he loved nobody more than money.

Q[ueen] proud and fickle and prudent; and ⟨comes⟩ to hoard everything she could. Her manner very pleasing and obliging with dignity.

False from constitution, not to serve his purpose but to make mischief.

K[ing] to break all connect[ions] for enter[tainment] and for pleasure of breaking them.

Saturday morning.

MR ELLIS presents his compliments to Mr Walpole, and requests the favour of a ticket for Mr Fisher[3] and three more of his family to see Strawberry Hill.[4] Mr Fisher is a very worthy

1. (1713–1802), cr. (1794) Bn Mendip; M.P.
2. These are apparently notes for a character sketch of George III and Queen Charlotte. Those crossed out by HW were probably used, but the sketch is missing.
3. John Fisher, under secretary of state (American Department) 1781–2; secretary

to the Board of Excise, 1784 (J. C. Sainty, *Officials of the Secretaries of State 1660–1782*, 1973, p. 78; *London Calendar*, 1784, p. 152).
4. HW's 'Book of Visitors' records that 'Mr Fisher and 3' were admitted at SH on 28 Aug. 1788 (BERRY ii. 231).

gentleman whom Mr Ellis found a commis⁵ in Lord Sackville's⁶ office and continued him in that station,⁷ and he is now Secretary to the Board of Excise.

To John Pinkerton, Wednesday 29 October 1788

Printed for the first time from a photostat of the MS inserted in vol. I of a copy of Pinkerton's *Walpoliana*, [1799], now in the University of Delaware Library. This copy was sold Swann Galleries 25 Feb. 1965 (Miscellaneous Sale), lot 293, to the University of Delaware Library; its earlier history is not known.

HW's acquaintance with Pinkerton began in 1784. The only year between 1784 and 1794 when 29 October fell on Wednesday was 1788. See n. 1 below.

Address: To Mr Pinkerton.

Berkeley Square, Wednesday, Oct. 29.

Dear Sir,

I AM returning to Strawberry Hill, where I shall be glad if you will pass next Sunday, and come as early as you please.¹ Be so good as to let me known by a line,² if I do not find you at home now.

Yours etc.

H. W.

5. 'A deputy, delegate, clerk; used chiefly of foreign officials' (OED).

6. Lord George Sackville (after 1770, Germain) (1716–85), cr. (1782) Vct Sackville; M.P. He was secretary of state for America 1775–Feb. 1782.

7. Ellis was secretary of state for America Feb.–March 1782.

1. Pinkerton was beginning work on his *Medallic History of England to the Revo-* *lution* (published anonymously in 1790) and sought HW's advice and assistance. HW wrote to him 15 Oct. 1788: 'Should you be impatient, will you come and search those MSS [of George Vertue] yourself? Next, will you come next Sunday hither, and pass the whole day, if you please, in the examination?' (Chatterton 299).

2. No reply to this letter has been found.

From THOMAS HOLCROFT,[1] late November 1788

Printed from *Memoirs of the Late Thomas Holcroft, Written by Himself, and Continued to the Time of his Death* [by William Hazlitt], *from his Diary, Notes, and Other Papers,* 1816, iii. 290–2, where the letter was first printed. Reprinted in later editions of Holcroft's *Memoirs.* The history of the MS and its present whereabouts are not known.

Dated approximately by HW's reply *post* 28 Nov. 1788.

Sir,

THE politeness with which I was received on my accidental visit to Strawberry Hill,[2] in company with Mr Mercier,[3] and the pleasure I felt not only in viewing so rare a collection of the works of art, but in the very kind manner in which they were shown, will not easily be forgotten. As a small testimony of the truth of this, I then projected, and having received them from the binders, now take the liberty to send you copies of such dramatic works of mine, as have been already played and published,[4] which I beg you to accept, not as a task imposed upon you to read them, nor yet with an expectation of praise, but as an acknowledgment of as much thankfulness as I dare express. I have also enclosed a copy of a manuscript comedy,[5] for which I can give no better reason, than that though every motive of delicacy would make me avoid laying you under the least restraint, yet it may happen that the perusal of it may afford you an hour's amusement, which is the best return I am at present able to make for the attention with which you were pleased to treat me, and the invitation you gave me to revisit Strawberry Hill in a more favourable season.

I am, Sir,

Your very respectful, humble servant,

T[HOMAS] H[OLCROFT]

1. (1745–1809), dramatist, novelist, and translator.
2. The date and circumstances of this visit are not known.
3. Charles-André Mercier (d. 1823), younger brother of the dramatist Louis-Sébastien Mercier and friend of Lady Craven (*post* 11 Dec. 1788 and n. 2). In 1799 Holcroft married his daughter, Louisa (*Memoirs of the late Thomas Holcroft,* 1816, ii. 237).
4. This collection of plays included

Duplicity, 3d edn, 1782; *The Noble Peasant,* 1784 (a comic opera); *The Follies of a Day,* 1785; *The Choleric Fathers,* 1785 (a comic opera); and *Seduction,* 1787. The bound volume, now in the Victoria and Albert Museum, is Hazen, *Cat. of HW's Lib.,* No. 1853. HW had already acquired copies of these plays for his 'Theatre of Geo. 3.'
5. Possibly *The German Hotel,* adapted from J. C. Brandes's *Der Gasthof;* first acted at Covent Garden 11 Nov. 1790 and

To Thomas Holcroft, Friday 28 November 1788

Printed from a copy by the late Sir Shane Leslie, Bt, in 1941 of the MS then in the possession of the Hon. Mrs Clive Pearson, Parham Park, Pulborough, Sussex. First printed in *Memoirs of the late Thomas Holcroft, Written by Himself,* 1816, iii. 292–3. Reprinted in later editions of Holcroft's *Memoirs;* Cunningham ix. 158; Toynbee xiv. 96. The MS is untraced until sold Sotheby's 22 May 1897 (Important Autograph Letters and Historical Documents Sale), lot 94, to Barker; resold Sotheby's 6 July 1900 (Autograph Letters and Historical Documents from Various Collections Sale), lot 381, to Maggs; *penes* G. Beresford Fitzgerald, of London, in 1902; resold Sotheby's 26 March 1904 (property of G. Beresford Fitzgerald), lot 397, to W. V. Daniell; later acquired by Sir Herbert H. Raphael, Bt, who inserted it in an extra-illustrated copy of Cunningham's edition of HW's *Letters,* 18 vols, folio; this copy was sold Sotheby's 4 Feb. 1919 (Raphael Sale), lot 311, to Bumpus for Lord Cowdray, the father of the Hon. Clive Pearson; bequeathed by his widow, the Hon. Mrs Pearson, to her daughter, Mrs P. A. Tritton, of Parham Park, in 1974.

Address: To Thomas Holcroft Esq. at No. 45 in Upper Mary le bone Street.

Berkeley Square, Nov. 28, 1788.

THE civilities, Sir, which you are pleased to say you received from me at Strawberry Hill, were no more than were due to any gentleman, and certainly did not deserve such acknowledgment as you have made;[1] and I should be ashamed of your thanking me so much, if the agreeable manner in which you have greatly overpaid them by the present of your works, did not make me easily swallow my shame, though it will not dispense me from assuring you how much I am obliged to you. I shall read them with pleasure as soon as I am settled in town.[2] Just at present, I live between town and country, and should not have leisure but to read them by snatches.

It is for this reason, that if you are not in haste for it, I shall beg leave to keep your MS comedy, till I can peruse it with proper attention.[3] If you should want it soon, I will return it and ask for it

published the same year (Elbridge Colby, *A Bibliography of Thomas Holcroft,* New York, 1922, pp. 62–3). HW's copy (now WSL) is Hazen, op. cit., No. 1810:49:4.

1. See previous letter.

2. HW apparently 'settled in town' for the winter on 2 Dec., when he returned to Berkeley Square from SH (OSSORY iii. 30).

3. See following letter.

again, for it would be unjust to the merit of your works to run through them too rapidly.

I am Sir

Your obliged and obedient humble servant

Hor. Walpole

To Thomas Holcroft, Thursday 4 December 1788

Printed for the first time from the MS now wsl. The MS is untraced until sold Sotheby's 30 July 1930 ('Other Properties'), lot 627 (with two other items); acquired from W. T. Spencer by wsl, Sept. 1932.

Berkeley Square, Dec. 4th 1788.

MR WALPOLE has read Mr Holcroft's comedy[1] with great pleasure, and shall be glad to see him on Sunday morning next at eleven o'clock, if not inconvenient;[2] and names that hour as the least liable to interruption.

To Lady Craven, Thursday 11 December 1788

Printed from *Works* v. 666–8, where the letter was first printed. Reprinted in *Elegant Extracts . . . Originally Compiled by the Rev. Vicesimus Knox D.D.*, ed. J. G. Percival, Boston, [?1826], iv. 299–300 (closing and signature omitted); Wright vi. 307–9; Cunningham ix. 160–2 (last paragraph, closing, and signature omitted in Wright and Cunningham); Toynbee xiv. 99–102. The history of the MS and its present whereabouts are not known.

Berkeley Square, December 11, 1788.

IT IS agreeable to your Ladyship's usual goodness to honour me with another letter[1]—and I may say to your equity too, after I had proved to Monsieur Mercier,[2] by the list of dates of my letters,

1. See *ante* late Nov. 1788 and n. 5.
2. We have found no account of Holcroft's visit.

---

1. Missing.
2. See *ante* late Nov. 1788, n. 3. Mercier began his career as an engraver and pic-

ture dealer. He was *maître d'hôtel* of the Hôtel de l'Empereur in Paris when Lady Craven made his acquaintance. In 1787, when Lady Craven was living at the court of Ansbach in Germany, she persuaded Mercier to come there to be secretary of the Literary Society of Triesdorf and Ans-

that it was not mine but the post's fault, that you did not receive one[3] that I had the honour of writing to you above a year ago—Not, Madam, that I could wonder, if you had the prudence to drop a correspondence with an old superannuated man, who, conscious of his decay, has had the decency of not troubling with his dotages persons of not near your Ladyship's youth and vivacity.[4] I have long been of opinion that few persons know *when* to die—I am not so English as to mean when to dispatch themselves—no, but when to go out of the world. I have usually applied this opinion to those who have made a considerable figure, and consequently it was not adapted to myself. Yet even we ciphers ought not to fatigue the public scene when we are become lumber. Thus, being quite out of the question, I will explain my maxim, which is the more wholesome, the higher it is addressed. My opinion then is, that when any personage has shone as much as is possible in his or her best walk (and not to repeat both genders every minute, I will use the male as the common of the two), he should take up his Strulbrugism,[5] and be heard of no more. Instances will be still more explanatory. Voltaire ought to have pretended to die after *Alzire, Mahomet* and *Sémiramis,*[6] and not have produced his wretched last pieces. Lord Chatham should have closed his political career with his immortal war[7]—And how weak was Garrick, when he had quitted the stage,[8] to limp after the tatters of fame by writing and reading pitiful poems, and even by *sitting* to read plays which he had acted with such fire and energy![9] We have an-

bach; he also became the Margrave of Ansbach's librarian. He was in London in Nov. 1788; HW met him during his 'accidental' visit to SH in company with Thomas Holcroft (F. Baldensperger, 'Notes sur le frère de Sébastien Mercier,' *Revue d'Histoire littéraire de la France*, 1912, xix. 411–13; T. V. Benn, 'Charles-André Mercier et sa part aux ouvrages de son frère Louis-Sébastien,' *Revue d'Histoire littéraire de la France*, 1927, xxxiv. 582–8; *Memoirs of the Margravine of Anspach. Written by Herself*, 1826, i. 191–99.

3. Missing.

4. HW was then seventy-one years old, Lady Craven thirty-seven.

5. The Struldbrugs were inhabitants of Luggnagg, an island in Book Three of *Gulliver's Travels.* They had the privilege of eternal life without immortal vigour,

strength, or intellect. HW wrote Lady Ossory 6 July 1777: 'Few persons know when they should die—I mean when they should have done living. I have taken up my strulbrugship, only reserving a comfortable annuity of cheerfulness and amusement, as monarchs do, who resign their crowns, and intend to have all the pleasures of royalty without the cares' (Ossory i. 364).

6. HW wrote Robert Jephson *ante* late Feb. 1775 *bis:* 'I admire [Voltaire] infinitely, especially in *Alzire, Mahomet,* and *Sémiramis.*'

7. The Seven Years' War.

8. On 10 June 1776.

9. 'Garrick has been *reading* plays at Althorpe à la Texier, and been adored as usual; yet I do not believe he succeeded half so well in the women. He goes on

other example in Mr A[nstey];¹⁰ who, if he had a friend upon earth, would have been obliged to him for being knocked on the head the moment he had published the *first* edition of the *Bath Guide;* for even in the second he had exhausted his whole stock of inspiration,¹¹ and has never written anything tolerable since.¹² When such unequal authors print their works together,¹³ one may apply in a new light the old hacked simile of Mezentius, who tied together the living and the dead.¹⁴

We have just received the works of an author¹⁵ from whom I find I am to receive much less entertainment than I expected, because I shall have much less to read than I intended. His *Memoirs,* I am told, are almost wholly military, which, therefore, I shall not read— and his poetry, I am sure, I shall not look at, because I should [not] understand it.—What I saw of it formerly¹⁶ convinced me that he would not have been a poet, even if he had written in his own language; and though I do not understand German, I am told it is a fine language; and I can easily believe that any tongue (not except- ing our old barbarous Saxon, which, a bit of an antiquary as I am, I abhor) is more harmonious than French. It was curious absurdity, therefore, to pitch on the most unpoetic language in Europe, the most barren and the most clogged with difficulties. I have heard Rus- sian and Polish sung, and both sounded musical—but to abandon

writing his wretched epilogues too, for he cannot sit down with the *strulbruggism* that he had the sense to take up' (HW to Mason 24 Jan. 1778, MASON i. 347).

10. Christopher Anstey (1724–1805), au- thor of *The New Bath Guide,* 1766, which HW greatly admired.

11. HW wrote Lord Holland 29 July 1766: 'I am sorry to tell you that there is a new edition of the *Bath Guide* with most execrable additions. I shall adhere to the old copy' (SELWYN 229).

12. HW disparaged *The Patriot,* 1767, *The Priest Dissected,* 1774, and *An Elec- tion Ball,* 1776, among other pieces by Anstey. See COLE i. 310; OSSORY i. 196; MASON i. 242. 'Since the *first* edition of *The Bath Guide,* never was a duller goose than Anstey!' (HW to Lady Ossory 28 Sept. 1786, OSSORY ii. 527).

13. Anstey's *Poetical Works* were pub- lished posthumously by his son John Anstey in 1808.

14. The tyrannical Mezentius, king of Caere in Etruria, would link dead bodies with the living, fitting hand to hand and face to face, and thus slay them by a lin- gering death (*Æneid* viii. 485–8).

15. *Œuvres posthumes de Frédéric II, Roi de Prusse,* Berlin, 1788. Henry Con- way lent HW his set of the *Œuvres* to read. HW found the three volumes (VIII–X) of Frederick's letters to Voltaire 'pedantic . . . tiresomely flattering . . . utterly void of variety, with . . . bushels of vile verses' (OSSORY iii. 33). The earlier volumes included Frederick's history of his own times, his history of the Seven Years' War, memoirs from the Peace of Hubertusberg, etc.

16. HW owned a copy of *Œuvres du philosophe de Sans-Souci,* Potsdam, 1760, containing odes, verse epistles, and 'L'Art de la guerre' by Frederick (Hazen, *Cat. of HW's Lib.,* No. 1295).

one's own tongue, and not adopt Italian, that is even sweeter and softer and more copious than the Latin, was a want of taste that I should think could not be applauded even by a Frenchman born in Provence. But what a language is the French, which measures verses by feet that never are to be pronounced, which is the case wherever the mute *e* is found! What poverty of various sounds for rhyme, when, lest similar cadences should too often occur, their mechanic bards are obliged to marry masculine and feminine terminations as alternately as the black and white squares of a chessboard! Nay, will you believe me, Madam? Yes, you will; for you may convince your own eyes, that a scene of *Zaïre*[17] begins with three of the most nasal adverbs that ever snorted together in a breath. *Enfin, donc, désormais* are the culprits in question.[18] *Enfin donc,* need I tell your Ladyship, that the author I alluded to at the beginning of this long tirade is the late King of Prussia?

I am conscious that I have taken a little liberty when I excommunicate a tongue in which your Ladyship has condescended to write[19]—but I only condemn it for verse and pieces of eloquence, of which I thought it alike incapable, till I read Rousseau of Geneva.[20] It is a most sociable language, and charming for narrative and epistles. Yet, write as well as you will in it, you must be liable to express yourself better in the speech natural to you; and your own country has a right to understand all your works, and is jealous of their not being as perfect as you could make them. Is it not more creditable to be translated into a foreign language than into your own? and will it not vex you to hear the translation taken for the original, and to find vulgarisms that you could not have committed yourself? But I have done, and will release you, Madam; only observing, that you flatter me with a vain hope when you tell me you shall return to England sometime or other.[21] Where will that time be for me?—and when it arrives, shall not I be somewhere else?

17. A tragedy by Voltaire, first performed in 1732.

18. HW is mistaken; there is no scene in *Zaïre* that begins with these words.

19. Lady Craven does not appear to have published any work in French before 1790, when her comedy *Le Philosophe moderne* was privately printed. HW's copy of the play is Hazen, op. cit., No. 2365.

20. While admitting that Rousseau had a 'masterly genius,' HW maintained that

'Boileau and Rousseau have succeeded so little in odes, that the French still think that ballad-wright Quinault their best lyric poet—which shows how much they understand lyric poetry!' (MASON i. 276, 426).

21. Lady Craven's next visit to England was in the summer of 1791 (*The Beautiful Lady Craven*, ed. A. M. Broadley and Lewis Melville, 1914, i. lxxiv; BERRY i. 342).

I do not pretend to send your Ladyship English news, nor to tell you of English literature. You must before this time have heard of the dismal state into which our chief personage is fallen![22] That consideration absorbs all others. The two Houses are going to settle some intermediate succedaneum, and *the obvious one*,[23] no doubt, will be fixed on.[24]

This letter, I hope, will be more fortunate than my last. I should be very unhappy to seem again ungrateful, when I have the honour of being with the greatest respect,

Madam,

Your Ladyship's most obliged and most humble servant,

Hor. Walpole

To Lord Buckinghamshire, Sunday 14 December 1788

Printed from Hist. MSS Comm., *Lothian MSS*, 1905, pp. 437–8, where the letter was first printed (salutation, closing, and signature omitted). The MS passed to Buckinghamshire's eldest daughter and coheir, Lady Henrietta Hobart, who in 1793 married, as her second husband, Lord Ancram, later 6th Marquess of Lothian; *penes* the 10th Marquess of Lothian, Blickling Hall, Norfolk, in 1905; not further traced.

[Berkeley Square, Dec. 14, 1788.]

I AM quite confounded by your Lordship's goodness and by the honour you have done me which I esteem as much as the great curiosity[1] your Lordship has been pleased to send me; and I beg

22. For a detailed account of the King's incapacitating illness which lasted from October 1788 to February 1789, precipitating the Regency crisis, see Ida Macalpine and Richard Hunter, *George III and the Mad-Business*, New York, 1969, pp. 14–86.

23. The Prince of Wales.

24. On 10 Dec. in the House of Commons William Pitt presented the report of the committee appointed to examine the King's physicians concerning his state of health. Pitt then engaged in a debate with Charles Fox on the need to consider precedents and on the alleged right of the Prince of Wales to 'assume the reins of government, and exercise the power of

sovereignty, during the continuance of the [King's] illness and incapacity' (Cobbett, *Parl. Hist.* xxvii. 692–716). The Parliamentary debates of Dec. 1788 are fully discussed in J. W. Derry, *The Regency Crisis and the Whigs 1788–9*, Cambridge, 1963, pp. 67–119.

1. An undated letter in French by Peter III (1728–62), Czar of Russia Jan.–July 1762, to his mistress, the Countess Elisaveta Romanovna Vorontsova, inquiring about her health. The MS, described by HW as an 'Original letter from the Czar Peter III to his mistress Elizabeth Woron-

leave to return you my most grateful thanks for both. I should bring them myself to your Lordship's door were I not confined to my house by a great cold,[2] but I shall have that honour the first moment I am able.

The letter will be very valuable in my little collection though certainly it was more worthily placed in such a seat as Blickling;[3] but as your Lordship is more pleased in conferring favours than in possessing curiosities, I will only say that you could not have honoured any man with such a present who would be more sensible of such a distinction and who is more proud of being with the greatest respect and gratitude . . .

To Richard Cosway, 1789

Printed for the first time from the MS now wsl, acquired from Mrs A. H. Hallam Murray, of Hythe, Kent, in Feb. 1938; its earlier history is not known.

Dated approximately by the birth of Cosway's only child in 1789; the month and day of the birth are not known.

Address: To Rich[ar]d Cosway Esq.

Dear Sir,

I AM delighted to hear Mrs Cosway is so well delivered,[1] and wish her and you a thousand joys.

Yours etc.

H. Walpole

---

zow. Given to me Dec. 14, 1788 by John Hobart 2d Earl of Buckingham, formerly ambassador in Russia,' is now wsl. See Mann vi. 55 n. 30 and Hazen, *Cat. of HW's Lib.,* No. 2576, *sub* Peter III.

2. HW wrote Lady Ossory 26 Dec. 1788: 'I have been confined to my house for some days by the worst cold and cough I ever had in my days. I treat it as ill as possible, and do not give it a morsel; still it will not leave me. In revenge it will not let me speak' (Ossory iii. 33).

3. Blickling Hall, Buckinghamshire's seat in Norfolk.

---

1. The Cosways' only child, Louisa Paolina Angelica, was born in 1789. She was named for her godmother, the Countess of Albany; her godfather, General Paoli; and her mother's friend, Angelica Kauffmann (Berry i. 285 n. 16). She died 29 July 1796 (gm 1796, lxvi pt ii. 705).

To Lord Charlemont, Wednesday 11 March 1789

Printed from a photostat of the MS in the Royal Irish Academy, Dublin. First printed, Toynbee xiv. 121. For the history of the MS see *ante* 20 Oct. 1770.
Address: To the Earl of Charlemont at the Hotel in Albemarle Street.

Berkeley Square, March 11th 1789.

MR WALPOLE is infinitely sensible of and grateful for the great trust with which Lord Charlemont has so kindly honoured him, and which he repeats his promise of never abusing. He has only to wish that he had dared to ask what from such a specimen of poetic wit he was tempted to solicit, a communication of more instances of such a talent.[1]

To Thomas Pennant, Monday 30 March 1789

Printed for the first time from the MS now wsl, purchased in Sept. 1947 from Henry Stevens, Son and Stiles by Henry C. Taylor, who gave it to wsl 22 Sept. 1947; its earlier history is not known.
Address: To Thomas Pennant Esq. at Downing, Flintshire. *Postmark:* MR 30 89.

Berkeley Square, March 30th 1789.

Dear Sir,

THE weather has been so very bad and severe, that till yesterday I could not go to Strawberry Hill to look for the poem you wanted an account of, on the Duchess de Chevreuse.[1] It is in a thin volume less than a duodecimo, and called, 'Musarum Deliciæ, or the Muses Recreation, conteining severall pieces of Poetique Wit.' The

---

1. Charlemont enjoyed translating epigrams from the Italian, French, Latin, and Greek. A folio volume of his translations in MS is in the Royal Irish Academy (Maurice Craig, *The Volunteer Earl*, 1948, pp. 219–20). The 'specimen of poetic wit' that he sent for HW's perusal may have been one or more of these translations.

1. Marie de Rohan (1600–79), m. 1 (1617) Honoré d'Albert, Duc de Luynes (d. 1621); m. 2 (1622) Claude de Lorraine, Duc de Chevreuse (*Dict. de biographie française* viii. 1113–15).
2. Sir John Mennes (1599–1671), Kt, 1642; admiral. He was comptroller of the Navy 1661–71, and is frequently mentioned in Pepys's *Diary*.

second edition. By Sir J. M.[2] and Ja. S.[3] London, Printed by J. G.[4] for Henry Herringman,[5] at the signe of the Anchor in the new Exchange, 1656.[6]

For the *poetique wit*, there is neither wit nor poetry. At page 49 are forty-six bombast lines, 'Upon Madam Chevereuze swimming over the Thames.'[7]

Mr Granger,[8] I believe, had his information of those lines from me—but I do not know who told him the author was Sir J. Mason.[9] It might be so. However at p. 63 it is said that a Sir John Mennies wrote to *me* (one of the authors, I suppose) to desire me to go to a condemned priest, whom the King had reprieved, and persuade him to be hanged, without which the Parliament denied the King to pay the army.[10] To that letter is a reply[11] in verse, as bad as the other poems, which might be composed by Ja. S.—but in truth, it matters little who wrote wretched verses! The only curious fact is the Duchess's swimming, which no doubt happened in the reign of Charles I[12] and was an event worthy of being recorded in better memoirs, considering what a remarkable personage the Duchess

3. James Smith (1605–67), D.D. (Oxon.), 1661; poet and divine. Poems by Smith and by his friend Sir John Mennes appeared in several other anthologies besides *Musarum Deliciæ* (see DNB *sub* James Smith).

4. Perhaps John Grismond II, printer in Ivy Lane ?1639–?1666 (H. R. Plomer, *A Dictionary of the Booksellers and Printers . . . in England, Scotland and Ireland from 1641 to 1667*, 1907, p. 87).

5. (d. 1704), bookseller, at the Blue Anchor in the Lower Walk of the New Exchange 1653–93 (ibid. 96–7).

6. HW's copy of the book is Hazen, *Cat. of HW's Lib.*, No. 1970. The first edition was published in 1655.

7. HW quotes six lines from the poem in his letter to Pennant *post* 10 April 1789.

8. Rev. James Granger, HW's occasional correspondent (*ante* 24 April 1764, n. 1).

9. Sir John Mason (1503–66), Kt, 1547; statesman. In the *Supplement* (1774) to his *Biographical History of England*, Granger included an entry (pp. 269–70) on the Duchesse de Chevreuse, noting that she

possessed 'a constitution which enabled her to swim across the Thames.' Granger added in a footnote: 'In a little volume of poems, by Sir J. M. is a copy of verses complimenting her on this talent, which is not mentioned among her political or amorous adventures in the "Memoirs of De Retz."' On 'Sir J. M.' Granger wrote: 'Quere if Sir John Mason.'

10. 'A letter to Sir John Mennis, when the Parliament denied the King money to pay the army, unlesse a priest, whom the King had reprieved, might be executed. Sir John at that time wanting the money for provisions for his troop, desired me by his letter to goe to the priest, and to perswade him to dye for the good of the army' (*Musarum Deliciæ*, 2d edn, 1656, p. 63).

11. 'The Reply' is on pp. 63–5.

12. Probably during her second visit to England in 1638–40 (Victor Cousin, *Madame de Chevreuse*, 1869, pp. 144, 171–3).

13. HW mentions the verses on the Duchesse de Chevreuse in his letter to Daniel Lysons 22 Aug. 1795 (DALRYMPLE 265 and n. 4).

was.[13] Her daughter,[14] one [of] the heroines of the Cardinal de Retz,[15] was, I think, born in England.[16]

I remember Queen Senauki, as she was called, and who was brought over from Georgia by General Oglethorpe[17] with her husband Tomo Chachi,[18] when I was a boy at Eton School, where I saw them,[19] was said to have swum from Chelsea to Fulham—one of her eyes she had lost in battle. She wore a red paduasoy gown and petticoat, but no shift—her hue was very black.[20]

I hope you had a good journey home, and am, Sir,

Your most obedient humble servant

HOR. WALPOLE

14. Charlotte de Lorraine (1627–52), called Mlle de Chevreuse, second dau. of the Duc and Duchesse de Chevreuse (Cousin, op. cit., 34).

15. Jean-François-Paul de Gondi de Retz (1614–79), Cardinal de Retz. Charlotte de Lorraine is frequently mentioned in Cardinal de Retz's *Mémoires;* HW's copy of the Cologne, 1718, edition is Hazen, op. cit., No. 962.

16. Charlotte was apparently born in Lorraine; her elder sister Anne-Marie (1625–52) was born at Hampton Court during the Duchesse's first visit to England (Cousin, op. cit. 34; Louis Batiffol, *La Duchesse de Chevreuse,* 1913, p. 73).

17. James Edward Oglethorpe (1696–1785), general, philanthropist, and trustee for the colony of Georgia.

18. Tomochichi (d. 1739), chief of the Yamacraw Indians, a band of outlawed Creek Indians settled near Savannah, Georgia (L. F. Church, *Oglethorpe: A*

Study of Philanthropy in England and Georgia, 1932, p. 112).

19. In June 1734 Oglethorpe arrived in England with a small party of Yamacraw Indians that he had brought from Georgia. Their visit, which lasted four and a half months, created a considerable stir in London. HW doubtless saw Tomochichi, his wife Senauki, and the other Indians when they were taken to Eton on 16 Sept. 1734 (ibid. 116–20; A. A. Ettinger, *James Edward Oglethorpe: Imperial Idealist,* Oxford, 1936, pp. 144–6; SELWYN 94 nn 2, 3).

20. The 1st Earl of Egmont described her in his diary as 'an old ugly creature, who dresses their meat.' She and the other Indians wore their native dress until they were provided with new clothes; according to Egmont, 'the Queen's was a sort of scarlet Rosetti in the make of our English wrappers' (Hist. MSS Comm., *Egmont Diary,* 1920–3, ii. 114, 117).

To Richard Bull, Monday 30 March 1789

Printed for the first time from the MS now WSL. The MS was probably given by Bull to Mrs Agneta Yorke (n. 2 below) and descended in the family of the Earls of Hardwicke until their seat, Wimpole Hall, was acquired by the 2d Baron Robartes (6th Viscount Clifden, 1899) in 1891; sold by the 7th Viscount Clifden, through William H. Robinson Ltd, to WSL, August 1954.

Address: To Richard Bull Esq., Stratton Street.

Berkeley Square, March 30, 1789.

Dear Sir,

I AM much concerned for any accident that affects you, and still a little more when it deprives me of the pleasure of seeing you. I hope you are better and that we shall meet soon. I should be glad to wait on you any morning, or, if it were not inconvenient to you, early in an evening, any day after Thursday next.

Many thanks for the last prints you was so kind as to send me, and for those[1] I found today on my return from Strawberry Hill. They are truly very meritorious, and have much more spirit, strength and chiaroscuro than are almost ever seen in etchings. I beg you will be so good as to let Mrs York[2] know how sensible I am of the honour she has done me by so curious and valuable a present; and pray tell me where she lives, that I may leave my name and grateful thanks at her door:[3] it is the least I can do in return for so great a favour, as, I assure you, I think it.

Yours most sincerely

Hor. Walpole

1. Four views of scenery in Hampshire and the Isle of Wight, etched 'by Miss Yorke, daughter of Charles Yorke, 2d son of Lord Chancellor Hardwicke, and of Miss Johnson, Mr Yorke's second wife, who drew the views' (HW's MS note on the etchings, which he pasted in his *Collection of Prints, Engraved by Various Persons of Quality,* now WSL). Two more prints by Miss Yorke (an etching after a drawing by William Gilpin and another impression of the 'View on Beaulieu River' drawn by her mother) are included in HW's *Collection* but were possibly acquired at a different time. Bull, like HW, formed a collection of prints by amateur artists; his two folio volumes of their works are in the British Museum.

2. Agneta Johnson, dau. and coheir of Henry Johnson of Great Berkhamsted, Herts, m. (1762), as his second wife, the Hon. Charles Yorke, second son of the 1st E. of Hardwicke (Namier and Brooke iii. 675).

3. See following letter.

To Mrs Yorke and Miss Yorke,[1] April 1789

Printed for the first time from the MS now WSL. The MS descended in the family of the Earls of Hardwicke until their seat, Wimpole Hall, was acquired by the 2d Baron Robartes (6th Viscount Clifden, 1899) in 1891; sold by the 7th Viscount Clifden, through William H. Robinson Ltd, to WSL, August 1954.

Dated approximately by HW's letter to Richard Bull *ante* 30 March 1789, in which he asks for Mrs Yorke's address so that 'I may leave my name and grateful thanks at her door.'

MR WALPOLE came to thank Mrs Yorke and Miss Yorke for the great honour they have done him in being so good as to send him by Mr Bull the beautiful and very masterly etchings by Miss Yorke.[2] Mr Walpole has been out of town,[3] or should have expressed his gratitude sooner.

To Thomas Pennant, Friday 10 April 1789

Printed for the first time from a photostat of the MS in the National Library of Wales, Aberystwyth, kindly furnished by Mr Evan D. Jones (National Library of Wales MS 15, 423c). The MS is in a collection of Pennant papers acquired by the National Library, through Lowe Bros. of Birmingham, from Newnham Paddox, Warwickshire (the seat of the Earl of Denbigh), in Sept. 1949; its earlier history is not known.

Address: To Thomas Pennant Esq. at Downing, Flintshire. *Postmark:* AP 11 89.

Strawberry Hill, April 10th 1789.

Sir,

THERE is not a single incident of time or place mentioned in the verses on the Duchesse de Chevreuse's natation over the Thames than what I sent you,[1] except that it was in the month of July, as follows,

1. Caroline Yorke (1765–1818), dau. of the Hon. Charles Yorke by his second wife (see previous letter, n. 2), m. (1790) John Eliot, 2d Bn Eliot, 1804, cr. (1815) E. of St Germans.

2. See previous letter and n. 1.

3. HW did not return to Berkeley Square until after 10 April, on which day he wrote to Thomas Pennant from Strawberry Hill (see following letter).

———

1. See HW to Pennant *ante* 30 March 1789.

But her chaste breast, cold as the cloyster'd nun,
Whose frost to crystal might congeal the sun,
So glaz'd the stream, that pilots then afloat
Thought they might safely land without a boat.
July had seen the *Thames* in ice involv'd,
Had it not been by her own beams dissolv'd—²

This wretched nonsense will suffice, and I believe you will not wish for more.

If you looked into the list of our Bishops of London, I do not wonder that you did not find old Rawlinson's³ name there.⁴ He was the nonjuring titular Protestant bishop,⁵ and died twenty years ago or more. I have often seen him at sales of books and prints, when I used to frequent them. His library was sold by auction,⁶ and consisted chiefly, I think, of black-lettered and other old English books. His antiquities (of little value) he bequeathed to the University of Oxford.⁷ I have some faint recollection that he left some orders about the disposal of his heart,⁸ but I really forget what. You might perhaps learn from Oxford, if you have any correspondent there—though, if I mistake, I should be sorry to set you on a scent of so little importance.

2. *Musarum Deliciæ: or, The Muses Recreation*, 2d edn, 1656, p. 50 ('Upon Madam Chevereuze swimming over the Thames,' ll. 27–32).
3. Richard Rawlinson (1690–1755), collector, topographer, and nonjuring bishop.
4. Pennant had perhaps consulted the *Companion to the Royal Kalendar*, issued annually, which contained a list of the archbishops and bishops since the accession of George III in 1760.
5. Rawlinson was consecrated a bishop among the nonjurors by Bishops Gandy, Doughty, and Blackbourne in Gandy's chapel on 25 March 1728, but he always concealed his episcopal and even his clerical character (DNB).
6. The first part of his library of printed books and books of prints was sold by S. Baker, beginning 29 March 1756 (fifty days); the remainder of the library and more than 20,000 pamphlets were sold by Baker, beginning 3 March 1757 (ten days). Single prints, books of prints, and draw-

ings were sold by Baker 15–23 March 1757 (eight days) (Nichols, *Lit. Anec.* v. 498; *List of Catalogues of English Book Sales 1676–1900 now in the British Museum*, 1915, p. 66; Frits Lugt, *Répertoire des catalogues de ventes publiques*, The Hague, 1938– , No. 946).
7. His benefactions to Oxford included 'a number of books with and without MS notes, all his English and foreign seals, his antique marbles, and other curiosities; his copper-plates relative to several counties, his ancient Greek and Roman coins and medals, part of his collection of English medals, his series of medals of Louis XIV and XV, a series of medals of the Popes . . . and a great number of valuable MSS' (Nichols, *Lit. Anec.* v. 493). These bequests were divided between the Bodleian Library and St John's College, where he had been an undergraduate.
8. His heart was bequeathed to St John's College; it was placed in a marble urn in the College chapel (ibid. v. 497).

The books of the Pinelli Library⁹ I hear sell well; a Durandus on vellum¹⁰ went for above an hundred pounds. The MS on papyrus¹¹ is a true and very great curiosity and in perfect preservation. Cardinal Ximenes's Bible,¹² for which they say £500 had been offered, and which it is supposed the Duke of Wirtemberg¹³ is come over to buy (no wise way I should think of getting it cheap) has no beauty in my eyes. Some coat of arms that had been illuminated at the bottom of the title-page,¹⁴ is effaced.

If you have any old ashes on your estate,¹⁵ Sir, it may amuse you to look if there is any branch beautifully curled. I saw one yesterday at Sir George Beaumont's¹⁶ that is wreathed so exactly like the most

9. The celebrated library formed by Maffeo Pinelli (1736–85) of Venice, consisting chiefly of printed books by Greek, Roman, and Italian authors (many incunabula and early editions printed on vellum), with a number of Greek and Latin manuscripts and a collection of Bibles. A six-volume catalogue of the library, compiled by Jacopo Morelli, was published at Venice in 1787 as *Bibliotheca Maphæi Pinellii Veneti magno jam studio collecta*. In 1788 the London bookseller James Edwards purchased the library from Pinelli's heirs. The books and manuscripts were sold at auction by Edwards in two sales, the first lasting from 6 April to 20 May 1789 and the second, in thirty-two days, beginning 1 Feb. 1790 (GM 1789, lix pt ii. 837).

10. A copy of the first edition (printed on vellum, with illuminated letters) of the *Rationale divinorum officiorum*, Mainz, 1459, by Guillaume Durand (or Durant) (ca 1230–96), Bishop of Mende (*Bibliotheca Maphæi Pinellii Veneti* i. 129–30, No. 782). It was sold for £101.17.0 (*Bibliotheca Pinelliana. A Catalogue of the Magnificent and Celebrated Library of Maffei Pinelli, Late of Venice*, [1789], p. 214, lot 5693).

11. A Latin MS on Egyptian papyrus, written in A.D. 572 during the reign of the Byzantine emperor Justin II. The MS is the subject of Girolamo Francesco Zanetti's *Dichiarazione di un antico papiro scritto nell' anno settimo dell' impero di Giustino il Giovine*, Venice, 1768, folio (*Bibliotheca Maphæi Pinellii Veneti* iii. 343–5, No. 7895; engraved facsimile iii.

following p. 367). The MS is described on the title-page of Edwards's sale catalogue as 'the completest specimen hitherto known to exist, of an instrument written upon the ancient Egyptian papyrus, A.D. 572'; it was sold for £43.1.0 (*Bibliotheca Pinelliana*, p. 531, lot 12801).

12. The famous Polyglot Bible produced under the patronage and at the expense of Cardinal Francisco Ximenes de Cisneros (1436–1517), Abp of Toledo, grand inquisitor, and regent of Castile. This, the earliest of the great Polyglot Bibles, was printed at Alcalá (Complutum), Spain, in 6 vols, folio, 1514–17, although not circulated until 1522; it is often referred to as the Complutensian Polyglot (T. H. Darlow and H. F. Moule, *Historical Catalogue of the Printed Editions of Holy Scripture in the Library of the British and Foreign Bible Society*, 1903–11, ii. 2–6). The Pinelli copy was printed on vellum (*Bibliotheca Maphæi Pinellii Veneti* i. 1, No. 1). It was sold for £483.0.0 (*Bibliotheca Pinelliana*, p. 183, lot 4909).

13. Karl Eugen (1728–93), D. of Württemberg 1737–93.

14. The title-page in each volume bears the arms of Cardinal Ximenes; the arms are generally printed in red in all of the volumes except for the fifth (Darlow and Moule, op. cit. ii. 5).

15. Downing, 3 miles NW of Holywell, Flintshire.

16. Sir George Howland Beaumont (1753–1827), 7th Bt, 1762; M.P.; amateur artist, collector, and patron of art. His country seat was Coleorton Hall in Leicestershire. .

picturesque old grotesques, that probably they were originally taken from nature.

I am Sir

Your most obedient humble servant

Hor. Walpole

To Treadway Russell Nash,[1] Friday 1 May 1789

Printed from the MS now wsl. First printed, Toynbee *Supp.* ii. 30. The MS is untraced until it was acquired by Bertram Dobell, the London dealer, before 1918; not further traced until sold Parke-Bernet 19 April 1943 (property of Mr and Mrs Harris Hammond, of Bordentown, New Jersey), lot 12 (with five other items), to the Brick Row Book Shop, from whom wsl purchased it in April 1943.

Berkeley Square, May 1st 1789.

Good Sir,

I HAVE perused your notes and think them very just and proper and useful, and that the edition[2] will be a very fine one.

I have taken the liberty of suggesting (with a pencil) one emendation in p. 10[3] that I think would make much better sense of the couplet,

> Call fire and sword a desolation
> A godly thorough reformation.

The first line standing thus is a contradiction to the second; Butler could not mean that the Dissenters intended to give a horrid idea of their warfare; no, they

> Call'd fire and sword *and* desolation
> A godly thorough reformation.[4]

1. (1725–1811), of Bevere, Worcs; D.D., 1758; F.S.A., 1773; historian of Worcestershire.

2. Of Samuel Butler's *Hudibras*, edited by Nash and elegantly illustrated with plates after Hogarth and others, 3 vols, quarto, 1793. The third volume contains Nash's extensive notes on the poem. Only 200 copies of the edition were printed;

HW's copy is Hazen, *Cat. of HW's Lib.*, No. 3179.

3. Of the MS, presumably, submitted for HW's perusal.

4. Nash adopted HW's emendation (Part I, Canto i. ll. 201–2):

> Call fire, and sword, and desolation,
> A godly-thorough-Reformation,

(*Hudibras*, ed. Nash, 1793, i. 14).

In the former couplet too there would want the copulative *and* at the beginning of the second verse. I am with great respect and gratitude, Sir

Your most obedient humble servant

H. Walpole

From Richard Gough, Wednesday 27 May 1789

Printed from Nichols, *Lit. Anec.* vi. 281, where the letter was first printed. The history of the MS and its present whereabouts are not known.

Enfield, May 27, 1789.

PERMIT me, Sir, to solicit a place in your library for a new edition of Camden's *Britannia.*[1] A work long wanted: how executed is submitted to your impartial examination, which it is hoped will not be withheld from it; and the result of it, as it will point out all its errors with rigorous justice,[2] will render its corrections a genuine offspring of friendship, and confer a lasting obligation on, Sir,

Your obedient and obliged humble servant,

R. Gough

1. *Britannia: or, A Chorographical Description of the Flourishing Kingdoms of England, Scotland, and Ireland. . . . By William Camden. Translated from the Edition Published by the Author in MDCVII. Enlarged by the Latest Discoveries, by Richard Gough,* 3 vols, folio, 1789. The publication of Gough's edition was first announced in the *London Chronicle* 4–6 June 1789, lxv. 541. HW's copy (one of fifteen presentation sets) is Hazen, *Cat. of HW's Lib.,* No. 424. For his opinion of Camden's *Britannia,* in a letter to Lord Buchan 11 Feb. 1787, see Dalrymple 194.

2. See following letter.

To Richard Gough, Thursday 28 May 1789

Printed from a photostat of the MS in Thomas Kirgate's hand in the Bodleian Library (MS Eng. letters d.2, f.154). First printed, Nichols, *Lit. Anec.* vi. 282. Reprinted, Toynbee xiv. 127–8. The MS presumably came into the possession of John Nichols about the time of the publication of *Literary Anecdotes,* vol. vi (1812), and descended in the Nichols family; sold Sotheby's 18 Nov. 1929 (John Gough Nichols Sale), lot 239 (with HW to Gough 15 March 1792), to Last; acquired by the Bodleian Library before 1957.

Endorsed by John Bowyer Nichols: Printed in "Literary Anecdotes."

Berkeley Square, May 28th 1789.

MR WALPOLE is extremely ashamed of receiving so magnificent a present[1] from Mr Gough, and yet thinks it would be a want of the respect and gratitude he owes him, not to accept it with a thousand thanks, and with the admiration it deserves, and to which the voice of the public will certainly give its deserved praise, and in which Mr Gough's well-known judgment and accuracy is not likely to have left any errors, and none Mr Walpole is very sure that he is capable of finding.

Mr Walpole begs pardon of Mr Gough for not thanking him with his own hand,[2] but has been very ill with the gout for this month,[3] and is not yet able to write himself.

1. See previous letter and n. 1.
2. The MS is in the hand of HW's secretary, Thomas Kirgate.
3. See CHATTERTON 246 n. 2.

TO ELIZABETH CARTER,[1] Saturday 13 June 1789

Printed from Montagu Pennington, *Memoirs of the Life of Mrs Elizabeth Carter*, 1808, i. 480–2, where the letter was first printed. Reprinted, Cunningham ix. 179–80; Toynbee xiv. 128–9; extracts printed in J. L. Clifford, *Hester Lynch Piozzi (Mrs Thrale)*, Oxford, 1941, pp. 343–4. The MS passed into a collection of letters and documents formed by Elizabeth Carter's niece, Miss Hannah Carter; sold Sotheby's 22 Dec. 1919 (property of Hannah Carter), lot 102, to Edgar; resold Anderson Galleries 29 April 1921 (George D. Smith Sale), lot 363, to unknown; not further traced.

Berkeley Square, June 13th 1789.

Dear Madam,

DR DOUGLAS[2] has been so good, at your desire, as to inquire after me, and will let you know that I mend, though slowly, as is very natural at my age, and with my shattered limbs.[3] I cannot however content myself, though your kindness would be so, with a mere answer that is satisfactory enough. You must allow me to add my own thanks, as I feel much obliged, and am proud of your thinking me at all deserving to interest your sensibility, though I am not conscious of sufficient merit. I do not mean, however, to misemploy much of your time, which I know is always passed in good works, and usefully. You have therefore probably not looked into [Mrs Piozzi]'s *Travels*.[4] I, who have been almost six weeks lying on a couch, have gone through them. It was said that Addison might have written his[5] without going out of England.[6] By the excessive vulgarisms so plentiful in these volumes,[7] one might suppose the writer had never stirred out of the parish of St Giles.[8] Her Latin, French, and Italian

1. (1717–1806), poet, translator of Epictetus, and miscellaneous writer.

2. Andrew Douglas (ca 1736–1806), M.D. (MORE 360 n. 9). His first wife, Mary, was Mrs Carter's half-sister.

3. See previous letter and n. 3. HW was then seventy-one years old.

4. '——'s travels' in Pennington, who intentionally omitted the name. *Observations and Reflections Made in the Course of a Journey through France, Italy, and Germany*, 2 vols, published 4 June 1789, by Hester Lynch Salusbury (1741–1821), who m. 1 (1763) Henry Thrale; m. 2 (1784) Gabriel Piozzi. HW's copy is Hazen, *Cat. of HW's Lib.*, No. 3138.

5. Joseph Addison, *Remarks on Several Parts of Italy*, 1705.

6. HW makes the same remark in his letter to Henry Zouch 20 March 1762; see CHATTERTON 52 and n. 5.

7. In his letter to Mary Berry 30 June 1789, HW particularly objects to Mrs Piozzi's use of 'though,' 'so,' and 'I trow' (BERRY i. 21 and n. 22).

8. 'I hope you will discover that *my* style is much improved by having lately studied Madame Piozzi's travels—there I dipped, and not in St Gyles's Pond, where one would think she had been educated' (HW to Hannah More 23 June 1789, MORE 302). Mrs Carter found Mrs Piozzi's

too, are so miserably spelt, that she had better have studied her own language before she floundered into other tongues.⁹ Her friends plead that she piques herself on writing as she talks¹⁰—methinks then she should talk as she would write. There are many indiscretions too in her work, of which she will perhaps be told, though B[aretti]¹¹ is dead.¹²

I shall remove to Twickenham next week,¹³ to enjoy my roses at least, since I have lost my lilacs and nightingales. I ought, I know, dear Madam, to beg you not to take the trouble of answering this;¹⁴ but when you have had the great good nature of remembering my gout, how ungrateful it would be to deny myself the pleasure of hearing that you have not suffered much lately by your headaches.¹⁵ I dare not flatter myself that they are cured, for when are constitutional evils quite removed? We who have intervals, and still more, on whom Providence has showered comforts even when we are in pain, must recollect what more durable sufferings exist, and how many miserable beings have no fortunes to purchase alleviations. This I speak for myself, who know how far I am from deserving any of the blessings I enjoy. You, my dear Madam, have led a life of

style 'sometimes elegant, sometimes colloquial and vulgar, and strangely careless in the grammatical part' (*Letters . . . to Mrs Montagu*, ed. Montagu Pennington, 1817, iii. 314).

9. Throughout the book Mrs Piozzi makes use of numerous phrases and quotations in Latin, French, and Italian; English translations are frequently supplied in footnotes.

10. Mrs Piozzi's friend the Rev. Leonard Chappelow observed that 'to read 20 pages [of *Observations and Reflections*] and hear Mrs P. talk for 20 minutes is the same thing,' and he insisted that 'should anyone say to me, that 'twas a desultory publication, I shall immediately reply—'Twas intended to be so' (Chappelow to Mrs Piozzi 18 June 1789, quoted in J. L. Clifford, *Hester Lynch Piozzi (Mrs Thrale)*, Oxford, 1941, p. 345 and n. 1).

11. 'B——' in Pennington. Giuseppe Marc' Antonio Baretti (1719–89), Italian linguist, lexicographer, and miscellaneous writer.

12. He died 5 May 1789. His obituary in GM 1789, lix pt i. 469–70, begins: 'Mrs Piozzi has reason to rejoice in the death

of Mr B. for he had a very long memory, and malice enough to relate all he knew.' In 1773 Baretti had been engaged by the Thrales as a language teacher for their eldest daughter, Queeney; after three years of employment in their household, he had a falling out with the Thrales and left abruptly. Thereafter Baretti harboured a resentment against Mrs Thrale, and in 1788 three long, vindictive 'Strictures' by him attacking her appeared in the *European Magazine* xiii. 313–17, 393–9, xiv. 89–99 (Clifford, op. cit. 109, 142–4, 322–4).

13. HW was at SH by Saturday, 20 June, when he dined there with George Selwyn, Lady Ossory, and the Hon. Caroline Fox (BERRY i. 13 and n. 7).

14. No reply from Mrs Carter has been found.

15. 'Her unwearied application [to her study of languages] injured her health, and probably laid the foundation of those frequent and severe headaches, from which she was never afterwards wholly free' (Montagu Pennington, *Memoirs of the Life of Mrs Elizabeth Carter*, 1808, i. 9).

virtue, and never forget your duties; it would be strange then if I confounded you with

Your very respectful, and obliged humble servant,

Horace Walpole

To Richard Gough, Saturday 27 June 1789

Printed from a photostat of the MS in the Bodleian Library (Gough Prints 223b). First printed, Toynbee xiv. 138–9. The MS was bequeathed by Gough to the Bodleian Library with his collections relating to British topography.

Address: To Richard Gough Esq. at Enfield. *Postmark:* JU 27 89. ISLE-WORTH.

Strawberry Hill, June 27,1789.

MY PORTRAIT of Humphrey Duke of Gloucester,[1] Sir, from which Thane[2] made his print,[3] is on the door of an altar-table, which came out of St Edmundsbury,[4] and belonged to Peter Leneve,[5] Norroy, and by his widow[6] went to Martin, at whose sale[7] Mr Ives[8] bought it, as after his death I did,[9] since Mr Granger published his catalogue.[10] The portrait agrees extremely with and confirms another that I always concluded represents the same prince in my Marriage of Henry VI[11] as another side of one of the doors corresponds too

1. Humphrey (1390–1447), D. of Gloucester; youngest son of Henry IV.

2. John Thane (1748–1818), engraver and printseller.

3. Several portraits in HW's collection at SH were engraved for Thane's *British Autography. A Collection of Fac-Similes of the Hand Writing of Royal and Illustrious Personages, with their Authentic Portraits,* 3 vols, [1788–?93], but no engraved portrait of Humphrey, Duke of Gloucester, is included in this work.

4. That is, the abbey church at Bury St Edmunds, Suffolk. HW was probably mistaken about this; see Chatterton 184–5 and n. 14.

5. Peter Le Neve (1661–1729), Norfolk antiquary; Norroy King-of-Arms, 1704.

6. Frances Beeston (or Berston), m. 1 (1727), as his second wife, Peter Le Neve;

m. 2 (1731), as his second wife, Thomas ('Honest Tom') Martin (1697–1771), of Palgrave, Le Neve's executor.

7. Martin's 'pictures and lesser curiosities' were sold by auction at Diss in 1773.

8. John Ives (1751–76), antiquary and herald. Ives was a principal purchaser at the various sales of Martin's collections.

9. The 'altar tablets' (the folding doors hinged to the altar-piece) supposed to have come from Bury Abbey were purchased by HW at the sale of Ives's collection 13–14 Feb. 1777, lot 75, for £20. HW had the 'tablets' sawn into four pieces, and placed them in the Chapel at SH ('Des. of SH,' *Works* ii. 507–8). They were sold SH xxi. 44 to the Duke of Sutherland for £63.10.0.

10. See *ante* 3 April 1764, n. 2.

11. See *ante* 14 June 1784, n. 11.

with the portrait of Archbishop Kempe[12] in the same marriage. Another side has Cardinal Beaufort,[13] less striking, but not quite unlike
his head, as I suppose, in my picture.[14]

I cannot give you equal satisfaction, Sir, on the portrait of Duchess
Jaqueline.[15] I do not even remember it in Mr West's[16] possession,
nor can I say I recollect ever to have seen a portrait in enamel so
early as her time. In truth Mr West's authority was not very good.
His knowledge, judgment, and I will not say more, were not to be
depended on. In his large picture of Henry VIII and his family,
which I bought at his sale,[17] are Philip[18] and Mary[19] bringing in
War; Elizabeth, Peace and Plenty, two emblematic figures with their
emblems, and with naked feet. These Mr West called the Countesses
of Shrewsbury and Salisbury—though there was no Countess of Salisbury in the reign of Elizabeth—he might as well have called Mars,
Guy Earl of Warwick.[20] Moreover he put the name of Antonio

12. John Kemp (ca. 1380–1454), Abp of
York, 1426, and of Canterbury, 1452.

13. Henry Beaufort (d. 1447), Bp of
Winchester, 1405; cardinal, 1426.

14. HW's conjectures concerning the figures represented on the 'altar tablets' and
in the 'Marriage of Henry VI' were first
aired in his letter to William Cole 20 Feb.
1777 (COLE ii. 30–2). See also Cole's reply
23 Feb. 1777 (ibid. ii. 35–9).

15. Jacoba (or Jacqueline) (1401–36), Cts
of Holland, m. 1 (1406) Jean, Dauphin of
France; m. 2 (1418) Jean, D. of Brabant;
m. 3 (1422) Humphrey, D. of Gloucester
(annulled); m. 4 (1432) Frank van Borselen, Graaf van Oostervant.

16. James West, HW's occasional correspondent (ante 31 March 1764, n. 1).

17. HW bought the picture on the third
day of West's sale, 31 March 1773, lot 66,
for 80 gns. It hung over the chimney in
the Great North Bedchamber at SH ('Des.
of SH,' Works ii. 494), and was sold SH
xx. 86 to John Dent for £220.10.0; it is
now owned by Mark Dent-Brocklehurst at
Sudeley Castle, Glos. HW describes the
picture in his Anecdotes of Painting: 'Another curious picture painted about the
same time [in the reign of Queen Elizabeth], I know not by what hand, was in
the collection of James West, Esq. It represents Henry VIII sitting under a canopy
supported by pillars, and delivering the

sword to Prince Edward. On the right
hand of the King stand Philip and Mary;
Mars is coming in behind them. Queen
Elizabeth, too large in proportion to the
rest, stands forward on the other side, and
leads Peace and Plenty, whose faces are
said to be portraits of the Countesses of
Shrewsbury and Salisbury; but the latter
must be a mistake in the tradition, for
there was no Countess of Salisbury at that
time. Lady Shrewsbury I suppose was the
famous Elizabeth of Hardwicke. . . . This
picture was brought from Chislehurst,
whither it had been carried from Scadbury, the seat of the Walsinghams, and is
now at Strawberry Hill' (Works iii. 115n).
The painting was formerly attributed to
Hans Eworth but is now thought to be
the work of Lucas de Heere (1534–84),
who lived in England 1567–77. It was commissioned by Queen Elizabeth as a present
to Sir Francis Walsingham (Roy Strong,
The English Icon: Elizabethan and Jacobean Portraiture, 1969, pp. 139–41, No.
95). See COLE i. 305 and n. 10; OSSORY ii.
472 and n. 25.

18. Philip II (1527–98), K. of Spain
1556–98.

19. Mary (Tudor) (1516–58), Q. of England 1553–8, Philip II's wife.

20. Guy de Beauchamp (ca 1271–1315),
10th E. of Warwick, 1298.

More[21] on the picture, though More certainly did not paint here in the same Queen's time.[22] The real painter, I have no doubt, was Otho Venius,[23] the master of Rubens,[24] whose colouring it resembles, though in a much weaker style; and the two ends of the picture are exactly in the manner of Venius's emblems.

Of the MS[25] after which you inquire, Sir, I know nothing at all, nor ever heard of it. What little information is within my narrow compass, I am always ready and happy to give you, Sir, as everybody should for the sake of the public as well as for your own satisfaction, though nobody owes it more to you, Sir, nor has more respect for you, than

Your much obliged and obedient humble servant

Hor. Walpole

To the Rev. Joseph Warton, Sunday 19 July 1789

Printed for the first time from the MS now wsl. For the history of the MS see *ante* 18 Jan. 1788.
Endorsed by Warton: Mr Walpole's letter respecting the picture.

Strawberry Hill, July 19, 1789.

Sir,

I HAVE received the favour of your two letters,[1] and am very sorry it is impossible for me to inform you who was the painter of the portrait of my father that you have purchased. He was Knight of the Garter thirteen or fourteen years before he was Earl;[2] and as he was Prime Minister during all that period,[3] you may be sure that ⟨var⟩ious pictures were drawn of him by various painters; and as I was at school, at the University and abroad during the greatest part

21. Anthonis Mor (1519–75), Flemish painter.

22. Mor is said to have visited England in 1554, possibly arriving in 1553 (Strong, op. cit. 117).

23. Otto van Veen (or Venius) (1556–1629), Flemish painter.

24. Rubens received his later training in Venius's studio, and shows his influence.

25. Not identified.

1. Both missing.

2. Sir Robert Walpole became a Knight of the Garter in 1726; he was created Earl of Orford in 1742.

3. He was chancellor of the Exchequer and first lord of the Treasury from Oct. 1715 to April 1717 and again from 1721 to 1742.

of that time,[4] I could neither know, nor remember if I had known, many of those portraits, and yours was probably one which I never saw. Richardson,[5] Jervase,[6] Sir Godfrey Kneller, Gibson,[7] Hyssing[8] and Wootton[9] I do know painted him,[10] and Vanloo[11] and Zincke.[12] There are prints of him from Kneller among the Kitcat Club,[13] from Richardson,[14] Wootton,[15] Zincke[16] and Vanloo,[17] and I believe from other painters.

This is all the satisfaction, Sir, I am able to give you; and if I attempted more, it would be a vague guess, and from the circumstances I have mentioned, not to be esteemed authentic. I am with great regard, Sir,

Your most obedient humble servant

HOR. WALPOLE

---

4. HW was at Eton 1727–34, at King's College, Cambridge, 1735–8, and on the Grand Tour 1739–41 ('Short Notes,' GRAY i. 4–11).

5. Jonathan Richardson, the elder.

6. Charles Jervas (ca 1675–1739).

7. Thomas Gibson (ca 1680–1751).

8. Hans Hysing (1678–1752 or 1753).

9. John Wootton (ca 1682–1764).

10. The known prototypes and later versions of the portraits of Sir Robert Walpole by these painters are recorded in John Kerslake, *Early Georgian Portraits*, National Portrait Gallery, 1977, i. 198–205. See also *ante* Nov. 1772.

11. Jean-Baptiste Van Loo (1684–1745).

12. Christian Frederick Zincke (1685–1767).

13. Kneller's portraits of members of the Kit-Cat Club, commissioned by Jacob Tonson, are now in the National Portrait Gallery; see David Piper, *Catalogue of Seventeenth-Century Portraits in the National Portrait Gallery 1625–1714*, Cambridge, 1963, pp. 398–403. The portrait of Sir Robert Walpole was engraved in 1733 by John Faber, junior, with the Garter ribbon and star added (J. C. Smith, *British Mezzotinto Portraits*, 1878–84, i. 381, No. 208:28). George White's mezzotint of 1715 is probably based on the Kit-Cat portrait, with variations (ibid. iv. 1589, No. 54; Piper, op. cit. 257).

14. In his letter to Lord Hardwicke *ante* Nov. 1772, HW states that a print in which Sir Robert wears the Garter robes was taken from a painting 'by Richardson [of Walpole] in a green frock and hat, and the dogs and landscape by Wootton.' This print has not been otherwise identified.

15. No print after a portrait painted exclusively by Wootton has been identified.

16. Zincke's miniature of Sir Robert in Garter robes, painted in 1744, is now on loan to the Manchester Art Gallery from the collection of the Earl of Derby; it was engraved by George Vertue in 1748 for the frontispiece to the 1752 edition of HW's *Ædes Walpolianæ* (Kerslake, op. cit. i. 204).

17. Van Loo's original portrait of 1740, now in the Hermitage Museum, Leningrad, was engraved by John Faber, junior, in 1741 (ibid. i. 199; Smith, op. cit. i. 440, No. 372).

To Elizabeth Carter, Saturday 25 July 1789

Printed from a photostat of the MS in the Harvard College Library. First printed in Montagu Pennington, *Memoirs of the Life of Mrs Elizabeth Carter*, 1808, i. 482–5. Reprinted, Cunningham, ix. 198–200 (closing omitted); Toynbee xiv. 168–70 (closing omitted); Toynbee *Supp.* ii. 64 (postscript only, misdated); extract printed in R. A. Smith, 'Walpole's Reflections on the Revolution in France,' in *Horace Walpole: Writer, Politician, and Connoisseur*, ed. W. H. Smith, New Haven, 1967, p. 100. The MS is untraced until sold Sotheby's 28 July 1899, lot 151, to Barker; inserted in an extra-illustrated copy of Austin Dobson's *Horace Walpole. A Memoir*, New York, 1890 (vol. II, facing p. 7), owned by Sir Herbert H. Raphael, Bt; later acquired by R. G. Shaw, who presented it to Harvard in 1915.

Endorsed in an unidentified hand: Lord Orford.

Strawberry Hill, July 25, 1789.

Dear Madam,

I HAVE the pleasure of sending you a little present,[1] that I venture to say will be very agreeable to you. It was written by Miss More at her late visit to the Bishop of London.[2] Mrs Boscawen[3] showed it to me, and I was so charmed that I wrote immediately to the authoress[4] and insisted on printing a few copies, to which with much modesty she consented,[5] though she had not had any such intention. The more I read it, the better I like it;[6] it is so perfect that I do not think a word could be amended, and yet it has all the ease and freedom of a sketch. The sense, satire, irony and compliments have all their complete merit.

As I love to extract some satisfaction out of grievances, I hope that this bad summer has been favourable to your headaches.[7] I hope too that the almost incessant rains have not damaged the corn and hops in your county.[8] It ought to be a consolation to us too that the

1. A copy of Hannah More's *Bishop Bonner's Ghost*, printed earlier in July at the SH Press in an edition of 200 copies (Hazen, *SH Bibl.* 137–40).

2. Beilby Porteus (1731–1809), Bp of Chester 1776–87, of London 1787–1809. See MORE 301 n. 5.

3. Frances Glanville (1719–1805), m. (1742) Hon. Edward Boscawen (1711–61), Adm. and M.P. (BERRY i. 34 n. 32).

4. See HW to Hannah More 23 June 1789 (MORE 300–2).

5. See her reply to HW 27 June 1789 (ibid. 303–4).

6. HW wrote Lady Ossory 22 July 1789 that he hoped she 'admire[d] *Bonner's Ghost*, which will not lose of its beauties even if you read it often' (OSSORY iii. 56).

7. See *ante* 13 June 1789, n. 15.

8. In his letter to Lady Ossory 1 July 1789 HW mentions that his hay 'has been sopping these twelve days,' and in his letter of the 22d to her he refers to 'the late deluges' (OSSORY iii. 50, 55).

badness of the season has been ⟨our greatest calami⟩ty,⁹ while such
tragic scenes have been acting in ⟨France,¹⁰ and perhaps may⟩ continue and be extended in that country. Were they to stop now, it
would not be without such a humiliation of the House of Bourbon
as must be astonishing. Their government was certainly a very bad
one; but I cannot conceive that such a sudden and tumultuary revolution can at once produce a good and permanent constitution, when
not only all the principles and spirit of the nation must be changed,
but the whole system of their laws and usages too, and where the
rights and privileges of the various provinces are so discordant and
so different. The military, though that is extraordinary, may have
been seized with this rapid enthusiasm—but are as likely to revert
to their old spirit—and if the royal power is in a manner annihilated, will the nobility and clergy escape? If they are preserved from
fear, will the people be much relieved? And if those two bodies are
crushed, how long will the popular government be tranquil?—I pretend to no authentic information on what is passing, and less to
penetration—but I do not conceive that the whole frame and ma-
chine of a vast country can be overturned and resettled by a *coup de
baguette,* though all the heads in it have been changed as much as
when millions of Goths invaded nations and exterminated the inhabitants.

Excuse this vague speculation, but for this last week I have heard
of nothing else but this strange revolution. Nobody can talk on any
other subject. I am with the greatest regard, Madam,

⟨Your most obedient and humble servant

Horace Walpole⟩

PS. I must add a few words of reflection. What a lesson ought
this great convulsion to be to politicians! France, esteemed the most
stable of all governments, has plunged itself into this catastrophe by

9. HW's signature has been cut away
from the MS; the resulting lacunae have
been filled up using the text of the letter
printed in Pennington's *Memoirs* (see
headnote).
10. HW learned of the fall of the Bastille and 'the horrible scene at Paris' on
19 July (Berry i. 38–41). During the following weeks, as he received further ac-

counts of the events in France, he filled
his letters to Lady Ossory and others with
similar comments that express his strong
aversion to the Revolution. His views are
fully discussed in R. A. Smith, 'Walpole's
Reflections on the Revolution in France,'
in *Horace Walpole: Writer, Politician,
and Connoisseur,* ed. W. H. Smith, New
Haven, 1967, pp. 91–114.

its intrigues. By wasting its treasures to embroil other countries, it embarrassed its finances; the war to deprive us of America increased its debt: the pursuit of a marine to rise on our fall, swelled that debt—A reform became expedient,[11] and disgusted the nobility, who were at the head of all regiments. Soldiers only make risings and riots; they are generals and colonels who make rebellions—I need pursue my reflections no farther.

To Edward Jerningham, Thursday 30 July 1789

Printed from a photostat of the MS in the Henry E. Huntington Library. First printed in Lewis Bettany, *Edward Jerningham and his Friends*, 1919, pp. 48–9. Reprinted, Toynbee *Supp*. iii. 55. For the history of the MS see *ante* 13 Feb. 1778.
Address: To Edward Jerningham Esq. in Green Street, Grosvenor Square, London. *Postmark:* JY 31 89.

Strawberry Hill, July 30, 1789.

Dear Sir,

I SHALL be extremely glad to see you on Saturday, and thank you for proposing it and for staying all night; but alas! I am sorry that your Muse is not pregnant, for my Apollo is so old, though not troubled with the rickets like the Emperor,[1] that I fear he will not be able to impregnate her. However I have some hopes of your finding Lady Ailesbury and Mr Conway here,[2] and he is still so vigorous a poet, that who knows but he may do your Madam Clio's business?[3] I can at worst be your *accoucheur,* or my assistant Kirgate[4] shall, who

11. HW had taken seriously the efforts to reform France into a limited monarchy. He wrote Lady Ossory 15 Jan. 1788: 'the Parliaments of France . . . are aiming at wrenching from the crown some freedom for their country' (Ossory iii. 2).

1. Joseph II, Holy Roman Emperor 1765–90. Beginning in the summer of 1788, Joseph suffered intermittently from a fever and various other ailments. According to a report from Vienna dated 17 June, 'The accounts of the Emperor are not very consoling; the night sweats still continue, the spitting of blood has come on him again, and that prince is almost reduced to a skeleton' (*Daily Adv.* 7 July 1789). He died

20 Feb. 1790. 'Particulars, collected from the papers, respecting the last illness and death of the Emperor' were printed in GM 1790, lx pt i. 261–2.

2. Conway, Lady Ailesbury, and their daughter Mrs Damer were at SH on Saturday and Sunday, 1–2 August; they left on Monday for Ealing (Berry i. 48).

3. The only piece published in 1789 by Jerningham was *Enthusiasm: A Poem. In Two Parts,* but Jerningham apparently also composed a poetic tribute on *Bishop Bonner's Ghost* (n. 5 below). See *post* 9 Aug. 1789.

4. Thomas Kirgate, HW's secretary and printer.

has just delivered the Virgin Hannah of a divine babe, of which she fell in labour on fancying she saw a ghost.[5]

Yours most sincerely

H. Walpole

To Joseph Cooper Walker,[1]
Wednesday 5 August 1789

Printed from the MS now WSL. First printed, Toynbee xiv. 179–81. The MS is untraced until sold Sotheby's 20 Dec. 1877 (Collection of Autograph Letters Sale), lot 51 (with six other letters from HW to Walker, 1787–92), to Naylor; *penes* Mrs Alfred Morrison in 1904; resold Sotheby's 15 April 1918 (Morrison Sale, Part II), lot 896 (with HW to Unknown 25 June 1796), to Maggs; offered by Maggs, Cat. Nos. 370 (autumn 1918), lot 2096; 399 (Christmas 1920) lot 3445; acquired by Quaritch and offered by them, Cat. No. 415 (April 1928), lot 987; sold by Quaritch to WSL, Aug. 1936.

Strawberry Hill, Aug. 5, 1789.

Sir,

I HAVE received from Mr Ouseley[2] the parcel and letter[3] with which you have been so good as to favour me. I am not only extremely obliged to you, Sir, but much ashamed that my trifling writings should have taken up so much valuable time of a gentleman who generally employs it so much better for the information and entertainment of the public, and I am sure for mine, who have received both from your *Essay on the Irish Dress*,[4] and now from that on the Irish stage.[5]

Happy would it have been for me, Sir, to have received your communications and instructions a few years ago, when I should gladly have made use of them, which I can scarce flatter myself now I shall have an opportunity of doing. I have no thoughts of reprinting my

5. Hannah More's *Bishop Bonner's Ghost* was printed earlier in July at the SH Press. The speaker in the poem is the ghost of the inquisitorial Roman Catholic Bishop of London, Edmund Bonner (ca 1500–69).

1. (1761–1810), Irish antiquary.
2. Probably Sir William Ouseley (1767–1842), Kt, 1800; orientalist.

3. Missing. For the contents of the 'parcel' see n. 5 below.
4. *An Historical Essay on the Dress of the Ancient and Modern Irish*, Dublin, 1788. HW's copy is Hazen, *Cat. of HW's Lib.*, No. 3390.
5. HW presumably means *Historical Memoirs of the Irish Bards*, 1786. HW's copy is ibid., No. 3212.

Catalogue of Royal and Noble Authors;[6] and as I republished my *Anecdotes of Painting* in five small volumes but three years ago,[7] it would be too much vanity and presumption at the age of 72,[8] to expect that another edition could be wanted during my life.[9] However, as the latter may be useful to artists, and consequently may some time or other be wanted, I will insert in my own copy the notices that will improve it, and especially your corrections, which are always most welcome to me.[10]

On some passages in your letter, I will trouble you farther with a few words.

The picture of Petitot by himself was perhaps the very fine one which Mr Welbore Ellis[11] procured from Ireland not many years ago for the late Duchess of Portland, and which her Grace bequeathed to her friend Mrs Delany,[12] who has since left it to her nephew Mr Dewes.[13]

The inedited poem of Lord Essex[14] Mr Ouseley has been so obliging as to offer me a sight of;[15] a favour I shall gladly accept when I go to London.

The anecdotes of Jervas[16] I shall be happy to see whenever you are at leisure, Sir, to oblige me with them.

6. *A Catalogue of the Royal and Noble Authors of England,* 2 vols, SH, 1758; 2d edn, 2 vols, 1759; quarto edition printed at SH in 1787 as part of HW's *Works* (*ante* 11 Feb. 1764, n. 2).

7. See *ante* 28 Nov. 1786, n. 1.

8. HW was actually seventy-one, his date of birth being 24 Sept. 1717 OS.

9. A reprint of the fourth edition in four vols, octavo, was undertaken by James Dodsley in 1796 but was apparently never published (Hazen, *SH Bibl.* 66).

10. In his letter to Walker *post* 21 Dec. 1790, HW thanked Walker 'for your notes on two publications of mine, though, as I have told you, Sir, I am too old to think of making any additions to them.'

11. (1713–1802), cr. (1794) Bn Mendip; M.P.

12. See *The Duchess of Portland's Museum,* ed. W. S. Lewis, New York, 1936, p. 9; *ante* 28 Nov. 1786, n. 2.

13. Mrs Delany had three nephews with the surname of Dewes: Court Dewes (1742–93), of Welsbourn, Warwickshire; Bernard Dewes (1743–1822); and the Rev. John Dewes (after 1786, Granville) (1744–1826), of Calwich, Staffordshire (*The Autobiography and Correspondence of Mary Granville, Mrs Delany,* ed. Lady Llanover, 1861–2, vi. facing p. 1, 'A Pedigree of the Granville Family'). All of them received bequests from Mrs Delany, but the Petitot self-portrait was left to Lady Weymouth (ibid. vi. 485–6, 490).

14. Doubtless Robert Devereux (1566–1601), 2d E. of Essex, 1576.

15. In a letter to Bishop Percy 2 April 1797 Walker writes: 'The poem of which he [Ouseley] is possessed is a curious original poem of the Earl of Essex, written while he was confined in the Tower' (Nichols, *Lit. Illus.* vii. 739). The poem is not mentioned among the 'Pieces omitted in the foregoing Catalogue of Royal and Noble Authors, and discovered since the volume was printed' in *Works* i. 526–33.

16. Charles Jervas (ca 1675–1739), painter. For HW's account of him in *Anecdotes of Painting* see *Works* iii. 410–12.

I am not acquainted with a painter called *Miles* Hussey; it is perhaps a mere error of a letter for *Giles* Hussey,[17] a great draftsman, who, I believe, died since my last edition,[18] and whom I have briefly mentioned in the Addenda to my fourth volume of that impression.[19]

The lady's[20] opinion of Simnel[21] and Warbeck[22] being the same person, I must beg leave, Sir, to question. The first was spared, and disgracefully employed in the kitchen of Henry VII.[23] As the King got both into his power,[24] had Simnel escaped or died, would not Henry have urged it on the appearance of the latter? If Simnel survived till then, they could not be the same. I mention these objections, Sir, as they occur to me, but with the utmost respect to the noble lady who suggested the opinion, and who I find, like you, Sir, is too favourable to my tragedy,[25] which I did not intend should become so public, when I imprudently printed a small number of copies of it.[26] The subject[27] is inexcusably disgusting, and I can only prove that I am sensible of that and other faults, by suppressing it as far as is now in my power.[28]

17. (1710–88), painter and draftsman. There is a short biographical account of him in HW's 'Book of Materials,' 1771, p. 82 (now WSL), printed in Toynbee *Supp.* ii. 180–1.

18. Hussey died at Beaston, near Ashburton, Devonshire, in June 1788 (GM 1788, lviii pt ii. 751–2; Nichols, *Lit. Anec.* viii. 181).

19. In his notice on —— Hussey (d. 1769), a painter of racehorses and other subjects, HW pointed out that 'this was a different person from Mr Giles Hussey, whose drawings are so deservedly admired' (Addenda to *Anecdotes of Painting*, 4th edn, 1786, iv. following p. 316).

20. Not identified. Mrs Toynbee suggested (xiv. 180 n. 3) that the lady is 'probably the Countess of Moira, whose letters to Bishop Percy, printed in Nichols's *Illustrations of Literature* . . . , testify to her interest in historical subjects.' See Nichols, *Lit. Illus.* viii. 1–23.

21. Lambert Simnel (ca 1477–living 1525), pretender to the English throne (GRAY ii. 163 n. 14).

22. Perkin Warbeck (ca 1474–99), another pretender, whom HW believed to be the true Duke of York, younger son of Edward IV (ibid. ii. 163 n. 15; *ante* 29 Dec. 1767, n. 23).

23. The story that Lambert, after being pardoned for his imposture, was employed as a scullion in the royal kitchen derives from Polydore Vergil's *Anglicæ historiæ libri xxvi*, but HW probably read it in Francis Bacon's *Historie of the Raigne of King Henry the Seventh*, 1622 (Hazen, *Cat. of HW's Lib.*, No. 886; DNB *sub* Simnel).

24. Lambert was taken prisoner during the battle at Stoke in Nottinghamshire on 16 June 1487. Perkin, after proclaiming himself Richard IV at Whitesand Bay on 7 Sept. 1497, surrendered two weeks later at Beaulieu in Hampshire, where he had taken sanctuary.

25. *The Mysterious Mother.*

26. Fifty copies of the play were printed at the SH Press in the summer of 1768 (Hazen, *SH Bibl.* 79).

27. Incest.

28. For two earlier instances of HW's efforts to suppress the play see *ante* 16 April 1781, 8 Nov. 1783. An unauthorized edition was undertaken at Dublin in 1790; when Walker and Lord Charlemont were unable to forestall publication, Walker took it upon himself to oversee the printing of the play. See *post* 6 Nov. 1790.

The Marchioness of Buckingham,[29] I know, has also done signal honour to my little romantic story. I was last year on the point of going to visit her Ladyship's picture[30] on that subject of which I have heard great encomiums, but was unluckily prevented by the gout, to which I am very subject, and which added to my age confines me much at home, and warns me not to indulge any distant views. Still less could I expect the very flattering[31] civilities that, though a total stranger to both,[32] I have received from you, Sir, and Mr Ouseley. I am extremely grateful to both, though conscious of their being much too partial, and am with great respect and esteem, Sir, his, and

Your most obedient and obliged humble servant

Hor. Walpole

To Edward Jerningham, Sunday 9 August 1789

Printed from a photostat of the MS in the Henry E. Huntington Library. First printed in Lewis Bettany, *Edward Jerningham and his Friends*, 1919, p. 49. Reprinted, Toynbee *Supp.* iii. 55–6. For the history of the MS see *ante* 13 Feb. 1778.
Address: To Edward Jerningham Esq. in Green Street, Grosvenor Square, London. *Postmark:* AU 10 89.

Strawberry Hill, Aug. 9, 1789.

Dear Sir,

YOU HAVE the genteelest way in the world of calling whore and rogue, for a constable is no better, who stops a young woman[1] on King Apollo's highway and *presses* her to own her bastard child.[2] You then almost lay it to me; and then, as if I were a god, my illegitimate babe becomes immortal![3] Well, you verify the old saying,

29. Mary Elizabeth Nugent (d. 1812), m. (1775) George Grenville (afterwards Nugent Temple Grenville), 2d E. Temple, 1779; cr. (1784) M. of Buckingham; she was cr. (1800) Bns Nugent, s.j.
30. Not located.
31. The MS reads 'flatteries.'
32. HW may not have been a 'total stranger' to Walker at this date. Among the seven letters from HW to Walker sold at Sotheby's 20 Dec. 1877, lot 51, was one

said to be dated 1787, but this letter has not been further traced (see headnote).

———

1. Hannah More.
2. HW had 'insisted' on printing Miss More's poem *Bishop Bonner's Ghost* at the SH Press (*ante* 25 July 1789).
3. Jerningham wrote a poetic tribute in which he apparently implied that HW was partly responsible for the composition of *Bishop Bonner's Ghost*. Jerningham's verses are not known to have been preserved.

that extremes meet:[4] it is difficult to be more distant in quantity of person than Falstaffe and I—yet like him, I am the cause of wit in other men;[5] and though you have laid a child to me, you slyly laugh at my age[6] and meagre figure, and tell me I could beget nothing but a ghost. My phantom issue however is not so very incorporeal, for it has propagated by your Muse; and if the bantling did not cajole its grandpapa so immeasurably, I should be very proud of producing Master Fitz-Bonner, and suckling him in the nursery[7] of

Your most obliged humble servant

H. WALPOLE

From JOHN CRANCH,[1] Monday 17 August 1789

Printed for the first time from a photostat of the MS inserted in HW's copy of William Habington's *Castara*, 1640, now in the Dowse Collection, Massachusetts Historical Society. For the history of this copy see Hazen, *Cat. of HW's Lib.*, No. 2388.

London, 17 Aug. [17]89,
No. 1, Old Broad Street.

I HAVE made much inquiry, and can neither find any other copy of this book,[2] nor (which still more surprises me) any further account than the book itself furnishes, of so fine and amiable a wit as its author. My present information therefore tempts me to suppose the fame of both to have sunk in that oblivious gulph, which probably overwhelmed so many other (cotemporary) men and monuments of genius—the public distractions of this country,[3] which so soon followed the production of *Castara;* and I should not have presumed to request from Mr Walpole the condescension of accepting this

---

4. HW also uses this proverbial phrase in his letter to Lady Ossory 10 June 1780 (OSSORY ii. 196).

5. 'I am not only witty in myself, but the cause that wit is in other men' (*2 Henry IV* I. ii. 8–9).

6. HW was then seventy-one years old.

7. That is, printing Jerningham's verses at the SH Press.

---

1. (1751–1821), painter.

2. *Castara*, 3d edn, 1640, a collection of poems in three parts by William Habington (1605–54). The book was first published anonymously in two parts in 1634, with a second edition, corrected and augmented, in 1635. For HW's copy see headnote; on the verso of the title-page he wrote some biographical notes about Habington.

3. The events leading up to the English civil war.

book (curious as I think the matter of it) but under a persuasion of its being likewise extremely *scarce;*⁴ or had any less exceptionable mode occurred of expressing my gratitude for the favour of having been permitted to contemplate that sanctuary of curious literature and of the delicate arts at Strawberry Hill.⁵

J. CRANCH

To JOHN SIMCO, Thursday 20 August 1789

Printed for the first time from a copy of the MS then (ca 1930) in the possession of Miss Elizabeth Daley, of New York City; not further traced. On the second and third sides of the letter is written, in an unidentified hand, a list of one hundred names (including those of many Scottish kings), beginning with Dongardus and ending with James IV; it is possibly a list of prints owned by Simco.

Address: To Mr Simco, No. 11 Great Queen Street, Lincoln's Inn Fields, London. *Postmark:* AU 21 89. ISLEWORTH.

Strawberry Hill, August 20th.

MR WALPOLE is sorry he cannot give a ticket¹ for any day next week, as every day is engaged till Monday se'ennight,² but Mr Simco may have a ticket for any day in the week after next, if he lets Mr Walpole know by next Saturday's post.³

4. In his copy of the *Description of SH*, 1774, p. 23 (now WSL), HW noted that 'the 3d edit. of [*Castara*], now very scarce, was printed in 1640, small duodecimo.'
5. Cranch had visited SH the day before; HW's 'Book of Visitors' records that 'Mr Crank from Mrs Marsham' was there on 16 August (BERRY ii. 234).

1. A ticket to visit SH, in the form of a note addressed to HW's housekeeper.
2. 31 August. There may have been a cancellation, as HW's 'Book of Visitors' contains no record of a visit on Tuesday, 25 August (BERRY ii. 234).
3. No reply from Simco has been found, but the 'Book of Vistors' shows that he visited SH on Tuesday, 1 Sept. (ibid.).

To Richard Gough, Monday 24 August 1789

Printed from the MS now WSL. First printed, Nichols, *Lit. Anec.* iv. 712–13. Reprinted, Wright vi. 341–2; Cunningham, ix. 212–13; Toynbee xiv. 197–8 (closing and signature omitted in Wright, Cunningham, and Toynbee). The MS presumably came into the possession of John Nichols about the time of the publication of *Literary Anecdotes*, vol. iv (1812), and descended in the Nichols family; sold Sotheby's 6 Nov. 1951 (property of the children of John Bowyer Buchanan Nichols [1859–1939]), lot 428 (with HW to Gough 5 Dec. 1796 and HW to George Hardinge 9 July 1777), to Maggs for WSL.

Endorsed in an unidentified hand: This letter has been printed in Gent. Mag.[1]

Address: To Richard Gough Esq. at Enfield. *Postmark:* AU 24 89. ISLE-WO⟨RTH⟩.

Strawberry Hill, Aug. 24, 1789.

I SHALL heartily lament with you, Sir, the demolition of those beautiful chapels at Salisbury.[2] I was scandalized long ago at the ruinous state in which they were indecently suffered to remain. It appears as strange that when a spirit of restoration and decoration has taken place, it should be mixed with barbarous innovation. As much as taste has improved, I do not believe that modern execution will equal our models.

I am sorry that I can only regret, not prevent. I do not know the Bishop of Salisbury[3] even by sight, and certainly have no credit to obstruct any of his plans.[4] Should I get sight of Mr Wyat, which

---

1. We have found no printing of the letter in the *Gentleman's Magazine.*

2. As part of the alterations to Salisbury Cathedral undertaken 1789–92 at the direction of James Wyatt, the Beauchamp and Hungerford chapels on either side at the eastern end were demolished and the monuments removed to the nave. Gough's *Sepulchral Monuments in Great Britain,* 1786–96, ii. 186–91, contains an account of the Hungerford chapel, with illustrations (plates LXX–LXXII).

3. Hon. Shute Barrington (1734–1826), Bp of Llandaff 1769–82, of Salisbury 1782–91, of Durham 1791–1826. He visited SH in 1792 ('Book of Vistors,' BERRY ii. 240).

4. Wyatt's proposed 'improvements' to the cathedral were in general sympathetically received by the Bishop and Chapter (Howard Colvin, *A Biographical Diction-ary of British Architects 1600–1840,* 1978, p. 942). According to William Dodsworth, the verger of the cathedral, 'Mr Wyatt was perfectly sensible of the great beauties of these chapels, but it was found necessary to remove them for the safety of the building. It was done, however, with proper caution, and with the consent of the descendants of the founders. The ornamental parts, many of which were defaced, are perfected and judiciously arranged. . . . In changing the sites of monuments, the greatest delicacy and precaution was observed' (Dodsworth, *A Guide to the Cathedral Church of Salisbury. With a Particular Account of the late Great Improvements Made Therein, under the Direction of James Wyatt, Esq.,* 2d edn, Salisbury, 1792, p. 32).

it is not easy to do,[5] I will remonstrate against the intended alteration; but probably without success, as I do not suppose he has authority enough to interpose effectually—still I will try.

It is an old complaint with me, Sir, that when families are extinct, chapters take the freedom of removing ancient monuments, and even of selling over again the site of such tombs. A scandalous, nay, dishonest, abuse, and very unbecoming clergymen! Is it very creditable for divines to traffic for consecrated ground, and which the church had already sold?—I do not wonder that magnificent monuments are out of fashion, when they are treated so disrespectfully. You, Sir, alone have placed several out of the reach of such a kind of simoniacal abuse,[6] for to buy into the church or to sell the church's land twice over, breathes a similar kind of spirit.

Perhaps, as the subscription indicates taste, if some of the subscribers could be persuaded to object to the removal of the two beautiful chapels, as contrary to their view of beautifying, it might have good effect; or if some letter were published in the papers, against the destruction,[7] as barbarous and the result of bad taste, it might divert the design. I zealously wish it were stopped—but I know none of the chapter or subscribers. I have the honour to be with great regard

    Sir

        Your much obliged and most obedient humble servant

                            HOR. WALPOLE

5. See the following letter to Wyatt.
6. By documenting their historical importance in *Sepulchral Monuments in Great Britain*, the first volume of which had appeared in 1786.

7. Gough strongly criticized Wyatt's proposals in letters of 21 Oct. 1789 and 7 Jan. 1790 published in GM 1789, lix pt ii. 873–5, 1194–6.

To James Wyatt, Monday 31 August 1789

Printed from a photostat of the MS inserted in an extra-illustrated copy of James Boaden's *The Life of Mrs Jordan,* 1831 (vol. I, facing p. 81), now in the Harvard Theatre Collection, Harvard College Library. First printed, Toynbee *Supp.* iii. 449. The extra-illustrated copy of *The Life of Mrs Jordan* was presented to Harvard by R. G. Shaw in 1915; it was formerly in the collection of Sir Herbert H. Raphael, Bt.

Endorsed in an unidentified hand: A letter from Horace Walpole to Mr James Wyatt.

Strawberry Hill, Aug. 31, 1789.

Dear Sir,

I HAVE determined at last to build my offices next spring, and wish much to have them executed under your direction.[1] I know how much you are most deservedly employed; but whenever you have a morning to spare in the two next months, I shall hope you will bestow it on me here, and if you will take a bed here, I shall be more glad.

Be so good as to let me know by a line a few days beforehand, when I may be so fortunate as to expect you,[2] that I may not be out of the way, as I sometimes go to town for a day. I am Sir

Your obedient servant

Hor. Walpole

---

1. Wyatt apparently accepted HW's commission, and the Offices were built under his direction in 1790 from the designs drawn by James Essex (1722–84) in 1776. The cost of building the Offices was £1,855; they were the last important addition to SH (*Strawberry Hill Accounts . . . Kept by Mr Horace Walpole from 1747 to 1795,* ed. Paget Toynbee, Oxford, 1927, pp. 16, 18, 175–6; W. S. Lewis, 'The Genesis of Strawberry Hill' *Metropolitan Museum Studies,* 1934, v pt i. 82 and fig. 29; Berry i. 74).

2. The date of Wyatt's meeting with HW is not known.

To Richard Bull, ca September 1789

Printed for the first time from the MS pasted in Bull's extra-illustrated copy of the *Description of SH*, 1784, now WSL. For the history of this copy see Hazen, *SH Bibl.* 128, copy 13.

Dated approximately by the reference to the second edition of Pinkerton's *Essay on Medals*, 1789, which was reviewed in the *Monthly Review*, Aug. 1789, lxxxi. 139–40, and in the GM, Sept. 1789, lix pt ii. 837 ('Review of New Publications').

THOUGH you will not come to me, nor can I ever find you at home, I cannot forget all the honour you have done to my trifles, nor that I ought to make them as perfect as I can: I therefore send you a plate from Mr Pinkerton's new edition of his *Essay on Medals*,[1] in which he has given my unique gold medal of Antony and Octavia,[2] and which is mentioned in my case of 25 rare coins.[3] It is No. 4 of this plate.[4]

Yours etc.

H. WALPOLE

1. An *Essay on Medals*, 2d edn, 2 vols, 1789, by John Pinkerton, HW's friend and correspondent. HW had declined the dedication of the 1784 edition (*ante* 8 Aug. 1784), but accepted that of the second edition. HW's copy (the dedication copy), now in the British Museum, is Hazen, *Cat. of HW's Lib.*, No. 3823. See CHATTERTON 254 n. 5.

2. Described by HW in his letter to Conyers Middleton 9 April 1743 (DALRYMPLE 14).

3. The medal is No. 13 in HW's 'Catalogue of the 25 most precious coins and medals in the rosewood case': 'Gold medal of Marc Antony: reverse, the head of Octavia, the only one of her known, which makes this medal of the highest value' ('Des. of SH,' *Works* ii. 450).

4. Plate 2 in the first volume of Pinkerton's *Essay on Medals*. The 'Explanation of the Plates' says (i. 301): '4. Antony, reverse his wife Octavia; an aureus formerly Cardinal Quirini's, now Mr Walpole's. The same is known in large brass, but in gold it is believed unique, and unpublished.' See DALRYMPLE 14 n. 26. The engraved plate is pasted in Bull's extra-illustrated copy of the *Description of SH* next to HW's letter, with a label below that reads: 'Mr Walpole's unique gold, is No. 4 of this plate.'

To William Parsons,[1] ?1790

Printed from the MS pasted in Parsons's presentation copy of HW's *Essay on Modern Gardening*, SH, 1785, now WSL. First printed in Hazen, *SH Bibl.* 131–2, where the history of Parsons's copy is given.

Dated conjecturally by HW's letter to Parsons *post* 21 Feb. 1790.

MR WALPOLE has the pleasure of sending Mr Parsons the book[2] he promised him, of which he has but two more copies left.[3]

To John Wilkes,[1] 1790

Printed for the first time from a photostat of the MS in the British Museum (Add. MS 30874, f. 38). The correspondence and papers of Wilkes were acquired by the British Museum in 1878.

Dated by the printing of Wilkes's edition of Theophrastus in 1790 (see n. 2 below).

MR H. WALPOLE returns Mr Wilkes many thanks for the honour he has done him in sending him his beautiful edition of Theophrastus.[2]

---

1. (ca 1764–1828), poet; F.R.S., 1787; member of the literary 'Della Cruscans' at Florence, along with Bertie Greatheed, Robert Merry, and Mrs Piozzi (GM 1828, xcviii pt i. 92; W. N. Hargreaves-Mawdsley, *The English Della Cruscans and Their Time, 1783–1828*, The Hague, 1967, pp. 87, 300). This group produced *The Arno Miscellany*, Florence, 1784, and *The Florence Miscellany*, Florence, 1785; HW's copies are Hazen, *Cat. of HW's Lib.*, Nos 3803 and 3810. HW also owned Parsons's *Poetical Tour in the Years 1784–6*, London, 1787 (ibid., No. 2916). Parsons visited SH 14 May 1788; the 'Book of Visitors' records the visit as 'Greatheads, Siddonses, Kembles, Mr Parsons etc. *Myself*' (BERRY ii. 229).
2. HW's *Essay on Modern Gardening*, translated into French by the Duc de Ni-

vernais, SH, 1785. Parsons's presentation copy, now WSL, is inscribed by him 'From Mr Walpole' (see headnote).
3. 400 copies were printed, of which 200 were sent to Paris for Nivernais' use (Hazen, *SH Bibl.* 129). 'Mr Parsons' is the last name in HW's list of persons to whom he presented copies of the book (BERRY ii. 260).

---

1. (1725–97), politician; M.P.
2. ΘΕΟΦΡΑΣΤΟΥ ΧΑΡΑΚΤΗΡΕΣ ΗΘΙΚΟΙ. *Johannes Wilkes, Anglus, recensuit. Londini, Typis Johannis Nichols*, 1790. 120 copies of this edition of Theophrastus's *Characters* were printed, in addition to four copies on vellum, for private distribution (Nichols, *Lit. Anec.* ix. 68–9). The book does not appear in the SH records.

To Sir William Musgrave, 1790

Printed for the first time from a photostat of the MS fragment in Sir William Musgrave's collection of autographs in the British Museum (Add. MS 5726B, f. 73).
Dated by the endorsement.
Endorsed in an unidentified hand: 1790 Mr Horace Walpole afterw[ar]ds E. of Orford.

. . . at seven o'clock?

Yours etc. etc.

H. Walpole

To Mrs Archibald Alison,[1] Saturday 16 January 1790

Printed for the first time from the MS now wsl, acquired (with HW to Mrs Alison 18 Feb. 1790) in Dec. 1951 from Miss Dorothy Robinson, of Bath, who had inherited it in a collection of letters; its earlier history is not known.
Address: To Mrs Alison at Woodhouse lie near Edinburgh. *Postmark:* JA 16 90.

Berkeley Square, Jan. 16, 1790.

Dear Madam,

FROM the character I have heard of Mr Alison's[2] abilities I should always have been glad to learn that he had written a book,[3] and that I should have the pleasure of reading it; but I am doubly delighted, as it procured me the satisfaction of receiving a letter from you,[4] and so very obliging an one. It is most true that I have long had a most sincere regard and esteem for you[5]—but that

1. Dorothea Gregory (ca 1755–1830), dau. of Dr John Gregory of Edinburgh University, m. (1784) Rev. Archibald Alison; friend of Mrs Montagu, with whom she lived after the death of her father in 1773 until the time of her marriage.

2. Rev. Archibald Alison (1757–1839), LL.B. (Oxon.), 1784; curate of Kenley, Shropshire, 1790; prebendary of Salisbury, 1791; vicar of High Ercall, Shropshire, 1794; rector of Rodington, Shropshire, 1797; minister of the Episcopal Chapel, Cowgate, Edinburgh, 1800; author and divine.

3. *Essays on the Nature and Principles of Taste*, Edinburgh, 1790. HW's presentation copy (untraced) is Hazen, *Cat. of HW's Lib.*, No. 549.

4. Missing.

5. HW wrote Lady Ossory 23 Oct. 1784: 'I am acquainted with Mrs Allanson, and have very great esteem for her' (Ossory ii. 446).

was your merit, not mine. If I have any towards you, it was for speaking, perhaps more freely than I ought to have done, on your subject; but it was from zeal and truth, and with no intention of its reaching you. From the same ardour I have inquired after you, whenever I have had an opportunity, and the returns were just what I expected, encomiums on you; for the world is pretty just to the good, when it has no interest to be otherwise.

I wish I had a twentieth part of as just a title to your regard, and to the honour Mr Alison does me in sending me his book. I will impute the latter very willingly to the respect he may know I have for you, Madam; and in that point he will not be deceived. I beg to return him my thanks, and am impatient for his present.[6]

There was but one phrase in your letter, Madam, that, though all were flattering, I could dislike. You say you may never have another opportunity of writing to me.[7] I know but one reason that can prevent my receiving such a pleasure whenever you are inclined to make me so happy, and, that is my age, which forbids my expecting such satisfaction often, though it does not at all diminish my taste for it. Nay, I even indulge a visionary hope of living to enjoy a greater pleasure, that of seeing you again; for though threescore years and ten are pronounced to be a scene of sorrow,[8] I flatter myself the denunciation was but a reflection of experience, and not an invariable sentence—at least I, who have passed the term by two years, should be most ungrateful to Providence, if I did not avow that, in my own case at least, old age is by no means an uncomfortable season; as I hope you and Mr Alison will prove together, with the additional blessing of seeing happiness extended to your children.[9] I have the honour to be with the utmost respect and gratitude

     Madam
       Your most obliged and obedient humble servant

                   Hor. Walpole

6. HW praises the book but voices some 'objections' in his letter to Mrs Alison *post* 18 Feb. 1790.

7. No letters from Mrs Alison to HW have been found.

8. Psalms 90.10: 'The days of our years are threescore years and ten; and if by reason of strength they be fourscore years, yet is their strength labour and sorrow; for it is soon cut off, and we fly away.'

9. The Alisons had six children (two sons and four daughters), not all of whom were born by this time (Sir Archibald Alison, Bt, *Some Account of My Life and Writings: An Autobiography*, ed. Lady Alison, Edinburgh, 1883, i. 2, 9, 23, 32, 62–4).

To Thomas Astle, Saturday 30 January 1790

Printed from a photostat of the MS in the possession of Messrs Maggs Bros., London. First printed, Toynbee xiv. 246. The MS is untraced until sold Sotheby's 15 April 1899 (Important and Valuable Autograph Letters and Historical Documents Sale), lot 199, to Dr H. T. Scott; offered by Maggs, Cat. No. 360 (autumn 1917), lot 2345; later owned by Percival Griffiths, from whom it passed to his niece by marriage, Philippa, Countess of Galloway (d. 1974); sold Sotheby's 24 July 1979 ('Other Properties'), lot 335, to Maggs.

A MS written in the first person (signed and dated), but otherwise identical to this one in its wording, is now wsl; it is apparently an imitation of the letter to Astle made by an unidentified copyist.

Endorsed in an unidentified hand: 221. L[or]d Orford.

Address: To Thomas Astle Esq. at Battersea Rise. *Postmark:* JA 30. PENNY POST NOT PAID.

11 Berkeley Square, Jan. 30, 1790.

MR WALPOLE begs Mr Astle's pardon for the trouble he is going to give him, but shall be extremely obliged to him if he can let him know what Mr West[1] gave at Lord Oxford's[2] sale[3] for the seal of *Edmund King of Sicily,*[4] or what Mr Brander[5] gave for it at Mr West's.[6] A line will be sufficient.

1. James West (1703–72); M.P.; politician and antiquary.

2. Edward Harley (1689–1741), styled Lord Harley; 2d E. of Oxford, 1724; collector.

3. Lord Oxford's collection of Greek, Roman, and English coins, medallions, and medals was sold by Mr Cock of Covent Garden 18–24 March 1742. The 'gold seal of Edmund King of Sicily, brother of King Henry III of England' was lot 176 on the third day of the sale (20 March); it was purchased by West for £4, according to George Vertue's priced copy of the sale catalogue, which had been in HW's possession since 1757 (see Hazen, *Cat. of HW's Lib.,* No. 2359).

4. Edmund (Plantagenet) (1245–96), called Crouchback; E. of Leicester and of Lancaster; titular K. of Sicily, 1254. The seal was ordered engraved 25 May 1254 (gec vii. 378).

5. Gustavus Brander (1720–87), F.R.S., F.S.A.; merchant and antiquary (Nichols, *Lit. Anec.* vi. 260–1; dnb). His library, prints, and manuscripts were sold by Leigh and Sotheby on 8 Feb. 1790. HW's inquiry was doubtless made in connection with this sale.

6. West's collection of medals, medallions, and coins was sold by Langford 19–26 Jan. 1773. The 'gold seal, which had been annexed to a grant of King Edmund' was lot 83 on the third day of the sale (21 Jan.); it was purchased by Astle ('Astley') for £18.7.6, according to HW's priced copy of the sale catalogue (now wsl).

From RICHARD FRENCH,[1] Sunday 14 February 1790

Printed from the MS now WSL. First printed, Toynbee *Supp.* iii. 296–301. Damer-Waller; the MS was sold Sotheby's 5 Dec. 1921 (first Waller Sale), lot 127, to Wells; given by him to Thomas Conolly, of Chicago, from whom WSL acquired it in 1937.

Derby, Feb. 14th 1790.

Dear Sir,

ENGAGEMENTS which entirely diverted my attention from concerns of taste and literature, have prevented my acknowledging sooner the favour of your very just observation on the Apollo,[2] for which my friend[3] holds himself much obliged to you.[4] The lines are altered, and in my opinion improved: the Venus[5] you will think highly so. She is now described as a model of ideal beauty; which is precisely what I believe the sculptor intended to express. The passage you will recollect is in the future tense.

Onward with step sublime Apollo spring,
And mark the arrow on unerring wing:[6]
In Beauty's bashful form, the veil unfurl'd,
Ideal Venus win the gazing world.

The explanation of the Barberini vase[7] is transcribed by a schoolboy, and as I have not time to examine it may probably contain some inaccuracies, which you will be so good as to overlook.[8] I have

1. Of Derby; friend of Erasmus Darwin.
2. The Apollo Belvedere.
3. Erasmus Darwin (1731–1802), physician, botanist, poet, and evolutionist. He lived in Derby from 1783 to 1802 (Desmond King-Hele, *Doctor of Revolution: The Life and Genius of Erasmus Darwin,* 1977, pp. 155, 284). At this time he was working on his long 'philosophical' poem *The Botanic Garden. Part I. . . . The Economy of Vegetation,* published in 1791. Part II of the poem, *The Loves of the Plants,* had appeared in 1789, with a second edition in 1790. HW's copy is Hazen, *Cat. of HW's Lib.,* No. 3809.
4. HW's letter to French, in which he apparently suggested some alterations to Darwin's poem, is missing.
5. The Venus de' Medici.
6. In the printed poem this couplet reads:

Onward with loftier step Apollo spring,
And launch the unerring arrow from the string;
(*The Economy of Vegetation* ii. 105–6).

7. The celebrated Portland Vase, now in the British Museum. It had long been in the possession of the Barberini family in Rome, from whom it was acquired by the art dealer James Byres and sold to Sir William Hamilton; the Duchess of Portland purchased it from Hamilton in 1785, only a few months before her death.

8. *The Economy of Vegetation* ii. 320 refers to 'Portland's mystic urn.' Note XXII of the 'Additional' Notes' to the poem (following p. 214) is a seven-page discourse on the Portland Vase, illustrated with four engraved plates (pp. 53–9). The 'explanation . . . transcribed by a schoolboy' was doubtless returned to French after HW had read it.

read Messrs King's and Marsh's explanation of this enigma in the last vol. of the *Archæologia;*[9] neither of which are at all satisfactory to me. They are both feeble attempts to reconcile it with the life of Severus[10] by Lampridius;[11] with an ostentatious display of a mighty little learning, and not a trait of genius. I think you will allow my friend's solution to be not only ingenious, but if you will take the trouble to study the 80th and 81st plate of Bartoli's *Admiranda* etc.[12] which is taken from a sarcophagus in the Pamphilii palace,[13] you will scarce hesitate in admitting the probability of it. It being too voluminous for a letter I have enclosed it in two covers to Lord Geo. Cavendish;[14] to whom if you think it will afford amusement, I beg it may be shown; for of all human beings I know no one whose happiness I am more desirous of promoting: and I am inclined to believe that since mankind have taken it into their heads to walk on their hind legs, and cultivate their imagination these trifles do constitute no small part of their happiness. *Vitam quæ faciunt beatiorem*[15] somebody has said of them.

It was impolitic in me to mention the frontispiece, which I now find that I have not sufficient skill to execute tolerably. The author wishes to have it an allegory of the whole work, and not descriptive

9. 'Observations on the Barberini Vase. By John Glen King [1732–87], D.D. . . . Read Nov. 30, 1786,' in *Archæologia,* 1787, viii. 307–15; 'An Essay on the Elegant Ornamental Cameos of the Barberini Vase, with a View to an Explanation of them, and their Reference to History. By Charles Marsh, Esq. [1735–1812] F.A.S. . . . Read May 13, 1784,' in *Archæologia,* 1787, viii. 316–20.

10. Alexander Severus (208–35), Roman emperor 222–35.

11. Ælius Lampridius (fl. 4th cent. A.D.), historian. His life of Alexander Severus is included in the collection of biographies of Roman emperors, Cæsars, and usurpers known as the *Historia Augusta.*

12. *Admiranda romanarum antiquitatum ac veteris sculpturæ vestigia anaglyphico opere elaborata ex marmoreis exemplaribus quæ Romæ adhuc extant in Capitolio ædibus hortisque virorum principum ad antiquam elegantiam . . . ,* Rome, 1693. The plates in this oblong folio were designed and engraved by Pietro Santo Bartoli (ca 1635–1700); the text was supplied by Giovanni Pietro Bellori (ca 1615–96).

13. Darwin's Note XXII on the Portland Vase (n. 8 above) concludes as follows: 'I beg leave to add that it does not appear to have been uncommon amongst the ancients to put allegorical figures on funeral vases. In the Pamphili palace at Rome there is an elaborate representation of Life and of Death, on an ancient sarcophagus. In the first Prometheus is represented making man, and Minerva is placing a butterfly, or the soul, upon his head. In the other compartment Love extinguishes his torch in the bosom of the dying figure, and is receiving the butterfly, or Psyche, from him, with a great number of complicated emblematic figures grouped in very bad taste. Admir. Roman. Antiq.' The two relevant plates in Bartoli's *Admiranda* are numbered 66 and 67, not 80 and 81.

14. Lord George Augustus Henry Cavendish (1754–1834), cr. (1831) E. of Burlington; M.P.

15. 'The things that make life happier' (Martial, *Epigrams* X. xlvii. 1).

of any particular part. This he thinks may be intelligibly enough expressed in a picture of *Flora attired by the Elements*.[16] He has made use of the Rosicrucian doctrine of salamander nymphs, gnomes, water nymphs, and sylphs, as proper machinery for his philosophic poem, they having been originally intended [as] hieroglyphic representations of the elements, or as genii presiding over their operations.[17] But how shall I who am deficient in drawing the human figure design divinities, and such beings as are thus described in the 1st canto?

> She comes! descending through the whispering air
> The glowing Goddess guides her beamy car;
> Each circling wheel a wreath of flowers entwines,
> And gem'd with flowers the silken harness shines;
> The golden bits with flowery studs are deck'd,
> And knots of flowers the crimson reins connect.
> And now on earth the silver axle rings,
> And the shell sinks upon its slender springs;
> Light from her airy seat the Goddess bounds;
> And steps celestial print the pansied grounds.
> Fair Spring advancing calls her feather'd quire
> And tunes to softer notes her laughing lyre;
> Bids her gay hours on purple pinions move,
> And arms her zephyrs with the shafts of love.
> Pleased *gnomes* ascending from their earthly beds,
> Play round her graceful footsteps as she treads;
> Gay *sylphs* attendant beat the fragrant air
> On winnowing wings, and waft her golden hair;
> *Blue nymphs* emerging leave their favourite streams
> And *fiery forms* alight from orient beams.
> Pleased as they pass, she counts the impatient band,
> And stills their murmur with her waving hand.
> First the fine forms her dulcet voice requires
> Which bathe or bask in elemental fires;

16. This was the title adopted for the frontispiece, designed by Henry Fuseli and engraved by Anker Smith, with the publication date 1 June 1791. In Fuseli's design, the seated figure of Flora is surrounded by four other female figures, the Elements, in an oval format.

17. Darwin's 'Apology' for his poem (p. vii) states that 'The Rosicrucian doctrine of gnomes, sylphs, nymphs, and salamanders, was thought to afford a proper machinery for a botanic poem; as it is probable, that they were originally the names of hieroglyphic figures representing the elements.'

From each bright gem of day's refulgent car,
From the pale sphere of every twinkling star,
From each nice pore of ocean, earth, and air,
With eye of flame the sparkling host repair,
Mix their gay hues, in changeful circles play,
Like motes, that tenant the meridian ray.—etc.[18]

The Goddess of Botany then begins her address to the salamander
nymphs with a sublime description of the creation of the universe;
not of our comparatively small system, but of the infinity of systems
beyond the reach of Herschel's[19] telescopes.

Nymphs of primæval fire! whose dazzling train
Hung with gold tresses o'er the vast inane,
Pierced the drear reign of silence and of night,
And charm'd young Nature's opening eyes with light,
When *love divine* with brooding wings unfurl'd
Call'd from the rude abyss the living world.
—'Let there be light!' proclaim'd the Almighty Lord,
And trembling Chaos heard the sacred[20] word.—
Through all his realms the kindling Ether runs,
And the mass starts into a thousand suns:
Earths round[21] sun with quick explosion burst,
And second planets issue from the first;
Bend as they journey with projectile force,
In bright ellipses their reluctant course;
Orbs wheel in orbs, round centres centres roll,
And form self-balanced one revolving whole.
—Onward they move amid their bright abode,
Space without bound, the bosom of their God.—
Ethereal forms! who chase the shooting stars,
Or yoke the volleyed lightenings to your cars;
Cling round the showery bow with prisms bright,

18. Several of these lines were revised
for publication in *The Economy of Vegetation* i. 59–88.

19. Sir William Herschel (1738–1822),
Kt, 1816; astronomer. He had recently
(1789) discovered the sixth and seventh
satellites of Saturn using the great reflect-
ing telescope that he had built under the
patronage of George III.

20. HW has written 'potent' above this
word in the MS. In the printed poem the
line (i. 104) reads: 'Astonish'd Chaos heard
the potent word.'

21. In the MS the word 'their' has been
inserted (probably by HW) above the line
after 'round.' In the printed poem the
line (i. 107) reads: 'Earths round each sun
with quick explosions burst.'

And pleased untwist the sevenfold threads of light;
Eve's silken couch with gorgeous clouds adorn,
Or fire the arrowy throne of rising Morn.
—Who plumed with flame in gay battalions spring
To brighter regions borne on broader wing;
Where lighter gases, circumfused on high,
Form the vast concave of exterior sky;
With airy lens the scatter'd rays assault,
And bend the twilight round the twinkling vault;
Ride with broad eye and scintillating hair
The rapid fireball through the dusky air,
Dart from the North on pale electric streams,
Fringing Night's sable robe with transient beams,
Or call the star which leads the milky morn,
And fill with lucid flame her golden horn;
Illume with comet-blaze the sapphire plain,
Pale planets glimmering through its silver train;
Pearl the white zodiac; gem the glowing pole;
Or give the sun's phlogistic orb to roll.—etc.[22]

You see, Sir, that these young ladies perform grand offices, and are not to be painted by a common dauber. Perhaps your ingenious friend Mrs Damer,[23] who has all the forms of ancient Greece at her finger's ends, or that rising genius, young Mr Locke,[24] might design these 'nymphs with broad eye and scintillating hair.' But *I* must relinquish the task to some common designer of book-prints, who possibly may find his models in the Strand or Drury Lane.

You expressed so much gratification from the first quotation I sent you[25] that I will venture to refer to Lord Geo. Cavendish for another extract from the third canto addressed to the water nymphs. It is a tribute to the memory of a deceased friend of his Lordship's, who had a great taste for botany and natural history.[26] To me it must ever be the most interesting part of the poem.

22. As with the previous quotation, several lines were revised for publication in *The Economy of Vegetation* i. 97–136.

23. See *ante* 27 June 1772, n. 3. She was an accomplished sculptor.

24. William Lock, the younger (1767–1847), amateur painter, whose work HW greatly admired (BERRY i. 111 n. 8).

25. French's letter to HW is missing.

26. In ll. 297–320 of the third canto 'The Nymphs of the river Derwent lament the death of Mrs French' ('Argument of the Third Canto,' p. 111). A footnote to line 308 ('And bow'd his alders o'er Milcena's tomb') states that this is 'In memory of Mrs French, a lady who to many other elegant accomplishments added a proficiency in botany and natural history.'

I am much afraid that you will repent that you have encouraged me to be troublesome; but I cannot conclude without expressing my concern at your intimations of following soon your great and excellent father *quo pius Æneas, quo Tullus dives, et Ancus.*[27] No, Sir, that must not be till a distant day, till you are incapable of receiving or communicating pleasure. Where the flame is brilliant, the vital spark must still be strong.

Believe me to be Sir with great respect

Your most faithful servant

RICH[AR]D FRENCH

PS. As the Doctor's poem will scarcely be out before midsummer,[28] I will endeavour to send a few more extracts shortly; and if you will have the goodness to permit me, I will then take the liberty of requesting you to procure for me Mrs Damer's observations on a monumental bas-relief[29] in which I am too deeply interested.

To Mrs Archibald Alison, Thursday 18 February 1790

Printed for the first time from the MS now WSL. For the history of the MS see *ante* 16 Jan. 1790.

Address: To Mrs Allison at Woodhouse lie near Edinburgh. *Postmark:* FE 18 90.

Berkeley Square, Feb. 18, 1790.

Dear Madam,

I WAS in the right to assert that old age has its satisfactions:[1] you perhaps would not write to me if [I] were fifty years younger. I do not say but that it would be a different kind of pleasure if you did; yet it would not make so lasting an impression, for youth has so many joys, that it seldom reflects on any, and thence does not taste

27. 'Whither righteous Æneas, whither rich Tullus and Ancus [have gone]' (Horace, *Odes* IV. vii. 15).

28. Although some of its plates are dated 1 Dec. 1791, *The Economy of Vegetation* was published 10 May 1792; see *post* 14 May 1792, n. 4.

29. Not identified.

1. See HW to Mrs Alison *ante* 16 Jan. 1790. Mrs Alison's reply to this letter is missing.

them so sensibly. I feel all your kindness, Madam, but when you compliment me: a daisy in a meadow is much such an ornament as I am to the world; it is not quite so common as the blades of grass, but there are a thousand other daisies of equal value, or rather of none, and while there are violets and roses, we daisies are but weeds.

I should have thanked you and Mr Allison for his obliging present[2] sooner and more particularly than I did, but I will tell you sincerely what prevented me. I began it immediately, did read part of it and liked it much; but here in town, I was so often interrupted, that I found I could not pay due attention to the thread of the argument, nor was it to be taken up and laid down, like Mr Boswell or Mrs Piozzi.[3] I therefore waited till I could go to Twickenham for a few days and read it at my leisure, without being diverted from it. I have now done so, begun it again and finished it without any intervening distraction, and very attentively.

I can say with truth that it has pleased me much: there is a great deal of ingenuity, and the subject seems to have been meditated intensely. With equal sincerity I will confess that in some points I do not agree with Mr Allison, and he is so modest as not to demand universal acquiescence. It would be impossible to detail my objections without writing an essay, for which I have neither time nor am young enough. In general, I think he does not go back far enough, or, in other words, that he states *the effects* of taste for *the principles* of taste, by making taste the source of imagination in proper recipients—but does not taste exist, though it meets not with objects capable of receiving its impressions?[4] And is there not a native and inherent taste in an artist, of whatever description, who impresses taste on his works and foresees what effect they will have? Does not a statuary or painter conceive and produce sublimity, grace, beauty and harmony? Can those ideas be sensible to the original mind, be put into execution, and, be productive of correspondent ideas in another person, and not exist, independently, though not always attended by effect, from defect in the receiver?

2. A copy of Alison's *Essays on the Nature and Principles of Taste*, Edinburgh, 1790. HW's copy is Hazen, *Cat. of HW's Lib.*, No. 549.

3. HW probably has in mind Boswell's *Journal of a Tour to the Hebrides, with Samuel Johnson, LL.D.*, 1785, and Mrs Piozzi's *Anecdotes of the late Samuel Johnson, LL.D.*, 1786. HW's copies are, respectively, Hazon, op. cit., Nos 3069 and 3826 (both now wsl).

4. Chapter I of Alison's first essay 'Of the Nature of the Emotions of Sublimity and Beauty' concerns 'the Effect produced upon the Imagination, by Objects of Sublimity and Beauty' (pp. 1–48).

May I venture to ask if Mr A. does not confound taste and subsequent imagination too much? and does he not attribute too much to the association of ideas, and thence destroy the simplicity of ideas?[5] Methinks he does so, particularly in architecture, on which I differ with him the most. He seems to resolve all our admiration into that of a proper strength of a building, and into our prejudice to antiquity[6]—but can he really think that walls and columns only please when adequate to what they support? Nay, does one man in ten thousand on seeing an edifice consider whether the walls are of a proper strength and heighth? Forgive me if I say that he seems to be in an error about columns. We do not admire a column because its shaft and base are sufficient to support the entablature: on the contrary all three are parts of *one* support, and destined—not two of them to support the third and uppermost part, but all three to support something else, as the pediment or roof of a temple, etc. When Mr Allison shall behold the wondrous colonnade before Carleton House,[7] he will be struck at the absurdity of its supporting nothing!

I might not probably be able to prove by words the reality of *proportion*, though I have some notion that it can be proved by numbers and figures. I cannot define taste active or passive, though persuaded of both; no more can I define wit, yet is wit less real? So do I think proportion, and of its being a beauty, distinct from collateral ideas.—But to finish my answer at once, I cannot help believing, that the Great Author of all things had types or standards of sublimity, beauty, grace, harmony, and proportion in his mind, or knew that they would be necessary consequences of certain arrangements when he diffused all those excellencies both over or through the grandest as well as through the minutest of his works. This may not be a philosophic way of cutting the knot, but at least it releases

5. Section III, pp. 15–29, of the first chapter considers the effect that is produced by 'associations' in increasing the emotions of sublimity or beauty.

6. See especially the sections 'Of the External Proportions of Architecture' and 'Of the Internal Proportions of Architecture,' pp. 355–89 of Alison's second essay 'Of the Sublimity and Beauty of the Material World.'

7. The official residence of George, Prince of Wales, in Pall Mall. Alterations to the building began in 1783 under the direction of Henry Holland, who added the Corinthian portico and the Ionic screen fronting Pall Mall and remodelled the interior. The *European Magazine*, 1788, xiv. 384, reported that 'The screen of columns in the front is about 200 feet in length, and of the Ionic order of architecture. They certainly have a most grand and elegant appearance, but, we thought, seemed to require some ornaments at top to take away from that plainness unavoidable in an erection of such length.' Ornaments of artificial stone were later added. An engraved view of the front elevation appears ibid. xiv. facing p. 384.

me from the uneasiness of contradicting Mr Allison, and gives him an opportunity of confuting me. Indeed it is a kind of confession of being vanquished, when I fly to belief, and desert argument.

I own I have hinted my cavils very unwillingly, dear Madam, and in mere obedience to your commands. I do not love disputes or metaphysics, and it is one of the greatest compliments I can pay, when I enter on them; and it is certainly a compliment, too, for does one contest parts of a book that has not a great deal of merit? I will not even take it ill, if *you* should be displeased with my trifling criticisms; it will but give me a higher opinion of your virtues, and make me, if possible, be with greater esteem,

> Dear Madam
> Your most sincerely devoted humble servant
>
> HOR. WALPOLE

To William Parsons, Sunday 21 February 1790

Printed from a photostat of the MS bound in William Parsons's presentation copy of *The Mysterious Mother*, 1781, in the possession (1952) of Mr William Zimmerman, Jr, Arlington, Virginia. First printed in N & Q 1863, 3d ser., iv. 284 (dateline omitted). Reprinted, Toynbee xv. 446 (dateline omitted); Toynbee *Supp.* ii. 38 (misdated 'Feb. 24, 1790'); extract printed in N & Q 1850, 1st ser., i. 273. Parsons apparently bound the MS in his presentation copy of *The Mysterious Mother*. Spencer Hall on 25 Feb. 1850 (when he sent to N & Q HW's letter to Edward Louisa Mann, *ante* 28 July 1771, 'found among the papers of the late William Parsons, one of the Della Cruscan poets') said he had authenticated HW's handwriting by comparison with 'a note sent with a copy of *The Mysterious Mother* to Mr Parsons'; not further traced until offered by Quaritch, Cat. No. 328 (Jan. 1914), lot 196; later acquired by Mr Zimmerman (d. 1967). A copy of this letter (made by 'S. W.' on 31 March 1793) is in the University of Glasgow Library (MS Murray 502/101).

Berkeley Square, Feb. 21, 1790.

MR WALPOLE is afraid of thanking Mr Parsons as he ought for his kind compliments,[1] lest he should seem to accept them as due, when he is conscious of deserving more blame than praise; and though he obeys Mr Parsons's commands in sending him the tragedy,[2] and begs his pardon for his mistake and the trouble it has

1. Parsons's letter in answer to HW's letter *ante* ?1790 is missing.

2. *The Mysterious Mother*, SH, 1781; see headnote.

occasioned,[3] he is unwilling to part with a copy without protesting against his own want of judgment in selecting so disgusting a subject,[4] the absurdity of which he believes makes many faults, of which he is sensible in the execution, overlooked.

To William Fermor, Monday 22 March 1790

Printed for the first time from the MS in the Yale University Library. The MS was in the possession of the Rev. Thomas Prater (rector of Hardwicke and Tusmore, Oxon., 1841–56; Fermor had lived at Tusmore) in 1849; sold Puttick and Simpson 20 July 1855 (Very Interesting Collection of Autograph Letters Sale), lot 113, to unknown; resold Sotheby's 3 June 1893 (Bateman Sale), lot 160, to Burke; resold Anderson Galleries 22 October 1915 (Adrian H. Joline Sale, Part VII), lot 764, to George D. Smith; resold Anderson Galleries 30 Nov. 1920 (John L. Clawson Sale), lot 515 (bound with HW to Lord Ossory 23 June 1771), to Walter M. Hill, of Chicago; both letters later acquired by George E. Vincent, of Greenwich, Connecticut, who gave them to the Yale Library in Feb. 1933.

Endorsed in an unidentified hand: March 22d 1790. Honourable Mr H. Walpole on Lady Browne's death to Wm. Fermor Esq.

Berkeley Square, March 22d 1790.

Sir,

AS I am extremely concerned for the loss you have had of my dear old friend,[1] so I am very sensible, Sir, to your great goodness in thinking so soon of notifying our misfortune to me. I had a most sincere regard for Lady Browne and for her amiable qualities and excellent temper. I have long seen with great grief the dangerous state of her health, and for some months despaired of her recovery.[2] The last time I saw her, about ten days before her death, I found her worse than I had yet seen her, and when I called on her the night before she died, I was not surprised, though much shocked, to learn so bad an account of her.

3. HW had previously sent Parsons a copy of the French translation of the *Essay on Modern Gardening*, SH, 1785; see HW to Parsons *ante* ?1790. HW seems to be apologizing for having sent the wrong book.

4. Incest.

————

1. Lady Browne, HW's Twickenham neighbour and correspondent. She died 20 March 1790 (*European Magazine*, 1790, xvii. 240). William Fermor was her son by her first marriage to Henry Fermor (ca 1715–47).

2. Lady Mary Coke noted in her journal that she passed the evening of 20 Dec. 1788 'with Lady Browne who is always in a suffering state' (Coke, 'MS Journals' *sub* 24 Dec. 1789).

As you yourself, Sir, must have been prepared for the fatal event, and have so great comfort in the tranquillity of her last moments and Christian resignation, I hope the blow will have no bad effects on your own health.

I was at Twickenham when the honour of your letter[3] arrived here, and before I came away, I sent my servant[4] to Richmond to inquire after you, not then knowing you was in town.

I beg, Sir, you will accept my thanks and sincere condolence, and I hope you will give me leave for Lady Browne's sake to profess myself with the greatest respect and attachment

> Sir
>> Your most obedient and devoted humble servant
>>> HOR. WALPOLE

To LORD CARLISLE,[1] Saturday 10 April 1790

Printed from a photostat of the MS in the possession of Mr George Howard, Castle Howard, Yorkshire, kindly furnished by the archivist, Miss Judith Oppenheimer. First printed in Hist. MSS Comm., 15th Report, App. vi (*Carlisle MSS*), 1897, p. 680 (salutation, closing, and signature omitted). Reprinted, Toynbee xiv. 249. The MS passed by family descent to the 9th Earl of Carlisle (1843–1911); on the death of the 9th Earl's widow in 1921, the family estates were divided and Castle Howard (and its collection of family papers) went to her only surviving son, the Hon. Geoffrey Howard (1877–1935); his second son, Mr George Howard, inherited Castle Howard on the death of his older brother in 1944.
Endorsed by Carlisle: Mr Walpole, April 11th [17]90.

Berkeley Square, April 10, 1790.

My Lord,

I HAD sent my servant to the other end of the town to Mr Pinkerton's[2] bookseller,[3] or I should not have been so late before I acknowledged the great pleasure I received from the beautiful and genteel lines[4] with which your Lordship was so very good as to

3. Missing.
4. Perhaps James Colomb, HW's footman.

———

1. Frederick Howard (1748–1825), 5th E. of Carlisle, 1758; K.T., 1767; K.G., 1793.
2. John Pinkerton, HW's friend and correspondent.

3. John Nichols (1745–1826), bookseller and printer at Cicero's Head, Red Lion Passage, Fleet Street (H. B. Wheatley, *London Past and Present*, 1891, iii. 154–5). See n. 7 below.
4. *To Sir Joshua Reynolds on his late Resignation of the President's Chair of the Royal Academy*, 1790. HW's copy of

honour me yesterday. It is very fortunate for Sir Joshua that the justice you have done to his merit will long survive his works, and will convince posterity that he was the real founder of an English school—if such a school shall continue.

Your Lordship has as justly described his foreign predecessors[5] and the characters of their works; and you have said in few lines, what I had attempted in far too many in prose.[6] Yet I am so pleased, that allow me, my Lord, to say, that you will be very blameable, if, with so poetic a talent, you do not employ it oftener to vanquish competitors more worthy of you.

I have the honour to be, my Lord, with the greatest respect, admiration and gratitude

> Your Lordship's
> Most obedient and most obliged humble servant
>
> Hor. Walpole

PS. Your Lordship has but half a guinea more to pay for the volume[7] that accompanies this.

To Thomas Pennant, Monday 19 April 1790

Printed for the first time from the MS now WSL. For the history of the MS see *ante* 25 May 1773.

April 19, 1790.

MR WALPOLE sends Mr Pennant an old impression of Queen Elizabeth's coin;[1] it is not on the paper he wished, but is better than could be obtained now from the plate.

Carlisle's poem has not been traced in the SH records.

5. Among the foreign-born painters whom Carlisle mentions are Van Dyck, Rubens, Lely, Kneller, Verrio, Van Loo, and Dahl (ll. 19–48).

6. HW alludes to his accounts of these painters in *Anecdotes of Painting in England*, SH, 1762–71.

7. *Vitæ antiquæ sanctorum qui habitaverunt in ea parte Britanniæ nunc vocata Scotia, vel in ejus insulis,* 1789. John

Pinkerton was the editor of this work, of which only one hundred copies were printed; the publisher was John Nichols. Both HW and Carlisle were subscribers to the work. HW's copy (untraced) is Hazen, *Cat. of HW's Lib.,* No. 2450.

———

1. Described by HW in his *Catalogue of the Royal and Noble Authors of England:* 'I have in my possession . . . a fragment of one of her [Queen Elizabeth's] last broad pieces, representing

Mr W. thanks Mr P. for the print,[2] and will send him a Lambert[3] as soon as he can find one, but believes he has not one in town, but may have at Strawberry Hill.

To ?Thomas Astle, Friday 30 April 1790

Printed from a copy (furnished by the owner to Mrs Toynbee and now wsl) of the MS in the possession (1905) of John D. Enys, Enys, Penryn, Cornwall. First printed, Toynbee xiv. 250 (salutation omitted). The MS is untraced until sold Sotheby's 12 Dec. 1894 (Autograph Letters and Historical Documents Sale), lot 322, to Steele; resold Sotheby's 5 May 1900, lot 237, to Barker; *penes* John D. Enys in 1901 but not further traced.

The addressee is conjecturally identified as Thomas Astle, the most likely one of HW's antiquarian friends at this date who had a 'most precious treasury of MSS' that included 'several antique Scottish charters and other documents' (see n. 4 below).

Berkeley Square, April 30, 1790.

Dear Sir,

YOU have for many years been so very obliging to me[1] that I presume on that kindness to recommend to you the bearer Mr Pinkerton,[2] whose great abilities, various knowledge and indefatigable industry in the pursuit of literary truth, cannot want so poor and inferior countenance as mine to introduce him to one of congenial zeal in the cause of erudition. Mr Pinkerton, Sir, is engaged

her horridly old and deformed: an entire coin with this image is not known: it is universally supposed that the die was broken by her command, and that some workman of the mint cut out this morsel, which contains barely the face. As it has never been engraved, so singular a curiosity may have its merit, in a work which has no other kind of merit' (*Works* i. 321). A small engraving of the coin is given in the text. The coin is listed (No. 10) in the 'Catalogue of the 25 most precious coins and medals in the rosewood case,' 'Des. of SH,' *Works* ii. 450. HW purchased it at the sale of Lord Oxford's collection in 1742.

2. Possibly a separate impression of the engraved portrait of Sir Henry Lee that is the frontispiece to Pennant's *Of Lon-*

don, published 22 April 1790 (Berry i. 93 n. 13). See HW to Pennant *ante* 10 Oct. 1787 and n. 4.

3. Perhaps John Lambert (1619–84), the parliamentary general. Robert Walker's portrait of him was engraved by Alexander Bannerman for HW's *Anecdotes of Painting*, SH, 1762–71, ii. facing p. 155. Pennant may have requested a separate impression of this print.

———

1. Astle's assistance to HW in his antiquarian pursuits began as early as 1767, when HW was working on *Historic Doubts on . . . Richard the Third;* see *ante* 3 Aug. 1767.

2. John Pinkerton, HW's friend and correspondent.

in elucidating the very ancient history of Scotland from the most authentic memorials that exist.[3] He has been informed that in your most precious treasury of MSS[4] are several antique Scottish charters and other documents. And he could not receive that information, without learning at the same time how benevolent and indulgent a patron you are of the devotees to historic antiquities. Mr Pinkerton is a man of strict honour and I will answer that he will not abuse your condescension if you will favour him with a view of whatever may suit his object. On me you will confer a new and particular obligation, and it will be a pleasure to me too to have formed an acquaintance between two gentlemen to whom this island are [sic] and will be so much indebted.

I have the honour to be with great regard, Sir

Your very grateful and most obedient humble servant

HOR. WALPOLE

3. Pinkerton's *The History of Scotland from the Accession of the House of Stuart to that of Mary. With Appendixes of Original Papers*, 2 vols, was published in 1797. In the Preface (i. v) he calls it 'the greatest labour of his life.'

4. According to the biographical notice of Astle printed in Nichols, *Lit. Anec.* iii. 202, 'his MS library [was] accounted to exceed that of any private gentleman in England; and his liberal utility to men of science their acknowledgments abundantly testify.' Astle bequeathed his MSS conditionally to the 1st Marquess of Buckingham, who built a library at Stowe to receive them; many of the most valuable items are among the Stowe MSS now in the British Museum.

To Richard Gough, Monday 17 May 1790

Printed from a photostat of the MS in the Henry W. and Albert A. Berg Collection, New York Public Library. First printed, Nichols, *Lit. Anec.* vi. 291. Reprinted, Toynbee xiv. 251. The MS presumably came into the possession of John Nichols about the time of the publication of *Literary Anecdotes*, vol. vi (1812), and decended in the Nichols family; sold Sotheby's 18 Nov. 1929 (John Gough Nichols Sale), lot 235, to E. J. Heise; later acquired for the Berg Collection.

Endorsed by John Bowyer Nichols: To R. Gough Esq. (Printed in Literary Anecdotes).

Endorsed in an unidentified hand: (?) Sent 29.

Address: Richard Gough Esqr.

Berkeley Square, May 17, 1790.

Dear Sir,

I HAVE the pleasure of telling you that Lord Monson has acquainted me with his having brought his old portraits to town,[1] and that you may see them at his house in Albemarle Street, but they are so much decayed, that he does not propose to have them repaired.

If you should be coming to town, I will beg you to give me previous notice, and I will be ready to attend you to his Lordship's house; but I must know it overnight, that I may apprise Lord Monson; and I should wish to hear from you in time, that I may not be at Strawberry Hill, whither I go frequently now the season is so fine. I am Sir, with great regard

Your much obliged humble servant

HOR. WALPOLE

---

1. These 'old portraits' had formerly been at Broxbournbury, Monson's seat in Hertfordshire, which he sold in 1789. See *ante* 8 May 1788 and n. 15. Gough's particular interest in the portraits is not explained.

From RICHARD BULL, Friday 28 May 1790

Printed from a photograph of the MS written on the old mount of a drawing by Marcellus Laroon, now in the Courtauld Institute of Art, Sir Robert Witt Collection (see n. 1 below). First printed in Robert Raines, *Marcellus Laroon*, 1967, p. 141, No. 80. Reprinted in Raines's exhibition catalogue *Marcellus Laroon*, Aldeburgh and London, June–July 1967, No. 57. The drawing is untraced until sold Sotheby's 30 June 1920 (Francis Wellesley Sale), lot 505; resold Sotheby's 11 Feb. 1947 (Randall Davies Sale), lot 266 (with another Laroon drawing), to Colnaghi; acquired from Colnaghi by Sir Robert Witt, who bequeathed it to the Courtauld Institute in 1952.

In 1790 the 28th of the month fell on a Friday only in May.

Friday, [May] 28, 1790.

MR BULL found this drawing[1] in a lot bought for him,[2] some little time since—it may *possibly* be of some use to Mr Walpole; 'tis of none at all to Mr Bull, nor did he know till yesterday that it was in the lot ordered to be bought for him.

1. A pencil drawing by Marcellus Laroon (1679–1772), signed and inscribed by him 'Mat Ashton the Painter at Chester.—Carigatura,' now in the Courtauld Institute of Art, Sir Robert Witt Collection (No. 4384). The drawing depicts three men jeering at a fourth (presumably Ashton), who wears an oversized hat, coat, and boots; the words 'miserable Goths' are contained in a balloon issuing from Ashton's mouth. Matthew Ashton (fl. 1725–50) was a portrait painter who worked in London and in Ireland (Robert Raines, *Marcellus Laroon*, 1967, p. 141, No. 80; illustrated p. 160, pl. 6).

2. Neither the lot nor the sale in which it was included has been identified.

To George Nicol,[1] Sunday 27 June 1790

Printed for the first time from the MS now wsl. The MS is untraced until sold Wheatley 8 Dec. 1836 (George Sigmond Sale), lot 848, to unknown; resold Sotheby's 10 May 1875 (Pocock Sale), lot 183, to Webster; resold Sotheby's 1 Dec. 1892 (property of a Gentleman), lot 195, to Pearson; resold American Art Association—Anderson Galleries 25 Oct. 1934 (Thomas Hughes Kelly Sale), lot 571 (with HW to ?Dalrymple 3 July 1792), to wsl.

Address: To Mr Nichols at the Shakespeare Gallery in Pall Mall, London.
Postmark: JU 28 90.

Strawberry Hill, June 27, 1790.

Sir,

AS YOU and Mrs Nichols[2] and Mr Boydel[3] were so obliging as to promise me a morning, I shall be very glad of the favour of your company either on Saturday or Sunday next[4] whichever will be more convenient to you, and at twelve o'clock, which is the hour most favourable for seeing my house, which depends much on the sun.

If this is too early in the season, a week later will be the same to me, but after that I shall be absent for a little time. If young Mr Boydel[5] will accompany you, I shall be very glad to see him.

I am

Your much obliged humble servant

Hor. Walpole

1. (or Nichol) (ca 1740–1828), bookseller to George III and to other notable collectors. He was associated with his uncle, David Wilson, in the Strand until 1777, later removing to Pall Mall, where he became associated with the Boydells in printing their edition of Shakespeare. He established the Shakespeare Press about 1790 with William Bulmer (1757–1830) (GM 1828, xcviii pt ii. 279–81; Nichols, *Lit. Illus.* viii. 501).

2. Mary Boydell (d. 1820), m. (1787), as his second wife, George Nicol; print collector (GM 1787, lvii pt ii. 836; 1820, xc pt ii. 574; 1824, xciv pt i. 236).

3. John Boydell (1719–1804), engraver and publisher of prints; alderman 1782–1804, sheriff, 1785, and lord mayor 1790–1

of London. He and his nephew Josiah Boydell (n. 5 below) were partners in the printselling business and in the Shakespeare Gallery, which they built in Pall Mall to house the paintings they commissioned to illustrate Shakespeare's plays (Nichols, *Lit. Anec.* iii. 411–17; BERRY i. 80–1 n. 27; DALRYMPLE 206 and n. 16).

4. HW's 'Book of Visitors' records that the 'Boydels and Nichols' were at SH on Saturday, 3 July; HW showed them the house himself (BERRY ii. 236). See following letter.

5. Josiah Boydell (1752–1817), painter and engraver; alderman of London 1805–9; Master of the Company of Stationers, 1811 (GM 1817, lxxxvii pt i. 376–7).

To GEORGE NICOL, Tuesday 6 July 1790

Printed from the MS now wsl. First printed, Toynbee *Supp.* ii. 39–42. The MS is untraced until it was acquired by F. T. Sabin, the London dealer, before 1918; sold by Gabriel Wells to wsl in July 1932.

Strawberry Hill, July 6, 1790.

IT GIVES me great pleasure to hear, Sir, that my house and collection entertained you so well.[1] They have many visitants, for I refuse none,[2] though frequently not very conveniently; yet I never regret that disturbance, when it is not idle curiosity and the fondness for making a party that draws spectators hither—but to persons of taste and knowledge like you and your friends, I am happy to show the collection myself.

You express so much kind satisfaction,[3] Sir, in what you did see, that I will venture to say you saw my assemblage of curious trifles very imperfectly. I am not only afraid of tiring my company, for a virtuoso is apt to set a value on things that appear errant baubles to others, but from my age[4] and lameness it is impossible for me to go through the whole collection even with a small number of persons: but if you will give me another day alone and take a bed here,[5] at your leisure, I flatter myself I could amuse you for good part of the time, and even with what you are a better judge of than I am, a few singular books, which I had not time to produce last week.

This is but a preface, Sir, to the gratitude I owe you for the very obliging offers of service you make me[6]—but as you have so much modesty yourself, I hope you will excuse my saying that you wound mine by the far too civil terms in which you speak of my very shallow literary merit, which has never aimed at more than amusing myself. There was a time when I should have been proud of receiv-

1. HW wrote Mary Berry 3 July 1790 (apparently after midnight): 'The Boydels and Nicholses breakfasted here yesterday, in return for their civilities at the Shakespeare Gallery' (BERRY i. 80–1). The visitors were George Nicol, his wife Mary, John Boydell, and Josiah Boydell. See previous letter and n. 4.

2. HW's Rules for admission to SH stated that 'Mr Walpole is very ready to oblige any curious persons with the sight of his house and collection; . . . he re-

fuses a ticket to nobody that sends for one' (Hazen, *SH Bibl.* 226).

3. Nicol's letter to HW is missing.

4. HW was then seventy-two.

5. There is no record of another visit by Nicol until 16 Aug. 1791, when Nicol was accompanied by Edmund Lodge ('Book of Visitors,' BERRY ii. 239).

6. Nicol, a bookseller, had perhaps offered to publish any future work that HW might write. See *post* 30 Aug. 1792.

ing both assistance and information from you—now, at near seventy-four, I have neither the presumption to look forwards to duration, nor the vanity to imagine that old age, additionally enfeebled by between thirty and forty years of gout, is fit for anything but repose. My best wisdom has consisted in forming a baby-house full of play-things for my second childhood, and I fear they do me more honour, especially as they amused you, than what Pope so well has called

—the rattles of the Man or Boy.[7]

I am extremely thankful, Sir, both to you and Mr Lodge[8] for his offer of inspection of the roll exhibiting a portrait of Richard III.[9] I shall be glad to see it, but will certainly not trespass on his too great indulgence—on the contrary, when I come to town, I will wait on him and look at it at the College of Arms. I imagine it is a dupli-cate of one drawn by Rous of Warwick, which was in the possession of the late Duke of Manchester,[10] and I suppose is still at Kimbolton. The late Duke was so good as to lend it to me, and I had some of the portraits not only copied but engraved for a second edition of my *Historic Doubts*,[11] though I have been too indolent to put my intention in practice. I will show them to you, when I have the pleasure of seeing you here again.

The proposals[12] you kindly enclosed were most welcome, and I

7. Farewell then Verse, and Love, and
    ev'ry Toy,
    The rhymes and rattles of the Man
    or Boy:
(*Imitations of Horace*, Epistle I. i. 17–18).

8. Edmund Lodge (1756–1839), Blue-mantle Pursuivant-at-Arms, 1782; F.S.A., 1787; Lancaster Herald, 1793; Norroy, 1822, and Clarenceux, 1838; K.H., 1832 (BERRY i. 278 n. 46). Nicol was the pub-lisher of Lodge's *Illustrations of British History* (see n. 12 below).

9. The Latin or 'Lancastrian' version of the so-called Rous Roll, one of two ar-morial roll chronicles executed by the an-tiquary John Rous (?1411–91) to celebrate the history of the earls of Warwick. It has been in the possession of the College of Arms since 1786. See *ante* 17 Feb. 1768, n. 2; A. G. B. Russell, 'The Rous Roll,' *Burlington Magazine*, 1917, xxx. 23–31; A. R. Wagner, *A Catalogue of English Medieval Rolls of Arms*, Oxford, 1950, pp. 116–18.

10. George Montagu (1737–88), 4th D. of Manchester, 1762. His seat was Kim-bolton Castle in Huntingdonshire. See *ante* 17 Feb. 1768, n. 1.

11. A second edition of *Historic Doubts on the Life and Reign of King Richard the Third* was published 12 Feb. 1768, only eleven days after the first edition; it is a page-for-page reprint (Hazen, *Bibl. of HW* 72). The ten portraits in the Rous Roll that HW had engraved were in-cluded in the third edition of *Historic Doubts, Works* ii (printed in 1771, pub-lished in 1798), between pp. 166 and 167, on two large folding plates.

12. The proposals (not preserved with the letter) were for Lodge's *Illustrations of British History, Biography, and Man-ners, in the Reigns of Henry VIII, Ed-ward VI, Mary, Elizabeth, and James I, Exhibited in a Series of Original Papers, Selected from the Manuscripts of the Noble Families of Howard, Talbot, and Cecil*, 3 vols, 'Sold by G. Nicol, Bookseller

beg you, Sir, to set me down as a subscriber. I had barely heard of an intended publication of Shrewsbury papers, but in so vague a manner that I concluded them letters belonging to the *Duke* of Shrewsbury;[13] and as the Duke of Montagu[14] is lately dead, in whose possession I have formerly heard the Duke of Shrewsbury's papers existed, I supposed those were the papers in question. We do much want authentic documents for the reign of King William:[15] still those Mr Lodge promises[16] may be as valuable—and as I have told you my age, you will not wonder that I am impatient; and for that reason, as much as I respect, Sir, your great improvements in typography,[17] I would be content to have the Shrewsbury papers worse printed, provided I could see them soon.

The demolishing reformers in France, I hear, have ordered all monkish property to be sold[18]—what pity if some Englishman does not purchase the British MSS in the Jacobin College at Paris,[19] where

to his Majesty, Pall Mall'; published 27 May 1791 (BERRY i. 278 n. 46). HW's copy is Hazen, *Cat. of HW's Lib.*, No. 455. Plans for the intended publication are mentioned in letters between John Charles Brooke and Richard Gough of 16 and 17 Jan. 1790; see Nichols, *Lit. Illus.* vi. 424–5.

13. Charles Talbot (1660–1718), 12th E. of Shrewsbury and E. of Waterford, 1668; cr. (1694) M. of Alton and D. of Shrewsbury. At his death the Dukedom of Shrewsbury and the Marquessate of Alton became extinct. For a genealogical table of the Earls of Shrewsbury see GEC xi. 731.

14. George Montagu (before 1749, Brudenell) (1712–23 May 1790), 4th E. of Cardigan, 1732; cr. (1766) D. of Montagu. HW's one surviving letter to him is *ante* 20 Nov. ?1759.

15. William III, K. of England 1689–1702.

16. As the title-page states, Lodge's *Illustrations of British History* contains 'a great part of the correspondence of Elizabeth, and her ministers, with George, the sixth Earl of Shrewsbury, during the fifteen years [1569–84] in which Mary Queen of Scots remained in his custody.'

17. Nicol employed William Martin 'to cut sets of types after approved models in imitation of the sharp and fine letter used

by the French and Italian printers.' He also set up a private foundry to cast the types and a printing-house to produce the Boydell *Shakespeare* (1791–1802) and Milton's *Poetical Works* (1794–7) (D. B. Updike, *Printing Types*, 3d edn, Cambridge, Mass., 1962, ii. 123, 144–6).

18. The French National Assembly, which had nationalized the landed estates of the Gallican church on 2 Nov. 1789, decreed on 14 May 1790 that the estates should be sold by auction to the highest bidder.

19. The Scots College, founded in 1569, at this period located in the rue des Fosses-Saint-Victor, now rue du Cardinal Lemoine (DALRYMPLE 107 n. 6). On 5 June 1790 a 'remonstrance' from the British minister plenipotentiary, Lord Robert Fitzgerald, was delivered to the National Assembly, claiming 'in favour of the Irish and Scotch colleges at Paris, an exemption from the operation of the decree of the National Assembly, by which the property of all lands, etc. of the church and clerical corporations, is declared to belong to the state' (GM 1790, lx pt i. 560). But in 1793 the revolutionary government confiscated the Scots College property, and after that the College existed only intermittently as a separate institution, until finally it was sold in 1846.

King James's,[20] Bishop Atterbury's,[21] and other *dark* papers were deposited—I saw there the will of Mary Queen of Scots written by her own hand,[22] and one word effaced by a tear—it was written on the eve of her death—Do not let this hint sleep.

You say you are not apt to write long letters (the greater obligation to me) I fear *I* am apt to write long ones; an old man and an old scribbling pen are subject to babble. Still I think I could not say less in return for the number of obliging expressions in yours to

Your very grateful and obedient humble servant

HOR. WALPOLE

PS. I need not inform you, Sir, of the many valuable conventual libraries in Paris alone. At St Germain des Prés is also a great collection of antiques and other rarities.[23] The French may sell them, but certainly no French will purchase them at this crisis, when they not only want money, but when no man can be sure of any property.

---

20. James II.

21. Francis Atterbury (1662–1732), Bp of Rochester 1713–23.

22. Accompanied by Adam Smith, HW visited the Scots College on 15 March 1766 and was shown the treasures of the College library by the Principal, John Gordon. 'I saw the papers of King James II. . . . He [Gordon] showed me also three other boxes, the first of which he told me contained the papers of Bishop Atterbury, the second of the Duke of Ormond, and the largest, other papers belonging to the Pretender and his affairs, which he said were very curious. He showed me another volume of letters written by the Queen of Scots and James I to the Bishop of Glasgow. . . . There is also her will, dated Feb. 7 [1587] and her codicil of requests, dated Feb. 8 *le matin de ma mort.* . . .

He showed me several very ancient charters of the Kings of Scotland, with the seals finely preserved' ('Paris Journals,' DU DEFFAND v. 307, 358–9). James II's autograph memoirs remained at the College until about 1793, when they were destroyed (CONWAY ii. 443 n. 12).

23. HW wrote Conway 29 Oct. 1774: 'The convent and collection of St-Germain, I mean that over against the Hôtel du Parc Royal, is well worth seeing' (ibid. iii. 204). HW had visited the Abbey on 26 Dec. 1765 and noted in his 'Paris Journals': 'Fine library. Many bronze busts, some of which antique, as Minerva. Fine one of Louis XIV by Bernini. Cabinet of antique shells, precious stones etc. Some fine small bronzes. Nothing good in the church' (DU DEFFAND v. 290).

To John Pinkerton, Tuesday 10 August 1790

Printed from a photostat of the MS in the Stanley Withers Collection, Manchester Central Library, by kind permission of the City of Manchester Cultural Services. First printed in R. S. Woof, 'Some Horace Walpole Letters,' N & Q 1965, ccx. 26. The Stanley Withers Collection of autograph letters was acquired by the Manchester Central Library on Withers's death in 1927; the earlier history of the MS is not known.

Dated by the postmark.

Address: To John Pinkerton Esq. at Kentish Town.[1] *Postmark:* AU 10 90. ISLEWORTH.

Dear Sir,

I HAVE been in London for a few days,[2] and not returning till yesterday afternoon, did not receive your letter[3] till then, which was too late for the post. I now send this for Friday,[4] which is the first day I have unengaged.

Yours etc.

H. W.

PS. Please to tear off this half of the paper.

---

1. In Middlesex, 3 miles from London. Pinkerton lived at Mansfield Place, Kentish Town (CHATTERTON 302, 305, 308).

2. HW assured Mary Berry of his intention to visit her in Somerset Street on Thursday, 5 Aug. (BERRY i. 107).

3. Missing.

4. A ticket to visit SH on Friday, 13 Aug. HW's 'Book of Visitors' records the visit of 'Mr Buckland, from Mr Pinkerton' on that date (ibid. ii. 236).

To John Nichols, Thursday 26 August 1790

Printed from the MS in Thomas Kirgate's hand and signed by him, now WSL. First printed, Nichols, *Lit. Anec.* viii. 438–9. The MS descended in the Nichols family until sold Sotheby's 18 Nov. 1929 (John Gough Nichols Sale), lot 242, to Ludford; not further traced until resold Sotheby's 29 Oct. 1962 (property of a Gentleman), lot 264 (with Richard Gough to Joseph Cooper Walker 24 Oct. 1787), to Maggs for WSL.

Strawberry Hill, August 26, 1790.

Sir,

IN A note at the bottom of p. 832, in No. 51 of *Bib. Topog. Brit.*[1] you have said Mr Walpole has in his collection 'the Battle of Bosworth enamelled on a jewel, usually worn by King Henry VIII and sold among King Charles the First's pictures.' Mr Walpole ordered me to inform you, Sir, that he has no such thing; never saw it; nor knows no more about it, but that he thinks it is mentioned in the catalogue of King Charles's pictures.[2] He begs, therefore, you will correct the note if inserted in the *Hist. of Leicester.*[3]

Mr Walpole will be much obliged to you, Sir, for the portraits of Mr and Mrs Stavely,[4] from the *Bib. Topog.*,[5] which he begs may

1. John Nichols, *Additional Collections towards the History and Antiquities of the Town and County of Leicester,* 1790, p. 832n [*Bibliotheca Topographica Britannica,* 1790]. HW's set of the *Bibliotheca* is Hazen, *Cat. of HW's Lib.,* No. 3348.

2. *A Catalogue and Description of King Charles the First's Capital Collection of Pictures* . . . , 1757, pp. 47–8: 'a golden jewel . . . at the top on the outside enamelled, the Battle of Bosworth Field, between King Henry VII, and King Richard III. . . . On the other side is the red and white roses joined together; done also in enamel work.' See also *Abraham Van der Doort's Catalogue of the Collections of Charles I,* ed. Oliver Millar, *Walpole Society* 1958–60, xxxvii. 116; *ante* 15 Dec. 1760, n. 1.

3. Nichols inserted the following notice in his *History and Antiquities of the County of Leicester,* 1795–1815, iv pt ii.

557: ' "The Battle of Bosworth, enamelled on a jewel, usually worn by King Henry VIII" was sold among King Charles the First's pictures; and is said by Sir Joseph Ayloffe, in 1770 [*Archæologia,* 1775, iii. 190], to have been then in the possession of the Hon. Horace Walpole.' In a footnote (n. 6) Nichols added: 'But I have Lord Orford's express authority, in a letter to myself, for saying that it was not there.'

4. Mary Onebye (d. 1669), m. (1656) Thomas Staveley (1626–84), antiquary, of Belgrave, Leics.

5. The engraved portraits of Thomas Staveley and his wife are pls XXVIII and XXIX in Nichols's *Collections towards the History and Antiquities of the Town and County of Leicester,* 1790, facing pp. 613, 615 [*Bibliotheca Topographica Britannica,* No. 50, in vol. vii of the collected *Bibliotheca,* 1790]. HW doubtless wanted separate impressions of the engravings for his collection of English 'heads.'

be left at his house in Berkeley Square, when you send that way.
I am, Sir,

Your humble servant,

T. Kirgate[6]

From Frances Burney,[1] ca Tuesday 19 October 1790

Printed from *Diary and Letters of Madame d'Arblay*, ed. Charlotte Barrett,
1842–6, v. 158–9, where the letter was first printed. Reprinted in later editions
of the *Diary and Letters*, including that edited by Austin Dobson, 1904–5, iv.
423–4; extract printed in Toynbee xiv. 308 n. 1. The original letter is missing.
The text in *Diary and Letters* is apparently only an approximate version of the
letter actually sent, reconstructed by Fanny Burney from memory.

Dated conjecturally by HW's reply *post* 20 Oct. 1790.

IF Mr Walpole has still the goodness to remember an old acquaintance, long lost to all apparent claim for that honour, he
is requested to spare his servant, James Columb,[2] to call at her
apartment next Thursday, at St James's Palace,[3] about two o'clock;
as she wishes to learn from said James Columb what he would have
her do with the small sum of money still remaining in her hands of
her late servant, Jacob Columb,[4] his cousin. She received his message
ten days ago requiring her not to pay it to one Peter Bayond, but
this morning she has had a letter from an attorney with reverse directions.[5]

6. Thomas Kirgate (1734–1810), HW's
printer and secretary.

1. (1752–1840), m. (1793) Alexandre
d'Arblay; novelist and diarist.

2. James Colomb, HW's footman.

3. 'Yesterday their Majesties and the
three eldest Princesses arrived at St
James's Palace from Kew. At two o'clock
the Drawing Room commenced. . . . afterwards the Royal Family returned to
Kew' (*Daily Adv.* Friday, 22 Oct.). As Second Keeper of the Robes to Queen Charlotte, Fanny Burney would have accompanied the Queen on all her journeys.

4. Jacob Columb (or Colomb), Fanny
Burney's servant, had died in September
1790. Miss Burney was informed by Moses

Hugenien, a Swiss friend of Columb, that
'poor Columb, in the last quarter of an
hour, desired to leave everything to his
sisters [in Switzerland]. He certainly meant
everything of his wearing apparel, watches,
etc., for what money he had left in my
hands he would never tell anybody.' Miss
Burney was preparing to make this disposition when a man named Peter Bayond
came forward with a will, probated at
Doctors' Commons, naming HW's servant
James Colomb and himself as joint heirs.
Miss Burney, however, was convinced that
the will 'must be a forgery' (*Diary and
Letters of Madame d'Arblay*, ed. Austin
Dobson, 1904–5, iv. 420–1).

5. The day after her interview with
Peter Bayond, Miss Burney 'had a message

ANNE SEYMOUR DAMER, BY RICHARD COSWAY

And now can Mr Walpole pardon this abrupt and troublesome intrusion from one who seemed at least consigned to silence and quiet?[6] she will not say to oblivion, lest a quotation should occur for an answer—'Seemed, Madam? nay, you were!'[7] She trusts, however, there can be no local impropriety in bringing herself again to life, purely to speak for the dead; yet her courage of renovation does not amount to expecting a place in the memory of Mr Walpole without calling to its aid that she has the honour to be, etc. etc.,

F. Burney

To Richard French, Wednesday 20 October 1790

Printed for the first time from a copy of the MS in the possession of Lt-Col. John Chandos-Pole, Newnham Hall, Daventry, Northants, kindly furnished by Mr H. M. Colvin. The MS is inserted in an extra-illustrated copy of Daniel Lysons and Samuel Lysons's *Magna Britannia; Being a Concise Topographical Account of the Several Counties of Great Britain*, 1806–22 (Derbyshire, vol. IV, f. 103). This copy was extra-illustrated by Mrs Isabella Thornhill (d. 1878), of Stanton Hall, Stanton-in-the-Peak, Derbyshire; the earlier history of the MS is not known.

Address: To Richard French Esq. at Derby.

Strawberry Hill, Oct. 20, 1790.

I MUST again thank you, dear Sir, for game, and so I must in Mrs Damer's name, as she charged me to do. She has had a fall, slipping from her pedestal[1] and cutting her leg badly. It is almost

from James Columb, charging me not to pay this man, whom he believed a cheat, and honestly declining to share in any such perjury; but persisting all should go to the sisters. . . . I then settled . . . to pay nothing further but to Philip or James Columb, both servants of Mr Walpole.' Soon afterwards Miss Burney 'received a letter from an attorney, Mr F. Matthews, desiring me to pay forthwith to Peter Bayond the sum in my hands of the late Jacob Columb! It was now necessary to apply to the cousins. I therefore took the courageous step of addressing myself to Mr Walpole himself, that through him I might act with them. His former kindness to me was a secret stimulus to assure me he would not take amiss such a call upon his remembrance and his time' (ibid. iv. 422–3). See HW to Frances Burney *post* 20 Oct. 1790.

6. Miss Burney had been employed in her position at Court since July 1786 (*ante* 6 July 1786, n. 1).

7. 'Seems, madam? Nay, it is. I know not "seems" ' (*Hamlet* I. ii. 76).

1. Mrs Damer was a sculptor.

healed,[2] and Sir W. Fordyce[3] allowed her for the [first] time to dine here yesterday. He has ordered her a journey, very far from equally agreeable to me, and which I must approve however, as her health is too delicate for London winters, without now and then recurring to a much warmer climate. In short, she is to set out on Monday se'n-night for Lisbon and returns in April.[4]

As I hope, Sir, I forget none of your commands, I have prevailed on the Miss Berrys,[5] who are also gone abroad for similar reasons, but to Italy,[6] to sit to Miss Foldsone.[7] She is got into very great vogue, with much merit indeed, but the men, I believe, like better to sit to her than I should think the women do, for she is very pretty, and so young and fresh, that few London complexions find a foil in hers.

I am, dear Sir,

Your much obliged and obedient humble servant

HOR. WALPOLE

2. Mrs Damer wrote Mary Berry 11 Oct. 1790: 'Till my leg is healed I can answer for nothing as to time. This Fordyce told me this morning, though he believes, from the present appearance, that it will be soon well' (*The Berry Papers: Being the Correspondence Hitherto Unpublished of Mary and Agnes Berry (1763–1852)*, ed. Lewis Melville, 1914, p. 26).

3. Sir William Fordyce (1724–92), Kt, 1782; M.D. (Cantab.), 1770.

4. Mrs Damer's father, General Conway, wrote Sir William Hamilton 28 Nov. 1790 concerning her trip to Lisbon: 'She was not ill, but only not quite well; the harsh winters here generally affect her, and in point of climate I believe that is among

the first' (Percy Noble, *Anne Seymour Damer*, 1908, p. 119). Mrs Damer sailed for Lisbon ca 8 Nov., arriving seven days later; she stayed there until 20 Feb. (ibid. 118–19, 128).

5. Mary Berry (1763–1852) and her sister Agnes Berry (1764–1852), HW's correspondents.

6. They left London for Italy on 10 Oct. 1790 and did not return until 11 Nov. 1791 (BERRY i. 110, 372 n. 3). Most of their stay in Italy was spent in Florence.

7. Anne Foldsone (before 1775–1851), m. (1793) Joseph Mee; miniature-painter. For details concerning her portraits of the Berry sisters see BERRY i. 133–4 and n. 27.

To Frances Burney Wednesday 20 October 1790

Printed from Toynbee *Supp.* ii. 43–5, where the letter was first printed in full. An extract (first two paragraphs omitted) was printed in *Diary and Letters of Madame d'Arblay*, ed. Charlotte Barrett, 1842–6, v. 159–60, and in later editions, including that edited by Austin Dobson, 1904–5, iv. 424–5; and in Toynbee xiv. 308–9. The MS descended in the Burney family to Arthur G. Burney, who owned it in 1918; not further traced.
Address: To Miss Burney, at St James's Palace.

Strawberry Hill, Oct. 20, 1790.

HUMILITY modest and beautiful as yours, Madam, could alone make you express yourself to me[1] in terms that make me ashamed; and I should be twenty times more ashamed both of my heart and taste, were I capable of forgetting so much virtue, sense, and genius as Miss Burney's. Who can forget the prototype of Evelina and Cecilia?[2] I have had the pleasure and honour of conversing with her, of having her at my house;[3] and can I forget how amiable and agreeable she is? And yet I shudder to think how near she was to having reason to think, not only that I had forgot her, but that I was grown the most consummate ill-bred brute upon earth—in short, Madam, the postman dropped your letter on Twickenham Common, and by the most fortunate accident in the world for my character, a poor woman found it, and by another favour of fortune could read, and brought it to me two hours after the postman was gone by, and the post hence gone out.[4] Oh! Miss Burney, how justly you would have condemned me (though perfectly innocent) did you receive no answer from me, nor see my servant,[5] as now you will at the moment you appoint; and he shall bring you this, as it is too late, by the accident I have mentioned, to send it to Windsor.

I wish you could know all I have felt on the misfortune that was on the brink of happening to me; and then you would be certain of my very respectful memory, and of my happiness in having this opportunity of professing it to you with the deepest sincerity. With regard to the affair in question, give me leave to advise you for your

1. See *ante* ca 19 Oct. 1790.
2. The heroines of Fanny Burney's first two novels, *Evelina* and *Cecilia*, published respectively in 1778 and 1782.
3. See *ante* 6 Sept. 1785, nn. 2, 3.

4. The Twickenham post arrived at 12:30 and departed at 1 p.m. (CHATTERTON 296; BERRY i. 89).
5. James Colomb.

own sake to consult some lawyer before you pay the money, and to ask him how you may get security for it. The two Colombs[6] my servants, cousins to your late servant, have a very bad opinion of that Bayoud,[7] and suspect he forged the will, and are persuaded they can prove so. It is made to the prejudice of two very poor sisters of your servant, to whom even ten pounds would be of consequence. I know nothing but from them. The poor man, it seems, said he made no will—but I hear he felt a just sense of your virtues, Madam, and only wanted a fortune to pay a just tribute to your excellent qualities and goodness.[8]

As this will come to you by my servant,[9] give me leave to add another word on your most unfounded idea, that I can forget you, because it is almost impossible for me even to meet you. Believe me, I heartily regret that deprivation, but would not repine were your situation either in point of fortune or position equal in any degree to your merit—but were your talents given to be buried in obscurity? You have retired from the world into a closet at Court—where indeed you will still discover mankind, though not disclose it; for if you could penetrate its characters on the earliest glimpse of its superficies, will it escape your piercing eye, when it shrinks from your inspection, knowing that you have the mirror of truth in your pocket! I will not embarrass you by saying more, nor would have you take notice of or reply[10] to what I have said. Judge only that feeling hearts reflect, not forget. Wishes that are empty look like vanity—my vanity is to be thought capable of esteeming you as much as you

6. Philip Colomb (d. 1799), HW's valet, and James Colomb.

7. Spelled 'Bayond' in Miss Burney's letter *ante* ca 19 Oct. 1790. In his letter *post* 3 Nov. 1790 *bis*, HW says 'I am not sure I spell his name rightly' and writes 'Bayeux.'

8. See *Diary and Letters of Madame d'Arblay*, ed. Austin Dobson, 1904–5, iv. 417, 419.

9. 'A letter filled with the most flattering kindness was brought to me at St James's by his servant, Philip Columb' (ibid. iv. 424).

10. 'In my answer to Mr Walpole [missing], I told him that, even from that closet in which he had deposited me, I

could look for truth in words, and expect there might be meaning in professions; therefore, I ventured to rely upon his sincerity and crave his advice how to proceed. I then stated the case more fully. I received from him the kindest of answers [also missing] immediately, offering to join his own security with his servant's, to insure me from ever more being troubled upon this subject, and protesting that if, at any time, I could employ him "in any great or little service, it was a happiness I owed him," and finishing with warmest and most cordial professions of a regard with which I am extremely flattered' (ibid. iv. 425). See following letter.

deserve, and to be reckoned, though a very distant, a most sincere[11] friend, and give me leave to say, dear Madam,

Your most obedient humble servant

Hor. Walpole

Fanny Burney wrote HW ca 2 Nov. 1790, declining the 'generous offer of security' that he had made her in his previous letter (see *ante* 20 Oct. 1790, n. 10). 'I could not bear to involve in any such possible embarrassment a much nearer and dearer friend; but I thankfully accepted his counsel, and resolved upon paying the whole into the hands of his servants, the Columbs, assuring him, at the same time, that I had now in my possession a security much more valuable to me than any indemnity in money matters, namely, that of the kindness and the remembrance with which he honoured me.' In due course Miss Burney found it necessary to consult a lawyer, who settled the dispute with Peter Bayond 'in a manner the most friendly on his own part, though the most mortifying to Mr Walpole and myself; for Peter Bayond obtained half the property, from persisting he would else sustain a lawsuit, in which Mr Woodcock [the lawyer] assured me I must necessarily be involved in expenses that would double the whole of what my poor servant had left! The other half the cousin received. . . . I could not forbear concluding my letter [to HW] with telling him that the opinion I enclosed for him had almost petrified me, and that, if such was our chance of *justice* with *law,* we must agree never to relate this little history to the democrats abroad, lest we should all be brought forward to illustrate the necessity of universal reform, and the National Assembly should echo with all our names!' (*Diary and Letters of Madame d'Arblay,* ed. Austin Dobson, 1904–5, iv. 425–7). Fanny Burney's letter is missing. For HW's reply see *post* 3 Nov. 1790 *bis.*

---

11. This word was underlined for emphasis by Miss Burney and so printed in *Diary and Letters,* ed. Barrett, v. 160, and in later editions. In Toynbee *Supp.* ii. 45,

'dear' is italicized ('give me leave to say, *Dear* Madam'), but 'sincere' is not. HW apparently did not underline either word.

To Frances Burney, Wednesday 3 November 1790

Printed from a copy of the MS kindly furnished by its owner, Mr John R. G. Comyn, The Cross House, Vowchurch, Turnastone, Herefordshire. First printed, Toynbee xiv. 309. For the history of the MS see *ante* 6 Sept. 1785.

Endorsed in an unidentified hand: Hugenin, Perfumer, Haymarket. James Colomb at the Honourable H. Walpole's.

Address: To Miss Burney.

Nov. 3d 1790.

Dear Madam,

I AM exceedingly vexed for you, and sorry to have kept your servant[1] so long but I find I could not send you a definitive answer without keeping him much longer. All I can say at present is, that I trust I shall deliver you tomorrow from any further trouble—but not being a lawyer myself nor having one here to consult, I hope you will excuse my sending my servant[2] to you this evening, and he shall wait on you at St James's tomorrow at two o'clock[3] and bring you the result of my opinion, after I have considered the case as coolly and ably as is in my poor power to do this evening.[4]

Yours most cordially

HOR. WALPOLE

1. Probably William Moss, described by Fanny Burney as 'a former servant of Mrs Schwellenberg, whom I had hired for the present' (*Diary and Letters of Madame d'Arblay*, ed. Austin Dobson, 1904–5, iv. 418).

2. Philip Colomb.

3. When the Queen's Drawing Room was held at St James's Palace (*ante* ca 19 Oct. 1790, n. 3).

4. See following letter.

To Frances Burney, Wednesday 3 November 1790 *bis*

Printed from a copy of the MS kindly furnished by its owner, Mr John R. G. Comyn, The Cross House, Vowchurch, Turnastone, Herefordshire. First printed in *Diary and Letters of Madame d'Arblay,* ed. Austin Dobson, 1904–5, iv. 493–5. Reprinted, Toynbee xiv. 309–12. For the history of the MS see *ante* 6 Sept. 1785.

Strawberry Hill, Nov. 3d at night, 1790.

Dear Madam,

MR CAMBRIDGE[1] called on me this morning and prepared me for the vexatious subject of your letter,[2] which though it mortifies me horridly for the new trouble you have had, and for the triumph of villainy and injustice, yet I trust you will soon be delivered from your inquietude by those very defects of our law, which you feel, and which though glaring as they are in the present case, I agree with you in not wishing to see corrected by any National Assembly of tyrannic assassins.

It is very plain, Madam, from Mr Woodcock's[3] sober advice that it would be folly and extravagance to attempt to set aside the will at the expense at least of £80 to obtain at most less than half that sum for the poor claimants in Swisserland,[4] who would then be liable to pay their late cousin's debts, which are called about £24 though I cannot learn that they amount to quite eighteen. Give me leave to state both accounts as far as I can collect them from my two servants;[5]

Debts

In Miss Burney's hands	16–0–0	To his tailor	8–0–0
In the perfumer's[6]	10–0–0	Burial	3–5–0

1. Richard Owen Cambridge (1717–1802), poet; HW's neighbour at Twickenham.

2. Missing; see commentary on Fanny Burney's letter to HW ca 2 Nov. 1790.

3. Probably Elborough Woodcock, attorney at the Six Clerks Office and at No. 2 Lincoln's Inn, New Square (*The Universal British Directory of Trade, Commerce, and Manufacture,* 1791, p. 392; *Diary and Letters of Madame d'Arblay,* ed. Austin Dobson, 1904–5, iv. 426; MANN viii. 62 n. 24).

4. See *ante* ca 19 Oct. 1790, n. 4.

5. James and Philip Colomb.

6. Moses Hugenien, toyman at No. 33 Haymarket (*The Universal British Directory of Trade, Commerce, and Manufacture,* 1791, p. 188). Fanny Burney refers to him as 'M. Huguenon, who is a perfumer' (Dobson, op. cit., iv. 420). Hugenien had been instructed 'to superintend his [Jacob Colomb's] affairs, and when all was over to see that his poor remains were decently interred, and every attention paid that seemed right and kind. . . . I told

Two watches worth about	4–13–0	Perfumer's journey to	
Clothes .... about	4–0–0	Windsor for his effects	15–
	——————	Paid by perfumer at	
	34–13–0	the hospital	13–
			——————
			12–13–

There ought besides to be added to the lat Colomb's debts, five guineas which as he w: dying he desired might be given to a woma by whom he had had a child, and which woul make the debts amount to .... 17–18–0.

This being the state of your late servant's circumstances, or probably very near it, Madam, it is clear that my two servants cannot advise their cousins abroad, nor undertake for them, to contest the will, nor can any of them, in order to punish a rogue, afford to be at the expense of a suit—and thence it is as clear, Madam, that you must pay the money in your hands, and be freed from any farther trouble—except a little suspense, which I will now explain, and give you the best advice I am able, which again will be to take better advice.

Bayeux (I am not sure I spell his name rightly) to cover his fraud, we suppose, joined my servant *James* Colomb with himself as executor and *heir*. Now what I should propose is, that you, Madam, should offer Bayeux's attorney to pay the money in your hands to the two executors together, that is, half to one and half to the other, on each giving you a receipt before proper witnesses; and I should also advise you not to write to the attorney yourself, but get a lawyer to write for you and be present when you pay the money.

As Bayeux has got a probate of the will, I conclude he has also administered, and I do not know whether that will not entitle *him* to receive the whole sum from you—and he certainly will then never pay a farthing to James Colomb, who will be cheated as well as his cousins in Swisserland.[7]

M. Huguenon ... that all should be forthwith sent over to Switzerland, when the clothes, etc., were sold. I gave him an order to Kew and the Queen's house, as well as here at Windsor, for searching and collecting all his poor chattels' (ibid. iv. 419–20).

7. For the outcome of this affair see the commentary on Fanny Burney's letter to HW ca 2 Nov. 1790. Jacob Colomb's relations in Switzerland did not receive any of the money.

The will, such as it is, was written by an ignorant foreign school-master, and calls Bayeux and James Colomb *heirs* instead of residuary legatees.

Philip Colomb will bring you this letter tomorrow, Madam, and his brother James shall wait on you whenever you have settled to pay the money. I am obliged to go to Park Place on Saturday for three or four days, and cannot do without Philip. I do propose to be here again on Tuesday.[8] As business is much more easily transacted by word of mouth than by letters, if Dr Burney[9] could be so kind as to call on me here on this day or tomorrow se'nnight, I think we could save you, who have little, time and trouble. In the meantime, to save you both, you are very welcome to show this to your lawyer.

I will detain you, Madam, but by very few words more. I am ashamed that your partiality should have induced you to mention me in so very kind a manner to Miss Cambridge[10] for my behaviour in this affair. I have done nothing more than I should have done for an entire stranger; you yourself, who exercise every virtue so naturally, would not think you had any merit in doing the very same. I should be very happy to have any opportunity of serving or obliging you voluntarily from esteem and good will—but, dear Madam, is it praiseworthy to comply with what you had a right to ask of anybody? I sent my servant when you had business with him, and business that affected his relations: I must have been a brute to you, if I had not sent him; and he would have been in the right not to have minded me, but to have obeyed your summons. I am not a despotic democrat, but

Your most sincere humble servant

Hor. Walpole

8. HW visited the Conways at Park Place, Berks, as planned (BERRY i. 130–4).
9. Miss Burney's father, the music historian.

10. Charlotte Cambridge (1746–1823), only surviving dau. of Richard Owen Cambridge; friend of Fanny Burney (ibid. i. 80 n. 20).

To Edmund Burke, Thursday 4 November 1790

Printed from a photostat of the MS among the Wentworth Woodhouse papers in the Sheffield Central Library, by kind permission of the Earl Fitzwilliam and the Trustees of the Wentworth Woodhouse Estates. First printed in J. T. Boulton, 'Burke and Walpole,' *Times Literary Supplement,* 20 April 1951, l. 245. For the history of the MS see *ante* 3 Dec. 1777.

Endorsed by Mrs Burke: Horace Walpole November 4th 90.

Address: To the Right Honourable Edmund Burke at Beaconsfield, Bucks.

Postmark: NO 4 90.

Strawberry Hill, Nov. 4, 1790.

MR WALPOLE is extremely obliged to Mr Burke for his kind remembrance in sending him his most valuable book;[1] but as Mr Walpole cannot write like Mr Burke, he will not attempt to praise what deserves the noblest encomiums; and must be content to join his weak voice to the great choir of admiration[2] that such a work must excite.

---

1. *Reflections on the Revolution in France,* published 1 Nov. 1790. 'Mr Burke ordered Dodsley to send me his book, though I have not seen him three times in three years. Good breeding obliged me to thank him, and my real admiration called on me to avow it. . . . I might safely swear [the letter] did not contain six lines; and all it said was, that unless I could write as well as he does, I could not fully express my admiration, yet did not doubt but he would have that of mankind' (HW to Lady Ossory 9 Dec. 1790, OSSORY iii. 100). HW wrote Edward Jerningham *post* 10 Nov. 1790 that the *Reflections* was 'the wisest book I ever read in my life; and after that, the wittiest.' See also BERRY i. 132. HW's copy does not appear in the SH records.

2. See OSSORY iii. 100 n. 5.

To Joseph Cooper Walker,
Saturday 6 November 1790

Printed for the first time from the MS now wsl. The MS is untraced until sold Sotheby's 20 Dec. 1877 (Collection of Autograph Letters Sale), lot 51 (with six other letters from HW to Walker, 1787–92), to Naylor; resold Sotheby's 31 July 1885 (Naylor Sale), lot 972 (with two other HW letters), to Suyster; not further traced until acquired from Breaker by wsl, Sept. 1939.

Address: To Joseph C. Walker Esq. at No. 15 in Eccles Street, Dublin. *Postmark:* NO 6 90. NO 10.

Strawberry Hill, Nov. 6, 1790.

I AM extremely obliged to you, Sir, for your information of various kinds,[1] though the first article certainly gives me no pleasure;[2] but I cannot help myself now. I was to blame to let my tragedy go out of my own hands; but it has been dispersed too much to prevent its publicity. I only wonder how a bookseller can think it worth his while to reprint it;[3] and I more wonder and regret that you, Sir, should give yourself the trouble to superintend the press.[4] I give you many thanks for the honour you do me, and hope your time will never be so ill employed again, as by your letters and by what the newspapers tell me of a work[5] you have in hand (and which I shall be happy to see), I believe it never has been.

Your additional notices of engravers and engravings are very curious; and could I expect to see another edition of my *Anecdotes* wanted, would be very useful;[6] though were it wanted, I am much too old to think of improving it, especially as the volume of en-

1. Walker's letter to HW is missing.
2. Walker apparently informed HW that a spurious edition of his tragedy *The Mysterious Mother* was being printed at Dublin. Walker and Lord Charlemont tried to prohibit the publication of this edition without HW's approval, but the bookseller demanded recompense of £50. See Hazen, *SH Bibl.* 83; *post* 17 Feb. 1791.
3. The Dublin edition was published by John Archer, William Jones and Richard White, No. 30 Dame Street, in 1791. The title-page is a cancel, the original title-page being dated 1790 instead of 1791

(Hazen, *SH Bibl.* 83). Lord Charlemont's intervention probably delayed the publication. HW's copy of the Dublin edition is Hazen, *Cat. of HW's Lib.*, No. 2490.
4. For Walker's part in correcting the proofs of the edition see *post* 23 March and 4 April 1791.
5. Perhaps *Lives of the Painters, Sculptors, and Engravers of Ireland,* a work for which Walker gathered materials but which he never published (DNB). We have found no newspaper notice relating to this or any other work undertaken by Walker at this time.
6. See *ante* 5 Aug. 1789 and nn. 9, 10.

gravers,[7] is not only the most defective of the work, but so incomplete, that probably a more perfect and better history of that art will be undertaken by some[bo]dy else;[8] especially as the art is so much improved in this country, as well as its elder sister, painting. I have saved what Vertue had collected of the early history of both arts;[9] and it will be easy for better historians, now they both deserve better, to continue the work, and more fully, as notices, at least of the best artists, will be preserved.

I have seen the *Paradox* on Richard III,[10] but thank you for mentioning it, and for the account of the two portraits of Petitot.[11] In short, Sir, I have variety of obligations to you, and the chief is your kindness to a perfect stranger, but who is with great regard

Your very grateful and obedient humble servant

HORACE WALPOLE

7. The *Catalogue of Engravers*, SH, 1763 (published 1764); 2d edn, SH, 1765 (published 1767).

8. HW owned a copy of Joseph Strutt's *A Biographical Dictionary: Containing an Historical Account of All the Engravers*, 2 vols, 1785–6 (Hazen, *Cat. of HW's Lib.*, No. 254, now WSL). HW noted on the verso of the half-title in the first volume: 'This author makes many mistakes both in proper names and languages, probably from being little versed in the latter; but the book is useful.' HW also owned a copy of Pierre-François Basan's *Dictionnaire des graveurs anciens et modernes*, 2d edn, 2 vols, 1789 (ibid., No. 3705).

9. HW's collection of George Vertue's notebooks in thirty-eight volumes is ibid., No. 3704; most of the contents have been published by the Walpole Society.

10. 'The Prayse of King Richard the Third' in *Essayes of Certaine Paradoxes*, 1616, by Sir William Cornwallis (ca 1579–1614). In 1768, at HW's request, Thomas Gray sent him a summary of Cornwallis's essay on Richard III, calling it 'an idle declamation, the exercise of a schoolboy that is to be bred a statesman' (GRAY ii. 176–7, 178–80). HW apparently had the essay transcribed for his use; a MS in folio entitled 'A Paradoxe in Prayse of King Richard III, or the Life and Raigne of Richard III' is Hazen, *Cat. of HW's Lib.*, No. 2594.

11. Possibly the self-portrait of Jean Petitot, the elder (1607–91), the celebrated painter in enamel, and the self-portrait of Jean Petitot, the younger (1653–1702), also a miniaturist, that in 1929 were in the collection of Julia, Countess of Dartrey (1862–1938). The seat of the Earls of Dartrey was Dartrey House, near Cootehill, Co. Monaghan, and the portraits may have been acquired from descendants of the younger Petitot who settled in Dublin (Basil S. Long, *British Miniaturists*, 1929, pp. 340–1; *Anecdotes of Painting, Works* iii. 259).

To Edward Jerningham,
Wednesday 10 November 1790

Printed from a photostat of the MS in the Henry E. Huntington Library. First printed in Lewis Bettany, *Edward Jerningham and his Friends*, 1919, pp. 49–50. Reprinted, Toynbee *Supp.* iii. 61–3. For the history of the MS see *ante* 13 Feb. 1778.

The year of the letter is established by the postmark.

Address: To Edward Jerningham Esq. in Green Street, near Grosvenor Square, London. *Postmark:* NO 11 90. ISLEWORTH.

Strawberry Hill, Wednesday, Nov. 10th.

Dear Sir,

AS YOUR letter[1] has no date of day, week, month or year, and as I receive it today, I conclude next Tuesday does not mean yesterday but a certain Tuesday in next week, when, or any Tuesday, but those that are dead and gone, I shall be happy to have your company.[2] On Sunday next I believe I shall be in town myself.[3]

Delighted with Mr Burke?[4]—yes, so delighted that I have read him twice, and if I were not so old and had not lost my memory, I would try to get his whole book by heart. It is the wisest book I ever read in my life; and after that, the wittiest. It ought to be translated into all languages, and commented, and preached in all churches in portions—pray, has not Dr Price[5] hanged himself?

I have been reading at the Antipodes too—that is, Mrs Hervey[6] had *The Laurel of Liberty*[7] at Park Place,[8] and I dipped into it,

1. Missing.
2. HW wrote Mary Berry from SH 18 Nov. 1790: 'The Charming Man [Jerningham] passed Tuesday here and part of yesterday, and I carried him back to Lady Mount Edgcumbe' (BERRY i. 145).
3. HW was at SH on Saturday, 13 Nov., but supped at Miss Farren's in Green Street, Grosvenor Square, on Monday, the 15th (ibid. i. 138, 141).
4. Edmund Burke's *Reflections on the Revolution in France* had been published on 1 Nov. (*ante* 4 Nov. 1790 and n. 1).
5. Richard Price (1723–91), D.D., LL.D.; moralist and economist. His sympathy with the French Revolution was proclaimed in his *Discourse on the Love of Our Country, Delivered on Nov. 4, 1789*, to which Burke replied in the *Reflections*.

HW wrote Mary Berry 8 Nov. 1790: 'Mr Burke's pamphlet has quite turned Dr Price's head; he got upon a table at their club [the Revolution Society], toasted to our Parl[iament] becoming a National Assembly, and to admitting no more peers of their assembly' (BERRY i. 135; see ibid. n. 38 and MORE 343 n. 10).
6. Elizabeth March (b. between 1748 and 1756, d. ?1820), m. (1774) Col. William Thomas Hervey; novelist (BERRY i. 132 n. 18).
7. A poem written in defence of the French Revolution by Robert Merry (1755–98), leader of the 'Della Cruscan' circle at Florence.
8. Where HW visited the Conways 6–9 Nov. (ibid. i. 130–4).

and there I found *cobweb tears* and *lutestring oceans*⁹—new productions—if not of nature, at least of art, and I suppose to be had
at the new Birmingham warehouse of the original maker¹⁰—but
keep my secret; I don't desire to be hoisted *à la lanterne,* for modern
liberty is very captious, and since the new crime of Leze-Nation has
been invented, one may commit treason against anybody's majesty
in a whole country, or perhaps against their high and mighty allies
in any other country. Adieu!

Yours etc.

H. W.

To JOSEPH COOPER WALKER,
Tuesday 21 December 1790

Printed from the MS in Thomas Kirgate's hand, now WSL. First printed, Toynbee xiv. 345–7. The MS is untraced until sold Sotheby's 20 Dec. 1877 (Collection
of Autograph Letters Sale), lot 51 (with six other letters from HW to Walker,
1787–92), to Naylor; resold Sotheby's 23 March 1892 (Several Important Collections of Autograph Letters Sale), lot 440, to Barker; resold Sotheby's 14 July
1896 (Collection of Autograph Letters and Historical Documents Sale), lot 435,
to Maggs; offered by Maggs, Cat. No. 196 (1903), lot 977; sold by A. H. Reed,
Dunedin, New Zealand, to WSL, Oct. 1938.

Strawberry Hill, December 21, 1790.

Sir,

THOUGH I have had the gout in my hand for some time¹ and
am not able to write myself,² I will not delay any longer thank-

---

9. 'Della Crusca has published a poem
called *The Laurel of Liberty,* which . . .
has confounded and overturned all ideas
—there are *gossamery tears* and *silky
oceans*—the first time to be sure that
anybody ever *cried cobwebs,* or that the
sea was made of *paduasoy*' (HW to Mary
Berry 8 [11] Nov. 1790, ibid. i. 136).

10. Presumably an allusion to Joseph
Priestley (1733–1804), the theologian and
scientist, who was minister of the New
Meeting, Birmingham, 1780–91. His *Letters to the Right Honourable Edmund
Burke, Occasioned by his Reflections on
the Revolution in France,* a vindication
of the principles of the Revolution, was
not published at Birmingham until 1791,
but his views on the Revolution were already well known.

---

1. HW wrote Lady Ossory 6 Jan. 1791:
'I have been ill for these three weeks . . .
with some gout and a good deal of rheumatism, and this is the first day in which
I have been able to walk (with help) from
my bedchamber to the Blue Room' (OS-
SORY iii. 105).

2. The letter is in the hand of HW's
printer and secretary, Thomas Kirgate.

ing you for your last favours, particularly for your notes on two publications of mine,[3] though, as I have told you,[4] Sir, I am too old to think of making any additions to them. For my tragedy,[5] you do it too much honour, and give yourself a great deal too much trouble about it, and if the bookseller will print it,[6] I had rather he printed it faultily, than that you should take the pains to correct the press.[7] I much approve of your scheme for promoting painting in Ireland,[8] and heartily wish success both to your plan and to the art there. Indeed, as your country seems in earnest in setting about improving and aggrandizing itself, and has already done itself honour by its public buildings, I have no doubt but painting will flourish as well as architecture.

The college for old maids is a very benevolent idea, but I am not well enough acquainted with Ireland to judge whether it is a practicable one.

Dr Young's treatise[9] is very ingenious indeed, and his arguments very satisfactory. I never did believe that Gothic architecture was of Moorish or Saracenic origin, being very unlike to the drawings I have seen from buildings of either people; still less do I attribute Gothic to the Saxons,[10] who never invented anything but a barbarous mode of corrupting language. I have thought that the intersection of regular arches may have suggested the idea of pointedness, whenever or wherever that form was first adopted. Doctor Young's defence of its strength[11] pleases me extremely, and I wish his arguments may recommend it as successfully as I think they ought to do.

One opinion I have, which is, that the florid Gothic owes its beautiful improvements to England alone; nor do I know parallel samples but in some few cathedrals in France in provinces that were subject to us. Had the style originated in France, that nation is too

3. *A Catalogue of the Royal and Noble Authors of England*, SH, 1758, and *Anecdotes of Painting in England*, SH, 1762–71.

4. See *ante* 5 Aug. 1789.

5. *The Mysterious Mother*.

6. See *ante* 6 Nov. 1790 and nn. 2, 3.

7. For Walker's part in correcting the proofs of this unauthorized edition published at Dublin see *post* 23 March and 4 April 1791.

8. Nothing is known of this scheme, but it may have been proposed under the auspices of the Royal Irish Academy, of which Walker was an active member. For

Walker's work towards a history of Irish artists see *ante* 6 Nov. 1790, n. 5.

9. 'The Origin and Theory of the Gothic Arch,' *Transactions of the Royal Irish Academy*, 1790, iii. 55–87, by Matthew Young (1750–1800), D.D., Bishop of Clonfert 1798–1800. Neither the essay nor the *Transactions* appears in the SH records.

10. For Young's arguments against a Moorish, Saracenic, or Saxon origin for Gothic architecture, see ibid. iii. 58–61, 65–66.

11. See ibid. iii. 80–7.

apt to be partial to its own inventors not to have spread the taste more diffusively.

To Jane Pope,[1] Thursday 30 December 1790

Printed from a photostat of the MS in Thomas Kirgate's hand in the Bodleian Library (MS Toynbee c.1, f. 5). First printed, Toynbee *Supp.* ii. 45–6; extract printed in *Strawberry Hill Accounts . . . Kept by Mr Horace Walpole from 1747 to 1795*, ed. Paget Toynbee, Oxford, 1927, p. 177. The MS is untraced until it came into the possession of Mrs Serena Elizabeth Courtauld before 1918; later acquired by Dr Paget Toynbee, who presented it to the Bodleian Library.

Endorsed in an unidentified hand: H. Walpole 1790 /1790; *in a different hand:* Miss Pope.

Address: To Miss Pope in Great Queen Street, Lincoln's Inn Fields, London. *Postmark:* DE 31 90.

Strawberry Hill, December 30th 1790.

Dear Madam,

I HOPED before this to have been in town, and to have called on you, but I have been seized by the gout,[2] and cannot even write with my own hand;[3] but it is necessary to tell you that I have settled everything as far as I can.

Sir R. Goodere[4] gave up the house[5] on Christmas Day, but has not sent me the half-year's rent due to you,[6] but if he does not, he *shall* the moment I get to town, and then you shall have the thirty-five pounds.

I have settled with John Seth[7] about the furniture; he had one appraiser and I another, and their valuation of the goods came to an hundred and ninety-two pounds. I have agreed to take the goods

---

1. (1742–1818), actress, famed for her soubrette rôles; friend of Kitty Clive.

2. See previous letter, n. 1.

3. Except for the signature, the letter is in the hand of Thomas Kirgate.

4. Sir Robert Goodere (ca 1720–1800), Kt, 1762; lieutenant of the Band of Gentlemen Pensioners 1762–72; water bailiff of the Thames above Staines, 1760, 1762 (BERRY i. 124 n. 19).

5. Little SH ('Cliveden'). Sir Robert and Lady Goodere were HW's tenants at Little

SH from 1785 (the death of Mrs Clive) until 25 Dec. 1790. HW wrote Mary Berry 16 Dec. 1790: 'I came to town yesterday purely on your account and return tomorrow. Cliveden was this morning secured to you and your sister in form' (ibid. i. 160). The Berrys took possession of the house in 1791.

6. As Mrs Clive's legatee, Miss Pope apparently received the rent from the lease of Little SH that Mrs Clive had held.

7. Not identified.

and furniture at their valuation,[8] except the pictures, which John claims, but I said I understood that you claim them, and till that is settled between you and him, I would have nothing to do with the pictures. I do suppose they are valued at very little indeed. You, probably, Madam, would wish for the four oil portraits,[9] the rest are ordinary prints, and more ordinary drawings, and therefore, Madam, if you are not very earnest about it, and do not dispute them, I will take the whole at the valuation of the appraisers, and you shall have what pictures and prints you please from me, and the great basket of shell flowers, which poor Mrs Clive admired, but I own I do not.

I must beg you to send me your answer[10] hither, for I doubt I am not likely to be in town soon.

Yours most sincerely

HOR. WALPOLE

From PRINCESS CZARTORYSKA,[1] 1791

Printed from a photostat of the MS in the Central Library, Twickenham, Middlesex, kindly furnished by Mr T. V. Roberts. First printed, Toynbee *Supp.* iii. 305. The MS apparently passed on HW's death to Mrs Damer, who bequeathed it to Sir Wathen Waller, 1st Bt, but it was not sold in either of the Waller Sales held in 1921 and 1947; the date of its acquisition by the Central Library, Twickenham, is not known.

Dated approximately by the endorsement.

Endorsed by HW: From Pr[ince]ss Czartoriski 1791.

Address: Pour Monsieur Walpolle.

APRÈS avoir essayé trois réfus de votre part, Monsieur, sur le désir que j'avais de voir votre maison de campagne,[2] il y a

8. HW paid £192 for the 'purchase of Mrs Clive's goods' and £3 for the valuing of the goods (*Strawberry Hill Accounts . . . Kept by Mr Horace Walpole from 1747 to 1795*, ed. Paget Toynbee, Oxford, 1927, p. 18).

9. Possibly among them was one of John Mills (d. 1736), the actor; this portrait was 'in the collection of Miss Pope' in 1796 (*The Biographical Mirrour*, 1795–[1802], ii. facing p. 88).

10. Missing.

1. Izabela Elzbieta Flemming (1746–1835), m. (1761) her uncle, Prince Adam Kazimierz Joachim Ambroży Marek Czartoryski, Stanislas II's first cousin (MANN ix. 633 n. 31). She had visited England in 1768, 1773, and 1786 (OSSORY i. 96, 110; *Extracts from the Journals and Correspondence of Miss Berry*, ed. Lady Theresa Lewis, 2d edn, 1866, iii. 462–3).

2. No letters from HW to Princess Czartoryska have been found. There is no record of her having visited SH in HW's 'Book of Visitors' or his letters.

assurement plus de curiosité que d'amour-propre à revenir encore
à la charge.³ Cependant je ne puis m'empêcher de tenter encore
cette difficile entreprise, et j'ose réiterer ma prière pour avoir une
permission d'aller voir la maison charmante à votre campagne, et
surtout ce qu'il y a dédans. Si la chose est possible, je fais précéder
ma reconnaissance d'avance, si il est de ma destinée de ne pas
pénetrer dans ce sanctuaire, j'emporterai mes regrets en Pologne⁴
où j'aurais voulu n'emporter que le plaisir et l'admiration de tout
ce qu'il y a de charmant à voir à votre campagne.

To Lord CHARLEMONT, Thursday 17 February 1791

Printed from a photostat of the MS in the Royal Irish Academy, Dublin. First
printed in Francis Hardy, *Memoirs of the Political and Private Life of James
Caulfield, Earl of Charlemont,* 2d edn, 1812, ii. 254–7. Reprinted, Wright vi.
397–9; Cunningham ix. 287–8; Hist. MSS Comm., 13th Report, App. viii (*Charlemont MSS*), 1894, ii. 135–6; Toynbee xiv. 374–6 (closing and signature omitted
in Wright and all later printings). For the history of the MS see *ante* 20 Oct.
1770.

Berkeley Square, Feb. 17, 1791.

IT IS difficult, my Lord, with common language that has been so
much prostituted in compliments, to express the real sense of
gratitude, which I do feel at my heart, for the obligation I have to
your Lordship for an act of friendship as unexpected as it was un-
solicited; which last circumstance doubles the favour, as it evinces
your Lordship's generosity and nobleness of temper, without sur-
prising me. How can I thank your Lordship as I ought for interesting yourself, and of yourself, to save me a little mortification, which
I deserve, and should deserve more, had I had the vanity to imagine

3. HW's endorsement on the letter is
dated '1791'; the letter may have been
written in May. He wrote Sir John Sebright *post* 27 May 1791 that he planned
to settle at SH on 4 June; he entertained
Sir John, Lady Sebright, and Miss Sebright there on 6 June (BERRY ii. 238).

4. Princess Czartoryska and her son
Prince Adam had left Poland in 1789 to
visit Paris and London; they returned to
Poland in 1791 (*Memoirs of Prince Adam
Czartoryski and his Correspondence with
Alexander I,* ed. Adam Gielgud, 1888, i.
49–51). The Duke of Queensberry gave a
dinner in her honour towards the end of
August 1790 (Hist. MSS Comm., 15th Re-
port, App. vi [*Carlisle MSS*], 1897, p. 686).

that my printing a few copies of my disgusting tragedy[1] would occasion different and surreptitious editions of it?

Mr Walker has acquainted me,[2] my Lord, that your Lordship has most kindly interposed to prevent a bookseller of Dublin[3] from printing an edition of *The Mysterious Mother* without my consent[4]—and with the conscious dignity of a great mind, your Lordship has not even hinted to me the graciousness of that favour. How have I merited such condescending goodness, my Lord? Had I a prospect of longer life, I never could pay the debt of gratitude; the weightier as your Lordship did not intend I should know that I owe it.

My gratitude can never be effaced, and I am charmed that it is due and due with so much honour to me, that nothing could bribe me to have less obligation to your Lordship, of which I am so proud—but as to the play itself, I doubt it must take its fate. Mr Walker tells me the booksellers have desired him to remonstrate to me, urging that they have already expended fifty pounds;[5] and Mr Walker adds, as no doubt would be the case, that should this edition be stifled, when now expected, some other printer would publish one. I certainly might indemnify the present operator, but I know too much of *the craft*, not to be sure that I should be persecuted by similar exactions—and alas! I have exposed myself but too much to the tyranny of the press, not to know that it taxes delinquents as well as multiplies their faults.

In truth, my Lord, it is too late now to hinder copies of my play from being spread: it has appeared here both whole and in fragments; and to prevent a spurious one, I was forced to have some

1. *The Mysterious Mother*, first printed at the SH Press, 1768, in an edition of 50 copies; a second edition was printed by James Dodsley in 1781 to forestall unauthorized reprints but was never published (*ante* 23 Nov. 1785; Hazen, *SH Bibl.* 79-83).

2. Joseph Cooper Walker's letter is missing, but see HW's letters to Walker *ante* 6 Nov., 21 Dec. 1790.

3. John Archer, William Jones, and Richard White are the names of the booksellers that appear on the title-page of the Dublin edition, 1791. This title-page is a cancel, the original title-page (preserved

in a copy now WSL) being dated 1790 (Hazen, op. cit. 83).

4. The Dublin edition was already printed; Walker had read the proofs in November and December (*ante* 6 Nov., 21 Dec. 1790). See *post* 23 March and 4 April 1791 for Walker's part in supervising the publication. The Dublin edition was published by March 1791; a reprint of it was published in London with a Preface dated June 1791 (Hazen, *Cat. of HW's Lib.*, Nos 2490, 2491).

5. HW wrote Walker *post* 26 Feb. 1791 that he did not wish to indemnify the bookseller for his expenses and that the

printed myself;[6] therefore, if I consent to an Irish edition, it is from no vain desire of diffusing the performance. Indeed, my good Lord, I have lived too long not to have divested myself both of vanity and affected modesty. I have not existed to past seventy-three without having discovered the futility and triflingness of my own talents— and at the same time it would be impertinent to pretend to think that there is no merit in the execution of a tragedy, on which I have been so much flattered; though I am sincere in condemning the egregious absurdity of selecting a subject[7] so improper for the stage, and even offensive to private readers—but I have said too much on a personal theme; and therefore, after repeating a million of thanks to your Lordship for the honour of your personal interposition, I will beg your Lordship, if you please, to signify to the bookseller that you withdraw your prohibition; but I shall not answer Mr Walker's letter,[8] till I have your Lordship's approbation, for you are both my Lord Chamberlain and Licenser;[9] and though I have a tolerably independent spirit, I may safely trust myself under the absolute power of one who has voluntarily protected me against the licentiousness of those who have invaded my property, and who distinguishes so accurately and justly between licence and liberty. I have the honour [to be] with the utmost respect and infinite gratitude, my Lord,

Your Lordship's most obliged
and most devoted humble servant

Hor. Walpole

prohibition on the publication would be taken off.

6. See n. 1 above.

7. Incest.

8. See HW's reply to Walker *post* 26 Feb. 1791.

9. One of the duties of the lord chamberlain was to license plays for performance on the stage.

To Lady Charlemont,[1] Saturday 26 February 1791

Printed from a photostat of the MS in the Royal Irish Academy, Dublin. First printed, Toynbee xiv. 384. For the history of the MS see *ante* 20 Oct. 1770.

Berkeley Square, Feb. 26, 1791.

MR WALPOLE cannot help troubling Lady Charlemont with a few words, and begging her Ladyship to accept his most grateful thanks for the great honour of her letter.[2] Mr Walpole is extremely concerned to hear of Lord Charlemont's indisposition,[3] and is ashamed of having disturbed his Lordship by so long a letter[4] on a personal affair, but certainly knew nothing of his not being well, and shall inquire anxiously for a better account.

To Joseph Cooper Walker, Saturday 26 February 1791

Printed for the first time from the MS now WSL. The MS is untraced until sold Sotheby's 20 Dec. 1877 (Collection of Autograph Letters Sale), lot 51 (with six other letters from HW to Walker, 1787–92), to Naylor; not further traced until acquired from Breaker by WSL, Sept. 1939.

Address: To Joseph C. Walker Esq. in Eccles Street, Dublin. *Postmark:* FE 26 91.

Berkeley Square, Feb. 26, 1791.

Sir,

ON receiving the favour of your letter,[1] and not choosing to indemnify the bookseller for what he says he has expended

1. Mary Hickman (d. 1807), dau. of Thomas Hickman, of Brickhill, Co. Clare, m. (1768) James Caulfeild (1728–99), cr. (1763) Earl of Charlemont.

2. Missing.

3. Charlemont wrote Alexander Haliday, M.D., of Belfast, 18 Feb. 1791: 'The disorder which has for this fortnight past oppressed me, originated in a violent cold, which has fallen upon my breast, my head, my eyes, my nerves, and indeed, I believe, upon every part about me. In short, I have often felt pain, but never till now experienced the real oppression of malady; neither have two physicians as yet been

able essentially to relieve me' (Hist. MSS Comm., 13th Report, App. viii [*Charlemont MSS*], 1894, ii. 136). In April he wrote Thomas Prentice that he and Lady Charlemont were going to Bath for their daughter's health, 'and the physicians assure me that the waters will be serviceable to me also' (ibid. ii. 138). They stayed at Bath from June to mid-October.

4. *Ante* 17 Feb. 1791, concerning the spurious Dublin edition of HW's tragedy *The Mysterious Mother*.

———

1. Missing.

about my tragedy,[2] which would not secure me from its being printed at least by others; I wrote to Lord Charlemont to ask his Lordship's leave for taking off the prohibition,[3] which was the least I could do, after his Lordship had done me the honour of interesting himself so kindly about me. Lord Charlemont will no longer oppose the publication—but I believe the bookseller will not repay himself, if he laid out £50—and that will be his own fault, for doing what he had no right to do.

I am Sir

Your obedient humble servant

HOR. WALPOLE

To GEORGE NICOL, Sunday 13 March 1791

Printed from the MS now WSL. First printed, Toynbee *Supp.* ii. 47–9. The MS is untraced until acquired by F. T. Sabin, of London, by 1918; sold by Gabriel Wells to WSL, July 1932.

Berkeley Square, March 13, 1791.

Dear Sir,

I BEG you will tell Mr Lodge[1] that it is impossible to contest such solid reasons as he has produced for *Lord T. Howard* being the Earl of Suffolk,[2] both from Camden[3] and the confrontation of the dates; and it is far more likely that I should have been ignorant than Camden.

2. Walker had reported to HW that the bookseller at Dublin had 'already expended fifty pounds' in reprinting *The Mysterious Mother (ante* 17 Feb. 1791 and n. 2).

3. See *ante* 17 Feb. 1791. Lord Charlemont had asked the publishers to suppress the edition 'lest the feelings of the amiable author might be hurt' ('Advertisement from the Publishers,' *The Mysterious Mother*, Dublin, 1791, p. [v]). See *post* 4 April 1791, n. 3.

1. Edmund Lodge (*ante* 6 July 1790, n. 8).

2. Thomas Howard (1561–1626), styled Lord Thomas Howard 1561–97; summoned

to Parliament 5 Dec. 1597 as Lord Howard de Walden; cr. (1603) E. of Suffolk. Lodge identifies Lord Thomas Howard in his *Illustrations of British History, Biography, and Manners, in the Reigns of Henry VIII, Edward VI, Mary, Elizabeth, and James I*, 1791, iii. 29n, 386n. HW's engraved portrait of Lord Thomas Howard was sold London i. 106. HW identifies him correctly in *Anecdotes of Painting*, 1762–71, ii. 34n.

3. William Camden, in his *Britannia; or a Chorographical Description of Great Britain and Ireland, Together with the Adjacent Islands*, ed. Edmund Gibson, 1722, in the section on Suffolk, i. 453, states that 'King James . . . in the first

I rejoice in the discovery and authenticity of a portrait of George Earl of Shrewsbury⁴—but I must beg you will not venture getting the original for me to see. It is so great a curiosity, and being already a little chipped, that I own, if it was my own property, I should be very sorry to let it run such risks, which is too great for uniques, the loss or destruction of which cannot be repaired. I shall be quite content to see the print, and much obliged for three or four proofs.⁵

Mr Lodge knows to be sure that there is a print of the memorable Bess of Hardwicke,⁶ the wife of Earl George, in Collins's account of the families of Vere, Cavendish, etc.⁷ It was engraved, though but

year of his reign, created Thomas Lord Howard of Walden (second son of Thomas Howard Duke of Norfolk) Earl of Suffolk; whom, for his approved fidelity and valour, he had before made Lord Chamberlain' (HW owned this edition of *Britannia* and also Richard Gough's translation, 1789; see Hazen, *Cat. of HW's Lib.*, Nos 424, 563, and DALRYMPLE 194). In his *Annals, or, the Historie of the Most Renowned and Victorious Princesse Elizabeth, Late Queen of England*, trans. R. N., 3d edn, 1635, p. 481, in the chapter on 1597, Camden identifies Lord Howard as 'Thomas Howard also, the second sonne of Thomas Duke of Norfolke, who was lately chosen into the Order of the Garter, was called by writ to this Parliament, with the title of Baron Howard of Walden.' HW's copy of the English translation, 1688, is Hazen, op. cit., No. 2166. HW's remarks probably concern the identification of a portrait. When he visited Castle Howard in 1772, he was shown a portrait that was said to represent Henry Howard, 1st Earl of Northampton, but was actually a portrait of Lord Thomas Howard, Earl of Suffolk; portraits of both men at Castle Howard were engraved for Lodge's *Portraits of Illustrious Personages of Great Britain* (see SELWYN 258 and nn. 11, 12).

4. George Talbot (ca 1522–90), 6th E. of Shrewsbury, 1560. A portrait of him, dated 1580, from a painting in the possession of the Rev. Thomas Bancroft of Chester (Lodge, op. cit. i. x), is the frontispiece to vol. II of Lodge's *Illustrations;* it is described by Roy Strong, *Tudor and Jacobean Portraits*, 1969, i. 286–7, as the

original from which was made a 'watercolour on white paper . . . by an unknown artist' now in the National Portrait Gallery (ibid. ii. plate 557). John Charles Brooke wrote Richard Gough 11 March 1791: 'Mr Basire is engraving Arabella Stewart (from Mr Walpole's) for Mr Lodge; and has obtained, by means of the *Gentlemen's Magazine*, a fine original of old George Earl of Salop from Chester, for the like purpose. He has a very good subscription' (Nichols, *Lit. Illus.* vi. 426). Two similar portraits of the 6th Earl, which appear to be 'very early copies executed from a lost original,' are now at Hardwick Hall and at Welbeck Abbey (Strong, op. cit. i. 286, ii. plate 558). For a description of these portraits, see D. N. Durant, *Bess of Hardwick*, 1977, p. 261; Mark Girouard, *Hardwick Hall, Derbyshire*, The National Trust, 1976, pp. 8, 80; Lord Hawkesbury, 'Catalogue of the Pictures at Hardwick Hall,' *Journal of the Derbyshire Archæological and Natural History Society*, 1903, xxv. 107 and facing p. 106.

5. The engraving is by Thomas Cook (ca 1744–1818) (GM 1818, lxxxviii pt i. 475; Thieme and Becker vii. 348). There is no impression of the print listed in the London Sale Catalogue of 1842.

6. See *ante* 2 Sept. 1760, n. 6. Lodge gives a sketch of her character in his Introduction (*Illustrations* i. xvi–xvii).

7. Arthur Collins, *Historical Collections of the Noble Families of Cavendishe, Holles, Vere, Harley, and Ogle, with the Lives of the Most Remarkable Persons . . . Containing . . . Prints of the Principal Persons, engraved by Mr George*

indifferently, by Vertue in his old age, when his eyes almost failed, but, as I remember, pretty like, from the original still at Hardwicke[8]—where, by the way, I doubt very much whether the Queen of Scots ever was a prisoner—probably at most for very few days.[9] I never found any evidence for the tradition, and I am sure Mr Lodge's volumes produce none. The hangings of patchwork may have been of her Majesty's work, and seem so;[10] but the state in the hall, and I think the state bed, have not her arms, but those of the Earl and Countess of Devonshire. Moreover, Countess Bess, if I do not forget, does not mention any of the furniture as having served that Queen, much less as being of her work, though in her will the Countess is very circumstantial,[11] and even specifies a firescreen

Vertue, from Original Pictures, 1752. HW's copy, now in the British Museum, is Hazen, op. cit., No. 565.

8. HW presumably has in mind the portrait of 'Elizabeth of Hardwicke, in black velvet, chain of pearls, red hair, old, in the Drawing room' that he saw at Hardwick in Aug. 1760 (*Country Seats* 29). The same portrait, or a similar version of it, hangs in the Long Gallery at Hardwick today and is accepted as authentic; see Strong, op. cit. i. 287–8, ii. plate 562; Durant, op. cit. 260–1, No. 9; Girouard, op. cit. 78, 80, No. 9. George Vertue's engraving in Collins's *Historical Collections*, facing p. 14, is from a portrait then at Welbeck Abbey which was at that time believed to represent Bess and was said to have been painted by Cornelis Jonson van Ceulen (Vertue Note Books, *Walpole Society*, 1937–8, xxvi. 90); this portrait is recorded in R. W. Goulding and C. K. Adams, *Catalogue of the Pictures Belonging to his Grace the Duke of Portland, K.G.*, Cambridge, 1936, p. 387, as 'At Hardwick Hall. Formerly at Welbeck [Abbey]. . . . Given by the fourth Duke of Portland to the sixth Duke of Devonshire, January 1821.' See also *BM Cat. of Engraved British Portraits* iv. 95; Hawkesbury, op. cit. xxv. 138, No. 252.

9. In spite of later legend, there is no contemporary evidence that Mary Queen of Scots was ever at Hardwick Old Hall (now in ruins) or the new Hardwick Hall completed in 1597; see Girouard, op. cit. 11, 43–5, 97; Rev. Joseph Hunter, 'On the Claim of Hardwick in Derbyshire to

have been one of the Residences of Mary Queen of Scots during her Captivity in England,' *Archæologia*, 1847, xxxii. 73–82; Basil Stallybrass, 'Bess of Hardwick's Buildings and Building Accounts,' *Archæologia*, 1913, lxiv. 353–4, 387. In *Anecdotes of Painting*, 1762–71, ii. 2, HW accepts the tradition that the Queen of Scots was imprisoned at Hardwick.

10. 'The wooden screens at the end of the hall were inserted early this century to contain pieces from two sets of hangings originally made for Chatsworth in the 1570s. They are made out of a patchwork of pieces of velvet, cloth of gold and figured silk, partly cut out of medieval copes. . . . In the eighteenth and nineteenth centuries they were erroneously attributed to Mary, Queen of Scots' (Girouard, op. cit. 54). The only examples of the Queen's needlework now at Hardwick are two panels in the Paved Room (ibid. 27, 107), but there is no doubt that she and Lady Shrewsbury spent much time working on embroidery with the help of professional embroiderers (Durant, op. cit. 65–7).

11. Extracts from the Countess of Shrewsbury's will are printed in Collins, op. cit. 15–19; copies of the will are in the Public Record Office and at Chatsworth (Durant, op. cit. 244). Attached to the will is 'The Inventorie of the Plate and other Furniture of howshold stuff which is ment and appoynted by this my laste will and testament to be, remayne and contynewe at my howse or howses at Hardwick,' made in 1601, which does not

(which though shorter, is like a wooden traverse for brushing clothes) with a piece of red velvet, now grown tawny; which I saw a few years ago[12] when I was at Hardwicke.

I am so delighted with Mr Lodge's work, and his own knowledge, that I hope, dear Sir, you will persuade him to accompany you this summer on the visit you have promised me to Strawberry,[13] and take beds there. I have there a memorandum book, in which are the notes I took at Hardwicke[14]—but which indeed makes me not so accurate, for when I have set down anything to which I can refer, I am less careful to imprint it in my memory—apropos, I do not mean this as an excuse for loss of memory, which is too natural at seventy-three, especially considering the quantity of trifles with which I furnished mine.

I am dear Sir without compliments

Your much obliged humble servant

HOR. WALPOLE

mention furniture used by the Queen of Scots ('The Hardwick Hall Inventory of 1601,' ed. Lindsay Boynton and Peter Thornton, *Journal of the Furniture History Society*, 1971, vii. 2–5, 23–40; Girouard, op. cit. 97).

12. In August 1760; see *Country Seats* 29–30 and MONTAGU i. 297–8.

13. Nicol and Lodge together visited SH on 16 Aug. 1791 ('Book of Visitors,' BERRY ii. 239).

14. HW's 'Book of Materials,' 1759 (now WSL), pp. 89–91. See *Country Seats* 29–30.

From HENRY WILLIAM BUNBURY,
Wednesday 16 March 1791

Printed from the MS now WSL. First printed, Toynbee *Supp.* ii. 50 n. 7. An extract is printed in J. C. Riely, 'Horace Walpole and "The Second Hogarth,"' *Eighteenth-Century Studies*, 1975–6, ix. 40. Damer-Waller; the MS was sold 5 Dec. 1921 (first Waller Sale), lot 100, to Maggs; offered by Maggs, Cat. Nos 433 (Christmas 1922), lot 3018; 471 (1925), lot 2582; 501 (spring 1928), lot 91; sold by them to WSL in 1932.

Endorsed by HW (in the dateline): 1791.
Address: Honourable Horace Walpole, Berkeley Square.

Richmond,[1] March 16.

Dear Sir,

I HAD two drawings[2] which I had flattered myself, you would have done me the honour of accepting in return for many civilities I have received at your hands. But I am at this moment so situated, that I dare not send them to you, lest they should bear with them the appearance of *bribery and corruption*. I happened to pass today, Sir, a small house of yours[3] (where poor Mrs Clive[4] lived) which I have often looked at with an eye of envy: and was informed by a man[5] in the fields that the gentleman[6] who had it last, had quitted it. Mrs B.[7] and myself have long wished to meet with some small place about Twickenham: and having a very small fortune and now no prospect of it ever increasing,[8] if we should be so for-

1. The Bunburys were living at Richmond in Aug. 1789; Henry Bunbury visited SH on 20 Aug. 1789 (OSSORY iii. 62; BERRY ii. 234).

2. Not identified, but perhaps two drawings for Bunbury's *Annals of Horsemanship*, published in 1791, containing 16 plates. HW's copy of this work was bound with Bunbury's *An Academy for Grown Horsemen*, 1787, containing 12 plates (Hazen, *Cat. of HW's Lib.*, Nos 3913, 3914). For HW's albums of Bunbury prints (now WSL) see *ante* 28 April 1781 and n. 1; J. C. Riely, 'Horace Walpole and "The Second Hogarth,"' *Eighteenth-Century Studies*, 1975–6, ix. 38–40.

3. Little Strawberry Hill, situated on HW's property at Twickenham.

4. See *ante* 3 Dec. ?1748 OS, n. 1. She lived at Little SH ('Cliveden') from Nov. 1754 to Dec. 1785 (see Appendix 1; *Straw-*

berry Hill Accounts . . . Kept by Mr Horace Walpole from 1747 to 1795, ed. Paget Toynbee, Oxford, 1927, pp. 136–7, 176–7). Her brother James Raftor lived there with her from 1770 to 1785 (COLE ii. 373).

5. Not identified.

6. Sir Robert Goodere (*ante* 30 Dec. 1790, n. 4). He and his wife lived at Little SH from Dec. 1785 until 25 Dec. 1790 (BERRY i. 124 and n. 19).

7. Catherine Horneck (ca 1750–99), m. (1771) Henry William Bunbury (OSSORY i. 111 n. 34).

8. Bunbury was the second son of the Rev. Sir William Bunbury, 5th Bt, of Barton Hall and Mildenhall, Suffolk; his elder brother, Sir Thomas Charles Bunbury, had succeeded to the baronetcy in 1764.

tunate as to be acceptable as tenants and neighbours to you, we should be indeed most happy. We have never seen the house, but have been ever so delighted with the spot it stands on, that we are sanguine enough to be certain it would be the most desirable habitation in this country for us to settle contentedly at. I flatter myself you would at least find us very peaceable neighbours, and very careful of everything put into our possession. Although I cannot but say, we are very anxious that your answer, Sir, may be a favourable one, yet I hold myself bound to beg your acceptance of the drawings I intended for you, after I receive the answer,[9] whatever it may be. I have the honour to be with great regard, dear Sir,

Your very obliged and faithful humble servant,

HENRY WM BUNBURY

Hon. Horace Walpole.

To HENRY WILLIAM BUNBURY, Thursday 17 March 1791

Printed from Toynbee *Supp.* ii. 49–50, where the letter was first printed. The MS passed by family descent to Sir Henry Bunbury, 10th Bt; sold Sotheby's 13 May 1905 (property of Sir Henry Bunbury, Bt), lot 822, to Francis Harvey, of London, in whose possession the MS was in 1918; not further traced.

Berkeley Square, March 17, 1791.

I AM extremely sorry, dear Sir, that you should ask a favour[1] of me which for near six months it has been no longer in my power to grant. The house in question was let but from year to year, and the gentleman[2] who has left it, would have been very glad to have kept it, but I refused to accommodate him with a stable and coach-house, because I had destined the house for particular friends of mine,[3] to whom I engaged it the moment the last tenant went out

---

9. See following letter and BERRY i. 222–3.

———

1. Of leasing Little Strawberry Hill. See previous letter.
2. Sir Robert Goodere (*ante* 16 March 1791, n. 6, and Appendix 1).

3. Robert Berry, Mary Berry, and Agnes Berry. On 16 Dec. 1790 HW settled the house on Mary and Agnes Berry for their lives, but they did not actually live there until late Dec. 1791 (BERRY i. 160, 249, 263, 304, 377–8).

of it, and who are to come into it as soon as some alterations are made and new offices built—indeed, as it was, it would have suited nobody, so very bad the conveniences are.

When you say your drawings[4] would look like a bribe, I hope you think I am grateful enough to remember how amply you have bribed me already by your charming drawing of Richmond Hill.[5] Indeed, Sir, the purchase of prints from your genius are frequent bribes; and when you give them to the public, I reckon myself one of the obliged,[6] and therefore I shall be fully satisfied with purchasing prints from your two new drawings; for I cannot have the assurance to accept the originals, when I have the mortification of being forced to refuse your request (though out of my power), and of losing the satisfaction of having you and Mrs Bunbury for near neighbours. I have the honour of being with the greatest esteem, Sir,

Your most obliged and obedient humble servant,

Hor. Walpole

From Joseph Cooper Walker, Wednesday 23 March 1791

Printed for the first time from a transcript made by Thomas Crofton Croker, removed from Croker's extra-illustrated copy of the SH Sale Catalogue of 1842, now WSL. The original letter, apparently inserted by HW in his presentation copy of the Dublin edition of *The Mysterious Mother*, 1791, was sold SH iv. 162 (with another copy of the Dublin edition) to Money; this copy was later in the possession of Thomas Baylis, who acted as agent for Thomas Crofton Croker and John Wilson Croker at the SH Sale, and it passed from Baylis to T. C. Croker's son, Dillon Croker (see n. 2 below); not further traced. Another transcript of the letter in T. C. Croker's hand is bound in his copy of the SH Sale Catalogue, facing p. 53.

Dublin, Eccles Street, 23rd March 1791.

MR WALKER having been for some time dangerously ill of a nervous fever, and still unable to hold his pen, is therefore obliged to commit it to another hand[1] to inform Mr Walpole that he

4. See *ante* 16 March 1791, n. 2.
5. See *ante* 28 April 1781 and n. 3.
6. HW wrote Lady Ossory 6 Sept. 1787:

'I get everything I can of Mr Bunbury's' (Ossory ii. 572).

———

1. Not identified.

has now the honour of sending him a copy of the Dublin edition of his tragedy.[2]

The same cause which prevents him from writing, prevented him from reading the Preface, extract from Baker and Postscript;[3] he cannot therefore answer for their correctness; but Mr Walker hopes that Mr Walpole will not find any errors of consequence in the tragedy,[4] the sheets of which he read with a good deal of care.

2. *The Mysterious Mother*. The SH Sale Catalogue of 1842, iv. 162, lists 'The Mysterious Mother, 2 copies, the spurious edition printed in Dublin, 1791, unbound.' One of these was the presentation copy sent by Walker to HW and inscribed 'For the Honourable Horace Walpole from Joseph C. Walker' in Walker's hand, and 'The Irish Edition' in HW's hand. This copy contained MS corrections by HW (see Hazen, *Cat. of HW's Lib.*, No. 2490). The corrections were transcribed, with the text of the present letter, by Thomas Crofton Croker and laid in his copy of the SH Sale Catalogue, now WSL. HW's copy of the Dublin edition was later in the possession of Thomas Baylis, of Mayfield Lodge, who wrote to Dillon Croker: 'I have been looking all the morning for Horace Walpole's play for you, all I can find at present is the Dublin edition, the one considered by your father the most curious. Please refer to lot 162 in your Strawberry Hill Catalogue to see of what it consisted and if of more than what I send you, I will hunt after the remainder' (MS now WSL). See headnote.

3. The Dublin edition of 1791 contains the Author's Preface, dated 29 April 1781, which HW wrote for the edition printed in 1781 (never published); the Advertisement from the Publishers; a summary of David Erskine Baker's remarks on the play in his *Biographia Dramatica*, 1782 (ii. 247–9), followed by a justification of this publication of the play; and the Author's Postscript, which HW wrote for the SH edition of 1768. The 'extract from Baker' begins: 'Mr Baker, in his *Biographia Dramatica*, mentioning the following poem, tells us it was distributed by the author to his particular friends only; and with such strict injunctions of secrecy, that knowing its merits, much astonishment was excited at its being withheld from the public' (*The Mysterious Mother*, Dublin, 1791, p. vii). The London reprint, 1791, contains only the Author's Preface (dated June 1791) and the Author's Postscript.

4. HW communicated his corrections in his reply to Walker *post* 4 April 1791. Virtually the same corrections were made by HW in his copy of the Dublin edition (see n. 2 above).

To Sir Joseph Banks, Saturday 26 March 1791

Printed from a photostat of the MS in the Edinburgh University Library (MS La.III.514/7). First printed in George Chalmers, *The Life of Mary, Queen of Scots,* 1818, i. vi. The MS was forwarded by Banks to George Chalmers (1742–1825), the Scottish historian and antiquary, and became part of Chalmers's collections relating to the history of Scotland during the reign of Queen Mary, 1542–68; these collections later passed to David Laing, the Scottish bibliographer and antiquary, who bequeathed them to the Edinburgh University Library in 1878.

Address: To Sir Joseph Banks in Soho Square.

Berkeley Square, March 26, 1791.

I NEVER could ascertain the authenticity and originality of any portrait of Mary Queen of Scots, but of that[1] which is in the possession of the Earl of Morton,[2] and which was painted when she was prisoner at Loch-Leven.[3] There are copies of it at St James's, at Hatfield and Hardwicke.[4] Vertue did not think that the fine head in a black hat by Isaac Oliver in the King's collection, and which Vertue engraved when it was Dr Meade's,[5] was a portrait of her. He

1. This portrait, by an unknown artist, is of the so-called 'Sheffield' type, for which the original seems to be a miniature by Nicholas Hilliard. The picture was formerly at Dalmahoy, Midlothian, the seat of the 14th Earl of Morton; it was acquired by the Glasgow Art Gallery in 1926 (Lionel Cust, *Notes on the Authentic Portraits of Mary Queen of Scots,* 1903, pp. 83–7 and pl. XVIII; Roy Strong, *Tudor and Jacobean Portraits,* 1969, i. 220; Dalrymple 113 and n. 28).

2. George Douglas (1761–1827), styled Lord Aberdour 1768–74; 16th E. of Morton, 1774; F.R.S., 1785; F.S.A., 1786.

3. 'According to tradition this portrait is said to have been presented by the Queen at Loch Leven to her liberator, George Douglas, and from him to have passed to James Douglas, fourth Earl of Morton' (Cust, op. cit. 83). The tradition is now discredited because the painting is tentatively dated *post* 1603 (Strong, op. cit. i. 220–1; Dalrymple 113).

4. There are many versions of the 'Sheffield' type; the best of them is in the collection of Mrs Doris Herschorn, and there

is another at Windsor (Strong, op. cit. i. 220, ii. pl. 433; Cust, op. cit. 70–8). Most of these versions are now dated *post* 1603: the one at Hardwick Hall, not listed in the 1601 inventory, may have been painted ca 1613; the one at Hatfield House is first mentioned in an inventory of 1629; the one in the National Portrait Gallery was first recorded in 1637 (Strong, op. cit. i. 220–1). George Vertue wrote in his notebook *sub* 12 July 1731: 'at Hatfield Erl Salisburys I went to finish the picture of Queen of Scots a limning. I had begun. this picture is on board painted. the same as that at St. James. Windsor. at Hardwick Duke of Devonshire's. at Welbeck Ld Oxfords. all old pictures and undoubted genuine—and agrees with the Queens Monument Effigie at Westminster' (Vertue Note Books, *Walpole Society,* 1935–6, xxiv. 16). HW had a 'whole length in water-colours; by Vertue, from the picture at Hatfield' ('Des. of SH,' *Works* ii. 490).

5. The miniature of Mary Queen of Scots, dressed in a black dress with a high-crowned black hat over a white cap,

also doubted of that at Chiswick,[6] which he engraved for Lord Burlington,[7] and said to be painted for her by Zucchero,[8] when married to Francis II, but it is not clear, that Zucchero ever saw her; nor is the nose like that in Lord Morton's picture, which agrees with the figure on her tomb at Westminster;[9] in both[10] the nose rises a little towards the top; bends rather inwards at bottom and is thin. In Lord Burlington's picture it is fuller and rounder at bottom—but it is true that the profile on her medal[11] is rather full too. Yet I should think that Lord Morton's picture and the tomb are most to be depended on.

There is a whole length of Mary at Windsor;[12] but it must have been painted after her death, for in the background is a view of her

is attributed to Isaac Oliver; it was formerly in the collection of Richard Mead (1673–1754), M.D., and is now in the Royal Library at Windsor (Cust, op. cit. 140; Dalrymple 112–13 and n. 22). It is no longer considered an authentic portrait, but it was engraved as such by Vertue (BM Cat. of Engraved British Portraits iii. 195). Vertue mentions more than one picture of the Queen of Scots in Dr Mead's collection (Vertue Note Books, Walpole Society, 1929–30, xviii. 156; 1935–6, xxiv. 187).

6. This famous portrait (the 'Carleton' prototype) was purchased by Henry Boyle (d. 1725), cr. (1714) Bn Carleton. He bequeathed it to his nephew, Richard Boyle (1694–1753), 3d E. of Burlington, 1704, who removed it to his house at Chiswick, Middlesex; it is now at Chatsworth (Cust, op. cit. 133–5 and pl. XXXI; Dalrymple 113 and n. 25). Roy Strong has dated this picture 'certainly not earlier than the mid 17th century' (Strong, op. cit. i. 222–3). For Vertue's comments see Walpole Society, 1929–30, xviii. 70; for HW's doubts see Country Seats 30.

7. Three engravings by Vertue of the 'Carleton' portrait are listed in the BM Cat. of Engraved British Portraits iii. 196–7; the one showing the subject at half-length was published as the frontispiece to De vita et rebus gestis Mariæ Scotorum Reginæ, ed. Samuel Jebb, 1725 (Cust, op. cit. 135–6).

8. Federico Zuccari (ca 1543–1609) (Mann ix. 403 n. 11).

9. The monument in Westminster Ab-

bey was begun in 1606 by Cornelius Cure (d. 1609) and completed ca 1613 by his son, William Cure (d. 1632). It is said to have been taken from a death-mask and is considered an authentic likeness (Strong, op. cit. i. 216–17, ii. plates 439, 440, 441, 445; Cust, op. cit. 118–20 and plate XXVII; Dalrymple 113 n. 29, 139).

10. In the MS after 'both' HW crossed out 'and that'; he first wrote 'noses' and then crossed out the 's'.

11. A large medallion of uncertain date by Jacopo Primavera has a profile of Mary Queen of Scots which resembles the figure on the monument in Westminster Abbey; it is now in the British Museum (Cust, op. cit. 121–2 and pl. XIIb; Strong, op. cit. i. 215, ii. pl. 442). Two coins struck by John Achesoun (or Atkinson) at Paris in 1553 show the profile of the Queen at an earlier age (Cust, op. cit. 29–31 and pls I, no. 1, and XIIa).

12. This memorial portrait is a version of the portrait bequeathed by Elizabeth Curle to the Scottish College at Douai in 1620, now at St Mary's College, Blairs, Aberdeen. It contains a view of the Queen's execution on the right and shows her two ladies-in-waiting, Jane Kennedy and Elizabeth Curle, on the left. The Windsor version differs from the Blairs version only in the inscriptions; it has been at Windsor since 1684, and perhaps earlier (Cust, op. cit. 103–9 and pl. XXII; Strong, op. cit. i. 221–2, ii. pl. 438). It is described by Vertue in his notebooks (Walpole Society, 1929–30, xviii. 78).

execution. The picture in one of the company halls in the City,[13] from which there is a print,[14] and said to be Queen Mary with her son 3 or 4 years old, cannot be genuine, for I think she never saw James after he was a year old.

HOR. WALPOLE

To Sir James Colquhoun,[1] Thursday 31 March 1791

Printed from the MS now WSL. First printed in William Fraser, *The Chiefs of Colquhoun and their Country,* Edinburgh, 1869, i. 390. The MS descended in the Colquhoun family; it was subsequently bound in a volume of tracts that was owned in 1869 by Sir James Colquhoun, 4th Bt; later removed from the volume and sold Sotheby's 22 June 1955 ('Other Properties'), lot 732, to Maggs for WSL.

Berkeley Square, March 31, 1791.

Sir,

I YESTERDAY received the beautiful goat's horn[2] which you have been so good as to send me, with the inscription[3] with which you have been pleased to overhonour me. Indeed, Sir, I am ashamed that you should think that such a trifle as any writing of mine,[4] that was of no value to me, should deserve so curious a re-

13. Vertue wrote in his notebook: 'In drapers hall London. in the Court room. at whole length a lady and her son . . . this is falsely calld (Queen Mary of Scots) for the first reason against it she and her son never saw one another. after he was a 12 month old this boy is at least 6 years old—this picture is a woman very fair hair. the Queen of Scots was brown abourn.—' (ibid., 1935–6, xxiv. 94). The Draper's Hall portrait, ca 1610, is not accepted as authentic (Cust, op. cit. 143; Strong, op. cit. i. 222).

14. The engraving is by Francesco Bartolozzi (*BM Cat. of Engraved British Portraits* iii. 196).

1. (1741–1805), 2d Bt, 1786, of Luss, Dumbartonshire. At his seat, Rossdhu, on the west side of Loch Lomond, he formed a large collection of paintings, engravings, ancient coins and other antiquities, and Chinese porcelain (William Fraser, *The Chiefs of Colquhoun and their Country,* Edinburgh, 1869, i. 392).

2. 'A Scottish mull, made of a large ram's horn, and mounted in silver; a present from Sir James Colquhoun' ('Des. of SH,' *Works* ii. 512). It was sold SH xxiii. 13 to 'a London dealer in curiosities and antique relics, and the present Sir James Colquhoun [4th Bt, 1836] being informed of this by a friend who had seen it in the shop, purchased it, and it is now in his possession' at Rossdhu (Fraser, op. cit. i. 390 n. 1).

3. William Fraser (ibid. i. 389–90) describes the present as 'a beautiful goat's horn snuff-box, bearing the following inscription on the silver plate round the brim: "This trifle, given by Sir James Colquhoun of Luss, Bart, to the Honourable Horace Walpole, as a mark of respect." Below is a silver plate, on which are engraved the armorial bearings of Mr Walpole.'

4. Not identified. Fraser (ibid. i. 389) says only that 'Walpole . . . presented to Sir James Colquhoun of Luss a copy of some of his works.'

ward. The horn is a great rarity, and will be doubly valuable to me from the donor. I shall preserve it in my little collection with great care, and have the honour of being with the utmost gratitude and respect,

Sir

  Your most obedient and most obliged humble servant

HOR. WALPOLE

From RICHARD FRENCH, April 1791

Printed from an extract quoted in Thomas Thorpe's Catalogue of Manuscripts, 1834, pt iv, lot 1139. The MS is described as a letter 'respecting the portraits of Sir Robert Walpole and Horace Walpole'; it has not been traced.

The approximate date of the letter is that given in Thorpe's Catalogue.

. . . sensible that they will bestow the highest honour on the selection of distinguished characters which I am endeavouring to make.[1] . . .

---

1. French appears to have been selecting portraits of distinguished persons (including HW and Sir Robert Walpole) for use in a publication, but nothing is known of this project. Possibly in connection with the project, he visited HW in Berkeley Square on 25 May 1791 (BERRY i. 274).

To Joseph Cooper Walker, Monday 4 April 1791

Printed from a photostat of the MS in the possession of Hofmann and Free-man (Antiquarian Booksellers) Ltd, Sevenoaks, Kent. First printed, Toynbee xiv. 406–7. The MS is untraced until sold Sotheby's 20 Dec. 1877 (Collection of Autograph Letters Sale), lot 51 (with six other letters from HW to Walker, 1787–92), to Naylor; resold Sotheby's 31 July 1885 (Naylor Sale), lot 971 (with another HW letter), to Barker; *penes* John Boyd Thacher, of Albany, New York, in 1901; resold Anderson Galleries 11 Jan. 1916 (Thacher Sale), lot 1159; not further traced until acquired before April 1975 by John Fleming, the New York dealer, who sold it to Hofmann and Freeman in March 1976.

Address: To Joseph C. Walker Esq. in Eccles Street, Dublin.

Strawberry Hill, April 4, 1791.

I HAVE received the copy of my tragedy,[1] and am exceedingly obliged to you, Sir, for the care with which you have been so good as to see it printed[2]—but allow me to say, that I wish you had added another mark of kindness and prevented the editors from making me compliments to which I am so very ill entitled. To any *eminence in literature*[3] I am sure I have no pretensions; *an amiable character* I wish I deserved; and of *high rank* I certainly am not, nor ever aspired above being a private commoner, and have proved a very insignificant one. In short, Sir, I am ashamed at reading such things said of myself, and should be miserable if it could be supposed that I was aware of any such intention. I assure you I should

1. *The Mysterious Mother, a Tragedy,* Dublin, 'Printed for John Archer, William Jones and Richard White 1791' (see *ante* 23 March 1791, n. 2).

2. Walker wrote to HW's friend John Pinkerton 13 March 1797 (after HW's death): 'His friend Lord Charlemont and I exerted ourselves to prevent the publication of his "Mysterious Mother" in Dublin. Failing in this attempt, I attended the work through the press, and am happy in being able to say that the Dublin edition is one of the most correct editions of that incomparable drama' (Nichols, *Lit. Illus.* vii. 734).

3. The Advertisement from the Publishers states that 'The impression was just completed, when hearing accidentally, that some persons, to whose opinion we wish to pay every deference, had expressed the greatest anxiety lest the feelings of the amiable author might be hurt, we determined, without hesitation, to suppress the edition. The expense already incurred, was, after such a hint, a consideration beneath our notice; we were glad to embrace the opportunity of testifying our sincere regard for the high rank, excellent character and eminence in literature of the gentleman who is the reputed author. Finding, however, after an interval of several months, that our well-meant intentions could not be effectual, and that our interference had only delayed, but could not prevent a publication eagerly demanded, we have been induced, reluctantly, to comply with the general wish, and to deliver for sale a work that has been a considerable time in readiness' (*The Mysterious Mother*, Dublin, 1791, pp. v–vi).

have been more adverse to their being inserted, than I was even to the publication of the play.

The text is surprisingly correct. I have found some very immaterial errors,[4] or rather only literal alterations (probably from some MS copy) and one alone that affects the sense, and that not in the piece, but in the postscript, where in page 98, line 11, *terror* is printed for *horror*. I will just specify the rest, though of no consequence. In page 5, line the 6th should have been printed thus,

It knows not wherefore. What a kind of being
Is circumstance! (there the pause should be; and then)
I am a soldier etc.

In p. 10, line 11, Oh! he has played me etc. dele *how*. P. 12, line 2, for *the* staff, r[ead] *this*. P. 15, last line but two, after *tool*, dele the comma. P. 81, for effi*cacy* lost, r[ead] effi*cacy's* lost. P. 82, for pulse repl*y* not, r[ead] repl*ies* not. P. 94, for fellow being, r[ead] fellow being*s*. P. 97, for but I *am* willing to insinuate, r[ead] I *was* willing etc.

Now, Sir, I should blush to mention such very trifling inaccuracies, if I did not think it a just return for your trouble of overlooking the press, to prove to you that even the jealous eye of an author could discover no more, and no more material slips. Consequently I must again thank you, though again lament the Advertisement from the Publishers, of which I hope you will always bear me witness I was perfectly ignorant and innocent. For every other attention I shall always be, Sir

Your much obliged and obedient humble servant

HOR. WALPOLE

PS. Your health, Sir, I hope, is recovered and restored—on reading your letter[5] again, I observe that your indisposition prevented your seeing the unlucky preface that gives me so much concern; and the only word in the whole publication that hurts the sense, by your not overlooking the postscript.

N[ote] in my original, in the 2d line of the first scene, was *chill*, not *dull*, as *chill*ing is more productive of fear than *dull*ing is.

---

4. The corrections given here were apparently taken from HW's copy of the Dublin edition sent to him by Walker; a transcript of HW's annotations was preserved with the transcript of Walker's letter of 23 March 1791, laid in Thomas Crofton Croker's copy of the SH Sale Catalogue of 1842 (now WSL).

5. *Ante* 23 March 1791.

To Sir John Sebright,[1] Friday 27 May 1791

Printed for the first time from a photostat of the MS in the possession (1956) of Miss Olive Lloyd-Baker, of Hardwicke Court, Hardwicke, Glos. The MS passed by family descent to Miss Lloyd-Baker, a great-great-great-granddaughter of Sir John Sebright.

Berkeley Square, May 27th [1791].

MR WALPOLE did himself the honour of calling on Sir John Sebright yesterday, and particularly to ask when it will be convenient to Sir John and Lady[2] and Miss Sebright[3] to favour him with their company some morning at Strawberry Hill.[4] Mr Walpole goes thither tomorrow[5] to put up some of the small pictures and other baubles that are always removed in winter, and is obliged to be in town on Monday;[6] but thinks of settling there on Saturday 4th of June,[7] by which he hopes there will be some rain, as his little place is not at all in beauty at present. If Monday 6th will be agreeable, Mr Walpole will be much flattered with the honour of seeing Sir John and Lady and Miss Sebright at any hour they will please to name.

1. Sir John Sebright (1725–94), 6th Bt; M.P.

2. Sarah Knight (d. 1813), m. (1766) Sir John Sebright, 6th Bt, 1761 (GM 1814, lxxxiv pt i. 97; *Hertfordshire Families*, ed. Duncan Warrand, 1907, pp. 216–17).

3. Henrietta Sebright (1770–1840), elder dau. of Sir John and Lady Sebright, m. (1794) Henry Lascelles, 2d E. of Harewood, 1820 (BERRY i. 286 n. 22). HW wrote Mary Berry 8 June 1791: 'the daughter had given me a drawing, and I owed her a civility' (ibid. i. 286).

4. They came to breakfast at SH on Monday, 6 June (ibid.). HW wrote in his 'Book of Visitors' for that day: 'Sir J., Lady and Miss Sebrights. Myself' (ibid. ii. 238).

5. HW stayed at SH until Monday, 30 May, when he entertained General Conway and Lady Ailesbury, Lord and Lady Frederick Campbell, Miss Elizabeth Hervey, and Mrs William Thomas Hervey at breakfast (ibid. i. 280, ii. 238).

6. Mrs Damer wrote Mary Berry 29 May: 'I am to see him [HW] tomorrow, after his return from Strawberry, and to carry him to my mother's, who has a party for the Comtesse d'Albanie' (*The Berry Papers*, ed. Lewis Melville, 1914, p. 36). HW wrote Mary Berry 2 June 1791: 'Lady Ailesbury made a small assemblage for her [the Comtesse d'Albany] on Monday, and my curiosity is satisfied' (BERRY i. 280).

7. HW wrote Mary Berry 2 June: 'Such weather makes me wish myself at Strawberry, whither I shall betake myself on Saturday for three days; but shall not be able to settle yet' (ibid. i. 281; see also i. 283.)

To Lord Lansdowne, Thursday 16 June 1791

Printed from the MS in Thomas Kirgate's hand, now wsl. First printed, Toynbee, *Supp.* ii. 51–2. Damer-Waller; the MS was sold Sotheby's 5 Dec. 1921 (first Waller Sale), lot 29, bought in; resold Christie's 15 Dec. 1947 (second Waller Sale), lot 42, to Maggs for wsl.

Strawberry Hill, June 16, 1791.

My Lord,

THOUGH most unwilling to trouble your Lordship again, it is impossible to suppress the gratitude I feel for the letter you have been pleased to honour me with in answer to mine.[1] A testimonial to my father's character from so good a judge as your Lordship is the most flattering present I could receive, and convinces me of what I have long thought, that the more his conduct is weighed by great understandings, the more his genuine merit will be allowed.

Pardon me, my Lord, but I cannot so readily accept the praise your Lordship too liberally bestows on a son unworthy of such a father; and forgive me if I use a few words to prove that there was no merit in my patient silence on the diminution of my place in the Exchequer.[2]

When Sir Robert gave me that place,[3] it produced much less than it did afterwards by successive wars and other increasing expenses of government. If augmented burthens made your Lordship and others, and then the whole legislature, think it necessary to reduce the

---

1. Lansdowne's letter is missing. It was apparently a reply to a (missing) letter of HW's, similar to *ante* 19 June 1783, concerning his office of usher of the Exchequer.

2. As a result of the inquiry in 1782 by the Commissioners for Examining the Public Accounts, the House of Commons adopted the resolution 'That the income and emoluments arising from the several offices of auditor of the Exchequer, clerk of the Pells, tellers of the Exchequer, and usher of the Exchequer, have, from the late enormous issues of public money, become unreasonable and excessive, and that the same require some regulation in future' (Cobbett, *Parl. Hist.* xxiii. 120). By the Act of 23 Geo. III, c. 82, the office of

usher of the Exchequer was to be abolished after the death of the present holder (HW) and the holder of the reversion (Samuel Martin). See *ante* 19 June 1783 and n. 7; 7 July 1782, n. 8; 12 Aug. 1782.

3. In Feb. 1738 the income from the ushership of the Exchequer was estimated to be 'worth £900 a year,' as HW explains in his 'Account of My Conduct Relative to the Places I Hold under Government, and towards Ministers,' dated 30 March 1782 (*Works* ii. 364). In 1782, by averaging the annual income from the previous twelve years, HW reported that his average income from the office was £1800 (ibid. ii. 367).

charge on the public by abridging offices, I had no reason to think myself personally injured, nor the smallest services to plead that entitled me to exemption. Having no reason for complaint, I certainly did not complain. I should have blushed to have been excepted, when others in the like predicament suffered, and several of whom could less afford a diminution. I had felt the benefit of the augmentation of the public expense—was it just to profit by it, and not be equally liable to suffer by the retrenchment of that expenditure? Having received what I certainly had done nothing to deserve, with what face could I have demanded, or solicited to be indemnified for my loss? I blame nobody who acted otherwise; they might have claims of merit; I had none. Indeed, my Lord, I thought myself so over-fortunate, that the commissioners of public accounts having overcharged my receipt by part of the arrears of the preceding year being paid to me in the last year of their survey, and adding them to my receipt of that year (which swelled my income beyond its reality, not intentionally I am persuaded)[4] I did not complain of that mistake, lest I should seem to think myself injured, when I had none of the feeling of an injured man.[5]

This explanation, I trust, will satisfy your Lordship's mind, that my total silence has proceeded from principle, and not from any affectation of philosophy, which I despise. I could have no resentment to your Lordship, or to any man who thought himself serving the public: and if your Lordship should imagine (to which I can by no means agree) that you owed me any indemnification, you have infinitely over-recompensed me by the noble justice you have done

---

4. According to the report of the Commissioners, HW's ushership paid him £4200 net in the year 1780 (GRAY ii. 256–7, Appendix 7). HW wrote in his 'Account of My Conduct': 'When therefore I am charged as receiver of £4200 a year, it should be remembered, that though I was so in the year 1780 (though I shall show that even that is an arbitrary statement, and not calculated on any medium), yet I cannot equitably be reckoned *communibus annis* to receive so large a sum. . . . I have sometimes had large arrears due . . . and thence I may in one year receive four or five thousand pounds, because in the preceding I did not receive half so.

much, the commissioners of accounts having examined my deputy but on a single year, were just in their report of what I received *that year;* but, had they gone farther back, would certainly not have given in £4200 as my receipt *communibus annis*' (*Works* ii. 368–9).

5. 'This unintended misrepresentation I bore in silence, it having been my steadfast purpose not to interfere with the public examination of places, nor take the smallest step to mitigate my own fate, which I submit implicitly to the discretion of the legislature' (ibid. ii. 369–70). See also *ante* 18 Aug. 1782, n. 4, and 19 June 1783.

to my father,[6] and have sweetened the infirmities of 74,[7] by administering a cordial to the old age of

My Lord, your Lordship's
most obliged, most respectful,
and most obedient humble servant

HOR. WALPOLE[8]

Marquis of Lansdown.

From Dr Charles Burney, Friday 8 July 1791

Printed for the first time from Burney's MS draft now WSL, written on the verso of a letter from Lady Banks (the wife of Sir Joseph Banks) dated 'Thursday evening' and addressed 'Dr Burney.' The MS draft descended in the Burney family and was acquired after the death of Miss Mabel Burney (1870–1953) by James M. Osborn, who gave it to WSL in Dec. 1954. The original letter is missing.

Dated by Fanny Burney's return 'yesterday evening' (7 July 1791) to her father's apartments (see nn. 2 and 5 below).

Endorsed by Burney: Copy of letter to the Honourable Horace Walpole.

Endorsed by Fanny Burney d'Arblay: July 1791. To Horace Walpole afterwards Lord Orford.

Dear Sir,

YOU have done me the honour so long and so kindly to interest yourself about the fate of my daughter,[1] that my gratitude has presented *you* first to my thoughts, the moment it was decided.[2] And

---

6. In his 'Account of My Conduct' HW wrote: 'I have never yet thanked Mr Burke for the overflowing pleasure he gave my heart, when, on moving his bill [Cobbett, *Parl. Hist.* xxi. 51], he paid that just compliment to the virtues of my honest excellent father' (*Works* ii. 370).

7. HW was actually only seventy-three; he apparently means 'in my seventy-fourth year.'

8. The signature is in HW's hand (see headnote).

---

1. See *ante* 6 July, 20 July 1786; 20 Oct. 1790. HW comments on Fanny Burney's appointment at Court in his MS notebook of 1786–95; see *Horace Walpole's Miscel-*

lany 1786–1795, ed. L. E. Troide, New Haven, 1978, pp. 35, 75–6, 93.

2. Fanny Burney had resigned her post as Second Keeper of the Robes to Queen Charlotte. She left St James's Palace after the drawing room on Thursday, 7 July (*Diary and Letters of Madame d'Arblay*, ed. Austin Dobson, 1904–5, iv. 490–1). She had been enjoined to keep secret (except from her father) her impending departure until the last week of her royal attendance (ibid. iv. 476, 480–1). She later described her homecoming to her father's apartments in Chelsea College: 'But my Father did the honours for me amongst those who had been most interested in my resignation. He called instantly upon Sir

I hasten to acquaint you that, after innumerable delays and uncertainty as to acceptance of a necessary resignation, and a state of health very alarming, a successor³ has arrived from Germany to relieve my anxiety for her situation, and her own, lest after the long patience which had been practised, offence would be taken at a wish to retreat from so honourable an employment even to take physic, or to die.⁴ But thank heaven, all has been at length well taken, and yesterday evening she returned to her natural abode.⁵ Her royal mistress and the whole family have not only parted with her reluctantly, but with apparent sorrow; a circumstance that will contribute to gild the rest of her days and make her forget former sufferings. But matters have not ended merely in a gracious and amicable manner, for such other solid proofs of approbation⁶ have been given as wholly content and fill with sensibility the grateful heart of my daughter and of him who has the honour to be with the truest attachment and respect, dear Sir,

Your obliged and most devoted servant,

C[HAS.] B[URNEY]

Joshua Reynolds and Miss Palmer, and Mr Burke; and he wrote to Mr Walpole, Mr Seward, Mrs Crewe, Mr Windham, and my Worcester Uncle' (*The Journals and Letters of Fanny Burney (Madame d'Arblay)*), ed. Joyce Hemlow et al., Oxford, 1972– , i. 2–3).

3. Caroline Jacobi (fl. 1791–7), daughter of Johann Friedrich Jacobi of Hanover, arrived shortly before 3 July, when Fanny Burney wrote her father: 'Mademoiselle Jacobi, my destined successor, is come. This moment I have been told it by the Queen' (Dobson, op. cit. iv. 481). Mlle Jacobi served as Keeper of the Robes to Queen Charlotte until Oct. 1797, when she returned to Germany (Hemlow, op. cit. i. 68 and n. 3.)

4. In Oct. 1790 Miss Burney wrote a memorial stating her wish to resign her position because of ill health, but she did not present it to the Queen until Dec. 1790. 'I could not, however, summon cour-age to present my memorial; my heart always failed me, from seeing the Queen's entire freedom from such an expectation: for . . . I saw she concluded me, while life remained, inevitably hers' (Dobson, op. cit. iv. 437; see also iv. 427–45).

5. Miss Burney wrote in her journal: 'My dear father was waiting for me in my apartment at St James's, when their Majesties and their fair royal daughters were gone. He brought me home—and welcomed me most sweetly' (Hemlow, op. cit. i. 2). Dr Burney was organist of Chelsea College and had occupied apartments in the Royal Hospital, Chelsea, since 1787. In August Miss Burney set out with Anna Dillingham Ord on a month's tour in the country; their first stop was Winchester and their last stop was Bath (ibid. i. 2 n. 7, 6–61; Dobson, op. cit. iv. 454).

6. Miss Burney was granted an annual pension of £100 (ibid. iv. 484; Hemlow, op. cit. i. xxx, 2).

To Dr Charles Burney, Sunday 10 July 1791

Printed from Toynbee *Supp.* ii. 52–3, where the letter was first printed. The MS descended in the Burney family to Arthur G. Burney, who owned it in 1918; not further traced.
Address: To Dr Burney at Chelsea College.

Strawberry Hill, July 10, 1791.

Dear Sir,

I SAW with great pleasure in the papers that Miss Burney has quitted her post,[1] and I give you a thousand thanks for confirming that satisfaction,[2] of which I cordially wish you joy. You have regained and will save the most valuable of children. I rejoice too that the conclusion has proved so different from your expectation,[3] and as you seem satisfied, I hope I shall be contented with it too, though I own I shall not be so cheaply, or if at all below your daughter's desert.

I assure you, Sir, I wish myself much joy too, as I flatter myself I shall now be the better for Miss Burney's release. You once was so kind as to bestow a whole day on me here with her.[4] I will not be unreasonably impatient: I know how many, many friends want to have amends made to them for her long eclipse, and I am still more sensible that she ought to have much repose to recover and re-establish her health and spirits,[5] and that, though she has been a lost sheep, she must not at once be turned out upon *the Common.*— Whenever therefore you shall think it proper to indulge me with a

1. Miss Burney's resignation of her post as Second Keeper of the Robes to Queen Charlotte was announced in the *Gazetteer and New Daily Advertiser* 8 July 1791: 'Miss Burney attended the drawing room yesterday, and resigned her place as Joint Mistress of the Robes to the Queen; which resignation, we are sorry to hear, is occasioned by a bad state of health.' See also *London Chronicle* 7–9 July, lxx. 26; *St James's Chronicle* 7–9 July, *sub* 9 July.

2. See previous letter. Miss Burney wrote of HW's letter to her father: 'Mr Walpole wrote the most charming of answers, in the gallantry of *the old Court,* and with all its wit, concluding with a warm invitation to Strawberry Hill' (*The Journals and Letters of Fanny Burney* (*Madame d'Arblay*), ed. Joyce Hemlow et al., Oxford, 1972– , i. 3).

3. The King and Queen accepted Miss Burney's resignation reluctantly but with friendliness, and granted her an annuity of £100 (*Diary and Letters of Madame d'Arblay,* ed. Austin Dobson, 1904–5, iv. 478–91).

4. They spent the night of 8 Sept. 1785 and the following day at SH. See *ante* 6 Sept. 1785; OSSORY ii. 498.

5. She went on a tour of the western counties from mid-August to mid-September and then spent a month with her sister, Susanna Burney Phillips, at Mickleham, Surrey (Hemlow, op. cit. i. 2, 6–67; *ante* 8 July 1791, n. 5).

day,[6] and safe to bring her with you, you cannot imagine, dear Sir, how happy you both will make

Your faithful humble servant,

Hor. Walpole

From Lord Townshend, Wednesday 30 November 1791

Printed from Toynbee *Supp.* ii. 247 n. 2, where Townshend's MS draft of the letter was first printed. In 1918 the MS draft was among the Townshend papers in the possession of Sir George Faudel-Phillips (1840–1922), cr. (1897) Bt, of Balls Park, Herts; not further traced. The original letter is missing.

Rainham,[1] November 30th 1791.

Dear Sir,

HAVING been at Houghton yesterday to inquire after my friend Lord Orford,[2] where I heard of your great anxiety and displeasure at his treatment,[3] my wish to contribute to your satisfaction will I hope apologize for this letter. I found that the three gentlemen of the faculty,[4] however they had differed before, were of the same opinion as to the cause and nature of his disorder, and reconciled as to the place and future mode of proceeding. This I particularly heard from Dr Ash[5] and Dr Willis;[6] it was clear to me that

6. Dr Burney and Miss Burney were engaged to spend the evening with HW on 4 Jan. 1792, but she was unable to go (Hemlow, op. cit. i. 108–10). No other visit to SH has been recorded in HW's letters except for Dr Burney's visit on 16 Aug. 1796 (Berry ii. 203–4).

1. Raynham Hall, Townshend's seat in Norfolk.
2. George Walpole, 3d E. of Orford, HW's nephew. He suffered 'a new fit of frenzy . . . attended by total insensibility, and so violent a fever, that . . . I had dreaded an express with an account of his death' (HW to Lady Ossory 23 Nov. 1791, Ossory iii. 129).
3. No one informed HW of his nephew's illness until Lord Cadogan sent him word,

'the persons in the house with Lord O[rford] and his servants totally concealing his situation from me, and from both his steward and his lawyer in town' (ibid. iii. 129–30). HW was displeased that Lord Orford had been moved from Brandon, Suffolk, to Houghton, and had sent Dr Thomas Monro to inquire into his condition (ibid. iii. 129; *post* 2 Dec. 1791).
4. Dr John Ash, Dr Francis Willis, and Dr William Norford (see below).
5. John Ash (1723–98), M.D., 1754; F.R.S.; formerly physician to the General Hospital at Birmingham (Foster, *Alumni Oxon.* i. 34; GM 1798, lxviii pt i. 544; Chatterton 314 and n. 5).
6. Rev. Francis Willis (1718–1807), M.D., 1759, who had attended George III during his attack of porphyria in 1788 (GM 1807, lxxvii pt ii. 1180; Ida Macalpine and

N.º XXVI.

N.º XXVII.

The Engaging M.ʳˢ F——y.

The Constant Admirer.

London, Publish'd by A.Hamilton.Jun.ʳ Fleet Street Oct.ʳ 1. 1781.

LORD ORFORD AND HIS MISTRESS, 'PATTY' TURK

Dr Norford[7] had differed with Dr Willis, the latter as well as Mr Edgar[8] of Swaffham having thought that too much calomel[9] had been given his Lordship, which had reduced him very much.

The reason that is given for removing him from Brandon,[10] where he might have had a small private house, was that upon his first apprehensions of a relapse he desired he might not be put into a *shut up house,* and therefore they conceived this step would have increased his disorder and that upon his recovery he would find such a variety of amusements at Houghton. I must add that last Sunday, when I first saw Dr Willis at Houghton, he told me that he was clear Lord Orford's disorder was not insanity, but only a delirium arising from a fever occasioned by his grief on the loss of Mrs Turk[11] and that when the fever abated the delirium would also.

Richard Hunter, *George III and the Mad-Business,* 1969, pp. 269–76; John Brooke, *King George III,* New York, 1972, pp. 331–6). A copy of Lord Townshend's letter to HW was sent by Townshend to Dr Willis (Toynbee *Supp.* ii. 247–8 n. 2). It is possible that Dr Willis sent one of his sons, who were associated with him in his medical practice: Dr John Willis (1751–1835) and Dr Robert Darling Willis (1760–1821).

7. William Norford (ca 1721–93), surgeon at Halesworth and Bury St Edmunds (*Bury St Edmunds, St James Parish Registers, Burials 1562–1800* [Suffolk Green Books No. xvii], Bury St Edmunds, 1916, p. 335; *European Magazine,* 1793, xxiii. 320; Toynbee *Supp.* iii. 304). He apparently resisted moving Lord Orford from Brandon to Houghton during his fever; see *post* 18 Dec. 1791.

8. Not identified. Swaffham, Norfolk, is 15 miles SE of King's Lynn and has a seat named Swaffham Manor. Lord Orford had founded the Swaffham Coursing Society in 1776 (Thomas Goodlake, *The Courser's Manual or Stud-Book,* Liverpool, 1828, pp. xiv, xxix).

9. The use of 'purges' in treating any illness was not unusual. HW says that 'a mad-keeper had been sent for privately to an apothecary in St Albans Street' (OSSORY iii. 130); it is not clear which doctor ordered the first treatment of Lord Orford.

10. Lord Orford had apparently become

ill at the vicarage house of Eriswell, between Brandon and Newmarket, which he had leased from Thomas Ball, rector of Eriswell (R. W. Ketton-Cremer, *A Norfolk Gallery,* 1948, p. 178; MANN viii. 293 n. 6). Dr Burney, the music historian, had visited Lord Orford 'at Eriswell, his favourite villa' about three weeks earlier, and 'found his Lordship's head as clear, his heart as kind, and his converse as pleasing, as at any period of their early intercourse' (Mme d'Arblay, *Memoirs of Doctor Burney,* 1832, iii. 148).

11. Martha ('Patty') Turk (ca 1737–91), Lord Orford's mistress, who had died on 13 Nov. at Eriswell, 'most sincerely lamented by all who were acquainted with her excellencies; the poor in particular were much indebted to her benevolence' (*Norfolk Chronicle* 19 Nov. 1791; *Norwich Mercury* 19 Nov. 1791). Dr Burney attributed Orford's relapse to a fall from his horse and to the sudden death of Mrs Turk, 'to whom . . . he was more attached than ever, from her faithful and affectionate attendance upon him during the long season of his insanity; though, at this time, she was become a fat and rather coarse old woman' (D'Arblay, op. cit. iii. 149). In a codicil (dated 4 Dec. 1776) to his will, Lord Orford bequeathed £5,000 to Mrs Turk, 'my dearest friend and companion through life,' and also 'my furniture and effects of every kind at my houses at Eriswell and High Beach.'

The doctor's only apprehension was that it might turn out a putrid one, but I had the pleasure to hear yesterday that this was no longer apprehended, and that our friend was much better. It was not judged proper that anyone should see our friend; any attention that I can show him or you, Sir, on this occasion, I shall rejoice in, and if upon his amendment he can come to Rainham, Lady Townshend[12] as well as myself would endeavour to make it as agreeable to him as possible. Doctor Willis continues some time longer and Mr Gardiner[13] attends his Lordship, who is a very worthy and attached friend.

> With perfect regard,
> Your obedient humble servant,
>
> TOWNSHEND

12. See *ante* 24 Aug. 1773, n. 9.

13. Richard Gardiner (b. 1762), eldest son of Lord Orford's friend Richard Gardiner (1723–81); army officer (*ante* ca 12 March 1762, n. 12; Toynbee *Supp.* ii. 247 n. 2). On 20 July 1778 he 'received an ensigncy in the West Norfolk regiment, commanded by the Right Honourable the Earl of Orford, then lying on the coast of Suffolk. . . . In 1779, this young gentleman was promoted to the rank of lieutenant in the said corps, then in a *camp volant* at Aldborough in Suffolk. . . . In 1780, he was again encamped on Tenpenny Common, near St Osyth in Essex, and from thence was appointed by his Majesty an ensign in the 6th Regiment of Foot, cantoned at Lewis in Sussex, and in the December following promoted to a lieutenancy in a royal independent company, for which he raised 30 men at Norwich. November 17, 1781, he received a commission, as captain of a company in the 102d Regiment of Foot, then going to the East-Indies: to this rapid promotion (being little more than nineteen years old) he fortunately succeeded by the assistance of a noble friend [Lord Orford], whose munificence and benevolent disposition, on all occasions, is equalled only by his extensive charity, learning, judgment, and taste, for every polite and liberal art' (*Memoirs of the Life and Writings of R-ch-d G-rd-n-r, Esq. alias Dick Merry-fellow*, 1782, pp. 74, 183–4). See *Army Lists*, 1780, 'List of the Officers . . . of Militia, p. 46 (Lt, Norfolk militia); 1781, p. 76, (Ensign 6th Foot); 1782–4, p. 179, (Capt. 102d Foot); 1785, p. 140, (Capt. 102d Foot); 1786–93, (Capt. 25th Foot); 1794–7 (listed on half-pay, under disbanded Independent Companies).

To Lord Townshend, Friday 2 December 1791

Printed from a photostat of the MS in the Osborn Collection, Yale University Library, kindly furnished by the late James M. Osborn. First printed, Toynbee *Supp.* ii. 245–7. In 1918 the MS was in the possession of Sir George Faudel-Phillips, 1st Bt, of Balls Park, Herts; not further traced until sold by Winifred A. Myers (Autographs) Ltd to Mr Osborn in the spring of 1966.

Endorsed by Townshend: From Mr Walpole December 2d 1791.

Berkeley Square, Dec. 2d 1791.

My Lord,

I ACKNOWLEDGE with all due sensibility the great honour your Lordship has done me by condescending to relieve my anxiety and grief about Lord Orford;[1] and as I well know the sincerity and value of your Lordship's friendship for him, a word of comfort and assurance from your Lordship bears double weight—but alas! my Lord, since your letter, written while your Lordship was with Dr Ash[2] at Houghton and in a moment a little more favourable, I have seen the doctor himself, and he has been far from raising my spirits or giving me much hope. Should the blow come, it will be a heavy one indeed, for added to the insolent and injurious treatment I have received, and which I do resent as I ought, I shall have the grievous mortification of thinking that the life of my poor nephew has been thrown away, and that had he been under my care as he was twice before,[3] his valuable life might have been preserved. Neither time was there any such management as of late—there were no contests, no disorders, no impertinence of apothecaries; all went quietly; and as Lord Orford was conducted without a moment's danger to his person, and without being hurried abruptly from place to place, I will presume to appeal to your Lordship's candour and just partiality to Lord Orford, and ask whether your Lordship ever heard from my nephew or from anyone about him at either of the times, whether I treated him unkindly? I will go much farther, my Lord; I will defy any man, who has interested himself to be my enemy without having given any cause to be so, to produce an instance in which either time Lord Orford was treated unkindly by me. On the contrary it was well

1. See previous letter.
2. See ibid. n. 5.

3. In 1773 and 1777 (Mann vii. 460–1 and nn. 4, 5; vii. 540; viii. 293–4, 372; Family 117–20).

known that I told the physicians[4] both times that I would set an example of how gently persons in my Lord's unhappy situation might be treated. I went farther, as your Lordship knows; I firmly resisted both Dr Battie[5] and Sir Rich. Jebbe,[6] who insisted on secluding Mrs Turk;[7] I said, I understood she was his only comfort, and she should not be taken from him. She remained with him incessantly both times, and my Lord certainly was not the worse.

I will be silent on infinitely more that I have to say, and I beg your Lordship's pardon heartily for troubling you with complaints; but since they have reached your Lordship's ears, I am incapable of concealing or softening them. I do assert that both Lord Orford and myself have been treated in a manner unparalleled—and it is sufficient to alarm any family if such proceedings are to be tolerated![8]— but that will be a future inquiry—I have submitted, because *I* would not presume to act without authority from law.

May I beg leave, my Lord, after repeating my most grateful thanks for your Lordship's goodness, to offer my most humble respects to Lady Townshend? What a happy hour would it be, my Lord, if I could hear that my poor nephew was under her Ladyship's roof and protection.

---

4. The physicians who attended Lord Orford during his first illness were Dr Robert Glynn, Dr Russell Plumptre, Sir Richard Jebb, and Dr William Battie (MANN vii. 461 n. 9); those who attended him during his second illness were William Bewley, an assistant of Dr John Monro, Dr John Beevor, and Sir Richard Jebb (FAMILY 118 n. 3, 119, 120 n. 1, 121–2; MANN vii. 540; OSSORY i. 350).

5. William Battie (1703–76), M.D., 1737; F.R.C.P., 1738. He had attended Lord Orford in 1773 (HW to Lady Ossory 30 Dec. 1773, ibid. i. 175 and n. 2; to Sir Edward Walpole 25 April 1777, FAMILY 123–4).

6. Sir Richard Jebb (1729–87), cr. (1778) Bt. He had attended Lord Orford in 1773 and 1777 (OSSORY i. 175 and n. 3; FAMILY 122–3; MANN viii. 294). After Lord Orford's first recovery HW commented: 'Dr Jebbe is, I think, rather less sanguine than Battie; but being less a mad doctor, seemed unwilling to take much decision upon him' (HW to Mann 30 Dec. 1773, MANN vii. 540).

7. See previous letter, n. 11. The *World* 13 Dec. 1791 reported (after Lord Orford's death): 'The sensibility which occasioned the death of this nobleman does honour to his memory. The attentions of Mrs Turk had, at one period of his life, called him back to reason. Never had he forgotten this circumstance. On her death [13 Nov.], he relapsed into phrenzy, from which medical aid for a time relieved him; but the wound he had sustained at his heart, was not to be so cured. He lingered for a time on a bed of sorrow more than sickness—which at length proved too powerful for his constitution.'

8. See *post* 18 Dec. and 29 Dec. 1791.

I have the honour to be with the greatest respect,

> My Lord
>> Your Lordship's most obliged and
>>> most obedient humble servant

>>>> HORACE WALPOLE

Marquis of Townshend.

To UNKNOWN, after 5 December 1791

Printed for the first time from a copy of the MS pasted in a copy of HW's *Works*, 1798, vol. I, in the Old Library of Jesus College, Cambridge, kindly supplied by Dr F. Brittain through the good offices of the late A. N. L. Munby. The history of the MS is not known.

Dated after 5 Dec. 1791, when HW succeeded his nephew as 4th Earl of Orford.

LORD ORFORD is very sorry he cannot possibly oblige the gentlemen[1] who desire to see Strawberry Hill now. It is never shown to anybody but from the first of May to the first of October, nor is in order to be shown: much furniture, pictures etc. being taken down, and locked up in different rooms.[2]

---

1. Not identified.
2. HW's Rules for visiting SH stated that 'The House will never be shown . . . at all but from the first of May to the first of October' (Hazen, *SH Bibl.* [226]). HW wrote James Bindley *ante* 7 Sept. 1781: 'This month is the time when I take down the small pictures and curiosities, and pack them up against damp weather' for the winter.

To ?CARLOS CONY,[1] Tuesday 6 December 1791

Printed from a photostat of the MS kindly supplied by its owner, Mrs P. A. Tritton, Parham Park, Pulborough, Sussex. First printed, Toynbee *Supp.* ii. 54. A facsimile of the MS appeared in *Horace Walpole: A Descriptive Catalogue of the Artistic and Literary Illustrations Collected by Herbert H. Raphael . . . for the Extension of the Original Edition of Walpole's Letters into Eighteen Folio Volumes*, Bristol, 1909, facing p. iv. The MS is untraced until sold Sotheby's 13 May 1905 (property of Sir Henry Bunbury), lot 823, to Francis Harvey; *penes* Sir Herbert H. Raphael, Bt (d. 1924) by 1909; for the later history of the MS see *ante* 30 June 1782.

Carlos Cony is the most likely recipient of this letter (see n. 1 below).

Endorsed, apparently by Cony: The answer to my letter by express by Herbert[2] on the 5th.

Berkeley Square, Dec. 6, 1791.

Sir,

AFTER the misfortune that has happened,[3] and when I had been flattered with hopes of Lord Orford's amendment, you will not wonder that I am not able to write many words in answer to the honour of your letter.[4] I think myself much obliged to you, Sir, for

1. Carlos Cony (fl. 1774–91), son of Edward Cony, high sheriff of Norfolk, 1734; Lord Orford's steward and solicitor in Norfolk. He was the most likely person to inform HW of Orford's death and the plans for the opening of the will (MANN ix. 131; FAMILY 118 n. 4; OSSORY i. 133 n. 18; *Miscellanea genealogica et heraldica*, 1877, new ser. ii. 545; Hamon Le Strange, *Norfolk Official Lists*, Norwich, 1890, p. 24). The endorsement on the letter has been compared with Cony's signed note (dated 4 Feb. 1779) in a 'Bill of Costs' submitted to Lord Orford, now in the Norfolk Record Office; it appears to be in Cony's hand (Norfolk Record Office, Bradfer-Lawrence Collection, B-L VIb, vi). Cony was in charge of distributing the mourning rings after Lord Orford's death (Robert Mackreth to Anthony Hamond 27 March 1792, MS in the possession of Capt. Anthony Hamond). According to Toynbee *Supp.* ii. 248n, there are among

the Townshend papers letters written by Cony to Lord Townshend, Orford's doctors, and other friends, concerning Orford's last illness.

2. Thomas Herbert, Lord Orford's servant, to whom he bequeathed £300 for faithful service. Herbert had witnessed two codicils to Orford's will on 13 Nov. 1791.

3. Lord Orford died on 5 Dec. 1791. The *Norfolk Chronicle* 10 Dec. reported: 'On Monday last an express arrived at the house of R. Kerrison, Esq. in this city [Norwich], with the melancholy tidings of the death of George, Earl of Orford, who expired the same morning about four o'clock of a putrid fever at Houghton Hall, in his 62d year.' The same report appeared in the *Norwich Mercury* 10 Dec. 1791.

4. Missing; it was an express written 5 Dec. and delivered by Thomas Herbert (see headnote).

the marks of respect you mean to pay to Lord Orford's memory,[5] which I certainly applaud.

Mr Walpole[6] my cousin will set out directly to Houghton to be present with you, Sir, and any gentlemen of the neighbourhood that you wish should, or that will please to be present at the opening of his Lordship's will[7]—you will excuse, I flatter myself, my not detaining your servant[8] longer than to assure you that I am with great respect

Sir

Your obedient servant

The Uncle of the late Earl of Orford[9]

5. For an account of the funeral 20 Dec. at Houghton, attended by 'many of the principal characters in this county and city' and by 'a multitude of spectators,' see *post* 29 Dec. 1791, n. 11. 'John Dashwood, Esq. who, at the particular request of the present Earl, regulated the ceremonies of the funeral, justly merited the thanks of his Lordship's friends, not only from the unremitted attendance shown to his Lordship during his illness, but likewise from the manner in which he has discharged this mournful testimony of respect' (*Norwich Mercury* 24 Dec. 1791; *Norfolk Chronicle* 24 Dec. 1791).

6. Hon. Horatio Walpole (1752–1822), styled Bn Walpole 1806–9; 2d E. of Orford, n.c., 1809; M.P. HW called him 'my namesake, cousin and nephew' (MANN ix. 418 and 131–2). Dr Toynbee (*Supp.* ii. 54 n. 3) identified 'Mr Walpole' as prob-ably the Hon. Thomas Walpole (1727–1803), HW's cousin, but he was living in France (see FAMILY 248, 275). According to the newspapers, the 'chief mourners [at the funeral] were the Marquis Townshend and the Hon. Horatio Walpole' (*Norwich Mercury* 24 Dec.; *Norwich Chronicle* 24 Dec.).

7. See *post* 29 Dec. 1791.

8. Thomas Herbert (n. 2 above).

9. HW also used this signature in his letters to Thomas Coutts *post* 7 Dec. 1791 and to the Duke of Bedford *post* 8 Dec. 1791. HW wrote Sir John Fenn 13 Dec.: 'I wish to pay all regard to my late nephew's memory, and therefore do not care to assume his title till he is buried, but where I am forced to give legal orders' (CHATTERTON 248). But HW's letter to Anne Clement 10 Dec. 1791 was signed 'Orford' (FAMILY 279).

To Thomas Coutts,[1] Wednesday 7 December 1791

Printed from the MS now wsl. First printed, Toynbee *Supp.* iii. 73. The MS was in the possession of Francis Edwards, the London bookseller, in 1925; offered by Edwards, Cat. Nos 1 (n. s., 1929), lot 400, and 4 (n. s., 1929), lot 315; sold by them to wsl, Sept. 1932.

Address: To Thomas Coutts Esq.

Berkeley Square, Dec. 7, 1791.

THE uncle of the late Lord Orford[2] is extremely sensible of the kindness of Mr Coutts, in the letter[3] he has been so obliging as to write to him, and is very grateful for the friendship he shows and expresses so tenderly for his late nephew,[4] and which must justly impress the uncle with great esteem for Mr Coutts, though he has not the satisfaction of his acquaintance; yet he should be glad to cultivate it,[5] if great age and infirmities had not for some years confined Mr Walpole to a small circle, and did not forbid his forming any views beyond the moments he can actually call his own—while they last, he shall not forget the gratitude he owes Mr Coutts.

To the Duke of Bedford,[1] Thursday 8 December 1791

Printed from Toynbee xv. 91–2, where the letter was first printed. The MS was in the possession of the Duke of Bedford in 1905; Mrs M. P. G. Draper, of the Bedford Estates Office in London, informs us that the MS has not been located among the Bedford family papers in London or at Woburn Abbey.

Berkeley Square, Dec. 8, 1791.

I AM most sensible, my Lord Duke, of the great honour your Grace has done me in condescending to be content with my account of the portraits at Woburn Abbey,[2] though so inadequate to what I wished to make it, more worthy of your acceptance.

1. (1735–1822), founder (with his brother James Coutts) of Coutts & Co., bankers in the Strand; Lord Orford's banker. A codicil (dated 13 Nov. 1791) to Orford's will mentions 'all my money in the hands of Mr Coutts, banker in the Strand, amounting to upwards of £5,000' (Lord Orford's will; see also MANN ix. 355 n. 7).
2. HW used this signature in his letters to ?Carlos Cony *ante* 6 Dec. 1791 and to the Duke of Bedford *post* 8 Dec. 1791.

3. Missing.
4. George, 3d E. of Orford, who died 5 Dec. (*ante* 6 Dec. 1791, n. 3).
5. HW's 'Book of Visitors' records the visit of 'Coutts and family' to SH on 7 July 1793 (BERRY ii. 243).

1. Francis Russell (1765–1802), 5th D. of Bedford, 1771.
2. *Notes to the Portraits at Woburn Abbey*, written by HW in Sept. 1791 at

The picture of the Countess of Devonshire[3] is an additional favour, for which I feel, my Lord, the most pleasing gratitude. Were I not obliged to confine myself by a recent misfortune in my family,[4] it would be my first inclination as well as duty to wait on your Grace with my humble thanks. All I can yet do is to entreat your Grace not to think of troubling yourself to add a visit to the honour with which you have already overpaid me by your letter,[5] too flattering not to increase the great respect already felt for your Grace by,

My Lord,
>   Your Grace's most humble and
>   most gratefully obedient servant,

THE UNCLE OF THE LATE EARL OF ORFORD[6]

Lady Ossory's request. A MS copy by Thomas Kirgate was sent by her to the Duke of Bedford; HW wrote Lady Ossory 23 Nov.: 'The Duke of Bedford is too gracious, Madam, in being pleased to say he is content with my meagre account of his pictures' (Ossory iii. 125–6, 130; see ante 25 May 1773, n. 9). Another fair copy of the MS in Kirgate's hand, with the heading 'Notes to the List of Portraits at Woburn Abbey, the seat of his Grace the Duke of Bedford, in Bedfordshire; by Horace Earl of Orford,' was apparently made after 5 Dec. 1791, when HW succeeded as 4th Earl; it is now at Woburn Abbey (Ossory iii. 126 n. 9; Hazen, Bibl. of HW 87). The Notes to the Portraits at Woburn Abbey was privately printed in 1800, presumably from Kirgate's earlier copy, since after the heading on p. 3 appears 'By H. W. 1791' and on p. 16 'Finished Sept. 29, 1791.'

3. See HW to Thomas Pennant ante 15 Oct. 1781, n. 12. The portrait is by

Theodore Russell (HW's Notes, No. 40, pp. 8–9; George Scharf, A Descriptive and Historical Catalogue of the Collection of Pictures at Woburn Abbey, 1877, pp. 97–8). Through Lady Ossory, HW had asked to borrow this portrait so that it could be engraved for Daniel Lysons's The Environs of London, 1792–6; the engraving by Nicolas Schencker, after the copy drawing by Silvester Harding, appears in the Environs i. facing p. 432. See Ossory iii. 131 and n. 13.

4. Lord Orford's death on 5 Dec. (ante 6 Dec. 1791, n. 3).

5. Missing. In his letter to Lady Ossory 23 Nov. 1791, HW wrote that his Notes on the pictures 'do not deserve the honour of a visit from his Grace' (Ossory iii. 130). Earlier in the year, HW had evaded the suggestion of such a visit (ibid. iii. 111–12).

6. HW used this signature in his letters to ?Carlos Cony ante 6 Dec. 1791 and to Thomas Coutts ante 7 Dec. 1791.

To Lady Bristol,[1] Sunday 18 December 1791

Printed for the first time from a photostat of the MS in the Hervey Collection, Bury St Edmunds and West Suffolk Record Office, Bury St Edmunds, Suffolk, kindly furnished by Mr Patrick F. Doran. The MS descended in the Hervey family, Marquesses of Bristol, at Ickworth, Suffolk, until it was deposited, with other family papers, in the Bury St Edmunds and West Suffolk Record Office by the 4th Marquess of Bristol.

Berkeley Square, Dec. 18, 1791.

I AM not only extremely honoured, Madam, but delighted by the receipt of the letter[2] with which your Ladyship has been pleased to favour me. Nothing could be more flattering to Dr Norford[3] and me than a confirmation of his excellent character and abilities by the testimony of so very respectable authority as your Ladyship's, whose virtues give you the truest dignity, and being so universally known and allowed, are sufficient to quash the falsehoods[4] invented against Dr Norford, partly I believe from malice to me, of whom they pretend to think him an agent, though utterly unknown to me even by sight to this hour, and also by name till the 14th of last month;[5] and partly, because the skill, duty, and indefatigable attention and tenderness of the Doctor to my unhappy nephew made him resist the wicked, dangerous, and unprecedented as well as unauthorized violence of carrying poor Lord Orford against his will to Houghton[6] in

1. Elizabeth Davers (ca 1732–1800), m. (1752) Hon. Frederick Augustus Hervey, 4th E. of Bristol, 1779. HW wrote Mann 9 May 1779 that he was 'not at all acquainted with' Lady Bristol (MANN viii. 475); but in June 1794 she came to visit SH ('Book of Visitors,' BERRY ii. 246).
2. Missing.
3. See ante 30 Nov. 1791, n. 7.
4. Apparently spread by Lord Orford's servants on the basis of disagreement among the doctors attending Orford before his death. Lord Townshend wrote HW ante 30 Nov. 1791: 'it was clear to me that Dr Norford had differed with Dr Willis, the latter as well as Mr Edgar of Swaffham having thought that too much calomel had been given his Lordship, which had reduced him very much.'
5. When Lord Orford became ill at

Brandon, Suffolk, HW was not informed of his disorder until Lord Cadogan sent word; it was possibly Lord Cadogan who mentioned Dr Norford as one of the attending doctors. HW immediately sent Dr Thomas Monro to inquire into Lord Orford's condition; Dr Monro returned to London on Friday, 18 Nov. (OSSORY iii. 129–30).
6. Lord Orford was moved from Brandon to Houghton allegedly because 'upon his first apprehensions of a relapse he desired he might not be put into a *shut up house*' (ante 30 Nov. 1791). But Dr Willis's opinion was that 'Lord Orford's disorder was not insanity, but only a delirium arising from a fever occasioned by his grief on the loss of Mrs Turk,' who died on Sunday, 13 Nov. (ibid.). See also *post* 3 April 1792.

a putrid fever, and which, if not the original cause of his death, was, to say nothing harder, an impediment to his recovery. Your Ladyship's great justice and love of truth have called on you to defend Dr Norford; and as my own innocence was so strangely implicated in his,[7] I hope your Ladyship will not think me too presumptuous in offering you my most humble and grateful thanks for your good offices, as part of the benefit redounds to me.

My broken and weak state of health,[8] the mass of business fallen on me, and the lawyers whom I have had with me this whole morning, have left me but few moments to save the post, or say more, than that I preferred being too brief to losing the first minute of acknowledging the honour of your Ladyship's letter, which has made me, if possible, still more than I have long been, with the greatest respect, Madam

Your Ladyship's most obedient, humble,
and now most grateful and devoted servant

ORFORD

To LORD TOWNSHEND, Thursday 29 December 1791

Printed for the first time from the MS now WSL, who acquired it from Maggs in Aug. 1946; its earlier history is not known.

Endorsed by Townshend: From Lord Orford December the 29th 1791.

Berkeley Square, Dec. 29, 1791.

My Lord,

I THINK myself much honoured by receiving any commands from your Lordship,[1] and do assure you it is not from the least unwillingness that I do not obey them the moment I receive them as readily as I hope I have always paid respect and attention to your Lordship. I only beg your Lordship to allow me a little time before I take anything upon me. The loss of my nephew[2] has been a heavy blow to me: It found me in a bad state of health, which has been increased

---

7. HW was apparently accused of sending Dr Norford as his agent. In his letter to Lord Townshend *ante* 2 Dec. 1791, HW offers a justification of his own conduct in the care of his nephew.

8. See HW to Mary Berry 13 Dec. 1791, BERRY i. 377.

---

1. Townshend's letter to HW is missing.
2. On 5 Dec. (*ante* 6 Dec. 1791, n. 3).

by the grief of being prevented from trying to save him by the un-
warrantable violence of hurrying him to Houghton,[3] and by the load
of business and perplexity that has fallen on me. As Lord Orford had
always the look of health and strength, and as I am so old and
broken, nothing was more unforeseen by me than his rapid death,
and consequently since I last had the care of him,[4] I was totally ignorant of the state of his affairs; and though I had had no reason to
entertain a favourable opinion of some persons[5] too much in his
confidence, I could not conceive that he had been plundered to the
degree that I now suspect he has been.

In this situation, my Lord, I neither know what I have or am likely
to have;[6] and therefore have determined not to take any step till the
three very respectable gentlemen,[7] too respectable to be joined with
Macreth,[8] who are executors, have performed their office and made

3. See *ante* 30 Nov. and 18 Dec. 1791.

4. In 1777, during his second attack of insanity. See HW to Sir Edward Walpole 21–5 April 1777 (FAMILY 117–25) and to Mann 28 April 1777 (MANN viii. 292–6).

5. Presumably Carlos Cony, Lord Orford's steward and lawyer in Norfolk (*ante* 6 Dec. 1791, n. 1); William Moone, also a steward (*ante* 3 Dec. 1777, n. 6); William Withers, described in a 'Case' concerning a codicil of Lord Orford's will (MS now WSL) as a carpenter who managed Orford's woods and plantations, and took charge of his cellars; also kept his cash books from 1774 to 1780 (OSSORY i. 141 and n. 11); Charles Lucas, Orford's lawyer in London (*ante* 1 Feb. 1774, n. 1, and *ante* 3 Dec. 1777; MANN ix. 123, 131, 143); and Robert Mackreth (n. 8 below), whom Orford had brought into Parliament supposedly in return for money borrowed from him (MANN viii. 53 and n. 18).

6. HW wrote Jane Clement 10 Dec. 1791: 'I knew not a tittle of the contents of his will till yesterday noon, and now very confusedly. He has given me the whole Norfolk estate, but with great encumbrances on it' (FAMILY 278). Orford's will was summarized in the *Norwich Mercury* 17 Dec., the *Norfolk Chronicle* 17 Dec., and GM 1791, lxi pt ii. 1164–5. See also CHATTERTON 313 n. 3.

7. There were four executors besides Mackreth (appointed in a codicil, dated 4 Dec. 1776, to Lord Orford's will), but one had died: Sir Henry Peyton (1736–89), of Doddington, Cambs, and Narborough, Norfolk; cr. (1776) Bt; sheriff of Norfolk, 1778; M.P. Brigg Price Fountaine (d. 1825), of Narford Hall, Norfolk; sheriff of Norfolk, 1775 (COLE i. 171 n. 29; Burke, *Landed Gentry*, 1925, p. 674). Edmund Rolfe, Jr (1738–1817), of Heacham, Norfolk; sheriff of Norfolk, 1769 (Venn, *Alumni Cantab.*; Hamon Le Strange, *Norfolk Official Lists*, Norwich, 1890, p. 25). Anthony Hamond, of Westacre and Swaffham, Norfolk; sheriff of Norfolk, 1792 (Burke, *Landed Gentry*, 1965, i. 360; Venn, *Alumni Cantab.*; *Eton Coll. Reg.*; Le Strange, op. cit. 26).

8. Robert Mackreth (*ante* 3 June 1779, n. 8). At his death, Orford owed Mackreth £6000; Mackreth wrote Edmund Rolfe 28 March 1797: 'I . . . lent our revered friend the Earl of Orford in the lifetime of his mother £6000—the interest of which sum was not to be paid till her Ladyship's death, but his Lordship was to give me a bond for interest (£300) every year to bear an interest at 5 per cent' (Hamond MS, quoted in Namier and Brooke iii. 89; Namier concludes that 'at the market-price of seats Mackreth should have paid Orford about double that sum for his four elections 1774–90').

their report; and therefore till the late Lord's will has been performed with regard to the Houghton estate,[9] I do not know what
part of it will remain for me, nor what assets there will be to pay off
or lessen the load of debt:[10] nor what retrenchments I may be obliged
to make, should I live to come into possession.

My suspense, I hope, will be no inconvenience to your Lordship,
to whom I am doubly bound by your condescension in honouring
my nephew's funeral,[11] for which I beg your Lordship to receive the
humble and grateful thanks of

My Lord
Your Lordship's most obliged and
most obedient humble servant

ORFORD

Marquis of Townshend.

9. Lord Orford made two wills, the first dated 25 Nov. 1752 (P.C.C. 166 Fountain) and the second dated 31 March 1756; a codicil dated 4 Dec. 1776 refers to the will of 1752 but does not mention that of 1756. The will of 1752, with five codicils, was probated in London on 7 March 1792 by Robert Mackreth, on 24 June 1792 by Brigg Price Fountaine and Anthony Hamond, and on 11 February 1793 by Edmund Rolfe (Lord Orford's will; FAMILY 296 n. 1; DALRYMPLE 323–4). The provisions of the 1752 will were that the Houghton estate should descend first to Sir Edward Walpole, second to HW, third to the Cholmondeleys, and fourth to the Walpoles of Wolterton. The Devonshire and Cornwall estates and the barony of Clinton, which Lord Orford had inherited in 1781 from his mother, passed to a collateral branch of the Rolle family, that is, to Robert George William Trefusis (1764–97), Lord Clinton (GEC; MANN ix. 148 and n. 5).

10. 'He has given me the whole Norfolk estate, heavily charged I believe, but that is indifferent. . . . he has restored me to my birthright, and I shall call myself obliged to him, and be grateful to his memory' (HW to Lady Ossory 10 Dec. 1791, OSSORY iii. 134). A list among the Hamond MSS states that the mortgage

debts amounted to nearly £87,000 (see Namier and Brooke iii. 89, 90 n. 6). The correspondence of Anthony Hamond with the other executors (now in the possession of Capt. Anthony Hamond) reveals the difficulties of settling the debts and legacies and paying off some of the mortgages (see OSSORY iii. 136 n. 2, 145 and n. 14). Robert Blake, HW's lawyer, wrote Anthony Hamond 8 Nov. 1792: 'We were wrong in our idea that as there is likely to be a residue after payment of debts etc. no one is interested in the disposition of that residue but the present Lord Orford for the fact is that all the mortgages made by the late Earl are specially debts of his, and the residue must go to pay off some of the mortgages, so that is of importance to the person next in remainder after the present Earl that the mortgages should be diminished as much as possible' (Hamond MS). When HW made his will on 15 May 1793, the two mortgages then outstanding totalled £17,500 (OSSORY iii. 134 n. 3).

11. 'On Tuesday last [20 Dec.] the stately edifice of Houghton received the numerous friends that assembled to pay the last melancholy tribute of regard and respect to the late Earl of Orford, whose remains (after having lain in state) were conveyed to the family vault in Houghton

From Richard Gough, ca 1792

Printed from Nichols, *Literary Anecdotes* vi. 292, where the letter was first printed. The history and whereabouts of the MS are not known.

Dated after 5 Dec. 1791, when HW became 4th Earl of Orford; placed by Nichols between letters of 15 March and 14 Nov. 1792. Sinclair's *Statistical Account of Scotland,* mentioned by Gough, appeared as follows: vol. I in 1791, vols II and III in 1792, vols IV–VIII in 1793, vols IX–XII in 1794, vols XIII–XV in 1795, vols XVI–XVII in 1796, vols XVIII–XXI in 1797–99.

ALLOW me, my Lord, to add one other painter to your list:—De Wit,[1] who was brought from Holland by Patrick Earl of Kinghorn,[2] about the end of the last century, to paint the ceilings of several rooms, with that of the chapel and the altar-piece at Glammis

church, in a hearse and six, attended by above 200 gentlemen who had enjoyed the honour of his Lordship's acquaintance. . . . The chief mourners were the Marquis Townshend and the Hon. Horatio Walpole in a mourning-coach and six. The executors, Edmund Rolfe, Brigg Fountaine, Anthony Hamond and Robert Mackreth, Esqrs. were in another coach and six. . . . The utmost decorum was observed by a multitude of spectators, who testified their deep affliction for the loss of their noble patron and benefactor, whose extensive beneficence and liberality were among his distinguished characteristics' (*Norwich Mercury* 24 Dec. 1791; see also *Norfolk Chronicle* 24 Dec.). HW's friend Sir John Fenn, who was then High Sheriff of Norfolk, had apparently invited HW to come; see HW to Fenn 13 Dec. 1791, CHATTERTON 248.

1. Jacob de Wet (or de Wit) (1640–97), Dutch painter, who came to Edinburgh in 1674 with Jan van Santvoort, Dutch carver, to work on the decoration of Holyroodhouse at the request of James II

when Duke of York (Thieme and Becker xxxv. 458–9, xxix. 454). This work was finished in 1686, and Lord Strathmore, by a contract dated 18 Jan. 1688, engaged De Wet to paint ceilings and many wall panels at Glamis Castle (the contract and an account of payments due, with Strathmore's notations, are in *The Book of Record, a Diary Written by Patrick First Earl of Strathmore and Other Documents Relating to Glamis Castle 1684–1689,* ed. A. H. Millar, Edinburgh, 1890, pp. 104–9; see also pp. xli–xliv, 175). De Wet's paintings in Holyroodhouse are described in Sir Herbert Maxwell, *Official Guide: The Palace of Holyroodhouse Abbey and Environs,* Edinburgh, 1936, pp. 10–15, 34–5, 148. HW did not include De Wet in *Anecdotes of Painting.*

2. Patrick Lyon (1643–95), styled Lord Glamis until 1647; Earl of Kinghorne, Lord Lyon and Glamis, 1648, and by a new charter, 1672; Earl of Strathmore and Kinghorne, by letters patent, 1677 (GEC, *sub* Strathmore and Kinghorne; *Scots Peerage* viii. 299; Millar, op. cit. xi–xxx).

Castle,[3] as I learn from Capt. Grose's[4] description of that castle in his *Antiquities of Scotland*.[5]—I think I have met with this artist in some other part of Scotland, in the *Statistical Account*[6] now publishing by Sir John Sinclair.[7]

3. Glamis Castle, Angus, about 17 miles north of Dundee, is described in the *Book of Record* (Millar, op. cit. xxii–xxv). De Wet painted fifteen large panels in the ceiling of the chapel, as well as sixteen panels on the walls, a door-piece and altar-piece, all reproduced from engravings in a Bible still preserved at Glamis Castle. He also painted the ceiling of the dining room, an oval in the chief bed-chamber, many chimney-pieces, door-pieces, and family portraits. A considerable amount of De Wet's work still remains in the castle; see ibid. xliii–xliv, 92, 104–9.

4. Francis Grose (?1731–91), antiquary and draughtsman; F.S.A., 1757; Richmond herald 1755–63; captain and adjutant in the Surrey militia, ca 1778 (GM 1791, lxi pt i. 492–4, 581; Nichols, *Lit. Anec.* iii. 656n–659n; COLE ii. 148 n. 2).

5. *The Antiquities of Scotland*, 2 vols, 1789–91. 'The hall [of Glamis Castle] is adorned with family pictures; and behind the hall is a handsome chapel. . . . On the altar is a good picture of the Last Supper, and on the ceiling an Ascension, done by one De Wit, a Dutchman, whom Earl Patrick, this Earl's grandfather, brought from Holland, and who painted the ceilings of most of the rooms' (1797 edn, ii. 87).

6. *The Statistical Account of Scotland*, 21 vols, Edinburgh, 1791–9; no mention of De Wet has been found, but Grose's *Antiquities of Scotland* mentions De Wet in describing Holyrood palace: 'The walls of this gallery are adorned with one hundred and twenty portraits of the kings of Scotland, nineteen of which are whole lengths; they were all painted by a Flemish painter, named De Wit, who was brought over for that purpose by King James VII when Duke of York' (1797 edn, i. 31–2).

7. Sir John Sinclair (1754–1835), cr. (1786) Bt; M.P.

To J. R. Dashwood,[1] Tuesday 3 January 1792

Printed from a photostat of the MS in the Hyde Collection, Somerville, New Jersey. First printed, Toynbee xv. 101. In 1905 the MS was in the collection of Robert Borthwick Adam (1863–1940), of Buffalo, N. Y., who had inherited the collection from Robert Borthwick Adam the elder (1833–1904); after the death of the younger Adam, the collection was temporarily deposited in the University of Rochester Library; acquired by Mr and Mrs Hyde in 1948.

Address: To J. R. Dashwood, Esq.

Berkeley Square, Jan. 3d 1792.

Dear Sir,

MR BLAKE[2] tells me you wish to shoot on my estates in Norfolk,[3] which I not only desire you will do, but should have consented to with pleasure yesterday,[4] if you had mentioned it.

I am with great respect and gratitude Sir

Your most obedient humble servant

ORFORD

1. Probably John Richard Dashwood, of Cockley Cley, Norfolk; sheriff of Norfolk, 1794 (Hamon Le Strange, *Norfolk Official Lists,* Norwich, 1890, p. 26). He was active in organizing a volunteer corps to supplement the army and the militia in defence of the east coast: 'On the 12th April, 1794, a county meeting was held at Norwich, J. R. Dashwood, Esq., High Sheriff, in the chair, at which, notwithstanding some opposition, an association for the defence of the county was formed, and subscriptions received to cover the necessary outlay' (R. H. Mason, *The History of Norfolk,* 1884, p. 458). Dashwood was a friend of Lord Orford's and took charge of the arrangements for his funeral (see *ante* 6 Dec. 1791, n. 5).

2. Robert Blake, who belonged to the legal firm of John Blake, John Norris, and Robert Blake in Essex Street, the Strand (*Universal British Directory,* 1791, i. 371, 385; BERRY ii. 180 n. 11),

represented HW in the settlement of Lord Orford's estate, and attended meetings of the executors at Houghton. HW writes on 13 Jan. that 'my agent has been a whole week' at Houghton (to Hon. Hugh Seymour-Conway 13 Jan. 1792, CONWAY iii. 489), and on 3 April that 'my agent goes to Houghton tomorrow' (*post* 3 April 1792 and n. 10). In the correspondence of Anthony Hamond with other executors of Orford's will, Robert Blake is called 'young Mr Blake' and 'Mr Blake Junr' (see Hamond MSS, *passim*); this correspondence, now in the possession of Capt. Anthony Hamond, contains many letters between Robert Blake and Anthony Hamond.

3. On the death of his nephew 5 Dec. 1791, HW became 4th E. of Orford and inherited the Walpole estates in Norfolk.

4. HW was at Berkeley Square at this time, but there is no record of this visit.

To Sir Isaac Heard,[1] Saturday 21 January 1792

Printed for the first time from the MS now wsl. The MS is untraced until sold Sotheby's 30 July 1920 (Printed Books, Autograph Letters, and Manuscripts Sale), lot 863, to Rivington; resold Sotheby's 19 May 1926 (property of Mrs M. A. Rivington, of St Leonard's-on-Sea, Sussex), lot 602 (with two letters from HW to Mrs Garrick), to B. F. Stevens & Brown, Ltd, London; acquired by wsl from Crompton T. Johnson, Farmington, Connecticut, in October 1932.

Berkeley Square, Jan. 21, 1792.

Sir,

I RECEIVED the favour of your letter,[2] and return the Pedigree[3] with a few additions; but you need not hurry yourself about a fair copy, for I am much indisposed,[4] and at present have no thoughts of taking my seat immediately;[5] but will let you know in time when I intend it. I am, Sir, with great regard

Your obedient humble servant

ORFORD

Sir Isaac Heard.

---

1. Sir Isaac Heard (1730–1822), Garter king-of-arms, 1 May 1784–1822; Kt, 2 June 1786 (Sir Anthony Wagner, *Heralds of England*, 1967, pp. 425–32; GM 1822, xcii pt i. 466–9; W. A. Shaw, *The Knights of England*, 1906, ii. 299; Mark Noble, *A History of the College of Arms*, 1805, pp. 418, 422, 439, 441, 448).

2. Missing.

3. On 11 May 1767 the House of Lords adopted Standing Orders requiring the registration, in the College of Arms, of a pedigree certifying the descent of a peer as a preliminary to a peer's taking his seat on succession (*Journals of the House of Lords* xxxi. 583–4, 588, 594; Anthony R. Wagner, *The Records and Collections of the College of Arms*, 1952, p. 25). The second resolution stated, 'That Garter King at Arms do officially attend this House upon the day, and at the time, of the first admission of every peer, whether by creation or descent; and that he do then and there deliver in, at the table, a pedigree of the family of such peer, fairly described on vellum' (*Journals of the House of Lords* xxxi. 584).

4. HW had suffered gout and fatigue as a result of increased business and social commitments after he succeeded his nephew George as 4th E. of Orford on 5 Dec. 1791. As he wrote to Lady Ossory 26 Dec. 1791, 'the Lordship and its train of troubles have half killed me'; see OSSORY iii. 134–5, 136 and n. 2.

5. HW never took his seat in the House of Lords; see HW to Hannah More 1 Jan. 1792, MORE 363–4 and nn. 2, 3. He wrote to William Beloe 5 Aug. 1792, 'I have not set my foot in Norfolk since his death nor for many previous years, nor have taken my seat in the House of Lords since the unwelcome title came to me, nor intend it' (DALRYMPLE 216).

To ?Charles Lucas,[1] Monday 30 January 1792

Printed from Toynbee xv. 104–5, where it was first printed. In 1905 the MS was in the possession of Mrs Mary G. Fogg, of Boston, Mass.; not further traced.

Monday, January 30, 1792.

Dear Sir,

I HAVE received a very unpleasant letter[2] from Callington,[3] on which I wish to talk with you, and therefore I shall be glad if you can call on me for a quarter of an hour at any time most convenient to you tomorrow between ten and four.

Yours etc.

Orford

1. Charles Lucas, living in 1797, had been George, Lord Orford's lawyer 1781–91, and probably before that (Mann ix. 123; Ossory ii. 281 n. 2; *ante* 1 Feb. 1774, n. 1). Lucas had handled the boroughs of Callington and Ashburton for him; see *ante* 3 Dec. 1777 and Mann ix. 462. After Lord Orford's death Lucas was in charge of paying small debts, and investigating deeds for properties, for the executors. His correspondence with Anthony Hamond is preserved in the Hamond MSS, now in the possession of Capt. Anthony Hamond,

and many receipts for payment of debts are now wsl.

2. Missing.

3. In Cornwall; one of the boroughs controlled by Lady Orford until 1781, and then by George, 3d E. of Orford, until 1791 (Namier and Brooke i. 225–7; Sedgwick ii. 510; Mann viii. 46–7; Conway iii. 192). HW was M.P. for Callington 1741–54. In 1792 the members for Callington were John Call and Paul Orchard (Namier and Brooke ii. 176, iii. 231).

To Sylvester Douglas,[1] Wednesday 15 February 1792

Printed from a photostat of the MS in the possession (1936) of Mrs Scott-Murray (later Mrs Colin Davy), of Heckfield Place, Basingstoke, Hants. First printed by George Daniel in *The Illustrated London News* 22 Dec. 1855, xxvii. 723; re-printed, Cunningham ix. 370; Toynbee xv. 106 (salutation omitted in Cunningham and Toynbee). The MS was inserted in the presentation copy of *The Mysterious Mother* given by HW to Douglas (Hazen, *SH Bibl.* 85, copy 4); sold Samuel Baker 12 July 1823 (Douglas Sale), lot 1594, to Thorpe; *penes* George Daniel, of Canonbury, in 1855, who acquired the book 'from a private source'; sold Sotheby's 27 July 1864 (Daniel Sale), lot 1723, to Harvey; *penes* Mrs Scott-Murray (later Mrs Colin Davy) in 1936; not further traced.

Berkeley Square, Feb. 15, 1792.

Sir,

I HOPE my having been out of town for three or four days, will excuse my not obeying your commands[2] sooner—and now when I do acknowledge the receipt of them, I am at a loss to express the confusion I feel at your much too obliging compliments, which I am very happy to receive as marks of your kindness and partiality, but have no right to accept as due to me. A performance,[3] in which I am conscious of so many faults, and the subject of which is so disgusting, it is very indulgent in any reader to excuse; nor can the favour of such able judges as you, Sir, and the Duc de Nivernois,[4] reconcile me to my own imprudence in letting it go out of my own hands—but having fallen into that slip of vanity, it is too late now to plead modesty, and there is less affectation, I hope, in obeying you both, than in troubling you with more words about a trifle. I have therefore the honour, Sir, of offering you a correct copy,[5] which I had printed some years ago to prevent a spurious edition,[6] and as I succeeded, I did not publish mine. The edition printed in Ireland[7]

1. (1743–1823), cr. (1800) Bn Glenbervie.
2. Apparently in a letter (missing) which asked HW to send copies of *The Mysterious Mother* to Douglas and to the Duc de Nivernais.
3. HW's *Mysterious Mother*, begun in 1766 and finished in 1768 ('Short Notes,' GRAY i. 43; Hazen, *SH Bibl.* 79).
4. See *ante* 15 Feb. 1764, n. 13.
5. HW's presentation copy to Douglas, with this autograph letter from HW, is listed in Hazen, op. cit. 85; see headnote.
6. *The Mysterious Mother* was reprinted by Dodsley in 1781 to forestall unauthorized reprints, but after the announced publication had prevented the spurious edition, HW did not publish his edition (*ante* 23 Nov. 1785; Hazen, op. cit. 82).
7. Dublin, 1791; see *ante* 17 Feb., 26 Feb. (to J. C. Walker), and 23 March 1791.

lately is less exact; and though I stopped it for some time, it was to no purpose. Lord Cholmondeley[8] is returning to Paris in [a] few days, and will carry a copy to the Duc de Nivernois.[9] I have the honour to be with great respect, Sir,

Your most obedient humble servant

Orford

From the Duc de Nivernais, Wednesday 29 February 1792

Printed from the MS now wsl. First printed, Toynbee *Supp.* iii. 305–7. For the history of the MS see *ante* 30 April 1785. The MS (except the last two words and the signature) is in the hand of a secretary.

À Paris le 29 fevrier 1792.

Monsieur le Comte,

MY LORD Cholmondeley[1] a eu la bonté de m'envoyer avant-hier un exemplaire de la *Mysterious Mother*.[2] C'est un nouveau bienfait de Monsieur Horace Walpole qui m'est très précieux, et dont je rends mille grâces à Mylord Orford. J'ai lu trop rapidement ce bel ouvrage pour oser en parler avec quelque détail; je me permettrai seulement de dire à l'auteur combien j'aurai admiré l'art avec lequel il a pu rendre la Comtesse de Narbonne[3] intéressante jusqu'à la dernière scène de la pièce. Quand je dis l'art ce n'est pas ce que je veux et dois dire car cet art-là est du génie, plus encore que celui de Racine dans sa *Phèdre*.[4]

M. Douglas[5] qui m'honore de son amitié vous a donc dit que j'ai

8. George James Cholmondeley (1749–1827), styled Vct Malpas 1764–70; 4th E. of Cholmondeley, 1770; cr. (1815) M. of Cholmondeley; HW's grandnephew.

9. He did; Nivernais thanked HW *post* 29 Feb. 1792.

1. See *ante* 15 Feb. 1792, n. 8.

2. In his letter to Sylvester Douglas *ante* 15 Feb. 1792, HW promised to send a copy of *The Mysterious Mother*, 1781, to the Duc de Nivernais.

3. The heroine of the play; HW discusses his development of the central character in his 'postscript' to the play (*Works* i. 126–7). For Mason's criticism of her and for HW's response, see Mason i. 9, 11.

4. In his letter to Robert Jephson *ante* late Feb. 1775 *bis*, HW comments on Racine's *Phèdre* in comparison with his own theory of tragedy.

5. See *ante* 15 Feb. 1792, n. 1.

essayé de traduire le *Paradis perdu*[6] de Milton; mais Dieu me preserve d'oser communiquer une aussi faible traduction à un Anglais tel que Monsieur Horace Walpole. En général les traductions françaises de poèmes anglais ne sont que des estampes qui ne représentent que le squelette du tableau, et il ne faut pas présenter ces squelettes à ceux qui ont le tableau devant les yeux, qui en sentent vivement toutes les beautés et surtout à ceux qui sont capables d'en produire de pareils. Mon amour pour l'Angleterre et pour la littérature anglaise m'a fait traduire aussi en vers *L'Essai sur l'homme*[7] de Pope. C'est plutôt la matière que le stile qui en rend la traduction difficile. Je m'en suis tiré comme j'ai pu, c'est à dire fort chétivement, et j'ai trop d'amour-propre pour laisser passer la mer à de pareils essais qui ne sont à vrai dire que des thèmes d'écoliers. Ce jeune étudiant en langue anglaise est depuis deux mois âgé de 75 ans,[8] et vous savez, Mylord, dans quelles circonstances il voit se terminer sa triste carrière,[9] et je vous supplie d'être assuré qu'aucune circonstance ni personnelle ni publique ne lui feront jamais oublier un instant toute la reconnaissance qu'il doit aux bontés de Monsieur Horace Walpole ni tout l'attachement aussi sincère qu'inviolable qu'il lui a voué depuis si longtemps—for ever,

Le D. de Nivernais

M. le Comte Orford.

---

6. Nivernais translated HW's *Essay on Modern Gardening*, SH, 1785, in which HW quotes *Paradise Lost* iv. 134–42, 223–30, 237–47 (see *ante* 6 Jan. 1785, 21 June 1786). The translation by Nivernais of these lines in French couplets is included in his *Œuvres*, 1796. His intention to translate more of *Paradise Lost* is mentioned by HW *ante* 1 Feb. 1785. Further selections were published posthumously as 'Choix des plus beaux morceaux du Paradis perdu . . . traduit en vers par Louis Racine et Nivernois,' 1803 (Bibl. Nat. Cat. *sub* Mancini-Mazarini).

7. Included in his *Œuvres*, 1796; see *Biographie universelle*, 1811–62, xxxi. 297.

8. He was born 16 Dec. 1716.

9. Because of the loss of family and friends, the confiscation of his titles and estates, his sympathetic loyalty to Louis XVI, and the dangers of his own position (Lucien Perey [Clara Adèle Luce Herpin], *La Fin du XVIIIᵉ siècle: Le Duc de Nivernais 1763–1798*, 4th edn, 1891, pp. 351–84; Berry i. 268 and nn. 6–8, ii. 28 and n. 9).

To Richard Gough, Tuesday 15 March 1792

Printed from a photostat of the MS in Thomas Kirgate's hand in the Bodleian Library (MS Eng. letters d. 2, f. 156). First printed, Nichols, *Lit. Anec.* vi. 291–2. Reprinted, Toynbee xv. 107–8. For the history of the MS see *ante* 28 May 1789.

Endorsed by John Bowyer Nichols: To R[ichar]d Gough Esq. (Printed in Literary Anecdotes).

Berkeley Square, March 15th 1792.

LORD ORFORD is confined by the gout in his arm,[1] but has examined the MS catalogue,[2] and cannot possibly satisfy Mr Gough whether it is the original, or a copy from which Vertue made his extracts.[3] As well as Lord O. recollects Vertue extracted his list from a MS in the possession of Mr Bryan Fairfax;[4] but Vertue took out nothing but the pictures, and none of the plate, furniture, etc. And though Lord Orford observes that some of the same pictures are mentioned as at different palaces, yet there seem to be several more than are in the Catalogue of the Royal Collection published by Bathoe.[5] And this is all the information Lord Orford can give Mr Gough.

1. This letter was dictated to Kirgate. HW wrote to Lady Ossory 10 April 1792, 'Kirgate orders me to tell your Ladyship that his master is mending as fast, or rather as slowly, as the latter expected . . . he does not reckon upon more than recovering some limbs and joints, that at their best are of very little use to him (Ossory iii. 139).

2. Apparently a fair copy of the MS catalogue of Charles I's collection of pictures in the Cabinet Room at Whitehall, by Abraham Van der Doort, which HW had purchased in November 1786 ('Abraham Van der Doort's Catalogue of the Collections of Charles I,' ed. Oliver Millar, *Walpole Society* 1958–60, xxxvii. xviii, xxi).

3. George Vertue's Notebooks show that he had studied the Ashmole manuscripts of the Catalogue, and had a copy made, in preparing the edition published for William Bathoe in 1757: *A Catalogue and Description of King Charles the First's Capital Collection . . . Now first published from an Original Manuscript in the Ashmolean Musæum at Oxford* (Vertue Note Books, *Walpole Society* 1929–30,

xviii. 54, 104–5; 1937–8, xxvi. 81; Millar, op. cit. xxi; see also Hazen, *Bibl. of HW* 120–5).

4. Brian Fairfax, the younger (1676–1749), commissioner of customs 1723–49; collector. A catalogue of his library, which was to be sold at auction, was printed in April 1756, but the whole library was sold to Robert Child (1739–82), of Osterley Park, where it remained until it was sold Sotheby's 6–14 May 1885 (property of the E. of Jersey) (DNB; BERRY ii. 72 and n. 28; GM 1782, lii. 406). In *Anecdotes of Painting* HW wrote: 'A catalogue of the pictures, statues, goods, tapestries and jewels [of Charles I], with the several prices at which they were valued and sold, was discovered some years ago in Moorfields, and fell into the hands of the late Sir John Stanley, who permitted Mr Vice Chamberlain Cook, Mr Fairfax, and Mr Kent to take copies, from one of which Vertue obtained a transcript' (*Works* iii. 200–1).

5. HW noted concerning 'the fair copy of Vanderdort's catalogue' which he had bought: 'It contains a few articles that are

To Lady Bristol, Tuesday 3 April 1792

Printed for the first time from a photostat of the MS in Thomas Kirgate's hand in the Hervey Collection, Bury St Edmunds and West Suffolk Record Office, Bury St Edmunds, Suffolk, kindly provided by Mr Patrick F. Doran. For the history of the MS see *ante* 18 December 1791.

Endorsed in an unidentified hand: Lord Orford (Horace Walpole) to Countess of Bristol 3 April 1792.

Address: To the Countess of Bristol in Bruton Street.

Berkeley Square, April 3d 1792.

Madam,

I MOST humbly entreat your Ladyship's pardon for not answering the honour of your letter[1] immediately, and now, for not answering it with my own hand, which indeed I am not able to do from lameness and weakness;[2] reasons which have prevented me from paying my respects to your Ladyship. I have been ill, Madam, the whole winter, and seldom out of my own house since October.

I cannot express, Madam, my shock and indignation at hearing that Dr Norford[3] is yet unpaid. Almost the first order that I gave on my late nephew's death, was, that his executors[4] should immediately pay his physicians, and I was told they had done so, which I the more readily believed because I heard at the same time of the very liberal manner in which they had rewarded Dr Ash,[5] who had not attended a twentieth part of the time that Dr Norford did.

But in truth, Madam, I now see through this iniquity: only two days ago I received a like complaint from Dr Monro,[6] whom I had dispatched to Brandon on the first notice of my nephew's disorder, and whom the executors had also said they would pay, but upon

not in this printed Catalogue [Bathoe's]. It goes to the bottom of p. 78 of this Edition; the rest, to the end of p. 81 is wanting' (Millar, op. cit. xxi, n. 3).

1. Missing.
2. The MS is in Kirgate's hand; for HW's illness see *ante* 15 March 1792, n. 1.
3. Dr William Norford (*ante* 30 Nov. 1791, n. 7). Robert Blake wrote to Anthony Hamond 8 Nov. 1792, 'Lord O. also leaves it entirely to the executors to pay the physicians, and does not object to the sums fixed on in their resolutions. His

Lordship wishes that Dr Norford should be paid as soon as convenient to the executors' (Hamond MS, in the possession of Capt. Anthony Hamond).
4. Brigg Price Fountaine, Edmund Rolfe, Jr, Anthony Hamond, and Robert Mackreth (*ante* 29 Dec. 1791, nn. 7, 8).
5. Dr John Ash (*ante* 30 Nov. 1791, n. 5). He had returned to London from Houghton by 2 Dec., and had reported to HW on Lord Orford's condition (*ante* 2 Dec. 1791).
6. Dr Thomas Monro (*ante* 30 Nov. 1791, n. 3; Ossory iii. 129–30).

inquiry yesterday I found it had been prevented by Coney,[7] a rascally steward of my late nephew, whom I instantly dismissed on his death, and who was one of that execrable cabal who hurried my poor nephew out of his life, by forcibly carrying him, against his consent, from Brandon to Houghton,[8] in the height of his fever; nor have I any doubt but this new insult and injury to Dr Norford is indirectly levelled at one[9] too, whom in their aspersions they connected with the Doctor.

Fortunately, Madam, my agent[10] goes to Houghton tomorrow, to meet the executors, and shall carry to them a severe reprimand for this abominable treatment of Dr Norford, and a positive injunction to satisfy him.

My breast and breath will not permit me, Madam, to add more at present, but that, with many thanks, for the honour your Ladyship has done me, in communicating the pamphlet[11] to me. I will read it as soon as I can recover attention and judgment enough to bestow on whatever comes recommended by your Ladyship's excellent understanding and taste.

I have the honour to be, Madam, with the highest respect,

Your Ladyship's most obliged, and
most obedient humble servant

ORFORD

7. Carlos Cony, Lord Orford's steward and attorney (*ante* 6 Dec. 1791, n. 1). Cony's uncooperative attitude is mentioned in a letter from Mackreth to Hamond 27 March 1792: 'I am extremely sorry Mr Cony should trouble you, and Mr Fountaine on such trifling subjects, had any mistake arisen in his correspondence with Mr Lucas, or myself—had he been kind enough to have written, and pointed out the error, or impropriety of such a measure, his ideas would have been adopted, but if he will take offence, where none was meant to be given, it makes it very difficult, and unpleasant, to proceed in the trust with that equanimity of temper we all wish to preserve—I trouble you with two of Mr Cony's letters with my answer to his last, by which you will perceive that even the smallest indelicate treatment was not intended towards him' (Hamond MS).

8. Lord Orford became ill with a high fever at the vicarage house near Brandon, Suffolk, and was moved to Houghton (*ante* 30 Nov. 1791 and n. 10).

9. That is, HW, who says *ante* 18 Dec. 1791 that he did not know Dr Norford even by name before 14 Nov. 1791 and had never seen him.

10. Robert Blake (*ante* 3 Jan. 1792, n. 2). Mackreth wrote to Hamond 27 March 1792, 'I have just seen Mr Blake who informs me that Lord Orford is laid up with the gout, and he has not been able to do any business, but Mr B. is in expectation of seeing his Lordship in a day or two—Mr Blake will be at Houghton next week, when he will do himself the honour to wait on you and Mr Fountaine, or will be happy to see you at Houghton' (Hamond MS).

11. A pamphlet by the Hon. Frederick William Hervey (1769–1859), Lady Bristol's younger son; see HW to Lady Bristol *post* 5 April 1792.

From Le Fevre d'Ormesson,[1] Thursday 5 April 1792

Printed from a transcript of a copy made by Joseph-Basile-Bernard Van Praet,[2] presumably from the letter which d'Ormesson sent to HW. First printed (omitting the last two sentences) in Paget Toynbee, 'Horace Walpole's Gift to Paris,' *The Times* 29 Oct. 1929; extracts printed in Lucien Auvray, 'Horace Walpole et la Bibliothèque du Roi (1766–1792),' *Bibliothèque de l'École des Chartes*, 1929, xc. 230. The MS of Van Praet's copy is preserved in the Bibliothèque Nationale; the letter sent to HW is missing.

Address: Monsieur Horace Walpole, comte d'Oxford [*sic*], en son château de Shaberry [*sic*] hill près Twickenham, comté de Middlesex, par Londres.

J'AURAIS DU, Monsieur le Comte, vous adresser plus tôt[3] les témoignages de la plus profonde reconnaissance et ma sensibilité à vos bontés particulières pour le dépôt qui m'est confié. Tous ceux qui le fréquentent seront à portée de profiter de vos bienfaits, et vous ne serez sûrement pas oublié dans leur souvenir. La magnificence de la reliure[4] rend ce présent encore plus recommandable, et vous avez voulu ne rien laisser à désirer. Je souhaiterais que mes relations littéraires en ce pays pussent me mettre à même de vous y offrir personnellement mes services. Vous me trouverez aussi reconnaissant qu'empressé à vous offrir les sentiments etc.

1. Anne-Louis-François de Paule Le Fèvre d' Ormesson de Noyseau (1753–94), keeper of the Bibliothèque du Roi; deputy to the Estates General, 1789; condemned to death by the tribunal of the Revolution, 20 April 1794 (NBG; *Biographie Universelle*, 1811–62, xxxii. 150–1). D'Ormesson had apparently confused HW with an '*homme agé* . . . who Monsieur d'Ormesson says was frequently at the Royal Library, but has not been seen there for a whole year' (FAMILY 283). HW had not been in Paris since 1775.

2. (1754–1837), 'écrivain attaché à la garde des livres imprimés,' 1784; 'sous-garde des livres,' 1792; 'garde des livres imprimés,' 1795, in the Bibliothèque du Roi (NBG).

3. The MS reads 'plutot.' In November 1766 HW had made a gift of fifteen volumes of his works to the Bibliothèque du Roi, and eventually received an acknowledgment from the Abbé Pierre-Jean Boudot (1689–1771), assistant to Jean Capperonnier who was keeper of the Bibliothèque du Roi (see *ante* 17, 21 Nov. 1766; DU DEFFAND i. 262 n. 5). HW wrote to Thomas Walpole the younger 26 June 1792, 'You cannot wonder that I concluded it [d'Ormesson's letter] was not meant for me, when you find it was to thank me for a present made to the library of the late King of France six and twenty years ago' (FAMILY 280).

4. The fifteen volumes were handsomely bound in red morocco with Walpole's arms stamped on the sides; the set included the works printed at the SH Press 1757–64 and *Ædes Walpolianæ*, 2d edn, 1752, and *The Castle of Otranto*, 1765, printed in London (see Lucien Auvray, 'Horace Walpole et la Bibliothèque du Roi (1766–1792),' *Bibliothèque de l'École des Chartes*, 1929, xc. 230–1; *ante* 17 Nov. 1766, n. 6).

To Lady Bristol, Thursday 5 April 1792

Printed for the first time from a photostat of the MS in the Hervey Collection, Bury St Edmunds and West Suffolk Record Office, Bury St Edmunds, Suffolk, kindly provided by Mr Patrick F. Doran. For the history of the MS see *ante* 18 December 1791.

Berkeley Square, April 5th 1792.

I MUST not dare, Madam, to question the truth of anything that your Ladyship is pleased to say to me[1]—yet may I at least presume to tell you that you have set my faith and my reason at variance?

On the information you have condescended to give me, Madam, it was impossible not to read the pamphlet[2] directly—I do protest *solemnly* (and *solemnly* is a grave word at my age and under my own hand, as this is) that I should have concluded the pamphlet written by one of the ablest writers in the administration or under his inspection. The argumentation is sound, cogent, clear and short, and never, never run down. The knowledge is extensive and never superficial, and our various interests of commerce etc. seem to me, no adept, perfectly understood. So much information, so well applied, at Mr Hervey's age,[3] would, I own, appear incredible, if some recent instances of the most splendid abilities—unheard of in my former life, had not appeared of late.

To all this mass of possession is added as uncommon a phenomenon, in such early youth, and the moderation and command of temper; not one argument is ruffled or weakened by passion.

That these are the pure dictates of my opinion I attest the book itself, which will warrant my assertions. I hold it a serious crime against morality to flatter a young author who discovers no parts; nor

1. Apparently in a letter (missing) accompanying a pamphlet written by her younger son (see *ante* 3 April 1792).

2. Not identified. No pamphlets by Hervey appear in the records of HW's library (Hazen, *Cat. of HW's Lib.*); HW says *post* 9 April and after 9 April 1792 that he lent this pamphlet to a friend.

3. He was now 22. Hon. Frederick William Hervey (1769–1859), 2d son of the 4th E. of Bristol; styled Lord Hervey 1796–1803; 5th E. of Bristol, 1803; cr.

(1826) M. of Bristol. His mother wrote that at 18 he had passed his examinations at St John's, Cambridge, 'with such wonderful credit and *éclat* that he was declared first of his year in every subject' (W. S. Childe-Pemberton, *The Earl Bishop*, New York, [1925], ii. 429; Brian Fothergill, *The Mitred Earl*, 1974, p. 143; Venn, *Alumni Cantab.* iii. 343). He received the M.A. in 1788 and was admitted to Lincoln's Inn 1 May 1793 (Venn, loc. cit.).

could even my good breeding or tender respect for the feelings of a mother have prevailed on me to go beyond common civilities, if sincerity did not guarantee my sentiments. Though forced to write in my lap and very slowly, I would write with my own hand, Madam; because I will adhere to the truth of every word I have said. I do not pretend to be a judge; but I have faithfully described the impression the work made on me.

I most cordially congratulate your Ladyship on the possession of so valuable a son, and I congratulate my country on having so able a rising champion,[4] at a moment when I fear they will be so essentially necessary! It is a consolation to me, who am quitting the earth, to leave hopes that the abilities and good sense of our countrymen will yet preserve our unique and precious constitution—but vigilance is equally requisite. The enemies are as indefatigable as atrocious. Mr Hervey wants no spur—He has my most fervent wishes for his success; and may your Ladyship live to see him crowned with the fame, honours and prosperity I have no doubt but he will deserve!

I have the honour to be with the greatest respect and gratitude, Madam, your Ladyship's most obliged and most obedient humble servant

ORFORD

4. He became M.P. for Bury St Edmunds 1796–1803 and Under-Secretary of State, Foreign Department, Feb. 1801–Aug. 1803. He was a Whig, but later turned Conservative. In 1801 Count Semen Romanovich Vorontsov, the Russian ambassador, wrote of him: 'J'ai vu croître ce fils, je le connais intimement; il a la vanité, l'esprit, la légéreté et le déficit de jugement caracteristique de la famille. Il est Hervey, Hervey, et Archi-Hervey, de manière que je tremble que ce ne soit lui qu'on nomme [as minister to St Petersburg]; et si on le fait, je m'attends à mille follies de sa part ainsi qu'à mille regrets de la vôtre' (Hist. MSS Comm., Fortescue MSS, 1910, vii. 6). See also GM 1859, ccvi pt i. 318.

To Lady Bristol, Monday 9 April 1792

Printed for the first time from a photostat of the MS in the Hervey Collection, Bury St Edmunds and West Suffolk Record Office, Bury St Edmunds, Suffolk, kindly provided by Mr Patrick F. Doran. For the history of the MS see *ante* 18 December 1791.

Endorsed in an unidentified hand: Lord Orford (Horace Walpole) to Countess of Bristol 9 April 1792.

Address: To the Countess of Bristol.

April 9, 1792.

Madam,

I CAN only add to what I said[1] on the first pamphlet you did me the honour to send me, that if I *have* seen prematurity of abilities, I now see in Mr Hervey what is still more rare perhaps, prematurity of wisdom, which is very striking in *The New Friend*.[2]

I last night engaged Lord Harcourt[3] to carry the other with him to *Windsor*[4] today—but I am afraid no method will be adequate to Mr Hervey's name.[5] His rank and great youth would strike universally, and would operate to his preferment as well as to his reputation.

I must own, though an unreasonable wish, that when Mr Hervey returns he would flatter me exceedingly by honouring me with a visit.[6] To invite a youth to the couch of a decrepit old man past

1. In his previous letter to Lady Bristol, *ante* 5 April 1792.

2. *A New Friend on an Old Subject*, 1791, in which Hervey defends Edmund Burke against the comments of Thomas Paine, deplores the sweeping lawlessness of the French revolutionists, and praises the gradual establishment of the English constitution: 'Instead of dissolving society, and speculating on abstract propositions of the rights of man, in the midst of anarchy and confusion, we have made, for a succession of ages, a gradual and steady progress to the attainment of our present constitution. . . . In pursuit of freedom we have not madly overturned every barrier of gratitude, allegiance, and religion that obstructed our progress towards it' (pp. 14–15). Hervey regarded

Paine's *Rights of Man* as dangerous and destructive (p. 18).

3. George Simon Harcourt (1736–1809), styled Vct Nuneham 1749–77; 2d E. Harcourt, 1777; M.P.; Master of the Horse to the Queen Consort (*ante* ?16 April 1766, n. 3). HW became estranged from Harcourt ca 1784, but they were reconciled by 1794 (see MASON ii. 348, 350, 365–6).

4. Probably to the unidentified 'person of much sounder judgment' mentioned *post* after 9 April 1792.

5. HW thought that Hervey should acknowledge the anonymous pamphlets; see following letter, dated after 9 April 1792.

6. We have not found any record of this visit.

seventy-four, who was acquainted with his great-grandfather,[7] is holding out no temptation; but I will promise not to be troublesome, and being aware of my own defects, I am not likely, I trust, to importune Mr Hervey with them, for whom I have conceived so much respect.

Your Ladyship's most obliged humble servant

ORFORD

To Lady Bristol, after 9 April 1792

Printed for the first time from a photostat of the MS in the Hervey Collection, Bury St Edmunds and West Suffolk Record Office, Bury St Edmunds, Suffolk, kindly provided by Mr Patrick F. Doran. For the history of the MS see *ante* 18 December 1791.

Endorsed in an unidentified hand: Lord Orford (Horace Walpole) to Countess of Bristol 1792.

Address: To the Countess of Bristol, Bruton Street.

LORD ORFORD having lent *the pamphlet*[1] to a person[2] of much sounder judgment than his own, has the pleasure of having his opinion confirmed in the fullest manner, the gentleman declaring it one of the most excellent pamphlets he ever saw.

Lord Orford would not presume without Lady Bristol's permission, to name the author;[3] but does earnestly wish Mr Hervey would put his name to it; it would do him infinite honour and would excite notice, anonymous pamphlets from their multiplicity being overlooked. Thousands and thousands of Mr Hervey's ought to be dispersed as an incomparable antidote to the reigning poison[4]—though it is not armour, alas! against assassination!

---

7. John Hervey (1665–1751), cr. (1703) Bn Hervey of Ickworth and (1714) E. of Bristol, with whose son and daughter-in-law HW had corresponded (*ante* 21 Oct. 1735 OS; MORE 415–16 and *passim*).

1. The pamphlet written by the Hon. Frederick William Hervey, Lady Bristol's younger son, which she had sent to HW before 3 April (see *ante* 3, 5 April 1792).

2. Not identified; possibly someone of the Court at Windsor (*ante* 9 April 1792).

3. Hervey's second pamphlet, like *A New Friend on an Old Subject,* 1791, was anonymous.

4. That is, the violent republicanism of the French Revolution. Hervey in *A New Friend* writes, 'History will record . . .

To Thomas Barret, Monday 14 May 1792

Printed from *Works* v. 670, where the letter was first printed. Reprinted, Wright vi. 473–4; Cunningham ix. 372 (signature omitted in Wright and Cunningham); Toynbee xv. 110–1. The history of the MS and its present whereabouts are not known.

Berkeley Square, May 14, 1792.

Dear Sir,

THOUGH my poor fingers do not yet write easily, I cannot help inquiring if Mabeuse[1] is arrived safely at Lee,[2] and fits his destined stall in the library.[3] My amendment is far slower, *comme de raison* than ever, and my weakness much greater. Another fit, I doubt, will confine me to my chair, if it does not do more—it is not worth haggling about that.

the flame of faction and revenge, unfanned by religious zeal or civil war, blazing with more violence than ever it had raged with in the hottest moments of political convulsions—The people in full possession of their liberty, exercising upon their fellow-citizens, acts of more outrageous barbarity than ever had been offered to the most determined Infidels, by the most sanguinary and exasperated Bigots' (pp. 10–11). HW mentions the French barbarities in his letters to Lady Ossory 10 April, 29 May 1792 (OSSORY iii. 139, 141).

––––––––––

1. Jan Gossaert (1478–between 1533 and 1536), called John Mabuse. A *List of Pictures at Lee Priory*, privately printed, 1817, lists as hanging in the Tower Room 'A very beautiful and curious picture— *Mabuse*. Purchased at a high price, on the recommendation of Lord Orford, who mentions it in his letters' (see J. P. Neale, *Views of the Seats of Noblemen and Gentlemen*, 2d ser., 1824–9, vol. II). A MS note by HW in his copy of *Anecdotes of Painting*, 1762, i. between pp. 52–3 (now WSL, see Hazen, *SH Bibl.*, 1973, pp. xvi, 66) says: 'It was evidently a fragment of a larger [picture] and probably an altarpiece containing only two Bishops and two Monks, turning towards, it should

seem, the Virgin and Child, which are wanting. The heads are most admirable; the draperies and ornaments exquisitely finished. This most valuable picture was purchased by Thomas Barrett, Esq., and is now in his beautiful Gothic Library at Lee near Canterbury' (printed in M. W. Brockwell, *The 'Adoration of the Magi' by Jan Mabuse*, privately printed, 1911, App. B, p. 10). The painting, now in the National Gallery, London, was identified by W. H. James Weale as 'A Canon and his Patron Saints,' part of an altarpiece by Gerard David (Gheeraert Davit) (d. 1523) (see W. H. J. Weale, *Gerard David*, 1895, pp. 17–20, and plate facing p. 18; Brockwell, op. cit. 17, n. 10).

2. Lee Priory, Kent, Barret's house in the Gothic style, executed by James Wyatt (BERRY ii. 111 and nn. 28, 31). HW visited Lee in August 1780 (*Country Seats* 76–7).

3. HW thought Barret's library 'the most perfect thing I ever saw, and has the most the air it was intended to have, that of an abbot's library . . . but I am sorry he will not force Mr Wyat to place the Mabeuse over the chimney, which is the sole defect, as not distinguished enough for the principal feature of the room' (to Mary Berry 17 Oct. 1794, BERRY ii. 136–7 and n. 5).

Dr Darwin has appeared,[4] superior in some respects to the former part.[5] The *Triumph of Flora,* beginning at the 59th line,[6] is most beautifully and enchantingly imagined; and the twelve verses[7] that by miracle describe and comprehend the creation of the universe out of chaos, are in my opinion the most sublime passage in any author, or in any of the few languages with which I am acquainted. There are a thousand other verses most charming, or indeed all are so, crowded with most poetic imagery, gorgeous epithets and style—and yet these four cantos do not please me equally with the *Loves of the Plants.*—This seems to me almost as much a rhapsody of unconnected parts; and is so deep, that I cannot read six lines together and know what they are about, till I have studied them in the long notes, and then perhaps do not comprehend them— But all this is my fault, not Dr Darwin's—Is he to blame, that I am no natural philosopher, no chemist, no metaphysician?

One misfortune will attend this glorious work—it will be little read but by those who have no taste for poetry, and who will be weighing and criticizing his positions, without feeling the imagination, harmony and expression of the versification.

Is not it extraordinary, dear Sir, that two of our very best poets,

4. Erasmus Darwin (1731–1802) (see *ante* 14 Feb. 1790), *The Botanic Garden. Part I. Containing The Economy of Vegetation. A Poem. With Philosophical Notes,* 1791, published 10 May 1792; advertised in the *Morning Herald* 7 May as 'Next Thursday will be published' and 10 May as 'This day is published' (also in *St James's Chronicle* 5–8, 8–10 May 1792, and *London Chronicle* 3–5, 5–8 May 1792, lxxi. 430, 440). HW wrote Mary Berry 26 May 1791 that Richard French 'says we shall have Dr Darwin's stupendous poem in a fortnight' (BERRY i. 274), but on 17 Aug. 1791 he noted that canto II 'is not yet published' (ibid. i. 339). Darwin wrote to James Watt ?1791, 'As *The Loves of the Plants pays* me well, and as I write for pay, not for fame, I intend to publish *The Economy of Vegetation* in the spring' (Hesketh Pearson, *Doctor Darwin,* 1930, p. 115). HW's copy of Part I is Hazen, *Cat. of HW's Lib.,* No. 3809.

5. *The Botanic Garden, Part II. Containing The Loves of the Plants, A Poem. With Philosophical Notes,* 1789 (2d edn,

1790; 3d edn, 1791 bound with 1st edn of Part I).

6. 'She comes!—the GODDESS!—through the whispering air,
Bright as the morn, descends her blushing car;
Each circling wheel a wreath of flowers intwines,
And gem'd with flowers the silken harness shines;
The golden bits with flowery studs are deck'd,
And knots of flowers the crimson reins connect.—
And now on earth the silver axle rings,
And the shell sinks upon its slender springs;
Light from her airy seat the Goddess bounds,
And steps celestial press the pansied grounds' (canto I, lines 59–68).

7. Canto I, lines 103–14, beginning 'LET THERE BE LIGHT!' HW praises this passage in conversation with Joseph Farington in 1796 (see DALRYMPLE 328–9).

Garth[8] and Darwin, should have been physicians?—I believe they
have left all the lawyers wrangling at the turnpike of Parnassus.
Adieu, dear Sir!

Yours most cordially,

ORFORD

To Unknown,[1] Sunday 1 July 1792

Printed in full for the first time from the MS now wsl. An extract from the letter was printed in Toynbee *Supp.* iii. 75. The MS is untraced until sold Sotheby's
12 April 1921 (Autograph Letters and Historical Documents Sale), lot 401 (with
another letter), to Maggs; offered by Maggs, Cat. Nos 405 (summer 1921), lot 1387,
and 457 (Christmas 1924), lot 3064; sold by them to W. Marchbank, Brinkburn,
Gosforth, Northumberland, before 1930; sold Sotheby's 20 Dec. 1948 (property of
the late W. Marchbank), lot 249, to Maggs for wsl.

Strawberry Hill, July 1st 1792.

I AM very sorry, dear Sir, to hear that you are leaving us, but you
oblige me much by offering to come hither previously,[2] which I
most willingly accept. Friday I conclude will be your first day of
leisure from your presentations, and therefore that day I propose
to you, or Saturday,[3] if suiting you better, only let me know which,
that I may let nothing interfere with your visit, when I hope you
will accept a bed as well as a dinner.

Yours most sincerely

ORFORD

8. Sir Samuel Garth (1661–1719), Kt;
poet and physician, whose poem *The
Dispensary* was a favourite of HW's (HW
to Pinkerton 26 June 1785, CHATTERTON
272). HW's copy of Garth's *Works*, Dublin,
1769, now wsl, is Hazen, *Cat. of HW's
Lib.*, No. 371; see also No. 4005.

1. Possibly Charles O'Hara (ca 1740–
1802), Maj.-Gen., 1781, who had just been
promoted to the position of Lt-Gov. of
Gibraltar: 'Yesterday [Fri., 6 July] General
O'Hara kissed the King's hand at the
levee, on receiving his commission as
Lieutenant Governor of Gibraltar' (Lon-

don *Chronicle* 5–7 July 1792, lxxii. 21). He
was a close friend of Gen. Conway and
Lady Ailesbury, and later became Mary
Berry's fiancé (see BERRY i. 119 and n. 10,
201, 203, 236).

2. If this offer was made in a letter, it
is missing.

3. We have not found any record of
this visit. According to HW's 'Book of
Visitors,' on Thursday, 5 July, he received
the 'Bishop of Dromore and family,' on
Friday 'Mr Ellis's servants,' and on Saturday 'Mr Staveley, the painter' (BERRY ii.
241).

To Joseph Cooper Walker,[1] Saturday 4 August 1792

Printed from a copy made by the late Sir Shane Leslie, Bt, in 1941, of the MS then in the possession of the Hon. Mrs Clive Pearson, Parham Park, Pullborough, Sussex. First printed, Toynbee xv. 125. The MS is untraced until sold Sotheby's 20 Dec. 1877 (Collection of Autograph Letters Sale), lot 51 (with six other letters from HW to Walker, 1787–92), to Naylor; resold Sotheby's 13 March 1903 (Autograph Letters and Historical Documents Sale), lot 733, to Maggs; offered by Maggs, Cat. No. 196 (1903), lot 974; acquired after 1905, when it was *penes* Maggs, by Sir Herbert H. Raphael, Bt, who inserted it in an extra-illustrated copy of Cunningham's edition of HW's *Letters;* for the history of this copy see *ante* 28 Nov. 1788.

Address: À Monsieur Monsieur Joseph Cooper Walker aux soins de Messieurs Piregaux & Co. à Paris.

Strawberry Hill, August 4th 1792.

Sir,

AS I conclude by the notice[2] you was pleased to give me, that you are by this time arrived at Paris, I would by no means neglect thanking you for the Italian pamphlet[3] you was so good as to send to me, for which I am much obliged to you.

You have long been so prejudiced in favour of my tragedy,[4] Sir, that I doubt you think others are so too. I wish it deserved such partiality.

I have the honour of being with great regard and gratitude, Sir,

Your obliged and obedient humble servant

ORFORD

1. See *ante* 5 Aug. 1789, n. 1.
2. Walker's letter (missing) from Rome is mentioned *post* 20 Sept. 1792.
3. Not identified.

4. *The Mysterious Mother* (see *ante* 6 Nov. 1790, 4 April 1791). Walker sent the Dublin, 1791, edition to HW in March 1791; see *ante* 23 March 1791, and Hazen, *Cat. of HW's Lib.*, No. 2490.

From BISHOP PERCY, Saturday 11 August 1792

Printed from Nichols, *Lit. Illus.* viii. 289–90, where the letter was first printed. Excerpts reprinted in *The Correspondence of Thomas Percy & Richard Farmer*, ed. Cleanth Brooks, Baton Rouge, Louisiana, 1946, pp. 178–9, 185, and in *The Correspondence of Thomas Percy & Thomas Warton*, ed. M. G. Robinson and Leah Dennis, Baton Rouge, Louisiana, 1951, pp. 162–3. The history of the MS and its present whereabouts are not known.

London, Aug. 11, 1792.

My Lord,

I HAVE at length been able to collect for your Lordship the sheets of Lord Surrey[1] and the Duke of Buckingham.[2] They have been printed off about 25 years. Since the death of Jacob Tonson,[3] at

1. Unbound printed sheets for Percy's two-volume edition of the works of Henry Howard, Earl of Surrey, never published; for a complete account of these volumes see Brooks, op. cit. 175–89. The edition was undertaken in 1763 upon an agreement with Jacob Tonson, and Percy projected one volume based on Tottel's *Miscellany;* probably in 1775 he expanded his plan to two volumes (ibid. 176–7, 181; Nichols, *Lit. Illus.* vi. 560; see also *ante* 14 Dec. 1775, n. 5). These octavo volumes are represented by Thomas Park's copy, now in the British Museum, of which the final sheets of volume II are apparently proofs rather than finished sheets (Brooks, op. cit. 175–6, 186; for other extant copies see ibid. 193–4). The Bodleian Library owns a set of 'first' proofs and a 'revise' of the *Æneid* (ibid. 179). Volume I of the BM copy is 'an attempted reprint' of the 2d setting of the 2d edition of Tottel's *Miscellany*, 1557; volume II includes the Second and Fourth Books of Surrey's *Æneid*, the *Ecclesiastes*, the *Psalms*, and additional poems by Surrey, Wyatt's *Psalmes*, additional poems, and *Oration*, as well as works by other authors (ibid. 175–6).
2. Unbound printed sheets for Percy's two-volume edition of the works of George Villiers, 2d Duke of Buckingham, never published; for a complete account of these volumes see Robinson and Dennis, op. cit. 148–65. Percy's agreement with

Tonson for this edition was made 12 June 1761 (Nichols, *Lit. Illus.* vi. 556–7, 560; Robinson and Dennis, op. cit. 152). The two volumes were being set in type concurrently in 1762, when Percy wrote to Thomas Warton on 25 April, 'the Printer of *the Duke of Buckm's Works* begin[s] to press upon my heels' (ibid. 34–5, 155). Percy's edition is now represented by two octavo volumes in the British Museum which were purchased at the John Bowyer Nichols Sale in March 1865. Another copy described as '2 vol., both vol. without prelims. (presumably never printed)' was sold Sotheby's 23 June 1969 (Thomas Percy Sale), lot 79. Volume I in the BM copy ends in the middle of the 'List of Plays quoted in the foregoing Key'; Volume II ends in the middle of *Poetical Reflections on Absalom and Achitophel*, which was, according to Percy's 'Advertisement,' the first of three 'Doubtful Pieces' (ibid. 155; see also pp. 32–3 and n. 7). The Bodleian Library owns some corrected proofs of parts of both volumes, which include additional material for volume II.
3. Jacob Tonson the third died 31 March 1767. Percy had written 13 Dec. 1766 to Richard Farmer, 'Surrey's Works are almost printed off' (Brooks, op. cit. 118, 178). Of Buckingham's works the two volumes were partially printed (n. 2 above). After Tonson's death the printing was discontinued, but Percy continued to collect materials. He wrote 12 April 1783

whose instance they were undertaken, and who ought to have assigned them to other persons, they have been wholly discontinued.
My fondness for these pursuits declining, I laid both those works
aside, till I could offer them to some younger editor than myself,
who could with more propriety resume them. I have now an ingenious nephew,[4] of both my names, who is a fellow of St John's
College, in Oxford, and both able and desirous to complete them.
To him I have given all the sheets so long since printed off, and
whatever papers I had upon the subject.

A few leaves only are wanting to complete Lord Surrey's version
of the 4th *Æneid*:[5] which, with the 2nd ditto, and his *Songs and
Sonnets*, etc. will be sufficient for the text of that Lord's *Poems*, etc.
and the editor will be most gratefully thankful for any information
respecting the lives or characters of Lord Surrey and his coadjutors;
and for any illustrations that may throw light on their compositions.[6]

to John Nichols that the booksellers 'were
to deliver up to you all the sheets of two
former works, formerly projected by the
late Jacob Tonson, *viz*. The Works of
Villiers Duke of Buckingham, and the
Works of Lord Surrey and Sir Thomas
Wyat, etc. The delivery of all the sheets
of both these publications, so far as they
go, into your care, *bona fide* and without
reservation, must be performed without
delay' (Nichols, *Lit. Illus.* vi. 571). On 22
May 1788 Nichols wrote Percy, 'I many
years ago, at your Lordship's request, took
into my warehouse the whole impressions
of "Buckingham" and "Surrey," which if
I had not done, they would have been all
burnt in Tonson's old warehouse,' and
asked if these 'are at some time to be
turned to waste paper'; but Percy promised
to complete the 'unpublished books' (ibid.
viii. 74, 76). According to Nichols, the
printing was resumed in 1795 and 'nearly
brought to a conclusion' (*Lit. Anec.* iii.
161n), but both editions remained unfinished when a fire on 8 Feb. 1808 in
Nichols's warehouse destroyed all the
printed sheets stored there (*ante* 14 Dec.
1775, n. 5; Brooks, op. cit. 186–7; Robinson and Dennis, op. cit. 163).

4. Thomas Percy (1768–1808), Fellow,
1792, of St John's College, Oxford; vicar
of Grays Thurrock, Essex, 1793 (Foster,
Alumni Oxon. iii. 1098; Nichols, *Lit. Anec.*
viii. 147–8). After 1792 the younger

Percy was the nominal editor, but
George Steevens was looking for additional poems for the Surrey edition and
Henry Meen was reading proofs (Brooks,
op. cit. 185, 192–3). In 1803 Bishop Percy
considered turning over the edition to
Thomas Park; and in 1805 he engaged
his curate, Hannington Elgee Boyd, to
prepare a glossary and complete the edition of Surrey (ibid. 186–7).

5. After Tonson's death the printing of
Percy's edition of Surrey stopped 'probably with sheet e of what was to become
Volume II. Sheet e, like sheets c and d,
and B-S (Volume I), has no watermark.
The last five leaves of Surrey's *Æneid*
(f1ʳ–f5ʳ) are on watermarked paper' (ibid.
179). This conclusion is substantiated by
some 'early' proofs of Percy's edition of
Surrey's *Æneid* in the Bodleian Library,
which end 'twelve lines short of the end
of Book Four' (ibid. 179–80).

6. In 1775 HW had offered his material
on Sir Thomas Wyatt and also drawings
of both Surrey and Wyatt; see *ante* 14
Dec. 1775 and nn. 3, 4. In his reply *post*
20 Aug. 1792 HW refers Percy to his
Miscellaneous Antiquities, No. 2, Strawberry Hill, 1772, which includes HW's
'Life of Sir Thomas Wyat, the Elder,' and
Wyatt's 'Defence, after the Indictment
and Evidence,' at his trial for high
treason in 1541.

Correct transcripts had been obtained of Lord Surrey's version of *Ecclesiastes*,[7] of his *Psalms,* of one of his *Poems on the Londoners;* and the same to Sir Thomas Wyat's *Seven Penitential Psalms;*[8] but these were of inferior value, and seemed hardly to merit the revival.

Of the 'Duke of Buckingham' Tonson wished to have every thing collected which had ever been ascribed to him:[9] but I believe I shall only recommend to my nephew to publish what is numbered vol. I in the sheets now offered to your Lordship. Between the 'Rehearsal' and the 'Key' were once printed the 'Chances' and the 'Restoration':[10] but the intermediate sheets have been cancelled and consigned to the trunk-makers.[11] And the same fate awaits the smaller pieces, collected into what is herewith numbered vol. II. They are only submitted to your Lordship in confidence, and I believe you will think them scarcely deserving republication.

7. The earliest mention of Percy's having obtained transcripts of Surrey's *Ecclesiastes* and *Psalms* is the entry for 1 Nov. 1775 in Percy's *Journal:* 'I also revised Ld Surrey's Translation of Ecclesiastes and Psalms in MS' (Brooks, op. cit. 180–1). A Table of Contents drawn up by Percy between 1773 and 1775 does not include the *Ecclesiastes,* and shows that he was then planning his edition as only one volume (ibid.). Percy found the *Ecclesiastes,* the *Psalms,* and 'A Satire against the Citizens of London' in the Harington MS which is now BM Add. MS 36529; Percy borrowed this MS in 1791 and took his text from it (see Ruth Hughey, 'The Harington Manuscript at Arundel Castle and Related Documents,' *The Library,* 1935, 4th ser., xv. 408, 410 and n. 2, 411; Brooks, op. cit. 182–3).

8. *Certayne psalmes chosen out of the psalter of Dauid commonlye called thee vii. penytentiall psalmes, drawen into englyshe meter by Sir Thomas Wyat Knyght,* 1549, of which Richard Farmer wrote to Percy 18 Feb. 1773, 'I have luckily found for you *Wyatt's* Psalms' (Brooks, op. cit. 166). The Psalms are included in the Harington MS now at Arundel Castle and in another MS now BM Egerton MS 2711, both of which Percy used and annotated (see Hughey, op. cit. 388–9, 425).

9. Percy's agreement with Tonson 12

June 1761 states: 'Whereas the Rev. Thomas Percy . . . is preparing for the press a collection of the Works of George Villiers, Duke of Buckingham, with an account of his Life prefixed thereto, and a new key to the Rehearsal; now it is hereby agreed . . . that the said book shall forthwith be printed in two volumes octavo' (Nichols, *Lit. Illus.* vi. 556–7). Percy wrote to Thomas Warton 19 Nov. 1761, 'I believe I formerly mentioned that I was collecting all the tracts of Villiers Duke of Buck. with a view to publish a complete edition of his works, hitherto very imperfectly attempted'; and he asked help in locating some tracts and various editions of *The Rehearsal* (Robinson and Dennis, op. cit. 25–6).

10. 'The Chances' and 'The Restoration' remain in this position in volume I of the BM copy of Percy's edition; also the smaller poems remain in volume II (ibid. 148–9). The two volumes were sent to Francis Osborne, 5th Duke of Leeds, in 1795, who replied 22 July 1795, ' "The Chances" are certainly somewhat broad, but the "Restoration," I think, has great merit' (ibid. 163; Nichols, *Lit. Illus.* viii. 314).

11. 'One whose business is the making of trunks . . . often with allusion to the use of the sheets of unsaleable books for trunk-linings' (OED).

I am now going for some weeks to Tunbridge Wells; and if, at
my return, your Lordship will be pleased to honour me, for the
editor's use, with any remarks on the foregoing subjects, it will
exceedingly oblige,

My Lord,
Your Lordship's most devoted
and most obedient subject,

THO. DROMORE

To BISHOP PERCY, Monday 20 August 1792

Printed from the MS now WSL. First printed, Toynbee *Supp.* ii. 56–7. The MS
was in the possession of Mr F. T. Sabin, 172 New Bond St, London, in 1918; not
further traced until acquired by WSL in July 1932 from Gabriel Wells.

Strawberry Hill, Aug. 20, 1792.

My Lord,

I RECEIVED the books,[1] which your Lordship did me the honour
of sending to me. They will be handsome editions, and I should
have been proud of being able to contribute to them; but indeed
I have found nothing wanting,[2] at least within the compass of my
scanty knowledge—your Lordship's own notes to Buckingham have
supplied all that was necessary.[3]

My sketch of Sir Thomas Wyat's life,[4] printed in the two numbers

1. Three volumes (as HW says below)
of printed sheets of Percy's editions of
the works of the Earl of Surrey and Sir
Thomas Wyatt, and of the Duke of
Buckingham (see *ante* 11 Aug. 1792 and
nn. 1, 2). In the Harington collection at
Arundel Castle there is a copy of Percy's
edition of Surrey 'being volume I and a
portion of volume II bound together'
(Ruth Hughey, 'The Harington Manuscript at Arundel Castle and Related
Documents,' *The Library*, 1935, 4th ser.,
xv. 393). There is also a one-volume copy
of Percy's edition of Surrey in the Osborn
Collection, Yale University Library, the
gift of Professor Cleanth Brooks.

2. Apparently Percy complained that
HW did not contribute any additional
information; see HW's reply *post* 18 Sept.
1792.
3. The conclusion of M. G. Robinson
is that the extant volumes and fragments
of Percy's edition 'can fairly claim to be
the best and indeed the only critical
edition that we yet have of all the works
of Buckingham' (*The Correspondence of
Thomas Percy & Thomas Warton*, ed.
M. G. Robinson and Leah Dennis, Baton
Rouge, Louisiana, 1951, p. 165).
4. HW's 'Life of Sir Thomas Wyat, the
elder' was printed as the introduction to
his *Miscellaneous Antiquities*, Number 2,

of miscellaneous papers⁵ that I published several years ago, your Lordship is welcome to use, if you should give any preface; and you know to be sure that there are besides his *Defense,* many of his letters in the Museum.⁶

I shall send the three books to my house in Berkeley Square on Wednesday, with orders to be delivered to anybody your Lordship shall please to commission to call for them.

I have the honour to be with great respect,

My Lord,
    Your Lordship's
        most obedient humble servant

ORFORD

Strawberry Hill, 1772, pp. 4–20, which contained 'Sir Thomas Wyat's Defence, after the Indictment and Evidence,' printed from Thomas Gray's transcript of BM Harl. MS 78, No. 7 (*Catalogue of the Harleian Collection of Manuscripts . . . in the British Museum*, 1759, vol. I, item 78, nos 6, 7; GRAY ii. 116 and n. 62). Percy wrote to Richard Farmer 25 Jan. 1773, 'Pray have you seen Mr Walpole's New Numbers, published at Strawberry Hill. His 2d No., luckily for me, contains a long account of Sr Thomas Wyat' (*The Correspondence of Thomas Percy & Richard Farmer*, ed. Cleanth Brooks, Baton Rouge, Louisiana, 1946, p. 165).

5. *Miscellaneous Antiquities*, Strawberry Hill, 1772 (see *ante* 29 July 1773, n. 2; Hazen, *SH Bibl.* 103–5). Number 1 con-

tained extracts from Sir William Segar's *Honour Military and Ciuill*, 1602; Number 2 contained Sir Thomas Wyatt's *Defence* and HW's *Life*. Since Percy had Number 2, HW offers to send him Number 1 (*post* 18 Sept. 1792 and n. 6).

6. In addition to Wyatt's *Defence* and his *Declaration* to the Privy Council (BM Harl. MS 78, Nos 5, 7), there are in the British Museum eleven letters from Wyatt, when ambassador to the Emperor, to Henry VIII and thirteen to other correspondents (*Letters and Papers, Foreign and Domestic, of the Reign of Henry VIII*, [1539] xiv pt i, pt ii, [1540] xv, *passim*; GRAY ii. 116 and n. 63; printed in Kenneth Muir, *Life and Letters of Sir Thomas Wyatt*, Liverpool, 1963).

To George Nicol,[1] Thursday 30 August 1792

Printed from the MS now WSL. First printed Toynbee, *Supp.* ii. 57–60. Extract printed in *Journal of the Printing-Office at Strawberry Hill,* ed. Paget Toynbee, 1923, pp. 51–2. The MS was in the possession of Frank T. Sabin, 172 New Bond St, London, in 1918; not further traced until acquired by WSL from Gabriel Wells in July 1932.

Strawberry Hill, Aug. 30th 1792.

Sir,

I AM exceedingly ashamed that you should for one moment have thought it necessary to make an apology for having proposed to pay me a very distinguished compliment;[2] and I am ashamed too that you should hold yourself in any light obliged to me, who am conscious of nothing more than paying respect to a gentleman so respectable in every light for character, good sense, learning, and peculiar liberality in your profession, superadded to your other virtues. As a desultory retainer to letters, my own pretensions would have been very ill founded, if I had not been sensible of such merits; and the great civilities[3] I have received from you on every opportunity, would have left me very ungrateful if I had seemed insensible to them.

Indeed, Sir, the dignity you have attained in your profession is one strong reason, amongst others, why I could not for a minute listen to the noble and disinterested proposal you was so kind as to make to me by Mr Pinkerton.[4] I would no more hear of a splendid and ornamented edition of my trifling writings, than I would dress my old, emaciated, infirm person in rich and gaudy clothes—but to issue from *your* press, Sir, *in a superb manner!*—the little blood that remains in my veins would rush up to my face if I had the vanity to harbour such a thought! *Your* press that is paying the national

1. (ca 1740–1828), bookseller to George III; HW's occasional correspondent (*ante* 27 June 1790, n. 1; BERRY i. 81 n. 28).

2. Nicol made a proposal through John Pinkerton to publish an edition of HW's works (see below).

3. See *ante* 6 July 1790 and HW's letter to Mary Berry 3 July 1790 where he mentions the Boydells and Nicolses and

'their civilities at the Shakespeare Gallery' (BERRY i. 80–1 and nn. 28, 29).

4. See *ante* 8 Aug. 1784, n. 2. HW invited Pinkerton to visit him on 13 or 14 Aug.; the visit may have been later since HW thanks him for a medal on 27 Aug., and Mary Berry thanks him for a book on 25 Aug. (CHATTERTON 316–17, 381).

debt to the mighty names and works of Shakespear[5] and Milton[6] must not tumble down to me.[7] Consider, Sir, collectors (I do not mean readers) of books, and still more, of prints would hereafter place my things magnificently printed and illustrated, next to your Shakespear and Milton—think of the scorn and ridicule that would fall on poor me, the third in such company!—nay, it would turn sour the nectar you are pouring out on our two immortal men; it would be supposed you had intended to humble them,

———et sibi consul

Ne placeat, servus curru portatur eodem.[8]

I am aware, good Sir, that humility is as often the dialect of vanity as of modesty, and therefore I will not specify what I think of my own writings; and the less, as what I am going to say, would seem to contradict my depreciation of myself.

I did some years ago, not only collect but begin to print some of my pieces, and actually did print one volume, and a third part of a second[9]—and I will tell you what occasioned that design. I learnt that a little printer had actually prepared an edition of what I have

5. In 1786 John and Josiah Boydell and George Nicol proposed to publish 'a most magnificent and accurate edition of the plays of Shakespeare in eight volumes of their largest quarto size' (*Morning Chronicle* 29 Nov. 1786). They also proposed to publish a series of prints, engraved from commissioned paintings, which would then be hung in their Shakespeare Gallery. For HW's comment on this plan see Ossory ii. 546–7 and nn. 12–14. *The Dramatic Works of Shakespeare,* 9 folio vols, 1791–1802, were printed by W. Bulmer & Co. for John and Josiah Boydell, George and W. Nicol. HW subscribed to the prints, and had two incomplete sets (11 numbers, with 55 plates); see Hazen, *Cat. of HW's Lib.,* No. 3904.

6. *The Poetical Works of John Milton, With a Life of the Author by W. Hayley,* 3 folio vols, 1794–7, was printed by W. Bulmer & Co. for J. and J. Boydell and G. Nicol.

7. 'me' is written below the line in the MS.

8.   'et sibi Consul
Ne placeat, curru servus portatur eodem'

('and lest the consul should become too
pleased with himself,
a slave is carried in the same chariot with
him')
Juvenal, *Satires* x. 41–2.

9. In his *Journal of the Printing-Office* HW wrote *sub* 24 Aug. 1768, 'Began to print an edition in quarto of all my Works'; *sub* 24 April 1769, 'Finished them [Mr Hoyland's poems]; and the printer returned to the Edition of my works'; *sub* 6 July 1787, 'Resumed printing my Works in quarto, with additions to Royal and Noble Authors.—not continued' (pp. 13, 20, 51–2). Mary Berry in her Preface to HW's *Works,* i. v–vi, wrote: 'Lord Orford so early as the year 1768 had formed the intention of printing, and soon after actually began, a quarto edition of his works, to which he purposed to add several pieces, both in prose and verse, which he had either not before published or never acknowledged as his own. A first and part of a second volume printed under his own eye at Strawberry Hill were already in a state of great forwardness.' For detailed analysis of the volumes printed see Hazen, *SH Bibl.* 88–9.

published, which was to appear the moment the breath should be out of my body, like my ghost, and justly like the ghost of some of my pieces that have long been dead and buried—I could not doubt but that in a posthumous edition some babes that have been laid to me, but were no babes of mine, would be produced as my issue; and having had ill-formed brats enough of my own that I had left to the parish, I did not wish to be thought more abandoned than I have been; and therefore chose a method of avowing my own, without being answerable for the slips of other men. Idleness, other avocations, and a good deal of indifference about productions, of the little value of which I am conscious, made me quite neglect the prosecution of my purpose; and as I am now so ancient and have so little activity left, it is not probable that I shall have either time or industry sufficient to complete my intention.[10]

I should certainly, Sir, not have troubled you with two pages on so insignificant a subject as myself, if you had not, by making that subject of some little moment to you, rendered it a duty on me to explain my reasons for totally and absolutely declining your most kind, too partial, and generous offer—and I knew not how to express my deep sense of gratitude without frankly and sincerely laying open my sentiments to you—I beg your pardon, if too diffusely.

Agree with you I most certainly do, Sir, about the *Fiends* on the Continent—*French* I will not call them, for that would confound the innocent with the guilty; and though *Devils* are sometimes styled *Fallen Angels,* that term I will as little use, as it might imply that I have thought that the French have been *Angels,* which I assure you I never did, though I have had a few friends amongst them, and one[11] whom I had the strongest reason to love—but surely even national antipathy is justifiable against a country that has produced *two massacres of Paris.*[12] For Barnave the Butcher[13] and such

10. After HW's death *The Works of Horatio Walpole, Earl of Orford,* in 5 quarto vols, edited by Mary Berry (although her father, Robert Berry, was the nominal editor), were published in June 1798 (see Hazen, *Bibl. of HW* 75–85). Between 1818 and 1825 four more vols (VI–IX) containing letters to Montagu, Cole, Hertford, and Zouch, and the *Memoires . . . of George the Second,* were issued by different publishers (ibid. 84–5).

11. Mme du Deffand.
12. HW refers to the massacre of the Swiss guards and others at the Tuileries on 10 Aug. 1792, and the massacre of the French Protestants on St Bartholomew's Day 24 Aug. 1572; see HW to Lady Ossory 18 Aug. 1792 (Ossory iii. 151–2 and nn. 1, 4) and to Robert Nares 12 Sept. 1792 (Dalrymple 218–19 and n. 3).
13. Antoine-Pierre-Joseph-Marie Barnave (1761–93), President of the National As-

wretches, I rejoice in their fall: they have profaned the sacred names
of Liberty, Justice, Humanity, and of every other virtue and drowned
them in blood; and I only dread their coming hither to enjoy real
liberty, and at the same time to endeavour to destroy it. I have no
patience with English that go to Paris—unless our Lameths[14] would
follow Dr Priestly's[15] son[16] thither.

I am, Sir, with the sincerest gratitude and regard

Your most obliged
and obedient humble servant

ORFORD

George Nicoll, Esq.

sembly, 1790, was accused of conspiracy and treason in the Legislative Assembly 15 Aug. 1792, was arrested 19 Aug., and was imprisoned until he was tried and guillotined 29 Nov. 1793 (*Dictionnaire de biographie française* v. 498–501; OSSORY iii. 159 n. 18; BERRY ii. 86–7 and nn. 7, 8).

14. The three Lameth brothers were: Alexandre-Théodore-Victor Lameth (1760–1829), Charles-Malo-François (1757–1832), Comte de Lameth, and Théodore (1756–1854), Comte de Lameth, all of whom were deputies to the National Assembly but were forced to flee after defending the King (see CONWAY iii. 486–7 and n. 14; BERRY i. 345 and n. 7; OSSORY iii. 159 and n. 19). On 15 Aug. 1792 Alexandre and Charles and others were accused of treason in the Legislative Assembly (ibid.).

15. Joseph Priestley (1733–1804), scientist and theologian, whose *Letters to the Right Honourable Edmund Burke*, Jan. 1791, and other statements favouring the principles of the French Revolution had led to the burning of his house by rioters in Birmingham on 14 July 1791 (BERRY i. 314–15 and nn. 14, 15). In Aug. 1792 he was made a citizen of France and in Sept. was elected a member of the National Convention by the Departments of Orne and Rhône-et-Loire; he declined the latter in a letter to the National Assembly (see his *Works*, xxv. 118, 131; F. W. Gibbs, *Joseph Priestley*, 1965, pp.

216–17; J. T. Rutt, *Life and Correspondence of Joseph Priestley*, 1832, ii. 183–4, 190–1).

16. William Priestley (b. between 1769 and 1773, d. before 1835), 2d son of Joseph Priestley, went to Paris in 1791 to seek a position there with the help of Comte Antoine Français (known as Français de Nantes), and the Duc de la Rochefoucauld d'Anville (Joseph Priestley, *Memoirs of Dr Joseph Priestley, to the Year 1795 . . . With a Continuation . . . By his Son*, 1806–7, i. 71, 133–4, 147; Gibbs, op. cit. 212; NBG *sub* Français. On 8 June 1792 William appeared before the National Assembly and was naturalized as a French citizen; 'M. François, of Nantes, who introduced Mr Priestley, made a long speech in praise of the abilities of Dr Priestley and his son' (*Daily Adv.* 15 June 1792; *London Chronicle* 12–14 June 1792, lxxi. 564; GM 1792, lxii pt ii. 657). Dr Priestley wrote to William Russell 22 June, 'My first account of the business at Paris was from the public papers. I had no expectation of any such thing; but if it had been my own wish and procurement, what harm was there in it? This country is not likely to be a desirable situation for any child of mine, and therefore it is natural for me to look for a settlement for them elsewhere' (Rutt, op. cit. ii. 185; see also Gibbs, op. cit. 214–15).

To George Nicol, Sunday 12 September 1792

Printed from the MS now WSL. First printed, Toynbee *Supp.* ii. 61–2. The MS is untraced until *penes* Frank T. Sabin, 172 New Bond St, London, in 1918; acquired by WSL from Sabin in Dec. 1928.

Address: To Mr George Nicol, in Pall Mall, London. *Franked:* Isleworth September the twelfth 1792. Free, Orford. *Postmark:* SE 13 92.

Strawberry Hill, Sept. 12th 1792.

Sir,

I OWE you very many thanks for the beautiful heads of Holbein, and the as beautiful letterpress.[1] I will take great care of both, till you are ready to exchange the former.

I am not less obliged to you for the very ingenious pamphlet;[2] it is full of wit, and though justly severe, extremely delicate and genteel, and must hurt the more from the modesty and civility of the author, who has certainly shown himself—

non impar congressus Achilli.[3]

I wish with so poignant a pen he would attack the Jacobins on *this* side of the Channel—but I do not desire the same command of temper, the same moderation; one cannot combat hyænas in sheep's clothing. I confess the horror I have felt on the late massacres[4]

1. *Imitations of Original Drawings by Hans Holbein in the Collection of His Majesty for the Portraits of Illustrious Persons of the Court of Henry VIII. With Biographical Tracts,* 1792–1800; published by John Chamberlaine (1745–1812), Keeper of the King's drawings and medals. The engravings were by Francesco Bartolozzi (1727–1815), the letterpress printed by William Bulmer (1757–1830). HW had Nos 1–9 (out of 14 numbers) and an extra copy of No. 1 (Hazen, *Cat. of HW's Lib.,* No. 3500). In a codicil to his will HW left 25 guineas to Chamberlaine to pay for the heads already received (see SELWYN 371). In the Introduction, Chamberlaine thanks HW for 'several communications, and for the trouble he took in concerting, with Mr Nicol, the plan of this publication.' Lodge acknowledges HW in GM 1800, lxx pt ii. 916, for reading the proofs and supplying 'two or three facts.'

2. Apparently Robert Nares's *Principles of Government Deduced from Reason, Supported by English Experience, and Opposed to French Errors,* 1792 (GM 1792, lxii pt i. 550), on which HW comments in his letter of 12 Sept. to Nares (DALRYMPLE 220–1). Nares had visited HW at SH on 30 Aug. (ibid. 218 and 'Book of Visitors,' BERRY ii. 242).

3. 'Infelix puer atque impar congressus Achilli'
('Unhappy boy, and ill-matched in conflict with Achilles')
Virgil, Æneid, i. 475.

4. The 'Journées de Septembre,' 2–3 Sept., when the estimated number of people massacred was from 4000 to 12,000, according to the *London Chronicle* 6–8, 8–11 Sept., lxxii. 239, 246; later reports place the number around 1400 (see OSSORY iii. 160 n. 2 and DALRYMPLE 219 and n. 5).

shocked me so much, that I could think and speak on nothing else, which prevented my thanking you sooner. Too much industry cannot be used by all friends to humanity, to spread horror for such atrocious deeds, while it is fresh, especially on the common people; for though every feeling breast must shudder, there are so many agents of the Parisian monsters in this country,[5] who are endeavouring to propagate their bloody doctrines in alehouses and among the populace, that if they are not strictly watched, mischief may arise even in this good-natured island—indeed in no other country but France did I ever hear of *three* St Bartlemis![6] Adieu! Sir I am

Your ever obliged humble servant

Orford

To the Earl of Lisburne,[1] Monday 17 September 1792

Printed from a photostat of the MS now in the British Museum (Egerton MS 2137, f. 121). First printed, Toynbee xv. 145–7. The MS is untraced until acquired by the British Museum in 1871.

Endorsed in an unidentified hand: 17 Sept. 1792. Ld Orford.

Strawberry Hill, Sept. 17th 1792.

My Lord,

WITH the great respect I have had for your Lordship ever since I had the honour of your acquaintance, I must be much vexed, and indeed am much surprised that Mrs Keppel[2] forgot to repeat exactly the words I said to her when she delivered your Lordship's commands to me. I told her directly that I had offered the refusal of my burgage-tenures at Ashurton[3] to Mr Trefusis,[4] and therefore must

---

5. See HW to William Beloe 24 Sept. 1792, Dalrymple 223–4.
6. See *ante* 30 Aug. 1792, n. 12.

---

1. Hon. Wilmot Vaughan (ca 1730–1800), 4th Vct Lisburne, 1766, cr. (1776) E. of Lisburne; M.P. His seat was Mamhead House, Devon.
2. Laura Walpole (ca 1734–1813), m. (1758) Hon. Frederick Keppel, Bp of Exeter, 1762, Dean of Windsor, 1765; HW's niece.

3. Ashburton, in Devonshire, where some property owned by Margaret Rolle, Lady Orford, was inherited by her son George, 3d E. of Orford, from whom HW inherited the burgage-tenures (Ossory iii. 184 and n. 12; Namier and Brooke i. 249–50). The entailed estates in Devonshire which were inherited by the 3d E. of Orford from his mother descended to the Trefusis family.
4. Robert George William Trefusis (1764–97), summoned to the House of

give him the preference. Mrs Keppel, with the laudable zeal which
I know she has for your Lordship and your family, immediately
asked if I would promise your Lordship the next refusal, if I should
not agree with Mr Trefusis—I replied, 'My dear Madam, I do not
love to make promises; but I will tell you one thing: whoever pur-
chases my burgage-tenures, will buy them dear, for I have so little
left to me of the possessions of my family, that I am determined to
make the most I can of the outlying parts that are unconnected with
my estate in Norfolk.'⁵

This, if not the very words, was the precise substance of my answer to Mrs Keppel, which I concluded she had reported to your
Lordship. Mr Trefusis did accept my offer, and my agent⁶ is actually
gone into Devonshire to negotiate the sale with him.

I must repeat my concern that it is not in my power to oblige
your Lordship as I should have been happy to have done—I have
not the slightest acquaintance with Mr Trefusis, nor ever saw him;
but his becoming heir to my nephew in Devonshire naturally pointed
him out to me as the person who would wish to enjoy the rest of the
property there; and my own interest suggested that he would thence

Lords as Lord Clinton, 1794; he was a
descendant of Bridget (Rolle) Trefusis
(1648–1721), sister of Samuel Rolle (d.
1719) who was the maternal grandfather
of George, 3d E. of Orford (GEC iii. 321).

5. See Ossory iii. 145, 184.

6. Apparently Robert Blake, who was
HW's legal representative in the settlement of Lord Orford's will (see *ante* 3
Jan. 1792, n. 2). A paper in Anthony
Hamond's hand written ca 1 Sept. 1792
reports, 'On Tuesday the 28th of August
1792 Mr Cony's clerk received a letter
from young Mr Blake informing him that
there was to be a meeting of the executors
at Houghton on the Friday following
[31 Aug.]. I told him I was much surprised
as I had heard nothing of it and therefore desired him to write to Mr Blake to
let him know I thought it better for him
not to come at this time. Mr Cony was
then at Cromer and Mr Fountaine from
home. When I returned home in the
evening I found a letter from Mr Blake
and on the Thursday he came down; on
the Friday I received a letter from him.
I went immediately to Houghton where I
met Mr Mackreth, Mr Lucas, Mr Blake
Junr but as Mr Fountaine was not come
home but expected in the evening I told
them I did not mean to stay but would
go to Mr Fountaine and come with him
in the morning which we did. Mrs Sheene
being there we executed the deed and we
gave Messrs Couts & Co. power to buy
into the four percents with Mrs Sheene's
money. . . . Mr Blake is to let us know
whether Lord Orford will take the furniture [at Houghton] and it is to be
considered by whom it is to be appraised.
We made some resolutions and looked
over some of the London bills and the
West Country account which is very far
from being clear to me. We agreed to
meet again on the 29th October and
ordered all bills under ten pounds to be
paid likewise that the funeral and other
expenses incurred by us should first be
paid' (Hamond MS). There are two letters from Blake to Hamond 11, 27 Sept.
1792, but they do not mention the
Devonshire property.

give the best price; though there is a circumstance,[7] not necessary to trouble your Lordship with, which may occasion my making some abatement to him, which I should not allow to any other person.

This is speaking very frankly, my Lord, but I scorn disguise, and having no reason to be ashamed of my intentions, which are strictly just, it would be unbecoming my respect for your Lordship, and unbecoming myself, to conceal anything in this affair, in which you might think hereafter that I had been wanting to you or to my own sincerity and plain dealing.

I have the honour to be with the highest esteem,

> My Lord,
> Your Lordship's
> Most obedient humble servant

> ORFORD

To the Earl of Lisburne.

To Bishop Percy, Tuesday 18 September 1792

Printed from the MS now wsl. First printed, Nichols, *Lit. Illus.* viii. 290–3. Reprinted, Cunningham ix. 494–6 (verses omitted); Toynbee xv. 147–50. The MS was acquired by John Bowyer Nichols (1779–1863) between 1831 and 1848, and passed upon his death to his son John Gough Nichols (1806–1873); sold Sotheby's 18 Nov. 1929 (John Gough Nichols Sale), lot 236, to Francis Edwards, Ltd; acquired by wsl in Sept. 1932 from Walter T. Spencer.

Strawberry Hill, Sept. 18, 1792.

IT WAS not, I assure your Lordship, from any idleness or want of attention to the intended publications,[1] with specimens of which you was pleased to entrust me, that I did not contribute any hints or information: but I have formerly scribbled so much on the subjects in question,[2] and have of late been so much involved, since my

7. Not explained.

1. Printed sheets of Percy's editions of the works of Henry Howard, Earl of Surrey, and of George Villiers, 2d Duke of Buckingham, which Percy had sent to

HW 11 Aug.; see *ante* 11 Aug. 1792 and nn. 1, 2.

2. Both Surrey and Buckingham are included in HW's *Royal and Noble Authors;* see *Works* i. 299–306, 416–20. Also HW wrote an 'Advertisement' to *A Cata-*

nephew's death,[3] in much more disagreeable business, that I had not only exhausted what I knew, but have had no time to collect new materials, except one single article, which I will mention before I conclude this letter.

With regard to Sir Thomas Wyat's dispatches, I cannot satisfy your Lordship whether there are more than four in the Museum.[4] It was from Mr Gray's transcript that I published Sir Thomas's defence—at this distance of time I cannot recollect whether he copied the letters too.[5]

Give me leave to set your Lordship right about my *Miscellaneous Antiquities.* I never published but *two* numbers:[6] in the second (which you tell me, you have, my Lord)[7] is all I know or could recover relative to Sir Thomas, and consequently I never engaged to say more of him. The first number shall be at your Lordship's service when you come to town.

I am much obliged and gladly accept, my Lord, your kind offer of sending me at your return to Dromore a copy of the title-page of the Countess of Northumberland's[8] volume of prayers,[9] of which I never heard before. My friend Lady Suffolk,[10] her niece by marriage, has

logue of the Curious Collection of Pictures of George Villiers, Duke of Buckingham, 1758, published by William Bathoe (*Works* i. 240–1; GRAY i. 27–8 and n. 183). For HW's life of Sir Thomas Wyatt see *ante* 20 Aug. 1792, n. 4; COLE i. 255, 261–2.

3. George Walpole, 3d E. of Orford, d. 5 Dec. 1791, and his executors were in the process of settling his estate (*ante* 29 Dec. 1791 and nn. 9, 10).

4. For Wyatt's letters to Henry VIII and others see *ante* 20 Aug. 1792, n. 6.

5. In 1760 Gray made a transcript of MS Harl. 78, No. 7, which he described in his letter to Thomas Wharton 18 Sept. 1759 as 'Sr Tho: Wyat's Defence at his Tryal, when accused by Bp Bonner of high-treason' (*Correspondence of Thomas Gray*, ed. Paget Toynbee and Leonard Whibley, Oxford, 1935, ii. 642); he also copied 'four long letters of his to the King' (Gray to HW 2 Sept. 1760, GRAY ii. 116). HW published the *Defence* but not the letters (see *ante* 20 Aug. 1792, n. 4).

6. See *ante* 20 Aug. 1792, n. 5. No. 1 was printed 22–28 June 1772; No. 2, 21 Sept.–10 Dec. 1772; each printing was of 525 copies, and both numbers were pub-

lished simultaneously by John Bell 1 Jan. 1773 (*ante* 29 July 1773, n. 2; Hazen, *SH Bibl.* 103). John Pinkerton in *Walpoliana* [1799], i. 65–7, printed a list of items which HW had planned to publish, but HW discontinued the series because of disappointing sales (MASON i. 66). In the *Public Adv.* 24 June 1773 they were advertised with the note, 'These Tracts were by mistake advertised to come out monthly, which was never intended.'

7. Apparently in a missing letter. Percy acquired *Miscellaneous Antiquities* No. 2 in Jan. 1773; see *ante* 20 Aug. 1792, n. 4.

8. Lady Elizabeth Howard (ca 1623–1705), 2d dau. of the 2d E. of Suffolk, m. (1642) as 2d wife, Algernon Percy (1602–68), 4th E. of Northumberland, 1632.

9. *Meditations and Prayers to be used before, at, and after the Receiving of the Holy Sacrament of the Lord's Supper,* 1682, which Percy recommended including in HW's *Royal and Noble Authors* (see *post* 15 Oct. 1793; BERRY ii. 32 and n. 18).

10. Henrietta Hobart (ca 1688–1767), m. 1 (1706) Charles Howard (1675–1733), 9th E. of Suffolk, 1731; m. 2 (1735) Hon. George Berkeley (d. 1746); mistress of

talked to me of her, having on that alliance visited her.[11] She then lived in the house now White's at the upper end of St James's Street,[12] and was the last who kept up the ceremonious state of the old peerage: when she went out to visit, a footman bareheaded walked on each side of her coach, and a second coach with her women attended her.[13] I think too that Lady Suffolk told me that her daughter-in-law the Duchess of Somerset[14] never sat down before her without her leave to do so. I suppose old Duke Charles[15] had imbibed a good quantity of his stately pride in such a school.

Thank you much, my Lord, for taking the trouble to detail the account of Fuller's[16] pictures of the escape of Charles the Second.[17]

George II; HW's neighbour at Marble Hill. See HW's description of her in *Reminiscences Written by Mr Horace Walpole in 1788*, ed. Paget Toynbee, Oxford, 1924, pp. 65–7, 101–2. Charles, 9th E. of Suffolk, was the youngest son of Henry, 5th E. of Suffolk, who was Lady Elizabeth Howard's brother; therefore 'niece by marriage' is correct.

11. HW in his *Reminiscences* (p. 126) says that Lady Suffolk saw the Countess of Northumberland 'particularly at visits to Gunnersbury,' then a seat of the E. of Suffolk.

12. Nos 37 and 38 on the east side of St James's Street (H. B. Wheatley, *London Past and Present*, 1891, ii. 302–3). White's Club, also called Arthur's, in 1755 moved to 'the great house in St James's Street,' which Robert Arthur purchased from its owner, Sir Whistler Webster (W. B. Boulton, *The History of White's*, 1892, i. 116 and illustration on facing page; for illustrations of the earlier premises of White's see ibid. facing pp. 17, 24). When the Countess of Northumberland lived there, it was called Suffolk House (see Gerald Brenan, *A History of the House of Percy*, ed. W. A. Lindsay, 1902, ii. 317–18).

13. HW relates this anecdote in his *Reminiscences*, pp. 126–7. It is repeated in Brenan, op. cit. ii. 318, citing *State Papers (Domestic), Charles II*.

14. Lady Elizabeth Percy (1667–1722), dau. and heiress of Joceline Percy, 5th E. of Northumberland, was the granddaughter of the Dowager Countess of Northumberland. See *ante* 14 April 1764,

n. 13; Brenan, op. cit. ii. 316–17 and genealogical table facing p. 180.

15. Charles Seymour (1662–1748), 6th D. of Somerset, 1678; K.G.; known as 'the proud Duke' (see *ante* 14 April 1764, n. 14; MANN iv. 18).

16. Isaac Fuller (1606–72), painter, who painted portraits (many of which have survived), an altar-piece at Magdalen College and an altar-cloth at Wadham College in Oxford, and decorative murals, mainly in taverns, in London. HW includes him in *Anecdotes of Painting*, iii. 4–7; see also Vertue Note Books I, *Walpole Society*, 1929–1930, xviii. 101–2, 105, 135; Thieme and Becker xii. 581; David Piper, *Catalogue of Seventeenth-Century Portraits in the National Portrait Gallery*, Cambridge, 1963, pp. 131–2, 275). HW owned Fuller's portraits of Edward Pierce (or Pearce) (d. 1658), the sculptor, and of John Ogilby (1600–76), the poet (sold SH xx. 111, xxi. 14; 'Des: of SH,' *Works* ii. 506).

17. HW writes in *Anecdotes of Painting*, iii. 6: 'He painted five very large pictures, the history of the king's escape after the battle of Worcester [3 Sept. 1651]; they cost a great sum, but were little esteemed.' These five paintings, on wood, 'representing in full size the principal persons concerned in concealing the king at Boscobel, and in promoting his escape from thence' are described in GM 1809, lxxix pt i. 291–2. They were presented to the Parliament of Ireland and were hung in the Parliament House in Dublin for many years; they were discovered later in a state of neglect by the 2d Earl of

I have some imperfect recollection of having heard that they are in Lord Clanbrassil's[18] possession, and am glad they are so well preserved. Surely, my Lord, so entertaining and informing a letter[19] was too generous to be in want of an apology. To make some sort of return, I can acquaint your Lordship, that in Dr Harrington's very precious publication, called *Nugæ Antiquæ*,[20] there is a sweet poem written by the *Viscount* Rochford[21] (whom the Doctor by mistake calls *Earl,* and does not seem to know was) brother of Anne Boleyn. The composition is so easy and so approaching to the refinement of modern poetry, that I found no difficulty of turning it, with few alterations, into the style of the present age, as may be seen by comparing them. This was done on its first appearance,[22] and I had laid it aside, reserving it for a second edition of my *Noble Authors,*[23] if I should ever produce one, which now at my very advanced age is not mighty likely;[24] and therefore if your Lordship should think proper to add the original, as it deserves, to Lord Surry's poems,[25] I

Clanbrassill (see below, n. 18), who had them repaired and removed to his seat at Tollymore Park, co. Down (GM loc. cit.; Alexander Chalmers, *The General Biographical Dictionary,* new edn, 1812–17, xv. 166–7).

18. James Hamilton (1730–98), 2d E. of Clanbrassill, 1758; M.P. After his death his seat at Tollymore Park, where the paintings hung, was inherited by his sister's son, Robert Jocelyn (1756–1820), 2d E. of Roden, 1797 (GM loc. cit.; GEC).

19. Missing.

20. *Nugæ antiquæ,* vol. I, a collection of papers chiefly relating to Sir John Harington (ante 28 Dec. 1782, n. 25), was published anonymously in 1769; vol. II, 1775, gives the name of the editor, Henry Harington (ca 1755–91), a descendant of Sir John Harington (MASON i. 191 n. 7; *Tottel's Miscellany (1557–1587),* ed. H. E. Rollins, Cambridge, 1928–9, ii. 90–1). HW apparently had seen these two volumes of 1769 and 1775, but the two sets recorded in his library are of the 3-vol. 2d edition, 1779 (Hazen, *Cat. of HW's Lib.,* Nos 411, 3814).

21. George Boleyn (d. 1536), styled Vct Rochford, brother of Queen Anne Boleyn, cr. (before 13 July 1530) Lord Rochford (GEC x. 140–2). The madrigal attributed to him by Harington (*Nugæ antiquæ,*

1775, ii. 252–3) is 'My lute, awake,' first printed in Tottel's *Miscellany,* and now generally believed to be by Sir Thomas Wyatt (Rollins, op. cit. ii. 83, 91–2, 189; MASON i. 191 n. 8).

22. HW wrote to Mason 14 April 1775, 'I have dipped into the second volume of *Nugæ antiquæ,* and was lucky there too, finding a madrigal, not at all despicable, by the Viscount Rochford' (ibid. i. 191).

23. In *Royal and Noble Authors,* SH, 1758, i. 72–5, HW included an account of Vct Rochford although 'none of his works are come down to us.' In July 1787 HW was printing his *Works* in quarto 'with additions to *Royal and Noble Authors*' (Hazen, *SH Bibl.* 88–9, 135). In the supplementary material on Lord Rochford HW printed his modernized version of 'Awake, my lute' (*Works* i. 528–9).

24. The work was reprinted in London 1758 (dated 1759), Dublin 1759, Edinburgh 1792, Edinburgh 1796, and London 1796 during HW's lifetime (Hazen, *SH Bibl.,* 1973, pp. xi, 36). But the additions to *Royal and Noble Authors* were first printed in 1787 for *Works,* vol. I (see above, n. 23).

25. Percy had used the Harington MSS, which were in the possession of Dr Henry Harington (1727–1816), M.D., of Bath, in 1775, 1791, and 1792; the first volume of

should have no objection to your giving my version too; not that it would do me any honour, but as it would prove how a poet of taste and with a good ear could anticipate the elegance of a more polished age, though he could not work miracles, as some who are no conjurers themselves, believe Rowley did,[26] even though nobody knows that Rowley ever existed. I enclose the verses, and have the honour of being

Your Lordship's
Most respectful and
most obedient humble servant

ORFORD

PS. I have made a mistake, for I this moment recollect that the ancient Countess of Northumberland was second wife and widow of the Lord Admiral Algernon,[27] and consequently not mother-in-law, but grandmother-in-law of the Duke of Somerset.[28]

I am not sure that Lord Rochford's verses were in the first edition of the *Nugæ*,[29] which I have not here; I rather think not. I know the pages of the two editions are not the same.

[Enclosure][30]

Verses (a little modernized) by G. Boleyn Viscount Rochford
from Dr Harrington's *Nugæ Antiquæ*, vol. II. p. 252.

Awake, my Lute, perform the last
And only service we will waste;
Repeat the strain in sighs begun:

Percy's edition of Surrey is a reprint of Tottel's *Miscellany*, which included 'My lute, awake' (see *The Correspondence of Thomas Percy & Richard Farmer*, ed. Cleanth Brooks, Baton Rouge, Louisiana, 1946, pp. 182–3; Rollins, op. cit. ii. 45–6, 90–1). HW's copy of *Songes and Sonettes*, 4th edn, 1559 (Hazen, *Cat. of HW's Lib.* No. 1920), contains many marginal notes which are emendations from a later edition (Rollins, op. cit. ii. 25–6, 100–1).

26. HW refers to the numerous essays in the controversy over the authenticity of the poems ascribed to Thomas Rowley; for HW's collection of these pieces see CHATTERTON, Appendix 1. See also HW to Percy *ante* 11 Jan. 1779.

27. Algernon Percy (1602–68), 4th E. of Northumberland, 1632; Lord High Admiral of England, 1638; appointed by the House of Lords High Admiral, 1643; he m. 1 Anne Cecil (1612–37), m. 2 (1642) Elizabeth Howard (ca 1623–1705).

28. See above, n. 14. HW in his *Reminiscences* (p. 126) says that the Countess of Northumberland 'lived to the age (Lady Suffolk thinks) of 93, Collins says 97,' but GEC says that she died aged 82.

29. They were in vol. II; see above, n. 22.

30. The verses are in Thomas Kirgate's hand.

And when the vocal moment's past,
  Be still, my Lute, for I have done.

Is music heard, where ear is none?
Can crayons grave on marble stone?
  My notes may pierce her heart as soon!
Should we then sigh, or sing, or moan?
  No, no, my Lute, we must have done.

The rock unmov'd when ocean raves
As soon shall yield to dashing waves,
  As Juliet by my suit be won:
My vows she scorns, *thy* soothing braves;
  Then pray, sweet Lute, let us have done.

Yet Venus shall assert her reign,
Proud Nymph, and punish thy disdain;
  Thro' that cold breast a flame shall run,
And me revenge some other swain,
  Although my Lute and I have done.

Sad in thy turn, the live-long hour
Of solemn night shall hear thee pour
  Thy plaintive descant to the moon;
While thy fair face's fading flow'r
  Shall touch me not, for I have done.

Then Juliet shall perhaps repent
Of youth unprofitably spent,
  And sigh in vain o'er moments gone;
And finding beauty was but lent,
  Shall weep its scorn as I have done.

Then cease, my Lute; be this the last
And only service we will waste,
  Here end my love as it begun:
Be from my heart her name eras'd,
  As from thy strings when thou hast done.

To Joseph Cooper Walker,
Thursday 20 September 1792

Printed from Toynbee xv. 450–1. First printed in *Walford's Antiquarian: A Magazine and Bibliographical Review,* 1885, viii. 277; reprinted, Toynbee xv. 450–1. The MS is untraced until sold Sotheby's 20 Dec. 1877 (Collection of Autograph Letters Sale), lot 51 (with six other letters from HW to Walker, 1787–92), to Naylor; *penes* Dr H. T. Scott in 1905; not further traced.

Dated by the frank.[1]

Address: Joseph Cooper Walker, Esq., at Holyland Coffee House, in the Strand, London. *Franked:* Isleworth, September the twentieth, 1792. Orford.

LORD ORFORD did receive the favour of Mr Walker's letter[2] from Rome, and did answer it to Paris.[3] He now sends Mr Walker a ticket[4] as desired, and is very sorry he shall not be at home himself, as he is going to General Conway's[5] for some days; nor could give the ticket for sooner than Tuesday,[6] Sunday and Monday being already engaged; and Mr Walker will see by the rules[7] how strictly Lord O. is forced to adhere to them.

---

1. For this type of franking see DALRYMPLE 240 n. 1, OSSORY iii. 164, CONWAY iii. 491.

2. Missing; mentioned *ante* 4 Aug. 1792.

3. *Ante* 4 Aug. 1792.

4. For visiting SH; 'Mr Joseph Cooper Walker of Dublin' is listed in HW's 'Book of Visitors' (BERRY ii. 242) as coming to SH on 25 Sept. 1792.

5. HW wrote to William Beloc from SH 24 Sept., 'I am just going to General Conway's [Park Place] for a few days' (DALRYMPLE 225). He returned to SH by 30 Sept. (HW to Hamilton 30 Sept. 1792, CHUTE 443).

6. Tuesday 25 Sept.; there are no entries in the 'Book of Visitors' for Sunday and Monday.

7. For a copy of the printed Rules see Hazen, *SH Bibl.* 226, 275.

To the HON. FREDERICK NORTH,[1]
Thursday 4 October 1792

Printed for the first time from a photostat of the MS now in the Huntington Library. The MS is untraced until offered by Quaritch, Cat. No. 434 (1930), lot 301 (loosely inserted in a copy of the SH Sale Catalogue of 1842); later acquired by the Huntington Library.

Dated 'Thursd. Oct. 4th' and signed 'Orford'; the only Thursday, Oct. 4th between 1791, when HW became E. of Orford, and 1797 was in 1792.

Address (pasted on the MS, cut down): The Honourable Frederic North at Bushy Park.

Endorsed by North: Orig. letter of my deceased friend the Hon. Horace Walpole after he became Earl of Orford, at the age of 80. F. N.

Thursday, Oct. 4th.

Dear Sir,

YOU have most kindly prevented me,[2] as I did not know you was returned to Bushy;[3] and unluckily, as I was gone to London.[4] I am still unfortunate, for though very impatient for the honour of seeing you, I have company in the house that detains me a little,[5] but I will make myself amends as soon as I can—though without intending to forget that you are fifty years younger, and consequently ought not to be too much troubled

With your most obedient servant

ORFORD

1. Hon. Frederick North (1766–1827), brother of the 3d and 4th Earls of Guilford; 5th E. of Guilford, 1817; M.P. Banbury 1792–4. Hannah More wrote in May 1789, 'I sat two hours in the evening with Mr Walpole, who had a pleasant little party. Among others, Frederick North, a very agreeable and accomplished young man: so learned, so pleasant, and with so fine a taste' (William Roberts, *Memoirs of the Life and Correspondence of Mrs Hannah More*, 1834, ii. 157).

2. North's letter is missing.

3. Bushey House, Middlesex, Lady North's house as Ranger of Bushey Park 1771–97 (OSSORY i. 156, n. 40). Her

husband, the 2d E. of Guilford, had died 5 Aug. 1792, and on 4 Oct. her eldest son, 'the Earl of Guilford was introduced to the King for the first time since his coming to the title' (*London Chronicle* 2–4 Oct. 1792, lxxi. 323).

4. HW went to Park Place 24 Sept. 'for a few days' and returned to SH by 30 Sept. (*ante* 20 Sept. 1792, n. 5; BERRY ii. 242). He may have gone to London 1–3 Oct.

5. HW's company may have been Joseph Farington, the painter, for whom HW wrote a letter of recommendation, 4 Oct., to Lord Harcourt (see CHUTE 542).

To UNKNOWN, Thursday 8 November 1792

Printed for the first time from the MS fragment now WSL. The MS is untraced until sold Sotheby's 18 June 1979 (Autograph Letters, Literary Manuscripts and Historical Documents Sale), lot 23 (in a small miscellaneous collection of autograph letters), to John Wilson (Autographs) Ltd; acquired from Wilson by WSL, August 1979.

The MS fragment consists of two separate portions, both mounted on a leaf from an old album: the upper portion contains the dateline and salutation, and the lower portion contains part of the last sentence, the closing, and the signature. *Endorsed in an unidentified hand:* Horace Walpole Earl of Orford.

Strawberry Hill, Nov. 8, 1792.

Sir,

... and show this note to him, he will pay you that sum.

I am Sir

Your obedient humble servant

ORFORD

To RICHARD GOUGH, Wednesday 14 November 1792

Printed from a copy of the MS made by John W. Ford, of Enfield Old Park, Enfield, Middlesex. First printed in Nichols, *Lit. Anec.* vi. 292. Reprinted, Toynbee xv. 163–4. The MS is untraced until sold Sotheby's 6 Aug. 1884 (Collection of Autograph Letters Sale), lot 281, to Barker; *penes* John W. Ford in 1900; not further traced.

Address: To Richard Gough Esq. at Enfield. *Franked:* Isleworth November the fourteenth 1792. Free. Orford.

Strawberry Hill, Nov. 14, 1792.

Sir,

I HAVE a portrait of Law,[1] and should not object to letting a copy of it be taken, but I doubt that could not be done, being in crayons, by Rosalba, under a glass; and any shaking being very prejudicial to crayons, I fixed the picture in one of the niches of my gallery under a network of carving, whence it cannot possibly be removed without pulling the niche to pieces.[2] The picture too being

1. John Law (1671–1729), of Lauriston; Scottish adventurer; controller-general of French finance, 1720. A pastel of Law by Rosalba Carriera (1675–1757), presumably the one at SH, was drawn by her in Nov. 1720 at Paris (see DALRYMPLE 167 n. 10). HW in 1782 offered to allow Lord Buchan to have it copied, and wrote on

12 May 1783, 'I have two or three different prints of him, and an excellent head of him in crayons by Rosalba, the best of her portraits' (ibid. 167, 180–1; 'Des. of SH,' *Works* ii. 463).

2. For this reason the copy apparently was not made in 1782–3 (DALRYMPLE 167).

3. 'The eagle found in the gardens of

placed over the famous statue of the eagle,[3] there is no getting near to it, I certainly could not venture to let a ladder be set against the statue. Indeed, as there are extant at least three prints[4] of Law, there does not seem to be another wanting.

I am sorry, Sir, I cannot give you a more satisfactory answer about Lady Wallingford.[5] I have met her at two or three places,[6] but I did not visit her, nor have the least knowledge of her husband's family,[7] nor to whom she left anything she had;[8] nor can I direct you at all where to inquire. I did not even know that there is an Earl of Banbury living.[9]

Your account, Sir, of the Cornwall monument[10] is very curious. I never met with the painter's name,[11] and thank you for it.

I am with great regard, Sir,
Your obedient humble servant,
Orford

Boccapadugli within the precinct of Caracalla's baths at Rome, in the year 1742. . . . It stands on a handsome antique sepulchral altar, adorned with eagles too' ('Des. of SH,' *Works* ii. 463; see Mann iii. 65–6 and n. 10, 122).

4. The *BM Cat. of Engraved British Portraits*, iii. 24, lists engravings by G. F. Schmidt, E. Desrochers, J. Van der Gucht, and L. Schenk, undated. The one by G. F. Schmidt from a lost painting by Hyacinthe Rigaud, ca 1719, is the only one mentioned in the London sale catalogue of HW's prints, iv. 501 (Dalrymple 180–1 and n. 12). See also David Piper, *Catalogue of Seventeenth-Century Portraits in the National Portrait Gallery 1625–1714*, Cambridge, 1963, p. 196.

5. Law's daughter, Mary Katherine Law (ca 1711–90), m. (1734) her first cousin, William Knollys (ca 1695–1740), styled Vct Wallingford (see Dalrymple 167 and n. 11).

6. HW wrote to Lord Buchan 12 May 1783 of 'Lady Wallingford his daughter, whom I see frequently at the Duchess of Montrose's' at Twickenham Park (ibid. 181).

7. After the death of the 1st E. of Banbury in 1632, Lady Wallingford's grandfather, Nicholas Knollys (or Vaux) (1631–74) claimed to be his legitimate heir, and although the House of Lords disallowed the claim, his descendants assumed the title until 1813 (ibid. 180 n. 9; GEC i. 402 n. a, 404, 407).

8. She died 14 Oct. 1790 at her house in Park Street, Grosvenor Square (GM 1790, lx pt ii. 960–1). In 1785 the Duchess of Portland had left her a legacy of £100 a year for her life (see Ossory ii. 484 n. 28).

9. Thomas Woods Knollys (1727–93), titular 7th E. of Banbury, 1776, whose father was a half-brother of Lady Wallingford's husband.

10. Gough's *Sepulchral Monuments in Great Britain*, vol. II, 1796, pt ii. *78–86*, describes the monuments of the Cornwall family in the church at Burford, Shropshire, the oldest being the tomb of Elizabeth (1384–1425), daughter of John of Gaunt, D. of Lancaster, whose second husband was Sir John Cornwall (d. 1443), cr. (1432) Bn of Fanhope and (1442) Bn of Milbroke (see also GEC v. 199–200, 254; Ossory ii. 249). Gough says that he visited the monuments 10 July 1792, and found the church restored and 'all the monuments and inscriptions cleaned and painted' at the expense of the Rev. Foller Walker Cornwall, of Delbury, Shropshire (Gough, op. cit. ii. pt ii. *78, 86*; see also Lord Liverpool and Compton Reade, *The House of Cornewall*, Hereford, 1908, pp. 169–70, 178–9).

11. Gough (op. cit. 79*–*80, *82) de-

To William Seward,[1] Friday 15 February 1793

Printed from John Martin, *A Bibliographical Catalogue of Books Privately Printed*, 1834, p. 77, where the letter was first printed from HW's MS draft laid in a copy of Brook Taylor's *Contemplatio Philosophica* (n. 3 below), in the library of the 1st Duke of Buckingham and Chandos at Stowe; for the history of this copy see Hazen, *Cat. of HW's Lib.*, No. 3830. Reprinted in John Martin, *Bibliographical Catalogue of Privately Printed Books*, 1854, p. 121.

Berkeley Square, Feb. 15, 1793.

LORD ORFORD is extremely obliged to Mr Seward for the valuable present of Mr B. Taylor's[2] Life:[3] the preface is particularly good,[4] and the account of biography of learned men admirably drawn and expressed.[5]

Lord Orford will thank Mr Seward much for a duplicate print of the head of Mr Taylor,[6] for his collection of English portraits.

---

scribes a painting of three members of the Cornwall family, on boards, which was signed 'Melchior Salaboss. Fecit, An'o Domini, 1588.'

1. William Seward (1747–99), man of letters, F.R.S., 1779, F.S.A., 1779; friend of Dr Johnson, James Boswell, Fanny Burney. Michael Lort introduced him to HW in 1779; see CHATTERTON 189 and n. 5. Seward was instrumental in persuading Sir William Young to publish Taylor's *Contemplatio* (see below, n. 4).

2. Brook Taylor (1685–1731), mathematician; LL.B. St John's College, Cambridge, 1709, LL.D., 1714; F.R.S., 1712; Secretary of the Royal Society 1714–18 (Nichols, *Lit. Anec.* i. 171–3; GM 1793, lxiii pt i. 436–9).

3. *Contemplatio Philosophica: A Posthumous Work, of the late Brook Taylor, L.L.D. F.R.S. some time Secretary of the Royal Society. To which is Prefixed A Life of the Author, by his Grandson, Sir William Young, Bart. F.R.S. A.S.S.*, printed by W. Bulmer and Co., Shakespeare Printing Office, 1793, not published. 'One hundred copies only of this work are struck off for the use of his friends' (*Monthly Review* 1793, x. 322). HW's copy is Hazen, *Cat. of HW's Lib.*, No. 3830. Brook Taylor's grandson, Sir William Young (1749–1815), 2d Bt, 1788, of Delaford Park, Bucks, M.P., edited this essay with an appendix of letters from family papers.

4. The preface, addressed to Seward and dated 1 Jan. 1793, begins: 'Three years have passed since you applied to me for an account of the life and writings of my grandfather, Brook Taylor, on a requisition having been made to you by some of the French Academy, that you would make inquiries relative to the memoirs of that able and learned mathematician' (Young, op. cit. iii).

5. In his introduction, Young states that biography should 'in delineating one learned man, personify, as it were, *learning itself* . . . in an enlightened period of

To RICHARD GOUGH, Friday 29 March 1793

Printed from a photostat of the MS in the Bodleian Library (MS Top. Gen. d.3, f. 361). First printed, Toynbee xv. 184. The MS was bequeathed by Gough to the Bodleian Library with his collections relating to British topography.

Endorsed in an unidentified hand: Ld Orford.

Berkeley Square, March 29, 1793.

Dear Sir,

THE estate at Piddletown[1] is not mine, but belongs to Lord Walpole's[2] son.[3] I never was there but in the year 1745,[4] and did not recollect that the picture[5] was there; but I asked my niece Mrs Walpole[6] about it last night, and she says it is there, and does not

its career,' but that he will 'supply little more than domestic materials' from family papers and letters (ibid. 4–5).

6. The frontispiece to *Contemplatio Philosophica* is a mezzotint of Taylor, engraved, 1714, by Richard Earlom from a painting owned by Taylor's daughter, Lady Young (*BM Cat. of Engraved British Portraits* iv. 248). A separate impression is not listed in the London sale catalogue of HW's prints.

———

1. Piddletown manor descended through the Hastings and Roy families to Samuel Rolle's first wife; by his second wife, Rolle was the father of Margaret Rolle, wife of the 2d Earl of Orford, on whose death 'his relict Margaret Countess of Orford enjoyed it [the manor] till her death in her own right; it then devolved to her only son George, third Earl of Orford, who died in 1791 a bachelor. He gave this estate and manor to his first cousin Colonel Horatio Walpole' (John Hutchins, *History and Antiquities of the County of Dorset*, 3d edn, 1861–70 [74], ii. 580, 615; MANN ix. 148 n. 6). Joseph Farington said that George Lord Orford bequeathed Piddletown manor to Martha

Turk 'and after her death to Col. Walpole,' and that since Mrs Turk predeceased Lord Orford, HW 'confirmed the bequest' to Col. Walpole (DALRYMPLE 324).

2. Horatio Walpole (1723–1809), 2d Bn Walpole of Wolterton, cr. (1806) E. of Orford, n.c.; HW's cousin.

3. Hon. Horatio Walpole (1752–1822), 2d E. of Orford, n.c., 1809; Col. of the West Norfolk militia, 1792, and in the Army, 1794.

4. There is no record of this visit.

5. A portrait of Henry Hastings (1551–1650), of Woodlands, near Horton, Dorset, 2d son of George, 4th E. of Huntingdon. Hutchins says, 'There was a whole-length portrait of Henry Hastings formerly in this house [Piddletown manor], exactly similar to that at Lord Shaftesbury's' (op. cit. ii. 615). The portrait at Shaftesbury's seat at Wimborne St Giles, Dorset, was engraved by James Bretherton and is reproduced in Hutchins, op. cit. iii. facing p. 152; see also iii. 154, 599.

6. Sophia Churchill (d. 1797), m. (1781) Hon. Horatio Walpole, 2d E. of Orford, n.c., 1809.

doubt but Mr Walpole would willingly allow it to be copied; but it is a whole length and cannot be sent to town.[7] If Mr Hutchings's[8] representative will send a person down to make a drawing of the portrait, and will apply to me, I will obtain the permission. I am with great regard, Sir,

Your obedient humble servant

ORFORD

To RICHARD GOUGH, Thursday 2 May 1793

Printed from a photostat of the MS in the Bodleian Library (MS Top. Gen. d.3, f. 362). First printed, Toynbee xv. 187. For the history of the MS see *ante* 29 March 1793.

May 2d 1793.

LORD ORFORD has the pleasure of acquainting Mr Gough that the picture of Mr Hastings[1] is arrived; and may be seen whenever Mr Gough shall happen to be in town.

7. It was sent to HW's house in Berkeley Square; see *post* 2 May 1793.

8. John Hutchins (1698–1773), topographer of Dorsetshire (*ante* 22 Sept. 1765, n. 1). The 1st edn of his *History and Antiquities of the County of Dorset*, 2 vols, folio, was published in 1774 (HW's copy is Hazen, *Cat. of HW's Lib.*, No. 4). Gough was collecting material for the 2d edn, of which vol. I appeared in 1796, vol. II in 1803, and vol. III was in print, when all the unsold copies of vols I and II, and all but one copy of vol. III were lost in the fire at the printing house of John Nichols 8 Feb. 1808. In his proposal for continuing the publication (GM 1811, lxxxi pt i. 99–100) Nichols says that 'from the great increase of materials collected with indefatigable industry by Mr Gough, it

[the new edn] contains more than double the quantity both of letterpress and plates, and may therefore be considered, in some degree, a new work.' Vol. III was published, with Gough's name as editor, in 1813; vol. IV in 1815 (DNB; BM Cat.).

1. A portrait of Henry Hastings, one copy of which was in Col. Walpole's house, Piddletown manor, and the other in Lord Shaftesbury's house, at Wimborne St Giles, Dorset (*ante* 29 March 1793, n. 5). Whether an engraving of Col. Walpole's painting was made is not known, but Bretherton's engraving of Shaftesbury's version was in John Hutchins's *History and Antiquities of the County of Dorset*, 3d edn, 1861–70 [74], iii. facing p. 152.

From JOHN SINGLETON COPLEY,[1] Tuesday 21 May 1793

Printed from the MS now WSL. First printed, Toynbee *Supp.* iii. 308. Damer-Waller; the MS was sold Sotheby's 5 Dec. 1921 (first Waller Sale), lot 111, to Maggs; offered by them, Cat. No. 433 (Christmas 1922), lot 3117; *penes* Capt. Frank L. Pleadwell, M.D., USN, of Honolulu, in 1935; acquired by WSL from Capt. Pleadwell in April 1947.

George Street, Hanover Square, May 21st 1793.

MR COPLEY presents respectful compliments to the Earl of Orford with the enclosed proposal.[2] If his Lordship shall choose to subscribe he is requested to signify his opinion relative to the situation of the picture[3] on the proposal, which Mr Copley will send for on Monday next.

Mr Copley has authority to say that the Lords who interest themselves in the picture approve of the plan and will subscribe largely to it.

1. (1737–1815), painter.
2. No record of this proposal has been found. Earlier, Edmond Malone had asked HW for information about portraits of persons whom Copley intended to represent in his painting 'Charles I Demanding in the House of Commons the Five Impeached Members' (see HW to Edmond Malone ?early 1785). This painting was in progress from 1781; it was first exhibited in May 1795 (J. D. Prown, *John Singleton Copley*, Cambridge, Mass., 1966, ii. 343–5, 347–50).
3. The picture cannot be identified firmly since Copley was working on several projects at this time.

From GEORGE GOSTLING,[1] Sunday 28 July 1793

Printed for the first time from a copy of the MS provided by the Edinburgh University Library. The MS is inserted in HW's presentation copy of Gostling's *Extracts from the Treaties between Great Britain and Other Kingdoms and States*, 1792, which was sold SH vii. 55 to Strong; offered in Strong's Catalogue, 1843, lot 621; sold Fletcher 8 April 1846 (Britton Sale, Part 4), lot 653, to Palmer; offered in Lasbury's Catalogues in 1848 and 1849; acquired by the Edinburgh University Library, ca 1850 (Hazen, *Cat. of HW's Lib.*, No. 3697).

Whitton, 28th July 1793.

M R GOSTLING presents his respectful compliments to Lord Orford, and begs leave to request his Lordship will do him the honour to accept his book of extracts from the marine treaties.[2]

1. George Gostling (ca 1745–1820), son of George Gostling (ca 1714–82), of Whitton Park (see HW to Mrs Gostling *ante* ?Aug. 1781, nn. 1, 6; GM 1820, xc pt i. 570). In the *Court and City Register* the son is listed as a Deputy Register for Doctors Commons, while the father is listed as Proctor to the Admiralty and Deputy Register of the Royal Peculiar of St Catherine's from 1769 to 1780 (1769, pp. 101–2; 1770, pp. 114–15; 1775, pp. 105–6); from 1780 on George Gostling, Jr, is listed as both a Deputy Register and as Proctor to the Admiralty (*Royal Kalendar*, 1780, pp. 107–8; *Court and City Register*, 1782–1820, *passim*). Apparently after the death of the elder George Gostling, his widow moved to a house in Twickenham, and her son George lived at Whitton Park; in 1796 he bought back the house and grounds of Whitton Place which had been sold to Sir William

Chambers (R. S. Cobbett, *Memorials of Twickenham*, 1872, pp. 174–5, 293, 388; Edward Ironside, *The History and Antiquities of Twickenham*, 1797, pp. 110–11, 143, 147, 149; Daniel Lysons, *The Environs of London*, 1792–6, iii. 578; *Supp.*, 1811, 318–19).

2. *Extracts from the Treaties between Great Britain and Other Kingdoms and States of Such Articles as Relate to the Duty and Conduct of the Commanders of His Majesty's Ships of War*, 1792. The preface, dated 29 Dec. 1792, states, 'I submit to your Lordships the following collection from the *marine treaties* of Great Britain. The last publication of this kind was in 1758: the present, besides containing many articles of the former treaties, which were inserted in that collection, contains extracts from the treaties made since that period, with the various maritime powers.'

To UNKNOWN,[1] Wednesday 25 September 1793

Printed for the first time from the MS now WSL. The MS is untraced until offered by Maggs, Cat. Nos 253 (Christmas 1909), lot 793, and 256 (1910), lot 470; sold American Art Association 4 March 1925 (William F. Gable Sale, Pt VII), lot 1043; later sold by the Walpole Gallery, New York, ?1927, to the Strawberry Hill Press, 432 West 45th St, New York, from whom WSL acquired it by exchange in January 1934.

Strawberry Hill, Sept. 25, 1793.

Sir

I HAVE received safely and in perfectly good condition a very fine present of grapes,[2] quite ripe and very highly flavoured, for which I beg leave to return you my grateful thanks.

I am but too sensible, Sir, of the truth of what you say of the reduction of the prices of wool and sheep.[3] I have felt a very considerable diminution of my rents from my Crostwick Estate,[4] which though the best of what my late nephew or his lawyers[5] were pleased to leave to me in a most scanty proportion of the estates of my family, has this year turned out very inferior to the last, and considering how unjustly it came loaded to me,[6] it is little preferable to that at Houghton.

1. Possibly 'R. Lucas, Esq. of Twickenham Common,' who d. 1816 (GM 1816, lxxxvi pt i. 277); at this time he owned Gifford Lodge (formerly Gen. Gunning's residence) and also the next house (formerly Abraham Prado's residence) which was remarkable for its vineyards (see R. S. Cobbett, *Memorials of Twickenham*, 1872, pp. 338–9; Daniel Lysons, *The Environs of London, Supp.*, 1811, p. 318).

2. Perhaps from Lucas's vineyards, formerly Prado's (n. 1 above). Prado had sent HW a huge bunch of grapes in Sept. 1774 (see OSSORY i. 207 and n. 12).

3. T. Tooke and W. Newmarch, *A History of Prices and of the State of the Circulation from 1792 to 1856* (ed. T. E. Gregory, 1928, i. 178) records 'a very general fall of prices, from the close of 1792 to the commencement of 1794. . . . there were very few commodities which were not lower at the close of 1792, and at different periods in 1793 and 1794,

than they had been at the commencement of 1792.' See also G. E. Fussell and C. Goodman, 'Eighteenth Century Estimates of British Sheep and Wool Production,' *Agricultural History*, 1930, iv. 131–51; Phyllis Deane, 'The Output of the British Woolen Industry in the Eighteenth Century,' *Journal of Economic History*, 1957, xvii. 220, 222–3.

4. HW inherited his Crostwight ('Crostwick') estates in Norfolk (mostly bought by Sir Robert Walpole ca 1720) from George, 3d E. of Orford; they are listed in HW's will (SELWYN 344). On 3 Oct. 1793 HW wrote that his steward from Crostwight came 'with accounts and a lease to be signed' (BERRY ii. 21).

5. Carlos Cony and Charles Lucas; see *ante* 29 Dec. 1791, nn. 5, 9.

6. HW's nephew had burdened these estates with mortgages which at the time of HW's will, 5 June 1793, still amounted to £13,500 and £4,000 (SELWYN 345).

I will not trouble you longer at present, Sir, especially as I am forced to write very slowly and with difficulty, having been confined to my room above six weeks with the gout in both hands and all over one arm,[7] of which I am but just recovered enough to [go] out in my coach. I hope you and your family enjoy much better health than I do or can expect at my age. I have the honour to be with great regard, Sir,

Your most obedient and obliged humble servant

ORFORD

To Bishop Percy, Tuesday 15 October 1793

Printed for the first time from the MS now wsl. The MS was tipped in a copy of *Meditations and Prayers to be used before, at, and after the Receiving of the Holy Sacrament of the Lord's Supper. By Elizabeth, late Countess of Northumberland*, 1709, in the possession of Oliver R. Barrett, Kenilworth, Ill., in September 1934; sold Parke-Bernet 8 January 1952 (Roger W. Barrett Sale), lot 282, to Brick Row for wsl, who removed the letter from the book.

Strawberry Hill, Oct. 15, 1793.

My Lord

I THANK your Lordship for the notices and anecdotes with which you have been pleased to favour me.[1] For the Countess of Northumberland's meditations,[2] they might just be mentioned, were I to reprint my catalogue of R. and N. authors[3]—yet being able to give no account of the publication, and the piece seeming so little worth notice, perhaps only sentences selected by her or her chaplain[4] for the use of her and her household, it would be telling the public

---

7. The left arm (Ossory iii. 188; Chatterton 318).

---

1. Percy's letter is missing; HW wrote of it to Mary Berry 16 Oct. 1793: 'I have had a letter from the Bishop of Dromore of seven sides of paper, the object of which was, to induce me to add to my *Noble Authors* some meditations by a foolish Countess of Northumberland, and to set me to inquire after a MS tract of

Earl Algernon: with neither of which I have complied or shall' (Berry ii. 32).

2. See *ante* 18 Sept. 1792, nn. 8, 9; Berry ii. 32 n. 18.

3. In July, 1787 HW undertook to reprint his *Catalogue of the Royal and Noble Authors* with additions for a quarto edition of his *Works*, but he did not include the Countess of Northumberland (see Hazen, *SH Bibl.* 36, 88–9).

4. Not identified.

nothing worth knowing. Indeed it may not even be *compiled* by the lady, the title-page[5] leaving it doubtful whether it means more than meditations and prayers to be used by Eliz. late Countess of N., the printing off not being finished before she died.

The anecdote relating to Mr Thynne[6] was very unfortunate for him, but though Lady N. might be the indirect cause of his death, she was a most innocent cause, and no ways reprehensible for it.[7]

I am sorry I can give your Lordship no information of either painter or engraver of the name of Baillie or Balli.[8] I do not recollect such a name, and now, unless very sure, I do not love to have recourse to my memory, which I am conscious frequently fails, and is the weaker at present, as after a sharp fit of the gout, I have been out of order for three weeks with a bilious complaint,[9] of which I cannot say I am quite recovered, and which must plead my excuse to your Lordship for the brevity of this, as from the lameness of my fingers and my weakness, I write very slowly and can write but very few lines at a time without resting.

I am equally unacquainted with the name of Shee the painter.[10]

5. The first edition of the *Meditations and Prayers* was published in 1682, long before the Countess's death in 1705; Percy apparently enclosed in his letter a copy of the title-page of the 1709 edition which reads *Meditations and Prayers to be used before, at, and after the Receiving of the Holy Sacrament of the Lord's Supper. By Elizabeth, late Countess of Northumberland* (BM Cat.; 1709 edn now WSL; see also *ante* 18 Sept. 1792).

6. Thomas Thynne (1648–82), of Longleat, Wilts, called 'Tom of Ten Thousand' because of his great wealth; M.P. Wilts 1670–82 (Foster, *Alumni Oxon., 1500–1714*, iv. 1485; DNB). In 1681 he was privately married to Lady Elizabeth Percy (1667–1722), widow of Lord Ogle and granddaughter of the Dowager Countess of Northumberland. On 12 Feb. 1682 Thynne was shot while riding in his coach down Pall Mall, by three assassins allegedly hired by Charles John, Count von Königsmarck (1659–86), who was in love with Lady Elizabeth; for anecdotes about Thynne see Gerald Brenan, *A History of the House of Percy*, 1902, ii. 379–96.

7. The Dowager Duchess of Northumberland had apparently arranged the match between her granddaughter, aged 15, and Thynne, and was in favour of the marriage. Lady Ogle immediately after the ceremony fled from London and went abroad with Lady Temple, but was rumoured to have been indirectly responsible for the crime. There were attempts to annul the marriage by a Mrs Trevor, who allegedly had a pre-contract with Thynne before his marriage. In the end, the three friends of Königsmarck were tried and executed, and Königsmarck was acquitted (Brenan, op. cit. 382–5, 393–5, 413).

8. Not identified.

9. Mrs Damer wrote Mary Berry 8 Oct. 1793, 'I find by a letter of Lord Orf[ord] to my mother, that he has had a bilious attack, and been quite ill for some days. . . . He was taken ill, I understand, last Sunday sennight [29 Sept.], but on Monday or Tuesday last, when he wrote, was sufficiently recovered to be going to take the air' (*The Berry Papers*, ed. Lewis Melville, 1914, p. 106).

10. Sir Martin Archer Shee (1769–1850), painter of portraits and historical pictures, had four portraits exhibited at the Royal Academy in 1791 and seven in 1792;

Indeed, my Lord, my age and frequent gout have numbed all the pursuits that amused me formerly—and as there is no probability of my meddling any more with the press, noble authors and painters are alike no game for me. There were not many of either breed that deserved much attention; and unless one could discover treasures of genuine merit, it is not worth while to add now and then an insignificant article.

I have the honour to be with great respect, my Lord,

Your Lordship's obliged and obedient humble servant

ORFORD

To Lady Anne North,[1] Saturday 30 November 1793

Printed from the MS now WSL. First printed, Toynbee *Supp.* iii. 341. The MS is untraced until offered by Maggs, Cat. Nos. 433 (Christmas 1922), lot 3809; 486 (Christmas 1926), lot 2437, and 513 (Christmas 1928), lot 2880; sold by them to WSL, June 1932.

Berkeley Square, Nov. 30, 1793.

LORD ORFORD cannot say how much he is obliged to the goodness of Lady Anne North for the great honour she has done him in sending him such beautiful verses,[2] which are worthy of the original. He must not presume to ask the name of the author; but being left at liberty to guess, it will add to the pleasure he has already received, if, as his wishes direct, these very fine lines prove to be the composition of Mr Frederic North.[3]

elected Associate of the Royal Academy in 1798, full member in 1800, and president in 1830; Kt, 1830 (Thieme and Becker; Strickland, op. cit. ii. 329–47; Martin A. Shee, Jr, *The Life of Sir Martin Archer Shee*, 2 vols, 1860, *passim*).

1. Hon. (after 1790, Lady) Anne North (1764–1832), m. (1798) John Baker Holroyd, cr. (1781) Bn and (1816) E. of Sheffield (BERRY i. 114 n. 11). HW wrote of her to Mary Berry 10 Sept. 1795, 'to Lady Anne I shall be supposed to be making court for a legacy, though it is

only gratitude for the large cabinet of gold and silver medals which she insisted on giving to me, and which I was so overjoyed, when authorized to send back to her' (ibid. ii. 164).

2. Probably a verse translation from the Greek (see below, n. 3). In 1791 Frederick North wrote a Pindaric ode, Αἰκατερίνῃ Εἰρηνοποιῷ, in honour of the Empress Catherine II on the occasion of the Peace of Galatz, which was published in Leipzig (BM Cat., *sub* Catherine II and Frederick North).

3. Lady Anne's brother (*ante* 4 Oct.

LADY DIANA BEAUCLERK,
AFTER SIR JOSHUA REYNOLDS

To Lady Diana Beauclerk, Monday 2 December 1793

Printed from the MS copy in Thomas Kirgate's hand, now wsl. First printed, Toynbee *Supp.* ii. 68–9. Damer-Waller; the MS copy was sold Sotheby's 5 Dec. 1921 (first Waller Sale), lot 7, to Maggs; offered by them, Cat. Nos 525 (Autumn 1929), lot 1903, and 570 (Spring 1932), lot 463; sold by Maggs to Walter T. Spencer; acquired by wsl from Spencer (with other Walpolian items) in Sept. 1932. The original letter is missing.

Endorsed by HW: To Lady Diana Beauclerc.

Berkeley Square, December 2d 1793.

I AM going to ask a favour of your Ladyship,[1] with which you will comply or refuse as you think fit. Mr Trevor,[2] our minister at Turin, has had printed at Parma a magnificent edition of three Latin poems[3] written by his father the late Lord Hampden,[4] yet

---

1792, n. 1). He was an enthusiastic student of Greek at Christ Church, Oxford, and was created D.C.L. on 5 July 1793; he had travelled in the Greek Islands, was received into the Greek church at Corfu in 1791, and later founded an Ionian university and library in Corfu and served as its chancellor 1820–7. He was an accomplished linguist and was proficient in German, French, Spanish, Italian, and Romaic, as well as Latin and Greek (see DNB; GM 1827, xcvii pt ii. 461, 648). Mary Berry wrote of him in 1808 in her journal: 'Frederick North is always entertaining to the head, but less gratifying to the heart; and in this is much inferior to his sisters, who are often quite as agreeable as himself' (*Extracts from the Journals and Correspondence of Miss Berry*, ed. Lady Theresa Lewis, 2d edn, 1866, ii. 354).

---

1. Lady Diana Beauclerk was first cousin once removed to John Trevor, 3d Vct Hampden (see below, n. 2). Thomas Trevor (1658–1730), 1st Bn Trevor, who was John Trevor's grandfather, was also the grandfather of Lady Diana's mother, Elizabeth Trevor (d. 1761), who m. (1732) Charles Spencer, 3d D. of Marlborough.

2. Hon. John Trevor (1749–1824), 3d Vct Hampden, 1824; 2d son of Robert, 1st Vct Hampden; minister to the Diet at

Ratisbon 1780–3; envoy extraordinary to Sardinia 1783–9, and envoy extraordinary and minister plenipotentiary 1789–99 (D. B. Horn, *British Diplomatic Representatives 1689–1789*, 1932, p. 127; S. T. Bindoff, E. F. Malcolm Smith, and C. K. Webster, *British Diplomatic Representatives 1789–1852*, 1934, pp. 118–19; MANN ix. 398 and n. 4; GM 1824, xciv pt ii. 465). The Berrys had visited the Trevors in Turin 2–3 Nov. 1790 and were 'much pleased with our morning entertainment, and with her and Mr Trevor's politeness to us' (*Extracts from the Journals and Correspondence of Miss Berry*, ed. Lady Theresa Lewis, 2d edn, 1866, i. 236–9).

3. *Britannia, Lathmon, Villa Bromhamensis* (*Poematia Roberti Vicecomitis de Hampden . . . curante filio Johanne Trevor*), Bodoni, Parma, 1792, folio (BM Cat.); it was dedicated to George III. There are three copies in the British Library, one printed on vellum, from the library of Marshal Junot. HW's request was apparently granted, for the book was in his library; see Hazen, *Cat. of HW's Lib.*, No. 3537.

4. The 1st Vct Hampden died 22 Aug. 1783 (see *ante* ca June 1763, n. 1; GM 1783, liii pt ii. 718). He was a scholar of classical literature and a collector of prints and drawings; elected F.R.S., 1764. His Latin poems were written between

only a few copies, of which he makes presents. Were the book to be bought, I should certainly purchase it, not only for the merit of the work, but as having had the honour of being acquainted with the author, as I have with his son the editor.[5]

Your Ladyship, who knows my shyness about receiving presents, will perhaps smile at my begging one; but in the present case I have a singular claim, which I flatter myself Mr Trevor will be so good as to allow, especially if supported by your Ladyship's mediation; for though my title to Mr Trevor's favour be very fair, I would not plead it arrogantly, but had much rather have it admitted as an obligation to me; and I shall think it a great one.

In short, Madam, being door-keeper to *the House of Noble Authors,* it is my office to admit Lord Hampden[6]—and I will not take it ill, if you tell me that since I have become one of that assembly, I have learnt to take a fee for doing my duty. Nay, tho' most contrary to your nature to do anything harsh, you shall convict me of this act of corruption, if you please, by sending this petition itself to Mr Trevor, which will save your writing many words, the only works by your hand of which you are not most liberal.[7] Nor will I load your Ladyship with more words than are necessary on this occasion, being always

Your devoted humble servant

ORFORD

1761 and 1776. He also wrote notes on Martial and a long commentary on Horace's works, which his son said 'formed his favourite amusement during several years' (William Coxe, *Memoirs of Horatio, Lord Walpole,* 3d edn, 1820, ii. 151n).

5. The only surviving correspondence between HW and the Viscounts Hampden is *ante* ca June 1763, a copy of which was preserved in HW's *Fugitive Pieces in Verse and Prose,* presented to the Prince of Orange. Robert 1st Vct Hampden had been secretary of embassy at The Hague 1736–9, under HW's uncle Horatio Walpole, and their correspondence (including a few letters from Sir Robert Walpole to Vct Hampden) is printed in Hist. MSS Comm., 14th Report, App. Pt IX (*Buck-*

inghamshire MSS), 1895, pp. 1–154; see also Coxe, op. cit. i. 404–14. HW mentions John 3d Vct Hampden and his wife in letters to Mann; see MANN ix. 398, 595.

6. HW apparently intended to include Hampden in a later edition of *Royal and Noble Authors,* but did not print any further additions to that work after 1787, when he printed at SH the first volume of his *Works* including some additions to *Royal and Noble Authors* (see Hazen, SH Bibl. 88–9).

7. Since the MS of this letter has not been found, presumably Lady Diana sent the original on to John Trevor in Turin. HW's comment suggests that she is liberal with her paintings but not with her letters.

To WILLIAM SEWARD, Thursday 6 February 1794

Printed for the first time from a photostat of the MS in Thomas Kirgate's hand in the Huntington Library. The history of the MS is not known.

Berkeley Square Feb. 6th 1794.

LORD ORFORD sends Mr Seward[1] the two pieces[2] he desired, and thanks him for the sight of the picture,[3] the subject of which he owns he should never have guessed.

To JAMES EDWARDS,[1] Friday 21 March 1794

Printed from a photostat of the MS now in the Bodleian Library (MS Montagu d. 9, f. 55). First printed, Toynbee xv. 108 (wrongly assigned to Joseph Cooper Walker and misdated 1792); date corrected, Toynbee *Supp.* iii. 324. The MS was acquired by the Bodleian Library before 1905.

Berkeley Square, March 21, 1794.

Sir,

IF MY (in every sense) weak, and extinguishing voice has added a momentary spur to Mr Roscoe's activity,[2] I may have advanced, and shall rejoice, some minutes of pleasure to myself—but I shall have done better, if by the accidental but natural effusion of my

1. See *ante* 15 Feb. 1793, n. 1.
2. Not identified. Possibly some materials for Seward's *Anecdotes of Some Distinguished Persons, Chiefly of the Present and Two Preceding Centuries*, three volumes of which appeared in 1795, one in 1796, and a supplement in 1797. HW's copy is described in Thomas Thorpe's Supplement for 1842 (lot 13130) as 4 volumes, a presentation copy to HW, with some MS notes by him (Hazen, *Cat. of HW's Lib.*, No. 821). Sir Robert Walpole is included in the *Anecdotes*, ii. 333–7. Seward was also collecting material for his *Biographiana. By the Compiler of Anecdotes of Distinguished Persons*, 2 vols, 1799, which includes an article on Sir Robert Walpole (ii. 553–9).
3. Not identified.

1. James Edwards (1757–1816), bookseller and bibliographer. In 1786 at the Duchess of Portland's sale he bought the famous Bedford Missal, now in the British Museum, described by Richard Gough in *An Account of a Rich Illuminated Missal executed for John, Duke of Bedford, Regent of France*, 1794 (HW's copy is Hazen, *Cat. of HW's Lib.*, No. 3812, now WSL). Edwards was publisher of the revised issue of the Bodoni *Castle of Otranto*, Parma, 1791, and joint publisher of HW's *Works*, 1798; HW called him 'a very ingenious bookseller, and of much taste' (CHUTE 436; DALRYMPLE 212 and n. 1; Nichols, *Lit. Illus.* iv. 881–4). The rest of HW's correspondence with Edwards is printed in DALRYMPLE *passim*.
2. William Roscoe (1753–1831) was writ-

satisfaction to you,[3] Sir, I can flatter myself, that I have anticipated the judgment of the public, and have contributed to Mr Roscoe's tasting beforehand the applause which his abilities and talents deserve.[4]

I must not say more now that you have thought my opinion worth communicating to that gentleman—what I then said, with self-interested enthusiasm, would now sound like flattery or grateful return of compliment. The simplicity of Mr Roscoe's style[5] (as far as I have seen it) and his avoidance of all affectation and pretensions, convince me that he would despise anything but genuine and merited praise.

I am Sir

Your truly much obliged humble servant

ORFORD

ing *The Life of Lorenzo de' Medici, Called the Magnificent;* the printed sheets of part of Vol. I were sent to Edwards, the publisher of the book, in the spring of 1794, and he transmitted them to HW through Mary Berry (see DALRYMPLE 249 and n. 1).

3. In his letter of 12 March 1794 to Edwards (ibid. 249) HW praises 'this most able, informing and entertaining work' and regrets that he may not see the completion of it. HW's commendation encouraged Roscoe and contributed to the warm reception of the published volumes (ibid. 258–9, 262–3, 274 n. 1).

4. The two volumes were published ca 13 Feb. 1796 (title-page of both volumes reads 1795); but Roscoe sent volume I to HW in March 1795 and volume II in Feb. 1796 (see DALRYMPLE 258, 273 and n. 1, 274). HW's copy, now WSL, has a note by Kirgate: 'Bound under the direction of Mr Edwards, Pallmall' (see Hazen, *Cat. of HW's Lib.,* No. 3703); bound in the second volume is Roscoe's presentation letter, 9 Feb. 1796, which is printed in DALRYMPLE 273–4. HW's letter of thanks for volume I, 22 March 1795 to Edwards, is printed ibid. 259.

5. HW comments on Roscoe's style in his letter of 4 April 1795 (ibid. 260–2), and calls Roscoe 'by far the best of our historians, both for beauty of style and for deep reflections' in his letter to the Rev. Mark Noble *post* 12 Jan. 1797.

To George Nicol, Thursday 8 May 1794

Printed for the first time from the MS now WSL. The MS is untraced until sold Stargardt (Marburg, Germany) 30 May 1961, lot 339, to Maggs for WSL.

May 8th 1794.

Dear Sir,

I HAVE been going to answer your letter[1] and thank you, for these two hours, and have been interrupted every minute, and now have only time to obey you for the day you desired[2]—but am sorry to tell you that your friends will see my house to disadvantage, for the small pictures and curiosities are always taken down in winter and locked up,[3] and I have been so ill and am still so weak[4] that I have not been able to unlock my cabinets and replace them, and cannot send my keys—indeed as you see I can scarce write[5]—but shall be most glad to see you when you have leisure to call, which I have much wished you would—any day except next Sunday.[6]

Yours sincerely
ORFORD

1. Missing; apparently a request for a ticket to see SH.
2. HW's 'Book of Visitors' lists '4 from Mr George Nicol' on 12 May 1794 (BERRY ii. 245).
3. Strawberry Hill was open to visitors from May 1st to October 1st (HW's 'Rules,' Hazen, *SH Bibl.* 225–7) but, as HW writes to Cole 27 Feb. 1777, 'most of the small pictures and curiosities, which are taken down and packed up in winter, are not restored to their places, till the weather is fine and I am more there' (COLE ii. 40–1). See also *ante* after 5 Dec. 1791.
4. In April HW was 'now able to begin to take air' (CHATTERTON 319), and his neighbour, John May, wrote 'a rhapsody in verse on my recovery' (BERRY ii. 96). But on 15 May HW wrote Pinkerton, 'I cannot go up and down stairs without being led by a servant' (CHATTERTON 320).
5. His handwriting is very shaky in the MS.
6. 11 May; HW had been at Strawberry Hill on 1 May, and returned to town on 3 May (BERRY ii. 99). He apparently stayed in Berkeley Square until after 15 May (CHATTERTON 320).

To Unknown,[1] Tuesday 27 May 1794

Printed from a photostat of the MS draft now in the Pierpont Morgan Library. First printed in *Extracts from the Journals and Correspondence of Miss Berry*, ed. Lady Theresa Lewis, 2d edn, 1866, ii. 40–2; reprinted, Toynbee xv. 291–3. The MS, which is unsigned and contains several corrections, seems to be a draft of a letter which perhaps was never sent. The history of the MS is not known.

May 27, 1794.

Dear Sir,

AN IDEA has arisen in my thoughts, on which I have a great desire to consult you,[2] not minutely, but in general, and this for two reasons—the first, because I have not extended or weighed the idea sufficiently myself; and the second, because the season is not yet arrived to carry the design (supposing it should be proper and practicable) into execution.

My wish is, that all who live under our present unprecedentedly happy constitution,[3] composed of King, Lords and Commons, should be grounded from their earliest youth, in such a firm attachment to that matchless system, in such undivided ardour of patriotism for that trinitarian but one composition, that no monarchic or republican doctrines, no factious or interested views, no attachment to political leaders or dictators, may ever be able to detach them from the great principles of the constitution.

1. Not identified; possibly Hon. Frederick William Hervey, later 5th E. and 1st M. of Bristol, whose political pamphlets on the excesses of the French revolution HW had praised *ante* 5, 9, and after 9 April 1792. HW also urged his friend Robert Nares to write pamphlets against the French revolutionists in Sept. 1792, and invited him to talk over 'a multitude of projections' (DALRYMPLE 220–1, 232). HW was pleased when Nares and William Beloe became the editors of the newly founded loyalist *British Critic* in June 1793 (ibid. 234–5, 238–9). Another friend, Robert Jephson, published *The Confessions of James Baptiste Couteau, Citizen of France* in both French and English in 1794, against the French revolutionary leaders (BM Cat.; Sir James Prior, *Life of Edmond Malone*, 1860, pp. 201, 210).

2. No record of this meeting has been found. Joseph Farington in his diary records that on 23 May he, Sir John Blagden, Charles Churchill, Sr, and William Beloe were at HW's; on 5 June Samuel Lysons and Beloe were there (see DALRYMPLE 319).

3. In a letter to Lady Ossory 9 Dec. 1790 HW expresses his admiration for the English constitution apropos of Burke's *Reflections on the Revolution in France* (OSSORY iii. 101–2; see also HW to Burke *ante* 10 Nov. 1790). For a thorough study of HW's attitude toward the English constitution and the French Revolution see Robert A. Smith, 'Walpole's Reflections on the Revolution in France,' *Horace Walpole: Writer, Politician, and Connoisseur*, ed. W. H. Smith, New Haven, 1967, pp. 94–114.

It is undeniable that we have no system of education at all calculated for impressing such essential patriotism. Parents content
themselves with breeding up their children in their own principles,
that is, of talking before their children with a bias towards Whig or
Tory principles, and the masters or tutors appointed, are probably
chosen, if principles enter into the consideration, for being supposed of the same party as the parent. If the tutor or master be a
clergyman, he will doubtless instill into his pupil a due respect for
the Church, which though incorporated by law into the general
system, is not a specific part of our tripartite constitution, though admitted into it, and which I would preserve there for (perhaps a
singular) reason, I mean, looking on the complex body of higher
and lower clergy, as a pin that tends to support that third part of the
constitution, the Crown, which might be too much weakened, if deprived of that buttress, should a contest arise between the Crown,
and the two other branches of the legislature, who possessing the
whole landed property of the kingdom, might be an overmatch for
the third power; and since the union of the three has produced and
preserved our unexampled system, and raised this country to such
a summit of glory, and wealth, with perfect freedom, it would be
madness to shake an edifice so cemented, in order to try speculative
experiments and reforms, which might endanger, but could not
augment our general felicity: The happiness of the whole is not to
be risked to humour a few visionaries.

After this short introduction, I will sketch my novel idea.

I would have an exposition of our triformed constitution drawn
up, showing how in its contexture and consequences it is preferable
to all systems of government yet invented. (I do not detail more on
this head here) but when stated in the strongest and clearest manner,
and *then reduced to a corollary of implicit faith,* I would have all
schools, seminaries, colleges, universities, obliged to inculcate this
creed into all the youth committed to their care—a plan of education,
a little more necessary to a Briton than Greek and Latin, though I
do not desire to exclude or interfere with the instruction into those
languages—far from it—if a code of constitutional doctrine could
be formed, I would have it subdivided. I would have an accidence
of short aphorisms or axioms extracted for young beginners; larger
grammars for the adults—and these only taught in short lessons on
holidays and without punishments annexed, that the learners might

have no disagreeable sensations annexed to what I wish to have them love, the constitution. Lectures, in the manner of sermons might be delivered once a week to the disciples of all ages, and the *love of our country and its beautiful constitution* inculcated by every seducing⁴ art possible.

You, my dear Sir, would be infinitely more able than I am, to dilate these rude hints, into a valuable and practicable system. My object is to raise a spirit of enthusiasm for our constitution into <our> young and future countrymen; and as my plan would attach them to each branch of the legislature, not one of the three, can, or at least ought, to be averse from adopting it by law, if it were better digested, and a patriotic code formed, which it would be the interest of all the three powers to sanction. All opposition that should tend to annihilate any one of the three powers, would be baffled, if the bigotry of the nation to the established constitution were predominant.

4. 'Seducing' crossed out in the MS.

From MARY CARTER,[1] Tuesday 3 June 1794

Printed from the MS now wsl. First printed, Toynbee *Supp.* iii. 309–10. The MS was sold SH vi. 117 to Thomas Thorpe; offered by Thorpe, Catalogue of Autograph Letters, 1843, lot 642; not further traced until *penes* James Tregaskis in 1925; offered by Tregaskis, Cat. No. 934 (February 1927), lot 529; sold by Tregaskis to wsl in June 1928.

Endorsed by HW: From Miss Mary Carter to Hor. Earl of Orford.

Venice, June 3d 1794.[2]

IT IS not in the power of lakes, rivers, seas, to wash you and your *amabilità* away from my remembrance.[3] I have long wished to get this small parcel[4] conveyed but have never been able to find a person who really knew where they were going.

I have had a most pleasant and agreeable tour,[5] if anything could balance the loss of those many kind friends I have given up for so

1. Mary Carter (d. 1812), dau. of Thomas Carter of Robertstown and Rathnally, County Meath; HW's occasional correspondent and neighbour; she is listed as 'Miss Carter, 7, Hill Street Berkeley Square' in the *Directory to the Nobility, Gentry . . . for 1793* (see BERRY i. 95 n. 23).
2. Miss Carter was travelling with the 2d Vct Palmerston and his family (ibid. ii. 59 n. 37); his journal of their two years in Italy and Switzerland mentions her several times (Brian Connell, *Portrait of a Whig Peer: Compiled from the Papers of the Second Viscount Palmerston 1739–1802,* 1957, pp. 280, 281, 284, 287, 288). On their return journey, on 26 May, they 'arrived at Venice. Lodged at the Lion Blanc on the great Canal, near the Rialto' (ibid. 300). They stayed in Venice until after 8 June, then proceeded north and arrived at Harwich on 2 Oct. (ibid. 303–5). Lady Mount Edgcumbe wrote Edward Jerningham 9 July 1794, 'I have a letter from Miss Carter. . . . She has the maladie du pays upon her, and means to come home, whether the Palmerstons do or not. But how or which way is she to come, every country surrounded with these monsters?' (*Edward Jerningham and his Friends,* ed. Lewis Bettany, 1919, p. 215).

3. HW had given her a copy of his *Essay on Modern Gardening,* with a French translation by the Duc de Nivernais, 1785; this copy is now wsl (BERRY ii. 260; Hazen, *SH Bibl.* 1973, p. xxviii, copy 13). She also appears in HW's MS list of people to whom he bequeathed 'Des. of SH,' 1784. HW mentions her in a letter to Mary Berry 19 July 1790: 'I supped at my sister's last night with several Churchills, Miss Carter, and Mr Fawkener' (BERRY i. 95).
4. Containing two mineral specimens which she describes below. She also gave HW 'an ancient knife, with a curious handle of gold; a present from Miss Mary Carter' ('Des. of SH,' *Works* ii. 512).
5. Lord Palmerston and his party left London in July 1792, and reached Naples 23 Dec., where they stayed for four months; at the end of April they moved north to Rome, and eventually to Berne and Basle in August; in late Sept. they returned to Italy and reached Naples again by Christmas, 1793, where they spent the winter (Connell, op. cit. 260–300). Their sightseeing trips at each stop are described in Lord Palmerston's journal (ibid.).

long a time. I have scampered like a nannygoat over every mountain that was possible; from that of La Cavo[6] I dug up with my own hands this piece of marble, part of the remains of the Temple of Jupiter Latialis of which there is no vestige remaining. The horrid monks[7] upon the top have collected all the fine large marble squares to wall in their stinking cabbage garden. They know less of their delightful spot than myself. I have been used vilely by Sir William Hamilton[8] who promised me a little Jupiter L. to take it up by.

The other piece is the incrustation of the water and looks like that on a tea-kettle. I was determined to see how it would polish, and send you a specimen. Brick and mortar makes a very pretty marble.

These are sad times and casts a gloom over every place. I hope we shall meet in the autumn[9] to better but all the prophets assembled could not foretell the end of this distressing war. Monsieur[10] was expected at this place, but this last sad event in his family[11] sent him to Verona.

6. Monte Cavo, the ancient Albanus Mons, a mountain of Latium about 12 miles south of Rome, where there had been a Temple of Jupiter Latiaris ('Et residens celsa Latiaris Juppiter Alba,' Lucan, I. 198), where the holy days called Feriæ Latinæ were celebrated (see Saverio Kambo, *I Castelli Romani: Grottaferrata e il Monte Cavo*, Bergamo, n.d., pp. 119–23 and illustrations facing p. 114, and on pp. 115, 121, 123, 134). In 1783 whatever stone remained from the ruined temple was used by Henry Stuart, Cardinal York, to build the Passionist monastery (ibid. 128).

7. The Passionists, officially entitled 'Discalced Clerics of the Most Holy Cross and Passion of Our Lord Jesus Christ,' were founded in Italy in 1720 by St Paul of the Cross, and by 1775 had twelve houses in Italy, with 114 priests and 62 brothers (*New Catholic Encyclopedia*, 1967–74, x. 1066–7, xi. 23–4). A print by Piranesi depicts some marble ruins collected on Monte Cavo (illustrated in Kambo, op. cit. 125). The walls of the convent garden contain some blocks from

ancient buildings, but modern excavations have not found any trace of the Temple of Jupiter.

8. Sir William Hamilton, the English envoy, entertained the Palmerstons and Miss Carter in Naples; Miss Carter is mentioned in company with the King of Naples on an excursion to the Belvedere, his villa near Caserta (Connell, op. cit. 279–80).

9. Since she arrived in London in October, she probably saw HW in Berkeley Square; she is not listed in the 'Book of Visitors' to SH at that time.

10. Louis XVIII (1755–1824), Comte de Provence; King of France 1814–24; Louis XVI's brother. On 24 May he arrived in Verona, where the Republic of Venice allowed him to set up his Court; he lived in the Casa Gazzola there until April 1796, when Napoleon forced Venice to demand his removal (Duc de Castries, *Louis XVIII: Portrait d'un roi*, 1969, pp. 86–115).

11. The execution on 10 May 1794 of his younger sister, Élisabeth-Philippine-Marie-Hélène (1764–94) (BERRY ii. 61 n. 6).

I will not take up more of that precious stuff of which life is composed but to assure you that I am with great esteem and respect

Your most obedient

MOLL VOLATILE EVAPORATED

Alas! Alas! I am sadly grieved by report. I shall ever love and pity.[12]

To LADY DOUGLAS,[1] Wednesday 16 July 1794

Printed from a photostat of the MS now in the Scottish Record Office. First printed in *The Letters and Journals of Lady Mary Coke,* ed. J. A. Home, Edinburgh, 1889–96, iii. xxiv; reprinted, Toynbee xv. 293 (address omitted). The MS remained at Douglas House, Petersham, which passed after Lady Douglas's death in 1817 to her daughter Caroline (d. 1857), m. (1810) Adm. Sir George Scott; Lady Scott left Douglas House to Charles Stirling Home Drummond-Moray (1816–91), husband of her first cousin once removed, Lady Anne Douglas (d. 1899), where Mr Drummond-Moray found the lettter in a collection of papers between 1857 and 1889 (*Letters and Journals of Lady Mary Coke* i. cxxiii n. 1; iii. vii); later acquired by the Scottish Record Office.

Address: To the Right Hon[our]able Lady Douglas in Ham Walks.[2]

Strawberry Hill, July 16, 1794.

I AM heartily and sincerely rejoiced, my dear Madam, that you feel yourself better in health,[3] and trust you will soon be perfectly recovered; though I am not quite so confident as you seem to be, as your head appears to be still a little affected, by your thinking

12. This postscript, written in two lines on the left side of the signature, probably refers to the sad report of the death of Madame Élisabeth by the guillotine and the continuing imprisonment of the Dauphin (Louis XVII) and his sister Madame Royale.

1. Lady Frances Scott (1750–1817), sister of Henry Scott, 3d D. of Buccleuch; m. (1783) as 2d wife, Archibald James Edward Douglas (formerly Stewart) (1748–1827), cr. (1790) Bn Douglas of Douglas.
2. Daniel Lysons in *The Environs of London,* 1792–6, i. 566, says, 'The celebrated Duchess of Queensberry resided at Ham, in the house which is now the residence of Lady Douglas.' Lady Douglas was the great-niece of Catherine, Duchess of Queensberry (ca 1701–77). HW had written Conway 8 June 1747, 'Richmond Hill and Ham Walks bound my prospect; but, thank God! the Thames is between me and the Duchess of Queensberry' (CONWAY i. 269).
3. After the birth of a daughter 9 Dec. 1790 she was dangerously ill until the end of Jan. 1791 (BERRY i. 165, 172; Lady Mary Coke, 'MS Journals,' *sub* 1, 7, 11, 27 Jan. 1791); but no record of her illness in 1794 has been found.

mine to be so—I sit for my picture![4] I, an unfinished skeleton of 77,[5] on whose bones the worms have left but just so much skin as prevents my being nailed up yet. I am not even a curiosity; nobody takes his doctor's degree in antiquity till past an hundred, and I want a score of wrinkles before I can put in my claim. Old Parr[6] and old Jenkins[7] would call me a vain impertinent boy for sitting for my picture, and hoping to be ranged amongst prints of remarkable veterans—nay, I don't believe Lady Desmond[8] in the other world would venture to [be] left alone with such a stripling—to be sure one more fit of gout may do much, and make such a cripple of me that I may pass on many for an antediluvian—as yet, I can only pretend, like a man who applied to be placed by favour in the Hospital of the Quinze Vingts,[9] though not quite blind, and being reproached with that *defect,* replied, 'Hélas! il est vrai, je ne suis qu'un aspirant.' —so I, Madam, hélas! want a score of being fit to be in a bracelet on your Ladyship['s] arm,[10] which would be a delicious purgatory to your

Devoted humble servant

Orford

4. The only known portrait of HW taken from life after 1794 is a drawing in pencil by Sir Thomas Lawrence; it was described by Daniel Lysons (*Supplement to . . . the Environs of London,* 1811, p. 316 n. 14) thus: 'The original, which was made for Samuel Lysons Esq., is at his chambers in the Temple.' An engraving inscribed, 'T. Lawrence R. A. ad vivum del. 1796,' was made by T. Evans for the frontispiece of HW's *Works,* 1798. Sylvester Douglas, Lord Glenbervie, wrote in his diary 19 Sept. 1797, 'Miss Berrys today gave me the print of the late Lord Orford engraved from a sketch made by Lawrence a very short time before his death. It is a head, a mere outline, but the most striking likeness I ever saw, for the features and expression'; see *The Diaries of Sylvester Douglas (Lord Glenbervie),* ed. Francis Bickley, 1928, i. 140; C. Kingsley Adams and W. S. Lewis, 'The Portraits of Horace Walpole,' *Walpole Society,* 1968–70, xlii. 21.

5. He was in his 77th year, but would not have his 77th birthday until 24 Sept.

6. Thomas Parr (d. 1635), allegedly born in 1483, was brought to London by the 2d E. of Arundel and was presented to the King in Sept. 1635 as a human wonder; he was buried in Westminster Abbey with an inscription stating that he had lived under ten Kings and Queens. HW used Parr and Jenkins as examples of longevity in Ossory ii. 326, 567, iii. 218; Mason i. 28.

7. Henry Jenkins (d. 1670), called the 'modern Methusaleh,' claimed to have been born in 1501.

8. See *ante* 17 Sept. 1757, n. 3; HW said she was 140 years old, but she was probably not more than 95 (Ossory i. 317, 366).

9. The Hospice des Quinze-Vingts was founded in Paris in 1260 by Saint Louis for 300 blind people (Mann iv. 107 n. 7). 'On a dit, mais sans preuve, que ce fut en faveur des gentilshommes à qui les Sarrazins avaient crevé les yeux' (Charles-Jean-François Hénault, *Abrégé chronologique de l'histoire de France,* ed. Michaud, 1836, *sub* 1258–63).

10. Apparently she had asked for a miniature portrait to put in a bracelet.

To Edmond Malone, Monday 28 July 1794

Extract printed from Sir James Prior, *Life of Edmond Malone*, 1860, p. 211, where it was first printed; reprinted in James M. Osborn, 'Horace Walpole and Edmond Malone,' *Horace Walpole: Writer, Politician, and Connoisseur*, ed. W. H. Smith, New Haven, 1967, p. 320. The MS is missing; not traced until sold Sotheby's 17 Nov. 1908 (Mrs Julia Davies Sale), lot 311 (with HW to Pinkerton 27 Aug. 1792) to B. F. Stevens; not further traced.

[Strawberry Hill, July 28, 1794.]

. . . Lord Orford will be much obliged to Mr Malone[1] for a print of himself and another of Mr Jephson.[2]

---

1. In July 1794 Malone sent HW a copy of Robert Jephson's *Roman Portraits, A Poem, in Heroick Verse*, royal 4to, 1794, which is dedicated to Malone. HW's copy, now WSL, is inscribed 'To the Right Honble. the Earl of Orford, from the Author, with Mr Malone's respectful compliments' (Hazen, *Cat. of HW's Lib.*, No. 466). HW replied in a letter seen by Sir James Prior, who quoted only this sentence in his *Life of Edmond Malone*, 1860, p. 211; see also James M. Osborn, 'Horace Walpole and Edmond Malone,' *Horace Walpole: Writer, Politician, and Connoisseur*, ed. W. H. Smith, New Haven, 1967, p. 320. The letter is described in Sotheby's catalogue 17 Nov. 1908, lot 311, as 'thanking him [Malone] for Mr Jephson's poem.'

2. HW also wrote a letter (missing) to Jephson in Ireland, who wrote Malone, 'I expected rather more praise from Lord Orford, and much less from Lord Mornington (Marquis Wellesley). . . . With Lord Orford's letter you ought to be particularly pleased, as you see how much he is struck with the note on the Queen of France [*Roman Portraits*, pp. 247–8, n. 4], all the materials for which, and not a little in the wording, I had in letters from you' (quoted in Prior, op. cit. 211n). The frontispiece of *Roman Portraits* is an engraved portrait of Jephson by J. Singleton after B. Stoker; in Silvester and Edward Harding's *Shakespeare Illustrated, by an Assemblage of Portraits and Views*, 1789–93, there is an engraved portrait of Malone by C. Knight after Sir Joshua Reynolds (*BM Cat. of Engraved British Portraits* ii. 640, iii. 146). No separate impressions of these are listed in the London sale catalogue of HW's prints.

To Mrs Garrick, Saturday 25 October 1794

Printed for the first time from the MS now WSL. Not traced until sold Sotheby's 19 May 1926 (property of Mrs M. A. Rivington of St Leonard's-on-Sea, Sussex), lot 602 (with HW to Sir Isaac Heard 21 Jan. 1792 and HW to Mrs Garrick 1 April 1796), to B. F. Stevens and Brown, Ltd, London; acquired by WSL from Crompton T. Johnson, Farmington, in October 1932.

Address: To Mrs Garrick at Hampton.[1]

Strawberry Hill, Oct. 25th 1794.

LORD ORFORD has not been well or should have returned Mrs Garrick a thousand thanks sooner for her magnificent presents of fruit,[2] which he dares not commend as they deserve; on the contrary he begs her to overwhelm him with no more, for he can not resist them, and yet without making himself ill, he cannot consume such bounties before half are spoiled, nor can he give away what are so generously bestowed on him.

To Lady Mount Edgcumbe,[1] Saturday 29 November 1794

Printed from a copy made by William Henry Edgcumbe, 4th Earl of Mount Edgcumbe (1832–1917) for Mrs Toynbee 16 Sept. 1901. First printed, Toynbee xv. 329–30. The MS descended in the Edgcumbe family, but Mr Colin Edwards, Assistant Archivist, Cornwall County Record Office, has kindly advised that the letter is not now in the collection of Mount Edgcumbe documents in that Office and may have been destroyed by bombing during World War II.

Strawberry Hill, Nov. 29, 1794.

My dear Lady,

I KNOW I am late in my congratulations to you and your good Lord[2] on the birth of your grandson,[3] the Prince of Mount Richmond—but my delay was meditated. I not only was sure that your

1. See *ante* 3 Aug. 1757, n. 2; BERRY i. 33, n. 27.
2. HW wrote Hannah More 21 Aug. 1792, 'Mrs Garrick I have scarcely seen this whole summer. She is a liberal Pomona to me; I will not say an Eve, for though she reaches fruit to me, she will never let me in, as if I were a boy and would rob her orchard' (MORE 374).

1. Emma Gilbert (1729–1807), m. (1761) George Edgcumbe, 3d Bn Edgcumbe, 1761, cr. (1781) Vct Mount Edgcumbe, and (1789) E. of Mount Edgcumbe (see *ante* ca 2 April 1776, n. 10).
2. See *ante* 23 May 1767, n. 2.
3. William Richard Edgcumbe (19 Nov. 1794–1818), styled Vct Valletort, was born at Richmond, where Lord and Lady Valletort had a villa (BERRY ii. 134, 169).

Ladyship at least was happy enough, but I was aware that you would receive such a dose of compliments on the occasion that your poor fingers would be lamed with answering them; and as your Ladyship's hieroglyphics⁴ are never easily expounded, I would not risk their being carried to the King's decipherer on suspicion of their containing a new plot.⁵

Well, now that I hope you are a little composed, I do cordially rejoice with you on so felicitous an event, yes verily, and on the safety of Miss Edgcumbe,⁶ the poor babe! I doubt you love her at least a third less than you did; yet I must do you the justice to own that you have a stock of love that would set up a whole parish. The share I take in this good fortune is not confined to the four parents,⁷ but selfish too: I rejoice in having lived to see the worthy stock of Edgcumbe branch out again; and I glory in having been a true prophet. Did not I scold you black and blue, Madam, on your despair on the first mishap?⁸ did not I tell you you would have a flock of

4. The letters of the Countess of Mount Edgcumbe to Edward Jerningham are printed in *Edward Jerningham and his Friends*, ed. Lewis Bettany, 1919. Mr Bettany frequently notes illegible words, and comments, 'Lady Edgcumbe's characters are exceedingly hard to make out, "a" and "u," "r" and "i," "d" and "cl," "th" and "M" being written in the same manner' (pp. 203, 213, 215, 220).

5. A plot to assassinate the King by a poisoned arrow at Windsor (then postponed to take place in the theatre in London) was discovered 27 Sept. 1794; three conspirators were imprisoned for several months, and a fourth, the informer, was released (see BERRY ii. 115 and n. 4, 118 and n. 22 for newspaper references).

6. Emma Sophia Edgcumbe (28 July 1791–1872), first surviving child of Lord and Lady Valletort, had been dangerously ill of scarlet fever. HW wrote Mary Berry 14 Oct. 1794, 'I have been at Richmond this morning to inquire after the eldest girl of the poor Valetorts, who has a scarlet fever of the worst kind, and of whom Dundas had no hopes on Sunday' and on 17 Oct., 'The little Edgcumbe they hope is out of danger. I called there last night' (BERRY ii. 134, 138).

7. That is, the parents and the Edg-

cumbe grandparents. Richard Edgcumbe (1764–1839), styled Vct Valletort 1789–95; 2d E. of Mount Edgcumbe, 1795; m. (21 Feb. 1789) Lady Sophia Hobart (1768–1806), 3d dau. of John 2d E. of Buckinghamshire (who d. 3 Sept. 1793). HW is teasing Lady Mount Edgcumbe about her active interest in her grandchildren: she wrote Edward Jerningham 9 July 1794, 'Our young are all well, and the infants, dear souls, quite perfection. They have been showing all their airs to the King and Queen, who honoured them with their notice. Missy made a low curtsey to the Queen, and said "Ta, Ma'am," and to the King "How do, Majesty." Little Car insisted upon Prince Ernest's shaking her by the hand. If I am come to gossip, like Old Mother Goose, it is time to end' (Bettany, op. cit. 215).

8. A stillbirth in July 1790; HW wrote Mary Berry 13 July 1790, 'Lady Valetort was brought to bed of a dead daughter yesterday but Lady Mount Edgcumbe is more likely to die of the miscarriage than she' (BERRY i. 89). Lady Valletort may have had a miscarriage in 1789; Lady Mount Edgcumbe wrote Edward Jerningham 7 Nov. 1789, 'Our young folks make a digression to Bath, which is thought good for Lady Valletort, who has not quite recovered her strength and her looks

grandchildren?[9] Would you have had them all at once like the Flemish Countess,[10] three hundred and sixty-five at a birth? I believe from the rapidity of his proceedings that Lord Valetort, to punish you, intends that you shall grandamize two or three dozen.

Well, now I will conclude my felicitations with a little dose of lecture. Pray, my good Madam, dote on Lord and Lady Valetort, who have humoured you to your heart's content in your own way, though few young couples, that had been married four or five years, would have taken such unrelaxed pains to indulge a mother's fancy.

And pray, my good Madam, learn to moderate your transports both of grief and joy, and learn a spoonful of patience. Providence has gratified you in a thousand instances, few persons in so many —and as you have no considerable blessing to pray for till the new Master Edgcumbe shall be married,[11] enjoy your good fortune, comport yourself like a reasonable parent, and be prepared to bear the cuttings of teeth, whooping-coughs, smallpoxes and measles, of your babes, which will certainly happen to them, since the children you *would* have, and when those accidents do arrive, it will not prove that you are a more unfortunate woman than your neighbour.

I am sensible, my dear Madam, that I have been taking great liberties with you but you know that for above seventy years I have been attached to the house of Edgcumbe as my father was before me;[12] and having added seven more years to the seventy,[13] I can have

since *the accident* of the summer' (Bettany, op. cit. 209). No other letter from HW to Lady Mount Edgcumbe has been found.

9. The children of Lord and Lady Valetort were: Emma Sophia, b. 1791, Caroline, b. 1792, William Richard, b. 1794, Ernest Augustus, b. 1797, and George, b. 1800 (Collins, *Peerage*, 1812, v. 333; Burke, *Peerage*, 1928, p. 1682). HW was Caroline's godfather and went to her first birthday party (BERRY ii. 38, 39).

10. Margaretha, wife of Herman, Count of Hennenberg, and dau. of Floris, Count of Holland and Zeeland, was supposed to have given birth in 1276 to 365 children as the result of a curse; HW repeats this legend to Mann 30 April 1762 (MANN vi. 32), to Hamilton 23 Oct. 1775 (CHUTE 426), to Mason 17 Jan. 1780 (MASON ii.

4), and to Hannah More 20 Feb. 1790 (MORE 338).

11. He d. unmarried 29 Oct. 1818. His younger brother, Ernest Augustus (1797–1861), became 3d E. of Mount Edgcumbe in 1839; he m. (1831) Carolina Augusta Feilding (1808–81).

12. HW wrote to Mann 9 Aug. 1784, 'It is to recommend Lord Mount Edgcumbe's only son [Richard, 2d Earl], who is on his travels. The grandfather [Richard, 1st Baron] was my father's most intimate friend; and the late Lord [Richard, 2d Baron] a friend of mine; and with the present [George, 1st Earl] I have been much acquainted from a boy; consequently I should wish you to be kind to the son' (MANN ix. 518).

13. HW had his 77th birthday on 24 Sept.

few more opportunities of showing my friendship to the family. I know your Ladyship's many virtues, and that a meritorious zeal for those you love, is the sole cause of your impatience. I am sensible of and grateful for your great goodness to me which, with your extremely good nature and good heart will I am confident make you to take in good part this amicable freedom

Of your Ladyship's most sincere
and obedient humble servant

ORFORD

To Richard Bull, ca 1795

Printed in full for the first time from the MS pasted below Richard Earlom's engraving of George 4th E. Waldegrave, in Richard Bull's extra-illustrated copy of the *Description of SH*, 1784, p. 146, now WSL. An extract of HW's note was printed in Hazen, *Cat. of HW's Lib.*, No. 3475. For the history of Bull's copy of the *Description of SH*, see Hazen, *SH Bibl.* 128, copy 13.

Dated ca 1795 from the handwriting, which is similar to that of other letters of this year. After the death of George 4th E. Waldegrave in 1789, the engraved portraits of him were apparently given to friends, and by 1795 HW did not have any extra impressions (see below, n. 2).

LORD ORFORD is extremely obliged to Mr Bull for the two prints.[1] He has not the plate of Lord Waldegrave,[2] but he believes Lady Waldegrave[3] has; and if she has, he will get one for Mr Bull.[4]

1. Not identified.
2. George Waldegrave (1751–89), styled Vct Chewton; 4th E. Waldegrave, 1784; in peer's robes, left hand on a table; mezzotint, 14 x 11¼ in., by Richard Earlom (1743–1822), from the painting by Jean-François Rigaud (1742–1810). The mezzotint was prepared to provide private prints for presents (see Hazen, *Cat. of HW's Lib.*, No. 3475); ten impressions were sold SH v. 224; another impression was sold SH xix. 10.
3. Lady Elizabeth Laura Waldegrave (1760–1816), m. (1782) her cousin, George 4th E. Waldegrave, 1784.
4. Apparently HW had given the copper plate for the engraving to Lady Waldegrave, and at this time did not have any impressions left.

To UNKNOWN,[1] Monday 16 March 1795

Printed from a photostat of the MS in Thomas Kirgate's hand, now in the Princeton University Library. First printed, Toynbee *Supp.* ii. 72–3. The MS is untraced until sold Sotheby's 17 March 1876 (W. Ashley Sale), lot 446, to William Waller & Son; later acquired by Alexander M. Broadley (1847–1916), of The Knapp, Bradpole, Bridport, Dorset, who inserted the letter in an extra-illustrated copy of John Doran's *A Lady of the Last Century (Mrs Elizabeth Montagu),* 1873, iii. facing p. 74; this copy was sold Hodgson 21 July 1916 (A. M. Broadley Sale, Pt I), lot 204, to Francis Edwards; resold Scott and O'Shaughnessy 20 Feb. 1917 (Miscellaneous Collection Sale), lot 115; presented in 1924 by Dickson Q. Brown to the Princeton University Library. The MS was removed in 1950 from the extra-illustrated volume.

Monday evening, March 17th.[2]

My Lord,

I RETURN to your Grace, with many thanks, the handsome letter of Lord Lansdown,[3] which indeed does great honour to him, and I assure your Grace I have not suffered a word of it to be copied: I should have returned it instantly, but had sent my secretary[4] to attend the sale of Sir Joshua Reynolds's pictures,[5] and had nobody to write for me.

1. The Duke to whom the letter was addressed has not been identified. A possible candidate is William Henry Cavendish Bentinck (1738–1809), 3d D. of Portland, HW's occasional correspondent, who might have owned a letter written by Lord Lansdown among the Portland MSS (Hist. MSS Comm., *Portland MSS,* v, 1899, and vi, 1901, *passim*); but many Lansdown letters were preserved in other MS collections (see Elizabeth Handasyde, *Granville the Polite,* 1933, list of MS sources, p. 249).

2. In 1795 Monday was 16 March; the year is determined by the reference to the sale of Sir Joshua Reynolds's pictures (see below, n. 5).

3. George Granville (1666–1735), cr. (1712) Bn Lansdown; poet; playwright; M.P.; privy councillor 1712–14; comptroller 1712–13 and treasurer 1713–14 of the Household; imprisoned in the Tower 1715–17 (Handasyde, op. cit., pp. 7, 151,

155, 160). In 1710 when the Tories came into power Lansdown succeeded Sir Robert Walpole as Secretary of War. HW included Lansdown in *Royal and Noble Authors (Works* i. 441–2), and noted that he had been imprisoned in the same rooms that Sir Robert had occupied in the Tower. See also Roger Granville, *The History of the Granville Family,* Exeter, 1895, pp. 410–24. The letter of Lord Lansdown may have been written to Sir Robert Walpole.

4. Thomas Kirgate; the letter is in his hand.

5. The sale of part of Sir Joshua Reynolds's collection of Old Masters took place at Christie's 13–17 March 1795; it was attended by Joseph Farington (*The Diary of Joseph Farington,* ed. Kenneth Garlick and Angus MacIntyre, New Haven and London, 1978– , ii. 315; see also Frits Lugt, *Répertoire des catalogues de ventes publiques, 1600–1825,* The Hague, 1938, No. 5284).

Apropos to Lord L. I will take the liberty of telling your Grace a trifling anecdote of another remarkable person of his connection; viz. Keith Earl Marshal,[6] who about the same time (whether taken up, or only sent for, I do not remember) was examined by King George the First himself:[7] on coming out thence, his friends asked him what the King had said to him; he replied in the words of the old ballad,

> The King look'd over his left shoulder,
> And a grim look looked he,
> And cry'd, Earl Marshal but for my oath
> Or hanged thou shouldst be.[8]

I beg your Grace's pardon, but if you will dig in an old mine, you must meet with some dross.

                I have the honour to be,
                    with great respect and gratitude,
                        My Lord, your Grace's
                            most obliged and most obedient
                                humble servant,

                                            ORFORD

---

6. George Keith (ca 1693–1778), 10th Earl Marischal of Scotland 1712–16; attainted for participation in the Jacobite rebellion of 1715; fled to France and then to Spain; sailed in command of the Jacobite expedition to Scotland which was defeated at Glenshiel in 1719; entered the service of Frederick II of Prussia, 1747; Prussian ambassador at Paris, 1751; while Prussian ambassador to Spain, sent intelligence to England, and was pardoned by George II in 1759 (GEC viii. 485–6; CON-WAY ii. 9 and n. 19; Scots Peerage, vi. 62–4).

7. He received a commission in Jan. 1715 from George I as Capt. and Lt-Col. of the 2d (Scots) troop of Horse Grenadier Guards, who had attended the King on his landing at Greenwich; the commission was apparently cancelled on the advice of the D. of Argyll, who persuaded George I to remove many Scottish nobles from their positions. After being deprived of his commission, the Earl Marischal returned to Scotland, and became active in the Jacobite insurrection (see Scots Peerage vi. 62). The anecdote HW relates has not been found.

8. The ballad of Queen Eleanor's Confession was about Eleanor of Aquitaine who m. (1152) Henry II; the Earl Marshal was William Marshal (ca 1146–1219), styled E. of Strigoil, E. of Pembroke, 1199. In the ballad, the King and Earl Marshal, disguised as friars, hear the Queen's confession that 'Earl Marshall had my maidenhed' and that she loves the Earl Marshal's son more than the King's son; the final stanza is the one quoted by HW (The English and Scottish Popular Ballads, ed. Francis J. Child, New York, 1965, iii. 257–64).

From LADY ANNE CONOLLY,[1] Friday 20 March 1795

Printed for the first time from a photostat of the MS in the British Museum (Add. MS 9433, f. 181). This letter was apparently forwarded by HW to the Rev. Daniel Lysons (see n. 5 below) and was included with Lysons's papers relating to the *Environs of London* (Add. MSS 9431–6) acquired by the British Museum after his death in 1834.

Endorsed in an unknown hand: Twickenham.

Friday, March 20th 1795.

LADY ANNE CONOLLY presents her respects to Lord Orford, in obedience to his request she had the title deeds of her place at Twickenham,[2] looked out, and sent to a lawyer,[3] who has been two days in making out the enclosed,[4] which she doubts will be of no use to the gentleman[5] that wants it, being of no earlier a date than 1671.

Lady Anne Conolly wishes most earnestly to hear Lord Orford is recovered from his painful disorder.[6] She is better, but still far from well.

1. Lady Anne Wentworth (1713–97), sister and heiress of HW's friend and correspondent, William Wentworth, 2d E. of Strafford; m. (1733) William Conolly, of Castletown, Co. Kildare (BERRY i. 56 n. 8).

2. Lady Anne was at this time living in the 'elegant edifice' with which she had replaced the old house at Twickenham that she had inherited from her brother, the 2d E. of Strafford, in 1791 (R. S. Cobbett, *Memorials of Twickenham*, 1872, p. 249; Edward Ironside, *The History and Antiquities of Twickenham*, 1797, p. 79).

3. Not identified.

4. Missing; presumably an abstract of title.

5. Rev. Daniel Lysons (1762–1834), to-

pographer; HW's chaplain and occasional correspondent; author of *The Environs of London*, 4 vols, 1792–6. Lysons had apparently asked HW to obtain information about the manor of Twickenham for the third volume of *Environs*, which was published 2 June 1795 (DALRYMPLE 251 n. 4). See *post* 17 April 1795. That he made use of the records Lady Anne sent to HW is shown by p. 562 n. 26: 'From papers obligingly communicated by Lady Anne Conolly, who holds some of the lands demised by these leases.'

6. HW had been suffering from a paralyzing attack of gout in his right hand and arm since late January; his illness continued into early April (MORE 398; DALRYMPLE 260).

From WILLIAM HARRISON,[1] Friday 17 April 1795

Printed for the first time from a photostat of the MS in the British Museum (Add. MS 9433, f. 179). This letter was apparently forwarded by HW to the Rev. Daniel Lysons and was included with Lysons's papers relating to the *Environs of London* (Add. MSS 9431–6) acquired by the British Museum after his death in 1834.

Endorsed in an unknown hand: Twickenham.

Land Revenue Office, 17th April 1795.

Dear Sir,

THE lease of Twickenham Manor[2] from Queen Catherine[3] to W[illia]m Genew[4] Esq. bears date 2d July 1688, and was granted for 12 years from 1707 to £20.6.8 p[er] annum: and there is an exception in it of the fee farm rent of £20 p[er] annum for *Yorke's farm*[5] therein mentioned to have been formerly part of the said Manor, which I had not observed before.

All I can find about the alienation from Jay to Gapper is this: The purchase from the trustees of forfeited estates[6] in 1723 was in the following proportions: Wendover Jay[7] ¼th part, Thomas Jay[8] ¾th

1. Daniel Lysons describes William Harrison as 'of the land revenue office in Scotland Yard' (*Environs of London*, 1792–6, iii. 246 n. 16). Probably he was a minor official in this office. Lysons apparently had asked HW to obtain information about the manor of Twickenham for the third volume of *Environs*, which was published 2 June 1795 (DALRYMPLE 251 n. 4). See *ante* 20 March 1795 and n. 5. Lysons acknowledged Harrison's help on p. 560 n. 12.

2. The manor of Twickenham extended through the parishes of Twickenham, Isleworth, and Heston; the manor house, later called Arragon House, stood opposite the Twickenham parish church of St Mary the Virgin (R. S. Cobbett, *Memorials of Twickenham*, 1872, pp. 12–15). While HW was living in Twickenham the house was occupied by Samuel Scott (ca 1702–72), the landscape painter, and later by his pupil, William Marlow (1740–1813). See Appendix 1 and n. 16.

3. Catherine of Braganza (1638–1705), m. (1662) Charles II.

4. Possibly the William Genew of Ham, Surrey, who died on 30 Oct. 1729 (*Chronological Diary to the Historical Register*, 1729, xiv. 60).

5. Later known as York House, located near the Twickenham parish church; it was 'a capital house standing in seven acres of land' (Cobbett, op. cit. 217–19). During the years that HW was living at SH, James Whitchurch (d. ca 1785) owned this property (OSSORY ii. 81 n. 6; see also Appendix 1).

6. The first Vct Bolingbroke, having acquired the reversionary lease of the manor of Twickenham granted by Charles II to the E. of Rochester in 1675, forfeited this lease to the Crown in 1715 upon his attainder for his Jacobite sympathies. In 1723 the trustees for forfeited estates sold his interest in this lease (Cobbett, op. cit. 12; BERRY ii. 257 and n. 27).

7. Not identified.

8. Not identified.

parts, and John Rutt[9] ¼th. In 1727 (March 16th) Thomas Jay assigned his two undivided fourth parts to Robert Gapper[10] of Chancery Lane, Gent., subject to a mortgage, which in 1772 was paid off by his son, the present Mr Gapper.[11] John Rutt in 1731 bequeathed his fourth part to his nephew John Sanisbury,[12] the brother of the present Alderman Sanisbury.[13] But how the share which belonged to Wendover Jay was disposed of I have not discovered. The Gappers, father and son, were both attorneys. The latter, who has quitted business, resides, I believe, at Frome[14] in Somersetshire.

I am, dear Sir,

Your most obedient servant,

WM HARRISON

PS. I shall be much obliged to you if, when you come to town, you will let me see the minutes you took from the deeds which Lady Ann Connolly gave you the inspection of[15]—especially of any which relate to the Crown Lands.

9. Not identified.

10. The *London Magazine* 1767, xxxvi. 372, reported in its July issue the death 'lately' of 'Counsellor Gapper, of Charlton Hawthorn [Horethorne], Somersetshire.'

11. Robert Gapper (ca 1721–99), formerly an attorney in the Temple, died at Fonthill House, Wincanton, Somerset, on 5 March 1799 (GM 1799, lxix pt i. 259).

12. John Sainsbury (d. 1792), steward to the M. of Salisbury (GM 1792, lxii pt i. 91).

13. Thomas Sainsbury (d. 16 May 1795), alderman of the ward of Billingsgate 1778–95; sheriff of London, 1780; lord mayor of London, 1786 (GM 1795, lxv pt i. 445; *Royal Kalendar,* 1787, p. 218, 1795, p. 218).

14. He actually lived at Wincanton, about twelve miles north of Frome. See n. 11 above.

15. See *ante* 20 March 1795.

To Edward Jerningham, Thursday 18 June 1795

Printed from a photostat of the MS in the Henry E. Huntington Library. First printed, Toynbee *Supp.* iii. 77. For the history of the MS see *ante* 13 Feb. 1778.
Address: To Edward Jerningham Esq. in Green Street, Grosvenor Square, London. *Frank:* Isleworth June the eighteenth 1795. Free. Orford. *Postmark:* ISLEWORTH. JU 19 95. FREE.

Dear Sir,

I OBEY your commands[1] and wish you much joy of Lady Bedingfield[2] and her move—

Yours most sincerely

O.

1. Not explained.

2. Charlotte Georgiana Jerningham (d. 1854), daughter of Sir William Jerningham, 6th Bt, m. (16 June 1795) at St George's, Hanover Square, Sir Richard Bedingfeld (1767–1829), 5th Bt, 1795. After the bride left the Jerninghams' residence at 5 Upper Brook Street, her cousin, Frances Dillon, dau. of the 12th Vct Dillon, wrote in a letter begun 'Tuesday, you have been gone half an hour': 'Well, presently your Uncle Edward came, and, *wishing joy,* said he did not know anything of the wedding till it was over, and that by chance. He stayed but a minute and then set off for the opera with George and my Uncle' (*The Jerningham Letters (1780–1843)*, ed. Egerton Castle, 1896, i. 78, 84). For Lady Bedingfeld's letter to her mother 18 June 1795, from Oxburgh, Stoke, Norfolk, see ibid. i. 88–90.

To Edmund Lodge,[1] Friday 19 June 1795

Printed from the MS now WSL. First printed, Cunningham ix. 455–6; reprinted, Toynbee xv. 345–6 (signature omitted in Cunningham and Toynbee). The MS was given by Edmund Lodge to Charles Bedford (ca 1742–1814) in November 1802; later in the possession of Mrs Erskine (a first cousin once removed of Charles Bedford) of Milton Lodge, Gillingham, Dorset; sold Sotheby's 15 Nov. 1932 (property of Mrs Erskine), lot 486, to Maggs for WSL.

Endorsed in an unidentified hand: Lord Orford, June 19, 1795.

Strawberry Hill, June 19, 1795.

Dear Sir,

I HAVE been meditating how to execute in the best manner I am able the commands[2] with which the Duke of Norfolk[3] has too partially been pleased to honour me. His Grace's family has given rise to such a number of illustrious persons and great historic events,[4] that selection is the principal difficulty; and I am sure I have not the vanity to take upon me to decide what subject deserves best to be preferred for the third picture.[5]

1. (1756–1839), Bluemantle Pursuivant-at-Arms, 1782; F.S.A., 1787; Lancaster Herald, 1793; Norroy, 1822, and Clarenceux, 1838; K.H., 1832 (HW to Nicol *ante* 6 July 1790 and n. 8; BERRY i. 278 and n. 46).

2. Lodge wrote Charles Bedford 21 Nov. 1802, 'The Duke of Norfolk has furnished a gallery at Arundel with a series of large pictures of the most remarkable actions of his ancestors, and in 1795 desired me to apply to Lord Orford for a subject for one of them. I had afterwards the honour of introducing the Duke at Strawberry Hill, and of making the two great folks acquainted, and I know I have somewhere a letter from Lord O. to fix the day for that visit—I have rummaged in vain for it, but, should I find it in future, you shall have it—It is a long letter, in the most sublime strain of flattery (to the Duke) and exceeds all that I could have conceived possible in that way, till I witnessed a still further excess in the interview which followed it' (MS now WSL). The letter fixing the date of the visit is missing, but HW's 'Book of

Visitors' records for 23 June 1795, 'Duke of Norfolk and Lord Suffolk. Myself' (BERRY ii. 248); Lodge presumably was also present.

3. Charles Howard (1746–1815), styled E. of Surrey 1777–86; 11th D. of Norfolk, 1786; M.P.; President of the Society of Arts 1793–1815. HW wrote of him to Mary Berry 16 Aug. 1796, 'He came hither two years ago to consult me about Gothicizing his restoration of the castle; I recommended Mr Wyat, lest he should copy the Temple of Jerusalem' (see ibid. ii. 205 and n. 19).

4. See Gerald Brenan and E. P. Statham, *The House of Howard*, 1907, *passim;* M. A. Tierney, *The History and Antiquities of the Castle and Town of Arundel; including the Biography of its Earls*, 1834, *passim;* G. W. Eustace, *Arundel: Borough and Castle*, 1922, pp. 195–230.

5. Not identified. In *Anecdotes of Painting (Works* iii. 209) HW describes a projected painting, designed by Van Dyck, of the 14th E. of Arundel and his family, which included some of the events

All I will pretend to, is to offer to his Grace's consideration three or four subjects, and the Duke's own better judgment will determine which of them will furnish the most picturesque representation.

1. The Battle of Flodden Field with the death of James IV.[6]

2. The Defeat of the Spanish Armada, where so many Howards distinguished themselves.[7]

3. The Duke of Norfolk[8] at bowls on Richmond Green receiving the Treasurer's staff on the resignation of his father.

4. Henry VIII and his attendants[9] all masqued at a ball at Cardinal Wolsey's[10] where the King distinguished Anne Boleyn.

I do not forget the amiable Earl of Surry's tournament at Florence[11]

suggested below: 'The Earl and Countess are sitting under a state: before them are their children: one holds a shield presented by the Great Duke of Tuscany to the famous Earl of Surrey at a tournament; and two others bring the helmet and sword of James IV taken at the victory of Floddenfield, by the Earl of Surrey's father, Thomas Duke of Norfolk. Portraits of both those noblemen are represented as hanging up near the canopy.'

6. After the victory over the Scots at Flodden Field 9 Sept. 1513, when James IV of Scotland was killed, Thomas Howard (1443–1524), E. of Surrey, became 2d D. of Norfolk, 1 Feb. 1514.

7. Charles Howard (ca 1536–1624), 2d Bn Howard of Effingham, 1573; cr. (1597) E. of Nottingham; lord high admiral, 1585; commander-in-chief of the English navy which defeated the Spanish Armada 21–9 July 1588. Lord Thomas Howard (1561–1626), cr. (1597) Lord Howard de Walden and (1603) E. of Suffolk, displayed such valour against the Spanish fleet that he was knighted at sea and was later made captain of a man-of-war.

8. Thomas Howard (1473–1554), styled Lord Howard 1483–1514, cr. (1514) E. of Surrey; 3d D. of Norfolk, 1524–47, 1553–4; lord high treasurer 4 Dec. 1522 to Feb. 1547 in succession to his father, Thomas Howard, 2d D. of Norfolk (above n. 6).

9. Thomas Howard, 2d D. of Norfolk (above, n. 6), was Marshal of England for the coronation of Henry VIII; was cr. (1510) Earl Marshal of England for life; was Guardian of England, 1520, during the King's absence in France; and on 18

Nov. 1515 conducted Wolsey, after his reception of the cardinal's hat, from the high altar to the door of Westminster Abbey.

10. Thomas Wolsey (?1475–1530), cardinal; at his banquet on 4 March 1522 at York Place in honour of the Emperor Charles V's ambassadors, there was a masque called the Château Vert in which both Henry VIII and Anne Boleyn took part; this was said to be the occasion when the King first took special notice of Anne Boleyn (see M. L. Bruce, *Anne Boleyn*, New York, 1972, pp. 39–41, 344; George Cavendish, *The Life and Death of Cardinal Wolsey*, ed. R. S. Sylvester, Oxford, 1959, pp. 25–30, 34–6, 205; *Letters and Papers, Foreign and Domestic, of the Reign of Henry VIII*, ed. J. S. Brewer, vol. III (1867) pt ii. 1557–9).

11. Henry Howard, styled E. of Surrey (*ante* 14 Dec. 1775, n. 3), in Thomas Nash's *The Unfortunate Traveller*, 1594, meets the hero, Jack Wilton, in the Low Countries and travels with him to Italy. In Florence, Surrey is said to publish a challenge to defend the supreme beauty of his Faire Geraldine in a tournament (*The Works of Thomas Nashe*, ed. R. B. McKerrow, reprint, Oxford, 1966, ii. 269–79). This story, though fictitious, was repeated by Michael Drayton in his *Heroicall Epistles*, 1598, and by Anthony à Wood in *Athenæ Oxonienses*, 2d edn, 1721, i. 68, to which HW refers in *Royal and Noble Authors* (*Works* i. 304–5n). For a complete study of the rise of this tradition, see Edwin Casady, *Henry Howard, Earl of Surrey*, New York, 1938, pp. 244–50.

nor his improvement of our poetry, nor the Earl of Arundel's[12] introduction of taste for painting and antiques; nor a much earlier Earl of Arundel's marriage with Adeliza[13] the widowed Queen of Henry I, nor Thomas of Brotherton[14] and the Bigods and Mowbrays,[15] and the destined alliance of Edward IV's second son[16] with the young Duchess of Norfolk—and many other historic subjects in that great race—but those are themes for smaller decorations, yet deserving to be recorded in Arundel Castle, and which could not be equalled in any other seat in England—but I fear I am trespassing on the Duke's patience, though I hope his Grace will pardon what flows from a zeal awakened by his flattering notice of an old otherwise useless antiquary—and

Dear Sir
Your obedient humble servant

ORFORD

Mr Lodge.

---

12. Thomas Howard (1585–1646), 14th E. of Arundel, 1604, cr. (1644) E. of Norfolk (*ante* 20 Nov. 1768, n. 3). HW called him 'the first who professedly began to collect in this country' and described his collections in *Anecdotes of Painting* (*Works* iii. 205–9). His collections of paintings, books, sculpture, gems, medals and coins were dispersed after the death of his widow in 1654 (see DALRYMPLE 114, n. 33; Lionel Cust, 'Notes on the Collections formed by Thomas Howard, Earl of Arundel and Surrey, K.G.,' *Burlington Magazine*, 1911, xix. 278–86, 323–5; Tierney, op. cit. ii. 482–5).

13. Adeliza (Adela, Adelaide) (ca 1103–51) of Louvain, m. 1 (1121) Henry I (1068–1135), King of England 1100–35; m. 2 (1138) William d'Aubigny (d. 1176), 1st E. of Arundel (BERRY ii. 205 and n. 15).

14. Thomas (1300–38), styled 'of Brotherton,' 5th son of Edward I, cr. (1312) E. of Norfolk, and (1316) Marshal of England.

15. The Norfolk title was held by the Bigod family from 1141 to 1306, before Thomas of Brotherton, and by the Mowbray family from 1397 to 1481.

16. Richard (1473–83) 'of Shrewsbury,' styled also Plantagenet, 2d son of Edward IV, cr. (1474) D. of York, (1476) E. of Nottingham, and (1477) E. of Warenne and D. of Norfolk; m. (15 Jan. 1478) Anne (1472–81), *suo jure* Countess of Norfolk and Baroness Mowbray and Segrave.

To Bishop Percy, Sunday 26 July 1795

Printed from Nichols, *Lit. Illus.* viii. 293, where the letter was first printed; reprinted, Toynbee xv. 349. The history of the MS and its present whereabouts are not known.

Strawberry Hill, July 26, 1795.

LORD ORFORD is much obliged to the Bishop of Dromore for his Lordship's present of the new edition of *Ancient Poetry*,[1] which Lord Orford is persuaded will give him great entertainment.

To the Rev. Mark Noble, Saturday 22 August 1795

Printed from a photostat of the MS in the Bodleian Library (MS Eng. misc. d. 156, f. 54). First printed, Toynbee *Supp.* iii. 337–8. For the history of the MS see *ante* 1 Jan. 1785.

Strawberry Hill, Aug. 22d 1795.

Sir,

I SHALL be glad to see the work[1] on which you are employing yourself. My account of Sir Thomas Wyat the Elder is in the second number of my *Miscellaneous Antiquities*,[2] both of which shall be at your service if you will accept them; but they would be too heavy to send by the post; therefore you must tell me how to

1. *Reliques of Ancient English Poetry*, 4th edn, 1794, 3 vols, 8vo; HW's copy is now WSL (Hazen, *Cat. of HW's Lib.*, No. 2919). Charles Rivington, the publisher, wrote to Percy 31 May 1794, 'I trouble your Lordship for your directions respecting advertising. The work is now nearly completed, and therefore it should be announced as nearly ready'; and Percy replied 13 June 1794, 'I am so little interested about the amusements of my youth, that, had it not been for the benefit of my nephew [*ante* 11 Aug. 1792, n. 4], I could contentedly have let the "Reliques of Ancient Poetry" remain unpublished. Yet I cannot think they will be neglected by the public, if once announced to them in the most simple form; and, therefore, must desire that there be

no mention of *additions* in the Advertisement, as this edition contains only one trifling insertion that is perfectly new. . . . Below I send a sketch of the Advertisement' (Nichols, *Lit. Illus.* viii. 309–11).

1. Possibly his unpublished *Life of the Family of Boleyn, particularly of Queen Ann Boleyn, with the life of her Daughter, Queen Elizabeth*, the MS of which was sold with his other MSS in Dec. 1827 after his death (MSS listed in GM 1828, xcviii pt i. 252–3). Sir Thomas Wyatt the elder (?1503–42) had been an admirer of Anne Boleyn before her marriage to Henry VIII, and wrote love lyrics addressed to her (Cole i. 261, 269–70).
2. Described *ante* 20 Aug. 1792, nn. 4, 5; 18 Sept. 1792, nn. 5, 6.

convey them; or I will leave them at any bookseller's[3] in London that you will point out to me, whence you may get them.

I am Sir

Your obedient humble servant

Orford

To the Rev. Mark Noble, Saturday 29 August 1795

Printed from a photostat of the MS in the Bodleian Library (MS Eng. misc. d. 156, f. 55). First printed, Toynbee *Supp.* iii. 338–9. For the history of the MS see *ante* 1 Jan. 1785.

Strawberry Hill, Aug. 29, 1795.

I HAVE sent the *Miscellaneous Antiquities*[1] to the Golden Cross,[2] Sir, with orders to be consigned to you; and I shall be much obliged to you for communicating your new work[3] to me when you shall have put your materials together.

I am rather surprised, Sir, that you gave any credit to that most unfounded article[4] of my settlement of this place on Lord H.[5] It is very rarely indeed that newspapers deserve any faith at all. How they should know the intentions of my will is not very conceivable—and rightly they certainly have not guessed. Lord H. is one of my many cousins, and one for whom I have great esteem—but his fortune is far superior to mine, and he has no occasion for more seats[6] than he possesses, much larger than this small one. Nor have I the vanity of supposing I can *perpetuate* my little collection of trifles. The noble assemblage of pictures made by my father,[7] and which

---

3. HW sent them to the Golden Cross Hotel; see *post* 29 Aug. 1795.

———

1. See *ante* 22 Aug. 1795 and n. 2.

2. Golden Cross Hotel, Charing Cross, No. 452 West Strand (Henry B. Wheatley, *London Past and Present,* 1891, ii. 120).

3. *Ante* 22 Aug. 1795, n. 1.

4. In the *Times* 17 Aug. 1795: 'Strawberry Hill, with all its beauties and singularities, its Gothic weeds, and *Palatinus Græcumque recepit Apollo,* is to descend to the Marquis of Hertford, it is said, upon the express promise that it shall never be sold, and its cabinets

neither separated nor removed. We sincerely hope, however, it may long remain with the present possessor.' HW mentions this to Mary Berry 18 Aug. 1795 and comments that someone had written 'to inquire who put into the papers my settlement on Lord Hertford! You may guess at the writer from the indecency and folly of the inquiry' (Berry ii. 139–40, 143).

5. See *ante* 18 Aug. 1735 OS, n. 1.

6. His principal residences were Ragley Hall, in Warwickshire, and his house in Grosvenor Street, London.

7. Sir Robert Walpole's collection of

ought now to have been mine, I have seen vanish—can I build on
the durability of any thing?—if you wish, Sir, to pass another day
here, I shall be glad of your company when you come to town,[8] provided it should be before the end of this month, when I am to go
into Buckinghamshire.[9] Be so good as to give me some *previous*
notice, and a direction whither to answer your letter. I am, Sir,

Your obedient humble servant

Orford

To Dr Charles Burney, Tuesday 5 January 1796

Printed from a photostat of the MS in Thomas Kirgate's hand in the New York
Public Library (Berg Collection). First printed, Toynbee xv. 441 (date omitted).
The MS is untraced until *penes* Mrs Henrietta Chappel, East Orchard, Shaftes-
bury, Dorset, in 1900. Not further traced until presented in 1941 by Owen D.
Young to the Henry W. and Albert A. Berg Collection of the New York Public
Library.
Endorsed by Fanny Burney d'Arblay: Signature of the famous Horace Walpole,
youngest son of the more famous Sir Robert Walpole afterwards Earl of Orford.
Endorsed on the verso, probably by Dr Burney: Horatio Walpole Lord Orford.

Berkeley Square, Jan. 5th 1796.

LORD ORFORD is very sorry he was too ill[1] to see Dr Burney,
when he was so obliging as to call; but being a little recovered
now, shall be very glad to see Dr Burney, whenever he has half an
hour to spare.[2]

paintings at Houghton Hall, Norfolk, was
sold by HW's nephew, George, 3d E. of
Orford, to Catherine II of Russia in July
1779 (see Mann viii. 427, 502 and n. 8;
ix. 164). The collection was described by
HW in *Ædes Walpolianæ* (*Works* ii. [221]–
78).
8. Noble lived at Barming, Kent, where
he was rector 1786–1827. There is no
record of his visiting SH at this time.
9. HW's letters to Mary Berry show
that he was at SH in late Aug. and early
Sept. (Berry ii. 153, 155, 159); he may
mean that he is going away at the end of
Sept., when he did meet the Berry sisters
at Park Place, Berks, 26–9 Sept. (ibid. ii.
167 and n. 2, 170). We have not found any
record of a visit in Buckinghamshire in
the summer of 1795.

1. HW suffered a severe attack of gout
that began on 6 Dec. 1795, when he wrote
Mary Berry that 'I have various threats
of gout, both in the left wrist and foot'
(Berry ii. 183–4), and lasted through
February. On 15 Feb. he wrote William
Roscoe in a letter dictated to his secretary,
Thomas Kirgate, that he had been 'extremely ill with the gout for above eleven
weeks, and ten days ago was at the point
of death' (Dalrymple 274–5). By 4 March,
however, he was able to write to Lady
Ossory in his own hand (Ossory iii. 214–
16).
2. Dr Burney called on HW some morning before 20 Feb. (*post* 20, ?22 Feb. 1796).

To Mrs Garrick, Monday 11 January 1796

Printed for the first time from the MS in Thomas Kirgate's hand, now WSL. The MS is untraced until acquired by exchange from the Folger Shakespeare Library by WSL in June 1950.

Endorsed in an unidentified hand: Lord Orford 11 Jan. 1796.

Berkeley Square, Jan. 11th 1796.

LORD ORFORD is very sorry to trouble Mrs Garrick again on a subject on which she was so obliging as to comply with his request.[1]

She will not be surprised at a moment when so many impudent impostures are attributed to Shakespeare,[2] that she should be resorted to as possessed of the most genuine treasure belonging to our great poet. Lord Orford did formerly borrow of Mrs Garrick the deed containing Shakespeare's own handwriting: Mr Malone, suspecting that the handwriting was not authentically copied,[3] is very anxious to have that signature fully authenticated, and has desired Lord Orford to borrow the deed once more; and if Mrs Garrick will be so kind as to trust Lord Orford with the deed once more,[4] he will make it a condition that it shall be returned very soon, for he

1. In February 1788 Mrs Garrick had acceded to HW's request to borrow an original mortgage deed, signed by William Shakespeare and dated 11 March 1613, for the use of Edmond Malone in the preparation of his edition of Shakespeare published in 1790 (*ante* 3 Feb., 7 Feb. 1788; MORE 259–60 and n. 4).

2. On 24 Dec. 1795 Samuel Ireland (d. 1800) had published *Miscellaneous Papers and Legal Instruments under the Hand and Seal of William Shakespeare: including the Tragedy of King Lear, and a Small Fragment of Hamlet.* This was a facsimile reproduction of documents that had been forged by his son, William Henry Ireland (1777–1835), and which had been exhibited at the elder Ireland's house since February 1795 (BERRY ii. 174 n. 7; OSSORY iii. 213 n. 14).

3. Malone, who took the lead in exposing Ireland's forgeries, was at this time working on his *Inquiry into the Au-*

thenticity of certain Miscellaneous Papers and Legal Instruments . . . attributed to Shakespeare, Queen Elizabeth, and Henry, Earl of Southampton, which was published 31 March 1796 (*Morning Chronicle,* 31 March 1796; *The Oracle and Public Advertiser,* 31 March 1796; Bernard Grebanier, *The Great Shakespeare Forgery,* New York, 1965, pp. 206–9). HW's presentation copy is Hazen, *Cat. of HW's Lib.,* No. 1358.

4. Mrs Garrick was unable to find the deed. 'As I have not the pleasure of being acquainted with Mrs Garrick,' Malone explained, '. . . Lord Orford . . . very obligingly requested her to furnish me once more with the deed to which our poet's autograph is affixed: but that lady, after a very careful search, was not able to find it, it having by some means or other been either mislaid or stolen from her' (Malone, op. cit. 119–20).

remembers having been very uneasy at Mr Malone's detaining it a whole year.

Lord Orford would have waited on Mrs Garrick with this request in person, but has been confined above these five weeks by a sharp fit of the gout.⁵ He hopes Mrs Garrick herself is perfectly well.

To Dr Charles Burney, Saturday 20 February 1796

Printed from the MS in Thomas Kirgate's hand, now wsl. First printed, Toynbee *Supp.* ii. 73–74. The MS descended in the Burney family and in 1918 was in the possession of Mrs Charles Burney, widow of Charles Burney (1840–1912); acquired after the death of Miss Mabel Burney (1870–1953) by James M. Osborn (see Joyce Hemlow, *A Catalogue of the Burney Family Correspondence, 1749–1878*, New York and Montreal, 1971, p. xvi), who gave it to wsl in 1954.

Endorsed by Fanny Burney d'Arblay: H. Walpole (Orford).
Endorsed on the verso, probably by Dr Burney: Horace Walpole Orford.

Berkeley Square, Feb. 20, 1796.

Dear Sir,

I THANK you much for your books,¹ which I did not, nor do mean, to *ask* for as a present, but was impatient to see anything with the name of Burney to it, which I was sure must give me pleasure. Again I thank you, and am sincerely

Yours,

Orford

5. See *ante* 5 Jan. 1796 n. 1.

1. *Memoirs of the Life and Writings of* the *Abate Metastasio*, 3 vols, published on 18 Feb. 1796 (Hazen, *Cat. of HW's Lib.*, No. 2811).

From DR CHARLES BURNEY, ?Monday 22 February 1796

Printed for the first time from the MS draft now WSL. For the history of the MS draft, see *ante* 8 July 1791. The original letter is missing.

Dated by HW's letter to Dr Burney, *ante* 20 Feb. 1796, to which this letter is a reply. The draft is written on a leaf torn from a letter received by Dr Burney, on the verso of which appears the address 'Dr Burney, Chelsea College'; a postmark '12 O CLOCK, 18 <FEB> 96'; and an endorsement, probably by Dr Burney, 'Hetty.' The draft was much corrected, and, is, in spots, almost illegible.

Endorsed by Fanny Burney d'Arblay: Horace Walpole afterwards Lord Orford.

Endorsed in pencil in an unidentified hand: Lord Orford Horace Walpole.

My Lord,

FOR the ease of your Lordship's conscience concerning the books[1] of which I had the honour to send an early copy to Berkley Square,[2] I here solemnly protest that it was not in consequence of the conversation on the subject which passed the morning I was there,[3] but from a long and premeditated desire of entreating permission to number your Lordship among those (may I say friends) whom I have ever been most ambitious to please and of whom death has, alas! so cruelly diminished the number![4] If you knew, my Lord, how flattering the approbation of such readers as your Lordship is to an author, you would not grudge him the gratification of such a small manifestation of gratitude. I have nothing to do with the sale of the work of which the copyright is consigned to the publisher.[5] Nor shall I dispose of a single copy <nor gift> in the way of <traffic.> Had there not been a third person[6] in the room, I should have disclosed my intention of taking that liberty[7] which the purest respect and regard suggested, and which it is hoped will be pardoned, though to, my Lord,

Your Lordship's most obliged,

obedient and faithful servant,

CHAS. BURNEY

1. *Memoirs of the Life and Writings of the Abate Metastasio,* 3 vols, which Dr Burney published on 18 Feb. 1796.

2. See *ante* 20 Feb. 1796 and n. 1.

3. The date of Dr Burney's visit to HW is not known.

4. Among Dr Burney's friends and correspondents who had died were David Garrick (d. 1779), William Bewley (d. 1783), Dr Samuel Johnson (d. 1784), Sir Joshua Reynolds (d. 1792), and, most recently, James Boswell, who died on 19 May 1795.

5. *The Memoirs of the Life and Writings of the Abate Metastasio* was published by G. G. and J. Robinson.

6. Not identified.

7. That is, of making HW a gift of the *Memoirs of . . . Metastasio.*

To Bertie Greatheed,[1] Monday 22 February 1796

Printed from the MS in Thomas Kirgate's hand, except for the signature, now WSL. First printed, Toynbee xv. 394–5; extracts printed in William Parsons, *Travelling Recreations*, 1807, ii. 155. The MS apparently was given by Bertie Greatheed to the actress Sarah Kemble (1755–1831), m. (1773) William Siddons; she was a friend of the Greatheed family and in 1788 played the role of Dianora in Greatheed's play, *The Regent*. The MS descended in the Siddons family until acquired by K. D. Duval, Books and Manuscripts, Falkland, Fife, 'direct from a Scottish descendant'; sold by Duval to WSL in April 1971.

HW's MS draft of this letter was bequeathed by Mrs Damer to Sir Jonathan Wathen Waller, 1st Bt (1769–1853) in 1828; it descended in the Waller family until given by his greatgrandson, Sir Wathen Arthur Waller, 5th Bt (1881–1947), of Woodcote, Warwick, ca 1923 to Lord Algernon Percy (1851–1933), of Guy's Cliff, Warwick, from whom it descended to his grandson, Commander David Heber-Percy, R. N. (1909–71); sold Sotheby's 21 July 1970 (property of Commander David Heber-Percy, R.N. retired), lot 653, to Maggs; offered by Maggs Cat. Nos 927 (Autumn 1970), lot 200, and 949 (Winter 1972), lot 138; sold to Edward H. Spencer ca 1974.

HW also had Kirgate make a fair copy of this letter which he retained and bound in his copy of the 6th edition of the *Castle of Otranto*, printed in 1791 by Bodoni at Parma, together with copies in sepia of four drawings by Bertie Greatheed, Jr (see n. 3 below), and a letter from James Edwards (1757–1816), bookseller in Pall Mall 1784–1804 (DALRYMPLE 212). For the history of this volume, now WSL, see Hazen, *Cat. of HW's Lib.*, No. 3729.

Berkeley Square, Feb. 22, 1796.

Dear Sir,

I HAVE been debating with myself for two days whether I should trouble you with this letter or not—at last I find that I cannot resist indulging myself. The grateful part is certainly most due, and my thanks must be very sincere, when vanity is the source of them, and the spring of what I have to say besides.

My extreme surprise at your son's[2] drawings,[3] which you was so very kind as to show me the other night, and I hope a little modesty

1. (1759–1826), dramatist (GM 1826, xcvi pt i. 367–8). The Greatheeds were close friends of Mrs Damer and of the Berry sisters, who visited them frequently at Guy's Cliff (BERRY i. 223 n. 11, ii. 91, 96, 124).

2. Bertie Greatheed, Jr (ca 1781–1804), amateur artist (GM 1804, lxxiv pt ii. 1073, 1236).

3. Four illustrations for HW's novel, *The Castle of Otranto*, 1765, depicting Jacquez and Diego frightened by the giant foot in the great chamber of the castle; the appearance of the spectre of the holy hermit to Frederic in Hippolita's oratory; the death of Matilda at the tomb of Alfonso; the apparition of Alfonso, dilated to an immense magnitude, proclaiming Theodore the true Prince of Otranto.

on finding them so superior to the trifling and fantastic subjects on which they are grounded, prevented my expressing half of what I felt—but it would be unjust to a father's feelings to suppress the high ideas I have conceived of your son's genius.

Though he is so extremely young, I am perfectly sure his drawings are completely his own—and I will tell you, Sir, what certifies me. I have seen many drawings and prints[4] made from my idle—I don't know what to call it, novel or romance—not one of them approached to any one of your son's four—a clear proof of which is, that not one of the rest satisfied the author's ideas—It is as strictly, and upon my honour, true, that your son's conception of some of the passions has improved them, and added more expression than I myself had formed in my own mind; for example, in the figure of the ghost in the chapel, to whose hollow sockets your son has given an air of reproachful anger, and to the whole turn of his person, dignity. Manfred in the last scene has an uncertain horror, that shows he has not yet had time to know what kind of agony he feels at what he has done. Such delineation of passions at so very youthful a period, or rather in boyhood, are indubitable indications of real genius, and cannot have issued from the instructions or corrections of a master—I know no man but young Mr Lock[5] capable of such exertions. He, not quite so juvenile as your son, shone by foreshortening and muscling—generally amongst the last acquisitions even of an able master—your son approaches him even in those uncommon talents; and, as far as I can presume to judge, draws excellently.

I am so charmed and interested in what you showed me, that if I flatter myself, Sir, at least you will be sure that I am not flattering you—in short, I must speak out. I am so delighted, and think myself so much honoured, by having contributed to inspire young Mr Greatheed with such speaking conceptions, that you cannot be surprised, if after meditating for above two days on the pleasure they gave me, I cannot sit down contented with a transient view, and with the bare recollection of every circumstance and attitude that struck me—and yet could I design at all like your son, I am certain

4. Among others, HW had seen drawings or prints of scenes from *The Castle of Otranto* by Anthony Highmore (*ante* 28 June 1783), Johann Wilhelm Meil, Anne Melicent Clarke (Hazen, *Bibl. of HW* 63–64), and John Carter (W. S.

Lewis, *Rescuing Horace Walpole*, New Haven, 1978, pp. 184–7).

5. William Locke, the younger (1767–1847), amateur artist, pupil of Henry Fuseli.

SCENE FROM 'THE CASTLE OF OTRANTO,'
BY BERTIE GREATHEED, THE YOUNGER

that I could sketch out at least the disposition of every one of the four drawings, and of every one of the principal characters, indeed of all but three or four. Will it then be taking too great a liberty, Sir, to own how much you would add to the great obligation you have already conferred on me, to allow me to have copies made of those astonishing drawings—you can depend on the care my own vanity would make me take of the originals, which my gratitude would oblige me to restore as safely.[6]

I have the honour to be, Sir, with the strongest sense of your kindness, and with the greatest esteem,

Your most obliged,
And most obedient humble servant,

ORFORD

From SIR JAMES COLQUHOUN, Thursday 31 March 1796

Printed for the first time from the MS in the hand of an amanuensis, except for the signature, now WSL. The letter, which HW tipped in the copy of *The Dances of Death, through the Various Stages of Human Life* presented to him by Sir James Colquhoun, has been removed from the book by WSL. It was sold SH vii. 79 to Cribb of King Street; not further traced until *penes* William Henry Fosdick; sold by his daughter, Mrs K. T. Riggs, of Athens, Georgia, to WSL in October 1947.

Edinburgh, St Andrew's Square, 31st March 1796.

My Lord,

I TAKE the opportunity of a friend[1] going to London, of sending your Lordship two specimens of our Scottish engravings. The first, 'The Dances of Death,'[2] engraved from the original designs,

---

6. The original drawings were in the possession of Sir Richard Proby, Bt, at Elton Hall, Peterborough, Northants, in November 1953, bound in a copy of the 6th edn of *The Castle of Otranto*, together with a copy of this letter made by Greatheed and a letter from him to the person (unknown) for whom Bertie Greatheed, Jr, made the drawings, requesting permission for HW to have

copies made. The volume was acquired by Sir Richard Proby's great-uncle, William Proby, 5th E. of Carysfort (1836–1909), from the Reginald Cholmondeley Sale, Christie's 1 Apr. 1897, lot 114, through Quaritch.

1. Not identified.
2. *Le Triomphe de la Mort gravé d'après les Dessins originaux de Jean*

which were cut in wood,[3] and afterwards painted by Holbein.[4] They are done by one of our first seal-cutters, a Mr Deuchar,[5] who has a genius in that way. The binding[6] I think extremely neat also, which will give your Lordship an idea how both these arts are advancing in this country.

The second is a publication by a Mr McNeill,[7] called 'Scotland's Skaith':[8]—the composition of which has been much admired; and, at the same time, will give you a specimen of our Scots printing.[9] The designs of the engravings, and the engravings themselves, are also executed by Scots artists.[10]

I also send your Lordship, two engraved heads:—the one, of my late worthy friend, and your acquaintance, Lord Hailes[11]—the

Holbein par David Deuchar, with an English title page, *The Dances of Death, through the Various Stages of Human Life . . . exhibited in forty-six Copper-plates, done from the Original Designs which were cut in Wood, and afterwards painted by John Holbein*, small quarto, Edinburgh, 1788, now WSL (Hazen, *Cat. of HW's Lib.*, No. 3715). Thirty of the designs follow those of Wencelaus Hollar published in 1651; sixteen were drawn from designs of Arnold Birckmann published at Cologne in 1555 (L. P. Kurtz, *The Dance of Death and the Macabre Spirit in European Literature*, New York, 1934, pp. 199, 201, 203).

3. *Les Simulachres et Historiées Faces de la Mort*, consisting of 41 woodcuts was published at Lyons in 1538 by Kaspar and Melchior Trechsel. They have been attributed to Hans Holbein (1497 or 1498–1543) although his name did not appear in the edition. The designs, which are a synthesis of the Dance of the Dead with the 'memento mori' type of vignette, were cut in the wood blocks by Hans Lützelburger (d. 1526) from Holbein's drawings (ibid., pp. 190–1; W. L. Gundersheimer, 'Introduction,' *The Dance of Death by Hans Holbein the Younger: A Complete Facsimile of the Original 1538 Edition of Les simulachres & historiees faces de la mort*, New York, 1971, pp. ix–x).

4. It was widely believed that Holbein had painted a *Dance of Death* on a wall in the churchyard of the Predicants in the suburbs of St John at Basle, a view that HW considered erroneous (*Anecdotes*

of Painting, Works iii. 67–8). Modern scholars date the painting, which was destroyed in 1805, ca 1470 and attribute it to Konrad Witz (Angèle Baumeister, 'HAP Grieshaber: The Dance of Death at Basle,' *Graphis*, 1966, xxii. 540).

5. David Deuchar (fl. 1743–1808), of Edinburgh, seal-cutter and engraver.

6. The book was bound in mottled calf but has been rebacked.

7. Hector MacNeill (1746–1818), Scottish poet and writer of ballads.

8. *Scotland's Skaith; or, the History o' Will and Jean: Owre True A Tale!*, Edinburgh, 1795, a popular ballad on the evils of drink, which passed through many editions (Hazen, op. cit., No. 1357).

9. The 1st and 2d edns were printed in 1795 by Mundell and Son, R. Bank Close, Edinburgh.

10. The frontispiece was engraved by Robert Scott (1771–1841), of Edinburgh, after the drawing by David Allan (1744–96), of Edinburgh, often called the 'Scottish Hogarth' (G. H. Bushnell, *Scottish Engravers*, 1949, pp. 2, 46–7); the plates, also designed by Allan, were engraved by Paton Thomson (?1750–after 1821) (Thieme and Becker xxxiii. 80). Scott was highly regarded for his small book illustrations; Thomson later engraved MacNeill's portrait as a frontispiece for his *Works* (1801).

11. See *ante* 17 April 1764, n. 1. The portrait of Lord Hailes was probably the engraving made by John Beugo (1759–1841), of Edinburgh, after the portrait painted by John Thomas Seton (fl. ca

other, of the late President Sir Thomas Millar.[12] I cannot say, I admire the engraving much; but being the only engraved heads of these two worthy characters, I thought I might venture to send them. And I shall be proud if your Lordship will think the trifles I have sent worthy your acceptance.[13] I however fondly hope that this will at least be adding to your Lordship's collection, what you are not already possessed of.

I have the honour to be
With great esteem and respect, My Lord,
Your Lordship's much obliged
and very humble servant,

J. W. COLQUHOUN

1760–1806) (J. C. Guy, 'Edinburgh Engravers,' *The Book of the Old Edinburgh Club,* Edinburgh, 1916, ix. 96–7; J. L. Caw, *Scottish Portraits,* Edinburgh, 1903, portfolio iii. 28–9, plate lxxi; *BM Cat. of Engraved British Portraits* ii. 4; Paul Harris, *A Concise Dictionary of Scottish Painters,* Edinburgh, 1976, p. 63).

12. Sir Thomas Miller (1717–89), cr. (1788) Bt; president of the College of Justice of Scotland, 1787–89, as Lord Glenlee; M.P. The portrait of Lord Glenlee was probably the engraving made by D. Blackmore Pyet in 1793 after the portrait painted by Sir Joshua Reynolds in 1761 (Edward Hamilton, *The Engraved Works of Sir Joshua Reynolds: A Catalogue Raisonné of the Engravings Made After His Paintings from 1755–1822,* new edn, Amsterdam, 1973, p. 52; information kindly supplied by Miss Sara F. Stevenson, Research Assistant, Scottish National Portrait Gallery).

13. HW found the books and engravings an 'agreeable present'; see *post* 3 May 1796.

To Mrs Garrick, Friday 1 April 1796

Printed for the first time from the MS now wsl. Not traced until sold Sotheby's 19 May 1926 (property of Mrs M. A. Rivington of St Leonard's-on-Sea, Sussex), lot 602 (with HW to Mrs Garrick 25 Oct 1794, and HW to Sir Isaac Heard 21 Jan. 1792) to B. F. Stevens & Brown; not further traced until acquired by exchange by wsl from the Folger Shakespeare Library in June 1950.

Dated by the reference to the only performance of *Vortigern* (see n. 4 below). *Address in Thomas Kirgate's hand:* To Mrs Garrick, Adelphi Terrace.

April 1st.

LORD ORFORD has but a minute's time to write, but shall be much obliged of Mrs Garrick,[1] if she can be so good as to let Mr Malone[2] have a place in her box[3] tomorrow night for *Vortigern.*[4]

1. Eva Maria Veigel, widow of David Garrick (*ante* 25 Aug. 1757 n. 5).

2. Edmond Malone, whose *Inquiry into the Authenticity of certain Miscellaneous Papers and Legal Instruments . . . attributed to Shakespeare* exposing the Ireland forgeries had been published the day before (*ante* 11 Jan. 1796 n. 3). Malone probably asked HW to intercede with Mrs Garrick for a place in her box because he anticipated that it would be difficult to secure tickets for the play.

3. Mrs Garrick kept up her connection with the theatre and had her own box at the Drury Lane theatre long after her husband's death in 1779 (Percy Fitzgerald, *The Life of David Garrick*, 2 vols, 1868, ii. 450).

4. *Vortigern*, one of William Henry Ireland's forgeries alleged to be a newly discovered play by Shakespeare, was acted for the first and only time at the Drury Lane theatre on Saturday 2 April 1796 and published by Samuel Ireland in 1799. The theatre was filled for the performance; hundreds of people had to be turned away; but the play was a failure, branded by critics as 'dull,' 'ludicrous,' 'a palpable forgery,' 'silly trash,' and almost laughed off the stage by the audience (*The Times* 4 Apr. 1796; *The Oracle and Public Advertiser*, 4 Apr. 1796; *Morning Herald*, 4 Apr. 1796; Bernard Grebanier, *The Great Shakespeare Forgery*, New York, 1965, pp. 211–23).

From A. Gomes,[1] Monday 2 May 1796

Printed for the first time from the MS now wsl. The MS apparently was included with the family papers bequeathed by HW to his grand-nephew George, 4th Earl of Cholmondeley (1749–1827), cr. (1815) Marquess of Cholmondeley (Family 311), and descended in the Cholmondeley family until acquired by wsl, with miscellaneous receipts, from the Marchioness of Cholmondeley in August 1955.

Endorsed by HW: had before in the stocks 82000£
added 4500£

86500£

remain in Croft's shop[2] 300£

Address: The R[igh]t Hon[oura]ble Hor. Earl of Orford.

2 May [17]96.

BOUGHT for the Right Honourable Hor. Earl of Orford by the hands of Wm Harris[3] Esq.

£4500—3 p[er] c[ent.] Cons[ols] at 66 ⅝[4] £2998.2.6
Com[mission] 5.12.6

£3003.15.0

which stock I have accepted in your name and send the receipts by said Mr Harris. I am happy to hear your Lordship is better,[5] hope [for] the continuance, and remain

Your Lordship's most obedient humble servant,

A. Gomes

1. Probably Abraham Gomes, who appears in the annual applications for membership in the Stock Exchange from 1802, when the series begins, to 1811; in 1811 his address was No. 3, Castle Street, Houndsditch (Guildhall Library MS 17957). This may have been the Abraham de Morderai Gomes Soares who signed a marriage contract as A. Gomes in 1785 (*Bevis Marks Records*, Pt II, 1949, p. 107, entry 1204; information kindly supplied by M. V. Roberts, Keeper of Enquiry Services, Guildhall Library, London); an Abraham Gomes was also one of the executors of his uncle's will in 1784 (Colyer-Fergusson Papers, University College Library, London; information kindly supplied by Mrs Emilie R. Steinhaus, Assistant Librarian, University College Library).

2. That is, on deposit with HW's bankers, Croft and Backwell of Pall Mall (Ossory ii. 116 n. 4).

3. See *ante* 27 Feb. 1771, n. 2.

4. 3 per cent Consols sold at 66⅝–66⅞ on 2 May (GM 1796, lxvi pt i. 448).

5. See *post* 3 May 1796 and n. 2.

To Sir James Colquhoun, Tuesday 3 May 1796

Printed from William Fraser, *The Chiefs of Colquhoun and their Country*, 2 vols, Edinburgh, 1869, i. 390, where it was first printed. The MS descended in the Colquhoun family and in 1869 was bound up in a volume of curious tracts in the possession of Sir James Colquhoun, grandson of the recipient of the letter; not further traced.

Address: To Sir James Colquhoun, in St Andrew's Square, Edinburgh.

Berkeley Square, May 3, 1796.

LORD ORFORD should be ashamed of not having sooner acknowledged the agreeable present of two books and two engravings[1] from Sir James Colquhoun if he had not been dangerously ill, in consequence of a long fit of the gout,[2] which fell upon one of his legs and produced an abscess, for which he is still under the surgeon's hands, and which has reduced him to a state of extreme weakness, and he hopes will apologise for thanking Sir James so superficially at present.

To Thomas William Coke,[1] Tuesday 7 June 1796

Printed for the first time from a photostat of the MS in Thomas Kirgate's hand in the possession of the Earl of Leicester, Holkham Hall, Norfolk. The MS passed by family descent to the present owner.

Endorsed by Coke: 1796. Lord Orford. Election.

Berkeley Square, June 7th 1796.

I SHOULD little deserve your favour, Sir, of which I am very ambitious, if I had not hastened to employ the little credit I have in Norfolk to support your interest,[2] when I heard it was likely to

---

1. See *ante* 31 March 1796.
2. On 19 March 1796 HW wrote to William Mason that he had suffered 'a very bad fit of the gout for fifteen weeks in every limb,' and added, 'I still cannot walk across my room, but held up by two or three servants . . . ; besides all this, I was very near going off towards the beginning of my illness by an inflammation in my bowels' (MASON ii. 337). See *ante* 5 Jan. 1796, n. 1. On 27 May he

wrote to William Roscoe that 'I am daily under the surgeon's hands' (DALRYMPLE 284).

———

1. (1754–1842), cr. (1837) E. of Leicester of Holkham; M.P. Norfolk 1776–84, 1790–1807, 1807–32; M.P. Derby Feb.–April 1807. As 'Mr Coke of Norfolk' he had the reputation of being the first Commoner of England (GEC).
2. Coke was standing for reelection as

be attacked. I am glad it was only threatened,³ and yet, that that menace demonstrated the affection of the County for you. The only unnecessary trouble it has given you, was thanking me for my useless zeal. I have the honour to be, with the greatest regard, Sir,

Your most obedient
humble servant,

ORFORD

To Sir James Colquhoun, Monday 20 June 1796

Printed from the MS in Thomas Kirgate's hand, now WSL. First printed in William Fraser, *The Chiefs of Colquhoun and their Country*, 2 vols, Edinburgh, 1869, i. 391. The MS descended in the Colquhoun family and in 1869 was bound up in a volume of curious tracts in the possession of Sir James Colquhoun, grandson of the recipient of the letter; it was removed from the volume and sold Sotheby's 22 June 1955 ('Other Properties'), lot 733, to Maggs for WSL.

Address: To Sir James Colquhoun at Edinburgh. *Postmark:* JU 20 96. F.

Berkeley Square, June 20th 1796.

I AM infinitely obliged to you, Sir, for your very kind inquiries¹ after a poor old cripple, who is the more unfortunate at not being able to thank you with his own hand.²

I have been laid up for four months by a severe fit of the gout,

M.P. for Norfolk. HW had recently ordered his stewards at Crostwick and at Houghton to instruct his tenants to vote for Coke in the election held on 2 June 1796 (FAMILY 291). He also sent letters on Coke's behalf to Norfolk at the end of May (BERRY ii. 184–5).

3. By Thomas Leigh Hare (ca 1749–1834), cr. (1818) Bt, of Stow Bardolph, Norfolk, and his supporters, who inserted advertisements in the *Norfolk Chronicle* 28 May, criticizing Coke and stating that a candidate would be nominated to oppose him in the election. Hare's intended candidate was Robert John Buxton (1753–1839), cr. (1800) Bt, who had been M.P. for Thetford 1790–6 and an active supporter of the younger Pitt. But Hare

withdrew his opposition on 31 May, apparently because Buxton refused to contest the election with Coke, who was a close friend of Charles James Fox. Buxton had 'a determination never to accept a seat in Parliament, unless unanimously elected' (*Norfolk Chronicle* 4 June). The Tory candidate, Sir John Wodehouse, 6th Bt, was also averse to a contest (BERRY ii. 185 n. 3). Coke was reelected to his seat on 2 June.

1. Colquhoun's letter is missing.
2. On 27 May 1796 HW wrote William Roscoe that his protracted illness had weakened him so much that he could 'neither write . . . nor dictate but by snatches' (DALRYMPLE 283).

and it was scarce going off when the venom fell on one of my legs, and produced two very dangerous abscesses, yet they too closed in nine weeks, and I am assured that I am getting well;[3] though at near seventy-nine,[4] I am not so weak as to expect more than a partial recovery, for some short time.[5] During such a period, if it does happen, I shall not forget how very kind you have been, Sir, to one who has the honour to be, with great respect and gratitude,

Your most obliged, and obedient humble servant

ORFORD

To Robert Blake,[1] Monday 27 June 1796

Printed for the first time from a photostat of the MS in the British Museum (Add. MS 18204, f. 127). The MS is untraced until acquired by the British Museum in 1850 with a collection of autograph letters and signatures of royal and illustrious persons said to have been formed by Mrs Cockle, governess to the children of William IV.

Endorsed, probably by Robert Blake: 27 June 96.
Address: To Rob. Blake Esq.

SHOULD not the £200 reserved for the College have been specified in this receipt?[2]

ORFORD

3. 'I have for seven weeks been in great danger,' HW wrote Roscoe, 'by the gout falling in two abscesses on one of my ankles, and it is but within three days that I have had hopes of recovery' (ibid.).
4. HW was born 24 September 1717 OS.
5. In July HW was well enough to go to Strawberry Hill (see *post* ca 12 July 1796), but on 29 August he wrote Hannah More that 'though perfectly healed, and even without a scar, my leg is so weakened that I have not recovered the least use of it, nor can move cross my chamber unless lifted up and held by two servants' (MORE 402).

1. HW's attorney in the settlement of the estate of his nephew, the 3d E. of Orford. Blake was a member of the firm of John Blake, John Norris, and Robert Blake in Essex Street, the Strand (*ante* 3 Jan. 1792; BERRY ii. 180 n. 11).
2. The receipt is missing. Probably it related to a payment of rents on Midsummer Day (24 June) from HW's tenants for the lands belonging to Christ's College, Cambridge, the leasehold of which HW had purchased from the executors of the estate of his nephew George, 3d E. of Orford (SELWYN 347).

To William Roscoe,[1] ca Tuesday 12 July 1796

Printed from the MS in Thomas Kirgate's hand, now wsl. An extract was previously printed in DALRYMPLE 285. The MS descended in the Roscoe family until sold Christie's 22 Apr. 1918 (Sale of Autographs in aid of the British Red Cross Society), lot 2230 (presented by Mrs Roscoe), to Bittencourt; resold Sotheby's 17 Dec. 1973 (property of a Gentleman), lot 253, to Seven Gables for wsl. The rest of HW's correspondence with Roscoe is printed in DALRYMPLE 258–64, 273–86.

Dated by HW's letter from SH to Lady Ossory 12 July 1796 when he wrote that he was 'quite content with being here again' (Ossory iii. 216).

Endorsed by Roscoe: Lord Orford.

Dear Sir,

AFTER eight months of a painful, and for some time, very dangerous illness,[2] I am recovered enough to bear being brought hither,[3] though so weak and lame that I have little prospect of being able to walk again; and you will excuse my not doing more than directing my letter with my own hand,[4] as every effort fatigues me.

One of my first thoughts, on my arrival here, was to have the two Florentine pieces taken out of my cabinet,[5] and I send you two most exact delineations of them, made by Mr Samuel Lysons;[6] and as you must have had them drawn for the engraver, I am sure it would have been impossible to have had them executed more minutely faithfully in every circumstance, though with the help of the largest magnifier we cannot decide what the three objects are in the little shield on the silver coin[7] near the word Noster; they seem to be pistols.

The copper medal,[8] though well-designed, seems rather to be a

1. (1753–1831), of Liverpool, historian; lawyer; banker; M.P.; HW's correspondent (DALRYMPLE 258 n. 1).

2. See *ante* 20 June 1796.

3. That is, to SH.

4. No address appears on the letter. Apparently it was written on a wrapper that has become separated from the letter.

5. The silver coin and copper medal (see nn. 7 and 8 below) were kept in the rosewood case in the library at SH.

6. Samuel Lysons (1763–1819), antiquary; F.S.A., 1786; brother of the Rev. Daniel Lysons, HW's 'chaplain,' to whose topographical works he contributed many etchings. He exhibited views of old buildings at the Royal Academy occasionally from 1785 to 1796 and published anonymously *Views and Antiquities in the County of Gloucester Hitherto Imperfectly or Never Engraved,* 1791–[8] (DALRYMPLE 194 n. 1; BERRY ii. 59 and n. 35; Hazen, *Cat. of HW's Lib.,* No. 3435; DNB).

7. 'A silver coin struck by the Republic of Florence when they declared Jesus Christ their King, to keep off the Pope: from Baron Stosch's collection: extremely rare' ('Des. of SH,' *Works* ii. 451). See also MANN v. 201–2, 233 n. 11.

8. A 'copper medal of Lorenzo of Medici, who stabbed Duke Alexander: the reverse copied from Brutus's medal,

cast, and the outline of the nose to have been a little rubbed; probably there never was a medal really struck.

I hope these drawings will arrive safely, and that you will not have waited for them;[9] nor will I detain you longer now, Sir, than to thank you again for your portrait,[10] which gives me the highest satisfaction, as the moment I showed it to Mr Edwards,[11] he knew it, and assured me how very like it is, which I can easily believe, as the acute sense in the countenance is worthy of the author of the *Life of Lorenzo*.

I am, Sir, with all the respect due to that author,

His most obliged
humble servant,

Orford

with the cap of liberty between two daggers; the legend, VIII ID. JAN. Very rare' ('Des. of SH,' loc. cit.; see also Dalrymple 278 n. 2).

9. HW was so favourably impressed by Roscoe's *Life of Lorenzo de' Medici*, published ca 13 Feb. 1796, that on 17 March he wrote to Roscoe: 'I am glad you intend a second edition, to which I *can* add two little notices that had escaped you'; these were the coin and medal (Dalrymple 274, 277–8). Roscoe thanked HW for Lysons's drawings on 6 Aug. (ibid. 286), but they

were not included in later editions. In the third edition, published in 1797, Roscoe acknowledged HW's help (ibid. 277–8 nn. 1, 5; 286 n. 4).

10. A miniature portrait of Roscoe, 1795, by Matthew Haughton (fl. 1795–1810), was sent to HW 19 May 1796, and HW thanked him for it on 27 May (ibid. 280 n. 3, 281 and n. 1, 283–4).

11. James Edwards, publisher of Roscoe's *Life of Lorenzo*; see ante 21 March 1794 n. 1 and Dalrymple 249, n. 1.

From Mrs Anna Aufrere,[1] Tuesday 12 July 1796

Printed from Toynbee *Supp.* iii. 311–12, where the letter was first printed. Damer-Waller; the MS was sold Sotheby's 5 Dec. 1921 (first Waller Sale), lot 118, to Maggs (with two other letters); not further traced.

The year is supplied by HW's letter to Mary Berry 26 July 1796; see n. 11 below.

Address: The Earl of Orford.

Hoveton Hall, near Norwich, Norfolk. July 12th.

My Lord

AS I cannot flatter myself with being known to your Lordship and consequently my presumption in troubling you must appear the greater, I beg leave to say, I lay no claim to your Lordship's compliance with my request, but should you not be biased in favour of any who have hitherto solicited you for the living of Crostwick[2] and should be pleased to consider my son,[3] you would confer upon me a lasting obligation—my niece Miss Norris[4] has kindly given him Ridlington[5] and East Ruston,[6] but is debarred from doing more for him by my brother[7] (her father) having disposed of the living of Bacton[8] by will to a more distant relation[9]—this is a hardship, which may induce your Lordship to attend to my application, if I am not too late in it—having so large a family as twelve children[10] you will I hope pardon a mother's desire to promote their

1. Anna Norris (ca 1734–1816), m. (1756) Anthony Aufrere (BERRY ii. 196 n. 8). Her brother John (n. 7 below) married HW's cousin, Charlotte Townshend (FAMILY 337; GEC *sub* Kimberley).

2. 4½ miles NE of Norwich, Norfolk. HW had inherited the advowson of All Saints Church at Crostwick (Crostwight) upon the death of his nephew George, 3d E. of Orford, in 1791 (SELWYN 344).

3. Rev. George John Aufrere (1769–1853), B.A., Corpus Christi College, Cambridge, 1793; vicar of Ridlington and East Ruston, Norfolk, 1794–1836; vicar of Bacton, Norfolk, 1810–23 (Burke, *Landed Gentry,* 1879, i. 52; Venn, *Alumni Cantab.* Pt II, i. 100).

4. Charlotte Laura Norris (d. 1845), m.

(18 Nov. 1796) Hon. John Wodehouse, 2d Bn Wodehouse of Kimberley, 1834.

5. That is, the vicarage of St Peter's Church at Ridlington, 4½ miles E. of North Walsham, Norfolk.

6. That is, the vicarage of St Mary's Church at East Ruston, 4 miles SE of North Walsham, Norfolk.

7. John Norris (1734–77), founder of the Norrisian Professorship of Divinity at Cambridge.

8. That is, the vicarage of St Andrew's Church at Bacton, 4½ miles NE of North Walsham, Norfolk. The Rev. George John Aufrere did, however, become vicar of Bacton in 1810; see n. 3 above.

9. Not identified.

10. Mrs Aufrere had five sons and seven daughters.

interest—and as my son performs his duty in the Church with more than usual applause I do not fear your Lordship's being satisfied with him, should you honour him with your election[11]—I beg my Lord again to repeat my apologies for this liberty, and to assure you that whether successful or not,

> I shall remain your Lordship's
> most obedient—humble servant
>
> ANNA AUFRERE

To the REV. JOHN ELDERTON,[1] Thursday 4 August 1796

Printed for the first time from the MS in Thomas Kirgate's hand, now WSL. The MS was bound in a copy of *Copies of Seven Original Letters from King Edward VI to Barnaby Fitz-Patrick,* SH, 1772, presented by Lord Ossory to the Rev. John Elderton 29 June 1788, from which it was removed by WSL (Hazen, *SH Bibl.* 101); not further traced until sold Hodgson's 21 Oct. 1937 (Markham Sale), lot 473, to Maggs for WSL.

Endorsed in an unidentified hand on the verso: The Earl of Orford's Note to Reverend J. E.

Endorsed in a different hand on the recto: Earl of Orford (late Hon. Horace Walpole's) Note to Reverend J. E.

Strawberry Hill, August 4th 1796.

LORD ORFORD has been so ill with the gout ever since last year as not to be able to write himself, nor can he recollect now having seen Mr Elderton's pictures.[2] He has formerly, at different times, seen different sets of heads of kings and queens of England, but none of them by any eminent master: there were two sets at least at

11. HW wrote to Mary Berry 26 July 1796: 'The living of Crostwick, which . . . Mrs Aufrere . . . would have *carried off* from me, is not vacant, and if it were, . . . is a miserable pittance of not thirty pounds a year' (BERRY ii. 196). The rector may have been the Rev. Thomas Hutchinson (or Hutchesson) (b. ca 1726), who became rector of Crostwick in 1756 (Venn, op. cit., Pt I, ii. 441; Francis Blomefield and Charles Parkin, *An Essay towards a Topographical History of the County of Norfolk,* 1805–10, xi. 13).

1. John Elderton (ca 1755–1832), chaplain to the 7th Earl of Cork and Orrery; vicar of Aldbourne, Wilts, 1781–1832 (Foster, *Alumni Oxon., 1715–1886,* ii. 417; GM 1832, cii pt ii. 580).

2. Presumably a collection of portraits of kings and queens of England.

Kensington;³ one suite at Mr Sheldon's at Weston;⁴ another at the Duke of Devonshire's at Hardwick;⁵ but none of them by Holbein,⁶ who I never heard painted a set of kings. Lord Orford has mentioned in his *Anecdotes of Painting*⁷ what painters there were in the reigns Mr Elderton mentions.⁸

To Lady Anne Conolly, early December 1796

Printed for the first time from a photostat of the MS in Thomas Kirgate's hand in Trinity College Library, Cambridge (MS Cullum Q. 122). The MS is untraced until given by Mrs William Bradstreet, who had it among her family papers, to George Gery Milner-Gibson-Cullum, who bequeathed it, together with a collection of his family papers, to Trinity College, Cambridge, in 1921.

Dated by HW's reference to suffering from the 'very cold weather' (see n. 1 below).

LORD ORFORD was very desirous of waiting on Lady Ann Conolly before she went to town, but he has suffered so much by the very cold weather¹ that he does not dare to stir out of his room. He hopes her Ladyship will be much better for going to London.

3. The 'two sets' of portraits of English kings and queens at Kensington Palace are described in George Bickham, *Deliciæ Britannicæ; or, the Curiosities of Kensington, Hampton Court, and Windsor Castle, Delineated*, 2d edn [?1755], pp. 13–14, 33–52. The set in the Gallery included portraits of all of the monarchs from Henry VIII to George II except Edward VI and Charles I, painted by Holbein, Lely, Van Dyck, Kneller, and others; the second set, in Queen Caroline's closet, included portraits of all the monarchs from Henry VIII to Queen Anne except James II and William III, painted by Holbein, Boit, Cooper, and others. HW undoubtedly became familiar with these portraits at Kensington in 1764 when he 'had the superintendence of that palace during the absence abroad of my sister Lady Mary Churchill, then housekeeper' (CHATTERTON 322 and nn. 7, 9).
4. HW visited Sheldon Hall, the seat of William Sheldon (d. 1780) at Weston, Warwick, in September 1768, where he saw a collection of 'Kings of England from

Henry 5th to Edward 6th both inclusive' (*Country Seats* 62; GM 1780, l. 445).
5. HW visited Hardwick Hall, Derbyshire, in August 1760, where, he reported, among the 'wretched pictures' there was 'a whole history of Kings of England, not worth sixpence apiece' (MONTAGU i. 297–8).
6. Hans Holbein (1497 or 1498–1543), whose portraits of some of the Tudor kings and queens were included in the 'two sets' of portraits at Kensington Palace.
7. SH, 1762–71.
8. Elderton's letter to HW is missing.

———

1. On 6 Dec. 1796 HW's secretary, Thomas Kirgate, wrote Lady Ossory that 'Lord Orford was struck last Thursday night by the intense cold, which . . . gave him great pain in both legs, which turned into an inflammation the next day in the right leg. . . . In this state he was brought to town on Friday last . . . and . . . he is now lying on a couch in a state of weakness and age, that keeps him from seeing anybody' (OSSORY iii. 227).

To RICHARD GOUGH, Monday 5 December 1796

Printed from the MS in Thomas Kirgate's hand (except for the signature), now WSL. First printed, Nichols, *Lit. Anec.* vi. 292–3. Reprinted, Wright vi. 534–5; Cunningham ix. 477; Toynbee xv. 430–1 (closing and signature omitted in Wright, Cunningham, and Toynbee). For the history of the MS see *ante* 24 August 1789.

Endorsed by John Bowyer Nichols: To Richard Gough Esq. Printed in 'Literary Anecdotes.'

Berkeley Square, December 5, 1796.

Dear Sir,

BEING struck with the extreme cold of last week, it has brought a violent gouty inflammation into one of my legs, and I was forced to be instantly brought to town very ill.[1] As soon as I was a little recovered I found here your most magnificent present of the second volume of *Sepulchral Monuments,*[2] the most splendid work I ever saw, and which I congratulate myself on having lived long enough to see; indeed I congratulate my country on its appearance exactly at so illustrious a moment, when the patriotism and zeal of London have exhibited so astonishing marks of their opulence and attachment to the constitution, by a voluntary subscription of seventeen millions of money in three days.[3] Your book, Sir, appearing at that very instant, will be a monument of a fact so unexampled in history; the treasure of fine prints[4] with which it is stowed well becomes such a production and such a work, the expense[5] of which becomes it too. I am impatient to be able to sit up and examine it more, and am sure my gratitude will increase in proportion. As

---

1. See previous letter, n. 1.

2. The first volume of Gough's *Sepulchral Monuments* was published in 1786; see *ante* 21 June 1786 and n. 1.

3. On Thursday, 1 Dec., the Bank of England opened Pitt's 'experiment of a voluntary subscription' for a loan under which the government would issue four-year convertible debentures instead of stock in order to raise funds for carrying on the war with France. Despite the criticism that this plan departed from 'the good old practice,' 'at the close of the subscription at the Bank on Saturday, there were seventeen millions subscribed to the voluntary loan' (*Morning Chronicle,*

28 Nov. 1796; *Morning Herald,* 5 Dec. 1796). An additional million was pledged before noon on 5 Dec., and this rapid achievement of Pitt's goal was regarded as a demonstration of generosity and patriotism, since the subscribers could have made more advantageous investments (*The Times,* 2 Dec., 6 Dec. 1796; *Morning Herald,* 3 Dec. 1796; *The Oracle and Public Advertiser,* 6 Dec., 7 Dec. 1796).

4. Vol. II of *Sepulchral Monuments* contains 131 plates as well as many small engravings in the text.

5. According to Joseph Farington, the second volume of *Sepulchral Monuments* cost 2000 guineas (DALRYMPLE 334–5).

soon as I shall receive the complete sheets, I will have the whole work bound in the most superb manner[6] that can be; and though being so infirm now, and just entered into my eightieth year,[7] I am not likely to be able to wait on you and thank you, I shall be happy to have an opportunity, whenever you come this way, of telling you in person how much I am charmed with so splendid a monument of British glories, and which will be so proud an ornament to the libraries of any nation.

I am, Sir,
with the highest gratitude and respect,
Your most obedient
humble servant,

ORFORD

TO MARGARET PLANTA,[1] Tuesday 13 December 1796

Printed for the first time from a transcript made by WSL in Sept. 1932 from the MS copy in Thomas Kirgate's hand bound in his copy of the *Description of Strawberry Hill*, 1784, then in the possession of Lord Walpole of Wolterton Park, Norfolk. The history of this volume before 1932 is not known; the original letter is missing.

Address: To Miss Planter.

Endorsed by Thomas Kirgate: The new catalogue was MS; Lord Orford thinking some parts of the printed one improper for the perusal of the Princess.

Berkeley Square, Dec. 13, 1796.

Madam,

HAVING received some time ago, by Lord Harcourt,[2] the commands of her Royal Highness the Princess Elizabeth,[3] to send her a catalogue of my collection at Strawberry Hill, I have been

---

6. The Introduction to *Sepulchral Monuments* was not published until 1799, and HW's two-volume set was still in 'boards, uncut' when sold SH viii. 123 to H. G. Bohn for £10.5.0. See Hazen, *Cat. of HW's Lib.*, No. 3644.

7. HW was born 24 Sept. 1717 OS.

---

1. (1754–1834), English teacher to the royal princesses 1778–1812 (*The Journals and Letters of Fanny Burney*, ed. Joyce Hemlow et al., Oxford, 1972– , i. 11 n. 2).

However, Fanny Burney remarked that although 'Miss Planta's post in the court calendar is that of English teacher, . . . it seems to me, that of personal attendant upon the two eldest princesses' (*Diary and Letters of Madame d'Arblay*, ed. Austin Dobson, 1904–5, ii. 447).

2. See *ante* ?16 Apr. 1766, n. 3.

3. (1770–1840), 3d dau. of George III, m. (1818) Friedrich Josef Ludwig, hereditary prince and (1820) Landgrave of Hesse-Homburg.

extremely anxious ever since to obey so gracious a command in the best manner I was able, and which only my great weakness and infirmities (not being able to move about my house but in the arms of two of my servants) prevented my completing till now.[4] I have had a new catalogue drawn up, for the old one[5] had been made in great haste, and was very imperfect, material articles not having then been purchased, and the disposition of many changed, besides the insertion of several of no kind of value. Many that are specified are certainly not worthy of her Royal Highness's notice, but if a review of the list can amuse her for a moment, Lord Orford shall feel it as an addition to the very great honour which her Royal Highness has already been pleased to confer on him,[6] and shall no longer think that he has lost his time in collecting so many baubles.

He begs you, Madam, to lay this humble offering at her Royal Highness's feet with vows of his most respectful duty and gratitude, and he shall be,

Madam,
Your most obliged and obedient humble servant,

ORFORD

To the REV. MARK NOBLE, Thursday 12 January 1797

Printed from a photostat of the MS in Thomas Kirgate's hand, now in the Bodleian Library (MS Eng. misc. d. 156, f. 117). First printed, Toynbee *Supp.* iii. 339–40. For the history of the MS see *ante* 1 Jan. 1785.

Berkeley Square, Jan. 12th 1797.

I HAVE received, Sir, your *History of the Medici*,[1] and am much obliged to you for it; it is well, and judiciously, and impartially written, and a satisfactory supplement to Mr Roscoe's *Lorenzo*,[2]

4. Apparently the Princess's request for a catalogue had been received in the summer of 1796, for on 25 July HW was attempting to dictate it to Kirgate but had to leave off because of illness (BERRY ii. 194).

5. HW had printed 200 copies of *A Description of the Villa . . . at Strawberry Hill* in 1784 but withheld nearly all of them from distribution (Hazen, *SH Bibl.* 123).

6. The Princess had visited SH on 3 July 1795 and had been very enthusiastic about it (CONWAY iii. 511 n. 1).

1. See *ante* 22 March 1787, n. 1; HW had read Noble's *Memoirs of the Illustrious House of Medici* in manuscript. HW's presentation copy is Hazen, *Cat. of HW's Lib.*, No. 416.

2. William Roscoe's *Life of Lorenzo de' Medici* (*ante* 21 March 1794, n. 2, and HW to Roscoe ca 12 July 1796, n. 9).

who I think is by far the best of our historians, both for beauty of style and for deep reflections, and his translations of poetry are equal to the originals.

I am sorry, Sir, I missed the pleasure of seeing you when you called,[3] I was dangerously ill the greatest part of last winter, and was so lamed that I have not had the free use of my feet since; and had a new attack last month, but am recovered enough to be quite out of pain, though I seldom go out of my own house.

I should have been glad to see that coin or medal you mention[4] of Lord Arundel,[5] but you do not say where you saw it, nor whether it is still to be sold; nor am I acquainted with the tract about Sir Thomas Wyat,[6] that you mention, nor do I know of what authenticity it is.

I am, Sir,
Your obliged
humble servant

ORFORD

From the REV. MARK NOBLE, Monday 16 January 1797

Printed for the first time from the extract in Thomas Thorpe's Catalogue of Manuscripts, Pt IV, 1834, lot 1139. Not further traced. Thorpe's Catalogue states that Noble was 'concerned to hear the gout had been such an enemy to his Lordship.'

Barming Parsonage,[1] Jan. 16, 1797.

THE very flattering ideas which your character[2] of the Medici Memoirs have raised in my mind, has rewarded twenty years' labour. Praise from Lord Orford is praise indeed. I shall reflect

3. The date of this visit is not known.

4. Mentioned presumably in a letter accompanying the presentation copy of Noble's book. The coin or medal has not been identified.

5. In Noble's reply (post 16 Jan. 1797), he refers to an embossed plate of Lord Arundel.

6. John Proctor, The Historie of Wyates

Rebellion, 1554, identified in Noble's reply post 16 Jan. 1797 and n. 6; this concerns Sir Thomas Wyatt the younger.

1. Noble was rector of Barming, Kent, 1786–1827.

2. Ante 12 Jan. 1797, where HW praises Noble's Memoirs of the Illustrious House of Medici.

upon it with satisfaction as long as I live.[3] I think Mr Roscoe's work[4] deserving every commendation.[5] . . . The tract relative to Sir Thomas Wyat's Rebellion[6] was published by one Pryor,[7] immediately after the gentleman's unhappy death.[8] It is now in the British Museum.

From Richard Clarke,[1] February 1797

Printed for the first time from the extract in Thomas Thorpe's Catalogue of Manuscripts, Pt IV, 1834, lot 1139, where the letter is described as sending HW 'a few scenes of a tragedy, called Belisarius.' Not further traced.

George Street, Surrey Road, Feb. [17]97.

. . . At the age of 74 I teach the Hebrew and the Classics, and should be glad of a private tuition. As a Universalist[2] in my belief, and, I trust, in my spirit too, I can live with any family. Deists[3] have never had the Gospel, nor heard its sound yet by any publisher or preacher.

3. Noble in his *Memoirs of the . . . Medici*, 1797, pp. 287–8, in discussing Bianca Cappello writes, 'England boasts two likenesses of her, they are both at Strawberry Hill, the seat of the Earl of Orford, and where the writer of these memoirs spent one of his happiest days. The one is a miniature, the other a portrait. The former, when Bianca was at the height of her charms, the other not long before her death: they are both invaluable.'

4. William Roscoe's *Life of Lorenzo de' Medici (ante* 21 March 1794, n. 2).

5. Thorpe's Catalogue states that Noble 'promises to make inquiries respecting an embossed plate of Lord Arundel.' This refers to the 'coin or medal you mention of Lord Arundel' (*ante* 12 Jan. 1797).

6. John Proctor, *The Historie of Wyates Rebellion, with the order and maner of resisting the same, wherunto in the ende is added an earnest conference with the . . . rebelles for the serche of the cause of their daily disorder,* printed by Robert Caly, 1554; another edition in 1555 (BM Cat.) It was reprinted in Edward Arber,

An English Garner, vol. VIII, 1896 and 1903.

7. John Proctor (?1521–84), historian; B.A. (Oxon.), 1540, M.A., 1544; master of the school of Tunbridge, Kent; rector of St Andrew, Holborn, 1578.

8. Sir Thomas Wyatt the younger (?1521–11 April 1554) was beheaded on Tower Hill for treason.

———

1. Possibly Richard Clarke, son of Henry Clarke, of Winchester, who matriculated at University College, Oxford, 17 Dec. 1741, aged 18 (Foster, *Alumni Oxon. 1715–1886*, i. 257); he may have been the Mr Clarke who kept 'a respectable school at Twickenham' ca 1749 at which he gave instruction in the classics (Nichols, *Lit. Anec.* i. 300–1).

2. 'One who believes or maintains the doctrine that redemption or election is extended to the whole of mankind and not confined to a part of it' (OED).

3. 'One who acknowledges the existence of a God upon the testimony of reason, but rejects revealed religion' (OED).

The Bishop of Landaff,[4] who is an infidel without knowing it, says that infidelity is spreading in great families.[5] When was it not found in them?

The following undated letters are arranged alphabetically by the names of the correspondents. New information has made it possible to date some of the letters, but it came too late for them to be inserted in the preceding chronological sequence, and so they have been kept in this group.

To Mrs Abington, early June 1771

Printed from a photostat of the MS in the British Museum (Add. MS 9828, f. 144). First printed, Wright vi. 44 (misdated 1779). Reprinted, Cunningham vii. 195 (misdated 1779); *The Life of Mrs Abington,* ['By the Editor of the "Life of Quin"'], 1888, p. 49; Toynbee xv. 437 (undated); Harold Simpson and Mrs Charles Braun, *A Century of Famous Actresses 1750–1850,* 1913, p. 122. The MS was acquired before 1836 by the British Museum in a volume of letters written to Mrs Abington.

Dated by HW's letter to Mann 8–10 June 1771 in which he mentions his dinner for foreign ambassadors at SH on Sunday, 9 June (n. 2 below). HW left for Paris 7 July 1771 and Mrs Abington arrived there in late August (see n. 4 below; du Deffand v. 333).

M R WALPOLE cannot express how much he is mortified that he cannot accept of Mrs Abington's obliging invitation,[1] as he had engaged company to dine with him on Sunday[2] at Strawberry

4. Richard Watson (1737–1816), D.D. 1771; regius professor of divinity, Cambridge, 1771–87; Bp of Llandaff, 1782–1816.

5. 'Infidelity is a rank weed, it threatens to overspread the land; its root is principally fixed amongst the great and opulent' (Richard Watson, *An Apology for the Bible, in a Series of Letters, Addressed to Thomas Paine,* Dublin, 1796, p. 145).

1. Missing.

2. 9 June 1771. HW wrote Mann 8 June 1771: 'Some of their representatives are to dine here tomorrow . . . there will be a little *corps diplomatique,* the French, Spanish, and Austrian ministers,' i.e., the Comte de Guines, Principe di Masserano, and Conte di Belgioioso (Mann vii. 311). On 'Sunday night' HW wrote: 'My party has succeeded to admiration, and Gothic architecture has received great applause' (ibid. 312).

Hill, whom he would put off, if not foreigners[3] who are leaving England. Mr Walpole hopes however that this accident will not prevent an acquaintance which his admiration of Mrs Abington's genius has made him long desire;[4] and which he hopes to cultivate at Strawberry Hill when her leisure will give him leave to trouble her with an invitation.[5]

To Lady Diana Beauclerk, 1782–90

Printed for the first time from a photostat of the MS in the Penzance Library. The history of the MS is not known.

An autograph, 'Hor. Walpole,' is pasted at the bottom of the MS.

Dated between 1782 and 1790 when both Lady Diana Beauclerk and George Selwyn were HW's near neighbours at Twickenham and Richmond (see below, nn. 2, 3).

Endorsed in an unidentified hand: To Lady Diana Beauclerk.

Y OUR LADYSHIP said here t'other night that you wished to know where to get some Frontignac wine.[1] I have inquired and got some that I am assured is very good; but as I am no judge, I have taken only a dozen bottles for a trial, and those to be returned,

3. Adrien-Louis de Bonnières (1735–1806), Comte and (1776) Duc de Guines, French ambassador to England 1770–6 (Mann vii. 256–7 n. 16); Vittorio Filippo Ferrero di Biella (1713–77), Principe di Masserano, Spanish ambassador to England 1763–72, ca 1775–7 (ibid. vi. 441 n. 11); Lodovico Carlo Maria (1728–1801), Conte di Barbiano di Belgioioso, Austrian minister to England 1770–82 (More 152 n. 16).

4. HW called on Mrs Abington in Paris on 30 Aug., and she invited him to call on her in London; see *ante* 31 Aug., 1 Sept. 1771. He was present at the opening of Sheridan's *The School for Scandal* at Drury Lane 8 May 1777 and praised her performance in a letter to Robert Jephson *ante* 13 July 1777.

5. We have found no record of this invitation, but see *ante* 11 June 1780, when HW offers to show her and her

friends around SH on any day she may choose; this letter implies that she had been there before.

1. From Frontignan on the Mediterranean coast of France, 'its sweet, golden Muscat wine . . . is the best French wine of its type, a *vin de liqueur* of considerable distinction and real class. These qualities, rare in Muscatels, it owes to the fact that it is made from a special, much superior variety of grape, the Muscatdoré-de-Frontignan' (*Frank Schoonmaker's Encyclopedia of Wine*, 6th edn, New York, 1976, p. 143). 'The Muscat vines, named for a port in Arabia, were probably introduced by returning Crusaders'; and in the 1530's Rabelais was familiar with the Muscat wines from Mireval and Frontignan (*Alexis Lichine's Guide to the Wines and Vineyards of France*, New York, 1979, p. 286).

if they do not prove good; so pray do not say you like them if you do not, and I will get you some other, and a larger quantity.

Mr Selwyn brings this,[2] and will bring your answer.[3] Tell me at what hour I shall send them, I suppose early in a morning. If you please I will send you a smaller quantity, and can do this as often as you want them, that they may not go into the cellar.

I am not able to wait on you yet, as you see by my writing, my hand is still bad,[4] and the fog yesterday hurt me a good deal, and brought back some pain into my foot.

2. George Selwyn took a house in Richmond in 1782 and lived there most of the time until his death on 25 Jan. 1791 (his London house was in Cleveland Court, St James's; his family seat was Matson, near Gloucester). HW wrote Selwyn 5 July 1786: 'I think you quite in the right to prefer Richmond to Gloucestershire, or rather, to live most where you find yourself most amused' (SELWYN 279; see also S. Parnell Kerr, *George Selwyn and the Wits*, 1909, pp. 308–9, 311–19). Selwyn's letters from Richmond to Lord and Lady Carlisle 1786–90 are printed in Hist. MSS Comm., 15th Report, App. vi (*Carlisle MSS*), 1897, pp. 645–69, 674–94.

3. Missing. Lady Diana Beauclerk lived at Little Marble Hill, Twickenham, 1782–9, and had moved to Devonshire Cottage, Richmond, before 26 Nov. 1790, where she stayed until her death (OSSORY ii. 182–3 n. 16; BERRY i. 82 n. 34, 148 n. 5). HW's 'Note to the Postscript' of his manuscript *The Parish Register of Twickenham*

(bound in his copy of the *Des. of SH*, 1774) says: 'After Mr Beauclerc's death she bought the small but most beautifully situated house next to Marble Hill, and opposite to Ham House. . . . She left that house in 1789, and bought another, next to the Duke of Montagu's, at the foot of Richmond Hill.' HW wrote Mary Berry 26 Nov. and 17 Dec. 1790 of his 'agreeable society at Richmond,' including Lady Diana and Selwyn, who met almost daily at Mrs Bouverie's, at Lady Diana's, at the Duke of Queensberry's, or at other houses (BERRY i. 148, 163–4). Selwyn wrote Lady Carlisle in Oct. 1790: 'The Duke [of Queensberry] is here. . . . We went together last night, and sat an hour at Lady Di's with Mr and Mrs Bouverie' (*Carlisle MSS*, op. cit. 692; see also BERRY i. 152 and nn. 37, 39; OSSORY ii. 541 and nn. 29, 30).

4. HW had a bad attack of the gout in his hands in Dec. 1790; see ante 21 Dec. 1790 and BERRY i. 174, 176–8.

From the DUCHESS OF BEDFORD,[1] n.d.

Printed from the MS now WSL. First printed, Toynbee *Supp.* iii. 312. Damer-Waller; the MS was sold Sotheby's 5 Dec. 1921 (first Waller Sale), lot 92, bought in; resold Christie's 15 Dec. 1947 (second Waller Sale), lot 53 (with nine other letters to HW), to Maggs for WSL.

Address: To the Honourable Horace Walpole.

Sunday.

THE Duchess of Bedford's compliments to Mr Walpole, and if he happens to be at the auction[2] tomorrow when the bust of Faustina,[3] lot 92, is sold (and has no thoughts of it for himself), she should be much obliged to him if he will buy it for her, if it is tolerable.[4]

1. Hon. Gertrude Leveson Gower (1715–94), m. (1737), as his second wife, John Russell, 4th D. of Bedford, 1732.
2. Not identified.
3. Faustina the younger (ca 125–76), wife of the Roman emperor Marcus Aurelius.
4. A 'Bust of Faustina the Younger' is listed among the objects in the Sculpture Gallery at Woburn Abbey in J. D. Parry, *History and Description of Woburn and its Abbey,* [1831], p. 280, No. 149. Miss Gladys Scott Thomson has informed us that it is now accepted that the bust at Woburn is the one referred to in the letter.

To Grosvenor Bedford, ca Thursday 17 January 1760

Printed from Cunningham iv. 22, where the letter was first printed. Reprinted, Toynbee xv. 437. The history and whereabouts of the MS are not known.

Dated approximately by the reference to 'the subscription for the French prisoners' (see n. 1 below).

Dear Sir,

I WISH you would be so good as to give five guineas for me (but without my name) to the subscription for the French prisoners, which I see by the enclosed advertisement has taken place;[1] and put it into the next account.

It is at Mr Biddulph's, banker,[2] at Charing Cross.

Yours ever,

H. W.

---

1. Advertisements by a 'Committee of several Noblemen and Gentlemen' seeking subscriptions to provide warm clothing for French prisoners appeared in the *Daily Advertiser* frequently between 3 Jan. and 12 Jan. 1760. On 16 Jan. a longer advertisement, listing the members of the committee and the subscriptions already received at 'Mess. Biddulph and Cocks's,' was printed; it also appeared in the *London Chronicle* 15–17 Jan. 1760. More than £1782.17.3 was subscribed (ibid. 15–17 Jan., 17–19 Jan., 24–26 Jan. 1760).

2. The earliest record of the banking firm of Biddulph and Cocks, New Buildings, Charing Cross, appears in 1763, when the members of the firm were Francis Biddulph (d. 1800), James Cocks (1734–1804), and Thomas Somers Cocks (1737–96) (F.G.H. Price, *A Handbook of London Bankers,* 1890–1, p. 39; BERRY ii. 18 n. 8; GM 1800, lxx pt ii. 1110).

TO GROSVENOR BEDFORD, n.d. 1

Printed from Cunningham iv. 23, where the letter was first printed. Reprinted, Toynbee xv. 437. The history and whereabout of the MS are not known.

This letter and the three following letters must have been written while Bedford was HW's deputy at the Exchequer (21 Aug. 1755–4 Nov. 1771). HW often asked him to carry out personal commissions.

Strawberry Hill, Oct. 12.

Dear Sir,

THE next time you go that way, be so good as to drop two guineas for me, but not in my name, according to the enclosed advertisement.[1]

I hope your gout is quite gone off.

Yours ever,

H. W.

TO GROSVENOR BEDFORD, n.d. 2

Printed from Cunningham iv. 23, where the letter was first printed. Reprinted, Toynbee xv. 438. The history and whereabouts of the MS are not known.

For conjectural dating see *ante* HW to Bedford n.d. 1.

Arlington Street, Oct. 29.

Dear Sir,

AS YOU go into the City, I will be obliged to you, if you will give two guineas for me at the Poultry,[1] but it must be ordered to be laid out only for the comfort of the sick prisoners, according to this enclosed advertisement.[2]

Yours, etc.,

H. W.

---

1. Presumably a newspaper advertisement soliciting contributions to a charitable cause.

---

1. The Poultry Compter, Wood Street, was a sheriff's prison chiefly for debtors, although a few felons and petty offenders were also confined there. No surgeon attended poor prisoners who were ill, the only provision for their care being 'a close

To Grosvenor Bedford, n.d. 3

Printed from Cunningham iv. 23, where the letter was first printed. Reprinted, Toynbee xv. 438. The history and whereabouts of the MS are not known.
For conjectural dating of the letter see *ante* HW to Bedford n.d. 1.

Dear Sir,

I WISH that any morning as you go into the City, you would take the trouble of calling at the Poultry Compter.[1] The poor people there have advertised several times[2] to beg money to pay their fees of discharge. I would give them two guineas towards it if I could be sure it would be honestly employed for them, and will beg you, if you find that possible, to advance it.

Yours ever,

H. Walpole

To Grosvenor Bedford, n.d. 4

Printed from Cunningham ix. 496, where the letter was first printed. Reprinted, Toynbee xv. 438–9. The history and whereabouts of the MS are not known.
For conjectural dating of the letter see *ante* HW to Bedford n.d. 1.

A S SOON as ever you receive the enclosed advertisement, pray carry it yourself to G. Woodfall,[1] printer, next Craig's Court, Charing Cross, and have it put into the *Public Advertiser* of tomor-

darkish room for the sick' (John Howard, *The State of the Prisons in England and Wales*, 1777, pp. 170–1; John Stow, *A Survey of the Cities of London and Westminster . . . Brought Down to the Present Time by Careful Hands*, 6th edn, 1754–5, i. 567; see also H. B. Wheatley, *London Past and Present*, 1891, iii. 117–18).
2. The advertisement has not been found.

———

1. See *ante* HW to Grosvenor Bedford n.d. 2, n. 1.
2. The advertisements have not been found.

1. George Woodfall (fl. 1748–71), bookseller and dealer in pamphlets first at the Kings Arms, Charing Cross; by 1760 at the corner of Craig's Court, and by 1771 at No. 6 Silver Street, Whitefriar's. His brother was Henry Woodfall (d. 1769), editor and printer of the *Public Advertiser* until 1758, whose son, Henry Sampson Woodfall (1739–1805), succeeded him in 1758. George Woodfall presumably received items for insertion in the *Public Advertiser* (Nichols, *Lit. Anec.* i. 300–1; N & Q 1855, xi. 377, xii. 217–18; H. R. Plomer, G. H. Bushnell, and E. R. McC. Dix, *A Dictionary of the Printers and*

row. Be so good not to mention it to any mortal,[2] and take care he does not know you nor suspect that you are a friend of mine. If he makes any scruple of inserting the last words, offer him more money, and if he will not, propose to change *scandalous* into *abusive,* and then I think he will have no exception.[3] I will explain all this to you when I see you.

Yours, etc.,

H. W.

To Grosvenor Bedford, n.d. 5

Printed for the first time from a photostat of the MS in the Royal Institution of Great Britain, London, kindly brought to our attention by Professor James E. Tierney. The MS is untraced until bound in an album (John Barlow's Book of Letters XV A, 186, 3) by John Barlow (1799–1869), secretary of the Royal Society 1843–60; the album was presented to the Royal Institution of Great Britain by Mrs Barlow.

For conjectural dating, see *ante* HW to Bedford n.d. 1. The MS bears an endorsement '1756' which may have been written by John Barlow in the nineteenth century; the handwriting of the letter is very like HW's of the 1750s.

Dear Sir,

PRAY send me word exactly how both your children[1] do today; I hope better; and how Mrs Bedford is.

Yours etc.

H. Walpole

Booksellers Who Were at Work in England . . . from 1726 to 1775, Oxford, 1930, pp. 269–70).

2. HW also employed Bedford in 1757 to insert in the *Public Advertiser* anonymous verses that he had written in defence of his cousin Henry Conway (*ante* 26 Nov. 1757).

3. The advertisement has not been found.

1. Bedford had at least two sons by September 1761 (*ante* 23 Sept. 1761): Charles (ca 1742–1814), and another son about whom nothing is known, but who had died before 1814; see Appendix 2. Apparently Bedford's children had been ill.

To William Bewley,[1] n.d.

Printed for the first time from the MS now wsl. The MS was pasted by Bewley in his presentation copy of *Fugitive Pieces,* SH, 1758; not further traced until acquired by a Norfolk bookseller from the Constable family of Norfolk; sold by him to James C. and Mary Sullivan Antiquarian Books & Prints, of Carlisle, who sold the volume to the Petersfield Bookshop, Petersfield, Hants; acquired from them by Ximenes Rare Books, Inc., New York, in July 1976 and sold to wsl in Aug. 1976.

The letter was presumably written between April 1777 and 5 Sept. 1783. HW first mentions Bewley (then in attendance on Lord Orford) in a letter to Sir Edward Walpole 21 Apr. 1777 (FAMILY 118); Bewley first mentions HW in writing to Dr Burney 25 Apr. 1777 (MS in the Osborn Collection, Yale University Library). Bewley died 5 Sept. 1783 (GM 1783, liii pt ii. 805).

MR WALPOLE hopes Mr Bewley will do him the favour of accepting this trifling volume,[2] that he may sometimes remember one who has a very sincere esteem for him; and who would be very happy to see him at Strawberry Hill.[3]

1. (ca 1726–83), surgeon and apothecary of Great Massingham, Norfolk; friend of Dr Charles Burney and Joseph Priestley; contributor to the *Monthly Review* (CHATTERTON 121 n. 1).

2. HW's *Fugitive Pieces in Verse and Prose,* SH, 1758; only 200 copies were printed (Hazen, *SH Bibl.* 39).

3. We have found no record of a visit by Bewley to SH.

3458　　 FROM RICHARD BULL N.D.

From Richard Bull, n.d.

Printed for the first time from the MS now WSL. The MS was sold SH vi. 126 (in a portfolio of letters, proof sheets, and documents relating to HW's *Historic Doubts on . . . Richard III,* 1768) to Boone for the 13th Earl of Derby; resold Christie's 24 March 1954 (Derby Sale), lot 345, to Maggs for WSL. See Hazen, *Cat. of HW's Lib.,* No. 2620.

Bull must have acquired the lots bought at John Talman's sale 19 April 1727 from a later owner, possibly James West (1703–72), who had a collection of Talman's prints and drawings (Nichols, *Lit. Anec.* vi. 160); West's sale of prints took place in January 1773. We do not know when HW acquired his prints by William Pass (see n. 2 below).

Address: To the Honourable Mr Walpole.

MR BULL presents his compliments to Mr Walpole, and sends for his perusal, a lot or two bought at Talman's sale;[1] a very trumpery parcel indeed, and by no means worth the trouble Mr Walpole will have in looking them over, nor would they have been mentioned to him, but on account of the print by *W. Pass,*[2] which Mr Bull did imagine, *from the Anecdotes,*[3] that Mr Walpole had not got.

Should Mr W. happen to think any of these paltry things of the least curiosity, what part he pleases is extremely at his service.

1. Bull's note at the bottom of the MS: 'John Talman died at Hinxworth, Herts, in February 1726. By will he gave all his prints and drawings to Trinity Coll. Cambridge, but by a codicil revoked the legacy, on account of an increasing family, and ordered them to be sold by auction.' John, son of William Talman (fl. 1670–1700), was an amateur artist, antiquary, and first director of the Society of Antiquaries 1718–26 (DNB; Nichols, *Lit. Anec.* vi. 159–60); at his sale on 19 April 1727 some of his prints and drawings were bought by George Vertue for the Society of Antiquaries, others apparently by James West.

2. William Pass (ca 1598–ca 1637), engraver. HW's account of him in the *Catalogue of Engravers* (*Works* iv. 19–21) lists twelve prints by William Pass, three of which were then in HW's possession.

The prints by him listed in the London Sale Catalogue of HW's prints, 1842, are Nos 74, 75, 77, 84, 100, 103, 117, 126, 140, 147, 170. Whether one of these is the print Bull offered HW is not known. For a list of Pass's engravings and illustrations of them see Arthur W. Hind, *Engraving in England in the Sixteenth and Seventeenth Centuries,* Cambridge, 1952–5, ii. 285–301 and plates 172–81.

3. In *Anecdotes of Painting,* 2d edn, SH, 1765, iii. 151, in the account of William Talman, HW wrote that John Talman 'made a large collection of prints and drawings, particularly of churches and altars, many of which were done by himself.' But Bull apparently refers to the article on William Pass in the *Catalogue of Engravers* (2d edn, SH, 1765, v. 25–7), where HW lists some prints by Pass which he did not own.

TO LORD DACRE, n.d.

Printed for the first time from the MS now WSL, bound in Lord Dacre's copy of George Vertue's printed, but untitled, booklet known as 'Explanations of Historic Prints,' [1740]. This copy was apparently in the possession of Lord Dacre's family until sold Sotheby's 7 Nov. 1938 (Barrett-Lennard Sale), lot 33, to Maggs for WSL. Hazen, *Cat. of HW's Lib.*, No. 2772, lists HW's copy of Vertue's 'Explanations of Historic Prints' as sold SH v. 103, but says that this set may have been of the edition republished by the Society of Antiquaries 1774ff.

The letter must have been written after 1755, when Thomas Barrett Lennard became Baron Dacre of the South; it may have been written as late as 1783, because it is bound with Richard Gough's letter of June 1783 to Lord Dacre in the copy of Vertue's 'Explanations' cited above (the Gough-Dacre letters are printed in Nichols, *Lit. Anec.* vi. 274–7). HW's letter to Lord Dacre *ante* 31 Aug. 1783 shows that Dacre was sending materials for a later edition of *Anecdotes of Painting* and the *Catalogue of Engravers* at that time. It is also possible that HW's letter was written ca 1761–2, when he was preparing the first edition of volume III of *Anecdotes* and the *Catalogue of Engravers* (Hazen, *SH Bibl.* 55).

Endorsed in an unidentified hand: From the Honourable Horace Walpole; To Lord Dacre.

I RETURN your Lordship the books[1] with a thousand thanks. The MS[2] is very curious, and contains a good picture of the times in every particular it touches. The case of knighthood shows that corruption then carried money *to,* not *from* Court.

---

1. Apparently one of the books was George Vertue's printed, but untitled, booklet known as 'Explanations of Historic Prints,' [1740], which were his descriptions for prints of four historical paintings by Holbein and others on the following subjects: 'A royal family piece . . . with King Henry VIII,' 'The royal progress of Queen Elizabeth,' 'The cenotaph of the Lord Darnley,' 'The battle array of Carberry Hill.' Vertue mentions the first set of these descriptions in his autobiography *sub* Nov. 1740 (Vertue Note Books, *Walpole Society* 1929–30, xviii. 6, 20). HW included a list of three sets of historical prints in his 'List of Vertue's Works' at the end of the *Catalogue of Engravers*, 2d edn, SH, 1765, pp. 13–14. HW may have acquired a copy of Vertue's 'Explanations,' since the SH Sale Catalogue, 1842, lists 'Virtu's Explication des Peinteurs'; see Hazen, *Cat. of HW's Lib.*, No. 2772.

2. Not identified. Whether HW used material from Lord Dacre's MS in the *Anecdotes of Painting* is not known; his reference to the corruption of the tradition of knighthood has not been found there.

From WILLIAM HAMILTON, Tuesday 10 December 1771

Printed in full for the first time from a photostat of the MS in the Fitzwilliam Museum, Cambridge. An extract is printed in Brian Fothergill, *Sir William Hamilton, Envoy Extraordinary*, New York, 1969, p. 117. The MS is part of the bequest of Spencer George Perceval (1838–1922) to the Fitzwilliam Museum; its earlier history is not known. The letter came to our attention too late to be included in CHUTE or in its proper sequence in HW's miscellaneous correspondence.

The year of the letter is established by HW's letter to Lady Ossory 14 Dec. 1771 (see n. 4 below).

Address: To the Honourable H. Walpole, Arlington Street.

Tuesday, December 10,
King's Mews.¹

Dear Sir,

I HAVE no scruple in showing *you* my collection² though it is not yet in the order fit for the vulgar eye. I shall be at Lord Cowper's³ on Friday morning from 10 till 3 and shall be happy to give you some idea of what the collection will be when properly arranged.⁴

I am, dear Sir,
With a most sincere regard,
Your very obliged humble servant,

W. HAMILTON

1. The Mews, or the King's Mews, at Charing Cross (H. B. Wheatley, *London Past and Present*, 1891, ii. 531–2).
2. Of Greek and Roman antiquities, previously described in part in P. F. Hugues ('d'Hancarville'), *Collection of Etruscan, Greek, and Roman Antiquities from the Cabinet of the Honble Wm. Hamilton*, Naples, 1766–7. The collection was purchased for the British Museum by a Parliamentary grant of £8,410 in 1772 (OSSORY i. 70 n. 23).
3. George Nassau Clavering Cowper (1738–89), styled Vct Fordwich 1738–64; 3d E. Cowper, 1764; M.P. He had been living in Italy since 1759 (MANN v. 543 n. 5).
4. HW presumably viewed the collection on Friday, 13 Dec. He wrote Lady Ossory the next day: 'If Lord Ossory has a mind to enrich Ampthill, Mr Hamilton has brought over . . . a collection of Tuscan vases, idols, amulets, javelins and casques of bronze, necklaces and earrings of gold from Herculaneum, Pompeii and Sicily, sacrificing instruments, dice of amber, ivory, agate, etc. in short enough antiquity to fill your whole gallery at least' (OSSORY i. 70).

To Dr Henry Harington,[1] ca 1768–9

Printed for the first time from a photostat of a MS copy in an unidentified hand in the Bath Reference Library. The MS copy was transferred to the Reference Library from the Guildhall of Bath in 1940; its earlier history is not known.

Dated conjecturally by the reference to the portrait of Princess Elizabeth, which was printed as frontispiece to *Nugæ Antiquæ . . . With an Original Plate of the Princess Elizabeth, Engraved 1554*, London: Printed for W. Frederick, at Bath, 1769. Dr Harington apparently wrote to HW to ask his opinion of the authenticity and date of the engraving which was in the Harington collection. Hazen, *Cat. of HW's Lib.*, Nos 411, 3814, lists two sets of the 2d edn, 1779, of *Nugæ Antiquæ*, but argues that HW probably owned the 1769 volume and vol. II, 1775, because HW refers to the 1775 volume in a letter to Mason and in his 'Book of Materials.'

Endorsed in the same hand: The Honourable Horace Walpole to Doctor Harington, Bath.[2]

Sir,

THOUGH you are pleased to do my knowledge as an antiquary more honour than I fear it deserves[3] I wish it was great enough to give you full satisfaction. For my opinion, it is extremely at your service. The portrait[4] I have no manner of doubt is designed for

1. Presumably Henry Harington (1727–1816), M.D., 1762; physician, author, and amateur musician; father of Henry Harington (1755–91), D.D., 1788, prebendary of Bath and Wells, 1787, who edited *Nugae Antiquæ*, vol. I, 1769, vol. II, 1775, from MSS in the possession of the Harington family. They were descendants of Sir John Harington (1560–1612), Kt, 1599, the Elizabethan courtier and poet (see below, n. 7).

2. The endorsement was apparently added later by the transcriber at the top of the MS copy. In 1771 Dr Harington removed from Wells to Bath, where he later served as alderman, magistrate, and mayor; but the manor of Kelston, about 4 miles from Bath, was the chief seat of the Harington family from the time of Henry VIII's grant of lands there until the mid-18th century (Ruth Hughey, *John Harington of Stepney: Tudor Gentleman*, Columbus, Ohio, 1971, pp. 18–19; Ian Grimble, *The Harington Family*,

New York, 1957, pp. 103, 113–14, 233–6; John Collinson, *The History and Antiquities of the County of Somerset*, Bath, 1791, i. 128).

3. Harington's letter to HW is missing; it apparently enclosed an engraved portrait said to represent Queen Elizabeth as a young woman.

4. Note at the bottom of the MS: 'This print was taken from the original plate given by Queen Elizabeth to Sir John Harington in 1595.' The print appears as the frontispiece to *Nugæ Antiquæ*, 1769 (see headnote), edited by Henry Harington (1755–91), who states in the Preface: 'The print of the Princess Elizabeth is taken from an original plate given by herself to her attendant Isabella Harington, soon after her enlargement from the Tower, 1554, and is in the Editor's possession; mention of which is made in some of the following letters' (ibid. 4). In 1609 Sir John Harington wrote Henry, Prince of Wales: 'The picture of Lady Elizabeth,

Queen Elizabeth. I cannot say positively whether before, or after, she was Queen. I should think before she was so, as the face, though moderately executed, is a young one, and there are no traces of regality, or of the order of the Garter, and I believe there is scarcely any picture of her, without the one or the other, done after she came to the Crown.[5] You do not mention, Sir, whether the plate is silver or copper. Hilliard[6] did many pieces of her and her successor on silver, but I believe none so early as this; nor does it seem so neat as his manner; though by the size and want of that neatness, it may be one of his first works. These observations and the long possession of it, Sir, in your family[7] seem to affix it [to] the period when Elizabeth was Princess. I am Sir

Your obedient humble servant,

Hor. Walpole

our late glorious Queen, was printed from a copper, graved by a most skilful artist, and given by her, as a token of her affection to my mother; which I send your Highness as it was thought to be of rare workmanship, as it is cut in metal, which few did then ever attempt to do' (ibid. 62). The copper engraving, formerly in the possession of Miss Philippa Harington, a direct descendant of John and Isabella Harington, is now in the Municipal Libraries and Victoria Art Gallery, Bath; the portrait, no longer believed to be of Princess Elizabeth, is reproduced in Hughey, op. cit. between pp. 52-3, and in Arthur M. Hind, *Engraving in England in the Sixteenth and Seventeenth Centuries*, Cambridge, 1952-5, ii. 283 and pl. 171.

5. In *Anecdotes of Painting* (*Works* iii. 112) HW wrote: 'A pale Roman nose, a head of hair loaded with crowns and powdered with diamonds, a vast ruff, a vaster fardingale and a bushel of pearls are the features by which every body knows at once the pictures of Queen Elizabeth.'

6. Nicholas Hilliard (ca 1547-1619), miniature-painter, goldsmith, jeweller. For Sir John Harington's comment on him see *ante* 28 Dec. 1782. Hilliard's earliest miniature of Queen Elizabeth is dated

1572; he usually painted on smooth vellum pasted on a card, often a playing card; he also designed and executed many medals of Queen Elizabeth (Philip Norman, 'Nicholas Hilliard's Treatise concerning "The Arte of Limning,"' *Walpole Society* 1911-12, i. 5, 12-13, 28-9, 52; Erna Auerbach, *Nicholas Hilliard*, 1961, pp. 6-7, 147, 180-7, 193). HW owned the folio MS of Hilliard's *Treatise on the Art of Limning* which is now in the University of Edinburgh Library (Hazen, *Cat. of HW's Lib.*, No. 2560).

7. John Harington (d. 1582), of Stepney, is said to have married Ethelreda (or Audrey) (living, 1555), allegedly a natural daughter of Henry VIII; m. 2 (after 1 April 1559) Isabella Markham (d. 1579), daughter of Sir John Markham, Lieutenant of the Tower; she was a lady-in-waiting to Princess Elizabeth. In 1554 Harington was imprisoned in the Tower for eleven months, and was in attendance on Princess Elizabeth while she was there (18 March-19 May 1554). In August 1560, when John and Isabella's son, John, was christened, Queen Elizabeth acted as godmother (Hughey, op. cit. 17-19, 35-7, 43-6, 226-7; Grimble, op. cit. 90-101). For other gifts of Queen Elizabeth see Hughey, op. cit. 55, and Grimble, op. cit. 101.

To Ozias Humphry,[1] 1784

Printed for the first time from the MS now WSL. The MS was bequeathed by Humphry (d. 1810) to his natural son, William Upcott (1779–1845), the autograph collector, after whose death it was sold by Sotheby's June 1846 (GM 1845, xxiv n.s., pt ii. 540–1), probably to A. A. Smets, Savannah, Georgia; included in the sale of his autograph collection after his death by Leavitt, Strebeigh & Co. 1 June 1868, lot 307 (vol. xxii), where the MS is described as an 'autograph letter or note not signed'; not further traced until bound in 1884 by James O. Watson, of Orange, New Jersey, in his extra-illustrated copy of *Horace Walpole and his World*, ed. L. B. Seeley, 1884; the volume was presented to the Free Public Library, Orange, New Jersey, by Watson; not further traced until offered by Hacker Arts Books, New York, Cat. No. 34 (1973), lot 420; purchased from Hacker in Feb. 1974 by WSL, who removed the MS from the extra-illustrated volume.

The letter could not have been written before 12 Jan. 1784 when Lady Dysart became the owner of the Wimpole Street house (n. 3 below), nor could it have been written after 16 Nov. 1784 when Lady Charlotte Maria Waldegrave married the Earl of Euston, leaving only one Lady Waldegrave in residence at Gloucester House (n. 7 below). The Duke and Duchess of Gloucester were abroad from 1783 to 1787 (n. 6 below), making it necessary for their servant to 'show the picture' at Gloucester House; and Humphry, whose acquaintance HW may have made in Aug. 1783 (*ante* 13 Aug. 1783 and n. 3), sailed for India 15 Jan. 1785, a journey he had contemplated since July 1784; he returned to England in early Jan. 1788 (Hist. MSS Comm., *Report on the Papers of Ozias Humphry, R.A. (1743–1810)*, 1972, pp. 46, 64; G. C. Williamson, *Life and Works of Ozias Humphry, R.A.*, 1918, pp. 117, 121).

Address: To Mr Humphreys.

MR WALPOLE has the pleasure of sending Mr Humphreys the order from Lady Dysart[2] for seeing the pictures at her house in Wimpole Street;[3] but Mr Walpole desires he may know the day and hour that Mr Humphreys and the other gentlemen[4] will go to Gloucester House,[5] that his R[oyal] Highness's servant who has the

---

1. (1743–1810), portrait painter and miniaturist; R.A., 1791 (*ante* 13 Aug. 1783, n. 3).

2. Charlotte Walpole (1738–89), m. (1760) Lionel Tollemache (1734–99), styled Lord Huntingtower 1740–70, 5th E. of Dysart, 1770; HW's niece.

3. Sir Edward Walpole, who died 12 Jan. 1784, left his house in Wimpole Street, with its contents, to his daughter, Lady Dysart (Ossory ii. 432 n. 1; Violet Biddulph, *The Three Ladies Waldegrave*, 1938, p. 163).

4. Not identified.

5. Previously known as Grosvenor House, Upper Grosvenor Street, the house was purchased by the Duke of Gloucester in 1761 and was thereafter called Gloucester House (H. B. Wheatley, *London Past and Present*, 1891, ii. 162).

care of the house[6] may be in the way to show the picture, for the Ladies Waldegrave[7] will not be in town these ten days.

From Lord Huntingdon,[1] n.d.

Printed from the MS now wsl. First printed, Toynbee *Supp.* iii. 313–14. For the history of the MS see *ante* 13 June 1759.

The letter must have been written between 1774 and 1784, since the 1774 edition of the 'Des. of SH' does not mention the snuff box, whereas it is described in the 1784 edition (n. 2 below). The 1774 edition, now wsl, contains an addition in Walpole's hand on p. 93: 'a green and white snuff box of Dresden porcelain set in gold; a present from Francis Earl of Huntingdon' (see Hazen, *Cat. of HW's Lib.*, No. 2523).

Address: To Mr H. Walpole.

LORD HUNTINGDON with his compliments sends Mr Walpole, according to promise, a little Spanish snuff. Having left off taking any, from finding that it disagreed with him, he hopes Mr Walpole will be so much his friend as to keep possession of his box.[2]

6. The Duke and Duchess of Gloucester were abroad from 1783 to 1787 (Ossory ii. 581 n. 2).

7. Daughters of HW's niece, the Duchess of Gloucester, by her first husband, the 2d Earl Waldegrave. The eldest, Lady Elizabeth Laura Waldegrave, had married in 1782 and was therefore no longer living at Gloucester House. The other two were Lady Charlotte Maria Waldegrave (1761–1808), m. (16 Nov. 1784) George Henry Fitzroy, styled E. of Euston, 4th D. of Grafton, 1811; and Lady Anna Horatia Waldegrave, m. (1786) Hon. Hugh Seymour-Conway (see *ante* 21 Aug. 1786, n. 2).

1. Francis Hastings (1729–89), 10th E. of Huntingdon, 1746.

2. The snuff box was sold SH xv. 21 to Kelsall for £17.7.0. HW's MS description (see headnote) was printed in 'Des. of SH,' *Works* ii. 485.

To Daniel or Samuel Lysons,[1] n.d.

Printed for the first time from the MS in Thomas Kirgate's hand, now wsl. The MS is untraced until offered by the Rowfant Book Shop, New York, Cat. No. 7 (1954), lot 196, from whom wsl bought it in July 1754.

This letter must have been written before 5 Dec. 1791 when HW became Lord Orford, and probably was not written earlier than 14 Feb. 1787 when HW received the first known letter from either of the Lysons brothers (Dalrymple 194; the rest of HW's correspondence with Daniel and Samuel Lysons is printed in that volume). HW's letter to Samuel Lysons 29 July 1787 (ibid. 196) shows that he was then acquainted with both Lysons brothers. Between 1787 and Dec. 1791 HW had two attacks of gout requiring his secretary, Thomas Kirgate, to write for him: one in Feb. 1788 (Ossory iii. 4) and the other in Jan. 1791 (ibid. 106). This letter may therefore have been written at either of those times.

M R WALPOLE sends his compliments to Mr Lysons, and returns him many thanks for his obliging inquiries.[2]

1. Daniel Lysons (1762–1834), divine and topographer; F.S.A., 1790; F.R.S., 1797. His brother Samuel Lysons (1763–1819), antiquary and lawyer, became F.S.A. in 1786 and F.R.S. in 1797.

2. Presumably about the state of HW's health (see headnote).

From SIR GEORGE[1] and LADY LYTTELTON,[2]
?Friday 22 September ?1752

Printed from the MS now WSL. First printed, Toynbee *Supp.* iii. 314–15. Damer-Waller; the MS was sold Sotheby's 5 Dec. 1921 (first Waller Sale), lot 155, to Maggs; not further traced until acquired by WSL, Sept. 1933.

The conjectural assignment of the year 1752 to this letter is based on the assumption that HW would not have been invited to Hagley immediately after the death of Sir George's father, Sir Thomas Lyttelton, 4th Bt, on 14 Sept. 1751. On 27 Aug. 1752 HW wrote to Sir George (letter missing; see CONWAY i. 344); if this letter declined an invitation to Hagley, it would explain Lady Lyttelton's annoyance. Although HW did visit Hagley in early Sept. 1753 (n. 3 below), it is apparent from Lyttelton's letter to HW *ante* 30 Sept. 1754 that he did not visit Hagley in 1754. Moreover, Lady Lyttelton could not have missed the post on 22 Sept. 1754, since it was a Sunday. On 18 Nov. 1756 Sir George was created Baron Lyttelton; therefore the letter could not have been written after that date (see endorsement below). There is no record of any invitation to HW to visit Hagley during 1755 and 1756, when a new house was under construction (n. 3 below).

Endorsed in an unidentified hand: From Eliz. Rich 2nd wife of Sir G. Lyttelton and from Sir George.

Hagley Park, Sept. the 22d.

NOT that I am so stubborn I won't say it neither——but—— I don't know——it's so awkward when one's angry,——besides its encouraging people so much!——but I hate to be teased——well, ——if——Pshaw! Now somebody wants to speak with me. ——

———————————————————————

————— Well, don't be in such a hurry!——I hate to be hurried! ——I tell you, if you'll have patience I for————Phoo! This nasty pen always wants mending!————hang it!————Why no,—— I can't say there is much occasion to write it this post, only that I may be rid of him.————The post is just going out!——fiddle faddle, one has not time to do things,——well,——I forgi———— ——I forgive you,——hoh!

---

1. (1709–73), 5th Bt, 1751; cr. (1756) Bn Lyttelton; M.P.
2. Elizabeth Rich (ca 1716–95), m. (10 Aug. 1749), as his second wife, George Lyttelton; by the spring of 1759 they had separated (CONWAY ii. 14–15 and n. 10).

My poor wife being gone mad (as you will see by her style), I can only say that I hope you will come to Hagley next year[3] when I flatter myself she will have recovered her senses, and be fit to receive you.

From LADY LYTTELTON, n.d.

Printed from the MS now WSL. First printed, Toynbee *Supp.* iii. 315. Damer-Waller; the MS was sold Sotheby's 5 Dec. 1921 (first Waller Sale), lot 155, to Maggs; not further traced until acquired by WSL in Sept. 1933.

This letter must have been written between 14 Sept. 1751, when Lyttelton became the 5th Baronet on his father's death, and 18 Nov. 1756, when he was created Baron Lyttelton. It was possibly written in Sept. 1754, since Sir George wrote HW from Hagley (*ante* 30 Sept. 1754) that 'we shall not build our grotto this year, and therefore the shells you are so kind to offer to it may as well be brought to Lady Lyttelton in Hill Street [Sir George's house in London] as sent hither now.' The ormer shells were received by HW after 18 May 1754 (CHUTE 175–6), and this note may have been a reply to a missing letter from HW asking where the shells should be delivered.

Endorsed in pencil by HW: From Eliz. Rich 2d wife of Sir G. Lyttelton.

It's very well, Sir!

PS. Sir George is at Worcester,[1] I don't know what his answer is.

---

3. HW visited Hagley Hall, near Stourbridge, Worcs, Lyttelton's seat, between 1 Sept. and 11 Sept. 1753. He described the house as 'immeasurably bad and old' but found the park so filled with 'enchanting scenes' in 'extreme taste' that 'I wore out my eyes with gazing . . . and

my tongue and my vocabulary with commending!' (CHUTE 147–9 and nn. 7, 9). A new house was begun the following year but was not completed until ca 1762 (GEC viii. 311 n; CHUTE 103–4 and nn. 9–11).

---

1. Which was near his seat, Hagley Hall.

From ELIZABETH MONTAGU, Saturday 19 January 1782

Printed from the MS now WSL. First printed, Toynbee *Supp.* iii. 315–16. Damer-Waller; the MS was sold Sotheby's 5 Dec. 1921 (first Waller Sale), lot 162, bought in; resold Christie's 15 Dec. 1947 (second Waller Sale), lot 53 (with nine other letters), to Maggs for WSL.

Dated by Mrs Montagu's move into her new house, No. 22, Portman Square, in December 1781, and by HW's attack of gout which lasted from 8 Jan. 1782 until the end of the month (see below, nn. 1, 2). In 1783, 19 Jan. fell on a Sunday, which does not fit with the phrase 'her party for Sunday.' In 1784, HW was not ill in January, and in June Miss Gregory was married (see below, n. 4).

Portman Square,[1] Jan. 19th.

MRS MONTAGU presents her compliments to Mr Walpole, and begs leave to inquire after his health;[2] she does not doubt of his bearing this fit of the gout with more patience than she does, but wishes to hear that the gout does not act with the double malice of inflicting great pain on him, as well as depriving her, and her party for Sunday,[3] of a great deal of pleasure. If young ladies had the power attributed to them in romances, of curing the sick knight by a few kind words, she would send a more tender message from Miss Gregory[4] than her respects and her compliments.

---

1. No. 22 Portman Square, which was built between 1777 and 1781; Mrs Montagu moved in while the workmen were still there in December 1781, and gave several house-warming parties in December and January (*Mrs Montagu, 'Queen of the Blues,'* ed. Reginald Blunt, 1923, ii. 13, 82–4, 111–12). Mrs Boscawen wrote Mrs Delany 12 Nov. 1781: 'I met . . . Mrs Montagu, who is very busy furnishing her new house: part of her family is remov'd into it'; and on 19 Dec.: 'Mrs Montague is in perfect health and spirits in her *Chateau Portman*' (*The Autobiography and Correspondence of Mary Granville, Mrs Delany,* ed. Lady Llanover, 1861–2, vi. 65, 78).

2. HW had a severe attack of the gout beginning 8 Jan. 1782, which he described to Lady Ossory 12 Jan., to Mason 10 Jan., and to Mann 17 Jan. (see OSSORY ii. 322–3; MASON ii. 174–5; MANN ix. 235).

3. Presumably 20 Jan. 1782. We have found no other reference to this party, although on 24 Dec. Mrs Montagu wrote Elizabeth Carter of various post-Christmas dinners (Blunt, op. cit. 113). In a letter of March 1782 she mentions having some readings by Le Texier: 'Lord and Lady Harcourt, Mr Walpole, Lady Clermont and many of your friends are on my list of subscribers to Le Texier' (ibid. 118).

4. Dorothea Gregory (ca 1755–1830), dau. of Dr John Gregory of Edinburgh University, upon whose death in 1773 she became the companion of Mrs Montagu; m. (14 or 19 June 1784) Rev. Archibald Alison (1757–1839) (see OSSORY ii. 446 and nn. 5–10).

From LORD NORTH, n.d.

Printed for the first time from the MS now WSL (a printed card with only the names and three words filled in, not in North's hand), pasted in one of HW's copies of the *Des. of SH*, 1774. For the history of this copy see Hazen, *SH Bibl.*, 1973, pp. xxiii, 109–10, copy 3.

Dated before 4 Aug. 1790, when Lord North became 2d Earl of Guilford; possibly after 1786, when his sight failed and he suffered increasingly from stomach pains and sleepless nights (Alan Valentine, *Lord North,* Norman, Oklahoma, 1967, ii. 441–2, 446). HW might have called on him in Grosvenor Square or at Bushey House, about a mile beyond SH on the road to Hampton Court. HW wrote Mason 26 March 1782: 'In all probability I shall see much more of my neighbour at Bushy, Lord North, than of any minister. He is very good company. I cannot be suspected of paying court, which I never did in his power: and though I have a very bad opinion of him as a minister, he is so totally out of favour as well as out of place, that methinks that negative merit has its value' (MASON ii. 210; see also OSSORY i. 156, ii. 214, 235, 580–1).

LORD NORTH presents his compliments to Mr Walpole and returns many thanks for the honour of his obliging inquiries.

From the DUCHESS OF QUEENSBERRY,[1] n.d.

Printed from Toynbee, *Supp.* iii. 316, where the letter was first printed. Damer-Waller; the MS was sold Sotheby's 5 Dec. 1921 (first Waller Sale), lot 173, to Maggs; offered by Maggs, Cat. No. 421 (spring 1922), lot 629; offered by Trebizond Rare Books, New York, Cat. No. 13 (1980), lot 121, tipped into a copy of HW's *Anecdotes of Painting*, 2d edn, SH, 1765; not further traced.

THE Duchess of Queensberry will dine at Strawberry Hill next Saturday,[2] if she is alive; she can answer for nobody else in the world, but does verily believe the Duke of Queensberry[3] will also.

1. Lady Catherine Hyde (ca 1701–77), m. (1720) Charles Douglas, 3d D. of Queensberry; 'her mad Grace of Queensberry' (HW to Mann 3 Jan. 1746 OS, MANN iii. 195). She lived at Petersham, across the Thames from SH (CONWAY i. 269). HW wrote a stanza on her well-preserved beauty, entitled 'Left on the Duchess of Queensberry's Toilet, the Author Finding Her from Home,' in 1771 (see MANN vii. 299 and n. 17; *Works* iv. 403). Mrs Delany wrote 29 Feb. 1772 that HW proposed a toast to the Duchess of Queensberry, which was that he 'wished she might live to grow ugly,' and she replied: 'I hope, then, you will keep your taste for antiquities' (*The Autobiography and Correspondence of Mary Granville, Mrs Delany*, ed. Lady Llanover, 1861–2, iv. 423).

2. We have found no record of this dinner party. For another occasion when the Duke and Duchess of Queensberry dined at SH see CHUTE 454 n. 2.

3. Charles Douglas (1698–1778), 3d D. of Queensberry, 1711; gentleman of the Bed-

The Duchess of Queensberry does not know where Mr Walpole is, but wherever he is, he would not have waited so long for an answer if she had been at home.

From the ?DUCHESS OF RICHMOND,[1] ?1784–?1791

Printed for the first time from the MS now WSL. The MS was sold by the Waldegrave family to Richard Bentley, the publisher, ca 1843; resold from the estate of his grandson, Richard Bentley the younger, to WSL, 1937.

Dated conjecturally between Jan. 1784, when HW separated politically from the Duke of Richmond, and 5 Dec. 1791, when HW became 4th Earl of Orford.

Address: Honourable Horace Walpole [with a seal, a ducal coronet over 'M'].

Saturday noon.

THE Duke[2] has seen Mr D.[3] who is astonished at his thinking *it*[4] worth asking him his opinion upon; he says he cannot imagine how anybody can think it worth repeating such mere Court nonsense; which can only be fabricated to give uneasiness, for it is of no other consequence, and that when people say those things it is more their *wishes,* than their *fears* which they utter. Indeed he has made me quite easy, and I hope this will make you so too—in haste. Adieu.

chamber to Frederick, Prince of Wales, 1733–51; Lord Justice General of Scotland 1763–78. His residences were Queensberry House in Burlington Gardens, London, Douglas House at Petersham, and Amesbury, Wilts (OSSORY ii. 64 n. 20, 67 n. 26; GEC x. 699 n. b).

1. Probably Lady Mary Bruce (1740–96), m. (1757) Charles Lennox, 3d D. of Richmond. The handwriting of the MS is very similar to that of the Duchess of Richmond's letters in the Newcastle papers (e.g., BM Add. MS 32979, f. 52). The 'M' on the seal may stand for Mary, the

Duchess's first name. The informal style of this letter suggests a close friend of HW.

2. Probably her husband, Charles Lennox (1735–1806), 3d D. of Richmond, 1750 (*ante* 11 March 1766, n. 1).

3. Probably Henry Dundas (1742–1811), cr. (1802) Vct Melville (*ante* ?16 Dec. 1775).

4. Possibly some question about HW's sinecures. HW seems to have approached someone connected with the government; see HW's letters to Lord Lansdowne about his ushership of the Exchequer (*ante* 19 June 1783, 16 June 1791).

To Lady Talbot,[1] n.d.

Printed from *Letters between the Rev. James Granger . . . and Many of the Most Eminent Literary Men of his Time,* ed. J. P. Malcolm, 1805, pp. 404–5, where the letter was first printed. Reprinted, Toynbee xv. 449. For the history of the MS see *ante* 24 April 1764.

MR WALPOLE came[2] to have the honour of waiting on Lady Talbot, and to thank her Ladyship a thousand times for the sight of this curious book,[3] which he would not detain at all. It has many valuable and rare prints in it, and four or five that he never saw.[4]

1. Mary de Cardonnel (d. 1787), m. (1734) William Talbot, 2d Bn Talbot, 1737, cr. (1761) E. Talbot. Lady Louisa Stuart speaks of her 'great pretensions to knowledge and accomplishments' and 'her large size and . . . over-powering manner' (*Notes by Lady Louisa Stuart on George Selwyn and his Contemporaries,* ed. W. S. Lewis, New York and London, 1928, pp. 15–16).
2. We have found no record of this visit.
3. Apparently a book containing prints, mentioned in an undated letter signed 'D. H. Roberts' [presumably William Hayward Roberts (1734–91), B.A., King's College, Cambridge, 1757, M.A., 1760, D.D., 1773; assistant at Eton 1760–71, Fellow, 1771, and Provost of Eton 1781–91] to the Rev. James Granger: 'When I had the pleasure of seeing you at Eton, I mentioned to you that a relation of mine had some prints, done from portraits, which

were thought valuable; and that Mr Walpole had seen them. Upon my telling him that you wished to look on them, he immediately lent them to me; and, enclosed in the book which contains these, I find the following note: [HW's letter is here quoted]. Whenever Mr Granger will do Dr Roberts the favour to come over to Eton, he will show him the prints' (*Letters between the Rev. James Granger . . . and Many of the Most Eminent Literary Men of his Time,* ed. J. P. Malcolm, 1805, pp. 404–5). This letter may be dated between 1773, when 'Dr Roberts' became D.D., and 15 April 1776, when Granger died (*ante* 24 April 1764, n. 1). Lady Talbot apparently gave the book to Dr Roberts's kinsman before 1773.
4. HW had assisted Granger in collecting prints for his *Biographical History of England,* 1769, which was dedicated to HW; see *ante* 3 April 1764, n. 2, and COLE i. 151–2.

To LADY TYRCONNEL,[1] between 1784 and 1791

Printed for the first time from the MS now WSL. The MS is untraced until *penes* Professor Frederick W. Hilles, of Yale University, in Jan. 1934; given by him to WSL in June 1937.

Dated between 1784, when HW first printed the Rules for admission to SH, and 5 Dec. 1791, when he became Earl of Orford.

M R WALPOLE presents his compliments to Lady Tyrconnel and is very sorry he cannot possibly obey her Ladyship's commands in admitting more than four as she will see by his printed rules[2] which he has the honour of sending to her. If her Ladyship and three more choose to see his house today, she is very welcome.[3]

---

1. Hon. Sarah Hussey Delaval (1763–1800), m. (1780) George Carpenter, 2d E. of Tyrconnel, 1762. When Frederick, Duke of York, bought Oatlands Park, Weybridge, Surrey (about 9 miles from SH), in July 1788, HW commented in his 'Mem. 1783–91' (now WSL, *sub* July 1788, quoted in OSSORY iii. 7–8 n. 17): 'It was very near Claremont, the seat of Lord Tirconnel, whose wife was so notoriously the Duke of York's mistress.'

2. HW's Rules for obtaining a ticket to see SH, first printed in 1784 (Hazen, *SH Bibl.* 225–9).

3. Since a visit by Lady Tyrconnel and her friends is not recorded in HW's 'Book of Visitors' between 1784 and 1791, she probably did not come. A later visit is recorded on 12 Aug. 1794 (BERRY ii. 246).

To Unknown,[1] after January 1761

Printed for the first time from the MS now WSL. The MS was offered by Maggs, Cat. No. 215 (Nov. 1905), lot 988; not further traced until sold Sotheby's 24 Oct. 1972, lot 468, to Seven Gables for WSL.

Dated after 8 Jan. 1761, when HW published the SH edition of Lucan's *Pharsalia*. Since HW's known visits to the Duke of Richmond's seat, Goodwood, do not coincide with the departure of one of his French friends from London, we have not been able to identify with certainty the addressee or to assign a precise date.

Monsieur,

C'EST avec un très grand regret que j'apprends la nouvelle de votre départ, ayant si peu profité de votre séjour ici. J'ai été à la campagne[2] de M. le Duc de Richmond,[3] mais en retournant par la ville, je voulais reparer la perte que j'avais faite, mais on me dit que vous n'étiez plus à Londres. Vous allez nous quitter précisément à l'arrivée de notre belle saison, et vous ne rapporterez en France qu'une idée désagréable de notre climat. Ne serait-il pas juste, Monsieur, de nous en dédommager, en nous faisant encore l'honneur d'une visite? Que Lucain[4] vous en fasse ressouvenir—pour l'autre petit livre,[5] ce serait de mon intérêt que vous l'oubliassiez. Pensez au moins, Monsieur, que c'était une marque d'obéissance, et que l'auteur est

Votre très humble et très obéissant serviteur,

Horace Walpole

---

1. Possibly Jacques-Aimar-Henri de Moreton, Comte de Chabrillan; maréchal-de-camp, 1762 (La Chenaye-Desbois and Badier, *Dictionnaire de la noblesse,* 3d edn, 1863–76, xiv. 556). He left Paris 28 March 1767, reached London 1 April, and dined at SH sometime in April or May (DU DEFFAND i. 278, 295; SELWYN 244–5 and nn. 1, 2). By 7 June he had returned to Paris and had given Mme du Deffand an account of SH (DU DEFFAND i. 306). Per-

haps HW had intended to see him again before his departure.

2. Goodwood, Sussex, the Duke of Richmond's seat.

3. See *ante* 11 March 1766, n. 1.

4. The SH edition of Lucan's *Pharsalia* was published 8 Jan. 1761 (Hazen, *SH Bibl.* 46).

5. Possibly HW's *Fugitive Pieces in Verse and Prose,* SH, 1758.

To Unknown, n.d.

Printed for the first time from the MS now WSL, who removed it from a folio album containing a large collection of autographs formed by the Branfill-Harrison family. The album is untraced until sold Sotheby's 13 Dec. 1950 (property of Mrs Gwendolen Morris), lot 131, to Charles A. Stonehill for Carnegie Bookshop, New York; sold by them to WSL in May 1951.

Pasted on the same album page with this letter is a small cut-out address as follows: 'To Edmund Lodge Esqre, James Street, Buckingham Gate'; franked 'Orford.'

The addressee and the year are unknown; we have not been able to connect any of HW's known visits to Park Place with 'Wednesday 23d.' The date must be before 5 Dec. 1791, when HW became 4th Earl of Orford.

Strawberry Hill, Wednesday 23d.

Dear Sir,

I SHOULD be sorry to be disappointed today, if you did not offer me amends on Friday, which I willingly accept. Of Friday sevennight I could not be sure, as I am uncertain whether I shall not go to Park Place about that time.

Yours etc.

H. Walpole

APPENDICES

APPENDIX 1

Horace Walpole's Twickenham 1747–1797

THIS appendix includes a map of Twickenham, showing the houses of the residents that Walpole mentions in his letters while he lived there from 1747 until his death in 1797; a list of the residents, giving their dates of occupancy and the sources from which the dates have been ascertained; and the complete text of Walpole's poem 'The Parish Register of Twickenham.'

The owners and tenants identified on the map are Walpole's contemporaries; earlier residents are for the most part omitted. Where more than one person occupied a house during the period, the name next to the house on the map is that of the earlier occupant. The dates of occupancy encompass the earliest and latest dates for which we have a record, but in some instances occupancy may have begun earlier or extended beyond the dates given.

We are deeply indebted for the list to Mrs Warren G. Creamer, who has been a volunteer in the Print Room at Farmington from its installation in 1954 and who has made Walpole's Twickenham a special study. The map itself is based primarily on 'A Plan of Twickenham in the County of Middlesex from an Actual Survey by Samuel Lewis, 1784,' which appeared as the frontispiece to Edward Ironside's *The History and Antiquities of Twickenham,* 1797 (reproduced as the back endpaper to MORE). It has been adapted for our purpose and executed by Edith McKeon Abbott, of Brookline, Massachusetts.

A list of cue titles used in the documentation precedes the list of Twickenham residents. Numbers in boldface type refer to volumes in the Yale Walpole Edition.

CUE TITLES

BM Map, 1769	'A Plan of the Improvents [*sic*] and Encroachments upon Twickenham Common in the Year 1769,' British Museum MS Ps 2/4970, B. XIII 6.a.Deposit.

Brewer	*The Beauties of England and Wales,* ed. J. Norris Brewer *et al.,* 1801–15, 18 vols.
Cobbett	R. S. Cobbett, *Memorials of Twickenham,* 1872.
Coke, *Journals*	*The Letters and Journals of Lady Mary Coke,* ed. James A. Home, Edinburgh, 1889–96, 4 vols.
Cunningham	*The Letters of Horace Walpole, Earl of Orford,* ed. Peter Cunningham, 1857–59, 9 vols.
Davis	Bertram H. Davis, *A Proof of Eminence: The Life of Sir John Hawkins,* Bloomington, 1973.
DNB	*Dictionary of National Biography,* ed. Leslie Stephen and Sidney Lee, reissue, 1908–9, 22 vols.
Draper	M. P. G. Draper, *Marble Hill House and its Owners,* 1970.
Dudden	F. Homes Dudden, *Henry Fielding, His Life, Works, and Times,* reprint edn, 1966, 2 vols.
Finberg, 'Scott'	Hilda F. Finberg, 'Samuel Scott at Twickenham,' *Apollo,* 1932, xv. 276–8.
GEC	George Edward Cokayne, *The Complete Peerage,* revised by Vicary Gibbs *et al.,* 1910–59, 13 vols.
Halsband	Robert Halsband, *The Life of Lady Mary Wortley Montagu,* Oxford, 1956.
Hickey	*Memoirs of William Hickey,* ed. Alfred Spencer, 1913–25, 4 vols.
HW Parish Reg. notes	See HW's notes to 'The Parish Register of Twickenham,' printed below.
Ironside	Edward Ironside, *The History and Antiquities of Twickenham,* 1797.

'Jewish Residents'	Hilda F. Finberg, 'Jewish Residents in Eighteenth-Century Twickenham,' *Transactions of the Jewish Historical Society of England,* 1945–51, xvi. 129–35.
Lysons	Daniel Lysons, *The Environs of London,* 1792–96, 4 vols.
Lysons Supp.	Daniel Lysons, *Supplement to the First Edition of the Historical Account of the Environs of London,* 1811.
Rate Books	Rate Books, Church of St Mary the Virgin, Twickenham.
Scots Peerage	*The Scots Peerage,* ed. Sir James Balfour Paul, Edinburgh, 1904–14, 9 vols.
1784 Map	'A Plan of Twickenham in the County of Middlesex from an Actual Survey by Samuel Lewis, 1784,' reproduced as the back endpaper in *The Yale Edition of Horace Walpole's Correspondence: The Correspondence with Hannah More . . . ,* New Haven, 1961.
SH Accts	*Strawberry Hill Accounts . . . Kept by Mr Horace Walpole from 1747 to 1795,* ed. Paget Toynbee, Oxford, 1927.
Stirling	A. M. W. Stirling, *The Hothams,* 1918, 2 vols.
Thames-side	F. C. Hodgson, *Thames-side in the Past,* 1913.
Urwin	A. C. B. Urwin, *Twicknam Parke,* privately printed, 1965.
Works	Horace Walpole, *The Works of Horatio Walpole, Earl of Orford,* 1798, 5 vols.

RESIDENTS OF WALPOLE'S TWICKENHAM

1. Little Strawberry Hill ('Cliveden'):

Catherine Clive, 1754–85 (see also 25)	SH Accts 136–7; **35**. 185; **15**. 317
James Raftor, 1770–85	**2**. 373; Cunningham ii. 458n
Sir Robert and Lady Goodere, 1785–90	**11**. 124
Robert Berry and the Misses Mary and Agnes Berry, 1791–1810 (see also 28, 42)	SH Accts 176–7; **11**. 160; Cobbett 330, 332

2. Strawberry Hill:

Horace Walpole, 1747–97	SH Accts 1

3. Richard Francklin, before 1747–65 — SH Accts 130–1; *Works* ii. 399–400; **10**. 147–8

4. a. Thomas Pitt, 1762–63 — See n. 1
   b. Isaac Fernandez Nunez, 1762 — See n. 1
   Stafford Briscoe, ?1770–89 — See n. 1

5. Radnor House:

John, 4th E. of Radnor, before 1741–57	**20**. 382; *Thames-side* 214
Frederick A. Hindley, 1757–80	**32**. 75n; **33**. 180
Nathaniel Webb, 1780–ca 1784	**33**. 183; Rate Books
Samuel Potts, 1782	**35**. 365
Sir Francis and Lady Frances Bassett, ca 1784–ca 1794	**33**. 183n; Rate Books
Lady Anne and Lady Marjory Murray, ca 1794–99	**12**. 20; Rate Books; *Thames-side* 228

6. Joseph Hickey, 1756–ca 1769 Hickey i. 7–8, 128
 Richard Holden (Haldane), Rate Books
  1770–83
 Miss Holden (Haldane), Rate Books; Ironside 143
  1784–94

7. Samuel Scott, ca 1758–ca Rate Books; Cobbett 293; Fin-
  1760 (see also 16) berg, 'Scott' 276–8
 Mrs Anne Gostling, 1783– Ironside 143; Cobbett 74; Rate
  99 Books

8. Thomas Hudson, before **2**. 150; **35**. 234
  1756–79
 John May, 1779–after 1794 Cobbett 292; Ironside 143; **12**.
   96; Lysons iii. 574
 Earl and Countess of Sef- 1784 Map
  ton, ca 1784

9. Pope's Villa:
 Sir William Stanhope, Cobbett 284–5; GEC viii. 658n
  1744–72
 Welbore Ellis (cr. Bn Men- **29**. 178 n. 21; Cobbett 285; Rate
  dip, 1794), 1772–1802 Books

10. Hon. George Shirley, ca **35**. 358 and nn. 13, 14; Ironside
  1780–87 79; Brewer x pt iv. 391; 1784
  Map

11. John Blake, Cross Deep Ironside 143; Cobbett 261–2;
  Lodge, 1772–94 Rate Books

12. Dr William Battie, after Cobbett 259
  1734–before 1761
 3d Earl and Countess **12**. 74n; GEC x. 622n
  Poulett, before 1761–93
 Mrs Jane Osbaldeston, **12**. 74n; Cobbett 260; Rate Books
  1793–7 (see also 15)

13. Edmund Waller, ca 1721–71 Cobbett 257–8; **33**. 200
 Matthew Duane, 1780–5 **25**. 216, 568; **33**. 200
 Mrs Matthew Duane, **12**. 102; Rate Books; Ironside 78;
  1780–ca 1797 Cobbett 258

14. Mary, Dowager Countess of　10. 216
    Shelburne, 1766–80
    Hon. Thomas Fitzmaurice,　Rate Books; Cobbett 254–5
    1780–91
    John Symonds, 1791–2　Cobbett 254–5; Rate Books

15. The Parsonage:
    Rev. Philip Duval, 1792–　12. 75n; Cobbett 123; see n. 2
    1808
    Mrs Jane Osbaldeston 1793　12. 74–5
    (see also 12)

16. Samuel Scott, ?1749–65 (see　Ironside 74; Rate Books; Fin-
    also 7)　berg, 'Scott' 276–8
    William Marlow, ca 1785–　Ironside 144; DNB
    1813
    John Curtis, ?1785–1813　See n. 3

17. York House:
    James Whitchurch, ca 1740–　33. 81; Cobbett 219
    ca 1785

18. Edward Ironside, after 1736–　Cobbett 251; Lysons Supp. 319
    80

19. William, 2d E. of Strafford　35. 293; 11. 283; 32. 192
    (n.c.) 1739–91
    Lady Anne Conolly, 1791–　11. 283; Cobbett 249; Coke,
    7 (see also 33)　*Journals* i. 215n

20. Henry Probyn, 1770–80　31. 199; Rate Books

21. Isabella, Dowager Countess　35. 307; Cobbett 248–9
    of Denbigh, before and
    after 1761
    Frances, Lady Browne, ca　31. 49n; 33. 472
    1766–85
    Thomas Forbes, 1788　31. 287; Rate Books
    Mrs Fitzherbert, 1789 (see　Ironside 144
    also 24)

22. Mr and Mrs George Morton Pitt, after 1737–56

9. 263n; Cobbett 213; Lysons iii. 563

Harriot Pitt, 1745–63 (m. 1762 Brownlow Bertie, later 5th D. of Ancaster)

Ironside 80, 145; Cobbett 213; GEC i. 129

Sir George Pocock, ca 1764–92

Ironside 80; Lysons iii. 599; Rate Books

23. Ragman's Castle:

John, 2d Duke of Montagu, ?–1749

Ironside 86; Cobbett 247

Mary, Dowager Countess of Pembroke, ca 1750

Cobbett 247; GEC x. 425

Mrs Hannah Pritchard, 1755–68

35. 234; Cobbett 247; DNB

Maria, Countess Waldegrave, 1763–before 1766

10. 69; 22. 136; 23. 415 n. 9

George, 3d Earl of Cholmondeley, after 1768– not later than 1770

Cobbett 247; Ironside 145; GEC iii. 203

Lady Bridget Fox-Lane, 1773–ca 1777 (m. 1773 Hon. John Tollemache)

32. 124; Rate Books

Mr and Mrs George Hardinge, 1783–1816

35. 624–5; Cobbett 247–8; Rate Books

24. Marble Hill:

Henrietta, Countess of Suffolk, 1729–67

22. 543; Draper 36–8

Henrietta Hotham, ca 1762–67 (see below and 25)

10. 93n; 35. 322; 40. 363n, 366n; Stirling ii. 93–4

John, 2d Earl of Buckinghamshire, 1767–93

Cobbett 244; Draper 48

John Halliday, 1768–69

Draper 48

Henrietta Hotham, 1793–1816 (see also 25)

12. 36n; 22. 544; Rate Books

Mrs Fitzherbert, 1795–6 (see also 21)

12. 138; Draper 50

Lady Bath, 1796–1808

Draper 50

25. Little Marble Hill ('Spencer Grove'):

Thomas Barlow, 1751–64	Draper 53
Catherine Clive, ?–1754 (see also 1)	15. 317n; Cobbett 245
Daniel Giles, 1764–78	33. 182; Cobbett 245; Draper 53; Rate Books
Raphael Franco, 1779–81	33. 183; Cobbett 245; Draper 53; 'Jewish Residents' 130–1
Lady Diana Beauclerk, 1782–89	33. 195 n.5; Cobbett 245; Draper 53; HW Parish Reg. notes
Lady Tollemache, 1790–91	Cobbett 246; Rate Books; Draper 53
Frederick Pigou, 1792–93	12. 36
Henrietta Hotham, 1793–1805 (see also 24)	12. 36; Lysons iii. 577; Draper 53

26. Mr and Mrs Richard Owen Cambridge, 1751–1806 — 11. 16n; Cobbett 95, 236–40; Rate Books

27. Twickenham Park House:

Diana, Countess of Mount-rath, 1743–66	31. 123; Lysons iii. 566; Urwin 81–83, 85, 90
Lucy, Duchess of Mont-rose, 1766–68, 1776–88	31. 123; Rate Books
Henrietta, Dowager Duch-ess of Newcastle, 1768–76	31. 123; GEC ix. 531; Rate Books
Lord Frederick Cavendish, 1788–1803	31. 123; 36. 252; Cobbett 231; Rate Books

28. Montpelier Row:

Charles Hamilton, 1770–84	33. 218; Cobbett 375; Rate Books
Sir Patrick Hamilton, ca 1777–80	33. 218
Robert Berry and the Misses Mary and Agnes Berry, 1790 (see also 1)	11. 79n; see n. 4

29. Rev. Samuel Hemming, 1761–85	Cobbett 143; Rate Books
Rev. Samuel Hemming, nephew of above, 1790–1805	Cobbett 144
30. Gen. and Mrs Henry Lister, Neville House, before 1770–85	31. 237; Cobbett 367; Rate Books
William, 2d Duke of Montrose, 1788–90	31. 286; Cobbett 367; GEC ix. 156
31. Stephen T. Cole and Lady 'Betty,' 1795	12. 159n, 161; Cobbett 363
32. Mary, Dowager Countess of Catherlough, after 1772–95	11. 65n; Ironside 144; GEC iii. 110
Mrs Gell, 1796	12. 250; Cobbett 256
33. Lady Anne Conolly, Copt Hall, 1771–91 (see also 19)	31. 196; 35. 346 nn. 4, 5; Cobbett 356–8; 1784 Map
Mr and Mrs Christopher D'Oyly, ca 1793–95	12. 58; Cobbett 358; Rate Books
34. Henry Fielding, 1747–48	Cobbett 359; Dudden i. 541–2
35. Selina, Dowager Countess of Ferrers, Heath Lane Lodge, ?–1762	Cobbett 354; Lysons iii. 599
Lady Frances Shirley, ?–1778	28. 412; Cobbett 354
Hon. George Shirley, 1778–ca 1780 (see also 10)	Ironside 78–9
Welbore Ellis, 1789–1802	Cobbett 355; Ironside 79; Rate Books
36. Vice-Admiral Francis Holburne, Laurel Lodge, ?1760s	Cobbett 355
Robert Baker, 1770–73	Cobbett 355; Rate Books
M. Augustine Noverre, 1773–84	Cobbett 355; Rate Books
Benjamin Green, 1784–94	Rate Books; 1784 Map

37. John Hierons, 1769–97   **12**. 223; Ironside 149; Rate Books; SH Accts 47; BM Map, 1769

38. Sir John Hawkins, 1760–71   Davis 66, 110; Ironside 85; Cobbett 346

    Paul Vaillant, 1772–97   Davis 110; Ironside 85, 150; Cobbett 348; Rate Books

39. Lady Mary Wortley Montagu, 1722–39   Halsband 97, 180; Cobbett 348

    Dr Charles Morton, 1772–99   Ironside 85, 142; Cobbett 75, 353; DNB xiii. 1047; Rate Books

40. Frances, Marchioness of Tweeddale, Gifford Lodge, before 1769–1788   Cobbett 338; Rate Books; BM Map, 1769; GEC xii pt ii. 80

    Gen. John Gunning, 1788–91   **11**. 365 n. 13; **34**. 17n; Rate Books; Cobbett 338; Ironside 141

41. Paul Whitehead, Colne Lodge, before 1756–74   Cobbett 340–2; **35**. 234

    Charlotte, Countess of Dunmore, after 1774–1818   Cobbett 342

42. Henry Collingwood Selby, 1784–97   **11**. 17; Ironside 108; Rate Books

    Robert Berry and the Misses Mary and Agnes Berry, 1788 (see also 1, 28)   **11**. 1, 17

    William, 10th Lord Cathcart, 1789–before 1793   **11**. 60; *Scots Peerage* ii. 526

43. Mr and Mrs Abraham Prado, 1769–82   **32**. 207; Rate Books; BM Map, 1769; 'Jewish Residents' 132–3

    Mrs Prado, 1782–88   **31**. 238; Lysons iii. 479

44. Mrs Francis Salvador, before 1763–after 1780   **22**. 72; Cobbett 339

    John Davenport, after 1780–96   **12**. 143; Ironside 107

45. Thomas Ash, before 1742– ca 1783	Cobbett 403; SH Accts 45; Rate Books
John Ash, 1786–96	SH Accts 45; Rate Books

Notes

1. On this property there were two houses. The smaller house was rented in March 1762 by Thomas Pitt, who named it 'Palazzo Pitti'; by early summer of 1764 he seems to have left Twickenham (**22**. 18, 25, 33, 152; **40**. 287–8, 328, 338). The larger house, known as Cross Deep House, may have been built by Isaac Fernandez Nunez, who committed suicide in its summer-house in August 1762. It was sold in October 1762 (**2**. 368; **38**. 167; 'Jewish Residents,' pp. 133–35). Later it was occupied by Stafford Briscoe, who apparently acquired it in 1770; he lived there until his death in November 1789 (**28**. 447; Rate Books; Ironside, pp. 70, 84; Cobbett, p. 294).

2. For a list of vicars from 1741 to 1808, see Cobbett, pp. 120–3.

3. According to information kindly supplied by Dr Michael Liversidge, William Marlow, who is listed as a ratepayer from 1775 to 1810, seems to have lived in this house from ca 1785 until his death in 1813. For the last three years of Marlow's life, his pupil, John Curtis, is listed as the ratepayer, but he and his family apparently had been living with Marlow since the early 1790s and possibly from ca 1785. The 1784 map of Twickenham identifies the house as being occupied by a Mr Shackerly, who may have been Marlow's tenant. See also M. H. Grant, *A Chronological History of the Old English Landscape Painters,* rev. edn, 1957–61, iii. 235.

4. Montpelier Row contained about 24 houses. Charles Hamilton and his nephew, Sir Patrick Hamilton, occupied No. 12. We do not know which house the Berrys occupied during the summer of 1790.

WALPOLE'S POEM ON TWICKENHAM

Printed in full for the first time from the MS pasted by HW in one of his copies of the *Description of Strawberry Hill,* SH, 1774, now WSL (Hazen, *Cat. of HW's Lib.,* No. 2522). First printed by Mary Berry in *Works* iv. 382–3, where most of the biographical notes are omitted; reprinted in *Horace Walpole's Fugi-*

tive Verses, ed. W. S. Lewis, New York, 1931, pp. 47–9. Although HW has noted that the poem was 'written about 1758,' he gives August 1759 as the date of this 'copy' in his 'Short Notes' of his life (Gray i. 33). An earlier draft of the poem in HW's hand is also now wsl. This draft contains a few alterations by HW in the text; his original title 'The Inmates of Twickenham' is crossed out and 'The Parish Register of Twickenham' substituted.

The Parish Register of Twickenham.
written about 1758.

Where silver Thames round Twit'nam meads
His winding current sweetly leads;
Twit'nam, the Muses' fav'rite seat,
Twit'nam, the Graces' lov'd retreat;
There polish'd Essex[1] wont to sport,
The pride and victim of a court!
There Bacon tuned the grateful lyre
To soothe Eliza's haughty ire;
Ah! happy, had no meaner strain
Than friendship's dash'd his mighty vein!
Twit'nam, where Hyde,[2] majestic sage,
Retir'd from folly's frantic stage,
While his vast soul was hung on tenters
To mend the world and vex dissenters.
Twit'nam, where frolic Wharton[3] revell'd;
Where Montagu[4] with locks dishevell'd
(Conflict of dirt and warmth divine)
Invok'd—and scandaliz'd the Nine.
Where Pope[5] in moral music spoke
To th'anguish'd soul of Bolinbroke,
And whisper'd, how true genius errs
Pursuing joys that pow'r confers;
Bliss never to great minds arising
From ruling worlds, but from despising.
Where Fielding[6] met his bunter muse,
And as they quaff'd the fiery juice,
Droll Nature stamp'd each lucky hit
With inimaginable wit.
Where Suffolk[7] sought the peaceful scene,
Resigning Richmond to the Queen,
And all the glory, all the teasing

Of pleasing one not worth the pleasing.[8]
Where Fanny[9] ever-blooming fair
Ejaculates the graceful pray'r,
And 'scap'd from sense, with nonsense smit,
For Whitfield's cant shuns Stanhope's wit.
Amid this scene of sounding names
Of statesmen, bards, and beauteous dames,
Shall the last trifler of the throng
Enroll his own such names among?
—Oh! no—enough, if I consign
To lasting types[10] their notes divine:
Enough, if Strawberry's humble hill
The title-page of fame shall fill.

H. WALPOLE

Postscript.
added in 1784.

Here Genius in a later hour
Selected its sequester'd bow'r;
And threw around the verdant room
The blushing lilac's chill perfume.
So loose is flung each bold festoon,
Each bough so breathes the touch of noon,
The happy pencil so deceives,
That Flora, doubly jealous, cries,
'The work's not mine—yet trust these eyes,
'Tis my own Zephyr waves the leaves.'

[HW's] Notes.

1. Twickenham Park belonged to Robert Earl of Essex, favourite of Q. Elizabeth, and he gave it to Sir Francis Bacon, to compensate for not having been able to make him Solicitor General. Bacon entertained the Queen there and presented a sonnet to her to intercede for the Earl's pardon, who was in disgrace—yet Bacon afterwards pleaded bitterly against the same generous patron on his trial.

2. Lord Chancellor Clarendon lived in the great house at Twickenham over against Ham Walks, and close to the church.

3. Philip Duke of Wharton lived in the great house in the middle of Twickenham fronting the street and between the two roads.

4. Lady Mary Wortley Montagu, the poetess, lived in the house now Dr Morton's, on the left hand as you go to the Common.

5. Lord Bolinbroke was often with Pope at Twickenham. See Pope's letters.

6. Henry Fielding, author of *Tom Jones, Tom Thumb*, etc. lived in a small house in the back lane behind Pope's garden.

7. Henrietta Hobart Countess of Suffolk, mistress of George II, built Marble Hill, and retired thither on leaving Court.

8. Madame de Maintenon complained of being obliged *to amuse a man, qui n'était pas amusable* (Louis XIV).

9. Lady Frances Shirley, a celebrated beauty, with whom Lord Chesterfield was in love, and on whom he wrote a well-known song, beginning, *'When Fanny, blooming fair,'* lived with her mother the Countess Dowager of Ferrers, at a very large house now pulled down, but the terrace of which towards the road next to Pope's, still exists. Lady Frances afterwards became a Methodist.

10. Mr Walpole had a printing press at Strawberry Hill where many books were printed.

Note to the Postscript.

Lady Diana Spencer, eldest daughter of Charles Duke of Marlborough, first the wife of Frederic St John Viscount Bolinbroke, and afterwards of Topham Beauclerc, had a most masterly genius for painting. After Mr Beauclerc's death she bought the small but most beautifully situated house next to Marble Hill, and opposite to Ham House. There she painted in the boldest style, though in watercolours, a room hung with green paper, which she adorned with large festoons of lilacs, and the surbase with wreaths of different plants, in a style superior to the greatest flower-painters. She afterwards painted another room there on brown paper with lunettes of peasants and children, chained together by garlands of different flowers, which were still more excellent and natural than even the lilacs here recorded.

She left that house in 1789, and bought another, next to the Duke of Montagu's, at the foot of Richmond Hill, and there painted another room with flowers on *treillage* in a style equally natural and masterly. The paintings on brown in the second room she gave to her sister the Countess of Pembroke. For her brother Lord Robert Spencer she painted a whole room in panels on velvet in Berkeley Square.

APPENDIX 2

The Bedford Family

GROSVENOR BEDFORD (d. 4 November 1771) served as HW's deputy at the Exchequer for sixteen years.[1] According to information supplied to Dr Paget Toynbee by one of Bedford's descendants, he was the son of Thomas Bedford (1673–1710), a clerk in Chancery, and his wife, Elizabeth, who was a daughter of William Grosvenor of Cheshire. Both Mrs Bedford and her unmarried sister, Anne Grosvenor, were intimate friends of HW's mother, and Sir Robert Walpole appointed Anne Grosvenor to the office of housekeeper at Somerset House, a post customarily held by ladies of good social position.[2] In 1732 Sir Robert appointed Grosvenor Bedford collector of customs at Philadelphia, a sinecure that he retained until his death.[3] Undoubtedly it was because of this long family association that HW offered the position of deputy usher of the Exchequer to Grosvenor Bedford the day after the death of the former deputy, William Swinburn.[4] Bedford, to whom the post had been promised, immediately accepted it (HW's deed appointing him, dated 21 August 1755, is now WSL). In October HW gave Bedford the use of a house in New Palace Yard that was one of the perquisites of the office of usher of the Exchequer.[5] At some later time he moved to Brixton Causeway, Surrey.[6] Grosvenor Bedford married before 1742, but we do not know the name of his wife. He had at least two sons,[7] one of whom died before 1814.[8]

His other son, Charles Bedford (ca 1742–1814), became a clerk in the office of the usher of the Exchequer in 1762[9] and continued in that capacity until 1774, even though his father, who died in 1771, had been succeeded as deputy usher by Joseph Tullie.[10] When Tullie

---

1. GM 1771, xli. 523; MANN vii. 343.
2. Paget Toynbee, 'Horace Walpole and "Mrs G",' *Times Literary Supplement*, 16 Dec. 1920, xix. 858.
3. HW to George Grenville 7 Sept. 1763; George Grenville to HW 8 Sept. 1763.
4. HW to Grosvenor Bedford 21 Aug. 1755.
5. HW to Grosvenor Bedford 16 Oct. 1755.

6. HW to Grosvenor Bedford 27 Feb. 1771; H. B. Wheatley, *London Past and Present*, 1891, i. 276.
7. HW to Grosvenor Bedford 23 Sept. 1761.
8. GM 1814, lxxxiv pt i. 701.
9. *Court and City Register*, 1763, p. 116.
10. *Court and City Register*, 1773, pp. 103–4.

died on 20 November 1774,[11] Bedford became deputy usher,[12] and he held the post until HW's death in 1797. Under his will, HW left Bedford a legacy of £2,000.[13] Charles Bedford lived for many years in the family villa at Brixton Causeway, but by 1808 he had moved to 9 Stafford Row, Buckingham Gate, London, where he died on 18 June 1814.[14] His wife, née Mary Page, died three years later on 14 April 1817.[15] The Bedfords had three sons: Grosvenor Charles Bedford, Horace Walpole Bedford, and Henry Bedford.

Grosvenor Charles Bedford (1773–1839) was educated at Westminster, being admitted on 2 March 1784. He entered Gray's Inn 26 January 1797. He served as assistant clerk in the Exchequer Office 1792–1803, clerk of the cash book 1803–6, clerk of the registers and issues 1806–22, and chief clerk in the auditor's office 1822–34. He was a lifelong friend of Robert Southey. He himself wrote poems, essays, reviews, and pamphlets. He lived with his parents and never married.[16] He died on 14 June 1839.[17]

Horace Walpole Bedford (ca 1776–1807) was also admitted to Westminster on 2 March 1784. He later held a post at the British Museum. Having a literary bent like his older brother, he contributed several sonnets to the *Monthly Magazine* in 1797. He died unmarried on 22 September 1807 at the age of thirty-one.[18]

Little is known about Charles Bedford's youngest son, Henry. Southey refers to him in several of his letters to Grosvenor Charles Bedford, calling him (in 1794) a 'wonderful child.' He mentions him again in 1825, when Southey saw him at the Admiralty; apparently Bedford held a post there. Southey mentions him for the last time in 1833.[19] The *Gentleman's Magazine* records the death on 27 July 1844 of a Henry Bedford of James Street, St James's Square, St James's Park, aged sixty-two; this was probably the youngest son of Charles Bedford.[20] Henry Bedford had a son, Henry Charles Grosvenor Bedford, who died in 1879.[21]

11. Ossory i. 217.
12. *Court and City Register*, 1776, p. 97.
13. Selwyn 359.
14. GM 1814, lxxxiv pt i. 701; *New Letters of Robert Southey*, ed. Kenneth Curry, 1965, i. 487 n. 1.
15. GM 1817, lxxxvii pt i. 473; G. F. Russell Barker and A. H. Stenning, *The Record of Old Westminsters*, 1928, i. 68.

16. *New Letters of Robert Southey* ii. 481–2; *Old Westminsters* i. 68.
17. GM 1839, xii n.s., pt ii. 98.
18. *New Letters of Robert Southey* ii. 482; *Old Westminsters* i. 68.
19. *New Letters of Robert Southey* i. 87; ii. 282, 389.
20. GM 1844, xxii n.s., pt ii. 327.
21. Toynbee, loc. cit.

APPENDIX 3

WALPOLE'S 'SHORT NOTES' OF THE DEBATES IN PARLIAMENT, 22 JANUARY 1752 OS

Printed from a photostat of the MS in the possession of the Duke of Bedford, Woburn Abbey, kindly furnished by the late Sir Lewis Namier. HW wrote John, 4th Duke of Bedford, 22 January 1752 OS: 'I have taken the liberty to send your Grace the enclosed short notes of the debates today. If they are of any use towards next Tuesday, by informing you on what foot the question has been put by the ministry, I shall be happy.' The text is printed without normalization to show how HW made the notes in the House of Commons. A summary of the debates appears in HW's *Mem. Geo. II* i. 242–3.

Jan. 22d 1752

Mr Pelham

THIS merely a defensive Treaty. If *Contrary to Expectation* there shd be a new War, the K. of Poland is to assist us: if there is a general War, this Country will be attack'd. In this Treaty no Stipulation of Levy money. The Proportions of money for us & Holland, not extraordinary, if the prudent Dutch come into this, We ought. Quære, whether this Extension of engagement & expence, prudent. Last year this kind of Measure was almost universally thought right. To prevent Dissentions among the Princes of Germany, by settling the Imperial Crown. If *I dislik'd this* Sort of Measure, wd have opposed it in it's beginning, not after agitated in Parl. & recommended by the Crown. This to be embracd, if it is right to separate Bavaria from France, & Saxony is only to be got by Subsidies. I disclaim all gaudy Ideas. By preserving the Equilibre between the Princes of the north, this Country may be safe. In private cases, if a person has a cruel neighbour, he balances him by joining with 2 or 3 other parishes. If what was done last year, was thought secure, but was not, it is a reason for seeking farther Strength. I *trust* this will be brought to an Issue before We meet again pro or con. You can only refuse this, by saying it is not a proper Way of bringing this Prince over to yr Interest.

Hor Walpole

How this differs from last year, tho the purposes the same: Everybody look'd even on that, as dangerous & unprecedented. This, to provide against Circumstances that nobody knows when they will happen. There were personal Reasons peculiar to the Elector of Bavaria, he had changed Sides; did not pretend to succeed his Father as Emperor, was in a ruin'd Condition, cd not over to us without assistance. The strongest reason for the Bav. Treaty, was an Intimation that a K. of the Romans wd be chosen before this Session. The King's Speech of this year founded on the Speech last yr, which had Words not understood; it mention'd *farther measures* to be taken, which nobody suspected meant *farther Subsidies*. Those *farther* are the same, only the Sum greater. I & many were even then concern'd. Some Conditions in this Treaty not worth a farthing a year. Cant guess how the money is to be divided among the Conditions. Who thought the K. of Poland wd act ag. us? had he any provocation? Who thinks he wd have acted ag. the two Imperial Courts? how shd his Son succeed to crown of Poland, but by their means? Cd France make him King there? cd they ever make a King there? They tried the Pr. of Conti & Stanislas, but failed. The Sum certain, the Performance uncertain. Before the Time comes, there may be alterations in German Princes & their Ministers: They have often Ministers, not their own Subjects. The Landgrave of Hesse's minister may next year be so at Cologne; & new Ministers may be for breaking Treaties of which They have not tasted the Fruits. The Storm cant break without Clouds gathering: you may get these Troops, in six Months, unless you are outbid. In German courts, Ministers have great advantages, & ought to have for their Trouble. France dont think these Troops an Object; but may be glad you spend yr money upon Them. It is *emere Spem pretio*. The Electors know it their Interest to have the Imp. Crown in the House of Austria. History of Charles 6, & 7th & present Emperor. There was no Occasion for our stirring now in time of peace, seeing the Duke of Lorrain was chosen, even ag. the Consent of France & Prussia. I wd be for this if the Empress has sent you word that She has discovered any new Machinations. if She has told you, her own Finances are out of order: for I cant beleive that We have engag'd in this Step officiously. *Continuing the Subsidy, will be a reason for their deferring the Election.* They will say, We shall all agree to choose the Arch Duke, but let us get as much Money as We can. Saxony will say to Bavaria, you have got a Subsidy; let me too. I dont love hopes & Trusts; however, if We are to pay no more—you had better deposit the Money, till the Election is over, & They have voted as you have a Mind. Bavaria engaged his Vote; the conditions of this Treaty are more Vague: This has the Words, *according to the fundamental Laws of the Empire,* which may be construed into an Objection if he has at any time a mind to evade performance. The Elector of Cologne, when he broke his Treaty, pleaded that there was no Specification of his Vote. Tis sd, that Elector is now gone to Munich, perhaps in order to get another Sum. The Dutch are so ruin'd, They can be of no use. Province of Holland alone owes 60 Million Sterl. Wish We were more strictly united with Prussia. It wd be wrong to give Russia a Subsidy, because her Interest the same as ours. Panegyric on the King, as *Author* of the Regency Bill: In the highest Point of Adoration & Respect at home & abroad. How he fear'd, when the Duke ill, who is our only Support & Security. Making the people uneasy, wd make the King so, & that might hurt his Health. Last year, the Report but of this Treaty, was calld a Calumny on the Ministry.—notwithstanding all these reasons, I shall be for it, as it is sign'd, & demanded, & wd lessen the King's credit abroad, & as I trust We shall have no more such. Dont mean to distress the Ministry, but to prevent their & our own Distress: nor to lay a Plan of Opposition, unless It were on more generous Motives than late Oppositions, which I abhorr. Advice to *Old Corps, who have had no great Encouragement,* to follow & act with Him, on this firm Persuasion that there will be no more such Measures. Shall give very little more Trouble, as perhaps my Parts decay, will confine myself to Wool, & such like Business, & follow the Advice of my namesake, Solve Senescentem maturè &c.

Soll. General.

H.W. has attack'd the Object, the View & the Foundation, & yet agrees to it. It has not been the Policy of this Country or Holland, to wait to give Subsidies, till you want Troops. Have a List in my pocket of the annual Subsidies pd by France in the year 1750. To Prussia, 300,000 £ Sterl. to Sweden Do. To Denmark, 100,000. To Elect. Pal. 25000; To Genoa 30000. To Modena 15000. To Parma, 120,000.

Saxony has refus'd to accept the Renewal of theirs, which was 96000, the Double of this Cologne has now about 50000. This is a preventive Measure. On all Elections of Kings, there have been Wars in Europe. If Some yrs ago Sweden had not agreed to choose Russia's K. of the Romans, It wd have caus'd War. Prudent, to have the Election in the Life of the Emperor. Wd you abandon the Measure because It did not succeed last yr? it was miss'd by loosing Cologne: This, to replace Him. When It is sd, they wd act as they do, out of their natural Interest, without Subsidies, It is Speculation ag. Fact. Did not Saxony join ag. us at the beginning of the last War? did not his Subsidy from France cease but in 1750? has not he connections with France by his Daughter? Saxony & Bavaria, most material Electors, as Vicars of Empire. This may prevent a War in Poland: Tho France has never made a King of that Country, yet She got Lorrain by trying. This not a temporary measure but for futurity. The King imitates King William, about the Succession of Spain. The Rightness of making a King of the Romans.

Potter & Sr H. Erskine two very bad Speeches *for* the Question. Sr Tho. Robinson a most absurd Mad Speech intended for the Question, but was on the Danger of Embden, with which he was proud of having alarm'd the World. very angry the newspapers had abused German Princes. Disclosed a great Secret of his own Discovery, that France has owd all it's Greatness for these 200 yrs to it's Treaty with the Swiss. Sr Walter Blacket & Beckford ag. the Question; the Latter sd you wd always have Enemies, while there remain'd any *Unsubsidiz'd Electors.* Sr W. Yonge for, Ld Strange against. Ld Hilsborough, for: thought we ought always to be concernd on the Continent, & by Subsidies only. While France subsidizes, We must. K. of Prussia supports Jacobitism.

Mr Fox expos'd the Doctrine of following France in Subsidies, which wd ruin us. look'd upon this Treaty as merely calculated to make a King of the Romans, which wd be worth ten times the Sum. The Electors not venal, for They might have much more from France if They did not follow the Interest of Germany.

Sr Peter Warren spoke ag. the Treaty for it's own Sake, voted for it for the King's. Mr Legge for it; Account of his own negotiations at Berlin, found by the Guarantee of Silesia that that King not to be reconcild. compar'd Prussia & Austria; the former accidentally great, the Latter always so, & of more use to us.

Ld Cobham.

Opposes This, because he had contributed to lay a great load of Debt
on this Country, during two foreign Wars, the most profuse in the
Management & most hazardous in the Execution. From Mr Pelham's
professions on the Peace, had hoped a new Æra, & beleiv'd it, from
the great Service he had done in reducing Interest, which was a
serious Pledge. Was drawn into the Measure last year, because he
was unwilling to turn Men's Eyes whither they are too apt to look
with Jealousy. Bavaria was a new Ally & to be encouraged. Prussia's
Rescript. Loss of Cologne. Dont desire to see Protest of Prussia back'd
by France. *Why did not We proceed to Election when We had a
Vote more than We have now? Woud consent to this, if I coud be
assured this Was the Last.* This was universally præcondemnd last
year. We are now for the 3d year labouring under a Land Tax of 3
Shillings, which more grievous than 4 Shillings at the beginning of
the War, by the Distemper among the Cattle. Want to ease the Load
of Debts, that the Crown may descend with Honour to the King's
Grandson: if these Measures are to be pursued, He must say, Non
hæc in Fœdera Veni.

Ch. Townshend, for.

Division
236, For.   54. against.

Ld Egmont was laid up with the Gout; Pitt was not there, Lord
Cobham went away. Brand, Aldworth, Rigby, in the Minority.

APPENDIX 4

WALPOLE'S LETTERS TO THE 'PUBLIC ADVERTISER,' AUGUST 1767

Printed from the MS now WSL. First printed in the *Public Advertiser* 28 Aug. 1767. For the history of the MS see *ante* 15 March 1763.

Before leaving London for Paris 20 Aug. 1767, HW doubtless turned over the MS to his deputy Grosvenor Bedford, to be copied and sent to the newspapers. HW wrote in 'Short Notes': 'In Sept. [1767] were published in the *Public Advertiser* two letters I had written on political abuse in newspapers. They were signed, *Toby*, and *A Constant Correspondent*' (GRAY i. 42). The publisher of the *Public Advertiser* was Henry Sampson Woodfall (*ante* ?Sept. 1766, n. 1). See following letter.

For the *Public Advertiser*

I DO not impute it to you, Mr Woodfall, but to the deadness of the season, that you now and then, on a dearth of news, adopt the railing epistles with which other papers abound. You may have another better-natured motive. Some mad doctors reckon that the privilege of venting our thoughts or abuse in print contributes to keep many a poor politician out of Bedlam; and that we never have had an administration which checked the liberty of the press, without a proportionate increase of lunatics in the hospitals. Thank God of late ministers seem determined not to hinder these wholesome evacuations. This therefore is a fit season for all the crazy, the disappointed and the malicious to *purge* themselves in the daily papers: nor ought you or your brethren, Mr Woodfall, to have the least objection to supplying these poor people with *paper*. Don't let any man persuade you that you are doing a wrong, uncharitable or prejudicial thing. Men of all sides have been so regularly abused, that calumny has lost its sting. Your only care should be to observe an exact neutrality. Print all that is sent you against every party. You please the writers, who love to read their own works in print, and you injure nobody. The very mob now neglects and despises all party writings. Abuse on politicians, in or out, is no more regarded than the puffs for quack medicines. Who, do you think, believes what is said by a writer that is ashamed or afraid to be known? One man undertakes to mend the ministry, another oversees Piccadilly, and several were still more busy to improve and widen the Devil's Gap,[1] or to speak politically, to put it on *a broader bottom*. What harm have any of these poor folks done? No ministry has been *written* out of place; the paviours go on in their own way in Piccadilly; and after all the controversies and labours of patriot writers since the days of Charles I, no one good has been obtained for this poor nation at the expense of so much ink and paper, but the single reformation of the aforesaid Devil's Gap.

One point I truly lament, for the sake of the public, and that is the melancholy degeneracy of writers in modern times. Our ancestors abused one another as much as we do, but then they made a point of diverting their readers at the same time. The Examiners employed as much Billingsgate as we do; but it was higher seasoned. Dr Swift and Lord Bolingbroke, who would not have disliked to have had a few throats cut in an insurrection, made their countrymen laugh, at the moment that they offered them daggers. But we are too idle, or inattentive to our readers. We never treat them with wit, humour, ridicule, sense or argument. Downright abuse, though an excellent ingredient, will not do alone, and we find it does not do. Who remembers one *letter* that has been written in the memory of man! It is here today, and gone tomorrow.

There is another point or two in which these worthy labourers of all sides have grievously wearied the public. For instance in the repetition of the same topics at certain seasons. Every summer we are assured that the administration for the time being will not dare to meet the opening of the session. This prophecy has been repeated so often without once proving true, that not a footman in opposition believes it. Other writers assure their readers that the administration, I do not mean the present, but every administration, is grown odious to the nation. This assertion is likewise worn threadbare. Some folks complain of the administration being changed so often. This like-

---

1. An archway and tenement at the west end of Great Queen Street, Lincoln's Inn Fields, known as 'Hell Gate' or the 'Devil's Gap'; it was taken down in Jan. 1765 (H. B. Wheatley, *London Past and Present*, 1891, i. 501; Walter Blott, *A Chronicle of Blemundsbury*, South Norwood, 1892, p. 370). 'The widening the Devil's Gap, at the entrance into Great Queen Street, is ordered to be carried into execution' (*London Chronicle* 24–6 Jan. 1765, xvii. 94).

wise is known to mean that the said plaintiffs wish to have it changed
once more, and consequently goes for nothing.

I have some objection also to the use of certain signatures frequently employed, because experience has shown that they mean the
very reverse of what they pretend, and thence destroy precision in
language. *Cato* and *Brutus* often write in behalf of arbitrary power.
Candour and *Candid* are assumed by authors of the most notorious
partiality; Æquus and *Æquitas* are full of *abuse;* and *Verus, Verax,*
and *Veritas* are seldom circumstantially exact in their assertions.
Tranquilus is generally in a passion, and *Moderation* foams at the
mouth. I could name many more, which for brevity I omit, but desire to be understood to favour no particular side, because I have
found them all equally faulty in their turns. It is invention and
novelty that I recommend, and those only in the method. A political
writer is allowed to invent what aspersions he pleases; but he owes
it to his readers to dress it up in some new form, or he may depend
upon it nobody will read his productions. The people want to be
diverted, not to believe; they don't trouble their heads about the
contentions among the great, because the people have seen over and
over, that there is not much difference. All love places, sinecures,
reversions and pensions. All are patriots when out, and courtiers
when in: and those only, whoever they are, who are content with
their places, and do not encroach on the liberties of their fellow subjects, are the men the people like. Factious gentlemen are neglected,
and nobody follows them: and for what private calumny they heap
on one another, nobody cares. In truth I believe they do not care
themselves. Abuse is the perquisitive of office, and passes like the
fees that they are forced to pay out of their salaries. It is said that
Cardinal Mazarine[2] preserved and bound up all the libels that were
printed against him, and left them in his hall for the amusement of
his footmen. He acted like a sensible man: and yet he was the sole
butt of abuse at that time. Every man in England who has had a public employment, might make a greater or less collection in proportion—and when that is the case, who can regard abuse any more
than a rainy day? It comes in its turn with the sunshine, and is as
soon forgotten.

Within these five years, we have seen the most common vices or

2. Jules Mazarin (1602–61).

foibles gravely urged as reasons why such or such a man should not be a minister. A man of this party and that keeps a girl. This man and that goes to Newmarket. This and that has not a grey beard. Are the writers serious when they hope the people will rise on such accusations? No: the writers at the time were disappointed, mortified and sore. Very likely they came from the bawdy house or the gaming table, with some additional disgusts, when they sat down to write their letters, which a week afterwards they would be the first to laugh at themselves. What then must the people do? why they laugh at the abusers, not at the abused, and things go on as they were. Yet it is very proper such writers should be indulged. They grow better-humoured when they have vented their spleen; and it were pity any man should be hindered from so innocent a discharge of his bile. It prevents their bearing malice; and accordingly we find that in six months they are capable of shaking hands with their bitterest enemies, and joining to write in concert with them against their late friends. How much better is this, than the deadly and lasting feuds that are kept up in other countries from generation to generation, where there is no liberty of the press?

Let me commend too our modern improvements in this art. Formerly we had nothing but pamphlets or weekly journals; not many men read the latter, and very few the former. How many celebrated libels, whose title-pages passed through several editions, when not a whole impression had been sold off! By stuffing letters into newspapers, the public are forced to read whatever anybody pleases to write. Moreover, a man who has not matter, or knowledge, or argument enough for a pamphlet, may write a letter. If he is too short-winded for a letter, he may be capable of penning an article of intelligence extraordinary, and has the satisfaction to boot of beholding it in a distinguished place of a newspaper. Who can grudge a poor man such a momentary joy! You, Mr Woodfall, I am sure have too much feeling to be so hard-hearted. Gratify your old customers, and your new. Your readers may be a little tired, but your writers never will be so; unless, as often happens, modes go out of fashion in the capital, while they are flourishing in the provinces. Ireland imitates its betters, and as fashions are always pushed to excess by imitators, exceeds even London in scandal and abuse. The colonies too, that used humbly to be content with the obsolete libels that could not find vent at home, have set up manufactures of their own, and it is said have already brought them to great perfection. Patriotism flourishes there, as it has done here, in beds of dung and filth, and I suppose from being a novel production, has, as yet, its admirers, who do not know how transient the bloom is.

I heartily wish you, Sir, and your customers well, and hope you will live to see many administrations abused, with the consciousness of not having done the least hurt to any of them.

Your constant reader,

Toby[3]

Printed from the MS now WSL. First printed in the *Public Advertiser* 2 Sept. 1767. For the history of the MS see *ante* 15 March 1763.
For the date see headnote to the previous letter.

To Mr Woodfall

Sir,

YOU are a good Christian, no doubt, and will be rejoiced to hear that you have contributed to the conversion of one sinner. The excellent letter in your paper signed Toby has opened my eyes, and made me ashamed of my past conduct, into which I will never relapse, if I can maintain my wife and eight children without it. You must know, Sir, I am a hackney-writer, but being a staunch Englishman, my principles have always inclined me to write against all administrations.

I had not left the charity school where I was brought up, before my natural disposition had carried me far into the study of *Examiners, Medleys, Craftsmen, Evening Posts,* and political magazines.[1] Italics touched my soul, and asterisks made me wild, though I own I seldom could discover the wit of the former, or the meaning of the latter; and what puzzled me still more was to find that many of the great personages whom I had seen so much abused in my favourite reading, are already purified from obloquy, and become the

3. The ninth and final volume of Sterne's *Tristram Shandy*, narrating the adventures of Uncle Toby with the Widow Wadman, had been published 30 Jan. 1767.

1. The chief periodicals alluded to are *The Examiner*, 1710–14, *The Medley*, 1710–12, and *The Craftsman*, 1726–50, although there were other periodicals with the same or similar names.

brightest names in our annals. I yet do not know how to believe that the Duke of Marlborough was a great general. Is it possible, think I to myself now and then, that such illustrious men (most of whose names indeed I do not know) as they were who abused him,[2] should have told a heap of lies?

Well! Sir, you will not be surprised to hear that I soon commenced author myself. I wrote a letter to a friend in the country, and after having shown it to one or two friends in town, who extolled it to the skies, I sent it to an evening post. Nothing could equal my impatience for the evening of its appearance. I did not dare to send for the paper, because I thought from the great noise it would make, that the minister would employ all his spies to find out the author, and that my having bought the paper, might discover me. But I went to all the coffee houses in the neighbourhood, an hour before the time, and could stay in none, where I did not find it. At last the waiter brought it. I had art and command enough of myself, though then very young, to take up another paper, both to disguise my interest in *the* paper, and to leave it to others to read. Judge of my mortification, when an old gentleman who first reached it, threw it aside, without reading my letter, and asked for another paper which generally had the best intelligence from Russia! I was cut to the soul; but impatience to see my own works in print was to me consolation. I eagerly catched up the paper, but before I had half finished my own letter, I saw another person who wanted a paper, and eagerly thrust mine into his hand. Sir, said I at the same time, here is a very stinging letter against the administration. I never read politics, said the gentleman dryly, and turned to the price of stocks. In short, Sir, neither there nor in seven or eight more coffee houses into which I entered successively, was the least notice taken of my letter, and yet I observed, with a mixture of joy, and of fear lest my countenance should betray me, three or four persons read my letter. I concluded they were all attached to the ministry. Next morning early, for I did not sleep a wink, I asked my washerwoman what news in town? She told me Black Bess was sent to Newgate—Upon suspicion, said I eagerly— No, no, said she, it was clear enough, she broke the watchman's head, and then was running on into a long story of a drunken fray, but I left her and affected to steal very carelessly out of my lodging. The

2. Swift, among others, wrote fierce attacks on Marlborough in *The Examiner*.

first person I met was a milkman, and him I asked if it was true that
the administration was changed—Damn the administration, said the
fellow, I am sure they all deserved to be hanged (oh! thinks I, I have
done their business), here have they gone, said he, and ordered us
to burn all the hides of the cattle that died of the distemper, and
then he told me a story of a cock and a bull and a man at Islington,
that had not a word of relation to my letter. In short, Sir, my mortifi-
cations were innumerable; I never heard one word of my letter,
though I was forced at last, in order to have it taken notice of, to
write an anonymous letter to the minister, to inform him that the
bitter letter of such a day, which had given such a blow to his power,
was written by a baker, who had threatened to arrest me. Nobody
was taken up; and though I continued my labours for the good of my
country, no material change happened for two years; and when it did,
the change had no relation to anything that had been written against
them.

To be short, Sir, I have written for and against every set of men in
England, but still with a tender regard to my honour, for I never
abused any man till he was in place: nay, I have always made him
amends, by crying him up to the skies, as the truest patriot upon
earth, the moment he was out again—so my conscience is clear on
that score. Sometimes when I have been pressed in time, I have reprinted the same satire on two succeeding ministers. My wife, who
was cruelly averse to my profession of author, has often, when she
could not cure me of my itch of writing and propensity to slander,
advised me at least to offer my pen to the administration, and I confess my weakness, did once prevail upon me to make the attempt. I
was rejected with scorn, though to raise my price, I owned myself
for the author of several virulent productions, of which the minister's secretary protested he had never heard. I went home, wrote one
ten times more bitter, and drew a character of my wife under that of
the minister's lady. My wife knew nothing of it, nor, I doubt, the
lady neither, for which now I am heartily glad.

Being grown desperate, I determined to write myself into a pension or pillory, and should certainly have obtained the latter at least,
by dashing into the new fashion of printing names at length—but a
check being put to that practice, I escaped before my turn came.

In the course of my labours, I have been acquainted with most of
the eminent writers in the political way, and you would be amazed,

Sir, if you knew how small the number is; as we write on all sides, and all subjects, you would think we are a great many; but in truth this branch of business lies amongst a very few. Now and then a gentleman condescends to visit Grub Street, but is very shy of our acquaintance everywhere else: and if they vouchsafe to set us to work, it is with so much caution, that it is plain they are ashamed of the vocation. And well they may be! Mr Toby's letter has made me ashamed of it myself. How indeed can the people believe the assertions of an anonymous writer, who stakes no character, and may tell what lies he pleases with impunity? If a statesman is guilty, would not he hear of it in other places than a newspaper? Could anything be proved, would not it be proved? Whatever appears only in a newspaper is most likely to be false. I own with contrition that most of my assertions have been of that nature. And were his M[ajesty], God bless him, to employ no ministers, till a perfect set could be found, or which is still more improbable, till nobody could be found to asperse them, this country would be in a fine state of anarchy.

Well! Sir, whatever my comrades may do, I blush for them and myself. I ask pardon of all those worthy gentlemen I have traduced, I advise my countrymen to treat anonymous writers with the contempt they deserve, and I promise never to offend in the same way again.

A CONSTANT CORRESPONDENT

N.B. In the course of the present reign I have written four hundred and thirteen letters against the Earl of Bute, two hundred and eighty-seven against the Earl of Chatham, six score against the Lord Holland, one hundred three score and odd against the Right Hon. G. Grenville, seventy against the Duke of Bedford, thirty-three against the Duke of Newcastle, eighty-eight against the Marquis of Rockingham, one against the Right Hon. Mr Dowdswell, one hundred and ten against the Duke of Grafton and the Right Hon. General Conway, above two thousand against the Scotch, and none against the Earl of Temple for which I humbly beg his Lordship's pardon; besides squibs, epigrams (though I have no talent for verse), prophecies, paragraphs of news, and intelligence extraordinary. I have appeared under the names of Modestus, Probus, Verus, Algernon Sydney, Russel, Impartial, and an hundred Antis. I have written for and against the Peace, general warrants and the Stamp Act, and sometimes have unbent my mind by entering into controversies, that were not absolutely ministerial, as the price of provisions, the Italian operas, the new pavement, London Bridge, the affairs of Corsica, and the monkey in the Haymarket. I have now and then given my opinion on new books and novels, but as I reserved the forte of my satire for politics, I found the gentlemen of the reviews excelled me at my own weapons, and treated poor authors with more acrimony than it was worth my while to do, and therefore I declined that province. I have however guarded the incognito so well, that I have still some spice of character left, and intend to live upon it for the rest of my days; for which reason, among others, you will excuse me, if like the rest of my brethren I conceal my name. Mem. I was excellent at an anecdote, or private family story, which I published without remorse or shame, and often without the least foundation of truth.[3]

3. These letters were printed; I think about 1767 (HW).

APPENDIX 5

WALPOLE'S UNSENT LETTER TO LADY CRAVEN, ?JULY 1786

Printed from an extract quoted in HW's 'Miscellany,' 1786–95, pp. 1–2, now wsl. First printed in *Horace Walpole's Miscellany 1786–95*, ed. L. E. Troide, New Haven, 1978, pp. 6–7, where the conjectural dating of the letter is discussed and the text fully annotated.

I QUESTION whether your voyage to the Greek Isles will answer your expectation, except in the beautiful but degraded scenes of nature. Very slight by all accounts seem to be the relics of Grecian art and taste. Defaced ruins of architecture and statuary, like the wrinkles of decrepitude of a once beautiful woman, only make one regret that one did not see them when they were enchanting. I never found even in my juvenile hours that it was necessary to go a thousand miles in search of themes for moralizing. Forty years ago I saw the *Angel, Goddess, Montagu* in her decay, and she was as striking a lesson of mortality, though still graceful, as the rubbish of what was once the Acropolis of Athens! When Turkish barbarism is added to the spectacle, it raises indignation—and why sail to the Ægean, only to be in a passion?